Fourth Edition

Human Motivation

Robert E. Franken
University of Calgary

Brooks/Cole Publishing Company
I(T)P® An International Thomson Publishing Company

Pacific Grove • Albany • Belmont • Bonn • Boston • Cincinnati • Detroit • Johannesburg • London • Madrid
Melbourne • Mexico City • New York • Paris • Singapore • Tokyo • Toronto • Washington

To Bob Earl
Teacher, mentor, friend

Sponsoring Editor: *Jim Brace-Thompson*
Marketing Team: *Lauren Harp/Christine Davis*
Editorial Assistants: *Terry Thomas, Drew Holzapfel*
Production Editor: *Keith Faivre*
Manuscript Editor: *Bernard Gilbert*
Permissions Editor: *Mary Kay Hancharick*
Interior and Cover Design: *Roy Neuhaus*

Cover Photo: *Thomas Ulrich / Adventure Photo & Film*
Illustration: *Jennifer Mackres, Laurie Albrecht*
Photo Editor: *Kathleen Olson*
Typesetting: *TBH/Typecast, Inc.*
Cover Printing: *Phoenix Color Corporation*
Printing and Binding: *R. R. Donnelley & Sons–Crawfordsville*

Credits continue on page 464.

COPYRIGHT © 1998 by Brooks/Cole Publishing Company
A division of International Thomson Publishing Inc.

I(T)P The ITP logo is a registered trademark under license.

For more information, contact:

BROOKS/COLE PUBLISHING COMPANY
511 Forest Lodge Road
Pacific Grove, CA 93950
USA

International Thomson Publishing Europe
Berkshire House 168–173
High Holborn
London WC1V 7AA
England

Thomas Nelson Australia
102 Dodds Street
South Melbourne, 3205
Victoria, Australia

Nelson Canada
1120 Birchmount Road
Scarborough, Ontario
Canada M1K 5G4

International Thomson Editores
Seneca 53
Col. Polanco
11560 México D.F., México

International Thomson Publishing GmbH
Königswinterer Strasse 418
53227 Bonn
Germany

International Thomson Publishing Asia
221 Henderson Road
#05–10 Henderson Building
Singapore 0315

International Thomson Publishing Japan
Hirakawacho Kyowa Building, 3F
2-2-1 Hirakawacho
Chiyoda-ku, Tokyo 102
Japan

Printed in the United States of America.

10 9 8 7 6 5 4 3 2 1

Library of Congress Cataloging-in-Publication Data
Franken, Robert E. [date]
    Human motivation / Robert E. Franken. — 4th ed.
        p.   cm.
    Includes bibliographical references and index.
    ISBN 0-534-34851-3 (alk. paper)
    1. Motivation (Psychology).   I. Title.
BF503.F7   1998
153.8—dc21
                                    97-37696
                                    CIP

Brief Contents

Part One   Issues and Organizing Principles in Motivation

Chapter One	What Causes Action: Themes in the Study of Motivation	1
Chapter Two	Components of Motivation	24

Part Two   Analyzing Some Basic Motivational Systems

Chapter Three	Hunger and Eating	55
Chapter Four	Sexual Behavior, Love, and Sexual Orientation	82
Chapter Five	Arousal, Attention, and Peak Performance	112
Chapter Six	Wakefulness, Alertness, Sleep, and Dreams	144
Chapter Seven	Drug Use and Drug Addiction	174
Chapter Eight	Aggression, Coercive Action, and Anger	208

Part Three   Emotions and Motivation

Chapter Nine	Emotions, Stress, and Health	239
Chapter Ten	Goal-Incongruent (Negative) Emotions: Fear and Anxiety, Pessimism and Depression, Guilt and Shame	273
Chapter Eleven	Goal-Congruent (Positive) Emotions: Happiness, Hope and Optimism, Attachment and Belongingness	305

Part Four   Growth Motivation and Self-Regulation

Chapter Twelve	Curiosity, Exploratory Behavior, Sensation Seeking, and Creativity	335
Chapter Thirteen	Predictability and Control, Achievement and Mastery, and Self-Esteem	365
Chapter Fourteen	Self-Regulation of Motivation	391

Contents

Part One Issues and Organizing Principles in Motivation

Chapter One
What Causes Action: Themes in the Study of Motivation 1

What Causes Behavior? 3

Approach and Avoidant Causes 3

Basic Themes of Contemporary Motivation
  Theories 4
  Behavior Represents an Attempt to Adapt 4
  *The Importance of Determining What Arouses and
    Energizes Behavior* 5
  *Understanding What Governs the Direction of
    Behavior* 5
  Understanding Persistence 6
  Understanding the Role of Feelings 6
  Accounting for Individual Differences 7
  The Question of Self-Regulating Behavior 7
  Do Humans Have a Will? 7

Theories of Motivation: A Historical Survey 8
  Instinct Theories 8
  Learning Theories 12
  Need Theories 15
  Growth and Mastery Motivation Theories 18
  Cognitive Theories 20

Biological, Learned, and Cognitive Forces 21

Main Points 22

Chapter Two
Components of Motivation 24

The Biological Component 25

Genetic Processes 25
Monozygotic and Dyzygotic Twins 26
*Learning and Genetic Processes: Hardwired and
  Softwired Behavior* 26
■ *Practical Application 2-1*
***The Biology of Obsessions and Compulsions* 26**
  Prewired Behavior 27
  Brain Circuits and the Disposition to Learn 28
  *The Predisposition to Experience Pleasure: Reward
    Systems in the Brain* 28
  *The Disposition to Process Information: The Reticular
    Activating System* 30
  Neurotransmitters 30

The Learned Component 33
  Attention and Learning 33
■ *Practical Application 2-2*
***Becoming Aware of Your Biological Processes* 34**
  Classical Conditioning 36
  Instrumental Learning 38
  Social Incentive Theory 39

The Cognitive Component 40
  Cognitive Theories 40
  The Nature of Cognitions 41
  Cognitive Dissonance Theory 43
  Implicit Theories 44
  Habits, Automatic Behavior, and Cognition 44
■ *Practical Application 2-3*
***Becoming Mindful of Your Cognitive Processes* 45**
  An Example: What Causes Happiness? 46
  Individual Differences 46
  Some Examples of a Components Approach 49

Main Points 53

Part Two   Analyzing Some Basic Motivational Systems

Chapter Three

Hunger and Eating   55

Eating and Digestion   56
The Biological Component   56
The Learned Component   59
The Cognitive Component   63

The Origins of Overweight and Obesity   63
The Biological Component   64
The Learned Component   67
The Cognitive Component   67

Theories of Overweight and Obesity   68
Internal-External Theory of Hunger and Eating   68
Boundary Theory of Hunger and Eating   72

Difficulties Confronting Dieters   74
The Biological Component   74
The Learned Component   75
The Cognitive Component   76

Health Implications of Weight Loss and
   Obesity   77

■ *Practical Application 3-1*
Some Rules for Dieting   78

Theories of Eating Disorders   78
The Spiral Model of Eating Disorders   79

Main Points   80

Chapter Four

Sexual Behavior, Love, and Sexual Orientation   82

Human Sexual Arousal (Passion)   83
The Biological Component   83
The Learned Component   86
The Cognitive Component   90

Love   93
The Biological Component   93
The Learned Component   93

The Cognitive Component   94
Sternberg's Interaction Model   95

■ *Practical Application 4-1*
Striving to Attain Consummate Love   96

Biological Differences between Men and
   Women   97
The Sex Hormones   97
Sexual Dimorphism in the Brain   101
The Politics of Biological Difference   103

Sexual Orientation   104
The Biological Component   104
The Learned Component   106
The Cognitive Component   108

Main Points   110

Chapter Five

Arousal, Attention, and Peak Performance   112

Definition of Arousal   113

Cortical Arousal   113
The Reticular Activating System (RAS)   113
Measuring Cortical Activity   114

The Autonomic Nervous System   115

Arousal, Affect, and Performance   117
Arousal and Affect   117
Arousal and Performance   117
Optimal Stimulation and Individual Goals   119
Conclusion   120

Arousal and Attention   120
Arousal and Selective Attention   120
Arousal and the Reorganization of Attention   121
Conclusion   121

Challenges for Performance Theory   122
Unexplained Arousal   122
*Reconceptualizing the Link between Arousal and
   Performance   122*

Systems Involved in Peak Performance   122
Trait Arousal (Anxiety)   124
   The Biological Component   124
   The Learned Component   126
   The Cognitive Component   127
   High Trait Arousal and Performance   128
State Arousal: Sensory Overload   129
   The Biological Component   129
   The Learned Component   130
   The Cognitive Component   131
   Dealing with Sensory Overload   131
   Sensory Overload and Performance   132
State Arousal: Cognitive Dissonance   132
   The Biological Component   133
   The Learned Component   133
   The Cognitive Component   133
   Cognitive Dissonance and Performance   134
State Arousal: Elevation Arousal   134
   Test Anxiety   134
   Competition Arousal   136
   Coping with Evaluation Arousal   140
   *State Arousal and Performance: Some Concluding
      Comments   140*
■ *Practical Application 5-1*
Using Guided Imagery to Overcome Distraction   141
Main Points   142

Chapter Six

**Wakefulness, Alertness,
Sleep, and Dreams   144**

Wakefulness, Sleep, and EEG Activity   145
   Correlates of Sleep and Wakefulness   145
   Paralysis During REM   145
   Sleep and Attention   145
   Jouvet's Model of Sleep   146
   Why We Fall Asleep and Why We Wake Up   147
   Individual Differences in Sleep Cycles   148
   Other Sleep Rhythms   149
   How Much Sleep Do We Need?   149

   Altering Sleep/Wakefulness Cycles   150
   The Effects of Sleep Reduction   150
■ *Practical Application 6-1*
Adjusting to Jet Lag   150
■ *Practical Application 6-2*
Shift Work, Sleepiness, and Catnaps   152
The Psychological Functions of Sleep   154
   *Experimental Procedures for Determining the
      Function of Sleep   154*
   REM Deprivation and Motivation   155
   The REM Rebound Effect   155
   *REM Sleep Deprivation and Psychological
      Health   156*
   REM Sleep, Learning, and Adaptation   157
   *Individual Differences in the Need for REM
      Sleep   159*
   Other Types of Sleep Deprivation   160
Dreaming   161
   Hobson's Activation/Synthesis Theory   161
   The Meaning of Dreams   162
   Lucid Dreaming   165
■ *Practical Application 6-3*
How to Become a Lucid Dreamer   166
   REM, NREM, and Sleep Onset Dreams   165
   Hartmann's Theory of Sleep   168
Sleep Disorders   169
   Insomnia   169
■ *Practical Application 6-4*
Some Common Reasons for Insomnia   170
   Sleep Apnea   172
Main Points   172

Chapter Seven

Drug Use and Drug Addiction   174

Some Basic Terms and Concepts   175
   *Drug Addiction: The World Health Organization
      Definition   175*
   Substance Abuse   175
   Psychoactive Drugs   175
   Dependency   175

Tolerance   176
Solomon's Opponent-Process Model of Tolerance   176

Why People Become Addicted   177
Approach and Avoidant Motivation   177
A Motivational Model   178

The Initial Motivation to Use Drugs   179
The Biological Component   179
The Learned Component   180
The Cognitive Component   181

Why Drugs Are Addictive   182

Heroin and Morphine   182
The Biological Component   182

■ *Practical Application 7-1*
Endorphins and Motivation   182
The Learned Component   184
The Cognitive Component   186

Stimulants: Cocaine and Amphetamines   188
The Biological Component   188
The Learned Component   188
The Cognitive Component   189

Relaxants: The New Antianxiety Drugs   190
The Biological Component   190
The Learned Component   191
The Cognitive Component   191

The Hallucinogenics: Cannabis (Marijuana, Hashish) and LSD   193
The Biological Component   193
The Learned Component   193
The Cognitive Component   193

Nicotine   194
The Biological Component   194
The Learned Component   195
The Cognitive Component   195

Alcohol   196
The Biological Component   196
The Learned Component   198
The Cognitive Component   199

■ *Practical Application 7-2*
Factors That Influence Drug Use   202
■ *Practical Application 7-3*
How People Quit Addictions   204
Main Points   205

Chapter Eight

Aggression, Coercive Action, and Anger   208

Kinds of Aggression   209
The Traditional Definition of Aggression   210
Research on Aggression   210
Early Laboratory Research   210
Aggression in the Real World   212

New Concepts Regarding Aggression   212
The Need to Control   212
A Working Definition of Aggression   212
Anger and Aggression   212

Measuring Human Aggression   213
The Biological Component of Aggression   213
Genetic Processes   213
Hormones and Aggression   214
Neuromechanisms   216

The Learned Component of Aggression   219
Frustration   219
Social Learning Theory   221

The Cognitive Component of Aggression   223
A Model of Coercive Action   224
Justice   225
Interpersonal Violence   228

Youth Violence   229
The Biological Component   229
The Learned Component   230
The Cognitive Component   231

Aggression and Health Issues   232
The Type A Personality and Coronary Heart Disease   232
Hostility and Heart Disease   233
Hostility and Anger in Hypertension and Coronary Heart Disease   233
Cynical Hostility   234
Hostility, TABP, and Plasma Lipids   234

■ *Practical Application 8-1*
Learning to Manage Anger   235
Main Points   236

Part Three   Emotions and Motivation

Chapter Nine

Emotions, Stress, and Health   239

Emotions and Motivation   240
  The Definition of Emotions   240
  The Universal Nature of Emotions   241
  The Role of Appraisal in Emotions   241
■ *Practical Application 9-1*
Using Emotions to Identify Goals, Motives, and Concerns   242
What Is Stress?   243
  The Definition of Stress   243
  Stress as a Fight-or-Flight Response   243
The Biological Component of Stress   244
  The Sympathetic/Adrenal and the Pituitary/Adrenal Responses   244
  Stress and the Immune System   246
The Learned Component of Stress   249
  Unpredictability and the Stress Response   249
  Learning How to Respond to Stress   252
  Social Factors and Stress: The Workplace Example   252
The Cognitive Component of Stress   254
  Problem-Focused and Emotion-Focused Coping   254
  Situational Factors and Personal Control   255
Moderators of Stress   256
■ *Practical Application 9-2*
Pet Ownership and Health   256
  The Biological Component   257
  The Learned Component   257
■ *Practical Application 9-3*
Becoming a Constructive Thinker   260
  The Cognitive Component   262
■ *Practical Application 9-4*
Some Rules for Dealing with Stress   264
Stress and Health   267
The Cancer Model   267
  The Biological Component   268
  The Learned Component   268
  The Cognitive Component   269
Main Points   271

Chapter Ten

Goal-Incongruent (Negative) Emotions: Fear and Anxiety, Pessimism and Depression, Guilt and Shame   273

Fear and Anxiety   274
  The Biological Component   274
  The Learned Component   275
  The Cognitive Component   277
Pessimism and Depression   280
  The Biological Component of Depression   281
■ *Practical Application 10-1*
Modern Individualism and the Rise of Depression   282
  The Learned Component of Depression   284
  The Cognitive Component of Depression   288
■ *Practical Application 10-2*
Cognitive Theory and Depression: Learning the Art of Constructive Thinking   294
Guilt and Shame   296
  The Biological Component   297
  The Learned Component   298
  The Cognitive Component   299
■ *Practical Application 10-3*
Managing Excessive Guilt and Shame   300
  Negative Emotions and Goal-Directed Behavior   302
Main Points   302

Chapter Eleven

Goal-Congruent (Positive) Emotions: Happiness, Hope and Optimism, Attachment and Belongingness   305

Hedonism and Happiness   306
  Hedonism   306
  Cognitive Theories of Happiness   307
  Hedonic Enjoyment and Hedonic Happiness   307

Happiness and Coping Behavior   308
   The Biological Component   308
   The Learned Component   309
   The Cognitive Component   309

Happiness from Confronting Fear and
   Uncertainty   310
   The Biological Component   311
   The Learned Component   312
   The Cognitive Component   312

The Motivation for Thrill-Seeking   313
   *The Interaction of Biological, Learned, and Cognitive
      Variables   313*
   *Self-Efficacy and the Dual Route to Anxiety
      Control   313*
   Self-Efficacy Theory and Thrill Seeking   316
   Some Concluding Remarks   316

Optimism and Hope   318
   Introduction   318
   The Biological Component   319
   The Learned Component   319

■ *Practical Application 11-1*
**How to Become an Optimist:
The ABCDE Method   320**
   The Cognitive Component   324
   Optimism and Competence   326

Belongingness, Attachment, and
   Community   326
   The Biological Component   327
   The Learned Component   329

■ *Practical Application 11-2*
Belongingness and the Immune Response   330
   The Cognitive Component   331

Main Points   332

Part Four   Growth Motivation and Self-Regulation

Chapter Twelve

Curiosity, Exploratory Behavior, Sensation Seeking, and Creativity   335

Exploratory Behavior   336
   The Behaviorist Explanation   336
   Challenges to Behaviorism   336
   Variety, Novelty, and Complexity   338
   The Biological Component   339
   The Learned Component   339
   The Cognitive Component   341

Extrinsic Motivation   346
   Extrinsic Motivation and Exploration   346
   Individual Differences and Extrinsic Motivation   347

Sensation Seeking   347
■ *Practical Application 12-1*
Facilitating Intrinsic Motivation   348
   The Biological Component   349

Practical Application 12-2
Are You a High or Low Sensation Seeker?   350

   The Learned Component   350
   The Cognitive Component   352

Creativity   353
   The Biological Component   354
   The Learned Component   355
   The Cognitive Component   357

■ *Practical Application 12-3*
Motivating Creativity by Asking, "What If?"   360
Main Points   363

Chapter Thirteen

Predictability and Control, Achievement and Mastery, and Self-Esteem   365

The Need for Predictability and Control   366
   Control and Health   366
   The Biological Component   367
   The Learned Component   367
   The Cognitive Component   368
   Control and Mastery   369

Mastery and Achievement Motivation   369

Achievement Motivation   370

  The Biological Component   370

■ *Practical Application 13-1*
Competence: Lessons for Parents and Teachers   371

  The Learned Component   372

  The Cognitive Component   373

■ *Practical Application 13-2*
Inducing People to Accept Challenges   376

Self-Esteem   379

  The Definition of Self-Esteem   380

  The Origins of Self-Esteem   381

  The Perpetuation of Low Self-Esteem   382

  *Self-Esteem and Reactions to Success and
    Failure   383*

  The Development of Self-Esteem   383

■ *Practical Application 13-3*
***Managing Self-Doubt after Failure: Downward
Comparison   384***

■ *Practical Application 13-4*
Learning Not to Overgeneralize after Failure   388

Main Points   389

Chapter Fourteen

Self-Regulation of Motivation   391

The Self-Regulation of Behavior   392

Setting Goals   393

  Proximal and Distal Goals   393

  Setting Difficult but Attainable Goals   394

  Feedback   394

  *Self-Set Goals, Assigned Goals, and
    Commitment   394*

  The Need for Challenging Goals   395

  Discrepancy Hypotheses   395

  Self-Efficacy Theory   396

  *Strategy Development: Making Plans and Making
    Adjustments   397*

Managing Emotions, Moods,
  and Self-Doubt   398

  Dealing with Self-Doubt   399

  Developing Good Thinking Habits   400

  Dreams, Images, and Visualization   400

■ *Practical Application 14-1*
Preparing for Setbacks and Hard Work   401

  Aspiration as Distal Goals   402

Self-Regulation and the Self-Concept   402

  Self-Knowledge and Self-Regulatory Functions   403

  Possible Selves   404

  Implicit Theories   407

■ *Practical Application 14-2*
How to Create Possible Selves   408

An Overview: Becoming a Process-Oriented
  Person   414

Main Points   414

References   416

Author Index   450

Subject Index   459

Preface

For centuries, scholars from diverse backgrounds and disciplines have speculated about what motivates humans. Explanations have ranged from those that suggest that human behavior is totally determined—such as by our genetic structure—to those that suggest that humans have complete control over their destiny—they have a will. It wasn't until around the turn of the century that many of these diverse explanations were subjected to any scientific scrutiny. As a result, we now have a much clearer understanding of what motivates humans. It turns out that we are not born to play out a predetermined role in this universe, nor do we have complete freedom to do what we want. We are limited by our biology but interestingly we are also limited by our failure to dream; thoughts and ideas do make a difference. Sometimes by making small changes we not only alter the course of our own behavior but we can, at least to some degree, alter the course of behavior of others. One implication of this is that we can change the course of history—a controversial but exciting idea.

This book is divided into four parts. In Part 1 we examine the major issues and organizing principles that delineate the topic of motivation. Chapter 1 starts with a discussion of the major issues in motivation and ends with a brief overview of the major theories that have been proposed to account for motivated behavior. I argue, based on empirical research, that the best way to understand motivation is to analyze various motivation systems in terms of their primary components: biological, learned, and cognitive. In Chapter 2 we examine in detail what it means to take a components approach and what it means when we say that behavior has a biological basis, a learned basis, or a cognitive basis.

In Part 2 we analyze several basic motivational systems from a components perspective. We start in Chapter 3 by examining not only why people eat, but why some people are inclined to become overweight. We look at the fascinating and perplexing question of why people who become overweight find it so difficult to shed those excess pounds. In Chapter 4 we examine the whole issue of sexual behavior: Why is it that some people are promiscuous and others are not? Why do some people stay in love while others do not? Why are some people attracted to members of the same sex while others are attracted to members of the opposite sex? In Chapter 5 we analyze peak performance. As we all know, the ability to attain peak performance is often difficult. The reason is that peak performance requires that we simultaneously attain an optimal state of arousal, focus our attention on the task at hand, and rid our brain of thoughts that might undermine our performance. In Chapter 6 we look at the links between alertness, ability to process information, quality of sleep, and the tendency to dream. We will look at such questions as why our ability to process information is often impaired when we don't get enough sleep or the right kind of sleep, or don't dream. In Chapter 8 we look at the whole question of drug use, drug abuse, and drug addiction. Since drug use seems, at least on the surface, to be maladaptive, we examine what it is about our biology, the environment, and the way we think that leads individuals to take drugs. In Chapter 9 we examine the whole question of aggression and coercive behavior. It has been suggested that one of the things that has helped us to survive as a species is our aggressive nature. How do we reconcile this with the observation that human aggression is one of society's major problems?

In Part 3 we examine the role that emotions play in motivation. While it was common in the past to treat emotions as distinct from motivation, the current view is that emotions play an integral role in motivation. They can both sustain and undermine goal-directed behavior, for example. That means if we are to attain the goals we have set for ourselves, we need to insure that our emotions are congruent with our goals; otherwise we will find it impossible to reach our goals.

In this section on emotions, we begin with a discussion of stress. Psychologists have done a great deal of work on stress and have shown that the management of stress is perhaps one of the most important things that we need to learn if we want to live happy and successful lives. Research on this topic is abundant and the implications are clear: stress not only tends to undermine goal-directed behavior; it tends to undermine our health. Although health is not the main focus of this book, we will see that motivation and health are intimately linked.

In addition to stress, there are a number of other goal-incongruent emotions that we need to learn to manage. In Chapter 10 we examine fear and anxiety, which have been shown, over and over, to undermine goal-directed behavior. Fear and anxiety often paralyze people into inaction. We also examine pessimism and depression. It has been shown repeatedly that people who adopt a pessimistic attitude often become depressed, and when people become depressed, motivation virtually ceases. Recent work on guilt and shame indicate again that these emotions are highly debilitating and also undermine goal-directed behavior.

The main goal-congruent emotions are happiness, hope, optimism, attachment, belongingness, and empathy. In Chapter 11 we review research that shows being happy, hopeful, or optimistic helps us persist in our pursuit of goals. One of the main antecedents of achievement and success, it has been found, is a willingness to persist. In the course of examining goal-directed behavior, researchers have found that people who tend to succeed in achieving their goals are characterized by such qualities as relatedness. While some people adopt the view that they do not need other people, research indicates that people who accept and develop their social skills tend to be more successful than those who do not. Additionally, they tend to be physically and psychologically healthier. In this chapter we will also examine the motivation for risk-taking behavior. Risk-taking behavior is a sign of positive health and adjustment, whereas its absence is a sign of neuroticism.

In Part 4 we talk about growth motivation. The idea that organisms are motivated toward development and growth has captured the imagination of many motivation theorists. As more and more research is being done, it is becoming increasingly clear to many theorists that humans have an innate disposition to realize their potential.

If the motivation for growth is innate in humans (and perhaps in animals to some degree), then why do people not all grow at the same rate? Why do some people succeed while others do not? Why do some people have big dreams while others do not? The answer is starting to emerge. Not all people are equipped to the same degree with the ability to do at least two things: to manage their emotions and to set goals. The new focus in motivation is that people need to learn not only how to manage their emotions (such as the emotion of self-doubt), but they need to learn how to set appropriate goals. The exciting thing is that people can be taught these skills. This new focus for motivation has been called the self-regulation of emotion.

In Chapter 12 we examine the early work on growth motivation that came out of the research on curiosity and exploratory behavior. It was this early work on curiosity and exploratory behavior that led theorists to suggest that organisms are characterized by a tendency towards growth. People are innately motivated to find out all they can about the world in which they live. We will also examine creativity and attempt to show that creativity grows out of the motivation to discover all that life has to offer. Certain people called sensation seekers appear to be born with a stronger curiosity and exploratory drive. As a result of this strong drive, they tend, among other things, to be more creative and unconventional. In Chapter 13 we review research which shows that humans are motivated to become competent—something that has its roots in the need to control. It is from their sense of competency and achievements that people develop a sense of self-esteem and self-worth.

Finally, in Chapter 14 we review a portion of the research on self-regulation of behavior. We examine, among other things, the principles of goal setting, the principles for managing one's emotions, and the principles for fine tuning one's goal-directed behavior. In this chapter we look at the research pertaining to the way people can learn to manage their thinking so that they can become fully functional and fully self-actualizing. We also discuss how a person can develop a fully differentiated self-concept. It is out of a fully developed and differentiated self-concept that we set difficult goals and entertain the idea that there are possible selves. In the final analysis, it is from developing a highly differentiated self-concept that people come to achieve their true potential.

Although this book was written mainly for psychology majors, I have kept in mind that motivation is interesting to just about everyone. Over the years I have had students from business, counseling, education, engineering, nursing, physical education, and social work who took my course because they felt that knowing something about human motivation would help them in their chosen professions. Others students in such fields as art, history, and philosophy have said they simply want to know something about their own personal motivation. Because motivation courses often attract such a diverse population, I have tried to make the book easily understood by readers with little background in psychology yet challenging to those who are familiar with the subject.

Many people have contributed directly or indirectly to the preparation of this book. Students in the various motivation classes that I teach have given me inspiration and the feedback that helped shape the organization and the context. Discussions with colleagues and graduate students have helped sharpen my thinking. To all those people I say thank you. A special thanks to Dan Skarlicki, who helped sharpen my thinking on the topic of justice.

Two secretaries in my Department, Alison Wiigs and Elfrienda Koch, deserve special recognition for all their efforts. They have helped me in numerous ways, such as proofing and faxing and arranging for couriers.

I thank all the reviewers who gave me many wonderful suggestions. Had I incorporated all their wonderful ideas and suggestions, this book would have been twice its present length. They are: Caran Colvin, San Francisco State University; Donna Hardy, CSU–Northridge; Wayne Harrison, University of Nebraska at Omaha; Carol Hayes, Delta State University; Robert Johnston, College of William & Mary; Michael McCall, Cornell University; Donald Meltzer, Southern Illinois University at Carbondale; Ronald Ribble, University of Texas–San Antonio; Rex Wright, University of Alabama, Birmingham.

I want to thank my editor, Jim Brace-Thompson, for his help and support throughout this project, which at times seemed endless. Also thanks to all the people at Brooks/Cole in the production phase who did the figures, the layout, the cover, the permissions, the copyediting, and the proofing. Your efforts are greatly appreciated.

Finally, I thank my wife Helen, and my children Ryan and Renee, who have given me so much love and support over the years.

Chapter One

What Causes Action:
Themes in the Study of Motivation

■ *What causes behavior?*

■ *Do all behaviors represent an attempt to adapt? What about drug use?*

■ *Where does energy (motivation) come from?*

■ *What gives behavior direction?*

■ *Why do some people persist while others give up?*

■ *Why are some people more motivated than others?*

■ *Do humans have instincts?*

■ *How much of our behavior is learned?*

■ *Do humans really have a will?*

Chris looks at his watch. It is 8 A.M. Outside the window, the sky is clear and the sun is shining; it looks like it's going to be a great day. Suddenly, his thoughts turn to mountain climbing. He imagines himself executing a difficult move, while his friend looks on in admiration. This brief fantasy gives him a warm and satisfied feeling. As he heads towards the bathroom, he notices the pile of books on his desk, and the warm feeling fades. The philosophy paper he was assigned isn't falling into place, and he isn't sure what he should do. A feeling of tenseness begins to take hold. While he brushes his teeth, his thoughts turn back to climbing. If there is one thing Chris really likes, it's climbing. He has an idea: Why not go climbing for a few hours? It would help clear his head and help get his thoughts together. Then he could finish the paper later. Impressed by that logic, Chris picks up the phone and begins dialing his friend. The warm feeling begins to return.

We are constantly faced with choices. Should we do what our heart tells us, or what our head tells us? Should we think about our future, or should we enjoy life now? Chris decided to follow his feelings, but another person might think, "If I work hard on my paper I might be able to take some time off tomorrow to do some climbing." Still another person might reason, "If I do well in my classes, I can do some climbing in the summer."

These choices can have significant consequences. For example, research shows that the ability to delay short-term gratification is an important element of achievement and success. One study found that children who were better able to delay immediate gratification at the age of 4 were more academically competent and had greater ability to deal with stress when they reached adolescence (Shoda, Mischel, & Peake, 1990). The ability to delay immediate gratification seems to be linked to some underlying personality qualities that have a genetic basis. One such quality is impulsivity. People who are high in impulsivity tend to engage in activities that have an immediate short-term appeal (Zuckerman, 1994). Accordingly, they are likely to have difficulty in delaying short-term gratification. Likewise, there is evidence that some people are attracted to novelty; anything new or different tends to capture their attention. Like impulsivity, this tendency appears to be inherited. For example, even at

3 days old, children have been found to differ in their interest in novelty, and this difference can be linked to an enzyme that they have inherited (Sostek, Sostek, Murphy, Martin, & Born, 1981). The bottom line is that the ability to delay gratification involves something more than self-control.

The environments in which we have been raised also seem to shape our ability to delay gratification. In particular, environments that show there is a benefit to delaying gratification tend to produce children who are better at doing so (e.g., Bandura & Mischel, 1965). It makes sense that children who understand the advantage of delaying gratification in return for a later reward would tend to include that behavior in their repertoire.

What role does volition play in this process? A growing body of research indicates that people can actively learn to take control of their lives by learning how to self-regulate. As we will see in the last chapter, self-regulation involves altering patterns of thinking. It starts with learning to self-monitor. With self-monitoring, people learn to correct their faulty thinking. For example, let's look back at Chris. He told himself that climbing for a few hours would help clear his head, so that he could finish his paper later. Do we really believe that Chris is only going for a few hours? Is he really going to come right home afterwards, or will he and his friend celebrate their climb with a few beers? When he comes home, how likely is he to start on his paper? What about the effects of alcohol on his ability to think?

If Chris is trained to monitor his thinking carefully and to reflect on the likely outcome of his decisions, he can probably learn to delay gratification, at least to some degree. Because of his impulsive nature, he may never have as much self-control as others; nevertheless, he should be able to gain a great deal more control.

We are constantly faced with decisions of all kinds, and the decisions that we make often have far-reaching implications. In this book, we will examine the forces—biological, learned, and cognitive—that shape our choices.

We will begin by considering some of the themes that are central to the thinking of motivational theorists and then briefly survey some of the major theories proposed by motivational psychologists over the years. It will be easier to understand current theoretical explanations of behavior if we understand some of the concerns of past theorists.

Theories represent an attempt to make sense out of a certain body of facts. It is the goal of every theorist to account for the greatest number of facts with the fewest possible concepts. Thus, as we will see, most theorists attempt to organize facts around a few central constructs. The theories reviewed in this chapter were successful, at least for a period of time, because they were able to explain an existing body of facts. However, research is always producing new facts. When theories lose their power to explain the available data, they need to be modified or perhaps abandoned. Some of the theories that we will discuss have lost their explanatory power, but they have provided an important legacy of psychological constructs. If we understand the classic theories, we will better understand why current theories have taken their present form.

What Causes Behavior?

Motivation theorists start with the assumption that, for every behavior, there is a cause. Their goal is to identify those causes. Motivation theorists tend to be eclectic; they draw on findings and principles from different disciplines. In the past, books about motivation were written from a single disciplinary perspective. They might attempt to explain behavior solely from an analysis of biological mechanisms, for example. That tradition died because it was not possible to explain all behaviors in terms of a single underlying mechanism or system.

Motivation theorists want to know what instigates behavior. While it is important to show that behaviors change as a result of certain interventions—for instance, therapy or the administration of rewards—motivation theorists want to get to the root cause: What causes action? They want to know what role is played by biology, learning, and cognition.

In the 1960s and 1970s, when learning theorists were able to show that a wide variety of behaviors could be increased, decreased, or changed by administering rewards, many psychologists and laypeople came to believe that most—if not all—human behavior can be explained on the basis of learning principles. It was only after it was demonstrated that there are pervasive constraints on what we can and cannot learn

that psychologists began to moderate their extravagant claims about the role of learning in our lives. Finally, with the demonstration by cognitive psychologists that thinking causes behavior and does not merely accompany it, the argument that all behavior could be explained by the principles of learning was put to rest. Learning is central to understanding action but is not the only cause.

Approach and Avoidant Causes

Psychologists distinguish between approach causes and avoidant causes. In approach behavior, people do things because of something they want, desire, or need. This is often conceptualized in terms of a specific goal object; they may, for example, want to eat a sandwich because they are hungry. Sometimes the want, desire, or need does not immediately give rise to a specific goal object. If we want independence, for example, we cannot visualize a single object; we may think of a variety of things—for example, having our own room, having a car, or having money.

In avoidant behavior, people do things to avoid something. Once again, that can often be defined in terms of a specific goal object. Fear of insects or snakes falls in this category. Anxiety, by contrast, may not immediately elicit a specific goal object. People who are anxious are often unable to specify the source; they simply experience a generalized sense of dread.

Avoidant causes tend to be very compelling; that is, they are not only aversive and/or noxious but also difficult—or impossible—to ignore. People who are afraid of insects or snakes, for example, feel a strong and immediate need to distance themselves from those goal objects. Because people are often unable to specify the source of their anxiety, they attempt to deal with it by finding a safe place. For example, a person who experiences anxiety at a party, without knowing its exact source, may decide to leave. It seems that the reason avoidant causes are so compelling is that they often involve threats to our survival. From a biological perspective, two primary goals are to survive and reproduce. If anything poses a threat to our survival, we need to deal with it immediately.

Even avoidant causes that do not threaten our survival tend to evoke the same reaction. Some theorists (e.g., LeDoux, 1996) have suggested that humans and animals are designed (or have evolved) to err on the side of being cautious, because it is better to treat something as a threat and survive than to take the risk that it is not and die.

Not all people are equally anxious; some are more anxious from birth (Watson & Clark, 1984). As a result, they are more likely to engage in avoidant behaviors. Even the thought of certain activities is enough to make them anxious. They may avoid eating certain foods because they fear they will get sick; they may avoid traveling for fear of injury; or they may avoid meeting new people in the hope of avoiding conflicts of opinion. In contrast, extraverts and sensation seekers spend more time in approach behaviors. They see the world as a source of opportunities and excitement. They may go to new restaurants to savor different foods; they may talk to strangers in cafes to see how other people think; or they may take risks, such as hang gliding or traveling the world (Zuckerman, 1994).

Basic Themes of Contemporary Motivation Theories

As a preliminary overview of contemporary motivation theories, let's look at some fundamental concepts.

Behavior Represents an Attempt to Adapt

A central theme of contemporary motivation theory is that all behavior represents an attempt to adapt to the environment. Operating on that underlying assumption, motivation theorists then ask about the origin of that adaptive behavior: What mechanisms or principles will allow us to explain it? Scientists often determine whether they understand the cause of an event by asking themselves if they can predict the conditions under which it will occur. Over the years, psychologists have developed a very sophisticated methodology to help them identify causes.

If all behaviors represent an attempt to adapt to the environment, how do we account for behaviors—such as taking drugs—that do not seem to be adaptive? To answer that question, motivation theorists consider

Building a home represents an attempt to adapt to the environment.

whether behaviors such as drug taking involve some of the adaptive mechanisms involved in other behaviors. As it turns out, there is considerable evidence that taking drugs triggers certain adaptive mechanisms. Many drug researchers have concluded that people use drugs to trigger the release of chemicals that are normally released only when we engage in adaptive behavior. The drugs short-circuit the normal adaptive route, so that, instead of rewarding an adaptive response, as it was designed to do, the chemical acts as a reward for drug taking. Adopting this perspective, we begin to understand that drug taking may reflect, at least under certain conditions, an attempt by humans to adapt.

The Importance of Determining What Arouses and Energizes Behavior

Humans interact with their environment in two basic ways: They need to master the environment, on the one hand, while looking out for their survival, on the other (e.g., White, 1959). In addressing these needs, humans often experience a conflict: Do they put their survival needs first, or do they put their mastery needs first? A great deal of research suggests that survival needs will take precedence. If I am in the middle of learning something new and my survival needs are threatened, I will abandon learning in favor of survival.

Research suggests that I have no choice in this matter. My nervous system is designed to insure that I attend to survival needs. When I am threatened, the part of the brain that deals with survival takes over and runs my behavior. Sensory input into the brain simultaneously travels along two distinct routes: One route takes the message to the part of our brain that deals with threats; the other route takes the message to the part of our brain that deals with rational analysis. The survival route always gets the message first, and that is presumably why my initial reaction is often emotional (LeDoux, 1992). Since the system that analyzes threats is very crude, it can be wrong. When the rational brain analyzes the situation more carefully, it may decide that my survival is not being threatened and try to shut down the emotional system. For example, if someone criticizes a paper I have written, my nervous system may react as though that person has physically attacked me. Instead of reacting in a rational way (calm, cool, and collected, like Mr. Spock of *Star Trek*), I respond with an insult. At one level of awareness, I may know that this behavior is inappropriate, but I find it impossible to control myself. Psychologists have come to discover that our nervous system often reacts as though our survival is being threatened in our daily lives.

By knowing what events in the environment arouse survival circuitry in the brain, we can better understand why people react as they do. The arousal of brain circuitry and the energization of behavior are closely linked. Once activated, the neural circuitry related to survival often remains active until the arrival of feedback that the threat is no longer present. Knowing how to shut down this circuitry, therefore, is criti-

cal. We all know people who have carried anger about some event for years. Research shows that such anger not only gets in the way of new learning but has negative health implications. Obviously, for the motivation theorist, understanding what arouses and energizes a behavior is fundamental.

Understanding What Governs the Direction of Behavior

Without direction, we would not be able to survive. Getting food, for example, demands that we engage in goal-directed behavior. Not only must we focus our attention on one alternative rather than another, but we must sustain that focus until our hunger needs are met. Need theory suggested that needs are what give direction to behavior (e.g., Murray, 1938). According to this explanation, when a need is aroused, we are more or less automatically pushed in the right direction. Research has shown that this explanation is inadequate. Both past learning and how we think about things (our cognitions) also play an important role. For example, some people eat not only to get nourishment but also to entertain themselves or to escape; others become restrained eaters because they want to be thin. According to current thinking, needs are conceptualized as dispositions; that is, they may give the impetus and even some of the direction for certain behaviors, but by themselves they do not fully explain why people do what they do.

Goal theory suggests that goals give rise to actions (Locke & Latham, 1990). According to this theory, goals create a tension, individuals move towards the goal in order to reduce that tension. Thus, both the direction and the energy for behavior are due to the goals. Where do these goals come from? They may have their origins in our biology, our learning, or our thinking; typically, however, the goal that ultimately motivates us is a blend of all three. Though the need for energy may create the biological drive we call hunger, what we decide to eat (our goal object) is shaped by our past habits and our thinking. While our initial impulse might be to eat a hamburger (an old habit), we may decide instead to have a plate of pasta because we have come to be concerned about the amount of fat in our diet (a new cognition or way of thinking).

Understanding Persistence

It is perhaps the motivational psychologist's interest in persistence, more than anything else, that distinguishes motivation from other branches of psychology. For example, persistence is one of the main predictors of success (e.g., Seligman, 1990); it is often much more important than academic intelligence. Traditional reward theory suggests that we are inclined to repeat behaviors that make us feel good (positive reinforcement) and discontinue behaviors that make us feel bad (negative reinforcement). Withdrawal of rewards is normally sufficient to produce the extinction of a learned response. According to traditional reward theory, events that make us feel bad (aversive or noxious stimuli) will be avoided. We might assume, therefore, that experiencing adversity and failure would cause an individual to give up. Interestingly, while some give up, others persist.

Over the years, numerous theories have been advanced to account for persistence of behavior in the face of no reward, adversity, and failure. One of the early explanations suggested that frustration cues that arise when we are not rewarded after we reach a goal actually become conditioned to the approach response (Amsel, 1962). According to this explanation, negative feelings come to act as a signal that reward is forthcoming. This idea is analogous to the old maxim of aerobics instructors: "No pain, no gain." While this turned out to be a very powerful explanation, it was based on the idea that behavior must be rewarded intermittently. What about persistence when there are no rewards? A more cognitive explanation suggests that persistence grows out of intrinsic motivation (e.g., Deci & Ryan, 1991). According to intrinsic theories of motivation, people come to believe that engaging in a certain behavior will result in a certain outcome. Many intrinsic motivation theories propose that the reward comes from mastering or developing competence; that is, while the carrot at the end of the path provides the direction for behavior, the process of mastering or developing competence provides the immediate reward that sustains the goal-directed behavior.

One difficulty with such theories is they cannot fully explain why people persist when they seemingly are making no progress towards a goal. According to intrinsic motivation theories, progress towards the goal rewards or provides the motivation for behavior. Why, then, do individuals persist when they are making no discernible progress? It has been suggested that people who persist under these conditions have developed optimism or hope; that is, they have learned to dismiss or manage adversity and failure (Seligman, 1990; Snyder et al., 1991). We will be considering optimism and hope in a later chapter.

Beyond its theoretical interest, understanding the nature and origins of persistence is also important from an applied perspective. In order to succeed, people need to learn how to persist in the face of failure and adversity.

Understanding the Role of Feelings

Motivation theorists have always been interested in how people feel. As we'll see, most motivation theories have addressed the question in terms of how much positive or negative *affect* is associated with a particular event. A central assumption of affect theories is that people approach things in order to experience positive affect and avoid things in order not to experience negative affect.

The distinction between approach and avoidant motivation, which we discussed earlier, is based on the idea that feelings are an important determinant of behavior. Current research indicates that feelings are often due to chemical reactions in our body or brain (e.g., Zuckerman, 1994). In other words, they are real and not imagined. Some theorists have suggested that we should monitor our feelings in order to guide our actions, because our feelings are more closely linked to our survival than is rational thought (LeDoux, 1992). Others have argued that feelings represent a more primitive part of the brain at work. According to this perspective, our feeling brain hasn't caught up with the computer age, and therefore we need to learn to ignore our feelings.

Whether listening to our feelings is going to increase our chances of survival or make us more happy is not clear. What I think is clear is that negative feelings tend to undermine goal-directed behavior and positive feelings tend to sustain goal-directed behavior.

That is why motivation theorists today are interested in understanding feelings.

Accounting for Individual Differences

While evolutionary psychologists and others are interested only in general principles of behavior, motivation theorists are interested in why individuals behave the way they do. Evolutionary psychologists, for example, argue that the ultimate motivation for sexual behavior is an underlying biological inclination to insure that our genes survive in future generations. The immediate pleasure or reward that we get from sexual behavior is merely a mechanism in service of that goal. They further argue that, in order to insure that their genes survive in future generations, the best strategy for males is to mate with as many females as possible, in order to produce as many offspring as possible. Even if some die, others will survive. They go on to argue that the best strategy for females is very different. Since the female carries the offspring, she is more limited in her ability to produce large numbers of offspring. Instead of quantity, she must seek quality. It has been suggested that the female will look for mates who can provide qualities such as strength and intelligence that would help her offspring to survive (Buss, 1994).

Even though that principle may help explain gender differences, it does not explain individual differences within each gender. Both males and females differ greatly in terms of their promiscuity. Why are there such differences within the genders? According to motivation theorists, there are other forces at work that modify certain underlying biological tendencies. It appears that both learned and cognitive factors can modify, at least to some degree, the way individuals behave. The challenge is to understand how, when, and why learning can exert such a powerful role over our underlying biology.

The Question of Self-Regulating Behavior

Like clinical psychologists, motivation theorists believe that it is possible to help people regulate their behavior. While clinical psychologists tend to focus on how to make people more normal, motivational psycholo-

gists are more concerned with what makes people exceptional: How did this person become the President of the United States? How did this individual become a rock star? How did this person muster the energy and skills to climb the highest mountain in the world?

Motivation theorists are fascinated with discovering why someone of average talent unexpectedly succeeds or why someone of exceptional talent unexpectedly fails. For the motivational theorist, the answer can be found in motivational principles. If the underlying reasons can be identified, then people can be taught how to alter the course of their lives. In the last chapter of this book, we will look at the work of motivation theorists who believe that, at least to some degree, humans can learn to self-regulate their behavior and thereby control their lives.

Do Humans Have a Will?

One of the most controversial ideas in all of psychology is that humans have a will (volition). The idea of will implies that people can create their own destiny. It has been suggested, for example, that people can create new possible selves, and then construct paths that will enable them to become one of those possible selves (e.g., Markus & Nurius, 1986). In other words, humans can dream (fantasize) about possible selves—about achieving some goal, becoming a different person, or doing something they have never done before. Next, they can adopt one of these possible selves as their goal, and then, by coupling such a goal with knowledge of how to achieve goals, can make their dreams a reality. Such theories suggest that people are not mere products of biology or the environment in which they live. Instead of being passive individuals reacting to the forces about them, they can actively construct a world in which they see themselves succeeding and achieving. In Chapter 14, we will examine the research that allows us to entertain the possibility of rising above the forces that strive to control us.

The concept of volition suggests that there are few—if any—limits on what we can do and what we can become. Most psychologists believe that there are limits placed on us by our biology, our ability to learn, and our ability to think and solve problems. In order to change, we need to work within those limitations. For example, while individuals can often learn to play the piano with some proficiency, they may not have the underlying talent to become a concert pianist. Similarly, while individuals may learn to do certain arithmetic calculations with some speed, they will never be able to compete with computers.

Most psychologists hold to a more limited view of volition that has come to be called *self-regulation of behavior*. According to the concept of self-regulation, we can learn to do things that will enable us to make certain changes in our lives: for example, to better focus our attention, to set goals, to generate paths to goals, and to avoid negative thinking. In short, we can learn to maximize skills and abilities that we already possess or we learn to develop new skills through careful thought and practice.

Theories of Motivation: A Historical Survey

Over the years, many different motivation theories have been advanced. Each of these theories has grown out of a somewhat different focus or concern. While the theories that I will discuss are very different in many respects, they all have grown out of a similar concern, to account for the arousal, direction and persistence of behavior. Those three words are what define the focus of motivation. While other disciplines in psychology are also concerned about arousal, direction and persistence of behavior, it is these three that are at the core of any motivational analysis.

In this chapter, I will identify some of the major issues and concerns that have shaped the development of motivation as we know it today. There are at least six major lines of inquiry that can be identified. Each of these grew out of an attempt to conceptualize motivation from a somewhat different perspective. These are: (1) instinct theories, (2) drive/learning theories, (3) need/personality theories, (4) growth and mastery motivation theories, (5) humanistic theories, and (6) cognitive theories.

I should warn the reader that my presentation of the various theories is very brief. Many of the theories I present were modified and, therefore, had greater ex-

planatory scope than I suggest in my discussion. My goal here is to identify the key concepts that gave rise to each of these theories.

Instinct Theories

The idea of instinct can be traced to such early writers as Thomas Aquinas. In order to explain why animals tended to behave adaptively, he suggested that they were equipped with instincts that provided the energy, direction, and persistence of behavior. Instincts were conceptualized as "purposive activities implanted in the animal by nature or the creator for the guidance of the creature in the attainment of ends useful to it in its own preservation or the preservation of the species, and the avoidance of the contrary" (Wilm, 1925, p. 40). While we would use different language today, the underlying idea remains essentially the same.

Thomas Aquinas believed that animals had instincts, but he did not accept that humans had instincts. He argued that humans had a dual nature—physical and nonphysical, or body and mind (intellect)—but that the physical side of humans was governed by different laws than those governing animals. The reason for this distinction came from the idea that humans were a special creation of God. Among other things, they were equipped with a soul and rational thought, and consequently could be held responsible for their actions. The problem with instincts, as initially conceptualized, was that instincts, rather than the soul or rational thought, were believed to cause behavior. Consequently, Aquinas offered two distinct theories of motivation: one for animals and one for humans.

Many early scientists grappled with the profound similarity between animal and human motivation. Superficially, it appeared that humans and animals operated by the same laws. At the same time, there seemed to be profound differences. René Descartes (1596–1650) provided an explanation that reconciled these two views. He suggested that the behavior of the body, below the level of willed action, could be explained mechanically (instincts), but behaviors that had to do with such things as moral conduct were under the control of the will. Descartes argued that the body and the mind (will, soul) interacted, and he suggested that the site of the interaction was the pineal gland. Certain physical acts, such as sexual behavior, were under the control of the mind and not simply the product of some mechanical mechanism.

This dualistic conception appealed to both the scientists and the Catholic church. According to Descartes' explanation, humans could be held responsible for their moral actions, a position that was consistent with the church's idea of special creation. The Catholic church, apparently feeling threatened by the view that human motivation could perhaps be explained in terms of instincts, had forbidden scientists from pursuing this question. Having accepted Descartes' view, the authorities relaxed that ban.

Descartes' position raised an issue with which psychologists have grappled ever since: Exactly how do the biological and cognitive sides of a person interact? Is it true that our cognitive side has ultimate control? Are there times when the cognitive side loses control? In criminal proceedings, for example, the question of insanity has very important implications. Similarly, a finding of medical abnormalities can dramatically alter the question of whether a person can be held responsible for his or her actions.

Evolutionary Theory

Although Descartes suggested that humans may share some of the instincts observed in animals, he maintained that we, unlike animals, could control those instincts. Evolutionary theory aroused the wrath of the Catholic church by suggesting that human motivation was due to the same processes that give rise to animal behavior.

Charles Darwin argued that the physical features of animals and humans and also their behavior were due to their biological structure. He further argued that the underlying biological structure of all species was constantly undergoing change as a result of environmental pressures. This idea, of course, challenged the idea of special creation. He suggested that the mechanism or principle that caused this change was *natural selection*. According to natural selection, members of a species with physical or behavioral attributes that allowed them to better deal with environmental pressures would survive and reproduce; as a result, they would pass along this biological structure to their offspring. In contrast, members of the species that could not survive would not reproduce and their bio-

Charles Darwin

logical structure would, over time, be lost. For example, if certain members of a species could escape their predators because their coloration and patterning allowed them to blend into their environment, they would survive. As a result, their biological characteristics would also survive. However, if the environment changed and their coloration and patterning no longer protected them from predators, they would die before they reproduced and their biological characteristics would be lost.

Mendel, a contemporary of Darwin, advanced the idea of genetics. Although Darwin did not know about Mendel's theories, Darwin's ideas can be explained by genetic theory. According to genetic theory, new genes emerge through a process called mutation. Thus, over time, a species can evolve; it can become more intelligent or more aggressive. Obviously, according to genetic theory, change would take time.

Note that Charles Darwin's contribution was not the discovery of evolution, as people often think; it had already been well documented that selective breeding could be used to produce animals with certain physical characteristics. Darwin's contribution was the suggestion that natural selection is the mechanism by which evolution occurs.

Darwin's work prompted a radical reexamination of the causes and origins of human motivation. Darwin argued that what he had observed in animals also held true for humans; the principles governing humans and animals were the same (Darwin, 1872). Further, evolutionary concepts implied that the route to understanding human behavior lay through observation of humans in relation to their environment. Previously, human behavior had been thought to be largely independent of environmental and biological influences. What governed behavior, it was thought, was the rational mind, which was cultivated, in the growing child, through education and the positive influence of parents and other adults.

Instincts and Motivation

Under Darwin's influence, biologists began to look at motivation in terms of instincts. In their early writings, they compared them to reservoirs. As the reservoir began to fill, it was suggested, it created a force that must be reduced or the reservoir would overflow, perhaps with disastrous consequences. In the early theories of instinct, behaviors were regarded as predetermined or fixed by our biological structure. Instincts were thought to account not only for the arousal of behavior but for the direction and persistence of behavior as well.

Psychologists were also greatly affected by Darwin's ideas. Early psychologists such as McDougall attempted to explain behavior in terms of a limited number of instincts. While that attempt ultimately failed, psychologists have continued to pursue the study of biology. Originally called physiological psychology, this discipline came to be known as the neurosciences when research began to focus on the structure of the brain and nervous system. More recently, the emergence of evolutionary psychology has marked a return to the study of the biological side of behavior from an evolutionary perspective.

Over the years, both biologists and psychologists have come to recognize that beyond inherited factors, learning and cognition also play an important role in behavior. Because the concept of instincts is often understood to imply that the causes of behavior are innate, psychologists tend to avoid this term today. Instead, they speak of genetics or simply biology.

Freud's Instinct Theory

Freud viewed the biological side of humans as providing the energy, or impulse, for behavior (Freud, 1900/1953, 1911/1949, 1915/1934, 1915/1949, 1923/1947). He posited a group of instincts, each with its own source of energy and its appropriate goal object. Although each instinct was hypothesized to have its own source of energy, Freud suggested that they all drew their energy from a general source called *libido*. Unlike the biologists who saw instincts as providing not only the energy but the direction for behavior, Freud viewed instincts as basically an energy source, with the direction of behavior subject to some of the principles of learning and cognition. The process was assumed to work as follows. When the energy associated with one of the instincts built up, it would become a source of tension for the person. To reduce the tension, the person would be inclined to seek out the appropriate goal object. Freud suggested that instincts give rise to representations of the goal object. He suggested, however, that humans could, and often did, substitute goal objects that could partially drain off the goal energy. For example, certain artistic endeavors (dancing, painting, music) might be used to symbolically replace the real goal object. The problem, as Freud conceptualized it, is that, in the course of development, certain goal objects have been associated with punishment, and therefore, rather than approach the goal object, the person will tend to avoid it. For example, a child who has been taught that sex is dirty or bad may be inclined to avoid sex as an adult; a child taught that it is bad to show anger may inhibit the natural tendency to express aggression.

Two things can happen when goal objects have been blocked. First, the person can learn to make alternative plans for attaining those goal objects; this process leads to the development of the ego. Second, if the ego has not fully developed or the prohibitions associated with the goal object are excessively rigid or

Sigmund Freud

strong, the person may redirect the energy along routes that will reduce the tension but do not lead to the appropriate goal object. For example, a person with a strong sex urge may redirect the energy by reading about sex; a person who feels anger toward her boss may redirect that anger through aggression toward her husband and children. Although redirecting energy in this way may, for a time, reduce the tension associated with the instinct, Freud argued that such methods would never be satisfactory, because every instinct had an appropriate goal object. The tension would continue to surface from time to time in the form of neurotic anxiety. Neurotic people, according to Freud, constantly fear that their instincts will get out of control. Freud's goal as a therapist was to help people discover why they had redirected the energy for their instincts—in short, why they felt guilt or fear whenever

they considered satisfying their instincts. Freud believed that the instincts were not bad and that the only way to achieve a happy life was to satisfy them. He argued that many young children learn inappropriate ways of dealing with their instincts or learn that the gratification of certain instincts is inherently bad. He believed that people could get rid of the guilt and fear associated with instincts if they gained insight into the conditions surrounding the acquisition of these feelings. Since such feelings were often learned very early in life, it was necessary, Freud argued, for the analyst to help patients rediscover their childhood.

Although Freud believed that insight into the origins of a problem—in other words, a new cognition— was sufficient to alter the course of behavior, many therapists have concluded that this is often not so. Wolpe (1969), for example, has argued that extensive relearning is often necessary.

Summary

There has been a long and heated debate about the role of biology in human behavior. The debate has revolved around the idea that humans are special. The Catholic church has argued that, because humans are special, they can be held responsible for their behavior, while animals cannot. Increasingly, research shows that, while biology plays an important role in governing our behavior, it does not account for all our actions. Learning and cognition often interact with biological dispositions to shape the final behavior.

Instinct theory not only accounts for the energy that gives rise to action but accounts for the direction of behavior as well. An exception to this is Freud's theory. Freud viewed the direction of behavior as largely due to the interaction of biology, learning, and cognition. Instinct theory also accounts for the adaptive nature of human and animal behavior. Again, Freud was an exception. Freud was interested in accounting for what can, and often does, go wrong when instincts clash with the values or practices of society.

In psychology, instinct theories of behavior have fallen out of favor for a number of reasons. First, in order to account for the wide range of behaviors that animals and humans exhibit, it was necessary to postulate more and more instincts. In the end, the number of instincts required simply became too unwieldy. Second, a growing body of evidence indicates that learning and cognition play an important role in behavior.

Nevertheless, there is an abundance of evidence that biology plays an important role in causing action. The influence of biology is currently conceptualized in somewhat different terms than in the instinct theories. According to current thinking, biology creates a disposition to action, while learning and cognition refine and shape the final course of action.

Learning Theories

Watson's School of Behaviorism

Learning theories grew out of the belief that behavior could be better explained by principles of learning than by instinct. John B. Watson, who later founded the school of behaviorism, concluded that there were only three innate emotional reactions—fear, rage, and love—from which all other emotions were learned or derived (Watson & Morgan, 1917). One of the most compelling arguments that learning, rather than instinct, is the basis of behavior is that people raised in different cultures behave quite differently. The existence of cultural differences suggests that behavioral patterns are shaped by the environment (for example, by modeling) and are not hardwired (Boring, 1950). While early learning theorists such as Watson did not completely abandon the idea that biology plays a role in behavior, their aim was to show that behavior can be largely explained by the principles of classical conditioning or instrumental learning (sometimes called reward learning).

Hull's Drive Theory

One of the most influential learning theorists was Clark Hull. Central to Hull's theory was the idea that the wide variations in human behavior can be explained in terms of the principles of learning. According to Hull, the activation of a drive leads to random behavior. In the course of that behavior, the organism accidentally performs a response that reduces a drive. When that happens, the behavior leading to drive reduction is strengthened. Over time, with repeated reduction of that drive, a habit is formed. For example, if

a hungry dog discovers, while in that deprived state, that knocking over a garbage can leads to food, the dog will develop a habit of knocking over garbage cans. Thus, unlike Freud, who suggested that instincts give rise to representations of goal objects, Hull suggested that the goal object is discovered in the course of random behavior.

According to Hull, the reduction of a drive produces reinforcement. In his theory, drives activate habits. Hull suggested a multiplicative relationship between drives and habits:

$$Behavior = Drives \times Habits$$

According to this formulation, when a habit is weak, it takes a strong drive (such as hunger) to produce behavior (such as knocking over garbage cans). However, if the habit is highly developed, then a weak drive can activate it. Thus, his theory can explain why even a well-fed dog will knock over garbage cans and eat garbage. In Hull's theory, drives provide the energy for behavior; without drives, there would be no behavior.

For a time, Hull's theory was widely accepted by psychologists. It took from instinct theories the basic idea that behavior is caused by drives, but it was also able to account for individual differences. One of Hull's important contributions was his explanation of how weak drive states can activate a strong habit and thus produce action. We are creatures of habit; Hull was able to tell us why.

Skinner's Reinforcement Theory

In the 1960s and 1970s, B. F. Skinner's theory came to replace drive theory. Skinner suggested that it was not necessary for a drive to be reduced in order for learning to occur. A number of experiments during that era showed that animals and humans will learn a behavior even if no biological drive was reduced. For example, rats learned to press a bar in order to drink a nonnutritive substance such as saccharin. According to Hull, the rats could not learn this behavior without reinforcement, and reinforcement can only occur if a biological drive is being reduced. In other studies, male rats maintained a high level of sexual interest and activity even if prevented from ejaculating during in-

B. F. Skinner

Even though the main construct in his theory was reward, he was not particularly interested in whether it made people feel good or bad.

Skinner was able to demonstrate that persistence is often greater if an organism is only rewarded some of the time, rather than each time it makes a desired response (partial reinforcement). While other psychologists constructed theories to explain why partial reinforcement leads to persistence (Amsel, 1962), Skinner was content to show that different types of partial reinforcement contingencies (what he called *schedules of reinforcement*) produce different forms of persistence. In this way, he demonstrated that such things as persistence can be explained without reference to biology.

While Skinner claimed he did not have a theory, others have argued that he did. The essence of his theory is that it is possible to radically change behavior. In his two books *Walden II* and *Beyond Freedom and Dignity*, Skinner describes how people can be happy and how emotions such as aggression can be eliminated by the principles of reinforcement. The theme of *Beyond Freedom and Dignity* is that we can create a perfect state by arranging reward contingencies in a certain way. In order to do that, we need to give up certain ideas, such as the need for dignity and freedom; and to surrender control to a benevolent superstate.

Research stimulated by Skinner's ideas has shown that it is possible to radically alter behavior through the systematic application of rewards. This line of research, called *behavior modification*, showed that it is often possible to alter widely diverse behaviors associated with, for example, drug use, eating patterns, family relationships, delinquency, and the acquisition of skills.

According to Skinnerian thinking, the energy, the direction, and the persistence of behavior are due to reinforcement contingencies; it is not necessary to postulate anything more. Psychologists have since demonstrated that rewards are only part of the story. Nonetheless, Skinner's legacy was to demonstrate that behavior is often under the control of rewards and can be altered simply by altering reward contingencies.

Social Learning Theories

According to Skinner's theory, rewards are external. Social learning theorists challenged that view by demonstrating that people can also learn by modeling

tercourse. If sexual behavior is for purposes of reproduction, then ejaculation would be essential for reinforcement to occur; by Hull's theory, the rats should lose interest in sexual activity.

Skinner's theory represented a major shift away from the biological basis of behavior. According to Skinner, behavior is under the control of external rewards. Positive rewards increase the probability of a behavior, and negative rewards decrease its probability.

Skinner described himself as an empiricist. He said he did not believe in constructing theories; he was only interested in talking about observable behavior. He deliberately used such phrases as "increasing the probability of a response" to emphasize that he was talking about observables. For him, words like "strengthen" were mentalistic constructs that could not be observed.

another person. They went on to suggest that we can acquire a new behavior simply by observing that it produces some desired outcome for another person. This argument explains why people will engage in a behavior for which they have never personally received a reward. Thus, two of the main features that distinguishes social learning theory from the theories of Hull and Skinner are: (1) the tendency to view behavior as occurring independently of environmental contingencies and (2) the assumption that organisms can acquire experiences (habits) in the absence of direct experience or reward.

Social learning theorists were not concerned, for the most part, with determining how such behaviors were functional or instrumental for the individual's survival. They were intent on showing that much, if not all, human behavior comes from information that humans process about the environment. For example, numerous studies have addressed the question of vicarious motivators (Bandura, 1986). These studies demonstrated that by observing others, individuals can often determine ahead of time what actions will bring pain (punishment) and what actions will bring satisfaction (reinforcement). Moreover, individuals can learn not only to avoid making certain mistakes, but they can learn to design an optimal course of action for achieving desired ends.

Social learning theorists were able to explain a wide range of behaviors that had no immediate survival value. At the height of social learning theory, it was popular to say that for example, aggression was nothing more than imitative behavior due to watching aggression and violence on television. In that case, one way to get rid of aggression would be to eliminate aggression and violence from television. As it turns out, it's not that simple. Individuals seem to be born with different dispositions toward aggression. Nonetheless, television does contribute indirectly to aggression. (We'll return to this topic in Chapter 8.)

According to social learning theory, information can account for the source (energy), the direction, and the persistence of behavior. Like Skinnerians, social learning theorists did not view the underlying biology as important. While they relied mainly on principles of learning to explain behavior, they did introduce rudimentary cognitive concepts (Berkowitz, 1990). In particular, they suggested that people develop expectations. As the result of watching aggression, for example, individuals develop ideas about what aggressive behaviors would be appropriate in certain situations. Such expectations can be thought of as if/then learning: "If this situation arises, then this is the appropriate behavior." According to social learning theory, people not only learn behaviors from observing others but also learn about consequences. An individual who sees, for example, that acting aggressively produces certain desired results might develop the expectation: "If I act aggressively, then I will get such and such." According to social learning theory, seeing another person engage in a certain behavior and attain a desired goal provides vicarious reinforcement to the observer. As a result of vicarious reinforcement, the likelihood of the observer imitating a certain behavior will increase.

Perhaps the most lasting legacy of social learning theory is the idea that much of human behavior arises out of information that we have passively observed. As we'll see in Chapter 14, we do indeed use such information to guide our actions.

Summary

Early learning theorists such as Watson and Hull suggested that biology provides the energy for behavior but that the direction is mainly due to learning. They argued that persistence has it roots in our biology but even persistence can be modified. The main advantage of these theories over instinct theories was their ability to account for individual differences.

Although John B. Watson founded behaviorism, Hull and Skinner were its two most influential proponents. Hull argued that the energy and persistence of behavior derive from drives, but the direction of behavior comes from learning (habits). Instincts, by contrast, provide not only the energy and persistence of behavior but also the direction.

Skinner abandoned the concept of drives. In doing so, he also abandoned the idea that our biology is a main determinant of our behavior. Skinner went so far as to suggest that, in order to produce adaptive behaviors, we merely need to arrange appropriate reinforcement contingencies. In two popular books, he argued that it is possible to create a utopian society by systematically employing principles of reinforcement.

Social learning theory has shown that humans process a great deal of information about the environment and that such information provides the source (energy) and direction of our actions. Both Skinner's theory and social learning theory represent a movement away from motivation theorists' initial focus on behavior as an attempt to adapt to the environment. Adaptive behavior is typically viewed within the context of the underlying biology, which was of no particular interest to Skinner or the social learning theorists.

Need Theories

According to the learning theorist, individual differences are due to learning. But how do such differences arise? Is our destiny as individuals simply the result of being in the right place at the right time? Surely the orderliness of the universe is due to something more than the whims of reinforcement. Consider siblings who grow up to be very different. How can that be if they have been exposed in the family to similar types of reinforcement and similar information? Note that Hull attempted to deal with this problem by linking learning to drives; he firmly believed that biology was important.

An obvious way to deal with individual differences is to argue that we are born with them. Need theory grew out of the idea that the energy, direction, and persistence of behavior are due to the existence of needs. Abandoning the unworkable idea that there must be an instinct for each different behavior, need theorists suggested that we are born with a limited set of needs that can be modified through learning.

Murray's Need Theory

Murray (1938) proposed that humans can be characterized by a limited set of needs (Table 1-1). He explained individual differences in terms of differences in the strength of the individual's needs, in striking contrast to Hull's view that individual differences are due mainly to learning.

Murray was not particularly concerned with whether needs were innate or learned; he accepted the idea that they could be acquired. His aim was to see if all human behavior could be explained by a limited number of needs.

As we see, Table 1-1 lists psychological needs, rather than more physical needs such as the need for food or water. Murray spent much of his life attempting to measure these needs. He invented the Thematic Apperception Test, a projective test in which people were presented with a picture and asked to tell a story about it. These stories were then systematically analyzed to determine the degree to which they reflected the needs that Murray had proposed.

Currently, the main proponent of need theory is David McClelland, who has worked for over 40 years to validate the need for achievement and, to a lesser extent, the need for affiliation and the need for power. His work shows that the need to achieve plays a fundamental role in behavior; we will return to this topic in Chapter 13.

Maslow's Need Hierarchy

Maslow is perhaps one of the best known need theorists. He argued that the basic physiological needs are associated with deficiency, and the higher-order needs with growth. This is consistent with the distinction between avoidant and approach motivation. In Maslow's view, needs can be grouped in categories, which are arranged in a hierarchical fashion, with the more basic or primary needs at the bottom (Figure 1-1). Only when the needs at the most basic level are satisfied does the next set of needs become relevant; people will be concerned about safety needs only when their physiological needs (for food, water, and warmth) have been met. Likewise, before they address their belongingness and love needs, their need to feel secure, safe, and out of danger must be met. As we see in Figure 1-1, people are ultimately motivated by the need for self-actualization, but only after their other needs have been met. We'll return to Maslow's ideas in a later chapter.

Acquired Needs

Like the instinct theorist, need theorists were faced with the problem of how to account for the diversity and complexity of behavior on the basis of a limited

Table 1-1.   Murray's list of basic human needs.

Human Need	Description
Abasement	To surrender. To seek and enjoy injury, blame, criticism, punishment. Self-depreciation. Masochism.
Achievement	To overcome obstacles and attain a high standard. To rival and surpass others. To strive and to master.
Affiliation	To form friendships and associations. To greet, join, and live with others. To cooperate and converse sociably with others.
Aggression	To assault or injure another. To fight. To oppose forcefully. To belittle, harm, blame, accuse, or depreciate another. To revenge an injury.
Autonomy	To resist influence or coercion. To defy conventions. To be independent and free to act according to impulse.
Counteraction	To master or make up for a failure by renewed effort. To overcome a weakness. To maintain honor, pride, and self-respect.
Defendance	To defend oneself against blame, criticism, belittlement. To offer explanations and excuses. To resist probing.
Deference	To admire and willingly follow a superior allied other. To cooperate with a leader. To praise, honor, or eulogize.
Dominance	To influence or control others. To persuade, prohibit, dictate, command. To restrain. To organize the behavior of a group.
Exhibition	To attract attention to one's person. To make an impression. To excite, amuse, stir, amaze, intrigue, shock, or thrill others.
Harm avoidance	To avoid pain, physical injury, illness, and death. To escape from a dangerous situation, to take precautionary measures.
Infravoidance	To avoid failure, shame, humiliation, ridicule. To refrain from action because of the fear of failure.
Nurturance	To nourish, aid, or protect a helpless other. To express sympathy. To take care of a child. To feed, help, support, comfort, nurse, heal.
Order	To arrange, organize, put away objects. To be tidy and clean. To be scrupulously precise.
Play	To relax, amuse oneself, seek diversion and entertainment. To have fun, to play games. To laugh, joke, and be merry. To act for fun without further purpose.
Rejection	To snub, ignore, or exclude another. To remain aloof and indifferent. To be discriminating.
Sentience	To seek and enjoy sensuous impressions.
Sex	To form and further an erotic relationship. To engage in sexual activity.
Succorance	To seek aid, protection, or sympathy. To cry for help. To plead for mercy. To adhere to an affectionate, nurturing parent. To be dependent, to have support.
Understanding	To analyze experience, to abstract, to discriminate among concepts, to define relations, to synthesize ideas.

Source: From *Explorations in Personality*, by Henry A Murray. Copyright © 1938, renewed 1966 by Henry A. Murray. Used by permission of Oxford University Press, Inc.

number of needs. To deal with this problem, many need theorists stressed the importance of rewards. They suggested that needs do not lead directly to behavior but are merely a disposition to action; and rewards strengthen those dispositions. This idea has been warmly received by psychologists. David McClelland's (1985) work on the achievement motive is based on this proposition. He argued, among other things, that children rewarded for achievement would grow up to have a strong achievement motive.

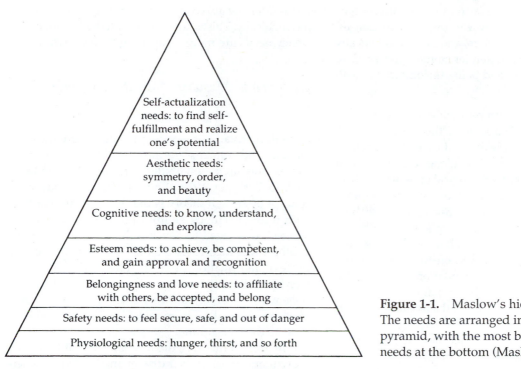

Figure 1-1.   Maslow's hierarchy of needs. The needs are arranged in the form of a pyramid, with the most basic or primary needs at the bottom (Maslow, 1943, 1970).

Self-actualization needs: to find self-fulfillment and realize one's potential

Aesthetic needs: symmetry, order, and beauty

Cognitive needs: to know, understand, and explore

Esteem needs: to achieve, be competent, and gain approval and recognition

Belongingness and love needs: to affiliate with others, be accepted, and belong

Safety needs: to feel secure, safe, and out of danger

Physiological needs: hunger, thirst, and so forth

The Factor Analytic Tradition

As research in need theory continued, the number of supposed needs steadily grew. Since one of the basic principles of science is to explain phenomena on the basis of the fewest possible concepts, the proliferation of needs was a concern for motivation theorists. They began to wonder whether this wide range of needs grew out of a smaller set of underlying needs or dispositions. This question was addressed by factor analysis, a statistical procedure that establishes whether different people group a certain set of items in the same way. If different people group things in a similar way, it may be because they are operating out of similar psychological structures. Using factor analysis, Cattell proposed a 16-factor model. That was followed by Eysenck's three-factor model. More recently, Costa and McCrae (1992) have suggested a five-factor model. One reason that different numbers of factors emerged in these studies is that the researchers began with different sets of items. The items that are used in factor analyses normally come from existing personality tests. To measure a certain personality trait, researchers design items that will measure this trait at different points along a theoretical continuum that goes from high to low. One reason different numbers of factors emerge in these studies is because researchers initially select different items for inclusion in the test they give to participants.

According to Costra and McCrae (1992), five basic factors underlie all personality measures:

1. Extraversion (also called positive emotionality), characterized by gregarious, assertive, and excitement-seeking tendencies.
2. Neuroticism (also called negative emotionality), characterized by anxiety, angry hostility, depression, and self-consciousness.
3. Agreeableness, characterized by warmth, compassion, and sympathy versus critical, distrustful, and skeptical attitudes.
4. Conscientiousness, characterized by productivity, ethical behavior, and responsibility versus self-indulgence and inability to delay gratification.

5. Openness to experience (also called intellect), characterized by having a wide range of experiences, valuing intellectual matters, and being aesthetically reactive (versus being gender stereotyped, holding conservative values, and being uncomfortable with complexities).

By assuming there can be a wide range of interactions between these five factors, this model can account for both the complexity and diversity of behavior. There is also considerable evidence that each factor can be linked to particular biological systems. In short, they tend to reflect underlying biological dispositions.

However, theorists still do not agree as to how many factors are necessary to adequately describe behavior. Recently, Benet and Waller (1995) suggested that seven factors are needed to ensure cross-cultural generality using a Spanish population. There is also disagreement on how to define or name these factors. As we see from the description of the five factors, a certain degree of complexity must be reintroduced in order to define these factors so that they are meaningful to nonspecialists. Nonetheless, the principle that human behavior can be described on the basis of a common underlying set of dispositions has now been widely accepted.

Summary

The measurement of needs has occupied psychologists for some time. The idea that needs give rise to action is no longer accepted in psychology. The present position is that needs lead to dispositions. Whether these dispositions lead to action depend on circumstances such as past rewards and how we think about the world. Factor analysis has provided psychologists with a more empirical way to establish the underlying psychological structure of human motivation. Currently, research suggests that all of human behavior can be explained in terms of 5–7 basic needs and that each of these needs can be linked to biological differences.

Maslow argued that the basic physiological needs are related to deficiency and the higher-order needs to growth. This distinction is consistent with the idea that human action is due to both avoidant and approach needs. Maslow also contended that needs are arranged hierarchically. This is consistent with the idea that deficiency needs are more compelling than growth needs.

Growth and Mastery Motivation Theories

Exploration, Curiosity, and Mastery

Growth motivation theories grew out of the idea that animals and humans are motivated by their need to successfully interact with the environment (Dember & Earl, 1957; Piaget, 1970; White, 1959). One underlying concept of growth theory is that humans are not born with fully developed abilities. In order to adapt and succeed, they need to develop those abilities. Central to all growth theories is the idea that humans need to process information and acquire skills—in other words, to develop *mastery.* To successfully deal with the environment, organisms need to learn as much as they can about the environment and to develop their skills to their maximum.

In growth theories, the mechanism that motivates growth and mastery is a discrepancy between where the individual is and where the individual needs to be in order to successfully adapt to the environment. This discrepancy creates a tension inside the organism. To reduce this tension, the individual needs to reduce the discrepancy, by developing skills and intellect. According to Piaget, organisms must develop cognitive structures that enable them to process vast amounts of information quickly and efficiently.

According to growth theorists, animals explore because the environment is a source of novelty. That novelty creates a discrepancy, which in turn creates a tension. To reduce that tension, organisms explore their environment and process all the information contained in it. When the environment is no longer novel, the tension subsides and exploratory behavior stops. Some theorists have gone on to suggest that organisms are designed to feel best when there is an optimal level of incoming stimulation for them to process (Berlyne, 1960). If the immediate environment does not provide enough stimulation, they will seek out a novel environment in order to satisfy their need for stimulation.

The idea of tension is reminiscent of Hull's drive concept. Like drives, tensions have a compelling quality. Tensions motivate the organism to do things that will return it to a homeostatic level. In the case of growth motivation, these tensions are only reduced when the individual develops skills or cognitive structures sufficient to deal effectively with the environment.

Growth theorists do not fully agree on whether it is best to account for growth motivation in terms of approach or avoidant mechanisms. Many growth theorists suggest that the discrepancy between what is out there in the environment and what is inside the individual (such as knowledge or skills) creates motivation. However, discrepancies can be conceptualized as the basis for experiencing challenge (an approach state) or tension (an avoidant state). In fact, a growing body of data suggests that some people react to a discrepancy as though it were a challenge (approach motivation), whereas others react to a discrepancy as though it were a threat (avoidant motivation). On this basis, theorists have made a distinction between people who are mastery-oriented and those who are ego-oriented (Nicholls, 1984). As it turns out, this distinction has far-reaching implications for explaining the differences in individuals' reactions to the same situation.

Why do people react so differently? It has been suggested that a mastery orientation can only flourish in a supportive environment. If we are constantly threatened in some way, we may come to develop a very different orientation—what has been called an *ego orientation*. Further, some theorists suggest that individuals may be born with a disposition to develop a mastery orientation or an ego orientation. Thus, the final outcome depends on how dispositional factors interact with environmental factors. Other research suggests that our reactions are also affected by how we label our experiences; that idea will be addressed in Chapters 12 and 13.

In the next section, we consider humanistic theories, which were also concerned with the question of growth.

Humanistic Theories

The humanistic approach was originally proposed by Abraham Maslow (1943, 1970) and Carl Rogers (1959). Humanistic psychologists base their theories on the premise that humans are basically good and possess an innate (biological) tendency to grow and mature. They further believe that each of us is unique. A central humanist concept is the need for self-actualization, which depends on a highly developed self-concept. The main focus of the humanistic theories was to understand and develop the self-concept.

Carl Rogers (1951) suggested that organisms have one basic tendency, which is to "actualize, maintain and enhance the experiencing self." While Rogers recognized that humans have needs, he stressed the inherent tendency of the individual to coordinate those needs in order to develop the self. He saw the self as constructed from basic sensory experiences and from the individual's interaction with the world. While the tendency to actualize was seen as innate, he recognized that the route to self-actualization is frequently characterized by pain and suffering.

Rogers believed that people have within themselves the capacity to judge what is good for them and what is not. Individuals value positively those experiences perceived as maintaining and enhancing the self and value negatively those perceived as undermining growth. Thus, what we approach and what we avoid depends on our perception of what promotes the development of the self.

Rogers suggested that, as we interact with the environment, we develop the *need for positive regard*—the need to receive approval, to be accepted, and to be loved. The need for positive regard also makes us sensitive to the criticism and praise of others. He suggested that positive regard eventually becomes internalized and, as a result, we come to develop *positive self-regard*. Rogers believed strongly that people need to have positive self-regard in order to realize their potential.

However, Rogers pointed out a potential problem with internalizing positive regard: If we determine our behavior on the basis of what pleases others, we lose sight of what is good for the development of the self. Rogers believed that the movement towards socialized worth and away from inherent worth was antithetical to self-actualization. People need to listen to their inner voices—to their innate capacity to judge what is good for the self; he called this the *organismic valuation process*. His childrearing advice to parents was that, rather than offering conditional love—that is, withholding love until children comply with behaviors that the parents value—they should embrace unconditional love; in other words, they should love their children for all their choices and behaviors, out of respect for their inherent ability to do what is best for themselves.

While Maslow and Rogers were never part of mainstream empirical psychology, their ideas received wide acceptance outside the mainstream. In recent years, as psychologists have begun to explore the nature of the self and the possibility that people can self-regulate their behavior, there has been a resurgence of interest in the ideas of Maslow and Rogers.

Summary

The idea that people are motivated by the need for mastery has had a profound impact on motivation theory. It implies that humans are intrinsically motivated; they do things because it gives them pride and satisfaction. In other words, goal-directed behavior does not depend on external rewards. Growth theories suggest that people undergo change as a result of their need to interact with the environment.

Most growth theories embrace the concept that growth is natural. It is interesting, therefore, to find that some people are more prone to grow (have a mastery orientation), while others are more prone to maintain the status quo (have an ego orientation). Although some research suggests that this difference is rooted in our biology, the humanists have argued that it is associated with our self-concept. They contend that we come into this world with a unique potential self that needs the right environment in order to grow and develop. Part of our job as individuals is to learn how to create an environment that will enable the self to grow. Like seeds, we will grow and blossom in the right soil and moisture.

Cognitive Theories

Cognitive theories of motivation have their roots in work done by learning theorists such as Tolman (1932), personality theorists such as Lewin (1938), and developmental theorists such as Piaget (1970). These theorists argued that mental representations formed by humans and animals play a central role in guiding their behavior. Traditional learning theorists such as Watson and Hull argued that behavior could be explained simply by the strengthening of a habit or association, without invoking the idea of mental representations; for many people, the idea that animals—especially rats—have mental representations was simply going too far. The early cognitive theorists designed a number of studies that were difficult to explain on the basis of traditional learning theory. For example, in the latent learning studies, one group of animals (typically rats) was allowed to explore a maze in the absence of any rewards (preexposure phase), while the control group was not provided with the opportunity to explore. Both groups of animals were then made hungry and rewarded when they got from one point to another. The animals given the preexposure learned the correct path much more quickly than did the controls. Cognitive theorists argued that the rats formed some type of mental map during the preexposure phase and used that map to find their way around when the rewards were introduced.

Expectancy-Value Theories

The idea of mental representations took hold in the 1950s and was incorporated into a number of theories in the field of motivation and elsewhere. One type of mental representation is an *expectancy*, a judgment about the likely outcome of some behavior, formed on the basis of past experiences. If I ask my boss for a raise, for example, what is the likelihood that I'll get it?

Expectancy is not a motivational construct by itself. However, it proves very useful when coupled with the motivational construct called *value*. The resulting expectancy-value theories (also called cognitive-choice theories) suggest that people not only have expectations about what might happen in response to a particular behavior but can also assign a value to the outcome. According to expectancy-value theories, people choose between different tasks by simultaneously assessing expectation and value for each. Suppose I want a game of tennis. I might form an expectation about my likelihood of beating my neighbor, as against the likelihood of beating her five-year-old son. If I conclude that I might be able to beat both of them, would it be more satisfying (of greater value) to beat my neighbor or her son?

Expectancy-value theories are hedonistic. They assume that we will select the alternative likely to arouse the greatest feeling of pleasure (positive affect). If the alternatives are all perceived as unattractive, we might select the option that produces the least pain. Expectancy-value theories were also called cognitive-choice theories or decision theories (Edwards, 1961). Tests of the expectancy value theory involved determining which of two or more alternatives a person would select given the probability of achieving a certain outcome (winning the lottery) and the reward magnitude (amount of money). In other words, what are the trade-offs that an individual makes when confronted with these two variables.

Goal-Setting Theories

The idea that humans can form expectations about the future played a key role in the development of goal-setting theories. According to Locke and Latham (1990), humans can motivate themselves by setting future goals. They suggest that goals affect behavior in four ways: (1) they direct attention; (2) they mobilize effort to the task; (3) they encourage persistence; and (4) they facilitate the development of strategies (Locke, 1968). Their research indicates that goals should be both difficult and specific; saying "Do your best" is not an effective way to motivate people. An important underlying moderator of goal setting is commitment. Unless we are committed to our goals, we will not put forth the effort necessary to achieve them. Psychologists have found that one way to increase commitment is to allow people to set their own goals.

Social-Cognitive Theories of Goal Setting

Whether people will set difficult goals for themselves (or commit themselves to such goals) depends on whether they perceive that they have, or can develop, the abilities they will need to attain the goals. Albert Bandura (1991) writes about people's *self-efficacy*, defined as expectations that focus on beliefs about their capabilities to organize and execute the behaviors requisite for attaining the outcome. Notice that, in expectancy-value theories, expectancy relates to outcomes corresponding to a specific level of effort,

whereas self-efficacy expectations focus on our beliefs about our capacities. Ultimately, such beliefs relate back to our self-concept. In other words, in Bandura's theory, the nature of the self plays a role in goal setting. As we'll see in Chapter 14, the visualization of possible selves can play an important role in determining the kinds of goals that people set.

Summary

Cognitive theories grew out of the idea that humans can form mental representations of their environment, which they can then use to guide their behavior. Moreover, humans can make choices between alternatives. According to cognitive theorists, behavior is not merely the result of a habit that propels us blindly forward.

Cognitive-choice theories were designed to explain how and why people make immediate choices. One of the most prominent early motivational theories was expectancy-value theory, which suggested not only that humans have expectations about outcomes, but that they attach values to these outcomes. According to expectancy-value theories, expectancies and values are multiplicative.

Goal theories grew out of the idea that humans have expectations about the future and that one way to make these expectations happen is to set goals. According to Locke and Latham (1990), these goals help provide the direction and persistence that characterizes goal attainment.

Social-cognitive theories of goal setting incorporate the idea that people have perceptions not only about their present level of skills, but also about their ability to develop skills. Thus, the future goals that people set for themselves depend on their self-concept.

Biological, Learned, and Cognitive Forces

In this review of some major theories of motivation, we have seen that motivation theorists have viewed the cause of behavior in terms of biology, principles of learning, and principles of cognition. In this book, we will examine a number of motivational systems. In each system, we will see that the expression of the underlying biology is modified by learning and cognition. Freud recognized a long time ago that human biology does not automatically aim a person in the right direction. Forces of society also play a role. For example, there is considerable evidence that one of the causes of bulimia (the tendency to binge and purge) in North American society is our obsession with thinness and dieting. There is also evidence that learning can short-circuit adaptive behavior. People sometimes use alcohol, for example, to help them block out the pain of loneliness or poor self-esteem. As a result, they develop the habit of drinking when faced with loneliness or feelings of inadequacy.

The focus in this book is to explain not only why people do what they do but also how they can change through self-regulation. A growing body of research indicates that people can change their behavior if they learn how to set goals and to ward off self-doubt. Advice based on research showing that people can change is presented throughout the following chapters; much of it involves principles of learning and cognition.

Main Points

1. There are two types of motivation: approach and avoidant motivation.
2. Neurotics tend to be dominated by avoidant motivation.
3. Extraverts and sensation seekers tend to be dominated by approach motivation.
4. Eight themes underlie contemporary motivation: Behavior represents an attempt to adapt; it is important to determine what arouses and energizes behavior; it is necessary to understand what governs direction; it is important to understand persistence; feelings are important; there are individual differences; humans often can self-regulate their behavior; humans have limited volition.
5. In the 16th century, it was thought that animals have instincts but humans do not.
6. René Descartes suggested that both humans and animals have instincts but that humans can control their instincts.

7. Charles Darwin suggested that the behavior of animals and humans is due their underlying biology.
8. Early psychologists such as McDougall attempted to explain all human behavior in terms of a limited set of instincts that provided not only the energy but the direction of behavior.
9. Freud was an early instinct theorist; he believed that instincts provided the energy for behavior but that the direction of behavior was due to various principles of learning and cognition.
10. Clark Hull suggested that the energy for behavior was due to drives and went on to suggest that behavior is due to the multiplicative effect of drives times habit (B = D X H).
11. B. F. Skinner abandoned the idea of drive but retained the concept of reinforcement.
12. Skinner believed that external rewards were the main determinant of behavior and suggested that society could be radically altered simply by altering reinforcement contingencies in the environment.
13. Social learning theorists suggested that many behaviors (habits) can be acquired in the absence of rewards. They suggested, for example, the people could learn to be violent simply by watching violence on television and by seeing the consequences of this behavior (vicarious reinforcement).
14. Need theorists such as Murray suggested that humans can be characterized by a set of needs that not only provide the energy for behavior but the direction as well.
15. Maslow suggested that needs can be arranged in a hierarchical fashion.
16. Murray and others suggested that these basic needs could be modified through learning.
17. Recently, it has been shown through factor analytic procedures that there are five basic personality factors: extraversion, neuroticism, agreeableness, conscientiousness, and openness to experience.
18. Growth motivation theories grew out of the idea that organisms need to learn how to successfully interact with their environment.
19. Growth theorists suggested that the reason animals explore their environment is to gain mastery over it.
20. According to goal-orientation theories, people adopt different orientations to the environment depending on whether they are threatened. When

threatened, they adopt an ego orientation; otherwise, they adopt a mastery orientation.

21. According to expectancy-value theories, organisms have expectations about whether they are likely to attain particular goals. They will choose the option with the best combination of expectancy and value.

22. According to social-cognitive theories of goal setting, whether people are inclined to set specific attainable goals depends on their feelings of self-efficacy.

23. Humanistic theories of motivation are growth motivation theories that suggest humans are motivated to self-actualize.

24. A central feature of all humanistic theories is the idea that humans need to develop the self.

25. The current focus of several motivation theorists is understanding the nature of the self.

Chapter Two

Components of Motivation

- ■ *What are the components of motivation?*
- ■ *Why is it necessary to talk in terms of components?*
- ■ *Why have scientists tended to study behavior from a single perspective?*
- ■ *What are the implications of adopting a single perspective?*

- ■ *What are some of the implications of viewing behavior from multiple perspectives (biological, learned, and cognitive)?*
- ■ *How does a multiple-perspective (components) approach help us understand such things as why people run or why people listen to rock music?*

Motivation theorists are concerned with the origins or causes of action. They are interested in why people do any number of things—eat, seek out sexual partners, take drugs, retaliate when threatened, make friends, care for children, set goals, solve problems, create. Early motivation theorists hypothesized that needs cause action (e.g., Murray, 1938). Their main focus was the identification and measurement of needs. It soon became apparent, however, that two different people with the same need—such as the need to achieve—did not expend the same energy nor did they persist equally. Obviously other factors were at work. Over the years, it has become apparent that a number of factors may moderate and enhance needs. Self-esteem, for example, plays an important role in determining whether people persist in the face of adversity or give up. In response to these findings, psychologists have reconceptualized needs not as direct causes of action but rather as dispositions to action (Atkinson & Birch, 1978; de Rivera, 1982; Raynor, 1974; Weiner, 1974a). Needs give us a push or nudge in a certain direction but they do not, by themselves, supply all the energy, nor do they fully provide the direction. The energy and the final direction come from other processes or systems.

These other processes or systems can be classified as biological, learned, or cognitive. Brain circuits are activated; learned responses are triggered; or we take control by making plans. I refer to these processes as *components of behavior* or *components of motivation*. Research shows that behavior is not due solely to a biological, a learned, or a cognitive process but rather to the interaction of all three (Kleinginna & Kleinginna, 1981b). Thus, the basic approach adopted in this book is that, in studying motivation, we are concerned with understanding how dispositions lead to action through the joint operation of biological, learned, and cognitive processes.

The Biological Component

All human action has a biological basis. It arises out of, for example, genetic predisposition, the activation of biological circuits, and the release of various chemicals and hormones. Without biological processes, there would be no action or life. While the main focus of the biological sciences has been to account for the uniformity of behavior within various species by identifying common underlying mechanisms, the focus of motivation theorists has been to explain individual differences by identifying subtle differences in those underlying mechanisms. These subtle—and sometimes not so subtle—differences help to explain why members of the same species act in different ways.

Genetic Processes

Humans differ in their desire to travel, to engage in risky sports, to spend time with friends, to have many sexual partners, to seek out conflict or excitement, and so forth. Many of these differences, it has been shown, can be linked to differences in biological regulators, such as enzyme levels. Further, these enzyme levels are inherited (Zuckerman, 1994). Enzymes are proteins in the body that regulate other chemical reactions but themselves remain unaltered.

Genes not only cause certain physical features to emerge; they also cause certain behaviors to emerge. In producing these physical features and behaviors, however, genes act in conjunction with the environment. As a result, we make a distinction between *genotype*, which refers to the constitution of an individual, and *phenotype*, which refers to the visible properties produced by the interaction of the genotype with the environment. Although genes set the stage for behavior, the environment shapes the final behavior. What genes often do is create a disposition to engage in certain behaviors. They may, for example, alter the chemical balance of the brain or the reactivity of a certain brain structure so that engaging in a certain behavior will produce a strong positive affect. Thus, genes do not cause you to engage in risky sports; they merely insure that, should you happen to engage in risky sports, you are likely to find them very exciting and rewarding. For a wide variety of reasons, including friends' admonitions about the dangers involved, you may never experiment with certain risky sports or discover the pleasure associated with them. Alternatively, you may decide to forego the pleasure or to seek out some other source of pleasure.

Monozygotic and Dizygotic Twins

The main technique used by scientists to determine whether certain behavior is due to genes is to compare monozygotic twins with dizygotic twins. Monozygotic twins result from a division of a single egg and, as a result, have exactly the same set of genes. Dizygotic twins, in contrast, result from the fertilization of two different eggs by two different sperm. As a result, they are just like any two siblings from the same family; that is, while some of their genes may be the same, others are different. By comparing monozygotic twins with dizygotic twins, it is possible to control for the effects of the environment, the effects of having two children that are exactly the same age, and gender-related differences. For each set of twins, the environment is going to be largely the same. In the case of siblings, there may be differences due to parents' experience in child-rearing, parents' job-related stress, marital conflict, the political climate in society, and so forth. Also, there are gender-related differences due to different genes on the X and Y chromosomes and to differences in socialization. Finally, since there is evidence that twins react differently to each other than to older or younger siblings, it is important to control for this effect as well.

To determine if individual differences have a genetic basis, rates of obesity, for example, are calculated for monozygotic and dizygotic twins. If obesity is due to genetic processes, the weights of monozygotic twins should be closer than the weights of dizygotic twins. Indeed, this is what has been found. Nevertheless, there is still considerable variability among monozygotic twins, especially if they have been raised in different environments. This suggests that, along with genetic processes, the environment also plays an important role.

Learning and Genetic Processes: Hardwired and Softwired Behavior

When we are born, certain behaviors are more or less fully developed (for example, the sucking response, the startle response, the orientation response). Other behaviors, in contrast, are not present at birth, and require various amounts of practice at a later stage (for example, walking, certain social responses). We refer to behaviors that occur without the benefit of practice (learning) as *hardwired* and behaviors that require practice as *softwired*. Further, hardwired behavior generally cannot be altered. For humans, most behaviors require some

Practical Application 2-1

The Biology of Obsessions and Compulsions

In *The Boy Who Couldn't Stop Washing*, Judith Rapoport (1989b) describes Sergei, a 17-year-old who was transformed almost overnight into a lonely outsider, incapacitated by his psychological disabilities. Haunted by the idea that he was dirty—in spite of evidence to the contrary—Sergei began trying to wash away imaginary dirt. At first, his ritual was confined to weekends and evenings, but eventually it began to consume all his time, and he was forced to drop out of school. His condition was diagnosed as obsessive-compulsive disorder (OCD).

Obsessive-compulsive disorders have been a major challenge to psychologists, because they have proven resistant to various forms of therapy, including the application of learning principles. Judith Rapoport has proposed a biological (ethological) model for the ori-

gins of OCD. This intriguing example illustrates how it is possible to view some OCDs in terms of biology.

The central element of Judith Rapoport's theory is that certain behavioral subroutines, related to grooming and territory, have been programmed into the brain over the course of evolution. Ordinarily, our senses tell us that we are clean or safe, and this is sufficient to suppress those subroutines that have to do with cleaning or safety. If, on account of a malfunction, higher brain functions fail to suppress these subroutines, however, they are replayed over and over, and the individual is a slave to behaviors such as washing or checking to see if the door is locked. One patient whom Judith Rapoport treated was a woman who felt compelled to pull out her hair, one strand at a time, presumably because of a breakdown in the subroutine associated with grooming.

level of practice before they are executed with perfection. Even the sucking response benefits from practice. At the same time, virtually no behavior is without some biological basis. In other words, virtually all behaviors we observe in humans are softwired to some degree. Even social responses are deeply rooted in our biology.

In practice, we rarely find a behavior that is truly hardwired or softwired. So why do we make this distinction? First, it is important for theoretical reasons—in order to understand where a behavior comes from, for example. Second, this distinction is important in practical situations—when assessing interventions, for example. If a behavior is mainly due to genetic processes, attempts to change it may not be cost-effective. On the other hand, if it is due to learning and cognition, we may decide, at least under certain conditions, that some form of intervention would be desirable. If a person has a speech problem, for instance, we might decide to intervene, because learning plays a very large role in speech.

Distinctions between hardwired and softwired behavior are also important in assigning responsibility. The question of responsibility is complex but is taken very seriously in our society. As an example, consider the debate over the human rights of gay men and les-

bians. If sexual orientation is hardwired, then gay men and lesbians cannot be held responsible for their sexual orientation and the argument that their human rights should be protected by legislation would probably be broadly accepted. If sexual orientation is softwired, it is quite a different matter. To what degree do we accept or tolerate certain deviations from the norm? While government might decide it has no business in citizens' bedrooms, does that mean that gay men and lesbians should be granted the same rights as heterosexual couples? If they are granted certain rights, what are the implications for others—for example, cult members?

It appears that genetic processes do play a significant role in sexual orientation. In fact, twin studies indicate that genetic inheritance accounts for about 25% of the variance. Since it does not account for 100% of the variance, learning and cognition must also play a major role; see Chapter 5 for a more detailed discussion of this issue.

Prewired Behavior

Prewired behavior is largely due to biology, but learning plays a critical role in its development. For example, it has been shown that people are prepared

While individuals with OCD often know that their behaviors are irrational, they feel helpless to control them. However, they often go to great lengths to hide them. When they can no longer conceal them, they may retreat from public view or public encounters. A good example is Howard Hughes, who became a recluse following the development of his obsession that contact with other people was a source of germs (Rapoport, 1989b).

Approximately 2% of the population has OCD. While OCD is resistant to psychotherapy, it seems to be treatable by antidepressants. Judith Rapoport argues that drugs such as clomipramine alleviate OCD symptoms because they affect the production and regulation of the neurotransmitter serotonin. Neurotransmitters are important in governing behavior because they carry messages across the synapse (the gap between two nerve cells) in the brain.

Whenever their concentration levels change, they can dramatically affect the way people think, feel, and act.

While drugs have proven effective, learning principles have also been used to deal with OCD; specifically, it has been shown that, in some circumstances, these behaviors can be extinguished. While it may seem contradictory to claim, on the one hand, that a behavior is biologically based and to accept, on the other, that behavioral conditioning can reverse it, behavioral biologists have come to accept the idea that many fixed action patterns that stem in part from hardwiring can be altered through learning principles.

(prewired) to associate sickness with taste but not with visual or auditory stimuli. (See the section on the learned component in this chapter.) Thus, we cannot be induced to associate sickness with visual or auditory stimuli, but we are inclined to link sickness and taste after only a single experience of eating something that makes us sick. Avoiding foods that might poison us has obvious survival value, and so the ability to quickly link taste with sickness is highly adaptive.

This example illustrates that certain classes of stimuli, such as taste, are waiting to be associated with a particular response, should they be paired. When they are paired, it often takes only a single experience for an association to be formed. Thus, prewired behavior is distinguished from soft-wired behavior both by the speed with which learning takes place and by the fact that only certain classes of stimuli become associated.

Why not hardwire the brain for things that threaten our survival? For many animals—for example, certain monkeys—it appears that snakes and spiders are hardwired to produce fear. The main advantage of prewiring over hardwiring is that we can quickly learn to avoid new forms of threat that might arise. At the same time, we are not incapacitated by needless fears. The main disadvantage of prewiring with respect to hardwiring is that we could die before we learn the behavior that we need. Insuring that certain types of associations will take place with only one pairing helps with this problem. Modeling provides a powerful way of learning to avoid things that might cause us harm. Prewiring insures that such learning occurs very quickly. The downside of modeling is that, should we be the children of neurotic parents, we might become disabled by useless conditioned fears. If we are raised by reckless parents, we might take chances that will endanger our survival.

Brain Circuits and the Disposition to Learn

Our brain contains a number of structures linked together by nerve pathways. When our sensory receptors are stimulated, these nerve pathways carry the incoming information to various parts of the brain. This incoming stimulation typically triggers memories, which allow us to recognize things that are familiar and important to us; they tell us how to respond appropriately to a given situation or a certain set of demands.

Brain structures generally work in conjunction with one another. When different structures, together with connecting pathways, are aroused simultaneously, we refer to them as *brain circuits*. The current view is that brain circuits cause emotions. For example, the activation of a certain circuit causes fear; the activation of another circuit causes anger; and still another causes euphoria. In other words, for each emotion there is a distinct brain circuit.

Usually, the activation of a certain brain circuit does not cause behavior or action but creates the disposition to action. Exactly how the individual acts will be influenced by both learned and cognitive variables. In the case of anger, for example, my disposition to retaliate might be modified by such things as memories of how my father dealt with provocations or rules of behavior that I have developed from my own experiences.

The Predisposition to Experience Pleasure: Reward Systems in the Brain

As well as brain circuits for specific emotions, others appear to facilitate the acquisition of adaptive behaviors. Over 40 years ago, James Olds (1955) found that animals would learn a wide variety of responses in order to receive electrical simulation to certain areas of the brain, initially called reward centers. The system of reward centers is now called the *reward pathway* (Figure 2-1). Experience with electrodes inserted in the brain to treat depression indicates that electrical activation of the reward pathway generally—although not always—produces very positive feelings in humans. Drugs such as amphetamines that activate this system are known for their ability to produce feelings of euphoria. Correspondingly, there is considerable evidence that activation of these pathways tends to reinforce behavior; that is, organisms will quickly learn behaviors that activate this system (Olds & Milner, 1954).

One of the most basic principles of psychology is that humans (and animals) are motivated to perform actions that produce positive feelings (positive affect). This mechanism helps humans to learn highly adaptive behavior, such as finding food, but also some less adaptive behavior. For example, recreational drug use

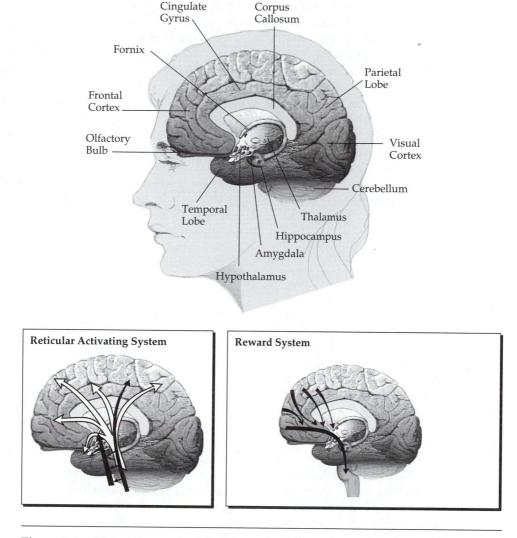

Figure 2-1.   Major structures of the human brain and their relationship to the reward pathway and the reticular activating system.

produces positive affect but is typically not adaptive (Chapter 7).

The reward pathway is not the only system that is responsible for producing feelings of pleasure. The *limbic system,* a structure deep within the brain that regulates emotions such as fear, love, and anger, is believed to be involved not only in the activation of behavior (dispositions) but also in its reinforcement. Note that the limbic system is triggered in somewhat different

circumstances than is the reward pathway. In other words, these systems help us adapt to different environmental demands. (For more details on the limbic system, see Chapter 5.)

It is important to identify and understand those biological systems because so much of human action seems to be motivated by the desire to experience positive affect. With an understanding of these systems, psychologists may be able to help people give up maladaptive behaviors by teaching them to substitute more adaptive ones. Rather than telling teenagers to say no to drugs, which they may find hard to do, it would be better to teach them to get high by engaging in behaviors that have less destructive outcomes.

Most psychologists regard the motivation to experience positive emotions as a disposition that people inherit. People are not compelled to take drugs or to have sex; those are merely options. One option may have greater appeal than another because of past experiences or expectations that have been created by the media or friends. The bottom line, however, is that humans are strongly disposed to seek pleasure in one form or another.

The Disposition to Process Information: The Reticular Activating System

From an evolutionary perspective, the most fundamental principle that governs behavior is the need to insure that our genes survive. In the past, evolutionary theorists suggested that we were motivated to insure our personal survival. However, human and animal behavior can be better understood by the idea that we are more motivated to protect our genes. One reason we attempt to survive is to reproduce and thereby increase the chance that our genes will survive. As parents, we are also inclined to protect our children because, if they survive, then our genes are likely to survive.

To survive, we need to be vigilant in detecting anything that threatens us. We also need to master our environment. We do that by processing information and developing skills. It is through mastery, for example, that we learn to obtain food and water and gain the opportunity to reproduce. Being vigilant and mastering the environment are generally viewed as highly incompatible activities. Because we only have a limited ability to process information, we don't have the resources to both scour the environment for potential threats and process new information. In addition, we don't have unlimited energy. Keeping two systems activated all the time would take an enormous amount of energy. Ideally, the brain's information-processing systems would respond to immediate demands and then shut down to conserve energy and to do routine maintenance such as rebuilding cells and restoring depleted chemicals.

This energy-saving arrangement is made possible by the reticular activating system (RAS), located at the top of the brainstem (Moruzzi & Magoun, 1949). When there is no incoming information, the RAS shuts down the brain. However, when the sensory receptors are stimulated, it activates the brain and insures that incoming information is analyzed. The RAS does not always activate the brain completely. When the incoming information is very familiar, for example, the brain is only partially activated. If a threat arises, however, the brain is fully activated to deal with it.

New or novel information of any kind almost always activates the brain. The brain analyzes new developments for any signs of a threat and also for purposes of gaining mastery over the environment. In this way, our brain maximizes our chances of survival.

During sleep, the brain often becomes very active—for example, when we dream. As we will see in Chapter 6, it appears that the brain often takes care of unfinished business during the night. The RAS makes this possible by periodically activating the sleeping brain.

Other systems within the brain that are devoted to arousal include the limbic system, which is thought to be more involved in rewards, whereas the RAS is more involved in neuronal organization (Routtenberg, 1968).

Neurotransmitters

To conclude our survey of the biological aspects of motivation, we need to consider brain chemicals called neurotransmitters. In motivational processes, neurotransmitters perform two distinct but complementary functions: information transmission and the regulation of moods.

Neurotransmitters and Information Transmission

Information is transmitted in the brain via nerve pathways. Interestingly, these nerve pathways are not continuous but are made up of short lengths of nerve fiber separated by gaps called *synapses*. In order to travel along the pathway, information must somehow cross these gaps. Researchers have found that, when the nerve pathway is activated, chemicals called neurotransmitters are released and carry the information across the synapse (Figure 2-2).

Figure 2-3 presents a classification of the many neurotransmitters in the brain. We will mainly be con-

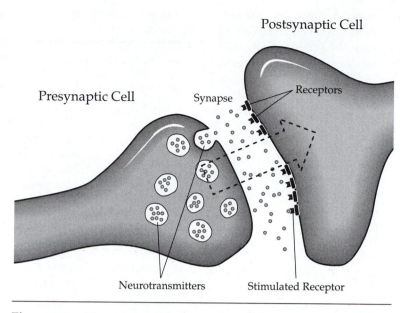

Figure 2-2. Neurotransmitters are released from presynaptic cells into the synapse to stimulate receptors on the postsynaptic cells.

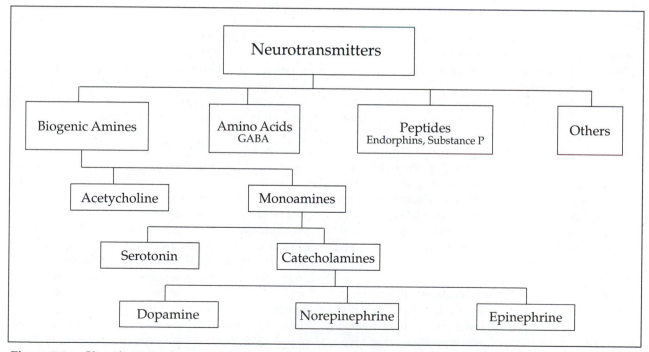

Figure 2-3. Classification of neurotransmitters.

cerned with the biogenic amines. Note that, for each type of neurotransmitter, there are several different receptors. For example, there are ten types of receptors for serotonin, at least five for dopamine, and several alpha and beta types for norepinephrine. The combination of different neurotransmitters and different receptors helps account for the ability of the brain to perform a wide range of complex functions (Kalat, 1995).

An important feature of neurotransmitters is that, once they have carried a message across the synapse, they are typically inactivated; this insures that they do not excite the postsynaptic neuron indefinitely. The inactivated neurotransmitter is resorbed by the presynaptic neuron, synthesized back into an active state, and stored in vesicles ready for release. In certain cases, the synthesis of a neurotransmitter involves proteins from foods that we eat. In other words, diet can play a role in the availability of neurotransmitters.

Neurotransmitters and Moods

Many neurotransmitters are directly involved in the regulation of moods. Norepinephrine, for example, has been linked to feelings of euphoria and depression. When the norepinephrine level at the synapse is high, we feel euphoric; when it is low, we feel depressed. Various drugs, such as the tricyclic antidepressants and cocaine, create a positive mood by maintaining a high level of norepinephrine in the synapse. Table 2-1 summarizes some of the mood effects linked to neurotransmitters.

GABA (gamma-aminobutyric acid), an amino acid neurotransmitter, plays an important role in regulating anxiety and information processing. (The relationship between anxiety and information processing is discussed in Chapter 5.) Two of the peptide neurotransmitters, endorphins and substance P, play an important role in the experience of pain. Endorphins have analgesic (painkilling) properties and have also been linked to positive moods. Heroin and morphine trigger endorphin release (Chapter 7). Substance P is involved in the transmission of pain information; painkillers block its action.

We are only beginning to understand how mood and adaptive behaviors are linked. In general, negative moods tend to be associated with attention to, or memory of, threatening stimuli, while positive moods tend to be linked to attention to, or memories of, opportuni-

Table 2-1. The effect of certain neurotransmitters on moods.

Neurotransmitter	Some Effects on Mood
1. Serotonin	Low levels linked to negative mood (depression); high levels linked to positive mood (euphoria).
2. Dopamine	Low levels linked to negative mood (depression); high levels linked to positive mood (euphoria). Many recreational drugs (such as amphetamine) trigger dopamine release.
3. Norepinephrine (also known as noradrenaline)	Low levels linked to negative mood (depression); high levels linked to positive mood (euphoria).
4. Epinephrine (also known as adrenaline)	High levels linked to brain activation; no direct link to mood.

ties and possibilities (for example, exploratory behavior). Which comes first is not clear. Perhaps both are triggered by the activation of a certain brain circuit.

Because they are relatively easy to monitor, moods can play an important role in helping us to understand and redirect our behavior. The ability to monitor moods is important in stress management, for example. By recognizing our moods and understanding what causes them, we can learn to alter our behavior or environment in order to regulate our moods and attention.

Depletion of Neurotransmitters

Neurotransmitters are manufactured and stored in various parts of the body and in the brain synapses. Stores of neurotransmitters can become depleted as the day progresses. Neurotransmitters stored in the synapses are replenished during sleep (Hartmann & Stern, 1972). Certain environmental factors tend to deplete these stores at a higher than normal rate; stress is a good example. Recreational drugs such as alcohol and cocaine can lead to the depletion of norepinephrine and other neurotransmitters. When these stores are depleted, our ability to think and process information is often impaired. Also, we tend to become depressed. Learning to regulate these neurotransmitters, therefore, has become a central focus for psychologists. Drug companies have invested billions of dollars in developing drugs that will regulate these neurotransmitters and hence our moods.

Neurotransmitters are central to attention, learning, mood, and motivation and, as psychologists, we need to have a solid grounding in their role. Understanding neurotransmitters is not peripheral to motivation; it is central.

Summary

Motivation is concerned with understanding how dispositions can lead to actions, through the interaction of biological, learned, and cognitive processes. These processes are known collectively as components of motivation. There is ample evidence from a variety of sources that human behavior is not infinitely flexible, as some learning theorists have argued, nor is it totally preprogrammed. The existence of general reward systems and arousal systems suggests that humans are capable of learning a number of new behaviors not specifically dictated by their genetic structure.

Not all new behaviors are adaptive. Whether adaptive or not, their persistence indicates that they are supported in some way by our biological structure. Our biological processes are not immutable, however; they can be regulated. In at least some cases, becoming aware of these biological processes is the first step toward learning how to control and regulate them.

The Learned Component

Attention and Learning

What we learn is governed, to a very large degree, by attention. For psychologists, attention consists of three interrelated processes. First, humans need to focus their sensory receptors on a source of information (stimulation) in order to analyze that information. We sometimes call this type of attention *attending* or *receptor orientation*. Second, even when organisms focus their attention on a given source of information, they selectively process only part of the incoming informa-

tion. This is called *selective attention;* it is related to the individual's mindset. If I'm hungry, for example, I'm likely to process food-related information, even though other information is present. Third, because we are limited in our ability to process information, we often cannot deal effectively with vast amounts of information or complex topics. One way we deal with vast amounts of information is to look for the underlying organization. Among other things, we look for things that can be grouped or chunked. One reason we hire guides when we travel is to help us deal with the complexity of the new environment. Guides help us to focus on what they think we should see and learn (selective attention). In addition, they often provide information that helps us to organize and make sense out of the information impinging on our receptors. We use words such as perception, meaning, and understanding to denote the idea that we are grasping the underlying organizational properties of the situation. What we remember are images, themes, and stories; rarely do we remember random, unrelated pieces of information (Kahneman, 1973; Navon & Gopher, 1979; Norman & Bobrow, 1975; Wickens, 1984).

Good teaching involves maximizing all three types of attention. First, a teacher aligns the desks towards the front of the room to insure sensory receptors are oriented on what the student is supposed to learn. Second, the teacher tells the students what they need to focus on and what to ignore. Finally, the teacher helps students to organize the material—for example, by providing lists or themes that link various elements of the material in some way. The teacher may also encourage her students to create their own organization by looking for personal meaning. A good way to link things together so that you can remember them is to create a story.

Associative and Cognitive Learning

Generally, when we talk about learning, we mean what psychologists call associative learning. Historically, psychologists have conceptualized these processes as *S-R learning*, the connection or association of stimuli and responses. Such learning processes depend on the first two types of attention and form the subject of the present section.

In the next section, I will discuss cognitive learning, which is the process of organizing information to construct meaning. This type of learning, studied by cognitive psychologists, depends on the third type of attention. As individuals, we often start to make sense out of the world through associative learning processes but, as things become more complex, we find it necessary to rely more and more on cognitive processes.

Let's now turn our attention to associative learning and the types of attention on which it depends: receptor orientation and selective attention.

Is Attention under Voluntary Control?

Attention is only partially under voluntary control. When something new is introduced into the environment, for example, attention will typically shift to that new source of stimulation. If we cannot process the information, because we lack the ability to comprehend it, our attention is likely to move on. Likewise, if

we have processed the same information on some previous occasion, our attention will shift to something else. When this happens, we subjectively report that we are bored. When our attention shifts, so does our learning. Thus, managing attention is the key to effective learning.

To the best of their ability, teachers attempt to present material at the optimum pace: not so fast that they lose the slow learner and not so slow that they lose the fast learner. Children with attention deficit/hyperactivity disorder are extremely distractible. Among other things, they seem unable to ignore most external stimuli. As a result, they often cannot learn in a regular classroom setting. Bright children sometimes have difficulty maintaining their attention in class, because they shift their focus to other things when they have extracted all the information presented to them.

Practical Application 2-2

Becoming Aware of Your Biological Processes

People can become aware of many of their biological processes. Peter Suedfeld (1975) found that people who spent long periods of time under conditions of sensory deprivation often became aware of some of their physiological responses, such as their heart rate and respiration (see Chapter 3). He suggested that, under conditions of sensory isolation, people begin attending to their physiological responses because they have nothing else to arouse their attention. More important, perhaps, he found that, as a result of their sensory isolation experience, they were less affected by stress at a later time. The reason they experienced less stress, he argued, was that they had learned to control those responses. In short, they had learned the basic techniques of relaxation, one of the main ways to alleviate stress.

Considerable research shows that one of the first steps in learning to control your physiological responses is to become aware of them. In relaxation training, for example, people are often first taught to contract a certain set of muscles (in their arm, for example) and then to relax them. In contracting and then relaxing a group of muscles, people typically become aware of those muscles and how to control

them. As a result, when they become tense, they can focus on those muscles and relax them at will. People can even learn to monitor and control their brain waves. When hooked to a machine that records brain waves (an electroencephalograph, or EEG) and allowed to monitor their brain waves on a screen, they can learn to produce alpha waves, which have been linked to a state of relaxed awareness. In order to produce alpha waves at will, people can learn to recreate the psychological state that is linked to alpha waves. Thus, when they are in a state of relaxed awareness, they know, on the basis of past learning, that their brain is likely to be producing alpha waves.

While we can become directly aware of our heart rate, respiration, and the tenseness of our muscles, we can only become indirectly aware of certain other biological processes. Take, for example, the reward pathway in the brain. This pathway has been linked to moods: When it is activated, we experience positive moods or feelings of euphoria, whereas when it is not active, we tend to experience negative moods or even feelings of depression. One way to become indirectly aware of your reward pathway is to monitor how positive or negative you feel.

Chemicals called neurotransmitters carry messages across synapses in the brain. Without them, it would be

Because attention is not always under our control, psychologists make a distinction between deliberate (intentional) and incidental (passive) learning. At times, we deliberately set out to learn something. For example, I may deliberately focus my attention on the way a person swings a golf club; or I may deliberately rehearse a phone number so that I can recall it at a later time. At other times, our learning is more incidental. Relaxing in front of the television, for example, I might learn how to rescue someone who has fallen in a fast-moving stream or how to cook squash. Neither of these two pieces of information may have any immediate interest to me; nonetheless, I may store them away and draw on them at some later time when I need them.

Because the amount of information we can process is limited, we often shift our attention back and forth in order to learn two things simultaneously. In a conversation, for example, we may shift our attention to a person entering the room and then shift back to the person talking. During that brief time, we may fail to process part of the conversation. Then we either try to fill in the missing portion or apologize for our lapse. We are not always aware that our attention is shifting in this way.

To some degree, we can learn to attend to two different sources of stimulation by this technique. For example, we can focus on something in the foreground while monitoring something in the background; or we can focus our eyes on one thing while listening to something else. Our ability to do so is limited mainly by the amount of information contained in the two sources of stimulation and the amount of time available. If the foreground provides considerably information to process, for example, we will not process

impossible to think or process information. These neurotransmitters tend to become depleted as a result of intense mental activity, stress, or even drinking alcohol. When this happens, thinking becomes sluggish. By monitoring your ability to think clearly, you can indirectly monitor the release of neurotransmitters in your brain. At various times throughout the day, estimate how well you can think or process information. This will give you some idea of the level of your neurotransmitters.

Another interesting exercise is to try to fire neurons in your brain by creating visual images (Crick & Koch, 1992). Because neurons fire only when an electrical threshold is crossed, you will be more likely to fire neurons in your visual cortex if your images are very detailed. First, create an image that you find very relaxing, such as sitting by a creek in summer, and then monitor your heart rate, your respiration, and your mood. Next, imagine a situation that would cause a stress response, such as seeing a spider walk across your arm or leaning over a balcony on the 40th floor of a building. Again, monitor your heart rate, your respiration, and your feelings. Try alternating between a relaxing and a stressful image and see how your reactions change. In this exercise, you are not only firing neurons in your brain, but also inducing the release of a variety of chemicals that have been linked to relaxation and to stress. The more you practice doing this, the more you will become aware of your own biology.

People in the western hemisphere are raised to ignore their biological processes or to treat them as distinct from mental processes. This is sometimes called the dualistic paradigm (Langer, 1989). We begin to become more aware of our biological responses when we understand that they are directly linked to our mental processes.

Extensive research suggests that many health benefits are associated with awareness of our own biological processes. Research in health psychology provides overwhelming evidence that how we think about things (especially adversity) affects not only our moods but also our immune system (Seligman, 1989). Perhaps one of the most powerful tools we have to affect our physiology and our health is humor (Carroll & Schmidt, 1990; Carroll, 1992). When you learn to put on a happy face, you can change your entire physiology (Chapter 9). Try experimenting to see what humor does to some of your biological processes.

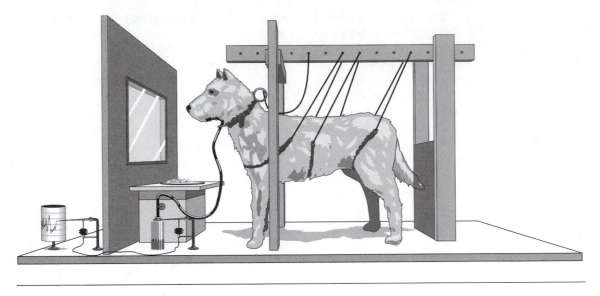

Figure 2-4.   A typical Pavlovian setup.

information in the background. If we are presented with complex visual information, we may have little attention left over for auditory stimulation. Given unlimited time, people will often demonstrate that they can readily do two or even more things simultaneously.

The point I want to emphasize is that learning depends on attention processes and therefore, in order to understand what people learn, we need to understand what controls and limits attention. Because attention is governed in part by motivational processes, what we learn can often be understood, at least in part, in motivational terms (Simon, 1994).

Now it's time to begin our survey of learning theories, with Pavlov's classic work on conditioning.

Classical Conditioning

Ivan Pavlov (1927) discovered classical conditioning when he found that dogs could be taught to salivate at the sound of a bell if the bell was rung whenever food was presented (Figure 2-4). According to Pavlov's analysis, food is conceptualized as an unconditioned stimulus (US) that naturally leads to the unconditioned response (UR) of salivation. The bell does not normally elicit salivation but, when paired with food (preferably a half-second before the food is presented), it acquires the ability to do so, because it is a reliable predictor

that food is forthcoming. Pavlov found that, after several pairings of bell and food, the bell elicited salivation even when no food was presented. In such circumstances, we say that the bell has become a conditioned stimulus (CS). The response elicited by the CS is called the conditioned response (CR). In general, the CR is not as strong as the UR. If the CS (the bell) is repeatedly presented in the absence of the US (the food), it will eventually lose its ability to elicit the response. The procedure of repeatedly presenting the CS in the absence of a reward or the US is called *extinction*.

Note that experiments demonstrating classical conditioning in the laboratory were arranged so as to increase the likelihood that the experimental subject (in this case, the dog) would attend to the relevant stimuli (in this case, the food and the bell). For example, animals were restrained so that they faced a given direction, and extraneous forms of stimulation were removed. Think of trying to replicate this experiment in the forest with rabbits running about.

Conditioning and Adaptive Behavior

Classical conditioning is crucial for adaptive behavior. Many organisms, including humans, depend on relatively innocuous signals to warn of threats to survival. Thus, it is imperative for them to accurately identify those signals. According to current thinking, classical conditioning involves more than simple S-R associations (e.g., Rescorla, 1988). The study of humans and animals suggests that organisms often act as sophisticated statistical evaluators of information; they select out those aspects of the situation that predict the presence or absence of other significant events (e.g., Basic Behavioral Science Task Force, 1996).

An interesting feature of conditioning is illustrated by a phenomenon known as *blocking*. If an animal is given a tone as a signal for a forthcoming electric shock, it will quickly learn to associate the tone with the shock. It will learn, for example, to make an avoidance response when the tone is presented. If a light is then presented together with the tone, the animal is inclined to treat the light as redundant and not to respond when the light is presented alone. In other words, the prior association of the tone and the shock will block the learning of the light-shock association (Kamin, 1968). This is consistent with other studies showing that the information value of the stimulus is what produces learning (Rescorla, 1988). The simple pairing of two events is not sufficient to produce classical conditioning. What is needed to account for learning is some additional concept—such as attention or information processing—that describes how organisms selectively attend or selectively process information (e.g., Kahneman, 1973; Navon & Gopher, 1979; Norman & Bobrow, 1975; Wickens, 1984).

Context and Conditioning

Associations are formed not just between the primary events that psychologists present, such as the CS and the US, but also between these events and the situation in which the conditioning takes place. This finding has helped us to understand a wide variety of findings, including data on drug addiction. Perhaps one of the most interesting findings about drug addiction is that drug effects are, to a very large degree, under situational control. The urge to use drugs, for example, appears to be triggered by the environment. Change the environment and the urge seems to disappear. Following the Vietnam war, only 15% of heroin users in the U.S. military became addicted again after returning to their homes (Basic Behavioral Science Task Force, 1996). It is also known that users need greater amounts of the drug to experience a high when they are in a familiar environment than they do in a new environ-

ment. In fact, heroin users taking their usual dose of the drug in a new environment have been known to die from an overdose. According to the opponent process theory of drug addiction, heroin and related drugs trigger an opponent process that neutralizes their effects. Research suggests that this opponent process can be conditioned to environmental cues. Thus, when a heroin user enters a familiar environment, the opponent process will immediately be triggered. This means the user will have to take greater amounts of heroin to override the opponent process. Should that same drug user inject heroin in an unfamiliar environment, the initial effects of the heroin would be strong, since the opponent process would not be in place. While the heroin itself would eventually trigger the opponent process, it might be too late to prevent an overdose.

Fear as a Conditioned Motive

The discovery of classical conditioning helped psychologists to understand many human fears. Because many fears, such as the fear of enclosed places (claustrophobia) or the fear of flying, are not universal, it has been suggested that they are learned. Claustrophobia may be the result of some traumatic experience early in life. As a child you may have been locked in a closet as a prank or by accident. While you were in that closet, you probably experienced some very negative emotions. You may have thought that whoever locked you in that closet had forgotten about you and you were doomed to starve to death. Or you may simply have been afraid of the dark and imagined that some monster was going to get you. According to the principles of classical conditioning, your emotional state was likely to become conditioned to that closet. Whenever you entered the closet, you would experience the same emotion. But the emotional experience would not be limited to that particular closet. Humans are inclined to generalize. Generalization refers to the tendency of organisms to react in a similar way to situations that appear similar. Thus, we are likely to experience the emotion again. That explains why a person might exhibit claustrophobia in an elevator, for example, even without any prior aversive experience in an elevator. According to the theory of classical conditioning, fear is simply a conditioned emotional response that has generalized to a variety of situations recalling that in which the negative emotional state was first elicited.

Reversing Classical Conditioning

According to the theory of classical conditioning, the only way to get rid of your fear is to extinguish the response or to use some kind of counterconditioning procedure. If the response is to be extinguished, the CS must be presented to you repeatedly in the absence of the US. According to the theory of classical conditioning, this procedure should weaken the fear response. In many cases it doesn't, for reasons that we needn't go into here.

In counterconditioning, the CS is paired with a more favorable response, such as relaxation or feelings of security. If the new response is strong enough, it should cancel out or replace the previously acquired response.

Instrumental Learning

In instrumental learning, organisms learn that certain environmental events, such as receiving rewards or punishments, depend on their own behavior. Certain foods can be rewarding (reinforcing) to an animal if it is hungry or if the food stimulates one of the sensory systems associated with food intake. Figure 2-5 compares classical conditioning and instrumental learning. What is particularly interesting about rewarded behavior is that, in many cases, the behavior will continue at a high rate even if the reward is removed. A nonrewarded response will eventually diminish in rate or strength. This process is called extinction. One way to make a response continue in the absence of reward is to offer *partial reinforcement* of the behavior—that is, instead of rewarding the behavior on every trial, to reward the behavior on only some of the trials.

Secondary Rewards and Instrumental Learning

If a reward is to be effective, it must be applied as soon as possible after the desired behavior has occurred. *Primary reinforcers* such as food are often very effective as rewards for behavior, especially in the training of animals. A primary reinforcer is something with the capacity to increase a response independently of any previous learning. Thus, we do not have to be taught the reward value of eating food, particularly when we are hungry. However, primary rewards are not very practical as reinforcers of many human behaviors. It's hard to imagine a university professor offering little pieces of candy to a student each time the student does well on a test. For humans, *symbolic* or *secondary rewards*—for instance, writing "Very good" or a big A on a test paper—often prove more effective than primary rewards.

Classical Conditioning

Teaching a dog to salivate to a bell

UCS (food)   →   UCR (salivation)
CS (bell)   →   CR (salivation)

1. The optimal conditions for producing conditioning are to present the CS (conditioned stimulus) about 0.5 sec before the UCS (unconditioned stimulus).

2. In this type of learning, the CS becomes a signal that the UCS is about to be presented. The UCR (unconditioned response) is automatically elicited by the UCS. The CR (conditioned response) is typically weaker, but it is the same response.

3. If the UCS (food) is not presented, the response will eventually extinguish.

Instrumental Learning

Teaching a dog to sit on command

S ("Sit")   →   R (dog sitting), reward

1. The optimal conditions for producing instrumental learning are to present the reward immediately after the desired R (response) is made.

2. In this type of learning, the S (stimulus) becomes the signal to perform an R. Getting the R to occur may require shaping (for instance, putting the dog into a sitting position).

3. If the reward is not presented, the response will eventually extinguish.

Figure 2-5. Comparison of classical conditioning with instrumental learning.

Why do these symbolic or secondary rewards actually work? There are at least two lines of thinking. One is that various forms of praise acquire reward value because they have been associated with the presentation of a primary reward. For example, when your dog sits up and you offer a little piece of meat as a reward, you may say, "Good dog." After a time, the phrase "Good dog" acquires reinforcing properties, through the principles of classical conditioning, because it has been paired with the presentation of the primary reward. When you were a child, your parents did the same thing when they fed you. As a result, when they express praise for you now, it makes you feel good, just as the food you ate as a child made you feel good. The second line of argument is simply that, as a thinking being, humans know that "Very good" or an A at the top of their paper means that they are acquiring a skill that has value. This skill can be used to earn money or simply to earn love and respect from people who matter to them.

Achievement as an Instrumentally Acquired Motive

According to the principles of instrumental learning, the strength of any response can be increased by means of a contingent reward. Suppose a child comes home with a score of 9 out of 10 on a math quiz and is rewarded in some way by the parents. A likely outcome is that the child would strive to do well on other math tests. If the parents then rewarded other good outcomes in the same way, the child might strive to do well in other subjects. Over time, the child might develop a tendency to work hard in every subject. This tendency might even generalize beyond school, to other situations. At that point, we might refer to this behavior pattern as achievement motivation.

Social Incentive Theory

The principles of classical conditioning and instrumental learning form the basis of social incentive theory. According to social incentive theory, positive (rewarding) experiences often occur when we do what others want us to do. For example, we often experience approval in connection with primary rewards such as money, food, clothing, affection (for example, hugging) and permission to watch television. Approval, in other words, takes on great significance; it signals that other primary rewards are forthcoming. Similarly, disapproval takes on great significance. Typically, we experience disapproval in connection with such things as withdrawal of money, having to go without dinner, physical punishment, and withdrawal of privileges such as watching television. As a result, we learn to avoid disapproval, because it signals the withdrawal of primary rewards (Bandura, 1991).

Seeking approval and avoiding disapproval are assumed to be central motivators for humans. One reason for their durability as motivators is that they are somewhat unpredictable (Bandura, 1991). Research has shown that, when reinforcement is intermittent, stimuli retain their ability to act as motivators. Later in life, we continue to seek approval and avoid disapproval. Disapproval can arouse in us the fear that we will lose our job or privileges, while approval arouses in us the expectation that rewards such as promotions or pay raises will be forthcoming.

Much of what we have called the learned component of motivation has its roots in social incentive theory. For example, some children learn to eat more than others because it earns them approval from a parent who eats too much. Some people use physical aggression to get their way because they received social approval for such behavior as children. We learn to control our sexual impulses, at least in part, out of a desire to please parents or significant others in society.

Intrinsic and Extrinsic Rewards

A distinction is often made between intrinsic and extrinsic rewards. When an activity itself provides the reward, we say that the activity is intrinsically rewarding. When an activity is performed in order to obtain an unrelated reward, we say that the activity is extrinsically rewarding. A child who does well in school simply to gain approval from parents or to acquire a skill that can be used to earn money or fame is pursuing extrinsic rewards. If, by contrast, the child finds the schoolwork motivating even in the absence of approval or other benefits, then the rewards are intrinsic. Note, however, that some theorists discount the role of extrinsic rewards in developing a strong achievement orientation and argue, instead, that achievement is linked to more intrinsic forms of motivation. Robert White (1959), for example, has suggested that achievement or mastery is linked to what he calls effectance motivation. David

McClelland (1985) contends that it grows out of curiosity or exploratory motivation. A number of motivation theorists believe that skill acquisition occurs partly for extrinsic reasons but largely for intrinsic reasons. Presumably different situations arouse different motives for learning.

Summary

Most learning theorists agree that all learning is governed by attention. Since we cannot attend to everything, we learn certain things and not others. Attention is only partially under our control; we have been programmed, to some degree, to attend to things that might threaten our survival.

Learning is an associative process. Two important forms of associative learning are classical conditioning and instrumental learning. Contrary to the assumption that only contiguity between stimulus and response is important for classical conditioning to take place, it has been shown that information value and not contiguity is the critical feature. This is consistent with the idea that attention is important in learning. However, the fact that context affects the strength of a conditioned response suggests that individuals are conditioned to the situation and not simply to a specific cue or to part of the situation.

Instrumental learning depends on administering a reward. Many things acquire the ability to reward (become secondary reinforcers) because they have been associated with a primary reward such as food.

Social incentive theory has its roots in classical conditioning and instrumental learning theories. According to social incentive theory, the desire for social approval is a powerful human motivator. Nonetheless, a great deal of research suggests that we also learn for intrinsic reasons.

The Cognitive Component

In psychology, cognitive processes are those associated with knowing. Cognition, therefore, involves thinking, perceiving, abstracting, synthesizing, organizing, or otherwise conceptualizing the nature of the external world and the self. Cognitive theories are typically framed in terms of having or developing cognitive structures that allow us to make sense of the complexity of the world.

Cognitive processes are often conceptualized in terms of the third aspect of attention discussed earlier. Humans are unable to process limitless amounts of information. Therefore, we need to develop cognitive structures that will reduce the complexity of the information we encounter. We do this by finding higher-order relationships, structures, principles, and rules. In other words, we process something other than the raw sensory information that falls on our receptors; we process the inherent order that summarizes that raw sensory information. Memories, therefore, have to do with order and structure.

Where do we get this organization and structure? Some is given to us by our sensory system; we are born with the ability to see figure as distinct from background, for example. Part of it comes from learning; we are taught relationships, structure, and rules. Much of it comes, however, from personal discovery. We are brilliantly equipped to find redundancy, for example; this allows us to discard everything but the essential elements. We are also equipped with the ability to create stories that link elements of our experience. It seems that, when we have a story, we don't need to remember the details; we can fill in the details on the basis of schemata stored in our memory.

Cognitive Theories

Piaget's theory of development is a good example of a cognitive theory. Piaget contended that children are motivated to develop cognitive structures because they need to interact with and master the environment. They begin, he suggested, by simply processing information in terms of whatever structures they have. Piaget called this process *assimilation*. When these structures are no longer complex enough for the child to make complete sense of his or her interactions with the world, the child begins to experience confusion or incomprehension, a state that Piaget simply called *disequilibrium*. He suggested that this state of disequilibrium motivates the child to develop new cognitive structures in order to make sense of the complexity, a process Piaget called

Jean Piaget

accommodation. Development, according to Piaget, is a lifetime process in which we continually move between disequilibrium and equilibrium.

Most, if not all, cognitive theories state or imply that the development of cognitive structures is linked to motivation processes. Most theories suggest that motivation can be conceptualized as some kind of discrepancy between what the individual can presently comprehend and what the individual needs to comprehend in order to make sense out of the world or simply to fully know. While early cognitive theorists focused on how we can come to know our external world, recently a number of cognitive theorists have focused their attention on how we come to know ourselves and how this can lead to the self-regulation of behavior, as we discussed briefly at the end of Chapter 1.

The Nature of Cognitions

In recent years, there have been numerous demonstrations that how we think about ourselves and the world has a profound impact on how we behave. Without attempting a complete overview of this work, the present section offers some basic examples of how cognitions affect behavior.

Note that cognitions are often based on past learning. As children, we learn to categorize, and we develop beliefs and attitudes by imitating and modeling our parents. As we develop, however, we often modify these cognitive structures. Using our own experiences, listening to the experience of others, or studying a carefully designed discourse (a lecture or a book, for example), we alter our beliefs. These changes are typically the result of a cognitive process. One interesting aspect of cognition is the tendency to make things consistent. We modify beliefs and attitudes so that they are consistent with our values. The result is a new set of cognitive structures that incorporate those values. While these cognitive structures may seem very similar to those we acquired as children, they often differ from our parents' in subtle but important ways.

This section is organized around the idea that humans are inclined to organize information according to certain rules, principles, and theories that allow them to see the world as consistent and predictable. According to attention theory, we see the world as consistent and predictable because we have developed structures for processing all incoming information. We do not wake up each morning and attempt to view the world in terms of the raw sensory information falling on our receptors; rather, we see it with the same eyes that saw it yesterday, last week, last year. It takes a great deal of change in the environment before we change our ideas. Sometimes, we need to be faced with some adversity before we will take a second look. The bottom line is that, once our cognitive structures are formed, they are very resistant to change. In a sense, we have learned to be lazy. We trust our cognitive structures even when they are no longer in harmony with the world.

Categories and Labels

The brain has evolved to identify the main characteristics of incoming stimulation. By this process, for example, infants learn to recognize the faces of their parents.

So that we can make sense out of the complex world in which we live, the brain has been designed or organized not only to isolate features (figure as opposed to background, for example) but to identify abstract qualities that define a thing or group of things. For example, the defining attributes of the category comprised of animals include life, legs, and a body. Horses, cows, and dogs are subsets of this category, each with their own defining characteristics. Behavioral neuroscientists suggest that, when a distinct combination of neurons is repeatedly fired, it forms an interconnection (or a pattern in the brain), to which we attach a name. These distinct patterns are not just the product of the external environment, but also involve memories. When we can't see something—perhaps because another object is blocking our view—we fill in the missing information by drawing on our generic memory (a collection of schemata), which contains the essential or defining features of a category (Crick & Koch, 1992). Categories, in other words, allow us to summarize complex information into more generic forms, thereby freeing us from the necessity of having to keep track of endless pieces of specific information. We label these categories appropriately as house, dog, mountains, and so forth. This is where learning enters the picture.

Categories and labels not only help us identify objects or things, but also help us identify dispositions, emotions, or behaviors—anger, happiness, sadness, or aggression, for instance. Think for a minute how important it is that we are able to do this. Let's say that I am standing in the hallway and someone steps on my toe. I ask myself how I should classify and label this behavior. If I label it as clumsy, I can forget it. If I label it as aggressive, however, it is quite a different matter. Humans, for the most part, feel that they must retaliate for an aggressive act. If I don't retaliate, I may be forced to regard myself as a victim. Thus, how I label someone else's behavior has important implications for how I react to them. If I label another person's behavior as selfish rather than altruistic, I might be inclined to provide a poor job recommendation for that person, especially if the job involved helping children with disabilities. If that same person were applying for a job as a construction worker, however, my perception of the person as more selfish than altruistic might have no effect on my recommendation.

Even more important, perhaps, is how I categorize and label my own behavior. Stanton Peele (1989) has argued that, when people label themselves as alcoholic, they begin to behave like an alcoholic; they lose control of drinking, for example. In his view, it is the label, and not the alcohol, that creates the behavior. Research has shown that people who drink as heavily but do not label themselves as alcoholic behave differently; they do not lose control of their drinking, for example. Peele argues that, in our culture, there is an association between being an alcoholic and the tendency to lose control when drinking alcohol. Thus, the label I use to describe myself can be very important, because labels carry with them a wide range of prescribed behaviors that I will unwittingly follow.

Cognitive psychology suggests that we have the power to select labels. That is, we can discover what is associated with a label and so determine whether it is useful. Thus, cognitive psychology does not deny past learning but contends that we need not be governed solely by it. We can redefine what a label means, just as we redefine our beliefs and attitudes.

Beliefs, Attitudes, and Values

As we develop, we learn many of our beliefs, attitudes, and values from our parents. We come to believe, for example, that a certain political party is best for us and our country because we have listened to the arguments of our parents and observed how they voted. We may come to value the family or the church because our parents valued them.

Many beliefs, attitudes, and values, however, are based on our own experiences and desires. Take, for example, the question of values—that is, those things that we believe are important to the achievement of success, happiness, health, and fulfillment. As we experiment with the values of our parents, we may be inclined to change them. We might come to believe, for example, that it is more important to live a full life than a long life. As a result of our new principle, we will begin to behave in very different ways.

Considerable evidence suggests that children and adolescents are actively involved in their own development (Lerner, 1984). An adolescent might, for example, come to appreciate that his or her behavior is leading to the destruction of the environment, which, in turn, will eventually reduce the length or quality of life. As a result, the teenager decides to adopt a lifestyle with a less negative impact on the environment—for example, to recycle bottles and cans, to buy products only from companies with good environmental practices, or to eat organic foods. By changing values, the individual hopes to achieve new goals, not only on a personal level but for society at large.

According to this distinction, some beliefs, attitudes, and values result from learning (imitation and modeling), while others result from cognitive processes (active construction). This distinction is important, although not always easy to make in practice. In order to change behavior, we often need to change beliefs, attitudes, and values. One way of doing this is to become more mindful of why we are doing or saying something (Langer, 1989). In particular, we may learn to make finer and finer distinctions. Instead of saying, "I hate person X," I might try to identify what it is about person X that I dislike. I may find that I dislike only a couple of things—X's habit of chewing gum and X's hairstyle. Once I can get past those things, I might notice some of X's more likable attributes—kindness and a sense of humor, for example.

One important feature of learning is the tendency to generalize a response learned in one situation to other situations. Generalization has obvious adaptive benefits, but it may also be highly nonadaptive. We can use cognitive processes to eliminate nonadaptive generalizations. Stereotypes (African Americans are good dancers; men are aggressive; women are complainers; Italians are criminals) are classic examples of response generalization. They arise when we try to generalize from a very limited number of instances. Because Michael Jackson is a good dancer doesn't mean that all African Americans are necessarily good dancers. Because we have been exposed to a rash of newspaper articles about homicidal men doesn't mean that all men are violent. Because women on a particular TV show complain a lot doesn't mean that all women are complainers. Because there is a predominance of Italians in the Mafia doesn't mean that all Italians are criminals. Stereotypes, in other words, are a special class of category.

Stereotypes typically often arise in the absence of relevant personal knowledge. We simply adopt the beliefs and attitudes of other people. Many of our stereotypes come from parents, teachers, and other significant people in our lives. We have stereotypes about many things, such as how people should or will act at different ages, how people will act if they are religious, and how people will act if they are rich or poor.

While stereotypes are often relatively stable, considerable research indicates that they can change. They disappear, for example, when we encounter new examples that do not fit the expected category. In that case, we are forced to make finer and finer distinctions. As this happens, the original stereotype (category) proves hopelessly inadequate and the brain rejects it. For a good description of what happens, see Langer (1989). The breakdown of a stereotype is also a good illustration of Piaget's theory of cognitive development.

Cognitive Dissonance Theory

Cognitive dissonance theory has its roots in the idea that people need to experience cognitive consistency (Festinger, 1957). It helps to explain why categories, beliefs, attitudes, values, and stereotypes are highly resistant to change. According to cognitive dissonance theory, humans are inclined to process information in such a way that it will be consistent with existing categories, beliefs, attitudes, values, stereotypes, and behavior—in other words, to ignore information that does not fit with existing beliefs and to seek out information that does fit. If we have a stereotype about old people, for example, we will be inclined to ignore exceptions and to process only those examples that are consistent with our beliefs.

One major area of research that grew out of cognitive dissonance theory concerns people's behavior when they have already committed to an action that is inconsistent with their cognitions. For example, what do people do when they have purchased a car and they discover that it is defective? Research has shown that they are inclined to disregard such information or to seek out more positive information. In other words, they are inclined to do whatever is necessary to make their beliefs and attitudes consistent with their actions. A study of smokers' reactions to evidence that smoking is linked to cancer provides a particularly good example. While nonsmokers were inclined to believe the evidence was reasonably conclusive, smokers were not (Festinger, 1957).

Cognitive dissonance theory has been able to explain, for instance, why people are inclined to become committed to an organization or an individual, even if that organization or individual does not treat them well. One study found that students' liking for a fraternity went up as the severity of the initiation increased. Having consented to behave in ways that are inconsistent with their beliefs about themselves and how they should be treated, individuals need to explain to themselves why they joined that fraternity (e.g., Aronson & Mills, 1959). Their reasoning, it has been suggested, goes something like this: "Why did I dress in that silly outfit and eat raw eggs, oatmeal, and hot sauce while they hurled insults as me? It must be because this is a great fraternity."

Implicit Theories

It has been suggested (Epstein, 1990; Dweck, 1991) that people develop *implicit theories*—hypotheses, models, and beliefs about the nature of the external world (world theories) and about what we need to do to satisfy our desires in this world (self theories). They are called implicit theories because they often exist at the preconscious level. In psychology, if we act at the conscious level, we are fully aware of the reasons for our actions. If we are operating at the preconscious level, by contrast, we could become conscious of the reasons for our actions given the right guidance or perhaps the right set of circumstances (Epstein, 1990).

Unlike scientific theories, which are rational and designed to make sense out of an existing body of facts, implicit theories often involve more irrational and intuitive thinking. Epstein has proposed that implicit theories often come out of a different system for processing information—the *experiential system.*

In the past, psychologists used the concept of expectations to explain why people with different desires, needs, or experiences would see things differently (Bruner, 1992). In recent years, it has become apparent that the concept of expectations is too narrow to explain the complex thought patterns that link individuals' actions to their perceptions of the external world and their conceptualizations of their skills and

abilities. As a result, emphasis has shifted to the concept of implicit theories.

Although they can be learned—at least in part—from modeling the behaviors of others, listening to the views of others, and reading what others have to say, implicit theories are thought to result mainly from our own experiences, our own interactions with the world, and our own successes and failures. In short, they are very personal. More important, perhaps, we think of them as constructed. Presumably, if we constructed them, we can change them.

Habits, Automatic Behavior, and Cognition

Psychologists make a distinction between habits and automatic behavior. *Habits* result from the repetition of some response or sequences of responses. While some theorists (for instance, Hull) have argued that a drive must be reduced in order for a habit to be strengthened, others argue that habits simply come from repeating a response over and over and that rewards merely act as an incentive for engaging in repetition (Hull, 1943).

Where do habits come from? According to learning theorists, they grow out of existing behavior. The ability to find food, for example, is assumed to grow out of some type of random behavior. When the organism consistently finds food in one location, the accompanying responses are strengthened over time, and a habit develops.

By contrast, *automatic behavior* has its origins in intentional or planned behavior (e.g., Langer, 1989; Bargh & Gollwitzer, 1994). If I am trying to find my way to a certain part of the city, for example, I might consult a mental map or even write out a set of instructions that tell me how to get there. Interestingly, after repeating the behavior over and over, I no longer need to think about what I intend to do; it becomes automatic. Alternatively, I might construct a set of implicit rules that I will follow when I meet someone new, so that I won't offend them. Again, over time I no longer need to think about my intentions.

Automatic behavior is highly adaptive. It allows me to use my limited attention to do other things. For example, while driving to some destination, I can think about what I am going to say when I get there. Sometimes, automatic behavior has amusing outcomes. I have, on occasion, left my house to go downtown and ended up in my parking spot at the university. Initially, the route is the same, and, if I happen to get absorbed in thought, automatic behavior takes me to the university.

Some theorists use automatic behavior as a more inclusive term to denote both habits and automatic behaviors that derive from planned behavior. According to current concepts regarding the nervous system, both types of behavior come from the strengthening of neural circuits in the brain. Existing technology cannot distinguish between circuits in the brain that had their origins in planned or intentional behaviors and those that came from the strengthening of some existing response; perhaps they are the same.

For people new to psychology, it may appear that the distinction between habit and automatic behavior is unnecessary. However, this distinction grows out of a long debate among scientists as to whether humans can actually create new behaviors or are simply creatures of conditioning. The concept of automatic behavior, with its aspects of planning and intention, implies that humans can take charge of their own behavior and create a new life for themselves.

Practical Application 2-3

Becoming Mindful of Your Cognitive Processes

In her book *Mindfulness*, Ellen Langer (1989) makes the case that our behavior is often mindless. We set out for work without thinking about how to get there, yet we arrive safely and on time. While mindless or automatic behavior is useful, because it frees our conscious mind to think about other things, it often means that we get into ruts; we don't change our habits even when we should. If we want to change, we need to become mindful of our cognitions. When we become mindful, we gain the power to change and to control things. As we'll see later, the ability to control or simply the belief that we can control our destiny is important for physical and psychological health.

How can you become mindful of your cognitions? Here's a simple step: Each time you decide to do something, ask yourself if there is something else you might do instead. Several things happen when you do this.

1. You learn to generate alternatives. Generating alternatives is a creative act and is the basis for all behavioral change. It makes you aware that you have choices.
2. You gain a sense of control. When you make decisions, you become aware that life is not just happening to you; you are making it happen.
3. You learn *how* to make decisions. Decision making takes practice. Once you learn to make decisions about simple things, you will eventually develop the ability to make decisions about important things.
4. You learn to take control of your thinking process. The more you analyze your thinking, the more you will become aware of your thinking and able to control it.

By forcing yourself to make a conscious decision about things that you do, you slowly become aware that you often do things for reasons. The next time you turn on the television, ask yourself: "Why am I turning on the television? Is there something else I could do?" You can use this technique in every area of your life. If you find yourself making a value judgment such as "I hate living in this city," ask yourself exactly what it is you don't like and if you want to do something about it. This forces you to make finer and finer distinctions. In doing so, you learn to identify what it is that you don't like. Using this approach, you might discover that you don't dislike the city you are living in but rather the neighborhood in which you live, the house, or even the level of traffic. If you come to realize that you hate your neighborhood, rather than the city, you have gained a great deal of power. Now, instead of having to quit your job and leave your friends in order to be happy, you only have to move to a new house or apartment. You have turned what appeared to be an insurmountable problem into a very manageable one. It all happened because you learned to become aware of your cognitions.

An Example: What Causes Happiness?

It has been suggested that happiness depends on whether or not the environment is providing us with satisfying rewards. According to this view, the way to increase happiness in the world is to create a perfect environment. This is one of the basic assumptions of Skinner's learning theory. But what is a perfect environment? To answer that question, you need to ask people what would make them happy. However, people do not agree on the answer.

Cognitive theorists do not focus on changing the environment. They argue that, while obviously important, the environment is often very difficult or even impossible to change. The best thing to do under those circumstances is to change the way you view the environment. This idea was summarized centuries ago by the Roman emperor Marcus Aurelius, who said: "If you are pained by the external things, it is not they that disturb you, but your own judgment of them. And it is in your power to wipe out that judgment now."

According to cognitive theories, what you see or feel depends to a very large degree on your beliefs, attitudes, values, and implicit theories. In our society, we often hold the view (an implicit theory) that we cannot be happy unless our stomachs are full. Yet in countries where there is a chronic shortage of food, people learn to be happy even though their stomachs are not always full. They take pleasure, for example, in being with their families or in laughing when their children tell jokes.

Happiness, in other words, is highly subjective. People often erect barriers that limit their ability to experience happiness. They say to themselves: "I will be happy when I retire" or "I will be happy when I have a sports car" or "I will be happy when I am married."

Many people have decided that they want to experience happiness as often as possible. As a result, they find happiness in simple things such as a cat chasing its tail, a wild flower, rainfall, children playing, a good night of sleep. Some of the happiest people in the world have come to appreciate simply being alive and experiencing the world after recovering from a serious accident or illness.

According to cognitive theories, happiness is a state of mind; it is the result of decisions we make. We know, for example, that optimists tend to be happier than pessimists. In general, optimists tend to see what is good, while pessimists tend to see what is bad. Research suggests that optimism can be learned. In his book *Learned Optimism*, Martin Seligman (1990), a leading psychologist, describes how we can become more optimistic. It may well be, as Seligman and others have argued, that optimism is the result of our learning a new way of explaining events to ourselves so that bad outcomes do not undermine self-esteem and good outcomes build self-esteem.

Does this mean the external world is not important? Quite the contrary. There is no question that we gain happiness through our senses, through exercising skills, through mastery, and through social interactions. But we each decide what aspects of the external world will make us happy. There are many ways to stimulate our senses, to exercise competency, and to experience the joys of social relations. If we accept the message of the advertising industry that happiness depends on wearing the right clothes, driving the right car, or drinking the right beverage, we cut ourselves off from many sources of happiness. Many people have found that happiness does not require an abundance of material things. They have learned that happiness can be found, for example, in enjoying nature, in developing friendships, and in helping other people.

Individual Differences

The main problem with most early theories of motivation was their failure to account for individual differences. Many theories of the 1950s were about so-called average humans. (A notable exception was Atkinson's theory of achievement motivation; see Chapter 13.) Data averaged from random samples of rats, pigeons, and humans were used to describe how the average person learned. Since then, we have come to realize that most of us don't behave in this way. Humans differ by gender, age, temperament, past conditioning, cognitive structures, momentary stress, goals, and recent failures and successes. These are the factors that we need to understand if we are to explain why different humans do quite different things under the same environmental conditions.

Attribution Theory:
Perceiving the Causes of Behavior

Attribution theory is concerned with how humans come to perceive the causes of behavior. To what cause does a person attribute a given behavior? How does a particular individual account for the fact that he failed? How does he account for the fact that he succeeded? When an individual notices that her heart is beating faster, how does she account for that? Will her interpretation affect her subsequent behavior? If someone's perceptions (interpretations) about the cause of behavior affect subsequent behavior, then we have good evidence that cognitive factors are not just secondary or incidental but play a central role in the arousal, direction, and persistence of behavior.

An experiment by Nisbett and Schachter (1966) illustrates how cognitive factors can affect behavior. They showed that humans could be made to tolerate high levels of shock by persuading them that their autonomic responses, such as fast heart rate, were due not to the shock but rather to a pill they had taken. In their experiment, Nisbett and Schachter asked subjects to take a series of electric shocks of steadily increasing intensity and to indicate (1) when the shocks became painful and (2) when the shocks became too painful to tolerate. Before receiving the shocks, the subjects were given a pill. Some were told that the pill would produce hand tremors, palpitations, and other autonomic responses. Others were told that the pill would produce a variety of symptoms that were not autonomic. Actually, the pill was a placebo; it had no physiological effects.

Attribution theory suggests that people are inclined to look for reasonable explanations for their behavior, including autonomic responses. If that is correct, then the subjects who thought the pill would increase autonomic activity would be inclined to attribute their autonomic responses to the pill, while the other subjects would be inclined to attribute their autonomic responses to the shock. Subjects who did not attribute their autonomic responses to the shock should be less sensitive to it and willing to tolerate higher levels of shock. Nisbett and Schachter found that, indeed, subjects who were told the pill would produce autonomic responses tolerated shock levels four times as great as did the other subjects. These results indicate that cognitive factors play an important role even in something as basic as the perception of pain.

Because people come from different backgrounds, because they have different experiences, and because they learn to think differently, they react very differently to the same event. Whether they are optimists or pessimists, for example, has important implications for how they will react. In this book, we will repeatedly address the question of individual differences. Let's begin by talking about the distinction between people known as internals and externals.

Locus of Control Theory:
Internal and External Causes

Heider (1958) suggested that people can be divided into two categories: those who tend to identify internal causes of their behavior (internals) and those who tend to identify external causes (externals). Internals perceive that the cause of behavior lies within themselves, whereas externals believe that it lies outside themselves. These two groups are said to differ in their locus of control.

One difference between external and internal determinants of behavior is that only actions with internal causes can be regarded as intentional. For example, if I step on your toe, you might arrive at two different conclusions: that I did it intentionally (internal causation) or that it was an accident (external causation). How you assess the situation will, of course, affect how you respond.

Externals are more likely to use an external frame of reference to label an event, while internals are more likely to use an internal frame of reference. Because of this difference, internals and externals often react differently to the same environmental event. We will return to this difference later.

Context and Cognition

Humans show a great deal of sensitivity to the situation or context (Bargh & Gollwitzer, 1994). The kinds of things I say, for example, are often tailored to the situation. What I say to my parents is often very different from what I say to friends. Beginning as an adolescent, I may take pleasure in provoking my parents. Later, I may decide I'd rather soothe them, on the grounds that they have a right to their opinions, just as I have a right to mine. Why not try to make our relationship as good as possible? What is interesting is that, over time, my new behavior becomes automatic. While I may fall back into my habit of provoking them, I become steadily better at making good on my original intention. According to the principles of cognition, my behavior could change because I developed a new way of viewing the situation (a new implicit theory).

Earlier, in discussing the learned component of motivation, we saw that drug effects and drug use are influenced by the context and that this could be understood in terms of the principles of classical conditioning. Could my attitudes to my parents also be explained by the principles of classical conditioning? No, because there is an important distinction between intentional and unintentional (or passive) learning. The learning was initially intentional in the parental example, whereas it was unintentional in the drug use example.

Not everybody is equally sensitive to situational or interpersonal cues. Snyder (1979) has suggested that some people, called *high self-monitors,* are much more sensitive to situational and interpersonal cues and, as a result, are inclined to adjust their behavior to the demands of the situation. *Low self-monitors,* in contrast, tend to be oblivious to situational and interpersonal cues; they tell inappropriate stories or bore you to death with their preoccupations. While we are not certain of the origins of these two approaches to the world, we do know that the tendency to be a high or a low self-monitor is habitual or automatic; it is something people do without having to think about it. According to self-regulation theories, we learn one pattern or the other (Bandura, 1991).

Social Incentive Theory and Cognitive Theory

There is a fine line between social incentive theory and cognitive theory. Seeking approval, which is the main theoretical construct within social incentive theory, is viewed as passively conditioned or learned, as opposed to being intentional. It is assumed that people simply imitate or model because they have been reinforced for such behavior. Cognitive theory, by contrast, assumes that people engage in forethought (Bandura, 1991); they think, analyze, create hypotheses, formu-

late plans, and set goals. Collectively, we refer to these activities as intentions. It is when behavior results from intention that we call it cognitive.

Summary

Cognition involves thinking, perceiving, abstracting, synthesizing, organizing, or any other process that allows the individual to conceptualize the nature of the external world and the self. According to attention theory, one reason that we develop cognitive structures is that we have limited ability to process information.

Cognitive processes give rise to categories, to which we attach labels. Cognitive processes also give rise to beliefs, attitudes, and values. Stereotypes are categories that develop out of limited information or the tendency to adopt the beliefs and attitudes of other people, especially role models. Beliefs, attitudes, values, and stereotypes are often very resistant to change. One explanation for this can be found in cognitive dissonance theory, which suggests that humans are inclined to process incoming information so that it is consistent with existing cognitions and behavior.

Implicit theories are hypotheses, models, and beliefs that we have about the nature of the external world (world theories) and about what we need to do to satisfy our desires in this world (self theories). Although we are often not fully aware of them, they guide our behavior. Implicit theories can, for example, play an important role in feeling happy or contented.

According to attribution theory, humans have a natural tendency to look for the causes of their behavior. Nisbett and Schachter illustrated the importance of the attribution process in their study of pain (shock). They showed that misattribution (mislabeling) of the source of increased autonomic activity was sufficient to decrease a person's sensitivity to pain (shock). Compared to controls, subjects who thought that their elevated arousal level was due to a placebo pill, rather than to the shock itself, tolerated shock levels four times as high.

Humans tend to differ with respect to their tendency to attribute events to internal factors as opposed to external factors. This tendency helps to account for the wide range of individual differences that we observe. The labels people use frequently provide a clue to the way they perceive or interpret the cause of an event. Research has shown that the way we label an event—such as having someone step on our toe—can affect not only how we feel but how we react.

Some Examples of a Components Approach

To illustrate a components approach to motivation, let's examine the motivation for running and the motivation for listening to rock music. We'll start by examining the current craze for running.

Motivation for Running

On the surface, running appears to be a straightforward activity. People state that they decide to run in order to get into shape, to lose weight, or to improve their health. However, there are also less obvious reasons. Some people run, they confess, in order to get away from their spouses or to avoid having lunch with their colleagues or to escape from the confines of their office or home. So far, all of these explanations are couched in avoidance terms. What about the positive reasons? It is hard at first for most people to see the pleasure in puffing and sweating on a hot day or freezing on a cold day but, after they have had a chance to experience the effects of running for some time, they tend to report that it makes them feel good and is a pleasant activity. The question that presents itself is how an activity that appears to demand so much effort—and sometimes pain—can be pleasant.

To answer this question, we need to understand that why people do something initially and why they continue to do it may be unrelated. For instance, most of us have good intentions that somehow fail to get translated into long-term behavioral change. I call this the New Year's resolution phenomenon. People will change their behavior for a day, a week, or even a month, but then fall back to their previous pattern. Once the initial motivation fades, there is nothing to maintain the new behavior.

What, then, is the motivation that maintains running, as distinct from the motivation for taking up running? While not everyone who tries running persists with it, some people develop signs of being addicted. If they stop running for a few days, they experience a negative physiological or psychological state analogous to drug withdrawal together with a compulsion to engage in the activity on a regular basis. The obvious question is whether running produces in this group of people some kind of chemical output that has motivating and possibly addicting properties.

The answer is a qualified yes. It appears that running or any aerobic exercise—such as swimming, cycling, walking, rowing, and cross-country skiing—stimulates the output of several chemicals. Norepinephrine output, for example, will increase to as much as 4.5 times normal levels (Davis, 1973; Howley, 1976). Since increased norepinephrine levels have been implicated in elation and euphoria, whereas low levels have been implicated in depression (Post et al., 1978; Schildkraut & Kety, 1967), it seems that people may run in order to experience increased outputs of this or related chemicals. Can people become addicted to norepinephrine? Again, the answer is a qualified yes. Addiction to amphetamines, which produce arousal and euphoria, has been documented for some time. Among other effects, amphetamines stimulate the output of norepinephrine and dopamine, and it has been hypothesized that people take amphetamines specifically for this purpose. It makes sense, therefore, that people will continue to perform a response, such as running, that stimulates the output of one of these chemicals.

A number of studies have shown that aerobic exercise alleviates anxiety (e.g., Morgan & Horstman, 1976) and depression (Greist et al., 1979). Although these studies must be considered preliminary, because several alternative explanations have not been completely ruled out, the results are consistent with a number of other physiological findings (Ledwidge, 1980). Concerning anxiety, exercise has been shown to be a muscle relaxant (Baekeland, 1970; Baekeland & Lasky, 1966) and to reduce lactate, an acid that plays a key role in anxiety symptoms (Clarke, 1975; Larson & Michelman, 1973; Pitts, 1969). In fact, there is evidence that aerobic exercise produces a general decrease in the adrenocortical response to stress (Tharp, 1975; White, Ismail, & Bottoms, 1976). This means that a person who engages in aerobic exercise will experience a less severe reaction to physical stress. As already noted, low levels of norepinephrine are implicated in depressive disorders. The finding that running increases norepinephrine output offers a compelling argument that exercise can alleviate feelings of depression. Further, there is evidence that chronic fatigue, a common

What motivates people to run?

complaint of depressives, is alleviated by aerobic exercise (Kraines, 1957). The fact that depressives exhibit less slow-wave sleep (Gresham, Agnew, & Williams, 1965), which aerobic exercise increases (Griffin & Trinder, 1978), suggests another important link between exercise and depression (Ledwidge, 1980). Finally, there is evidence that running improves short-term performance on mental tasks (Tomporowski & Ellis, 1986). The implication is that, for people who want to improve their cognitive functioning, running would have obvious reinforcing effects.

Over time, people who run tend to increase the amount they run. Returning to the analogy between running and drug addiction, we might say that they are showing a tolerance effect; that is, they are increasing their dosage level in order to experience the same effect. If people run to experience the effects of norepi-

nephrine or some other chemical, it makes good sense that they should tend to increase how much they run, for two reasons. First, as their bodies become conditioned, it is likely that they will have to run longer to get the same output of norepinephrine and dopamine. Second, human motivation may be characterized as an opponent process (Solomon, 1980). For every process set in motion, as we have seen, the body develops an opposing process, in order to return to its original state. Thus, when a drug stimulates one type of reaction, the body initiates an opposing reaction. For example, people often experience fatigue some time after they have taken an amphetamine. It is assumed that the opponent process occurs more quickly and becomes stronger each time it is activated by the drug, and a person would need to take larger doses of the drug to override this opponent process. Using this line of reasoning, we could argue that the body develops a tolerance for the chemicals produced by running, and so a runner needs to run more to get the same reaction.

If running is analogous to an addictive drug, why doesn't everybody who tries running become addicted to it? The most plausible explanation is that not everybody finds the chemical changes reinforcing. Schildkraut and Kety (1967) suggest that people who have a deficit of norepinephrine, including those who experience depression, would be inclined to find running rewarding. Likewise, Eysenck (1967) has argued that certain people (extraverts) tend to have subnormal arousal levels and are more inclined to seek out situations or drugs that increase their arousal level. Thus, the failure of some people to become addicted is not altogether unexpected.

Our explanation of why people run is, at this point, a hypothesis. Further research is needed to verify all facets of this explanation. Moreover, even if some people run for the reasons we have described, it does not mean that all do. It may be that some people run simply to lose weight and do not find running rewarding, aside from its results. I have talked to many people who run. Most say they enjoy the activity, but a number state that they do not and that they only run for extrinsic reasons: because their doctor prescribed exercise to control their blood pressure or because they want to get in shape for another sport, such as skiing or racquetball. If it is true that some people do not find the activity intrinsically rewarding while others do, these two groups may well differ in resting arousal levels, resting norepinephrine levels, or some other physiological mechanism that mediates the rewards associated with running.

So far, we have been discussing the biological component of motivation. If people run because they want to lose weight or because their doctor told them to, their motivation is cognitive; there is an intentional quality. Likewise, if people run not only because it makes them feel good but because they enjoy the attention they get when they look fit or if running makes them feel virtuous, because it requires effort, discipline, and determination, these would also be cognitive factors.

What about learning? If a person performs a response, such as running, at the same time each day, time of day could become a sufficient cue to elicit that response. Learning theorists have shown that, once a response has become a habit (usually because it has been rewarded for a period of time), that response will often be emitted for some time in the absence of a reward. Even if it is rewarded only occasionally, it will often continue at a steady and predictable rate for long periods. Therefore, it seems reasonable to suggest that some people run out of habit. Another possibility is that runners are motivated by rewards that are not directly linked to running but are contingent upon it; for example, the opportunity to enjoy the company of friends might induce some people to run. Because running itself does not provide the reward in this case but is only instrumental in its acquisition, the behavior would be regarded as governed by learning principles.

Note that the rewards for a given behavior may shift over time. For example, after a runner has become trim or tolerance has increased until the activity provides little biological reward, the behavior may be maintained by different rewards, such as enjoying the company of other runners. This primary motivation would then be the learned component.

Currently, there is great concern about the high rate of divorce and marital problems among runners (Lowther, 1979). Some therapists have noted that running often leads to a change in personality, which may contribute to marital breakdown. For example, people who take up running often gain self-confidence; such a change might motivate them to leave an already unhappy relationship. Why self-confidence should increase as a result of running is not clear; it could be due to chemical changes or to changes in self-image. Another possible reason for marital breakdown is that, once the addictive properties of running have taken hold, runners might leave their spouse alone for long periods. Finally, some people may have taken up running to escape their spouse. Thus, the marital breakdown might have begun long before the running, which was the result of the marital problem and not its cause.

This discussion illustrates several important points. First, what appears to be a simple behavior may be due to a complex set of processes working together. Second, the reason someone initially engages in a behavior may be quite different from the reason he or she continues that behavior. For example, a person may initiate a behavior for cognitive reasons (a doctor's recommendation), come to do it for biological reasons (norepinephrine and/or dopamine output) or psychological reasons (to reduce anxiety and/or depression), and finally maintain it out of habit or learning (to be with friends). In the final analysis, probably all three components are responsible for maintaining the response over a long period. People run for a variety of reasons. Indeed, the same person may run for different reasons at different times. We cannot infer motivation from simply seeing the behavior. The reasons that each individual runs can only be uncovered when we understand the individual.

The suggestion that running is largely maintained by chemical outputs is only a hypothesis. However, it is a good hypothesis, because the converging data all seem to point to chemicals such as norepinephrine as a common mediating variable. Frequently in psychology, converging data are used to formulate possible explanations about behavior. When more and more data point to the same mediating variable, we tend to view that variable as a good candidate to explain the behavior. An important question for the motivation theorist is whether such common mediating variables are motivational; that is, can they be considered important in the arousal, energization, and persistence of behavior?

Motivation for Listening to Rock Music

When people are asked about the most important sources of thrills in their lives, music will often rank highest (Table 2-2). Music is very pervasive in our lives.

Table 2-2. Some things that give people thrills.

Stimulus	Percentage of Respondents
Musical passages	96
Scenes in movie, play, ballet, or book	92
Great beauty in nature or art	87
Physical contact with another person	78
Climatic moment in opera	72
Sexual activity	70
Nostalgic moments	70
Watching emotional interactions between other people	67
Viewing a beautiful painting, photograph, or sculpture	67
Moments of inspiration	65
Something momentous and unexpected happening	63
Seeing or reading about something heroic	59
Sudden insight, understanding, solution to a problem	57
Particular moments in sports event	52
Success in a competitive endeavor	49
Particular fragrances	39
Physical exercise	36
Parades	26

Source: From "Thrills in Response to Music and Other Stimuli," by A. Goldstein, *Physiological Psychology,* 1980, *8,* 126–129. Copyright © 1980 Psychonomic Society. Reprinted by permission.

To explain why is a challenge to motivational theorists. Why is it that people buy tapes and CDs, go to concerts, learn to play instruments, or sing?

Presumably we come to appreciate music, at least in part, because of cognitive processes. We listen to new records because they have different lyrics, different melodies, and different combinations of notes and instruments. Hunt (1963) has argued that humans are motivated by newness or incongruity—by the difference between what we already know and what we have just experienced or are about to experience. Walker (1974) has suggested that a new piece of music can provide the psychological complexity that we seek after we have become familiar with other pieces. In *Emotion and Meaning in Music,* Leonard Meyer (1961) contends that, when we listen to music, we generate expectations about how things will proceed on the basis of our past experience. When the music conforms to our expectations, we relax; the more it deviates, the more we become tense. He goes on to argue that the artful juxtaposing of tiny expectations, frustrated and then fulfilled, is the basis of our emotional reaction to music. Others have extended this argument to suggest that the emotions we experience as we cognitively process music are due, in part, to unlearned reactions, which can be understood in terms of the link between cognitions and brain areas such as the limbic system (Rosenfeld, 1985).

In addition to motivation arising from cognitive variables, previous learning plays a role. We may like a piece of music because it stimulates pleasant memories or evokes pleasant fantasies. The voices of certain singers appear to be able to conjure up images of romance or just plain sex. Under certain conditions, a piece of music could conceivably evoke feelings of well-being or even self-confidence if, in the past, the music has been associated with this psychological state. Probably, at one time or another, all of us have suddenly remembered a pleasant experience associated with a particular piece of music. We may even deliberately play a piece of music in order to evoke the pleasurable state that it elicits.

For a number of people, mainly adolescents, rock music is best appreciated when it is played loud. Why is that? We know from several sources that sounds above a certain level (approximately 80 decibels, abbreviated dB) tend to produce some reliable physiological changes. Live rock music is often played at well over 100 dB in a closed room. If you happen to sit near a speaker, it may be as high as 120–140 dB—a level that can produce permanent hearing loss (Dey, 1970; Fern, 1976; Mills, 1975, 1978).

The main physiological change produced by high noise levels is increased arousal. From a motivational point of view, moderate levels of arousal are experienced as pleasurable. In fact, humans will often seek out stimulation in order to experience moderate levels of arousal. We might ask, therefore, whether listening to rock music is motivated, at least in part, by the desire to experience increases in arousal.

This seems plausible on the basis of information about the relationship of noise, arousal, and pleasure. A problem arises, however, if we try to explain why people often like to listen to loud rock music with friends as well as to dance to rock music. We know that social interactions and exercise also produce arousal. Consequently, if a person is listening to rock music to experience moderate arousal, then dancing and social interactions will increase arousal beyond a moderate level, and yet high levels of arousal have been hypothesized to be aversive (Hebb, 1955). Why, then, do people enjoy listening to rock music while dancing and socializing? Why do some people, in fact, actively seek out such situations? Perhaps adolescents need a great deal of stimulation in order to experience moderate arousal, or perhaps there are times when very high levels of arousal can result in pleasure (Berlyne, 1960). Schachter and Singer (1962) have shown that relatively high levels of arousal can intensify an already pleasurable reaction. If a person is already enjoying the company of friends, rock music together with dancing may enhance this already pleasurable state. Music and dancing have been an integral part of festivals and celebrations for thousands of years. Obviously, there is something about these activities that makes us feel good or possibly enhances an already festive mood.

Thus, as in the case of running, we see that the motivation for listening to rock music involves the interaction of three components, which may fluctuate over time. Research clearly indicates that some type of biological factor is involved in listening to rock music played at noise levels above 80 dB. However, the structure of the music and the associations it elicits are also important factors in the total reaction. We also see that the motivation for a particular activity may be enhanced or even changed by other activities with motivational properties. Specifically, rock music is often used in social situations that themselves are arousal-producing. Further, people often dance to music in social situations, and dancing has been implicated not only in arousal but in the output of norepinephrine. The combining—more precisely, the pooling—of motivation is a fascinating aspect of human behavior; it characterizes much of daily human activity.

Given that many factors contribute to motivation, can we ever know exactly which factors are involved in a particular person's motivation, and in what pro-

portions? Is it possible that one person is motivated mainly by biological components, another mainly by cognitive components, and yet another mainly by learned components? The answer is yes to both questions. It is possible, within limits, to determine whether one of these factors is more important for one person than for another. We could make this determination by designing a series of controlled experiments to compare the reactions of several people. It would be a good exercise for the student in experimental psychology to design just such an experiment; whether it would be worthwhile to carry out the experiment is another question.

Summary

The two examples discussed in this section—the motivation for running and for listening to rock music—illustrate why it is necessary to consider biological, learned, and cognitive factors when we try to explain a particular behavior. Although present in most—if not all—behaviors, biological factors can never be viewed as the sole determinants of human behavior. Humans are exposed to a wide variety of external rewards, which we know have a profound effect in modifying the direction of their behavior. Further, we must recognize that biological factors frequently find their expression because humans have learned a response that stimulates a biological mechanism. This pattern appears to reflect the fact that many human responses are not hardwired but can be acquired on the basis of general reward mechanisms. People who run, it can be argued, have learned to perform a response in order to experience a feeling of euphoria. Cognitions, too, play a profound role in human behavior. Our ability to appreciate music, for example, appears to be largely mediated by our ability to respond to the pattern of stimulation that music provides.

Main Points

1. In studying motivation, we are concerned with understanding how dispositions can lead to action through the interaction of biological, learned, and cognitive processes or components.

2. Three basic components are involved in all motivational systems: a biological component, a learned component, and a cognitive component.

3. The biological approach to motivation has traditionally assumed that behavior is ultimately tied to genetic structure.

4. Learning plays little or no role in hardwired behaviors but a very important role in softwired behaviors. Certain behaviors are prewired: The organism is biologically prepared to make the corresponding learned association very quickly—on the basis of even a single experience, in some cases.

5. It has been suggested that obsessive-compulsive disorders (OCDs) may be due to the activation of subroutines that evolved for grooming and territory.

6. The behavioral neurosciences have favored the idea that general reward systems evolved, rather than innate response patterns.

7. Even though reward centers have been located in the brain, behavior is nevertheless constrained by the nature or structure of the nervous system.

8. The reticular activating system plays a key role in controlling attention.

9. Information transmission in the brain depends to a very large degree on neurotransmitters.

10. Neurotransmitters also play a central role in creating the moods we experience.

11. The structure of the nervous system determines what we can and cannot learn.

12. The learning approach to motivation has traditionally assumed that behavior is the result of a person's reinforcement history and is governed by principles of learning.

13. What we learn is governed to a very large degree by attention.

14. Attention is not completely under our control and is limited.

15. There are two types of learning: classical conditioning and instrumental learning.

16. Social incentive theory suggests that we are motivated to seek approval from others.

17. Psychologists distinguish between two classes of rewards: intrinsic and extrinsic.

18. Psychologists use the term *cognitive* to refer to processes that have to do with knowing. Cognition, therefore, involves thinking, perceiving, abstracting, synthesizing, organizing, or any other process that allows the individual to conceptualize the nature of the external world and the self.

19. Many of our beliefs, attitudes, and values are often initially copied from our parents; however, they are also based on our own experiences and our own desires.

20. Cognitive dissonance theory has its roots in the idea that people need to experience cognitive consistency. According to cognitive dissonance theory, humans are inclined to process information in such a way that it will be consistent with existing categories, values, beliefs, and behavior.

21. Implicit theories are hypotheses, models, and beliefs that we have about the nature of the external world (world theories) and about what we need to do to satisfy our desires in this world (self theories).

22. We can learn to become aware (mindful) of our cognitive processes by, for example, thinking about why we make particular decisions and considering the alternatives available to us.

23. Automatic behavior refers to intentional behaviors that have become habitual.

24. Attribution theory proposes that humans are inclined to look for the causes of their behavior.

25. It has been suggested that there are two types of people: those who locate the causes of behavior within themselves (internals) and those who locate the causes of behavior outside themselves (externals).

26. Considerable evidence suggests that human behavior is under situational or contextual control. High self-monitors are more sensitive to the context than are low self-monitors.

27. Analysis of why people run and why they listen to rock music indicates that all three components—biological, learned, and cognitive—can be important in motivating a behavior.

Chapter Three

Hunger and Eating

- *What makes us feel hungry?*
- *Do we eat for psychological reasons?*
- *What makes us feel satisfied or full after we eat?*
- *Why are certain foods more appealing than others?*
- *Why do so many people tend to become overweight?*

- *What are the health implications of overweight?*
- *Why do people who have become overweight have difficulty shedding those extra pounds?*
- *Why do so many people exhibit eating disorders?*

Thousands of articles have been written about hunger and eating and about the relation between them. The abundance of research reflects the difficulty that has been encountered in providing a clear picture of the mechanisms involved. Let's begin our examination of hunger and eating by looking at five important issues.

1. *People eat for more than just biological reasons.* From a biological perspective, it seems that we should eat when we need to replenish depleted metabolic fuels and to replenish chemicals needed in the maintenance of the body. Humans and animals store two types of fuel—food in the gastrointestinal tract (which is immediately available) and reserves of fat. The problem is that we often feel hunger even though we have ample fat reserves (Friedman & Stricker, 1976). Researchers have therefore focused on the glucose level in the bloodstream, only to find that overall blood glucose levels do not correlate with reports of hunger (Mayer, 1955), even though glucose injections inhibit eating (Mook, 1963) and injections of insulin, which lower glucose levels, lead to reported feelings of hunger as well as stomach contractions (Goodner & Russell, 1965). Therefore, the reason that people report they are hungry must be more complex. In this chapter, we will examine the factors that govern hunger and eating.

2. *Obesity is a major problem.* In the United States, 31% of males are overweight and 24% of females are overweight (National Research Council, 1989). An abundance of anecdotal and experimental data indicates that organisms—and humans, in particular—often eat too much. The result of overeating is overweight; the extra food is simply converted to fat. Several biological systems have been implicated, along with certain learned habits and cognitions. We must consider all of these factors together if we are to account for obesity.

3. *Obesity has been linked to a variety of health problems.* Disorders linked to obesity include diabetes, hypertension, cardiovascular disease, and some cancers (Bray, 1992). The associated health costs have been estimated at $39 billion annually. In the past, overweight was simply seen in the context of personal appearance, but current research suggests much more serious consequences.

4. *Humans have difficulty getting rid of unwanted and dangerous fat.* People who are obese often wish they were not and are aware of the health implications of overweight. As a consequence, many pursue some form of dieting; the diet industry has been valued at $30 billion annually (Brownell & Rodin, 1994). The fact that people often have difficulty in curbing the amount they eat has provided us with a wealth of data about the role of learning and cognition in hunger and eating.

5. *Eating disorders have become a significant problem.* Bulimia—a pattern of binge eating followed by purging, which is typically a very secretive activity—has become a significant health problem in recent years. Bulimia has been linked to dieting, but it is not yet known whether dieting is the cause. Although the number of people who don't eat enough to maintain a normal weight is small compared with the number who overeat, the phenomenon is so dramatic that it has aroused wide attention. Why do some people restrict their food intake so much that they become emaciated? What does this disorder tell us about the biological mechanisms that normally control eating?

Eating and Digestion

In order to understand the complexity of hunger and eating, we will need a brief overview of the nature of food and some basic concepts relating to the digestion of food. In the process of eating, certain chemicals that shut down the eating response are normally released. Overweight is due to the failure of those mechanisms and/or the fact that humans often eat for other reasons.

The Biological Component

Food, Energy, and Energy Reserves

Fats, carbohydrates, and proteins.   When we ingest food, our stomach and intestines—the gastrointestinal (GI) tract—break down the food into more basic units that can be used for energy, as well as for rebuilding the body cells and manufacturing the chemicals needed to run the body. *Fats*, which we get from such foods as meats, milk products, and cooking oils, are broken down into fatty acids and glycerol. *Carbohydrates*, also referred to simply as starches and sugars, which we get from eating such foods as bread, pasta, cakes, desserts, and fruits, are broken down into glucose and fructose. *Proteins*, which we get from such foods as meats, beans, and vegetables, are broken down into amino acids. Once broken down into these more basic units, they are absorbed into the bloodstream. Most of the absorption takes place in the small intestine, with the exception of substances such as aspirin and alcohol, which pass more or less directly through the stomach walls into the bloodstream (Sherman & Sherman, 1989). The absorption of alcohol across the stomach wall accounts for the rapid effects of drinking. The intestines are an excellent storehouse for energy. After a big meal, it typically takes several hours for all the food in the intestines to be digested (Friedman & Stricker, 1976).

Energy and energy reserves.   Part of the glucose absorbed into the blood remains in circulation to be used as energy, but most is transported across the cell membranes and stored in the cells as glycogen, thereby providing an energy reserve. If we do not use all of the glucose generated by the digestive process, the liver converts some of it to fat, which is then stored as an energy reserve in our fat cells (also called adipose tissue). Fats are considered a quick form of energy; in earlier generations, most were burned off before they could be stored in the adipose tissue. Even today, when people engaged in manual labor need a steady source of energy, fats play an important role in supplying that energy. For people who do not engage in intense physical activity, however, weight gain is an inevitable by-product of a high-fat diet.

Amino acids and sugars go directly to the liver, which has the first choice of nutrients before passing them along to the rest of the body. The liver regulates the amino acid level in the blood. There are 20 different amino acids, which are used by the body for growth, repair, and energy. They are derived from proteins, and the best source is meat. Most plants are low in amino acids and many do not contain the full complement of the 20 amino acids that the body needs to function normally. Those who eat a meatless diet need to eat a variety of vegetables. Although beans are a good source of amino acids, they do not always contain the full complement; therefore, a mixture of beans and vegetables is generally recommended for vegetarians.

The need for a balanced diet.   A balanced diet should consist of protein (15%), carbohydrates (65%), and fats (15–20%), together with vitamins, minerals, trace elements, and water. Vitamins, minerals, and trace elements are normally found in sufficient quantities in the foods we eat. The reason we need to be concerned with a balanced diet is that too little or too much of one type of food can cause problems. For example, too much fat has been linked not only to heart disease but to cancer. Complete absence of fat, on the other hand, means that we lack one of the important foods that supply us with energy. The absence of protein is also problematic. While we can get along without carbohydrates and fats (which are stored in the body), we cannot get along without proteins. The amino acids contained in proteins provide the basic components that our body needs to manufacture, for instance, the neurotransmitters (such as norepinephrine and serotonin) that our brain needs to function (Wurtman, 1982). Amino acids also contain the components necessary for cell repair. Too much protein, on the other hand, is not only unnecessary but can lead indirectly to high fat levels. Red meats, in particular, have been linked to the high fat levels in our diet. Note that certain vitamins and minerals come mainly from proteins. For example, thiamine comes from pork and organ meat, vitamin B6 from meats, vitamin B12 from muscle meats, vitamin K from meats, vitamin A from milk and butter, and vitamin D from cod liver oil. Fruits are also a source of vitamins and minerals.

Carbohydrates are one of our main sources of energy. They also supply us with many vitamins, minerals, and trace elements. Unfortunately, the carbohydrates in junk foods have lost much of their nutritional value in processing. Since junk foods tend to be low in vitamins, minerals, and trace elements, they are sometimes referred to as empty calories. Alcohol, a carbohydrate that is high in calories but low in vitamins, can lead to weight gain, and is often regarded as a source of empty calories.

In order to lose weight, people sometimes cut down on carbohydrates or avoid them altogether. However, carbohydrates not only are an important source of energy, vitamins, and minerals but are also necessary for the proper digestion of other foods (they act as a catalyst); the absence of carbohydrates in the diet will eventually result in a dangerous toxic reaction in which ketone levels become very high. Consequently, dieters should not avoid carbohydrates but rather select those that are low in calories, such as potatoes.

Systems Involved in the Digestion and Regulation of Food Intake

In Table 3-1, the main systems involved in the digestion and regulation of food intake are summarized. In this section, we will examine those systems in some detail. Note, in connection with Table 3-1, that the inability to manufacture sufficient insulin results in a condition called diabetes. Normally, when glucose levels in the blood rise, the pancreas responds by secreting insulin. Insulin is important for converting glucose into energy and transporting glucose to the cells. Without insulin, glucose levels continue to rise, and the kidneys draw water into the urine, resulting in an excessive output of diluted urine. To compensate for the lack of available fuel (glucose) and energy for brain functioning, fat is mobilized, fatty acids are released, and protein is used as a source of energy. As a result, repair of injured tissue is slowed, and resistance to infection is low. Diabetics have particular difficulty breaking down carbohydrates, a condition that can be easily treated by daily injections of insulin and restricted intake of carbohydrates (Sherman & Sherman, 1989).

Some Biological Systems That Control Eating

Biological rhythms and food preference. One interesting feature of food intake is that it is linked to biological rhythms. In rats and in humans, preference for carbohydrates appears early in the activity cycle. Later in the cycle, the preference shifts to fats and proteins (Liebowitz, 1994). What this indicates, among other things, is that we do not have a generalized hunger but a number of specific hungers. This makes sense in that food intake is necessary not only to meet our energy requirements but also to provide the building blocks that enable us to repair cells and manufacture the chemicals needed for growth and day-to-day functioning.

Studies of the brain have shown that carbohydrate intake and fat intake are regulated by different neurochemical circuits. In other words, when levels of a certain combination of neurotransmitters and peptides are high, animals are inclined to ingest carbohydrates rather than fats; when levels of another combination of neurotransmitters and peptides are high, animals are inclined to eat fats. What is interesting is that the activation of these neurochemical circuits is governed by internal rhythms and is not simply due to the lack of energy or a certain nutrient.

Gender and age differences in eating patterns. There is evidence that gender differences in eating patterns can also be attributed to differences in activity of neurochemical circuits. In general, preference for carbohydrates is stronger in females than in males, a pattern that emerges shortly before and around puberty. Research with rats has linked this difference to a surge in a hypothalamic peptide.

Shortly after puberty, there is a dramatic increase in preference for fats, which has been linked to another hypothalamic peptide called galin. This preference for fat-rich diets is associated with a tendency to become overweight. The implication of this research is that we may not be able to change our eating habits as easily as the diet books say (Liebowitz, 1994).

Genetic Processes and Overweight. There appears to be a genetic component of obesity. Research suggests that the genes control the activity of the brain peptides, which in turn control the disposition to eat (Liebowitz, 1994); that is, brain peptides do not cause people to eat but set the conditions that will promote eating, should food become available. Because genes play a role in eating, some people take the position that there is nothing they can do about their weight. Consequently, they are inclined to become hopeless when they do experience weight gains.

The general implication of this research is that a number of chemicals in the brain exert a disposition not only to eat but to eat certain things. Thus, trying to substitute one food for another may not be as easy as dieters think, nor may it be easy to achieve some ideal weight. The important thing to remember is that these chemicals simply create a disposition; they are not the cause.

Table 3-1.   Endocrine glands and brain systems involved in hunger, eating, and energy mobilization.

Gland	Hormone	Action/Function
Endocrine Glands		
Stomach	Gastin	Stimulates release of hydrochloric acid. Increases gastric activity.
Duodenum (small intestine)	Secretin	Triggers release of pancreatic juices.
	Cholecystokinin	Digestion, absorption, and metabolism. Release linked to satiety.
Pancreas		Pancreatic juices essential for digestion of food.
	Insulin	Triggered by the intake of carbohydrates. Increases glucose uptake and converts to glycogen, which is then stored in the body cells. Promotes synthesis of fat and proteins. Release linked to satiety.
Adrenal cortex	Glucocorticoids	Convert stored fats and proteins to carbohydrates. Increases glucose levels in the blood. (Important in the mobilization of energy, especially under stress.)
Adrenal medulla	Epinephrine (adrenaline)*	Increases heart rate, oxygen consumption, and glycogen mobilization. (Again, important for the mobilization of energy.)
	Norepinephrine (noradrenaline)*	Increases blood pressure, constricts blood vessels.
Thyroid	Thyroxin (T4)	Regulates cell growth. Regulates metabolic rate.
Brain		
Hypothalamus	Various	The hypothalamus directs and monitors a number of endocrine functions.
Lateral		Monitors the taste and texture of food. Good taste and texture increases food intake.
Ventromedial		Monitors glucose levels (glucoreceptors). Lesioning presumably reduces the ability to detect low glucose levels.

*Also produced in the brain, where they act as neurotransmitters. Increased levels of norepinephrine in the brain have been implicated in positive moods.

The Learned Component

Hunger, Eating, and Satiety

We generally assume that people eat because they are hungry. However, as we will see, there are many reasons why people eat. Biologically, we eat because we need to restore energy reserves, to obtain the minerals and chemicals important in building and repairing cells or manufacturing neurotransmitters, and to provide the chemical catalysts involved in various complex chemical processes associated with digestion. There are also many psychological reasons for eating. We may eat out of habit—because it is lunch time, for example; we may eat because we want the pleasant sensory experience provided by food; we may eat because others are eating; or we may eat because we are bored.

Most researchers think it is important to distinguish between the concepts of hunger and eating. Hunger is a biological need. Since eating too much or the

Humans eat not only to satisfy hunger needs but for the sensory experience food provides.

wrong things results in overweight and the associated health disorders, it is eating that is the problem.

This distinction also involves issues of control. If we say that we only eat because we are hungry, we aren't taking responsibility for our behavior; we're blaming our biology. When we accept the idea that we eat for reasons other than hunger, we implicitly make the assumption that we have some control. At the same time, there is also a danger in assuming that we have complete control. It is important to know what we can and cannot change.

A common assumption is that people stop eating when they are full—in other words, that the state of satiety is what causes us to stop eating. Like hunger, satiety is a biological state. It has been linked to chemicals such as insulin and cholecystokinin that are released in the course of digestion (Table 3-1). As we will see, people often eat well beyond biological satiety. They continue to eat, for example, until they have finished what is on their plate.

Extensive research suggests that many people are insensitive to satiety cues or ignore them. For some people, the focus seems to be on the sensory experi-

ence. As a result, they overeat or eat the wrong foods. Again, as in the case of hunger, psychologists tend to focus on eating and not satiety. At one time or another, most of us have filled our plate to the brim. Sometimes we have paid the price later in stomach pains or indigestion. Our failure to respond to these cues contributes to problems of obesity.

To assess what guides people's eating behavior, psychologists typically monitor food intake under various conditions or at various times of the day. Because availability has been found to play an important role in how much we eat, researchers often present their participants with a buffet, in order to get an index of what and how much they eat when given a free choice. By comparing people under this standardized condition, it becomes possible to tease out some of the things that govern food intake.

Learning to Select a Balanced Diet

Do we instinctively know what foods we should eat in order to meet our nutritional needs, or is that a skill that we learn? From time to time, it has been suggested that humans are indeed born with this capacity, on the basis of a classic study in which children were presented with a wide range of foods and allowed to select what they wanted (Davis, 1928). Davis found that, over a period of time, the children selected a nutritionally balanced diet; they didn't just select sweet foods, for example. However, critics have pointed out that all the foods that Davis presented to the children were nutritious, and therefore his study fails to provide clear evidence. Note that the junk foods we know today were not available when Davis did his study.

Evidence that humans may select balanced diets under certain conditions must be weighed against an abundance of evidence to the contrary. In many instances, people have developed food preferences responsible for various forms of malnutrition, even when nutritious foods were readily available. The current popularity of junk foods, which have an appealing taste because they are sweet, salty, and high in fat, but are low in essential nutrients, is a good example. There is also evidence that the nutritional value of foods consumed is lower at lower socioeconomic levels of North American society (Adelson, 1968). Some commentators have attributed this difference to poor people's budget constraints. However, a more careful analysis shows that people at the lower socioeconomic levels buy more prepared foods and more snack foods, both of which tend to be low in nutritional value, although generally more expensive than fresh meat and vegetables. Therefore, poor people spend proportionately more money on food, but select foods that are less nutritious. It has been suggested that people at the upper socioeconomic levels of society tend to buy more nutritious foods because they are more knowledgeable about the nutritional value of food and more willing to spend time preparing it.

Selecting Foods on the Basis of Taste and Texture

An abundance of data indicates that humans are inclined to select foods on the basis of taste and texture rather than nutritional value (e.g., Schachter, 1971a). One consequence of this is that people will often select junk foods that taste good and have appealing texture but fail to provide essential nutrients that people need. Indeed, some junk foods, most notably popular breakfast cereals also load the body with unhealthy salt and sugar. If it were not for the milk in the bowl, many of these cereals would meet few of our basic nutritional needs.

As we have seen, one of the main criticisms of the Davis study is that in 1928 there were no junk foods as we know them today. The cakes and other sweets in his study were made from basic food products and not from the synthetic materials prevalent today.

The tendency to select foods on the basis of their sensory qualities has been linked to obesity. The role of sensory cues in the eating patterns of obese individuals was demonstrated in a study that compared extremely obese men and women with nonobese controls (Hashim & Van Itallie, 1965). The researchers prepared a bland, homogenized liquid diet similar in taste and composition to the vanilla flavors of commercial preparations such as Nutrament and Metrecal. The subjects, who were confined to a hospital, were allowed to eat as much of this diet as they wanted, but consumption was in a situation with no social interaction. The nonobese individuals continued to consume their daily average of about 2400 calories, but obese subjects reduced their intake to 500 calories a day, about 3000 calories less than their daily average before admission to the hospital (Figure 3-1).

Although other studies have not shown so dramatic an effect, the same general finding seems to hold even in very tightly controlled studies. In an experiment that asked subjects to evaluate taste (Nisbett, 1968), obese subjects ate significantly more than nonobese and skinny subjects when the food tasted good, but ate about the same amount when the food tasted bad. Again, this indicates that obese people are strongly influenced by the positive sensory qualities of food (Figure 3-2). Similar results have been obtained with cake and milk (Schachter, 1971b).

Cultural Preferences

The eating preferences of different ethnic groups provide compelling evidence that learning plays an important role in diet. The Italians are known for their love of pasta, the French for their garlic, the Mexicans for their hot peppers, the Japanese for their raw fish, and so on. Where do these different preferences come from?

From an evolutionary perspective, it would be highly adaptive if humans could learn to eat different foods depending on what was available. To do this, they would need to be able to identify not only which foods were nutritious but which ones would make them ill. There is considerable evidence that humans, as well as other organisms, quickly learn to avoid

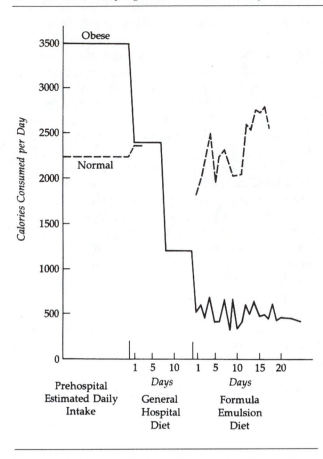

Figure 3-1. Effect of a formula emulsion diet on the eating behavior of an obese and a nonobese subject. (From *Emotion, Obesity and Crime*, by S. Schachter. Copyright © 1971 by Academic Press. Reprinted with permission.)

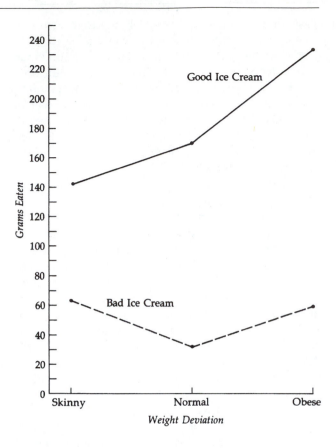

Figure 3-1. Effect of a formula emulsion diet on the eating behavior of an obese and a nonobese subject. (From *Emotion, Obesity and Crime*, by S. Schachter. Copyright © 1971 by Academic Press. Reprinted with permission.)

foods that are lacking in nutrition and are toxic (make you sick). However, learning to select foods that are nutritious takes considerably longer. Research by John Garcia and others suggests that, in order to detect that a food is not providing nutrition, the organism must develop a general malaise. In other words, food selection comes from learning to avoid all those foods that produce some type of aversive state (Nachman, 1970; Garcia & Koelling, 1966; Garcia, McGowan, Ervin, & Koelling, 1968). In these circumstances, the development of taste preferences in the early stages of food intake would be highly adaptive. Specifically, by model-

ing their parents and thereby developing preferences, individuals would eliminate the need to go through a long trial-and-error learning process with its attendant dangers.

Since the availability of foods changes, this learning process would need to be flexible, so that individuals could try new foods in the absence of their preferred diet. The fact that people develop new tastes, albeit over a considerable period of time, is consistent with this idea. Again, it can be shown that many of these new preferences are linked to taste and texture rather than to nutritional value.

The Cognitive Component

It appears that our disposition to eat fats and carbohydrates can be altered to some degree. Today, many people are learning to eat different foods on the basis of knowing what is healthy for them. Even though they might prefer a juicy hamburger, they slowly learn to eat foods that contain less fat, sugar, and salt. Interestingly, people often report that, after a time, they do not have to actively think about what they should or shouldn't eat, because their preferences have changed. People who have learned to eat less red meat or leaner cuts of meat, for example, often report that they come to prefer smaller amounts and that fatty cuts elicit an aversion sometimes bordering on revulsion. Such reports are encouraging, because they mean that, with time, we will develop taste and texture preferences in line with what we know is best for us.

Education plays an important role here. When people have a solid base of knowledge to work from, they can alter their behavior. The educational system plays a vital role in changing behavior by providing people with the information they need to make sound decisions.

Summary

When the three basic food types (fats, carbohydrates, and proteins) are ingested, they enter the gastrointestinal tract, where they are broken down into more basic chemical units and used as energy, to rebuild cells, and to manufacture the chemicals that are needed throughout the brain and body. One of the main sources of energy is the carbohydrates, which are broken down into glucose and fructose. While some of the glucose circulates in the blood, where it provides a source of immediate energy, much is transported across the membrane walls of the small intestines and stored in the cells as glycogen. Since carbohydrates are also our main source of vitamins, minerals, and trace elements, it is important to ensure that our diets contain about 65% carbohydrates. Fats can be an important source of energy but, when there is excess in the diet, much of it is transported to the fat cells (adipose tissue), where it is stored for future needs. Excess fat in the diet has been linked not only

to heart disease but also to cancer. Nevertheless, some fat, 15–20% of our diet, is generally recommended. Amino acids are important for rebuilding cells and for manufacturing many of the chemicals—such as the neurotransmitters in our brain—that our body needs to function. Even though proteins are important, they should account for only 15% of our diet. Insulin plays an important role in the conversion of glucose to energy. Without insulin, a condition called diabetes develops. Various biological systems that control not only how much we eat but what we eat have been identified.

Psychologists make a distinction between hunger and eating. Traditionally, hunger is regarded as a biological need. It is necessary to consider nonbiological factors that shape our eating habits, because they account, in part, for overweight and other concerns. Eating and digestion trigger various chemical processes that produce satiety in animals. Considerable research suggests that some people are inclined to ignore these biological cues and/or focus on sensory cues. As a result, they are inclined to overeat.

Humans are inclined to select what they eat on the basis of taste and texture of food. There is considerable evidence that these preferences for taste and texture are largely learned, probably in childhood. There is growing evidence that people can learn to change these preferences. In time, selection of food on the basis of understanding what is healthy for us can become a habit.

The Origins of Overweight and Obesity

If we continue to eat after we have ingested sufficient food to last until our next meal, the extra food will be stored as fat in the adipose tissue. This is as certain as the fact that the sun will rise tomorrow. Should we repeat this practice regularly, we not only will tend to gain weight but eventually will become obese.

Unfortunately, there is no easy way to define obesity. The term has been used to refer to people who have a very moderate amount of fat and to those who are extremely overweight. In many studies, individuals are categorized as obese if they exceed the average weight for their height, build, age, and gender by a given percentage—for example, 25%. This means that a person whose target weight is 150 pounds would be classified as obese at 180 pounds. Thus, among the people with whom we interact daily, some are obese. Many of us experience excessive weight gain sometime during our lives. Within us, there lives the potential obese person, ready to emerge if given the opportunity.

Why do people eat more than they need? Once again, we'll examine the biological, learned, and cognitive aspects of this question. As we'll see, at least three of the explanations assume some abnormality in the biological structure of obese people.

The Biological Component

The Genetic Factor

In order to distinguish what is inherited from what is acquired through experience, researchers need to control for either the environment or our genes. Since it is usually difficult to control the environment, scientists have traditionally studied adopted versus natural children and identical versus fraternal twins. These studies have shown that adopted children tend to resemble their biological parents in weight far more than they resemble their adoptive parents (Stunkard et al., 1985) and that identical twins, even when reared apart, are closer in weight than are fraternal twins or other siblings (e.g., Stunkard, Foch, & Hrubec, 1985). In other words, genes appears to play a central role.

One of the things that may be inherited is metabolic rate; a person with a high metabolic rate tends not to become obese. Other inherited factors were suggested by a study in which children of overweight parents not only preferred sweeter solutions but were more responsive to external cues in their environments (Milstein, 1980). People who are external are highly susceptible to the taste and texture of food; we'll return to this topic later in the chapter.

Energy Expenditure

The three components.   Energy expenditure has three main components: the basal metabolic rate (BMR), physical activity, and the specific dynamic action

(SDA) of food. About one-third of our energy use is attributable to exercise and about two-thirds to our BMR (Rodin, 1981). SDA is the increase in energy expenditure following the ingestion of food. It can increase the BMR by up to 20% for a few hours after a meal. Certain foods, such as proteins, produce the greatest increase (Powers, 1982). The actual proportions of energy expended in exercise and metabolism obviously depend on individual exercise patterns. The *basal metabolic rate* is the amount of energy we use in a given period of time in relation to our body size. It is measured as the number of calories we burn per square meter of body surface per hour when we are resting. What is interesting about basal metabolism is that it changes with age, varies markedly from individual to individual, and is affected by how large we are, what we eat, and how long we have gone without food.

Variation over the lifespan.   From birth to the age of 18–20 in females and a little later in males, our metabolic rate declines rapidly. As Figure 3-3 shows, at about the age of 20, the rate levels out, and from then on it declines much more slowly. This means that the amount of food we need to function at resting levels, in proportion to body size, declines rather sharply from birth until the age of 20 or so. From then on, we need approximately the same amount of energy to operate on a day-to-day basis. There is a sharp increase in food intake around puberty, because food is needed to build bones and muscles, which are developing rapidly at that time, and to supply the energy for the high level of activity typical of that stage.

Although obesity can occur at any age, humans often first encounter problems of overweight around the age of 20 or shortly thereafter. This is consistent with the idea that the amount we eat is controlled more or less by habit. First, because we have stopped growing, we no longer require as much food. Second, the reduction in metabolism rate means our bodies burn up fuel more slowly and the extra food is converted to fat. Finally, any reduction in exercise would further make us prone to overweight. The slow but continuous decline in basal metabolic rate with increasing age and the tendency to exercise less with increasing age are important factors in the tendency for humans to become overweight in their later years.

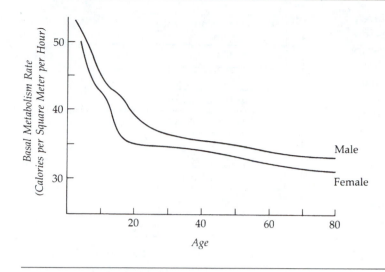

Figure 3-3.   Changes in basal metabolic rates with age. (From *Slim Chance in a Fat World*, by R. B. Stuart and B. Davis. Copyright © 1972 by the Research Press Company. Reprinted with permission.)

Individual differences in metabolic rates.   In a study, subjects who had wide differences in caloric intake were matched for height, weight, and level of activity. Even though their weights did not change over a period of weeks, it was often found that one member of the matched pair ate twice as much as the other (Rose & Williams, 1961). Such large individual differences in basal metabolic rate obviously play an important role in determining who will be prone to obesity and who will have difficulty dieting.

Obesity and Anorexia as Malfunctions of the Hypothalamus

A tiny brain structure called the hypothalamus is involved in a wide variety of motivational functions, including hunger and eating (see Figure 2-1). Two areas of the hypothalamus have been linked to eating behavior: Lesions of the ventromedial nuclei in the hypothalamus produce overeating, which leads to obesity (Teitelbaum, 1961); and lesions of the lateral hypothalamus lead to a failure to eat, a state called *anorexia*.

Lesions of the ventromedial nuclei.   Philip Teitelbaum (1961) noted that animals with lesions of the ventromedial nuclei (VMN) show the following characteristics.

1. They are unresponsive to normal satiety cues, which are presumably mediated by glucose.

2. They will not work as hard as normal animals to obtain food.
3. They will stop eating adulterated foods (such as food laced with quinine) sooner than animals with no lesions of the VMN.
4. They will eat large amounts of highly palatable foods.

Lesions of the lateral hypothalamus.   Lesions of the lateral hypothalamus (LH) have been shown to produce effects analogous but complementary to those in the VMN. Specifically, it has been shown that lesions of the LH result initially in the cessation of eating. After such animals have lost considerable body weight, they begin to eat again, but at a much reduced rate. This reduced rate of eating tends to be very stable. While palatable foods tend to result in increased eating and weight gain, as in animals with no lesions, animals lesioned in the LH continue to maintain their weight well below the prelesion level. The degree of anorexia that the animals display is related to the size of the lesion (Keesy & Powley, 1975).

The mechanism of hypothalamus operation.   Does the hypothalamus simply regulate the amount we eat or does it act as a monitor of, say, the level of body fat? The most widely held view is that the hypothalamus is involved in monitoring the store of adipose tissue. There is considerable evidence that VMN lesions produce a disruption in fat metabolism, which increases the amount of glucose converted to lipids; the lipids are then transferred to adipose tissue for storage (Frohman, Goldman, & Bernardis, 1972; Goldman, Schnatz, Bernardis, & Frohman, 1970, 1972a, b; Haessler & Crawford, 1967). It could be argued that the obesity resulting from a VMN lesion is due to the disruption of the normal metabolic process; that is, the lesion produces overeating because of the abnormally low glucose level that results from this disruption.

Set-Point Theory

On the basis of the findings from studies of the hypothalamus, Keesy and Powley (1975) have proposed a set-point theory of weight level—specifically, that the hypothalamus sets our weight. Some of us will have close to average weight, some will tend toward obesity, and some will tend toward anorexia. This hypothesis is summarized in Figure 3-4.

Keesy and Powley argue that their theory of weight level can readily account for the tendency of people who are inclined to overweight to fall off their diets. Because such people have a high set point, they would feel hungry, and in order to satisfy their hunger they would be inclined to overeat. Eventually, their weight would match their set point and, at that time, their food consumption would level off. Only by deliberately restraining their eating would they be able to keep their weight down. Any failure to restrain their eating would immediately result in a tendency to overeat.

The Yo-Yo Effect and the Famine Hypothesis

People who diet in order to achieve the slim figure that wins social approval often experience a phenomenon labeled the *yo-yo effect*. Once they have achieved their desired weight, they find it virtually impossible to keep the weight off and after a short time are again overweight, at least according to their standards. Obsessed with the desire to be slim, they again diet but again put on weight after achieving their desired weight. To their dismay, such dieters often find that, each time they put on weight following a diet, they not only regain all the weight they lost but put on a little more. Slowly but surely, they get heavier on each up-

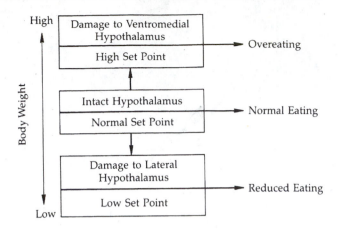

Figure 3-4. Damage (or lesions) to the ventromedial hypothalamus raises the set point, while damage (or lesions) to the lateral hypothalamus lowers the set point. (Based on R. E. Keesy and T. L. Powley, "Hypothalamic Regulation of Body Weight," *American Scientist*, 1975, *63*, 558–565.)

swing. Why do they put on more weight each time they diet? No one is certain, but one explanation comes from the famine hypothesis.

According to the famine hypothesis, obesity can be understood as an adaptive mechanism gone awry because we are no longer faced with periodic food shortages. By this theory, the adipose tissue evolved to protect humans against food shortages (Margules, 1979; Margules, Moisset, Lewis, Shibuya, & Pert, 1978) and, now that such shortages are rare, we tend to continue adding to an already adequate reserve. In short, people are inclined to progress from a comfortable reserve to a state of obesity. Extending this hypothesis, we can construct an explanation for the yo-yo effect: When people diet, the body responds as though it is going through a famine. If the weight loss due to the diet pushes the body below the set point, the body says to itself at the end of the diet: "I didn't have enough fat reserves to handle this last famine, so I must put on more weight than before, so that I'll be prepared for the next famine." When the person diets again and achieves his or her desired weight (again pushing the body below its set point), the body says: "The last time I put on extra weight it wasn't enough, so next time I'll have to put on even more." As a result, each time the individual's weight dips below the set point, the body becomes even more determined to prevent this from happening again and works to protect the individual against the next, inevitable famine by increasing the fat reserves even more. Obviously, the body doesn't talk to itself. There has to be some type of mechanism that signals the body to put on more weight.

The Yo-Yo Effect and Reduced Metabolism

One consequence of reduced food intake is a reduction in the rate of metabolism. It has been argued that this response to reduced food intake is highly adaptive, because it allows the individual to survive a famine. It may be that the yo-yo effect is simply the result of decreased metabolism. In other words, it may simply be that people tend to eat the same amount following a diet but, because the body's metabolism has slowed as a result of dieting, the same food intake produces greater weight gains.

The Learned Component

Statistics indicate that overweight children are likely to have overweight parents (Garn & Clark, 1976). Further, there is evidence that overweight children tend to become overweight adults (Eden, 1975; Hirsch, Knittle, & Salans, 1966). Although these findings support the idea that obesity may be genetically determined, there are reasons to question this conclusion. First, the child's weight tends to be more highly correlated with the mother's weight than with the father's (Garn & Clark, 1976). If the cause were purely genetic, the correlations should be equal. Second, the resemblance in the weight of siblings, even identical twins, decreases in later life. This suggests that factors other than the genes must be responsible for weight patterns.

How do we account for these findings? The reason that a child's weight tends to be correlated with the mother's may be that the mother largely controls the eating behavior of her children or simply the availability of food. Because of her own tendency to overeat, for example, the mother may fill her children's plates with more food than they require or simply make food available. If they are encouraged to eat all the food on their plates or to snack, the children will eventually convert the extra food into fat. If this behavior becomes a habit, it could help to explain their tendency to overeat in later life.

Another possibility is that fat mothers like to prepare appealing foods. Children who eat such foods may learn to associate eating with certain cues. Thus, foods with a particular taste, texture, or smell would tend to elicit the eating response. The presence or availability of such foods would determine whether such a person became obese. In any environment where such foods were readily available, the individual would be likely to overeat.

The finding that some people eat more when emotionally upset or under stress may be explained in a similar way. If a mother tries to comfort her children with food when they are upset, for example, the child may learn to eat under these conditions. Later in life, such people turn to food for comfort, just as they turned to their mother in childhood.

The Cognitive Component

Do we eat more when we are depressed, anxious, or stressed? No direct link has been established between emotional disorders and overeating. Typically, depression is characterized by weight loss rather than overeating. However, when a depressed state was induced in subjects high in self-restraint, they ate significantly more than did similarly depressed subjects who were low in self-restraint (Frost, Goolkasian, Ely, & Blanchards, 1982). This finding makes sense if we assume that the ability to control eating is greater in people who have more self-control and that they lose their ability or desire to exercise control when they become depressed. Typically, people who are depressed feel they have lost control of their lives.

There is considerable evidence that overweight people are more depressed than normal weight people. It cannot be concluded from such studies, however, that depression is the cause of overweight. It may well be that people who are overweight are more inclined to become depressed as the result of becoming overweight. The depression may be caused, for example, by feelings of loss of control, one of the known antecedents of depression. The only way to show that depression causes overweight is to undertake a prospective study. This involves selecting a sample of normal weight people and assessing levels of depression and then at a later time looking at the same people to see if the more depressed individuals of the sample have become overweight. One study using this design failed to confirm the widely held view that depression leads to weight gains. In fact, it was found that, as a rule, the overweight individuals were initially less depressed than normal weight individuals (Smoller, Wadden, & Stunkard, 1987). This finding is consistent with the general conclusion that depression results in an overall reduction in motivation, including the motivation to eat (see Chapter 10).

A recent study examined the effects of stress on eating. In one condition, a group of men and women were shown a film about industrial accidents (stress condition) or a pleasant travelogue (control condition) while they had access to sweet, salty, and bland snack foods. While stress markedly decreased food consumption in men, women under stress ate nearly twice as much sweet food as did their control counterparts, along with more bland food (Grunberg & Straub, 1992). The reason that, under stress, women ate more than did men may be associated with the fact that more women than men tend to be restrained eaters. As we'll see shortly, restrained eaters tend to consciously monitor food intake. If preoccupied with stress, they might fail to monitor their eating or simply not be motivated to control food intake. As a result, they would become disinhibited eaters.

Summary

Obesity is commonly defined as weight in excess of some norm, usually by approximately 25%. There is good evidence that the tendency to obesity is at least partly genetically determined. First, people who are overweight often come from overweight parents. Second, in terms of weight, adopted children are more likely to resemble their biological parents than their adoptive parents, and identical twins, even when raised apart, are closer than fraternal twins. Two possible explanations are that they inherit a similar metabolism rate or a propensity to eat in response to external cues.

Energy expenditure may also contribute to overweight. Energy expenditure has three main components: the basal metabolic rate (BMR), physical activity, and specific dynamic action (SDA). Our basal metabolic rate, which accounts for about two-thirds of our energy expenditure, decreases as we age. It slows fairly abruptly at around the age of 20; which may explain why some people tend to put on weight around that age.

Set-point theory suggests that the weight of each individual is governed by a set point determined by the hypothalamus. This theory is based on research showing that lesions in the hypothalamus can produce obesity and anorexia in animals. Margules has argued that obesity is an adaptive mechanism gone astray: We prepare for a famine that never comes. The famine hypothesis can account for the yo-yo effect. Each time individuals bring their weight below their set point, the body responds as though the famine has come. If food is available, as it tends to be in North America, individuals will be motivated to eat and prepare for the next famine.

Several factors suggest that overweight is due, at least in part, to learning. Since a child's weight is more likely to resemble the mother's weight than the father's, it has been argued that children of overweight mothers learn not only to overeat but to eat foods high in calories.

Individual differences in metabolism may account for differences in weight. BMR varies widely among individuals, so that some people can eat considerably more than others without putting on weight. Emotional disorders have not been linked to obesity.

Theories of Overweight and Obesity

Internal-External Theory of Hunger and Eating

One of the major theories about why people are overweight is linked to the observation that some people seem to eat in response to *external* cues, such as the sight and smell of food and the time of day, whereas other people seem to depend on *internal* cues, such as stomach contractions, glucose levels, and fat levels. This led Stanley Schachter to propose the internal-external theory of overweight and obesity. This theory generated a great deal of research and has been the cornerstone for much recent research.

Stomach Contractions and Hunger

One of the first systematic demonstrations that obese and nonobese people respond to different cues was made by Albert Stunkard (1959). He arranged for both obese and nonobese subjects, having gone without food overnight, to enter the laboratory at 9 A.M. Each volunteer was asked to swallow a gastric balloon (filled with water) that was attached to a mechanical device to record stomach contractions. Every 15 minutes for four hours, the volunteers were asked to report whether they were hungry. It was found that the nonobese were more likely to report hunger when the stomach was active than were the obese. This suggests that feelings of hunger are associated with internal stimuli for the nonobese but not for the obese. Since we would expect hunger to be associated with internal cues, the question is why the obese fail to respond to these cues. If they are not responding to internal cues, what cues are eliciting their reports of hunger?

Stanley Schachter (1971a) demonstrated that, whereas the nonobese person tends to respond to internal cues such as stomach motility or hypoglycemia (low blood glucose), the obese person tends to respond more to external cues. An obese person who is accustomed to eating at a certain time, for example, will feel hungry when the clock indicates mealtime. The nonobese person will be less influenced by the time on the clock, unless it happens to coincide with his or her internal cues. To test this prediction, Schachter had volunteers come to the laboratory under the pretense of studying "the relation between physiological reactions and psychological characteristics which require base level measurements of heart and sweat gland activity" (Schachter & Gross, 1968, p. 99). Electrodes were attached, presumably to measure heart rate and galvanic skin response. Half the obese and half the nonobese subjects were then left for a period of time (ostensibly to establish a baseline) with a rigged clock that over 50 minutes would be 15 minutes slow. The other half were left for the same period with a rigged clock that would be 30 minutes fast. The first group finished this phase of the study when its clock said 5:20 P.M., the second when its clock said 6:05 P.M. The experimenter returned at this point with a box of crackers from which

Table 3-2.   Amount of crackers eaten (in grams) by Schachter's subjects in four conditions.

Weight	Time	
	Slow	*Fast*
Obese	19.9	37.6
Nonobese	41.5	16.0

Source: From *Emotion, Obesity and Crime,* by S. Schachter. Copyright © 1971 by Academic Press. Reprinted with permission.

he was snacking and offered some to the volunteer. The experimenter also asked the subject to fill out an irrelevant questionnaire. If obese persons are more affected by clock time than by real time, they would be expected to eat more in the condition where the clock time was fast than in the condition where it was slow, because the apparent time in the fast-time condition was either near or past the subject's regular eating time. The results (Table 3-2) supported the hypothesis. On the average, obese subjects ate more crackers in the fast-time condition than in the slow-time condition, whereas the nonobese subjects ate more in the slow-time condition. Why was there a reversal for the nonobese subjects? Schachter notes that, when the nonobese subjects in the fast-time condition refused crackers, they said "No, thanks. I don't want to spoil my dinner." Apparently, cognitive factors were responsible in this case.

The Air France study.   These findings are consistent with those obtained by more naturalistic methods (Goldman, Jaffa, & Schachter, 1968). An airplane crosses several time zones when it flies from Paris to New York, so that a passenger's internal cues will fail to correspond with clock time after a flight. Because obese people respond to clock time rather than internal cues, they should adjust quickly to the local eating time. The nonobese, in contrast, should find it much more difficult to adjust their eating habits to local time. Interviews with Air France personnel assigned to transatlantic flights indicated that those who were overweight had less trouble adjusting to local eating time than those who were average in weight (Figure 3-5).

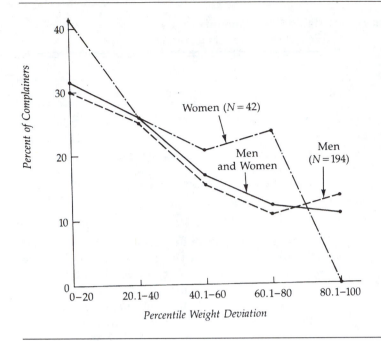

Figure 3-5. Relation of weight deviation among Air France personnel to complaints about the effect of time-zone changes on eating. (From *Emotion, Obesity and Crime*, by S. Schachter. Copyright © 1971 by Academic Press. Reprinted with permission.)

A further test of Schachter's theory: Fear, stomach contractions, and hunger. To determine more precisely whether nonobese people respond to an internal state—namely, stomach motility—a study in which stomach cues would be suppressed or eliminated was designed (Schachter, Goldman, & Gordon, 1968). Because fear is known to suppress gastric movement and researchers can easily manipulate fear by informing subjects that they will receive a shock, it was relatively easy to design a study in which nonobese subjects would experience little or no gastric movement. Subjects were told that the purpose of the experiment was to evaluate the effects of tactile stimulation on taste and that electrical stimulation would be used to stimulate the skin receptors. In the low-fear condition, subjects were told that the electrical stimulation would produce a mild tingling sensation. In the high-fear condition, subjects were told the shocks would be painful but would cause no permanent damage. They were further instructed that the experimenters wanted to get measures of taste before and during tactile stimulation. Hence the subjects started the tasting part of the experiment with the belief that they would shortly be experiencing shock in the next phase of the study. Actual

shock was not given; the instructions were used merely to induce fear. The tasting task involved judging some crackers in terms of several dimensions (salty, cheesy, garlicky, and so on). However, the actual behavior of interest was the number of crackers obese and nonobese volunteers ate. Subjects were told that they could eat as many crackers as they wanted in order to make their judgments. If nonobese subjects' tendency to eat is determined by gastric motility and the fear manipulation worked, the nonobese volunteers should have eaten less under the high-fear than the low-fear condition. This was, in fact, what occurred (Figure 3-6). The obese volunteers were not sensitive to the fear manipulation. They ate almost equal amounts under high- and low-fear conditions. This finding is consistent with the view that obese people are insensitive to internal cues.

Aspects of Externality

Is externality innate or learned? According to Schachter's theory, as we have seen, some people come to depend on external cues to tell them when to eat, whereas other people depend on internal cues to tell them when to eat. Whether this is an innate or learned

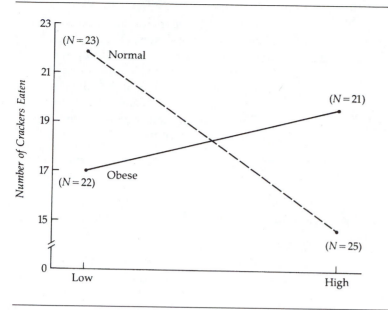

Figure 3-6. Effects of fear on number of crackers eaten by normal and obese subjects. (From *Emotion, Obesity and Crime*, by S. Schachter. Copyright © 1971 by Academic Press. Reprinted with permission.)

pattern of behavior has never been clearly established. Many diet clinics encourage their clients to listen to their bodies' needs (internal orientation) rather than allowing themselves to be controlled by the sensory qualities of food (external orientation). Despite this commonsense suggestion, there is evidence that, if you are an external, it is very difficult to learn to become an internal.

Externality and nonobese individuals. We might conclude from Schachter's work that only obese people are sensitive to cues in the environment associated with eating. Work by Judith Rodin and her colleagues indicates that this is not always true. They have shown that many nonobese people are sensitive to such environmental cues and that many obese people are not (e.g., Rodin, 1981; Rodin & Slochower, 1976). Further, they have shown that losing weight is not accompanied by a decrease in responsiveness to those cues (Rodin, Slochower, & Fleming, 1977). An obese person who salivates at the sight of a steak will have the same response even after losing considerable weight. Rodin's work indicates that, although externality may be associated with the motivation to eat, there is no one-to-one correspondence between that motivation and a person's weight. This lack of correspondence is

undoubtedly due to three factors: differences in metabolic rates; differences in self-control; and differences in the availability of food, especially palatable foods.

Sensory cues, externality, and the insulin response. In a series of studies, Rodin (1981) has explored the hypothesis that sensory cues such as taste and smell are sufficient to stimulate the release of insulin in externals. As we noted earlier, Rodin has argued that an elevated insulin level produces feelings of hunger. Note that Table 3-1 indicates a link between insulin and satiety. It appears from various studies that insulin at low levels may trigger feelings of hunger, while at higher levels it triggers feelings of satiety. If, indeed, sensory cues are capable of triggering the release of insulin in externally responsive people but not in internally responsive people, then we have a mechanism that can explain why externals tend to become obese. To test this hypothesis, Rodin first determined the subjects' degree of externality by a battery of measures that did not involve eating. Next, she asked the subjects to fast for a period of 18 hours. When they arrived at the laboratory, a steak was in the process of being grilled. They could see it, smell it, hear the crackling sound of it. At the same time, a blood sample was drawn in order to measure their insulin levels. The

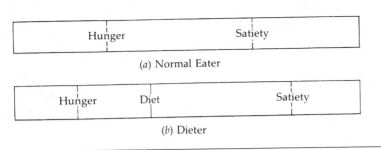

Figure 3-7. Hunger and satiety boundaries of dieters and nondieters. (The diet boundary is purely cognitive.) (Adapted from "A Boundary Model for the Regulation of Eating," by C. P. Herman and J. Polivy. In A. J. Stunkard and E. Stellar (Eds.), *Eating and Its Disorders.* Copyright © 1984 Raven Press. Reprinted with permission.)

externally responsive subjects, whether overweight or not, showed the greatest insulin response to the sight, smell, and sound of the grilling steak. In another study, Rodin examined whether the insulin response would increase as a function of palatability. As expected, the increase in insulin response was greater in externally responsive subjects.

Field studies of the insulin theory.   According to Rodin's theory, if different foods trigger different amounts of insulin, people might be able to control their weight and not feel hungry by carefully selecting the foods they eat. Since glucose triggers a greater insulin release than fructose, it follows from Rodin's theory that, if people eat food containing fructose (for instance, fruits) rather than food containing glucose (such as breads), they will feel less hungry at a later time. In a study by Spitzer (cited in Rodin, 1984), subjects were asked to drink lemon-flavored water that contained either fructose, glucose, or glucose made to taste as sweet as fructose. Two and one-quarter hours later, subjects were presented with a buffet containing a very large variety of foods and asked to eat whatever they liked until they were comfortably full. Subjects in both glucose conditions ate significantly more than did subjects in the fructose condition. Extrapolating to what might happen if subjects ate as they had done during the experiment over the course of a year, Rodin calculated that a given individual would gain (or lose) up to 50 pounds.

These results provide compelling evidence for the idea that insulin levels play an important role in governing food intake. If more insulin is present in the bloodstream when we load up our plate, we will put more on the plate.

Boundary Theory of Hunger, Eating, and Obesity

Janet Polivy and Peter Herman have proposed a boundary model of hunger and eating (Polivy & Herman, 1983; Herman & Polivy, 1984). According to this model, two separate mechanisms control hunger and eating, one for hunger and one for satiety (Figure 3-7a). Both mechanisms are assumed to have a physiological basis. Following the lead of other theorists, Polivy and Herman assume that, if we fail to eat or if we eat too much, we will experience an aversive state. Between these two boundary points is a range that is not under direct physiological control. Once we become hungry and begin to eat, the amount we eat will be controlled by such factors as social expectations and the taste and texture of the food. They argue that, within these boundaries, eating is under cognitive rather than biological control.

They further suggest that the upper and lower boundaries vary from person to person. They suggest that the lower hunger boundary is lower in dieters (Figure 3-7b) than in nondieters (Figure 3-7a), and the upper satiety boundary is higher in dieters than in nondieters. They further argue that, because dieters want to control their weight, they impose on themselves an upper boundary well below the biological satiety boundary. This is a purely cognitive boundary. This particular idea is an outgrowth of work on dieters and nondieters, which led Polivy and Herman to distinguish between restrained and unrestrained eaters.

Restrained and Unrestrained Eaters

Dieters, Polivy and Herman have found, tend to be *restrained eaters*. While they often feel hungry, think a great deal about food, and are readily tempted by the sight and smell of food, they consciously attempt to control their impulse to eat. If they do overeat or eat high-calorie foods (a no-no for dieters), they feel guilty. Nondieters, in contrast, tend to be *unrestrained eaters.* They do not experience persistent feelings of hunger, do not think about food as much as restrained eaters do, and are not so readily tempted by the sight and smell of food. More importantly, they are not constantly trying to control their food intake, nor do they feel guilty when they overeat.

Polivy and Herman have developed a scale to determine whether or not people are restrained or unrestrained (normal) eaters. They argue that the ideal weight, as prescribed by society, is often below the lower limit of a person's natural range. If such people are to achieve this ideal weight, they must constantly restrain their natural urges. In other words, the problem for the restrained eater is the need to deal more or less constantly with hunger and attraction to food. To see if you are a restrained eater, take the test in Table 3-3. The higher your score, the more restrained an eater you are.

The Preloading Studies

One of the most convincing lines of evidence for Polivy and Herman's theory comes from what can be called the preloading studies. They gave dieters and nondieters either one or two milkshakes (preloading) and then asked them to judge the tastes of three varieties of ice cream. Control subjects got no milkshake. Experimental subjects in the preloading condition were told that the purpose of the preloading was to determine how a previous taste affected subsequent taste perception. However, the real purpose was to determine whether preloading would affect the amount of ice cream that dieters and nondieters would eat. As dieters are restrained eaters who avoid such foods as ice cream, they should feel guilty and consequently make fewer taste tests (that is, eat less) than nondieters. The initial study (Figure 3-8) showed that, as preloading increased, the amount of ice cream the dieters ate in the course of the taste test also increased (Herman & Mack, 1975). In a subsequent study, subjects were told that the caloric content was high or low. When they were told that the caloric content was high, the effect was even greater (Polivy, 1976). These results are contrary to what we might intuitively expect. However, as

Table 3-3. Eating restraint scale.

1. How often are you dieting?
   Never; rarely; sometimes; often; always. *(Scored 0–4)*

2. What is the maximum amount of weight (in pounds) that you have ever lost within one month?
   0–4; 5–9; 10–14; 15–19; 20+. *(Scored 0–4)*

3. What is your maximum weight gain within a week?
   0–1; 1.1–2; 2.1–3; 3.1–5; 5.1+. *(Scored 0–4)*

4. In a typical week, how much does your weight fluctuate?
   0–1; 1.1–2; 2.1–3; 3.1–5; 5.1+. *(Scored 0–4)*

5. Would a weight fluctuation of 5 pounds affect the way you live your life?
   Not at all; slightly; moderately; very much. *(Scored 0–3)*

6. Do you eat sensibly in front of others or splurge alone?
   Never; rarely; often; always. *(Scored 0–3)*

7. Do you give too much time and thought to food?
   Never; rarely; often; always. *(Scored 0–3)*

8. Do you have feelings of guilt after overeating?
   Never; rarely; often; always. *(Scored 0–3)*

9. How conscious are you of what you are eating?
   Not at all; slightly; moderately; extremely. *(Scored 0–3)*

10. How may pounds over your desired weight were you at your maximum weight?
    0–1; 2–5; 6–10; 11–20; 21+. *(Scored 0–4)*

Source: From *Breaking the Diet Habit: The Natural Weight Alternative,* by J. Polivy and C. P. Herman. Copyright © 1983 by J. Polivy and C. P. Herman. Reprinted with permission.

we will see momentarily, they are consistent with the theory of Herman and Polivy.

The Disinhibited Eater

Herman and Polivy have suggested that, when dieters fail to restrain their eating (in this case, because they have agreed to serve in an experiment that requires them to break their usual strict rules), they adopt a what-the-hell attitude. They become disinhibited. They say to themselves, "As long as I've already lost control, I might as well eat as much as I want." What has happened, Herman and Polivy contend, is that, having for the moment abandoned their diet boundary, they are

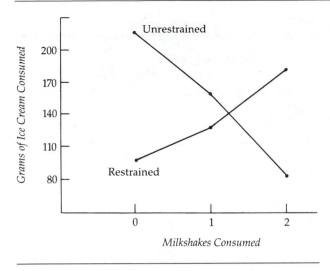

Figure 3-8. Effect of preloading (milkshake consumption) on subsequent ice cream consumption in restrained and unrestrained eaters. (From "Perception of Calories and Regulation of Intake in Restrained and Unrestrained Subjects," by J. Polivy. *Addictive Behavior*, 1976, *1*, 237–243. Reprinted by permission of the author.)

left with only their biological satiety boundary, which is higher than the nondieter's. That the effect increases when they are told that the preload is high in calories provides compelling evidence that the diet boundary is indeed cognitive rather than biological. How long does the dieter remain in this disinhibited state? Many dieters consider the next day a new beginning, and restrained eating is again the rule. However, the disinhibition effect can also be markedly reduced if their attention is called to their behavior (either by themselves or by someone else) (Polivy, Herman, Hackett, & Kuleshnyk, 1986).

While the boundary theory appears to be able to explain the behavior of dieters (especially the characteristic disinhibition effect) and of bingers as well, it has been criticized on the grounds that it fails to contribute to a better understanding of why people actually become obese (Ruderman, 1986).

Binge Eating and Anorexia

Herman and Polivy's theory can also account for binge eating and anorexia. In Figure 3-9, note that the binge

eater is not responding to the satiety boundary (or the satiety boundary is inoperative), whereas the individual with anorexia is not responding to the hunger boundary (or the hunger boundary is inoperative).

Summary

Internal-external theory grew out of the observation that obese people often eat in response to external cues, whereas nonobese people eat in response to internal cues. Several studies have shown that obese people tend to respond to time of day, palatability of food, and other external cues, whereas nonobese individuals tend to respond to internal cues. In a fascinating study, Judith Rodin has shown that the insulin response to the sight and smell of food is greater in externally responsive people than in internally responsive people. Field studies have shown that, indeed, insulin does seem to govern the amount we eat.

Boundary theory proposes that we have two boundaries, one for hunger and one for satiety. Polivy and Herman suggest that restrained eaters have a very high satiety boundary and, as a result, tend to overeat. In order to maintain their weight, they set a cognitive boundary. If circumstances should induce them to exceed their cognitive boundary, they tend to become disinhibited eaters for a time, usually the remainder of the day. Boundary theory can also account for binge eating and anorexia.

Difficulties Confronting Dieters

Anyone who has attempted to lose weight can attest to the difficulty and frustration involved. Why is dieting so difficult? Once again, let's consider the biological, learned, and cognitive components of this question.

The Biological Component

Anabolism (Caloric Thrift) and Catabolism (Caloric Waste)

According to the famine hypothesis, humans have developed several mechanisms to ensure survival in conditions where the food supply is unreliable:

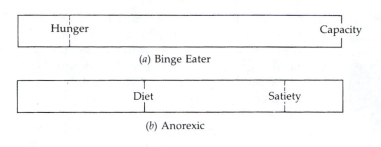

Figure 3-9. Failure of hunger and satiety boundaries in binge eaters and individuals with anorexia. (The diet boundary is purely cognitive.) (Adapted from "A Boundary Model for the Regulation of Eating," by C. P. Herman and J. Polivy. In A. J. Stunkard and E. Stellar (Eds.), *Eating and Its Disorders*. Copyright © 1984 Raven Press. Reprinted with permission.)

1. A mechanism to deal with the lack of food. This mechanism turns down the thermostat so that we don't use as much energy (Apfelbaum, 1975; Garrow, 1978). The deceleration of metabolism is referred to as *anabolism* or *caloric thrift*.
2. A mechanism to store food when it is available. The extra food is stored in the form of fat.
3. A mechanism to prevent the buildup of excessive amounts of fat. Excessive fat would hinder the individual's mobility and thus be nonadaptive. This mechanism is the acceleration of metabolism, which is referred to as *catabolism* or *caloric waste*. In this state, energy is spent more freely (Polivy & Herman, 1983).

While these mechanisms may have been adaptive in a world where food was scarce, they come to haunt the overweight person who decides to diet. When the dieter begins to cut down on food, the body responds with a reduced metabolic rate (anabolism), which hinders weight loss. To overcome this regulatory mechanism, the dieter must cut down intake still further. The body responds by further reducing the metabolic rate. Moreover, overweight individuals are used to eating fairly large quantities of food with relatively little weight gain, thanks to catabolism, and so dieting means they have to break entrenched habits of food consumption.

Dieters must also contend with the dynamics of insulin production. An individual with a considerable food intake will produce large amounts of insulin to digest that food. Over time however, insulin output tends to become independent of food intake; that is, the body gets in the habit of producing an increased amount of insulin. When a person cuts down on food intake, insulin output remains high, at least for a period of time; this condition is called *hyperinsulinemia*

(Rabinowitz & Zierler, 1962). In this condition, fat storage is enhanced, because insulin accelerates the conversion of sugar into fat. Also, as we noted earlier, an excess of insulin tends to increase feelings of hunger (e.g., Williams, 1960). Because of hyperinsulinemia, dieters tend to be hungry and, when they do eat, tend to be highly efficient in converting any unused food into fat; in other words, their bodies are unforgiving. Research with animals indicates that hyperinsulinemia may have a genetic component (Margules, 1979).

Cravings for Forbidden Foods

One way to make a diet more efficient is to stop eating high-calorie foods. The problem with this strategy is that, as our intake of these foods decreases, we crave them more (Striegel-Moore, Silberstein, & Rodin, 1986). Why should that be? Polivy and Herman (1983) have suggested that the body has a memory of the amount of food it normally gets. When an individual begins to eat fewer calories, the body responds by signaling the need for more food, especially foods high in calories, to restore the caloric intake to its previous level. It seems that hyperinsulinemia may also cause this preference, which would help explain why obese people crave high-calorie foods.

The Learned Component

The Cultural Ideal

Various researchers have noted that the ideal body enshrined in current cultural norms is extremely lean. Fashion magazines such as *Vogue,* for example, show the ideal female as very slim; typically, the models in fashion photographs are well below normative weight. Perhaps not surprisingly, about 70% of women in

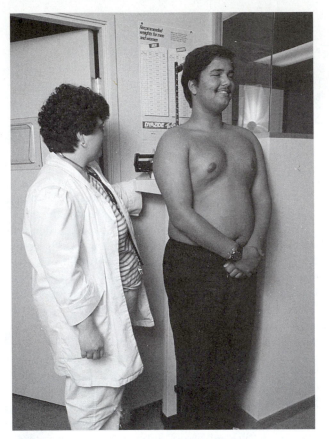

Many humans are faced with the problem of overweight early in life.

North America say they feel fat, but only 23% are truly overweight. The lean ideal is promoted by a diet industry valued at more than $30 billion per year, which supplies diet books, programs, videos, foods, pills, and devices (Brownell & Rodin, 1994). Can people actually lose weight to achieve this culturally ideal weight? And if it is possible, is it advisable for health reasons? As we have seen, there is considerable evidence that we are born with a set point that is difficult to alter.

Behavior Modification and Weight Control

Although the antidieting movement that has emerged recently argues that all diets fail (e.g., Garner & Wooley, 1991; Wooley & Garner, 1991), there is evidence that some diets can work. Programs combining very low-calorie food with intensive education and behavior modification seem to work best (e.g., Jeffery et al., 1993).

Behavior modification practitioners suggest that the main problem for the overweight person is to learn new patterns of eating that will not only lead to an immediate weight loss but also maintain the new weight. Dieters need a plan that will enable them to acquire a new set of habits. Many diets can result in weight loss; the problem is to keep from gaining the weight back again. Weight Watchers, probably the most famous behavioral program, was developed out of the belief that the best way to treat overweight is to teach new eating habits.

To illustrate this approach, Practical Application 3-1 presents a series of rules that a person in such a program might be required to follow and summarizes the reasons that these rules should lead not only to weight loss but also, over time, to a new set of eating habits that will maintain the weight loss. These rules, which are logical extrapolations from the research literature on hunger and eating, are similar in some respects to those in books on how to alter eating habits (e.g., Jeffrey & Katz, 1977; Mahoney & Mahoney, 1976; Stuart, 1978). There is nothing magical about these rules; they simply show how we may use our current knowledge to keep our weight under control. Note, however, that our knowledge about weight control is still incomplete. Not all overweight people are overweight for the same reason, as Rodin (1981) and others have repeatedly emphasized. Nevertheless, there is considerable agreement that, whatever the exact cause of the problem, overweight people must learn to reorganize their lives if they are to lose their unwanted weight and keep it off.

The Cognitive Component

Although individuals should not be held responsible for their weight and shape, there is considerable evidence that being a self-determined person—having a sense of autonomy—plays an important role in dieting. People with a stronger sense of autonomy tend, for example, to attend weight-loss programs more regularly, to lose more weight in the course of the program, and to maintain the weight loss longer (Williams, Grow, Freedman, Ryan, & Deci, 1996). Self-determination, therefore, plays an important role in dieting and dieting outcome. People in weight-loss programs need to be educated about their contribution to the outcome. Often dieters attribute their failure to the program, rather than to their own level of commitment or sense that change is possible.

Health Implications of Weight Loss and Obesity

Obesity has been associated with diabetes, hypertension, cardiovascular disease, and cancer (Bray, 1992). It is responsible for 5.5% of all health care costs in the United States—about $39 million annually (Colditz, 1992). At the same time, most researchers agree that current cultural norms regarding the ideal body put enormous pressure on people to become rigid, lean, and contoured. Indeed, there is considerable evidence that North Americans tend to be prejudiced against fat people (Crandall, 1994). For many dieters, achieving the cultural ideal is difficult, if not impossible, and consequently they are subjected to a great deal of physical and psychological stress.

Increasingly, psychologists are taking an active role in informing the public about issues surrounding weight loss and about behaviorally sound methods for losing weight (Brownell & Rodin, 1994). The following are some conclusions from existing research.

1. *Society needs to accept greater variability in shapes and weight.* We shouldn't assume that a lean person is a model of self-control, nor that a fat person is lacking in self-control. We need to see people for what they are and appreciate their diversity (Brownell & Rodin, 1994). Public education on this topic would be very helpful.

Trying to achieve the cultural ideal may be not only unrealistic but also a source of physical and mental stress. Dieters need to realize that there is a trade off between biology and self-control. Overestimating the role of biology can result in feelings of helplessness, while taking too much personal responsibility can lead to feelings of loss of control, guilt, and shame.

2. *Losing weight usually, but not always, prolongs life.* Recent studies on mortality have shown that losing weight is generally beneficial. In a prospective study, for example, it was found that a 10% reduction in

weight produced a 10% decrease in cardiovascular mortality. For obese men, the reduction in risk was 50% (Wannamethee & Shaper, 1990). In a study of Type II diabetes, a 10-kg loss in weight was estimated to restore 35% of the longevity loss associated with diabetes (Lean, Powrie, Anderson, & Garthwaite, 1990). However, other studies have shown that dieting can increase mortality in the obese (e.g., Pamuk, Williamson, Serdula, Madans, & Byers, 1993).

3. *Modest weight losses can have significant health benefits.* Until recently, researchers ignored the effects of modest weight losses, and focused instead on dramatic shifts from obesity to an ideal weight. There is considerable evidence that modest weight losses produce important medical benefits, including improvement in blood pressure, blood glucose control, blood lipids, and lipoproteins. Additionally, there is evidence that small weight losses are easier to maintain (Brownell & Rodin, 1994).

4. *Dieters should avoid drastic weight fluctuations.* When a diet ends, individuals often return rapidly to their original weight or even higher (the yo-yo effect). Early studies found that such fluctuations were extremely harmful. Recent studies have not been able to replicate these findings, and in many studies no harmful effects have been found. Nonetheless there appears to be a link between weight fluctuations and chronic disease (Brownell & Rodin, 1994).

Also, dieting and binge eating are often associated, but it has not been established that dieting is the cause of binge eating.

Summary

There are two primary obstacles to dieting. First, when the body is deprived of food, the metabolic rate tends to decline, thereby frustrating the dieter's attempt to lose weight. Second, dieting often produces a craving for restricted foods, often high-calorie foods.

The current cultural ideal calls for an extremely lean body, which is impossible for many people to achieve. However, weight loss is possible within limits. The best method for losing weight involves retraining our eating habits and exercising. Self-determination plays a central role in weight loss.

Society needs to accept people as they are and appreciate their diversity. Weight loss usually improves the health of obese people, but this is not always the case. Nonetheless, maintaining a normal weight often does have important health benefits. There is some evidence that drastic weight fluctuations may have negative health implications, but recent research suggests that this is not necessarily so.

Theories of Eating Disorders

There are two major eating disorders: bulimia and anorexia nervosa. *Bulimia* (literally "ox hunger") is often referred to as the binge-purge syndrome. Individuals with bulimia tend to be preoccupied with food and the urge to eat, but are also concerned with their weight; they often alternate between dieting and gorging (Schlesier-Stropp, 1984). *Anorexia nervosa* is characterized by a refusal to maintain body weight above minimum norms, a weight that is 25% below expected weight, an intense fear of gaining weight or becoming fat, and disturbances of body image. Both disorders primarily affect women. What causes these disorders? There is some evidence of a biological component, but most studies suggest that they have their roots in our obsession with thinness. Throughout our society, women are told that thin is in (Guy, Rankin, & Norvell, 1980). Fashion magazines link slenderness with beauty and femininity. Several studies have supported the observation that physically attractive women tend to be perceived as more feminine than unattractive women (e.g., Unger, 1985; Heilman & Saruwatari, 1979). In view of such attitudes, it is not

Practical Application 3-1

Some Rules for Dieting

Rule 1: *Eat in only one place and at regular times.* This rule is intended to help you stop snacking, by limiting the number of places where you eat and ensuring that you eat at appropriate intervals rather than by impulse. People are typically not good at monitoring their food intake and that many overweight people have become overweight because they snack. If you eat at regular times, your body will have the necessary calories and nutrients to keep you going. Eat *nothing* between meals.

Rule 2: *Use small plates.* Overweight people tend not only to fill their plates but to eat what is on them. Therefore, when you use a smaller plate, you tend to eat less.

Rule 3: *Eat slowly.* You should accomplish three things by eating slowly. First, the pleasure you get from eating will be maximized. Second, since the mouth provides feedback about the amount we have eaten, we can signal the brain that we have eaten a great deal by carefully chewing our food and making the eating process last as long as possible. Third, when we eat slowly, our digestive system has time to absorb some of the food, and this process should help to stimulate our satiety mechanism. I call this the *fondue phenomenon.* A meat fondue is made at the dining table, not in the kitchen. Each diner immerses little pieces of meat, one at a time, in a pot of near-boiling oil. When one piece is eaten, another goes into the pot. The process may take a couple of hours. People often report that they feel full long before all the meat is gone, even when the quantity of food eaten is quite small.

Rule 4: *Eat in the company of others.* People tend to eat slowly and to eat less when they are in the company of others. Besides, conversation tends to extend the eating time, an important factor in reducing food intake (see rule 3).

Rule 5: *If you eat alone, don't read or watch television.* The purpose of this rule is to help you learn to respond to internal cues as well as to help you monitor what and how much you are eating. When you are doing something else, you not only fail to monitor your intake but tend to eat quickly.

Rule 6: *Limit the availability of fattening foods.* If you can't resist cookies, candy, cake, and other high-calorie foods, surprising that many women become obsessed with thinness. Studies have yielded an abundance of evidence that individuals with bulimia and anorexia are motivated to diet by the belief that fat is ugly and must be eliminated. One study found that, by the age of 13, 80% of girls (but only 10% of boys) have already been on weight-loss diets (Hawkins, Turell, & Jackson, 1983).

In her book *Perfect Women*, Colette Dowling (1988) argues that many women with eating disorders have an overwhelming desire to achieve perfection. The drive to be perfect, she contends, comes out of women's feelings of inferiority, which result from the continuing disparagement of women in our society. These feelings of inferiority, she believes, are handed down from mother to daughter. In order to break this cycle, therefore, the communication between mother and daughter needs to be changed.

What is the solution? Since bulimia and anorexia nervosa seem to be related to our cultural values or practices, the real solution lies in coming to grips with our cultural values. Values do change. People not yet old can remember when women as thin as today's ideal were spurned as too skinny; those women tried to gain weight as desperately as contemporary women try to lose it. The answer to eating disorders, therefore, may lie in waiting for the pendulum to swing back to acceptance of a more realistic ideal for women to emulate.

The Spiral Model of Eating Disorders

To account for some of the diverse findings surrounding bulimia and anorexia nervosa, Heatherton and Polivy (1976) have developed the *spiral model.* This model starts with the finding that, in this society,

limit the amounts that are available. Remember that overweight people are often externals, and the mere sight of such food can stimulate the output of insulin.

Rule 7: *Allow for variety.* When we eliminate from our diet certain foods that we normally eat, we often develop a craving for those foods. When the craving becomes strong, we have a tendency to eat large quantities of those foods, if they are available. So if you are accustomed to eating pastas, for example, don't try to eliminate them altogether; just cut down.

Rule 8: *Don't try to lose weight too quickly.* When we do, our body often responds with a reduced metabolic rate. This response not only interferes with our ability to lose weight but may cause problems when we have reached our ideal weight. Another disadvantage of trying to lose weight very quickly is that, when we fail to meet our short-term goal, we tend to give up.

Rule 9: *Eat a balanced diet.* The goal of dieting should be not only to lose weight but to keep that weight off. Sometimes you can lose weight very rapidly by following a diet that requires you to eliminate certain types of food. Not

only do such diets often precipitate health problems, but they fail to teach us how we should eat after we have reached our desired weight. The goal of dieting is simply learning to eat less while staying healthy.

Rule 10: *Combine your diet with exercise.* Since basal metabolism can account for one-third of our energy expenditure, and exercise increases the BMR, exercise is useful not only for getting rid of excess fat but for maintaining our desired weight. The most effective program calls for at least 20 minutes of exercise three times a week and involves an activity that uses 300 calories and raises the heart rate to 60–70% of its maximum (McCardle, Katch, & Katch, 1991). Ideal activities are running, swimming, bicycling, walking upstairs, or any other aerobic activity that induces us to take in large amounts of oxygen. (Oxygen is required to burn calories.)

thinness is highly valued, especially for women. To become thin, people become restrained eaters. This means that many people constantly deprive themselves of food (restrain their food intake). However, dieters find themselves in an endless struggle with the body's regulatory mechanisms, which tend to keep each individual's weight at its set point. One by-product of this struggle, as we have seen, is the yo-yo effect, in which weight loss is followed by weight gains that may even surpass the previous high levels. According to the spiral model, when the body begins to win the battle and we begin to put on weight, our self-esteem begins to decline. With lowered self-esteem comes a *disinhibition effect;* we lose control over our food intake. One possible result is binge eating. According to this model, the obvious way to break out of the downward spiral is to abandon the unrealistic standards that we set for ourselves.

Summary

Bulimia is characterized by episodes of binge eating followed by purging. Anorexia nervosa is characterized by a refusal to maintain body weight above minimum norms, a weight level that is 25% below expected body weight, an intense fear of gaining weight, and disturbances of body image. In view of society's promotion of thinness as central to beauty and femininity, it is not surprising that some women become obsessed with weight loss. The most effective way of reducing the incidence of eating disorders might be to change society's attitudes towards body weight. According to the spiral model of eating disorders, a dieter's self-esteem begins to decline as efforts to control weight are frustrated, and then the dieter binges. This tendency to binge can be viewed as an attempt to escape from self-awareness.

Main Points

1. Carbohydrates, fats, and proteins are broken down into more basic units that can be used as energy and also to rebuild body cells and manufacture chemicals needed by the body and brain.

2. Most of the glucose absorbed by the blood is transported across cell walls and stored in the cells as glycogen; the remaining glucose is used for energy.

3. Unused glucose is converted into fat and stored in the adipose tissues.

4. Some of the proteins are converted into amino acids, which are important in rebuilding muscle and manufacturing essential chemicals.

5. A balanced diet should consist of protein (15%), carbohydrates (65%), and fats (15–20%).

6. Food intake has been linked to biological rhythms.

7. Gender differences in eating patterns have been linked to different activity in certain brain neuro-circuits.

8. Overweight is due in part to our genes.

9. People appear to eat for reasons that are not always linked to biological hunger.

10. People do not always stop eating when they reach the biological state called satiety.

11. There is no evidence that humans are equipped at birth to select a balanced diet.

12. Animals and humans tend to select foods on the basis of taste and texture.

13. Cultural differences suggest that, at least in part, food preference is learned.

14. Both animals and humans can learn to avoid foods that cause a general malaise.

15. Education can and does play an important role in determining what and how much people eat.

16. Obesity is defined as weight about 25% or more in excess of normal.

17. Twin studies suggest that genes play an important role in determining weight. We seem to inherit our metabolic rate.

18. Environmental factors also play an important role in overweight.

19. About two-thirds of our energy expenditure is due to the basal metabolic rate and one-third to exercise.

20. The basal metabolic rate decreases from birth until about the age of 20, when it tends to level off.

21. Lesions in the ventromedial nuclei of the hypothalamus lead to overeating and hence to obesity.

22. Lesions in the lateral hypothalamus cause the individual to reduce food intake.

23. Set-point theory suggests that the hypothalamus sets our weight.

24. According to Margules, the tendency to store fat is an adaptive mechanism that evolved to prepare us for periodic famines. Obesity, therefore, is linked to the fact that we no longer have to endure famines.

25. The yo-yo effect can be explained by the famine hypothesis.

26. A child's weight tends to be correlated more highly with the weight of the mother than with that of the father. This finding has led to the assertion that obesity may be due in part to the availability of food, which the mother tends to control.

27. Prospective studies of overweight have found them to be less depressed than normal weight.

28. According to internal-external theory, one reason that people become overweight is that their food intake is controlled by external cues, such as the sight and smell of food, rather than by internal cues, such as stomach contractions or the glucose level.

29. Externals show an increase in insulin output when palatable foods are available.

30. Field studies have linked insulin levels to quantity of food intake.

31. Boundary theory proposes that two separate mechanisms control our eating, one for hunger and one for satiety.

32. Dieters tend to be restrained eaters. They often feel hungry, think a great deal about food, and find it necessary constantly (and consciously) to control their food intake. In order to control their weight, they set a *cognitive boundary.*

33. Preloading studies have shown that, when this cognitive boundary has been overstepped, restrained eaters tend to become disinhibited eaters.

34. Metabolism tends to slow down during deprivation (anabolism).

35. Metabolism tends to increase after weight gain (catabolism).

36. Dieters often experience an increased desire for forbidden foods.

37. The cultural ideal calls for a lean body.

38. Behavior modification has been used to help people lose weight. This approach focuses on helping people to modify their eating habits.

39. Self-determined (autonomous) people are more successful at dieting.

40. Not everybody can or should lose weight.

41. For those who can and should lose weight, there are significant health benefits.

42. Excess weight has been linked to health problems such as diabetes, hypertension, and cardiovascular disease.

43. Even modest weight losses have benefits such as improvement in blood pressure, blood glucose control, blood lipids, and lipoproteins.

44. Weight fluctuation appears to increase certain chronic diseases.

45. North Americans' preoccupation with thinness has been suggested as a major determining factor in both bulimia and anorexia nervosa.

46. The spiral model accounts for some of the diverse findings associated with eating disorders.

Chapter Four

Sexual Behavior, Love, and Sexual Orientation

- From a physiological perspective, what constitutes sexual arousal or passion?

- Is sexual arousal the same for females and males? What produces sexual arousal in females and males?

- In what ways are orgasms the same and different for females and males? How do men and women differ biologically? What role do hormones play in sexual behavior?

- How do male and female mating strategies differ?

- Does learning play any significant role in sexual behavior?

- How is love different from sexual arousal or sexual passion?

- Why do people fall in love?

- Can we learn to fall in love or is that beyond our control?

- Why do some people fall in love suddenly, while others fall in love gradually?

- Is homosexuality biologically determined, is it learned, or does it comes from choices that people make? Can people change their sexual orientation?

The study of sexual behavior is a controversial topic. The controversy involves traditional values: Is it appropriate to discuss sex openly? Is sex only for reproduction? Is sex only for marriage? Or, perhaps, is sex merely to have fun? The controversy also involves the question of equity: Are males and females presented evenhandedly? Are stereotypes about male and female behavior being perpetuated? It involves women challenging the old male dogma and introducing their own. It involves debates about the role of biology and the environment.

In this chapter, we will examine four major topics. First, what is the underlying motivation for engaging in sexual behavior? Second, what is the basis of love? Third, what biological differences exist between men and women and what role do hormones play? Fourth, what is the origin of sexual orientation?

Human Sexual Arousal (Passion)

Prior to Masters and Johnson's pioneering book *Human Sexual Response* (1966), no solid scientific information was available about the nature of human sexual arousal—what we commonly call passion. This seems extraordinary in view of the vast number of publications purporting to inform the professional and the layperson about human sexual motivation. For example, a leading medical text stated unequivocally that women were nonorgasmic and but rarely, if ever, had sexual feelings (cited in Masters & Johnson, 1966). Two books by Alfred Kinsey and his associates—*Sexual Behavior in the Human Male* (Kinsey, Pomeroy, & Martin, 1948) and *Sexual Behavior in the Human Female* (Kinsey et al., 1953)—caused a storm of controversy. In these books, Kinsey objectively reported the results of interviews with male and female volunteers, which indicated not only that women enjoy sex, as do men, but that both sexes seem to enjoy a wide variety of sexual practices; that is, they like to have sex in different locations and in different positions. At the time, many people regarded the idea of variation in the sexual response as perverse. Among other things, Kinsey was attacked for the procedures he followed to obtain his sample. The basic argument was that his volunteers were not representative of the general population—that individuals willing to talk to strangers about their sexual practices must be deviant or abnormal. Although there were problems with Kinsey's sampling procedures, time has more or less vindicated him. Not only do humans enjoy sex, but a large number of them enjoy variations in their sexual behavior.

The Biological Component

The consensus that has emerged from Masters and Johnson's work is that human sexual behavior occurs in two major stages: a nontactile stage followed by a tactile stage. In the heterosexual paradigm, the person becomes interested in a member of the opposite sex because of visual, auditory, olfactory, or even cognitive cues. A woman, for example, may arouse the interest of a man by the shape of her body, her clothes, the way she smiles, the quality of her voice, the way she smells, or what she says. If she in turn finds the man attractive, she may agree to spend some time in proximity to him. They may go to a movie, have dinner together, walk together, and so on. If this first stage of proximity is satisfying for both, they move on to the second stage, which involves tactile stimulation. It usually begins with touching or holding hands, proceeds to petting, and gradually becomes more intimate unless inhibitions prevent the natural progression. The eventual aim is usually to have intercourse, with orgasm.

Masters and Johnson focused their research on the tactile phase of sexual behavior. In general, they held that human sexual behavior can be described as a sensory event. They argued that sex is rewarding because it provides a pleasurable sensory experience. Therefore, we need to understand exactly how the structure of this system facilitates the sensory events that motivate human sexual behavior.

Note that there is remarkable similarity between the female and the male sexual response. In other words, from a biological perspective, the sexual response seems to be organized in much the same way for males and females. Any differences seem to be due largely to learned and cognitive factors.

The Female Sexual Response

Masters and Johnson (1966) corrected certain misconceptions about the female sexual response: that women do not derive any pleasurable sensation from sex; and that women do not experience orgasm. In fact, they

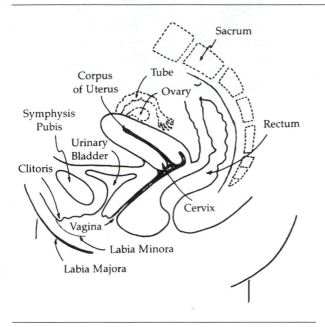

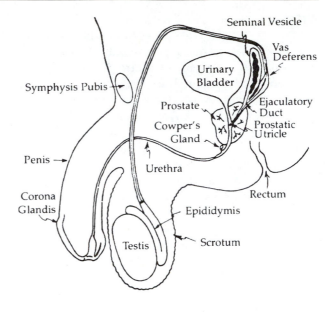

Figure 4-1.   Female pelvis: normal anatomy. (From *Human Sexual Response,* by W. H. Masters and V. E. Johnson. Copyright © 1966 by Little, Brown and Company. Reprinted with the permission of the publisher and authors.)

Figure 4-2.   Male pelvis: normal anatomy. (From *Human Sexual Response,* by W. H. Masters and V. E. Johnson. Copyright © 1966 by Little, Brown and Company. Reprinted with the permission of the publisher and authors.)

never found a case in which a woman who was properly stimulated did not experience an orgasm. Misconceptions about the female sexual response are probably due to comparisons with the male response. The differences that exist do not necessarily make a woman's response less intense or less satisfying than a man's response.

To describe the patterning of physiological and psychological responses, Masters and Johnson have divided the female sexual response into four stages: (1) the excitement phase; (2) the plateau phase; (3) the orgasmic phase; and (4) the resolution phase.

The female sexual response involves physiological changes that occur basically (1) outside the genital area, (2) in the clitoris, and (3) in the vagina. The diagram of the female pelvic area in Figure 4-1 will be useful in the following discussion.

It is beyond the scope of this chapter to describe all the varieties of stimulation that will produce a female orgasm. For most women, tactile stimulation in the

genital area is the most effective. Stimulation of the female genital area produces a more or less uniform pattern of physiological and psychological responses, as summarized in Table 4-1.

Note that, according to Masters and Johnson (1966), the clitoris is unique among organs in the human body in that its only function is pleasure. They argue that it exists solely for the purpose of receiving and transforming sensual information. Although no one denies that stimulation of the clitoris produces pleasure, some have argued that it is analogous to the penis (e.g., Morris, 1969). Masters and Johnson maintain that it is unique because it has nothing to do with reproduction and may not be necessary for orgasm, although it obviously plays some role in sexual pleasure and is usually involved in orgasm.

The Male Sexual Response

The sexual responses of males and females are very similar. Figure 4-2 shows a lateral view of the male

Table 4-1.   The human female sexual response.

Phase	Extragenital	Clitoris	Vagina
		Site of Reaction	
Excitement	Nipple erection Enlargement of breasts Sex flush (breasts) Involuntary muscle contractions Contractions of rectal sphincter	Size of clitoris increases (wide variation among individuals)	Vaginal lubrication Lengthening and distention of vagina Retraction of cervix and corpus of uterus into false pelvis
Plateau	Nipple erection continues Breasts enlarged Sex flush may spread to lower abdomen, thighs, buttocks Involuntary muscle contractions (hands and feet) Hyperventilation Increased heart rate Increased blood pressure	Entire clitoris retracts from normal overhang position	Marked vasocongestion near vaginal opening
Orgasm	Nipple erection continues Breast enlargement continues Sex flush terminates abruptly Involuntary muscle contractions Continued hyperventilation Peaking of heart-rate increase Peaking of blood pressure increase	Clitoris remains in retracted position	Rhythmic contractions near vaginal opening (area of vasocongestion)
Resolution	Decrease in all the above; also perspiratory reaction	Clitoris returns to normal overhang position	Rapid dispersal of vasocongestion Relaxation of vagina

Source: Based on W. H. Masters and V. E. Johnson, *Human Sexual Response*, 1966.

pelvic area; Table 4-2 summarizes male responses at various stages.

Although both the penis and the clitoris serve as important receptor systems for sensual stimulation, the penis has other functions not shared by the clitoris: It is essential for reproduction; and it plays an important role in stimulating the female.

One of the first signs of sexual arousal in the male is penile erection, which results from vasocongestion in the penis. The tissue structure of the penis is such that the increased supply of blood results in its elongation and distention. Continued stimulation of the penis typically produces ejaculation.

Mating Strategies of Males and Females

Evolutionary psychology has adopted the sociobiologists' view that the ultimate goal of our reproductive behavior is to maximize the survival of our genes in future generations. This hypothesis implies that males and females will adopt very different mating strategies. For males, the best strategy is to mate with as many females as possible; this is called the *quantity strategy*. Because females must bear the offspring, they need a different approach. Their best strategy is to be highly selective; this is called the *quality strategy*. They need to select mates who will provide: (1) characteristics such as strength and intelligence (or cunning) that will enable their offspring to survive and (2) help with raising the offspring. The evolutionary analysis gives rise to a number of predictions that can readily be tested. One study looked at six predictions that follow from the evolutionary analysis (Bailey, Gaulin, Agyei, & Gladue, 1994):

1. **Males will be more interested in uncommitted sex.** Obviously, if you are interested in quantity, you don't want to become involved.
2. **Males will be more interested in visual stimuli.** If you operate on a quantity strategy, it is to your benefit to be sexually aroused. If you work on a quality strategy, it is not to your benefit to become sexually aroused until you have assessed other important qualities.
3. **Women will be more concerned with status.** Status denotes possession or control of resources, which implies better ability to provide for offspring.
4. **Males will be more jealous.** If a male's partner is impregnated by another male, he has lost his ability to reproduce. Thus, being constantly vigilant is adaptive. Females do not have to be as jealous, it has been argued, because women are never burdened with unrelated children.
5. **Males are more concerned with physical attractiveness.** Even on a quantity strategy, you want to mate with a female who can successfully produce offspring. Physical beauty, it has been argued, includes the condition of the hips and breasts, which correlate with ability to carry and raise offspring.
6. **Males are more likely to prefer younger partners.** Youth, like beauty, is an indicator of a female's ability to carry and raise offspring.

To test these hypotheses, heterosexual participants—recruited through advertisements in various local papers—were asked to indicate, using a seven-point scale, the degree to which they agreed or disagreed with various sets of statements. The results are presented in Figure 4-3. In terms of d scores, the d score is the difference between the male means and female means, expressed in standard deviations. What Figure 4-3 shows is that, as compared to females, males are considerably more interested in visual sexual stimuli, have a much greater preference for younger sexual partners, are more jealous, are more concerned with physical attractiveness, and are less concerned with their partners' status.

Closely related to the hypothesis about status is another prediction from evolutionary analysis: that females will be attracted to dominant males. It appears that females are indeed attracted to the trait of dominance but only if dominance is accompanied by agreeableness (Jensen-Campbell, Graziano, & West, 1995). It makes sense that females would only be attracted to dominant males if they were agreeable, because the male must be willing to share in raising the offspring.

Summary

Masters and Johnson's pioneering work has provided us with a scientific description of the physiological events that result from sexual stimulation. The sexual response of both females and males can be divided into four phases: excitement, plateau, orgasm, and resolution. While important differences in the reactions of females and males have been known for some time, Masters and Johnson have shown that there are many similarities.

According to an evolutionary analysis, the quantity strategy of mate selection is best for males, whereas the quality strategy is best for females. Several predictions that follow from an evolutionary analysis have been confirmed through controlled research.

The Learned Component

Researchers have been interested in the question of what is sexually arousing for some time. They have found that pictures of nude members of the opposite sex can elicit sexual arousal and that pictures showing a member of the opposite sex in a state of sexual

Table 4-2.   The human male sexual response.

Phase	Site of Reaction		
	Extragenital	*Penis*	*Scrotum and Testes*
Excitement	Nipple erection (60% of males)	Penile erection (vasocongestion)	Localized vasocongestion
	Some sex flush	Urethra lengthens	Contraction of smooth-muscle fibers
	Involuntary muscle contractions		Thickening of scrotal skin
	Involuntary contraction of rectal sphincter		Testicular elevation
Plateau	Nipple erection	Vasocongestive increase in penile diameter	As in previous stage, plus greater elevation of testes and increase in testicular size
	Greater sex flush (25% of males)	Penile urethral bulb enlarges	
	Involuntary muscle contraction		
	Involuntary contraction of rectal sphincter		
	Hyperventilation		
	Increased heart rate		
	Increased blood pressure		
Orgasm	Continued nipple erection	Ejaculatory reaction (regular contractions of muscles)	As in previous stage
	Continued sex flush	Seminal fluid expelled through involuntary muscle contractions	
	Involuntary contraction of rectal sphincter		
	Hyperventilation	Urethra contracts in rhythm	
	Increased heart rate		
	Increased blood pressure		
Resolution	Very gradual retraction of nipples	Penile detumescence (two stages): rapid decrease in vasocongestion followed by slow decrease in vasocongestion	Either rapid or delayed return to normal state
	Rapid disappearance of sex flush		
	Perspiratory reaction		

Source: Based on W. H. Masters and V. E. Johnson, *Human Sexual Response,* 1966.

arousal or two persons engaged in sexual acts elicit sexual arousal more effectively than do simple pictures of nudity (e.g., Griffith, May, & Veitch, 1974; Mosher & Abramson, 1977). Several studies have shown that the stimulus does not have to be visual; verbal descriptions of sexual behavior are sufficient to elicit sexual arousal in most volunteer subjects (e.g., Heiman, 1977). The ability to fantasize may be an important mediator of this phenomenon, because subjects can become sex-

ually aroused through fantasy (e.g., Heiman, 1975, 1977; Masters & Johnson, 1966). People who are prone to fantasize or who have some sexual experience find it relatively easy to produce sexual fantasies (Carlson & Coleman, 1977).

Romantic themes and lust themes apparently produce the same amount of arousal (e.g., Fisher & Byrne, 1978; Heiman, 1977; Osborn & Pollack, 1977). It has long been held that women are not aroused by explicit

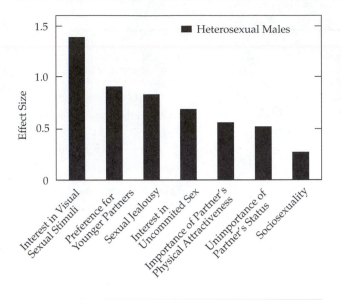

Figure 4-3. Sexual attitudes of heterosexual men compared with heterosexual women. The effect size is the difference between the means for men and women, expressed in terms of the standard deviation for men. (Adapted from "Effects of Gender and Sexual Orientation Evolutionary Relevant Aspects of Human Mating Psychology," by J. M. Bailey, S. Gaulin, Y. Agyei, and B. A. Galdue, *Journal of Personality and Social Psychology*, 1994, *66*, 1081–1093. Copyright © 1994 American Psychological Association. Reprinted by permission.)

erotic material, whereas men are (e.g., Abelson, Cohen, Heaton, & Suder, 1971), and that, compared to men, women are more sexually aroused by romantic themes. Research does not support these beliefs. It appears that, in the past, women have been reluctant to admit that they are aroused by pornography, because of cultural proscriptions (Gebhard, 1973).

The theme of chance encounter appears to increase sexual arousal in response to pornographic material. This finding is consistent with the literature on romantic attraction, which we will discuss later.

Why are nudity, romantic narratives, and the theme of chance encounter so arousing? Gagnon (1974, 1977) has suggested that these responses are learned—specifically through the creation of sexual scripts. Ac-

cording to Gagnon's analysis, all human sexual behavior is governed by sexual scripts.

Sexual Scripts

Sexual scripts are mental schemata of how an interpersonal sexual episode should be enacted (Gagnon, 1974, 1977; Simon & Gagnon, 1986). A sexual script is analogous to a movie script in which the actors have motives and feelings. Part of this movie script requires the actors to say certain things and to engage in certain nonverbal actions (Gagnon, 1974). Thus, in any sexual encounter, each individual is guided by a personal script.

Simon and Gagnon argue that sexual scripts initially arise out of information to which children are exposed, rewards and punishment they receive, and the process of imitation and modeling. Up until adolescence, they mainly involve gender-appropriate behaviors. Sexual scripts tell young boys and girls how they should react to and treat each other in a nonsexual encounter.

With the onset of adolescence, these scripts begin to incorporate sexual feelings. It has been suggested that, during masturbation, males coordinate or integrate their sexual feelings and activities with their gender roles. This coordination leads them to develop a sexual script that tells them how they should respond in actual sexual intercourse. As they experience each of the phases of the sexual response (excitement, plateau, orgasm, and resolution), they see themselves engaging in certain sexual behaviors (certain physical activities) and communicating (engaging in appropriate verbal and nonverbal responses). As the sexual script becomes more sophisticated, each phase becomes more clearly differentiated, so that the appropriate sexual behaviors (physical activity) and appropriate communication pattern coincide more closely to each of the phases of the sexual response.

It has been suggested that females have more difficulty learning to coordinate or integrate sexual feelings into their sexual scripts, because fewer females masturbate in early adolescence. Also, relative to male scripts, female sexual scripts in early adolescence contain less information that is purely sexual. Female scripts tend to focus on falling in love, while male scripts tend to focus mainly on sexual activity. Although falling in love may involve the excitement phase of the sexual response, it typically does not involve the other phases,

As the sex drive increases in adolescence, interest in sexual material also increases. Males have been found to be particularly interested in visual material.

which are more closely linked to sexual activity. Later in adolescence, female sexual scripts do incorporate the entire four-stage sexual response.

Gagnon (1974) suggests that, when adolescents begin to date, the script begins to shift from a fantasy-based masturbatory script to a more interpersonal and interdependent sexual script. In the course of petting, young couples begin to explore sexual arousal through touching each other while fully clothed. While this behavior is experienced as exciting, it does not typically produce orgasm. What is learned at this stage is to coordinate the feeling of being touched by another person with the excitement phase of the sexual response. In other words, the fantasy gives way to interpersonally instigated sexual excitement that comes largely through touch. Eventually, the female begins to adjust her script to include sexual arousal, which lays the groundwork for eventual orgasm.

As dating continues, the partners learn a number of other skills, such as mutual disrobing, how to obtain privacy, and how to better focus attention on the other person. Gagnon points out that, at this stage, sexual performance is often awkward, clumsy, and anxiety-ridden. With repeated practice and with greater mutual sensitivity, couples learn to coordinate their sexual scripts so that both can achieve sexual pleasure. Once a satisfactory solution has been worked out, sexual behavior often becomes semiritualized (Simon & Gagnon, 1986).

The Interaction of Biological and Learned Factors

Because of the important role of sexual scripts, it can be argued that sexual pleasure is the result of an interaction of biological (sensory) and learned factors. The pleasure that originally came only from self-stimulation eventually is shifted to the other person. According to this interpretation, sexual arousal comes to depend on sensory awareness of the sexual partner. Characteristics of the other person—including the sight, smell, and touch of that person—come to act as the source of sexual arousal. Through the process of generalization, other people can also act as sources of sensory arousal. Since images, fantasies, and scripts have also become linked to sexual arousal, the degree to which another person elicits these images, fantasies, and scripts will determine, in part, their potential for eliciting sexual arousal. In that respect, sexual arousal is in the eye of the beholder; people are aroused by what they perceive will happen.

The Reward Value of Sex

The reward value of sex seems to depend on participating in a satisfying sexual script. Women and men show a great deal of agreement on the typical sequence of heterosexual behaviors that lead to coitus. Fourteen behaviors have been identified as part of this script, including kissing, caressing, manual stimulation, oral stimulation, and penetration. Where the sexes differ is in the degree of arousal they experience from each of the fourteen behaviors in the script. While male arousal tends to build linearly with each subsequent step (behavior) in the sequence, culminating with the greatest arousal at penetration, female arousal does not build in this way but is highly variable. What females found most arousing was being stimulated by males, not penetration. Thus, even though males and females agree on the script, they tend to react differently to the same sexual behaviors (Geer & Broussard, 1990). This could account for the finding that females tend to show less interest in sex than do males (Hite, 1976; Zilbergeld, 1978).

Over the years, there has been continuing speculation about the nature of the female orgasm and conjecture as to why sexual arousal is different in women and men. Learning theorists suggest that differences in sexual arousal are linked to the individual's focus. Since females tend to focus on being stimulated by the male rather than on penetration, it follows that their greatest feelings of sexual arousal would be linked to being stimulated, rather than, as in the male, to orgasm associated with penetration.

Summary

Material that is sexually arousing for both males and females includes pictures of nude members of the opposite sex, people engaged in sexual acts, and verbal descriptions of sexual behavior. The ability to fantasize plays an important role in determining the degree to which different types of material will be sexually arousing.

Gagnon suggested that human sexual behavior is largely the result of sexual scripts. These mental representations or schemata help guide the individual through a sexual episode. It has also been suggested that, during masturbation, males and females coordinate or integrate their sexual feelings and activities with their gender roles. In this way, they develop a sexual script that tells them how they should respond during sexual activity with another person. With the onset of dating, the fantasy-based script is gradually transformed to a more interpersonal and interdependent sexual script. This transition is often characterized by awkwardness, clumsiness, and anxiety—by trial-and-error behavior. Because of the important role of sexual scripts, it can be argued that sexual pleasure is the result of an interaction of biological (sensory) and learned factors. According to this analysis, mature sexual arousal—sexual arousal that comes from others rather than the self—results from an increased awareness of the sexual partner's sensory characteristics.

The Cognitive Component

Adults' sexual scripts are influenced by the beliefs and attitudes they hold. Where do these beliefs and attitudes come from? They come in part from the society at large, from peer groups and from internalized values and ideals. Without reviewing all the data on the role of belief systems, let's look at a few interesting topics.

Attitudes to Sex

Liberal and conservative attitudes. From the 1950s to the early 1980s, North American society became more sexually permissive, especially towards premarital sexual experiences (D'Emilio & Freedman, 1988). Since then, sexual attitudes have become somewhat more conservative, perhaps as a result of a concern over sexually transmitted diseases and a broader cultural trend toward conservatism (Gerrard, 1987). The period from the 1950s to the 1980s was also characterized by a decline in the sexual double standard—the idea that premarital sex is socially acceptable for males but not for females (Brooks-Gunn & Furstenburg, 1989). As a result, despite the trend to conservatism, couples are having sex earlier and more frequently. They have become more open in their attitudes about sex.

Beliefs about the sex drive. Both males and females tend to believe that the sex drive is stronger in males than in females (e.g., Byrne, 1977) and consequently that sex is more important and more enjoyable for men than for women. This belief may account, in part, for the persistent double standard that sexual promiscuity is more acceptable in males than in females. As an exercise, think about some further implications of this belief.

The meaning of sexual experience. Perhaps one of the strongest differences between males and females is the meaning they attach to sex. While females tend to connect sex with feelings of affection and closeness, males tend to perceive sex as an achievement, an adventure, a demonstration of control and power, or a purely physical release. Consistent with this is the finding that men are less likely than women to be romantically involved with their first sexual partner. Women tend to value intercourse because it gives them a sense of shared feelings, emotional warmth, and being wanted. Men, in contrast, tend to isolate sex from other aspects of the relationship. They are more inclined to focus on arousal, for example (Basow, 1992).

Remember, however, that these general tendencies reflect statistical differences. Like men, women may sometimes perceive sex as an achievement, adventure, a demonstration of control and power, or a purely physical release; like women, men may associate sex with affection and closeness. Indeed, most men prefer that love and sex go together; like women, they value love far ahead of sex in terms of overall importance in their lives (Chassler, 1988: Pietropinto & Simenauer, 1977). As men get older, love and intimacy become the main motivators of sex (Sprague & Quadagno, 1987).

Individual Differences

To focus on differences between men and women can be misleading, because it leaves the impression that males and females comprise homogeneous groups. As we saw in discussing the meaning of sex, there are large differences among males, just as there are large differences among females. In fact, when the focus is on individual differences, males and females are often more similar than they are different.

My preference is to focus on individual differences whenever possible. This helps to avoid stereotyping females and males. Let's look at two theoretical approaches to individual differences. In these two approaches, we see that males and females often work from a common set of principles.

Introverts and extraverts. Eysenck (1967) has delineated two major types of people: introverts and extraverts. *Extraverts* are characterized by a high degree of sociability, impulsiveness, physical activity, liveliness, and changeability. *Introverts* tend to be less sociable, less impulsive, less active, and more stable in their responses to the external environment, and they can generally be characterized as more prone to fear and anxiety.

Questionnaires administered to introverts and extraverts have found several differences in their sexual behavior. For example, in a study of German students, Giese and Schmidt (1968), found that extraverts petted more and had intercourse more often, while introverts tended to masturbate somewhat more often. Eysenck's study of English students (1976) produced similar findings. He found, in addition, that extraverts tended to engage in a greater variety of sexual behaviors (such as cunnilingus, fellatio, and varied coital positions). These findings are summarized in Table 4-3.

Probably the most important finding from both Eysenck's study and Giese and Schmidt's is that extraverts tend to express more satisfaction with their sexual behavior. In fact, Eysenck reports that introverts are dissatisfied with their patterns of sexual behavior. He has suggested that this dissatisfaction results from inhibitions, worries, and guilt feelings that prevent introverts from fulfilling their desires. The introvert, Eysenck notes, tends to endorse Christian attitudes to sex in which virginity and fidelity are emphasized and the sensory aspects are downplayed. In sharp contrast, the extravert endorses the unorthodox permissive and promiscuous approach, in which frequency of sex and different partners are important to sexual satisfaction. Similar results were obtained in a study of Canadian college students (Barnes, Malamuth, & Check, 1984).

Unrestricted and restricted orientations to sex. People with an *unrestricted orientation* to sex have had many sex partners and plan to have many more, have had one-night stands, and endorse casual sex as a

Table 4-3. Sexual Practices of Extraverts and Introverts among unmarried German students.

	Males		Females	
Practice	*Extraverts*	*Introverts*	*Extraverts*	*Introverts*
Masturbation at present	72%	86%	39%	47%
Petting	78	57	76	62
Coitus	77	47	71	42
Long precoital sex play	28	21	18	21
Cunnilingus	64	52	69	58
Fallatio	69	53	61	53
More than three different coital positions	26	10	13	12

Source: From "Introverts, Extroverts and Sex" by H. J. Eysenck. *Psychology Today,* January 1971, 4(8), 48–51. Copyright © 1971 by the American Psychological Association. Reprinted with permission of the author.

comfortable experience. In contrast, people with a *restricted orientation* have had few sex partners, anticipate having few in the future, do not have one-night stands, and endorse the idea that commitment is a prerequisite for sex. An unrestricted view is more prevalent among men than among women (Snyder, Simpson, & Gangestad, 1986).

In terms of personality, a person with an unrestricted orientation is a high self-monitor, while a person with a restricted orientation is a low self-monitor. Low self-monitors base their actions on underlying dispositions and attitudes—for instance, that sex is only for marriage. High self-monitors tend to be responsive to the social and interpersonal cues of the situations in which they find themselves; that is, they make decisions on the basis of situational variables, and so their behavior tends to be different in different situations. While we do not know what causes variations in self-monitoring, it seems clear that an individual's degree of promiscuity is related to relatively stable personality factors (Snyder, Simpson, & Gangestad, 1986).

Low self-monitors tend to associate sex not only with love and romance but with long-term commitment. High self-monitors, in contrast, tend to view sex as a romantic encounter that does not necessarily imply any long-term commitment. If intimacy correlates

with long-term commitment, then low self-monitors are the people who form truly intimate relationships.

As we will see when we discuss love, intimacy and commitment are probably best viewed as independent processes. Individuals can experience intimacy without making a commitment. Conversely, being committed does not necessarily ensure intimacy.

Summary

Our sexual scripts are influenced by our beliefs, attitudes, and values. It is not surprising that, as a more liberal attitude towards sex became prevalent, premarital sex increased. The persistent belief that the sex drive is stronger in males than in females may help account for the double standard in our society with respect to sexual promiscuity.

One of the strongest differences between males and females is the meaning they attach to sex. While females associate sex with feelings of affection and closeness, males tend to perceive sex as an achievement, an adventure, a demonstration of control and power, or a purely physical release. Note, however, that these are statistical differences and do not reflect individual differences. Like women, most men prefer that love and sex go together and value love far ahead of sex in terms of overall importance in their lives.

The differences between the sexual practices of extraverts and introverts indicate that cognitive factors play a basic role in sexual behavior. The finding that extraverts pet more, have intercourse more often, and tend to engage in a wider variety of sexual behaviors is consistent with the ideas of Masters and Johnson and of Eysenck. According to Masters and Johnson, sex can be viewed as a sensory experience. According to Eysenck, extraverts tend to seek out more stimulation than introverts. That would explain why they tend to have sex more frequently and to engage in more varied practices. It is interesting that people who tend to let the situation determine their behavior (high self-monitors) are more likely to hold an unrestricted view of sex, whereas those who tend to let their beliefs and attitudes govern their behavior (low self-monitors) hold a more restricted view of sex. These findings seem to indicate that low self-monitors are more inhibited.

Love

Numerous writers have argued that it is important to distinguish between lust and love. Lust has more to do with short-term sexual attraction, and love with long-term psychological intimacy. Love generally involves lust (or passion), but it is more. Masters and Johnson (1966) acknowledged that pleasurable sex can occur without love and that a person can enjoy love without sex.

Love is our next topic. Once again, we will discuss its biological, learned, and cognitive components.

The Biological Component

When people are in love they experience a psychological state close to euphoria. Correspondingly, love has been linked to dopamine and norepinephrine, which have both been implicated in euphoria. In addition, love is especially linked to phenylethylanine (PEA), which "gives you that silly smile that you flash at strangers. When we meet someone who is attractive the whistle blows at the PEA factory" (Walsh, 1991). However, phenylethylanine does not last forever; after

two or three years, it begins to fall. This is consistent with the observation that, in 62 different cultures, the divorce rate peaks around the fourth year of marriage (Fisher, 1992).

Why do many marriages last beyond that point? It appears that the initial attraction stage gives way to an attachment stage, mediated by endorphins (Fisher, 1992). Endorphins (discussed in more detail in Chapter 7) are the equivalent of the body's own morphine; they not only reduce pain but produce feelings of well-being. There is growing evidence that endorphins are released not just in pain or fear, as originally thought, but also by other emotions; for instance, laughter is linked to endorphin release. Endorphins also play a critical role in maintaining the immune system. It is perhaps not surprising that the immune system tends to decline dramatically following the death of a spouse (Chapter 11).

Oxytocin has also been implicated in love. This chemical, produced by the brain, sensitizes nerves and stimulates muscles. It is thought to promote cuddling and to enhance orgasm. In a study of men, oxytocin levels increased by a factor of 3–5 during climax. Fisher (1992) suggests that oxytocin produces feelings of relaxed satisfaction and attachment.

The Learned Component

Falling In Love

When we fall in love, we are developing an emotional attachment to another person. This process can be rapid or gradual. Research shows that we frequently fall in love with somebody other than our ideal. In one study, only 40% of the subjects reported that their most intense experience of love was with a person close to their ideal (Averill & Boothroyd, 1977). In other words, falling in love depends on factors other than those we think we are looking for.

Certain common elements have been identified. Thoughts about the other person and dating frequency seem to be important factors (Kleck & Rubenstein, 1975; Tesser & Paulhus, 1976). Interestingly, chance meeting appears to be among the conditions most conducive to falling in love (Averill & Boothroyd, 1977), perhaps because the phrase itself suggests an accidental quality and so unexpected encounters make us more attuned to the possibility.

Sternberg (1991) argues that whether or not we fall in love is to a very large degree under our control. It has to do with our cognitive set. If we are set or prepared to fall in love, we will. According to Sternberg, love does not have to be accidental; it can be planned. You fall in love through your actions and you can stay in love through your actions.

Perhaps not surprisingly, falling in love tends to cause very positive changes in our self-concept. Among other things, people who have fallen in love are found to experience increased self-esteem and increased feelings of self-efficacy, which is a measure of individuals' perceptions of their ability to mobilize resources and meet a challenge (Aron, Paris, & Aron, 1995).

Attraction and Difficulty of Attainment

One good illustration of the importance of our own actions comes from research on attraction and difficulty of attainment. The question asked in one study was: "Are so-called easy-to-get women as attractive as hard-to-get women?" The results indicate that neither easy-to-get nor hard-to-get women are as attractive as women who are moderately hard to get. Apparently, when a woman is perceived as hard to get, men simply feel that the possible reward is not worth the time or the effort required to pursue it. In other words, they fail to become motivationally aroused. Easy-to-get women, it appears, also fail to arouse motivation. Very simply, it is not necessary to be highly motivated to win the easy-to-get woman. Moderately hard-to-get women, on the other hand, are perceived as potentially attainable goals if a reasonable amount of time and effort are devoted to the pursuit. Under these conditions, men appear to experience a high level of arousal, a condition that is assumed to enhance the attractiveness of the goal (Wright, Toi, & Brehm, 1984).

Why are goals that require some effort to attain more attractive to us than those we can have for the asking? There is no obvious answer. Apparently, the process of working towards a goal can be just as important as—or more important than—reaching the goal itself. As we have seen, the opportunity to experience a high level of arousal can be reinforcing. One reason that the romance goes out of marriage may be that the element of pursuit is lost; we value those things in which

we invest time and energy. As Sternberg (1991) argues, we can stay in love if we are willing to work at it.

Intimacy

Intimacy has to do with feelings of closeness, connectedness, and being bonded. It pertains more to the social and psychological aspects of love than to physical sex. Intimacy is something that people must learn. In the intimacy literature, long-term commitment is often used as one of the defining characteristics of true intimacy. Sternberg (1991) carefully distinguishes between intimacy and commitment. Commitment is a decision; it is a cognitive activity. Intimacy, on the other hand, is a skill; it is something that you learn.

It is often thought that intimacy takes time to develop, but this need not be the case. One way that people establish intimacy is to engage in self-disclosure. In self-disclosure, a person discloses something personal or private, in the expectation that, in return, the other person will disclose something personal or private. If self-disclosure proceeds rapidly, intimacy can quickly be established.

Research has linked willingness to self-disclose to a sensation-seeking personality type. According to Zuckerman (1979), sensation-seeking personalities need a high degree of novelty and complexity in their lives and are willing to take risks in order to meet this need. Research from a variety of sources has shown, among other things, that high sensation seekers tend to have more sexual partners than low sensation seekers. It is interesting to ask, therefore, whether high sensation seekers tend to engage in self-disclosure. Do they use self-disclosure or do they use some other strategy? A study on this question found that high sensation seekers are inclined to self-disclose information about their sexual motivation and behavior (Franken, Gibson, & Mohan, 1990). This suggests that sensation seekers not only use self-disclosure to establish intimate relationships but use a form of self-disclosure that signals their motives to the other person early in the relationship.

The Cognitive Component

According to Robert Sternberg (1991), staying in love depends on making the decision that you love someone, and that you are willing to invest the time and energy necessary to stay in the relationship. It is ultimately your decision whether you stay in love or fall out of love.

Commitment involves, among other things, the realization that love involves satisfying the needs of two distinct individuals. It also involves coming to accept that there are going to be differences or problems and that, if love is to endure, they must be resolved to the mutual satisfaction of both parties. In the final analysis, Sternberg contends, commitment is not just a desire or wish but rather the willingness to invest time and energy—in particular, the time and energy required to develop problem-solving skills. (We will return to this question in Practical Application 4-1.)

Having examined the biological, learned, and cognitive components of love, let's turn to a model that integrates all three.

Sternberg's Interaction Model

Sternberg (1991) suggests that love involves three primary components: passion, intimacy, and commitment. Sternberg's model of love (Figure 4-4) is a true interaction model. It is interesting to consider what happens to relationships that lack some of the three primary components in his theory. Sternberg has offered the following:

Passion alone = infatuated love. Infatuations often arise unexpectedly—simply as the result of a look, a touch, a word. They are characterized by bodily sensations, a tingling, a heightened heart rate, a warm sensuous feeling. Sometimes people act on their infatuations (also called attractions); sometimes they don't. Infatuations are often the grist for fantasies.

Sometimes infatuations become obsessive. Teens, for example, may become so infatuated with a movie star or a rock star that they cannot pursue a real relationship. Because infatuations are so limited, they are unfulfilling. Unless we can get beyond infatuation, we can never be truly happy.

Intimacy alone = liking. Liking occurs when you feel close and connected but without the need for passion or commitment. Relationships at work can be of this type; they are not important outside the context of work. Friendship is generally based on liking. We en-

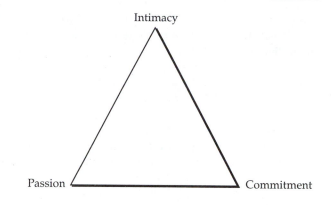

Figure 4-4. Sternberg's love triangle. (From *Love the Way You Want It,* by R. J. Sternberg. Copyright © 1991 by Bantam Books. Reprinted with permission.)

joy sharing our ideas and feelings, because it gives us a sense of being in tune with another person.

Commitment alone = sterile love. We often see commitment alone at the end of a long-term relationship, when partners are no longer physically attracted to each other and have lost their emotional involvement with each other. In societies where marriages are arranged, sterile love often characterizes the beginning of a relationship and is followed by the development of passion and intimacy.

Passion + intimacy = romantic love. Romantic lovers experience more than just physical attraction. They enjoy the emotion that comes with being together, experiencing the same feelings, sharing their closeness. They do not, however, have any sense that it will last or that they particularly want it to last. Sometimes romantic love starts with passion and the partners become close. Sometimes it starts with a friendship that over time grows into passion. It could be a shipboard romance or a summer fling.

Passion + commitment = fatuous love. Fatuous love is like the proverbial Hollywood marriage. After a whirlwind courtship, the couple gets married, without taking the time to develop intimacy. After a glorious honeymoon, they go their separate ways, in the conviction that their love will cross continents. But because there was no intimacy, true commitment never develops. When the passion fails, there is nothing to hold them together.

Intimacy + commitment = companionate love.   Companionate love might best be described as a long-term committed friendship. Sometimes, as the passion in marriage subsides, people retain a strong sense of intimacy and commitment. Family relationships are often characterized by both intimacy and commitment, as are cherished friendships.

Intimacy + passion + commitment = consummate love. Consummate love is the combination of intimacy, pas-

sion, and commitment. It is hard to attain and harder still to keep. It is what people strive for but often eludes them (Practical Application 4-1).

Summary

Love has been linked to dopamine and norepinephrine, because both have been implicated in feelings of euphoria. In addition, it has been found that attraction may be due, at least in part, to phenylethylanine (PEA). This initial attraction stage is believed to lead to an attachment stage, mediated by the endorphins. Oxytocin, a chemical that sensitizes nerves and stimulates

Practical Application 4-1

Striving to Attain Consummate Love

Sternberg argues that people can learn to attain consummate love. The first thing they need to recognize is that consummate love is like any other goal. They must consciously choose it as a goal and decide that they are willing to work towards it.

Many people in our society are not willing to commit themselves to this goal. They may decide, for example, that intimacy is not desirable or possible or that commitment to another person is inconsistent with their desire to be free or to be an individual. As a result, they may decide to satisfy their passion by pursuing endless sexual relationships. As one relationship fades, they look for another sexual encounter.

Sternberg points out that, if people commit themselves to the goal of consummate love, they need to recognize the obstacles and challenges that they must overcome. First, people have different tastes, different beliefs, and different habits. As a result, there are bound to be conflicts and problems. To deal with such differences, people need to learn problem-solving skills. One of the first things to learn is how to identify a problem. A good starting place is to simply identify the category to which it belongs. Does the conflict have to do with, for instance, money, running the household, sexual preferences, friends, religion, or political beliefs? Identifying the category helps to define the problem. Unless two people both agree on the problem, there is no point in trying to find the solu-

tion. Identifying the problem helps focus communication on the problem and prevents people from bringing in unrelated arguments. ("And furthermore, you never put the cap back on the toothpaste.") Sometimes it may be important to seek the help of other people. When people learn to focus on the problem and treat it as a mutual problem, they are less likely to blame each other.

Sternberg argues that people who have made the decision to attain consummate love need to learn to recognize the pitfalls—what he calls love villains—in relationships. All of us, he argues, hide behind a mask from time to time. When we feel vulnerable or afraid, we may try to hide our feelings, by putting forth an image that is the opposite of what we really feel. This is likely to cause problems in the relationship. Sternberg has identified ten villains or masks: the controller, the typecaster, the pious fraud, the procrastinator, the conflict avoider, the yes-sayer, the expert, the righteous accuser, the pretender, and the blamer.

People who wish to attain consummate love must accept that relationships are never perfect and are never cast in stone. Since people change, we must learn to accept such change. Since people make mistakes, we must learn to forgive. In the final analysis, we need to see obstacles as challenges and to see the future in terms of optimism and the possibility for growth.

muscles and seems to produce feelings of relaxed satisfaction and attachment, has also been implicated in love and orgasm.

Chance meeting has been found to be a major determinant of why people fall in love. Perhaps because the idea of falling in love suggests an accidental quality, some people seem predisposed to fall in love with an attractive person whom they meet by chance. The perceived availability of the imagined partner also plays a role. This suggests that calculations of the energy required to attain a goal may form part of feelings of attraction.

According to Sternberg, love—consummate love, as he calls it—has three major components: passion, intimacy, and commitment. Passion has to do with the physical and emotional aspects of love—with being attracted to another person and a desire for romance. Intimacy has to do with feelings of closeness, connectedness, and being bonded; it is a skill that people must learn if true love is to be achieved. Commitment involves a decision that your partner in love is worth the time and effort to make the relationship work. Much of that effort will be invested in acquiring the necessary problem-solving skills. Sternberg shows that relationships in which one or more of these components are missing are something less than consummate love. He argues that people can attain consummate love and offers several ideas about how to do it.

Biological Differences between Men and Women

There is no question that males and females are genetically different. But how genetically different are they? In 1990, British scientists identified a single gene of the Y chromosome that determines maleness. Without this gene all embryos would develop into females. The role of this gene is to activate a host of other genes, which guide the complex task of turning a fetus into a boy. The sex hormones are essential to this process.

Sex Hormones

Males and females have the same sex hormones but in different amounts. They play a critical role in ensuring that we have two sexes, male and female. They have also been implicated in a wide range of behaviors.

Some of the research on hormones grows out of work that is still in its infancy, though it has been going on for more than 25 years. This tremendously exciting research may eventually help us come to a better understanding of individual differences. Right now, much of the focus is on differences between males and females because, at least in animals, they are very stereotypical and therefore relatively easy to quantify. While this work does indicate that there are biological differences between males and females its significance relates, in my view, to the more basic question of how the brains of males and females develop.

Three Major Categories of Sex Hormones

The major category of hormones that govern male sexual behavior consists of *androgens*, the most important of which is testosterone. The two main categories of hormones that govern female sexual behavior consist of *estrogens* and *progestins.* The major estrogen is estradiol, and the major progestin is progesterone. Though we speak of androgens as male sex hormones and of estrogens and progestins as female sex hormones, this distinction is not entirely accurate. Androgens can be converted into estrogens and progestins, just as progestins can be converted into androgens. Estrogens and progestins circulate in the blood of men as well as women, and androgens circulate in the blood of women (Hoyenga & Hoyenga, 1979). Estrogen levels in males have been found to range from 2% to 30% of the level found in females, while the androgen levels in females has been found to range from 6% to 30% of the level found in males (Money, 1980). The main difference between the sexes, therefore, is simply the degrees of concentration of these hormones. One reason that the range is so large is that the levels of all hormones change constantly. As we shall see, both internal and external factors can dramatically alter these levels.

The Production of the Sex Hormones

The sex hormones are produced by the adrenal glands and the gonads. The male gonads are the testes; the female gonads are the ovaries. The male gonads produce mainly androgens, whereas the ovaries produce mainly estrogens and progestins. The adrenal glands produce mainly androgen. It has been estimated that about half of the androgen found in females is produced by the adrenal glands and about half by the ovaries.

The amount of each sex hormone present at any moment is governed by the pituitary gland, which is ultimately controlled by the hypothalamus. The pituitary releases as many as ten hormones that act in various ways to excite, inhibit, and generally modulate the complex patterns involved in the arousal and direction of the sexual response (Whalen, 1976). Most research has focused on the two gonadotropic hormones: FSH (follicle-stimulating hormone), which induces maturation of the ovarian follicles in the female and stimulates production of sperm in the male; and LH (luteinizing hormone), which induces ovulation in the female and stimulates the output of androgen by the testes of the male. Androgen influences the mating response of male animals and is generally regarded as one of the hormones that governs the arousal of sexual interest in the human male.

Androgen is produced more or less continuously in males. The output increases suddenly in early adolescence, which largely accounts for the sudden awakening of sexual interest in adolescent boys, and declines gradually through adulthood and old age. The decline in sexual interest with increasing age may be due to the decrease in androgen production (Bancroft, 1987), as well as other factors such as lack of variety and even the self-fulfilling prophecy that, as we grow older, we lose interest in sex.

The female hormones, in contrast, are produced in accordance with a 28-day cycle linked to egg production. It should be noted that the ovaries have a dual function: They produce both egg cells and hormones. The cycle begins when an anterior-pituitary hormone (follicle-stimulating hormone) initiates the growth of an ovarian follicle—an ovum and the surrounding cells. This growth continues for half the cycle. Because the follicle cells secrete estrogen, the amount of estrogen produced increases with growth of the follicle. About halfway through the cycle, the ovum breaks through the wall of the follicle and the ovary. This phenomenon is called *ovulation*. For the few days surrounding ovulation, the female is fertile; that is, the ovum is capable of being fertilized by male spermatozoa. In many lower animals, the female is at her peak of receptivity at this time, and consequently copulation generally occurs at the point in the cycle when conception is most likely. Research in which estrogen was injected at various times in the cycle indicates that estrogen is responsible for female receptivity. Thus, the

fact that estrogen production accompanies the development of the ovum ensures that the female is receptive when conception is most likely. Once the ovum breaks through the wall of the follicle and the ovary, estrogen production diminishes quickly, although estrogen continues to circulate in the bloodstream for some time.

Note that receptivity in the human female is relatively independent of estrogen levels. Various researchers, such as Masters and Johnson (1975), have argued that one of the primary functions of sexual behavior in humans is to create a pleasure bond. It is within the context of this pleasure bond that couples produce and care for their offspring (see also Morris, 1969).

In humans, ovulation ceases in the late 40s and early 50s, on the average. Simultaneously, of course, estrogen production dwindles. This change in physiological functioning is called *menopause*. As we have seen, estrogen is not closely tied to receptivity in humans and, although some women report a decline in sexual interest in the age range from 40 to 50, just as many report no decline or even an increase.

Sex Hormones and Differences in Physical Characteristics

For about one month after the egg has been fertilized, male and female embryos cannot be differentiated. In the second month, sex differences begin to appear. If the egg has been fertilized with an X chromosome, the gonads (the two collections of germ cells) begin to develop into ovaries. As the male ducts disintegrate, the female ducts thicken and become the womb, the fallopian tubes, and the upper two-thirds of the vagina.

If the egg has been fertilized with a Y chromosome, development moves in a very different direction during the second month. H-Y antigens, believed to be produced by the Y chromosome, change the ovaries into testicles, which produce various hormones: one that absorbs the female parts, such as the womb; testosterone, which thickens the spermatic cord; and dihydrotestosterone, which promotes the formation of the penis (Goy & McEwen, 1980; Haseltine & Ohno, 1981; Wilson et al., 1981; see also Durden-Smith & de Simone, 1983, for a very readable discussion of the material in this section).

To demonstrate that hormones are indeed responsible for the development of sex organs, female rats have been injected with the male hormone testosterone. Their female offspring are then found to be modified in several ways. They are born with an external vagina, often have a penis, and exhibit few mating responses in adulthood (Beach, 1976).

Ethical considerations prevent such manipulations with humans, but a great many data indicate that human hormones work in the same way. One line of evidence comes from observations of people who have undergone a voluntary sex change. Candidates for sex-change operations are injected with either testosterone (for a female-to-male change) or estrogen (for a male-to-female change). A male transsexual who receives estrogen (the family of hormones related to estradiol) can expect to grow breasts and add fat at the hips and thighs. Conversely, if androgen (the family of hormones related to testosterone) is given to a female transsexual, she develops an enlarged clitoris and grows facial hair, her voice deepens, and her musculature becomes more masculine (Rubin, Reinisch, & Haskett, 1981; CIBA Foundation Symposium, 1979).

Sex Hormones and Intellectual Functioning

While men and women do not differ in terms of intellectual functioning (for example, IQ scores), they do seem to differ in certain specific ways. Males tend to be superior on visual-spatial tasks such as tracking a moving object (e.g., Law, Pellegrino, & Hunt, 1993), mental rotation (e.g., Masters & Sanders, 1993), navigating their way through a route, and guiding or intercepting projectiles (Kimura, 1992). The difference may be as large as $d = 1.0$ standard deviation, depending on the test used (Voyer, Voyer, & Bryden, 1995). Females show superior performance on synonym tasks and verbal fluency (Gordon & Lee, 1986; Hines, 1990). The effect size is in the range $d = 0.5–1.2$ standard deviations. In addition, women do better than men on perceptual speed tasks—that is, identifying and matching items (Kimura, 1992). While females tend to have a clear quantitative advantage in the early years, this effect reverses itself before puberty (Hyde, Fennema, & Lamon, 1990). After puberty and into old age, males maintain their superiority.

Researchers have found that at least some of these differences can be linked to testosterone levels. For example, Kimura (1992) has found that women with high testosterone perform better on a spatial task (rotating figures) than women with low levels of testosterone, and that men with low levels outperform men with high levels (see top panel of Figure 4-5). Moreover, it has been shown that older men given testosterone improve their performance on visual-spatial tests (Janowsky, Oviatt, & Orwoll, 1994).

On tests of mathematical reasoning, men with low levels of testosterone perform better than men with high levels (e.g., Christiansen and Knussman, 1987; Kimura, 1992), but in women mathematical reasoning is unrelated to testosterone level (Kimura, 1992) (see middle panel of Figure 4-5). On perceptual speed tasks—tasks in which women are typically superior—there is no relationship between testosterone and performance (see bottom panel of Figure 4-5).

Kimura has not been able to find any differences on vocabulary tests and tests of verbal reasoning. This is consistent with the work of Hyde and Linn (1988), who did a metaanalysis of 165 studies involving about 1 million subjects and found no differences between the sexes. Kimura has, however, found differences between men and women in mathematical abilities. This topic is still controversial. In a metaanalysis of 100 studies, Hyde, Fennema, and Lamon (1990) concluded that "gender differences in mathematics are small" (p. 139). In particular, they found that this difference has decreased dramatically over the past two decades, which suggests the influence of environmental factors. The largest sex differences in mathematical ability tend to be at the upper end of the distribution (in the gifted population), where males outnumber females 13 to 1 (Benbow & Stanley, 1980, 1983). Hyde, Fennema, and Lamon (1990) have argued, however, that it is inappropriate to generalize from samples such as those studied by Benbow and Stanley. Benbow herself has acknowledged this point.

Intellectual functioning is influenced by many factors other than hormones. For an excellent summary of what is known and not known about intelligence, see Neisser et al. (1996).

Sex Hormones and Play

Some of the strongest evidence that sex hormones cause differences in behavior comes from research on play (for a review of these studies, see Collaer & Hines, 1995). The general finding is that females who have had prenatal exposure to high androgen levels show a tomboy pattern, characterized by rough, active outdoor play and by relatively high interest in practical

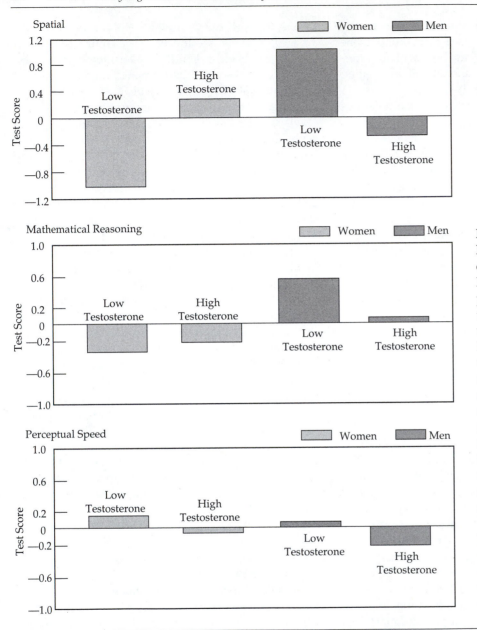

Figure 4-5. Testosterone levels can affect performance on some tests. Women with high levels of testosterone perform better on a spatial task *(top)* than do women with low levels; men with low levels outperform men with high levels. On a mathematical reasoning test *(middle)*, low testosterone corresponds to better performance in men; in women, there is no such relation. On a test in which women usually excel *(bottom)*, no relation is found between testosterone and performance. (From "Sex Differences in the Brain," by D. Kimura. *Scientific American*, 1992, *267*, 118–125. Copyright © 1992 by Scientific American. All rights reserved.)

clothing, in toys typically preferred by boys (cars, guns, building materials), and in boys as playmates. In addition, they show relatively low interest in feminine clothing, makeup, jewelry, doll play, and rehearsal of the adult maternal role. Males who have experienced prenatal exposure to progestin-based progesterone show the reverse effect, but less dramatically.

Summary

While males and females share the same basic sex hormones, they produce them in different amounts. These different concentrations of sex hormones appear to be responsible not only for many of the physical differences between males and females, but for some of the psychological differences as well. On the physical side, testosterone has a masculinizing effect. Among other things, testosterone is responsible for the development of the male penis, facial hair, and a deep voice. Injections of testosterone in females tend to produce an enlarged clitoris. Conversely, estrogen tends to have a feminizing effect. Among other things, it produces breast development and stimulates the body to store fat on the hips and thighs. In transsexual operations, estrogen is injected into males, with similar effects.

Kimura (1992) has shown that women with high levels of testosterone tend to perform better on certain spatial tasks (tasks in which men tend to outperform women) than women with low levels of testosterone. On mathematical reasoning tasks, men with low levels of testosterone tend to outperform those with high levels (Christiansen and Knussman, 1987; Kimura, 1992), whereas no relationship was found between testosterone levels and mathematical reasoning in women (Kimura, 1992). While this research is relatively new and needs to be replicated, it indicates that the study of hormones may be important in order for us to fully understand sex differences. Some of the clearest evidence for the role of hormones in sex differences comes from the examination of play in young children. As I will show in the next section, hormones have been strongly implicated in sexual orientation, a topic that has recently generated a great deal of interest in the media.

Sexual Dimorphism in the Brain

Dimorphism means the existence of two distinct forms. Evidence for sexual dimorphism comes from the observation that particular structures in the brain are different in size, number of neurons, and dendritic branching for females and males (Gorski, 1991).

Many researchers believe that these structural differences may be associated with certain behavioral differences. It is particularly noteworthy that these structures can often be altered by pre- or postnatal administrations of sex hormones. This suggests that differences in the male and female brain are due, at least in part, to the effects of sex hormones. Evidence that the environment can also alter these structures indicates a complex interaction between hormones and the environment.

Some Examples of Dimorphism

The hypothalamus. Considerable research indicates that the hypothalamus is involved in sexual and reproductive behavior. It has been found, for instance, that the number of neurons in an area of the hypothalamus called the sexual dimorphic nucleus is greater in male rats than in female rats. These nuclei are 5–7 times larger in the male than in the female. Prenatal injections of testosterone will increase the number of neurons in the dimorphic nucleus of a female rat, so that the hypothalamus more closely resembles that of a male, and prenatal administration of antitestosterone drugs to a male rat will reduce the number of nuclei in the dimorphic nucleus (Gorski, 1974, 1985, 1991; Haseltine & Ohno, 1981; Wilson et al., 1981).

Research has shown similar differences in the human brain (Swaab & Fliers, 1985). The hypothalamus is shown in Figure 4-6, together with some other brain structures in which sexual dimorphism has been found. Later in this chapter, when we discuss sexual orientation, we will review an interesting study by LeVay (1991) on dimorphism in the hypothalamus.

The cerebral cortex. It has been found that the right cortex is thicker than the left in male rats but not in female rats (Diamond, Dowling, & Johnson, 1981). The right hemisphere is thought to be involved in spatial abilities. We know that these differences are due, at least in part, to sex hormones, because they may be produced artificially by injecting testosterone in the female infant rat at a critical stage—usually at birth or shortly thereafter—or by castrating the male infant rat at birth (Beach, 1976; Haseltine & Ohno, 1981; Wilson et al., 1981). The work of Stewart and Kolb (1988) indicates that androgens suppress development of the left cortex. However, there is good evidence that the environment also affects the development of these structures in rats (Diamond, 1988). Animals provided with an enriched environment will show an increase in certain structures of the cortex.

Similar results have been obtained in human fetuses, where the right hemisphere is larger than the left in males but not in females (LaCoste et al., cited in Kimura, 1992). However, the evidence for humans is still meager and needs to be treated with caution.

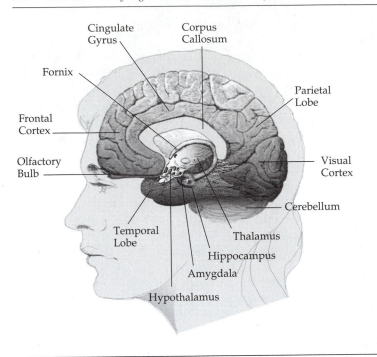

Cingulate Gyrus
Corpus Callosum
Fornix
Frontal Cortex
Olfactory Bulb
Parietal Lobe
Visual Cortex
Cerebellum
Temporal Lobe
Thalamus
Hippocampus
Amygdala
Hypothalamus

Figure 4-6. Cross section of the human brain, with some of the structures in which sexual dimorphism has been found.

The corpus callosum. The corpus callosum is thought to be involved in the coordination of the two sides of the brain. It has been suggested that, if one sex is found to have more connecting fibers in the corpus callosum, that sex should have a greater capacity to coordinate the two sides of the brain (e.g., Kimura, 1992). In humans, the corpus callosum—more precisely, the posterior portion—is larger and more bulbous in females than in males (Allen, Richey, Chai, & Gorski, 1991). It has been found that verbal fluency correlates positively with the size of a region of the corpus callosum (mainly defined by the splenium) and that another region of the corpus callosum (the posterior callosum) correlates negatively with language lateralization (Hines, Chiu, McAdams, Bentler, & Lipcamon, 1992). Since the area of the corpus callosum linked to superior language skills was larger in females, there is good reason to believe that the reason females often perform better than males on certain language tasks is due to the difference in the brain structure of females and males. This research makes use of a new method called magnetic resonance imaging (MRI), which permits measurement of the intact (living) brain. Previously, it was necessary to rely on patients with neural lesions, a method that is highly limited.

As yet, there is no clear evidence at what stage in development the corpus callosum becomes sexually dimorphic, nor has it been clearly shown to be affected by sex hormones. However, since all sexually dimorphic structures examined thus far have been influenced by prenatal hormones, Gorski (1991) suggests such effects will probably be found for the corpus callosum.

There is also evidence that early experience can alter this dimorphism (Berrebi et al., 1988; Juraska & Kopcik, 1988).

Other regions. The anterior commissure is larger in human females than in males (Allen & Gorski, 1991). There are also differences in subregions of the amygdala (Hines, Allen, & Gorski, 1992), a region in the brain that has often been linked to sex, aggression, gonadotropic secretion, and integration of olfactory information. Finally, recent brain imaging studies have found what may be differences in the lateralization of language (Shaywitz et al., 1995).

While these differences in brain structure may be of genetic or hormonal origin, they may also be due to experience. Certain patterns of thought or behavior could stimulate certain areas of the brain to develop. Further, as various theorists have suggested, there may be a bidirectional effect at work: Because a certain area of the brain is more highly developed, an individual may be disposed to engage in activities involving that area of the brain, and the increased use of that area may stimulate it to develop more.

Critical Periods of Sexual Differentiation

When does sexual dimorphism develop? Considerable research suggests that brain structures can be masculinized only at certain stages of development and that to reverse them at a later stage is impossible.* There is evidence, for example, that, after a certain critical period, injections of testosterone will no longer alter the hypothalamus (Haseltine & Ohno, 1981; Wilson et al., 1981). This critical period occurs either shortly before birth or shortly after birth. If the hypothalamus governs sexual orientation, as some people have suggested, the idea of critical periods means that, once sexual orientation has been established in the brain, it is very difficult, if not impossible, to alter that orientation.

In the case of the cerebral cortex, on the other hand, there is extensive evidence that sexual dimorphism can occur much later. This suggests a greater potential for environmental input to some structures than to others.

Sexual Dimorphism and Individual Differences

Gorski and others often point out, in connection with their work on sexual dimorphism in the brain, that there are large individual differences. Individual differences are generally larger than group differences (differences between males and females). In practical terms, this means that many female brains look more like typical male brains than like typical female brains and, similarly, that many male brains look more like

typical female brains than like typical male brains. As Figure 4-7 illustrates, the general finding is that most differences in brain structure and abilities between men and women are quite small compared to the large individual differences within the populations of men and of women. In some cases, such as the hypothalamus, these differences within each population are particularly large.

The Politics of Biological Difference

Research on differences between men's and women's brains is highly contentious (Eagly, 1995), because the existence of biological differences between men and women has sometimes been claimed as evidence of male superiority (Tavris, 1992). Research findings that males may be superior to females in certain areas might be used to buttress the argument for continued male dominance in certain occupations. This is sometimes characterized as the argument that biology is destiny. Many women scholars have taken issue with this line of argument and have pointed out that most of the differences are small and, in many cases, may be due to environmental factors rather than to biology.

When research shows that women are superior to men in certain skills and abilities, those skills or abilities are often devalued by males (Tavris, 1992). As a result, males claim superiority even in the face of a difference that seems to favor females.

Since biological differences between men and women are often small, some scholars have argued that they have no practical significance and may be ignored. That may not be true. Small biological differences are often responsible for large individual differences; by aiming an organism in one direction rather than another, they influence what the organism sees, hears, experiences, and thinks and even the self-schemata that are constructed. For an excellent review of the politics of comparisons between women and men, see Eagly (1995).

Summary

Substantial research indicates the existence of sexual dimorphism of the brain—differences in certain brain

---

* Masculinization is an unfortunate word. It's known that, without testosterone, the brain would tend to develop in its female form. However, females also produce small amounts of testosterone, and research with both animals and humans suggests that even small amounts of testosterone alter the development of the female brain. In other words, one reason why various structures of the female brain differ from those of the male brain is that the female brain was exposed to testosterone at some critical stage of development. Until someone suggests a better word, however, I will continue to speak of masculinization.

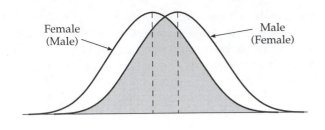

Figure 4-7. Normal distribution curves representing the differences between males and females. In most cases, the differences between males and females are small. These curves show that, when there are small differences, the vast majority of males and females tend to be alike rather than different (shaded area). Thus, when people talk about differences, they are talking about a very small proportion of the general population (unshaded area).

structures of males and females. Such sexual dimorphism appears to be due to the hormone testosterone. For example, prenatal injection of testosterone will increase the number of neurons in the female rat's hypothalamus, so that it more closely resembles that of a male. Injections of testosterone increase the thickness of the right hemisphere in the female brain, so that it more closely resembles that of the male. Interestingly, it has been shown that the environment can produce these differences as well. Recent evidence indicates that there may be sexual dimorphism of the corpus callosum and it may be linked to brain lateralization. Finally, there is ample evidence that such sexual dimorphism can only develop during critical periods of brain development.

Sexual Orientation

It has been suggested that all human beings have a sense of being female, male, or somewhere in between and that humans are inclined to publicly present themselves as female, male, or ambivalent. Our private inner experience is sometimes called our *gender identity* and our public outward expression is our *gender role* (Money, 1987). There is good reason to believe that gender identity and gender role arise in different ways.

In the following section, we will be talking mainly about gender identity.

Where do feelings about femaleness and maleness come from? Research on the sexual dimorphism of the brain suggests that such differences include a biological component. Hormones don't predetermine our feelings of femaleness and maleness, but they do seem to point us more in one direction than another. Whether we come to see ourselves as female or male also depends on learned and cognitive factors. Let's look at the biological, learned, and cognitive components of sexual orientation and, more specifically, homosexuality.

The Biological Component

Sexual Dimorphism of the Hypothalamus and Male Sexual Orientation

Some of the first hard scientific evidence that male homosexuality has a biological basis came from the work of Simon LeVay (1991), a neurobiologist at the Salk Institute in San Diego. LeVay examined a speck of neurons in the hypothalamus that is known to be linked to sexual behavior and is more than twice as large in men as in women. Since the area is too small to study in living humans, he used the autopsied brains of 19 homosexual men and 16 heterosexual men. He found the oval cluster in homosexual men to be half the size of that in heterosexual men; sometimes, it was even missing. His focus on the hypothalamus was prompted by the knowledge that, when the hypothalamus is damaged in male monkeys, they lose interest in females but they do not lose their sex drive, as indicated by their continued tendency to masturbate.

LeVay's research is consistent with evidence that male rats, if castrated at birth and thus deprived of testosterone, will never try to mate with females and will allow other males to mount them (Gorski, 1974, 1985, 1991). It is also consistent with evidence that testosterone is responsible for the development of the hypothalamus (Haseltine & Ohno, 1981; Wilson et al., 1981; Gorski, 1988). Note, however, that the nuclei that LeVay examined were not the same as the nuclei studied in the rat research. The significance of this difference has yet to be clarified.

Some researchers have called for further work to verify LeVay's findings. Because his sample of gay men consisted of men with AIDS, the differences observed in the hypothalamus might have been caused by AIDS. Concerns have also been expressed about the small size of the sample.

Despite LeVay's findings, neurobiologists do not believe that structural changes in the hypothalamus are the sole cause of homosexuality. First, other research indicates that the anterior commissure, a nerve network connecting the two hemispheres, is larger in females than in males and is larger in homosexual men than in heterosexual men (e.g., Allen & Gorski, 1991). Further, as we will see shortly, the environment also plays an important role.

Twin Studies and Male Sexual Orientation

Recent evidence indicates that genetic factors are important in determining individual differences in sexual orientation. Heritability estimates range from 31% to 74% (Bailey & Pillard, 1991). Using 110 fraternal and identical twins and 46 adoptive men and their brothers, this study found that, if one brother in a pair was homosexual, the likelihood that the other brother would be homosexual increased with the degree of genetic similarity.

The researchers advertised for homosexual and bisexual men who had a male twin or an adoptive or genetically unrelated brother with whom they started living by the age of 2. The brothers in 52% of the 28 sets of identical twins were both gay; those in 22% of the 27 sets of fraternal twins were both gay; and 11% of the adopted brothers were both gay. Since identical twins have the same genes, fraternal twins only share some genes, and the adopted brothers should have virtually none of the same genes, the evidence clearly points to a role of genetics in homosexuality.

Consistent with this is the recent discovery of a link between homosexuality in males and the long arm of the X chromosome (Hamer, Hu, Magnuson, Hu, & Pattatucci, 1993; Hamer & Copeland, 1994; Hu et al., 1995). If the gene for homosexuality were carried on the Y chromosome, homosexuality might be expected to disappear over time, because homosexuals tend to produce fewer offspring. If carried on the X chromosome, however, the trait would tend to be maintained over time. Research indicates that homosexuality has been prevalent for some time, exists independent of culture, and is behaviorally similar (Whitam & Mathy,

1986); these findings are consistent with the idea that it has a genetic basis.

Twin Studies and Female Sexual Orientation

Studies of twins have found similar results for lesbians (Bailey, Pillard, Neale, & Agyei, 1993). In a study of 71 sets of identical twins, 37 sets of fraternal twins, and 35 sets of adoptive sisters, it was found that 48% of the identical twins who said they were homosexual or bisexual had twins who were lesbian, as against 16% of the fraternal twins and 6% of the adopted sisters. Heritability estimates ranged from 27% to 76%. These results closely parallel those found for gay men. No linkage between homosexuality and the X chromosome has yet been found for lesbians (Hu et al., 1995).

Congenital Adrenal Hyperphasia and Female Sexual Orientation

When researchers deprived male rats of testosterone (for instance, by castration) and treated female rats with estrogen, which can have a masculinizing effect, they found that the genetic males behaved like females and the genetic females behaved like males (Williams, cited in Kimura, 1992). Since it is impossible to do this same research with humans, researchers have to depend on "experiments of nature" to determine whether or not hormones affect sexual orientation. Experiments of nature are much like laboratory experiments, except that the manipulation was not planned but occurred by accident. Because of a genetic defect, some women produce abnormally high levels of adrenal androgens—a condition called congenital adrenal hyperphasia (CAH). In order to assess whether the female offspring of these women tend to be more bisexual or homosexual, their responses to erotica have been examined. The reason for using responses to erotica grows out of the idea that erotica is perhaps less governed by social pressure to conform than is something like gender identity. Ehrhardt and Meyer-Bahlburg (1981) reported that in studies using such measures, approximately half the dreams of CAH-affected women were bisexual (none were homosexual). However, since there were no control groups, the researchers said they could not draw any definitive conclusions from this measure. Their conclusions were undoubtedly affected by the fact they also found that

CAH-affected women tend to adopt the gender identity they were assigned at birth; that is, they saw themselves as female. In a more highly controlled study, evidence was found for the idea that CAH-affected women tend to be more bisexual or homosexual (Money, Schwartz, & Lewis, 1984). In a sample of 30 CAH-affected women, 37% rated their sexual imagery and activity as bisexual or homosexual, 40% as heterosexual, and 23% were noncommittal. In a control group of 27 women with other endocrine disorders, 7% rated their erotic imagery and activity as bisexual whereas the remainder rated it as heterosexual.

Because CAH-affected girls often have more masculinized genitalia, there have been attempts to attribute the results to a more masculine upbringing of girls with CAH (Quadagno, Brisco, & Quadagno, 1977). This point has been contested by Ehrhardt and Meyer-Bahlburg (1981), who note that, if anything, parents of such children tend to encourage femininity—that is, stereotypical female behavior.

Ehrhardt and Meyer-Bahlburg (1981) also found that CAH-affected girls showed: (1) "a combination of intense active outdoor play, increased association with male peers, long-term identification as a 'tomboy' by self and others, probably all related to high energy expenditure" and (2) "decreased parenting rehearsal such as doll play and baby care, and a low interest in the role rehearsal of wife and mother versus having a career" (p. 1314).

Note that other researchers have shown that CAH-affected adult females score significantly higher than controls on tests of spatial ability (Resnick, Berenbaum, Gottesman, & Bouchard, 1986) and that, in highly controlled studies, CAH-affected girls have been found to play more with stereotypical boy toys and less with stereotypical girl toys (Berenbaum & Hines, 1992). Finally, note that prenatal exposure to sex hormones has been shown to affect certain immune systems (Geschwind & Galaburda, 1987; Halpern & Cass, 1994).

DES-Affected Women and Female Sexual Orientation

There is also data from women who were exposed prenatally to diethylstilbestrol (DES), a synthetic estrogen (formerly used to maintain pregnancy) that can have masculinizing effects on the brain but does not produce masculinizing effects on the genitalia (Dohler et al., 1984; Hines et al., 1987). In a sample of 30 DES-exposed women, 21% rated themselves as having bisexual or homosexual responsiveness compared to none in a control group (Ehrhardt et al., 1985). Since 12 of the DES-exposed had unexposed sisters, it was possible to compare them with their sisters. Whereas 42% of the DES-exposed rated themselves as bisexual or homosexual, only 8% of their sisters rated themselves similarly. Since DES does not masculinize the genitalia, it is difficult to argue that the effects are due to the parents' decision, based on the size of the genitalia, to raise their daughter more male-like (see section on sex assignment at birth for a more complete description of this hypothesis). The work on the CAH-affected and DES-exposed is not without critics. Fausto-Sterling (1985) has offered a detailed critique of the work on congenital-adrenal hyperphasia as well as other work that has been put forth as evidence for a biological basis for sex differences.

The Learned Component

For a long time, there has been a bias towards viewing sexual orientation as acquired. Historically, homosexuality was assumed to be the result of pathology. When researchers began to investigate this hypothesis, they could find no evidence to support it. In his study of 30 homosexual and 30 heterosexual men, Hooker (1957) concluded: "Homosexuality as a clinical entity does not exist. Its forms are as varied as those of heterosexuality" (p. 30). Lacking any evidence for the pathology hypothesis, the American Medical Association and the American Psychological Association no longer list homosexuality as a clinical disorder.

As research begins to show that there is a strong biological component, other learning interpretations have come under much closer scrutiny. It is no longer self-evident that homosexuality is acquired or is the result of choice. If homosexuality is acquired, as some people argue, what conditions lead to it? In the following section, I will examine some of the hypotheses that have been advanced over the years.

Psychoanalytic Theory

According to psychoanalytic theory, homosexuality in males grows out of a family constellation characterized by a close-binding overprotective mother and a detached, absent, or openly hostile father (Bieber et al., 1962). Such parents inhibit the expression of hetero-sexual feelings in the son. In addition, the absence of an effectual father means that the child has no good role model from whom to learn appropriate heterosex-ual behavior. The general consensus is that support for the psychoanalytic interpretation is not good; no re-search has been able to clearly link domineering moth-ers and ineffectual fathers to homosexuality.

Chance-Learning Hypothesis

According to this hypothesis, a young person seduced by someone of the same gender would learn to associ-ate the pleasures of sex with the gender of the seducer. No evidence has been put forth in support of this hy-pothesis; moreover, recent studies of young females and males who have been sexually seduced—or sexu-ally abused—indicate that, if anything, the result is the opposite. The following study by the Kinsey Institute suggests that there is little or no evidence to support the chance-learning hypothesis.

The Kinsey Institute Study

In one of the most extensive studies of the origins of homosexuality, a group of researchers at the Kinsey In-stitute interviewed 979 homosexual men and women and 477 heterosexual men and women (Bell, Weinberg, & Hammersmith, 1981). The researchers asked a num-ber of questions from a variety of theoretical orienta-tions. On the basis of their research, they drew the fol-lowing conclusions regarding the origins of sexual orientation.

1. Sexual orientation is determined prior to adoles-cence, even when youngsters have not been partic-ularly sexually active. (Numerous other studies have shown that most homosexual males become aware of their orientation during childhood or ado-lescence; Dank, 1971; Reiche & Dannecker, 1977; Whitam, 1977).
2. Homosexual behavior emerges from homosexual feelings—feelings that occur about three years, on average, before any overt homosexual experience.
3. Homosexual women and men tend to have a his-tory of heterosexual experiences in childhood and adolescence but have found these experiences not to be satisfying.

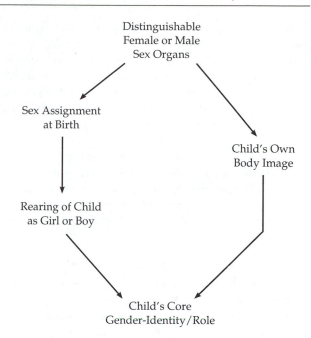

Figure 4-8. Environmental and cultural factors that influence the development of a child's gender identity/role. (From *Sexuality Today: The Human Perspective*, 3rd ed., by G. F. Kelly. Copyright © 1992 by The Dushkin Publishing Group, Inc., Guilford, CT. All rights reserved. Reprinted with permission.)

4. Identification with either parent played no signifi-cant role in the development of sexual orientation.
5. There was no evidence that any particular type of mother produces homosexual children. A slightly higher proportion of homosexuals had a poor rela-tionship with their fathers, but it was impossible to determine if this was a causative factor.

Sex Assignment at Birth

One of the main hypotheses regarding gender identity is the role of sex assignment at birth. This model is pre-sented in Figure 4-8.

According to this hypothesis, boys and girls are treated differently as they grow up. After dressing girls in pink and boys in blue, for example, parents give boys toy cars and trucks and reward them for boy ac-tivities but give girls dolls and reward them for girl activities. According to this hypothesis, sex assignment is the key to differences between men and women, because sex assignment determines how children are rewarded (Tavris & Wade, 1984). Although there is considerable evidence that boys and girls are rewarded differently, most of the studies are correlational. Next, we'll examine a noncorrelational study that relates to the hypothesis of sex assignment at birth.

Before we do so, it is important to make a distinction between sexual orientation and core gender identity. Whereas sexual orientation has to do with preference for a sexual partner, core gender identity has to do with the sense of being male or female. We will be mainly concerned with core gender identity (Hines & Green, 1991).

Rearing Boys as Girls and Core Gender Identity

Individuals with a genetic deficiency of the enzyme 5-alpha-reductase produce less dihydrotestosterone from testosterone, beginning in utero. This leads to female-appearing genitalia, because dihydrotestosterone is necessary for the prenatal development of the penis. In a sample of 18 such individuals, all raised as girls, 17 professed male identity in adolescence. Note that, at puberty, they developed male genitalia under the influence of testosterone (Imperato-McGinley et al., 1974, 1979). According to the hypothesis of sex assignment at birth, they should have adopted a gender identity corresponding to their assigned sex.

An enzymatic deficiency (17-beta hydroxysteroid dehydrogenase) produces female-appearing genitalia at birth; this is followed by considerable phallus growth and excessive hair growth in adolescence. A study of 25 such individuals found that they generally adopted a male identity during adolescence despite having been raised as females (Rosler & Kohn, 1983).

Status of the Learning Hypothesis

While there is still relatively little evidence for the three main hypotheses of sexual orientation—psychoanalytic, chance-learning, and sex assignment at birth—evidence from twin studies indicates that learning plays an important role. If biology is the main determinant of homosexuality, we would expect identical twins to be of the same orientation—either both homosexual or both heterosexual. That is clearly not the case. Only 30–70% of the variance in the study of male twins

can be directly attributed to heredity. This leaves considerable scope for the role of learning or cognition (Bailey & Pillard, 1991).

It seems clear at this point that, individually, none of the learning hypotheses provides a very complete explanation. To explore sexual orientation further, what we need, rather than studies that pit learning theories against each other or pit learning against biology, are experiments to elucidate the different kinds of learning experiences that might push an individual toward homosexuality.

Learning and the Expression of Sexual Orientation

Even if we knew beyond doubt that sexual orientation was completely biologically determined, it would still be important to consider the role of learning. There is substantial evidence that, like anyone else, gay men and lesbians select role models to help guide their development. One consistent complaint from the gay and lesbian community has been that the mainstream media do not offer them a range of role models. Gay men are often presented in the media as stereotyped effeminate individuals who are passive and often promiscuous. Lesbians complain that they are presented as very masculine, aggressive, and man-hating.

A particular sexual orientation can be expressed in many ways. Most likely, what determines its expression is the same for homosexuals as for heterosexuals. In other words, learning plays just as important a role in the expression of a homosexual orientation as it does in the expression of a heterosexual orientation.

Cognitive Component

Is homosexuality a choice? Do people decide to become homosexuals because it offers them an attractive and fulfilling lifestyle?

There is little or no evidence that homosexuality is actively chosen, except in unusual circumstances—in particular, in prison. In fact, many individuals have reported that, when they finally came to accept the possibility that they were gay or lesbian, they felt distraught and experienced psychological symptoms including anxiety, depression, suicidal ideation, and stress.

Nonetheless, there is extensive evidence that cognitive factors play an important role in how homosexuals come to think about themselves and express themselves. Cass's theory of homosexual identity formation provides a good summary of what we know about cognitive aspects of homosexual identity.

Cass's Six Stages of Homosexuality

Cass's (1990) description of the six stages of homosexual identity formation suggests that, in order for the process of homosexual identity formation to begin, the individual must experience some degree of sexual attraction or interest in someone of the same sex. As we see from the following account, the development of a homosexual identity involves a range of cognitive processes, including changes in attitudes, the development of new expectations, and the construction of a gender schema.

Stage 1: Identity confusion. In this stage, individuals begin to realize that information about homosexuality may somehow relate to them. They often experience persistent dreams and fantasies about members of the same sex but typically avoid homosexual behavior.

Stage 2: Identity comparisons. In this stage, individuals begin to examine the broader implications of what it means to be a homosexual. They deal with the question of how the acceptance of such an identity might affect their relationships with their family and their friends and how will they fit into society. They often experience a profound sense of loss, as they come to realize their alienation from heterosexual society. Some may devalue heterosexuality; others may turn their sexual identity confusion into antihomosexual attitudes and even exaggerated heterosexual behavior, while still entertaining homosexual fantasies.

Stage 3: Identity tolerance. As they come to accept their homosexuality, they begin to realize that sexual, social, and emotional needs go with being a homosexual. Typically, individuals become more involved with other homosexuals at this stage. As they come to accept that they have special sexual, social, and emotional needs, they develop a greater tolerance of their homosexual identity.

At this stage individuals must decide how open they wish to be about their sexual orientation. The pro-

cess in which individuals acknowledge their homosexuality and communicate it to others has been called coming out of the closet, or simply coming out.

Stage 4: Identity acceptance. In this stage, there is typically greater involvement with the gay and lesbian subculture and the development of a positive attitude towards other homosexuals. Individuals move from tolerating their homosexual self-image to fully accepting it.

Stage 5: Identity pride. As individuals come to accept the accomplishments of the gay and lesbian community and realize that there are standards of comparison other than those of the heterosexual community, they develop a sense of pride and abandon attempts to hide their homosexuality. This stage is often characterized by anger. As they become more conscious of the discrimination and homophobia that prevent them from living a full life, individuals often become politically active, in an attempt to change attitudes and laws that have a negative impact on gay men and lesbians.

Stage 6: Identity synthesis. In the last stage, individuals begin to accept that the world is not divided into warring factions of homosexuals and heterosexuals and that all heterosexuals need not be regarded as enemies. The anger that characterizes stage 5 gives way to a greater self-acceptance as a gay man or lesbian and the acknowledgment of a wide range of personality attributes and interests.

Sexual Plasticity in Humans

There is considerable evidence from cross-cultural work that the sexual behavior of humans is often highly plastic; humans adapt themselves to the conditions in which they find themselves. For example, when confined to prison, many men will engage in same-sex behavior even though they regard themselves as heterosexual. Money and Ehrhardt (1972) offer many examples of such plasticity. They point out that, in some cultures, young males go through a period in which they adopt a homosexual orientation, for example. This plasticity, however, applies only to behavior; it does not affect the individual's core gender identity.

Summary

Evidence from a range of sources indicates that there is a biological basis for a homosexual orientation. Specifically, sexual dimorphism of the hypothalamus appears to be responsible. Work on CAH-affected women and women exposed to DES suggests that exposure to androgens during critical stages of brain differentiation may be responsible, at least in part, for female homosexuality. That is not to say that homosexuality in men or women is hardwired, but biology points the individual in a certain direction. There is considerable evidence for the role of learning and cognition in the development of a homosexual orientation. The influence exerted by the selection of role models and value systems on individual development is undoubtedly as important for homosexuals as for heterosexuals.

There is little evidence that sexual orientation and core gender identity are the result of sex assignment at birth. There is good evidence, however, that core gender identity has a biological basis. Heritability estimates account for 30–70% of the variance. This leaves considerable scope for the contribution of learned and cognitive components.

A compelling argument that male homosexuality is not a conscious choice but is biologically based has been presented by some gay men. Who would willingly choose, they ask, a lifestyle characterized by job discrimination, homophobic violence, a high risk of AIDS, and wholesale rejection by friends, family, and society?

Main Points

1. Masters and Johnson have identified four more or less distinct phases in the sexual response of males and females.
2. Masters and Johnson suggest that the main motivation governing human sexual behavior is the pleasure derived from various forms of tactile stimulation.
3. Masters and Johnson argue that the clitoris is unique among human organs in that its only function is pleasure.
4. Masters and Johnson have found remarkable similarity between the sexual responses of males and females.
5. While males tend to adopt what has been called a quantity mating strategy, females tend to adopt a quality mating strategy.
6. As compared to females, males tend to be less interested in commitment, more aroused by visual stimuli, more jealous, and more concerned with the physical attractiveness and youth of potential partners. Females tend to be more concerned with the status of potential partners and are attracted to males who are dominant but also agreeable.
7. Sexual behavior in humans is thought to be largely the result of sexual scripts.
8. With the onset of adolescence, sexual scripts become coordinated with sexual feelings aroused through masturbation.
9. Females generally have more difficulty coordinating sexual feelings with sexual scripts than men do, perhaps because fewer adolescent females masturbate.
10. While heterosexual males and females agree on the sexual script that leads to intercourse, males focus more on penetration, while females focus more on being stimulated by the male.
11. The sexual scripts that people come to use are influenced by the beliefs and attitudes they hold. We examined liberal and conservative attitudes to sex, beliefs about the sex drive of females and males, and the different meanings that men and women attach to sex.
12. Women tend to value sexual activity because it provides a sense of shared feelings, emotional warmth, and being wanted, whereas men often focus more on arousal.
13. Compared to introverts, extraverts tend to pet more and engage in sexual activity more often.
14. People with an unrestricted orientation to sex, who typically have many sex partners, tend to be highly responsive to situational and interpersonal cues.
15. Variety and change tend to enhance sexual arousal.
16. It appears that attraction is due, at least in part, to phenylethylanine (PEA), whereas attachment is due, at least in part, to endorphins.

17. Oxytocin, which sensitizes nerves, stimulates muscles, and seems to produce feelings of relaxed satisfaction and attachment, has been implicated in love and orgasm.
18. According to Sternberg, love—what he calls consummate love—involves three components: passion, intimacy, and commitment.
19. In our society, people expect to fall in love and are attuned to unexpected encounters.
20. However, contrary to the idea that falling in love is accidental, Sternberg argues that we can make love happen.
21. Moderately hard-to-get women are perceived by men as more attractive than easy-to-get women.
22. It appears that people can learn intimacy.
23. Sternberg distinguishes between intimacy and commitment. There is evidence that people can be intimate without having long-term commitment.
24. Sternberg's model accounts for the complexity of love and provides an explanation of why people who do not share a common definition of love may find it difficult to maintain a long-term relationship.
25. There are three main categories of sex hormones: androgens (mainly male), estrogens (mainly female), and progestins (mainly female).
26. Both males and females produce hormones associated primarily with the other sex; thus, their behavior is governed by the joint action of male and female hormones.
27. Two important gonadotropic hormones are luteinizing hormone (LH) and follicle-stimulating hormone (FSH).
28. If an egg has been fertilized by a Y chromosome, H-Y antigens change the embryo's ovaries into testicles.
29. Testosterone, produced by the testicles, produces a variety of changes in the embryo, including the development of the penis.
30. While men and women do not differ in IQ, they have been found to differ in a variety of problem-solving abilities.
31. Men tend to be better at such tasks as rotating objects in space and mathematical reasoning; women tend to be better at perceptual speed tasks and arithmetic calculations and have greater verbal fluency.
32. Much of the sexual dimorphism of the brain has been linked to the presence of sex hormones during critical stages of development.
33. Three examples of sexual dimorphism of the brain can be found in the hypothalamus, the cerebral cortex, and the corpus callosum.
34. Most differences in brain structure and ability between men and women are smaller than the individual differences within each gender.
35. There is evidence that sexual orientation may be due in part to an area in the hypothalamus that has been linked to sexual behavior. The cluster of neurons in this area of the hypothalamus was found to be half as large in homosexual men as in heterosexual men.
36. Twin studies have provided further evidence for the biological basis of homosexuality.
37. CAH-affected women and women exposed to DES are more likely to have a homosexual orientation than are women in general.
38. The Kinsey Institute study collected evidence that is inconsistent with the psychoanalytic and chance-learning interpretations of homosexuality.
39. It has yet to be demonstrated that the core gender identity of an individual can be changed merely by rearing the child according to cross-gender norms.
40. Learning plays a major role in the expression of homosexuality.
41. Cass has described six distinct stages of homosexual identity formation: identity confusion, identity comparisons, identity tolerance, identity acceptance, identity pride, and identity synthesis.

Chapter Five

Arousal, Attention, and Peak Performance

- ■ What is peak performance?
- ■ Can people achieve peak performance in all areas of their lives?
- ■ What role does arousal play in peak performance?
- ■ Can anxious people ever achieve peak performance?
- ■ What role does attention play in peak performance?

- ■ Can people learn to control attention?
- ■ Can people achieve peak performance when they are threatened?
- ■ How does evaluation affect our ability to perform at peak levels?

P eak performance means doing the very best that we are capable of. It means being able to fully focus on the task in front of us and to persist in the face of distractions and adversity. For an athlete, it means being able to execute a skill while ignoring the presence of an audience, thoughts about failure, and feelings of fatigue.

One of the main things that prevents us from achieving peak performance is our inability to control our attention. The direction and organization of attention, it turns out, seems to be governed to a large degree by arousal. Research indicates that, when arousal shifts, attention tends to shift. Thus, to control attention, we need to gain control of our arousal.

The degree to which our attention is under voluntary control is a topic of great controversy. Those who argue that attention is controlled by arousal are saying that it is under involuntary control. They often go on to argue, however, that we can gain control over arousal and, thus, we are indirectly in control of attention.

Let's begin by discussing the nature and measurement of arousal.

Definition of Arousal

Arousal is the activation of the brain and the body. When we are aroused, they are in a state of readiness, so that we are prepared to engage in adaptive behaviors. Electrical activity in the brain increases, the heart beats more rapidly, and blood is redirected to the brain and muscles. Muscle tonus increases, in preparation for quick and efficient response. The activation of the brain and the body can be viewed as a state of energization. When we are aroused, the brain and the body are prepared to make use of chemicals—stored in various parts of the body—that facilitate information processing, planning, and the expenditure of physical energy.

There are two primary arousal systems: the cortical arousal system and the autonomic nervous system. The reticular activating system (RAS) is largely responsible for cortical arousal. The autonomic nervous system arouses the body.

Cortical and autonomic arousal often function independently (Neiss, 1988). It makes sense that there are occasions when we should be cortically aroused but not autonomically aroused—for example, when we are engaging in intellectual activities. At other times, we should be autonomically aroused but not cortically aroused—for instance, during routine but physically demanding activities. Finally, there are situations in which we need to be both cortically and physically aroused—for example, during a sporting activity, in battle, or during a musical or theatrical performance. To conserve energy and reduce wear and tear on the body, these systems are only activated when needed.

Let's begin our discussion of arousal with a look at cortical arousal.

Cortical Arousal

The Reticular Activating System (RAS)

Each of the various sensory receptors (visual, auditory, tactile, and so on) is connected to a sensory area in the brain via an afferent nerve pathway that ascends to the cortex via a specific projection system. Fibers branching from these pathways ascend to the reticular formation (Figure 5-1). When sensory information stimulates this system, it responds by activating the brain. Research on the RAS has shown that, unless the cortex is aroused, sensory signals going to the cortex will not be recognized or processed. If the cortex is optimally aroused, it will quickly recognize signals and efficiently process incoming information. In one study (Fuster, 1958), rhesus monkeys were required to learn to discriminate between two objects (to learn which object had a food reward hidden under it) when the objects were presented tachistoscopically (for a fraction of a second at a time). In the experimental condition, the animals were electrically stimulated in the RAS through a permanently implanted electrode; control animals received no stimulation. Not only did the experimental animals learn faster, but they had faster reaction times.

The RAS also has a descending tract, which influences motor functions. There is good reason to believe that the descending tract of the RAS may be in part responsible for the improvement in the speed and coordination of reactions under higher levels of arousal.

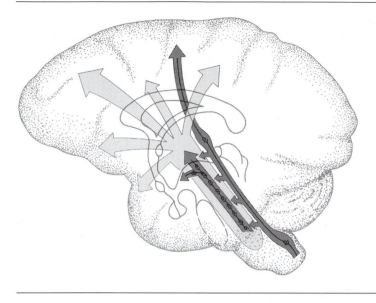

Figure 5-1. Ascending reticular activating system (reticular formation) schematically projected on a monkey brain. (From *Handbook of Psychology: Neurophysiology*, by D. B. Lindsley, Vol. 3, 1960. Copyright © 1960 by the American Psychological Society. Reprinted with permission.)

As a result of being put in this state of readiness, people are not only able to process more information (visual, auditory, tactile, and so on) but are able to process it better. Furthermore, they are able to better identify important features in the environment and integrate that information with memories or schemata stored in the brain. Finally, because the motor cortex has been activated, they are prepared to make an appropriate response or responses both rapidly and accurately.

Measuring Cortical Activity

Electroencephalograms

The brain is composed of many interconnecting nerve pathways. Electrical impulses generated by chemical processes travel along these pathways. The electroencephalograph (EEG) was designed to amplify these impulses so that a permanent record could be made of the activity of various brain structures. It is technically possible to obtain records of activity in any brain structure, but EEG recordings on humans are typically taken from structures on the outer perimeter of the brain.

EEG readings have shown that changes in brain activity are characterized by abrupt rather than gradual changes in the amplitude and frequency of the impulses (brain waves). In general, as a particular brain structure becomes more active, the amplitude (wave height) decreases and the frequency (number of peaks per second) increases. Figure 5-2 shows some examples of cortical activity corresponding to various behavioral and mental states.

Positron Emission Tomography

For about 100 years, it has been known that the regulation of blood supply to the brain is tightly coupled to local neuronal activity in the brain. About 40 years ago, researchers began tracing circulation by infusing radioactive material. Positron emission tomography (PET) is a refinement of this approach. A PET scanner is composed of hundreds of detectors that circle the brain. Using mathematical averaging techniques, the distribution of an isotope in the tissue can be measured. PET results in a very plastic and changing image that reflects neuronal activity in various regions of the brain (Raichle, 1988).

Let's look at a few of the important findings established by PET. Semir Zeki (1992) has used PET to explore which areas of the brain become active when people are exposed to various forms of visual stimulation. His work shows, among other things, that different regions in the brain become active in response to different dimensions of a stimulus—for instance, its color, form, and movement. From this we conclude

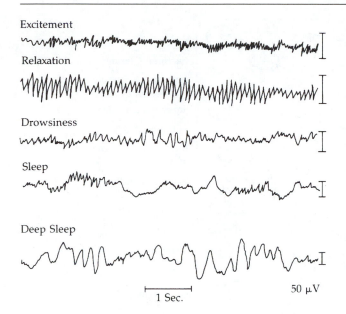

Excitement

Relaxation

Drowsiness

Sleep

Deep Sleep

1 Sec.   50 μV

Figure 5-2. EEG patterns ranging from sleep to wakefulness to excitement. (From "Electroencephalography," by H. H. Jasper. In W. Penfield and T. C. Erickson (Eds.), *Epilepsy and Cerebral Localization,* 1941. Copyright © 1941 by Charles C Thomas, Publishers. Reprinted with permission.)

that the brain tends to break down images into their component parts.

Other studies have been able to locate which area of the brain is used to detect signals. Through a series of converging experiments, it has been established that the right prefrontal cortex is part of an attentional system that is engaged when a subject is looking for a particular signal (e.g., Petersen, Fox, Posner, Mintun, & Raichle, 1988; Posner, Petersen, Fox, & Raichle, 1988). Richard Gur (1992) of the University of Pennsylvania has noted that men and women use different parts of the brain when solving problems and that men have difficulty detecting emotions in facial expressions, especially the facial expressions of women.

This work complements the work on the RAS. Not only does the brain as a whole become generally more active in response to external stimulation, but different areas of the brain become selectively more active in response to specific task demands. Perhaps even more important is the finding that, as people operate on in-

formation in certain ways, different areas of the brain become involved (e.g., Petersen et al., 1988; Posner et al., 1988).

The Autonomic Nervous System

Although cortical activity has frequently been used as a measure of arousal, many other physiological changes occur when a person is in a state of arousal. The autonomic nervous system is responsible for these changes. A wide array of stimuli trigger activity in the autonomic nervous system. For example, physical exertion, exposure to a loud noise or novel stimulus, injury to the body, anxiety, apprehension, or certain drugs will elicit a rather predictable pattern of responses. Heart rate increases, and blood vessels constrict. Together, these two reactions produce an increase in blood flow. The liver releases glucose for immediate energy, and the spleen releases red corpuscles, which are important for carrying oxygen. Digestion halts; however, fats are released into the bloodstream for conversion to energy. Perspiration increases, which is important for cooling when the person is expending great amounts of energy. Secretion of saliva and mucus decreases, giving a dry-mouth feeling. The muscles tense, the pupils dilate, and the senses are improved.

This pattern of responses, which is generally accompanied by increased cortical activity, is due mainly to the action of the hypothalamus, which triggers two parallel and complementary reactions: It stimulates activity in the autonomic nervous system and in the endocrine (glandular) system (Levine, 1960). Figure 5-3 shows the pathways in the sympathetic nervous system, a division of the autonomic nervous system. Most of the physiological changes associated with arousal can be traced to the activity of the sympathetic nervous system. In addition, the autonomic nervous system stimulates the adrenal medulla, which then secretes epinephrine or norepinephrine. Both epinephrine and norepinephrine produce RAS arousal. RAS activity is often associated with general arousal, which mediates sensory thresholds, muscle tonus, and other responses. It has been suggested that the release of epinephrine and norepinephrine provides a long-lasting chemical backup to the immediate action of the sympathetic nervous system. They have also been implicated in human emotional reactions.

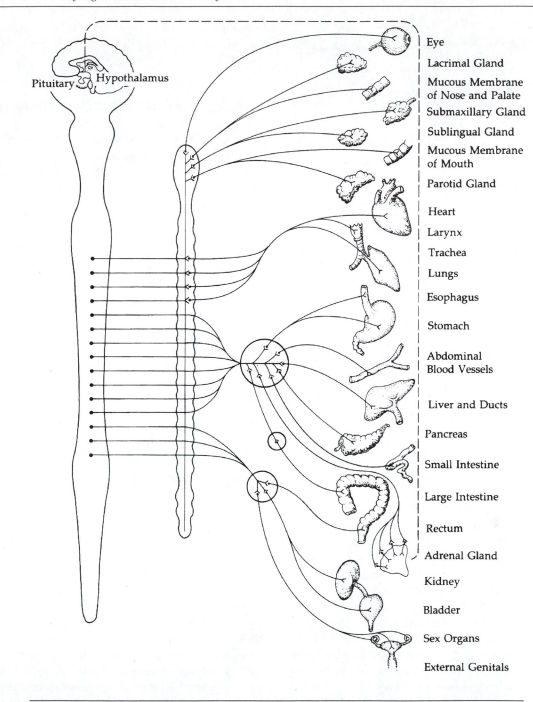

Figure 5-3.   Schematic diagram of the sympathetic nervous system (solid lines) and the action of the pituitary on the adrenals via the bloodstream (dashed line). (From "Stimulation in Infancy," by S. Levine. *Scientific American*, May 1966, *214*, 84–90. Copyright © 1966 by Scientific American, Inc. All rights reserved.)

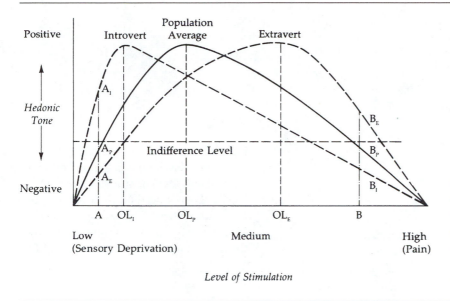

Figure 5-4. Relation between level of stimulation (arousal) and hedonic tone (affect) as a function of personality. (From *Experiments with Drugs,* by H. J. Eysenck. Copyright © 1963 by Pergamon Press Ltd. Reprinted with permission.)

Arousal, Affect, and Performance

Arousal and Affect

For some time, theorists have accepted the idea that arousal and affect are best described by an inverted U-shaped function (Figure 5-4). According to this theory, affect is negative or neutral at low levels of arousal, highly positive at some intermediate level of arousal, and negative (aversive) at very high levels of arousal. Further, it has been suggested that organisms are inclined to seek out new information that will produce positive affect. In other words, the motivation to explore, process information, and master the environment is assumed to be governed by a preference for moderate levels of arousal (Berlyne, 1960; Eysenck, 1967). Over the years this theory came to be called the *optimal stimulation theory* of behavior.

There is some evidence that the inverted U-shaped function describes the relationship between autonomic arousal and affect, but its relevance to cortical arousal has been disputed (Matthews, Davies, & Lees, 1990). Considerable evidence suggests that the relationship between cortical arousal and affect is linear; people often find high levels of cortical arousal highly pleasurable—for example, when they are thinking or problem solving or even in a sporting competition.

Even high levels of autonomic arousal can be quite pleasurable, at least for short periods, as in a sporting competition. It is when autonomic arousal remains high for long periods that it is experienced as negative. As we will see in Chapter 9, when autonomic arousal is prolonged, the stress response emerges.

Arousal and Performance

After reviewing all the data relating behavioral efficiency to arousal, Donald Hebb (1955) proposed an inverted-U-shaped function to describe the relation between arousal and performance (Figure 5-5). This is also commonly known as the Yerkes-Dodson principle, on the basis of 1908 observations by Yerkes and his student Dodson. Again, it has been disputed that the inverted U-shaped function always describes the relationship between arousal and performance (Matthews et al., 1990). Substantial research indicates that people are often better at detecting signals or identifying cues when cortical arousal is high. Similarly, it has been found that motor performance is often superior at high versus moderate levels of arousal.

To understand why theorists have postulated an inverted U-shaped function for both affect and performance, we need to consider two main lines of research: sensory deprivation and anxiety.

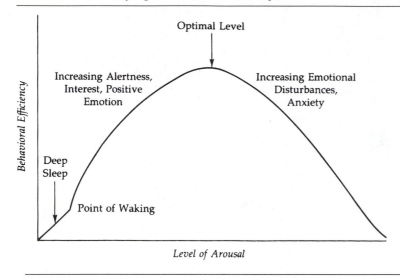

Figure 5-5. Hypothetical relation between behavioral efficiency (performance) and level of arousal. (From D. O. Hebb, "Drive and the C.N.S. (Conceptual Nervous System)." *Psychological Review,* 1955, *62,* 243– 254. Copyright © 1954 by the American Psychological Association.)

Research on Sensory Deprivation

Studies of sensory deprivation suggest that humans find low levels of stimulation aversive. Donald Hebb and his students at McGill University were the first to undertake systematic studies of sensory deprivation (Bexton, Heron, & Scott, 1954). Woodburn Heron (1957), one of Hebb's associates, paid male college students a substantial sum of money to lie on a bed for as many days as they could. To restrict visual stimulation, the students had to wear special translucent visors. To restrict auditory stimulation, they had to rest their heads on rubber pillows next to an air conditioner that put out a steady hum. To reduce tactile stimulation, the students were required to wear cotton gloves and cardboard forearm cuffs. The fingers are a rich source of stimulation and can be used to stimulate the body, by rubbing and kneading. The experimental setup is shown in Figure 5-6.

The effects of sensory deprivation began to show up after about a day. Subjects indicated that they had trouble thinking clearly. Many indicated that they simply ran out of things to think about. When they did try to think about something, they had trouble concentrating for any length of time. After 48 hours, most of the subjects found they were unable to do even the most basic mathematical computations ($12 \times 6 = ?$).

Many subjects found that they began to see images; nearly all reported that they had dreams or visions while awake. Hallucinations were common and

were likened to those produced by drugs. Most subjects tried to entertain themselves by thinking about certain things or activities, but many found it difficult to concentrate. Most of the participants welcomed activities that normally held no interest for them—having the opportunity to read stock market reports, for example. Such findings are consistent with Berlyne's (1960) view that, when people are underaroused, they will attempt to generate stimulation as best they can or focus on what is available.

All of the subjects found the experience very aversive. Even though they were being paid a substantial sum of money for each day of the experiment, most left after the second or third day.

This research is consistent with the inverted U-shaped function. However, it took a day or two for the lack of sensory stimulation to produce the intellectual deficits and for the aversiveness of the experience to emerge. The inverted U-shaped function suggests that the effects should have been experienced immediately. According to optimal stimulation theory, the moment-to-moment changes in arousal govern stimulation-seeking behavior.

Research on Anxiety

Research on anxiety indicates that chronically high levels of arousal are aversive (Barlow, 1988; Barlow, Chorpita, & Turovsky, 1996). There is also considerable evidence that, when people are anxious, their intellectual

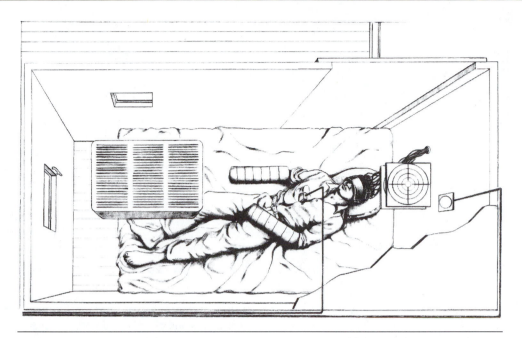

Figure 5-6. Sensory deprivation chamber used by the McGill University group. (Adapted from E. Mose, "The Pathology of Boredom," by W. Heron. *Scientific American*, January 1957, p. 52. Copyright © 1957 by Scientific American, Inc. All rights reserved.)

functioning becomes impaired. Among other things, they have difficulty in learning and concentrating and are easily distracted. Such research is consistent with the inverted U-shaped function.

Chronically high arousal does not mean that arousal is always high. People who have been classified as anxious often experience periods in which they do not experience high arousal. The research evidence seems to suggest that anxious individuals are more reactive than nonanxious people to certain types of environmental stimulation; that is, they show greater increases in arousal. Among other things, they are more reactive to novelty and to cues that signal dangers or threats. One consequence of this reactivity is that anxious people often experience high levels of arousal when there are high levels of stimulation.

Many theorists contend, however, that anxiety is not merely a state of hyperarousal (e.g., Barlow, 1988; Barlow et al., 1996). They argue that the difference between anxious and nonanxious people is more qualitative; that is, the reason anxious people experience more

negative affect is not simply because of high arousal but rather because they see the world in more negative terms (Watson & Clark, 1984).

Optimal Stimulation and Individual Goals

Apter (1982) has argued that the level of stimulation that people prefer depends on their goals. He has suggested that, rather than preferring some moderate level of arousal, people sometimes prefer high arousal and at other times prefer low arousal; that is, sometimes people like to experience excitement and at other times they like to relax. According to this theory, people tend to swing back and forth between these two states. Nevertheless, some people tend to be primarily in the high arousal state, while others tend to be primarily in the low arousal state (Apter, 1982).

Apter (1982) further argues that people also shift between two types of motivational goals. At certain times, people are motivated by the need for achievement; they focus on what are called *telic goals*. They plan their activities carefully and tend to complete

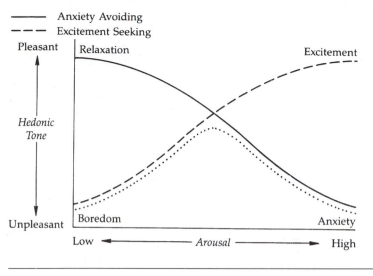

Figure 5-7. The hypothesized relationship between arousal and hedonic tone (affect) for the achievement state and the pleasure-seeking state. (From *The Experience of Motivation: Theory of Psychological Reversals*, by M. J. Apter. Copyright © 1982 by Academic Press. Reprinted by permission.)

them, in order to receive the satisfaction that comes from achieving a goal. Their behavior is marked by efficiency rather than pleasure. In this state, they are serious-minded and future-oriented; they plan. At other times, the same individuals are motivated by a desire to experience pleasure in the here and now; they focus on *paratelic goals*. They are inclined to prolong activities as long as they are producing high levels of pleasure. They tend to be playful and spontaneous (Svebak & Murgatroyd, 1985).

The crux of the theory is that the affect associated with arousal can shift abruptly, as individuals switch between telic and paratelic goals. In other words, satisfaction comes not from high or low arousal but the level of arousal appropriate to current goals (Figure 5-7). When we are in the achievement state, low arousal can be pleasant; we call it relaxation. When we are in the pleasure-seeking state, we call the same low level of arousal boredom. Similarly, high arousal can be very unpleasant (anxiety) in the achievement state and very pleasant (excitement) in the pleasure-seeking state. Note that, if you take the average of these two states, you come up with an inverted U-shaped function (the dotted curve in Figure 5-7).

Conclusion

There is no clear evidence that momentary high or low levels of arousal are aversive. It seems that prolonged periods of either high or low arousal are aversive.

While high arousal and negative affect seem to characterize anxious people, it does not automatically follow that arousal is the source of the negative affect or the poor performance that often characterizes anxious people. There is good reason to believe that the negative affect experienced by anxious people is due to their negative view of the world.

Arousal and Attention

Arousal and Selective Attention

Easterbrook (1959) has proposed that, at low levels of arousal, our attention is broad (we attend to many things) and inclusive (we process a great deal of information). At high arousal—beyond the optimal level—our attention becomes narrow (we attend to few things) and exclusive (we ignore everything but survival-related stimuli). At high arousal, in other words, we practice *selective attention*. According to Easterbrook, arousal governs attention and information processing. We are hardwired, so to speak, to perceive certain things when arousal is low and other things when it is high.

The environment is very complex, and humans have only a limited capacity to be aware of, and process, what is going on around them. To deal with their limited capacity, humans constantly shift their attention—not only the orientation of their receptors (eyes and ears) but the internal perspectives from which they examine incoming information. Piaget and other theorists have suggested that humans attempt to classify all incoming information using existing broad categories. As I watch someone execute a series of movements, for example, I look for an existing category that can summarize those movements. I might say the person is playing tennis, or running.

When we must devote our attention to some task, our ability to process information about the environment is further restricted. Suppose that I'm trying to find my way to a particular location in a strange city. Because I must concentrate on identifying key reference points on my route, I may not process very much about other things along my path—the buildings or the people I am passing.

Arousal and the Reorganization of Attention

According to Easterbrook (1959), high arousal can also lead to the reorganization of attention. According to his theory, when arousal become very high, our attention is directed towards the location and identification of things in the environment that might threaten our survival.

Easterbrook does not clearly indicate when attention will narrow and when it will become reorganized. Barlow (1988) and others suggest that, as arousal increases, attention first becomes narrower and eventually is reorganized. Barlow has suggested that arousal and the narrowing of attention may be mutually reinforced. Narrowing often increases arousal, which, in turn, provokes further narrowing of attention. Once reorganization begins, Barlow contends, there is a similar dynamic between reorganization and arousal. As people focus more and more on threat cues, they become more aroused, which makes them more inclined to focus on threat cues.

Conclusion

According to Easterbrook's theory, arousal directs attention. Attention is not governed by higher-order cognitive processes—such as the individual's implicit the-

ories about the world—but directly by arousal itself. In other words, arousal is more or less hardwired to attention processes. According to this view, the only way to gain control over attention is to gain control over arousal. Indeed, many theorists have approached the problem of attention from the perspective that humans need to learn how to control arousal.

There is considerable evidence that how we think about and conceptualize the world plays an important role in the activation of the various arousal systems. The implication of this research is that we are not completely at the mercy of arousal; rather, we can come to control arousal through the way we think about things. Nonetheless, such approaches generally accept Easterbrook's contention that arousal plays a directive role in attention.

Summary

Peak performance demands that attention be optimally directed. Since arousal plays a central role in the direction of attention, it is often necessary to manage arousal. There are two main arousal systems: the cortical arousal system and the autonomic arousal system.

Overall cortical arousal is due in large part to the reticular activating system (RAS). Studies using the electroencephalograph (EEG), which measures and records brain activity, have shown that changes in brain activity are abrupt rather than gradual. Research utilizing positron emission tomography (PET) indicates that not all areas of the brain are equally active.

Bodily arousal is due to the autonomic nervous system, which prepares the body to take action; it produces a number of bodily changes that prepare the individual to expend great amounts of energy. Most of the bodily changes are produced by a branch of the autonomic nervous system called the sympathetic nervous system. In addition, the pituitary gland activates the adrenal glands, which secrete epinephrine and norepinephrine. These chemicals provide the long-term backup for the more immediate action of the sympathetic nervous system.

Research from a variety of sources suggests that arousal and affect can be related by an inverted U-shaped function. Studies of sensory deprivation, for example, suggest that low levels of stimulation are aversive. Conversely, studies of anxious people suggest that high levels of simulation are aversive. Other research indicates, however, that whether high levels of stimulation are aversive depends on what goals people are pursuing and whether arousal is prolonged.

Arousal alters attention. Among other things, it has been argued that arousal restricts and even reorganizes attention. Specifically, under high arousal, our attention becomes directed towards survival-related cues in the environment.

Two of the main criticisms of arousal theory are that it has failed to treat the origins of arousal as important and that traditional arousal theorists have neglected the distinction between cortical and autonomic arousal.

Challenges for Performance Theory

In the remainder of this chapter, we will examine arousal within the context of individuals' attempts to obtain peak performance. As we begin, let's look at some of the challenges a theory of peak performance must face.

Unexplained Arousal

One of the central problems for performance theorists is to deal with the whole question of unexplained arousal (Neiss, 1988). There is a long line of research that indicates arousal has few psychological implications when people can explain the source of arousal, but has quite important psychological implications otherwise (Schachter & Singer, 1962). For example, if I have been running, I know that is why my heart is beating rapidly, and my heart rate is of no concern to me. However, if I notice that my heart is beating rapidly and I don't know why, I will begin at once to search for an explanation, and I may become quite alarmed.

Generally, people tend to look for explanations in terms of whatever motivational system is currently active. If I am with someone I love, I will tend to attribute any indicators of high arousal to my being in love. If

something I am doing frightens me, I will tend to attribute high arousal to my fears.

Reconceptualizing the Link between Arousal and Performance

Over the years, the concept of arousal has become central to our thinking about affect and performance. Recently, however, various researchers have come to question some of the traditional views on this topic. While accepting that arousal is important, they argue that we need to reconceptualize its role (e.g., Neiss, 1988; Reisenzein, 1994). One criticism is that, traditionally, arousal has been given too large a role and that we need to also consider the role of learned and cognitive variables (Neiss, 1988).

When people attempt to attain peak performance, they trigger increases in arousal that can both facilitate and undermine performance. We will find that whether arousal facilitates or undermines our performance is linked to how arousal interacts with learned and cognitive components. It interacts, for example, with how we explain the arousal that we feel.

Apter (1982) has pointed out that we can only make sense out of arousal if we consider it in terms of an individual's goals. Because peak performance is a goal-directed activity, it provides a fruitful context in which to analyze arousal.

Systems Involved in Peak Performance

Several systems have been implicated in peak performance. These systems are more or less functionally independent, according to the research literature. I refer to them as *arousal systems*. In order to attain peak performance, each of these systems must be operating optimally.

Traditionally, psychologists have made a distinction only between trait and state arousal. *Trait arousal* characterizes the individual more or less independently of the situation (or across situations), whereas *state arousal* arises out of the individual's interaction with the environment. Studies have shown that a wide variety of factors, both learned and cognitive, give rise

Table 5-1. Arousal systems that govern the performance of a skill.

Type of Arousal	Related Research Areas	Effect on Attention	Effect on Performance Outcome
Trait arousal			
Anxiety	Anxiety Timidity Emotionality Reactivity Negative affectivity	Restriction or narrowing Reorganization (to threat) Self-evaluative focus	Avoidant behavior Distraction of attention Apprehension
State arousal			
I. Sensory overload arousal	Sensory complexity Stress	Restriction or narrowing Reorganization (to threat)	Failure to process Inability to deal with complexity
II. Cognitive dissonance arousal	Cognitive conflict Counterattitudinal behaviors	Restriction or narrowing	Failure to process Inability to deal with complexity

III. Evaluation arousal
  A. Test anxiety
 	
  B. Competition
	
	Test taking
	
	Competition
	Interpersonal rivalry
	Self-focused attention
		
		Intrusive thinking
		
		Self-focused ego concerns
		Performance concerns
			
			Failure to focus on task
			
			Failure to focus on task
			Distraction
			Impaired judgments

to state arousal. We will limit our discussion to a few of the better-known systems.

Table 5-1 summarizes the main features of the most important systems that govern the performance of a skill. The first system in Table 5-1 is trait arousal. High trait arousal is often called anxiety or negative emotionality. The vast literature on anxiety and negative emotionality indicates that people differ in terms of whether they chronically experience low, moderate, or high arousal. In general, it appears that chronically high arousal is associated with negative affect. Further, research suggests that these individuals with chronically high arousal attend to very different things in their environment than do individuals with lower arousal. Not only do they focus on threats, but they tend to focus on their perceived lack of ability to deal with such threats. The negative affect and the accompanying shifts of attention are inconsistent with peak performance. As a result, such people are likely to engage in avoidant behavior or to experience apprehension.

The second system involved in peak performance is state arousal. *State anxiety* has been defined as a tran-

sitory emotional response involving feelings of tension and apprehension, whereas *trait anxiety* has been defined as a personality trait determining the likelihood that a person will experience anxiety in stressful situations (Spielberger, 1983). Stress comes from a person-environment interaction. It often comes from overstimulation and the inability to process the accompanying information. This corresponds to sensory overload arousal (Table 5-1). It has been shown repeatedly that environmental complexity tends to cause an increase in cortical arousal. When cortical arousal increases beyond some optimal point (beyond the individual's ability to process that information, for example), various mechanisms within the body automatically reduce information input. As we will see, individuals often learn to control input so that it matches their ability to process information. This is Easterbrook's (1959) narrowing concept.

A second type of state arousal involves cognitive dissonance arousal. When two pieces of information are in conflict, the individual responds, among other things, with increased arousal (Elkin & Leippe, 1986).

It has been shown that this increased arousal can alter performance on subsequent tasks. The research is consistent with Easterbrook's view that increases in arousal narrow attention.

A third type of state arousal involves evaluation arousal. This type of arousal is more or less specific to evaluative situations, such as taking a test or performing in a competition. Sarason (1984) and others have shown that, when put in a testing situation, many people show high levels of autonomic arousal. This is known as test anxiety. In this state, they experience *intrusive thinking*—thinking that focuses on themselves rather than on the task. Competition also leads to arousal. Competitiveness appears to be a learned orientation and has been linked with the need to win. Indirect evidence suggests that people with a strong need to win tend to become highly aroused in competitive situations (Franken & Brown, 1996). Other research indicates that people dislike competitive situations because they cause distraction and give rise to self-image concerns (Franken & Prpich, 1996).

Since test anxiety does not correlate significantly with dislike of competition, these might be viewed as two distinct systems, each with their own antecedents.

We will now consider trait arousal and the various types of state arousal in more detail.

Trait Arousal (Anxiety)

Biological Component

High arousal has been found to characterize people with negative emotionality, anxiety, and neuroticism, while low arousal has been found to characterize people who are low in emotionality, engage in meditation, or have mastered the relaxation response (Benson, 1975). Anxiety is a common emotion and is thought to be normal as long as it does not become completely debilitating. Estimates indicate that 7% of the U.S. population experiences debilitating anxiety (Katz, 1990). Anxiety is debilitating when there is no known cause and when it is completely out of proportion to the danger. Panic attacks, phobias, and obsessive-compulsive disorders are all examples of debilitating anxiety. On the average, twice as many females as males experience debilitating anxiety (11.0% of females and 5.1% of

males); most of that difference is due to the higher incidence of phobias (8.0% of females and 3.4% of males).

Twin studies of clinically anxious people have shown that there is a significant genetic component. Slater and Shields (1969) found, for example, that the concordance scores for generalized anxiety were 65% in monozygotic twins and 13% in dizygotic twins. Studies of normal personality, which typically isolate a factor referred to as anxiety, neuroticism, or negative emotionality, have also repeatedly shown that anxiety tends to be highly correlated in monozygotic twins but not in dizygotic twins (Young, Fenton, & Lader, 1971; Kendler, Heath, Martin, & Eaves, 1986). The underlying physiology that characterizes anxiety and negative emotionality is a state of hyperarousal (Lader, 1975, 1980a,b). This state that has been shown to be stable over time, which is another indication that it is a trait (e.g., Izard, Libero, Putnam, & Haynes, 1993).

Kagan's Timidity Theory

Kagan (Kagan & Snidman, 1991) has been studying timidity for over a decade. Studies of young children and infants indicate that, while some children are inclined to approach unfamiliar people and objects, others are not. He has made a distinction between inhibited and uninhibited children. One of the main features that distinguishes these two types is their sympathetic reactivity (autonomic arousal); inhibited children are characterized by higher levels. He argues that inhibited and uninhibited children possess different thresholds for excitability in the amygdala and its varied projections and that this difference results in their disposition to be inhibited or uninhibited. He points out that uninhibited and inhibited children represent not merely two ends of a continuum but two distinct types with a distinct genetic origin. He and his colleagues have taken the position that this is only a disposition and, therefore, it is necessary to consider the role of learning and cognition.

Eysenck's Extraversion/Introversion Theory

Eysenck (1967) has suggested that arousal, or activation, is one of the main continuums on which people can be differentiated. Some people, he has suggested, have an arousal level that is relatively low (extraverts), while others have an arousal level that is moderate to high (introverts). The key to understanding the difference between extraverts and introverts, according to Eysenck, is understanding how these two types of people maintain optimal stimulation. On the average, he argues, extraverts need more stimulation than introverts. Since socialization is a key source of arousal, extraverts would be more inclined to socialize than introverts. Because introverts tend to have a moderate to high arousal level, they are motivated either to maintain existing arousal levels or to reduce arousal levels. Therefore, in contrast to extraverts, who seek out social stimulation, introverts tend to avoid social contacts, in order to prevent any further increase in arousal (see Figure 5-4).

Another axis in Eysenck's theory runs from neuroticism to stability. Neurotic individuals are characterized by high autonomic nervous system reactivity, which would also influence limbic system activity. According to Eysenck, anxious individuals have high standing levels of cortical and autonomic arousal. Note that extraversion and neuroticism are the first two of the five factors isolated to describe personality by factor analytic procedures.

Even though Eysenck assumes that biology plays a central role, he believes that there is an interaction between biology and learning. As a result, the expression of personality involves understanding the nature of this interaction. Many of his experiments focused on changing behavior using the principles of learning and led others to credit him with being one of the founders of behavioral therapy.

Gray's Behavioral Inhibition Model

Extending Eysenck's theory, Gray (1982) proposed that personality and emotions are determined by two affective-motivational systems. The primary system is the behavioral inhibition system, which involves the septal-hippocampal systems of the brain, its monamine afferents, and the frontal cortex. Like Kagan (Kagan & Snidman, 1991), Gray argues that specific stimulus inputs such as punishment, nonreward, and novelty trigger the inhibition system, which suppresses ongoing behavior and redirects attention to relevant stimuli. According to Gray, people with an active behavioral inhibition system—anxious individuals—would reflect a combination of Eysenck's introversion

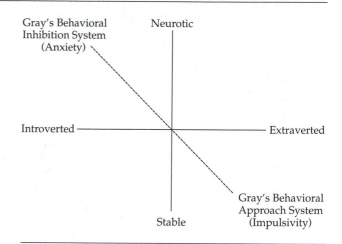

Figure 5-8. Eysenck's introversion-extraversion and neuroticism-stability axes, with Gray's anxiety-impulsivity axis superimposed. (Adapted from *The Biological Basis of Personality*, by H. J. Eysenck (Ed.). Copyright © 1967 by Charles C Thomas.)

and neuroticism. At the other end of Gray's axis is an approach system—sometimes called impulsivity—which reflects a combination of extraversion and stability (Figure 5-8).

Barlow's Anxious Apprehension Model

David Barlow has offered a model suggesting that anxiety tends to make people more and more dysfunctional as a result of a bidirectional effect between arousal and attention (Barlow, 1988; Barlow, Chorpita, & Turovsky, 1996). What happens, according to Barlow, is that the negative affect causes a shift in attention to a *self-evaluative focus*. This results in further increases in arousal and a further narrowing of attention. Instead of attention being broad and open, the individual shifts to a hypervigilant state in which attention becomes focused on the recognition of potential threats. The psychological state that accompanies this is intense worry. At this point, anxiety can take on a highly dysfunctional quality. Since intense worry is highly aversive, the individual may be consumed by avoidance behaviors. The most common avoidant response would be to leave the situation. Barlow's model of anxious apprehension is shown in Figure 5-9.

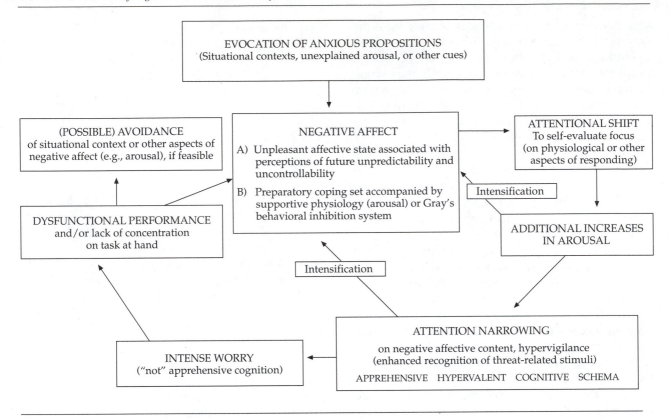

Figure 5-9.   Barlow's model of anxious apprehension. (From *Anxiety and Its Disorders: The Nature and Treatment of Anxiety and Panic,* by D. H. Barlow. Copyright © 1988 by Guilford Press. Reprinted by permission.)

In Barlow's theory, anxious people tend to account for unexplained arousal in terms of their negative view of the world. In other words, when arousal increases, the world takes on an even gloomier look.

Conclusion

Each of these theories uses slightly different language. What they have in common is the idea that, because of an underlying biological disposition, individuals react differently to the environment. The key factors in the theories—reactivity, timidity, inhibition, or apprehension—all have their roots in the individual's biological makeup. As we know, dispositions do not cause behavior. Accordingly, whether dispositionally high levels of trait arousal will direct attention in a certain way or provoke certain patterns of thought depends on the individual's underlying principles of learning and cognition. In short, trait anxiety interacts with learning and cognition to determine the final course of behavior.

The Learned Social Component

There is considerable evidence that most, if not all, of the anxiety disorders—such as irrational fears, phobias, panic reactions, and obsessive-compulsive behaviors—have their roots in generalized anxiety (Barlow, 1988). It has been suggested that, when people are anxious, they are prepared to make certain types of associations rather than others. Specifically, they are prepared to associate stimuli that signal things are threatening and dangerous. For example, people who experience their highly aroused (anxious) state as highly aversive will be inclined to associate a wide variety of stimuli with this state. It seems that certain classes of stimuli are more likely than others to become associated with this aversive state. This has been referred to as a state of preparedness (Seligman, 1971).

One of the key features of anxiety is the tendency to be constantly vigilant for potential dangers or threats. Various theorists have argued that, while our biology may predispose us to be alert to dangers and threats, the tendency to be chronically preoccupied with dangers and threats results from the interaction of biology and the principles of learning and cognition (Watson & Clark, 1984). According to Beck (1985), the affective system leads people to process the environment in a distorted way. When we are highly aroused or the behavioral inhibition system is activated, for example, we tend to focus on things that are potentially dangerous. The result is that we tend to process only negative information. This view is very similar to Barlow's view that high arousal tends to shift attention to threat and danger cues. Beck goes on to suggest that, if we process mainly negative information, we will be inclined to develop a schema or implicit theory of the world that involves more bad things than good things. The development of this negative schema would then determine how we are likely to process information in the future. In other words, even if arousal levels were lowered, we would continue to search for dangers and threats. Beck argues that anxious people not only distort information about the world but distort information about how effectively they deal with the world. Since it is a bad world and they are unable to make it good, they tend to see themselves as ineffective. Over time, anxious individuals come to believe that they lack the ability to deal with a bad world. This becomes the basis for depression.

Beck has argued that appraisal has its root in past information processing, which came about because of some affective system. By contrast, the social learning theorists can account, at least in part, for differences in information processing in terms of principles such as imitation and modeling. Living with parents who keep alerting us to dangers in our environment or telling us how bad things are could bias our information processing so that we tend to see more bad than good. Also, constantly being given a biased view of the world by the media could dispose us to develop an implicit theory of the world that is negative. There could even be a spiral effect: As our view of the world becomes more negative, we might be more inclined to buy papers that present a negative picture consistent with our view. This could induce publishers of papers to present even more bad news, on the principle that they are giving the public what it wants.

The Cognitive Component

Many theorists have argued that the experience of anxiety depends on how the individual appraises the world (e.g., Spielberger, 1985). Most of these theorists start with the idea that some event, often accompanied by autonomic arousal, causes us to carefully examine our situation. If the situation is appraised as dangerous or threatening, we will respond with fear or anxiety. If, on the other hand, we appraise the situation as challenging, we will respond with a very different set of emotions, such as mastery or involvement. According to cognitive theories, the affective reaction (arousal) is a very diffuse autonomic discharge that is experienced as neither good or bad. It is our appraisal of it that gives rise to our subjective experience.

According to cognitive theories, anxiety is a personality trait. While these theories are able to account for differences in anxiety provoked by different situations, they typically fail to say where these differences in appraisal come from. In Beck's theory, the different schemas or implicit theories are thought to have their origins in our affective reactions. One major problem for the cognitive theories is their inability to account for irrational anxiety. Often people know their reactions are inappropriate or irrational but are unable to control them.

Despite such problems, cognitive theories tell us something very important about the mental processes necessary in order to achieve peak performance. To deal with new challenges or with failure, we need to find ways of seeing the situation that will encourage us to redouble our efforts at learning and coping. How we appraise the situation determines whether we will engage in approach/adaptive behaviors or avoidant/nonadaptive behaviors.

While Beck suggests that schemas are learned, his methods for changing those schemas are cognitive. In working with clients, Beck teaches people how to think in more adaptive ways. He argues that, because people have developed faulty thinking, they are inclined to appraise situations in negative or nonadaptive ways.

In his research, he has shown that, when people are given cognitive retraining on how to appraise a situation, they respond in a more adaptive manner.

A large body of research links anxiety to cognitive judgments about the predictability and/or controllability of a situation. It indicates that the anxiety reaction is likely to vary in proportion to the degree that the situation seems predictable and controllable (e.g., Seligman, 1975). Consequently, broad belief systems involving hope and optimism are important in mitigating anxiety.

High Trait Arousal and Performance

High trait arousal is viewed as a major obstacle to attaining peak performance. One of the main problems for anxious individuals is not being able to focus their attention on the task. Instead, they tend to focus on potential threats and on their ineffectiveness in dealing with those threats.

To prevent such a reorganization of attention, anxious people must train themselves to appraise the world in positive terms. In other words, people born with a disposition to be anxious can learn to see the world in more positive terms. To do so, they need to change their schemata or implicit theories of the world. If anxious individuals develop a positive implicit theory in which the world is basically benign, they should be less inclined to respond to everything they encounter as a potential threat.

An aspect of anxious individuals' negative outlook is that they tend to overgeneralize following failure. Instead of accepting failure as the outcome of a specific situation and moving on, they are inclined to expect that all subsequent situations will also end in failure. Developing a positive implicit theory should help with this problem.

Anxious individuals also need to develop the belief that they can be effective in making changes. They need to believe that they can make a difference. Research has consistently shown that people with good coping skills experience far less anxiety than people with poor coping skills.

In addition, anxious individuals need to accept that high arousal is necessary for peak performance. Also, high arousal can be experienced as a positive emotion. Whether we experience high arousal as negative or positive often depends on whether we view the situation as a threat or a challenge. Peak performance involves rising to the challenge. Thus, learning to appraise the situation in more positive ways can help anxious individuals to deal with their high arousal.

Finally, individuals need to learn how to rest and relax. When our arousal level is too high for too long, we are likely to develop a stress reaction.

Summary

Twin studies indicate that there is a genetic component to anxiety. Kagan distinguished between inhibited and uninhibited children on the basis of their responses to unfamiliar situations and found that inhibited children are characterized by greater sympathetic reactivity (autonomic arousal). Eysenck has proposed that differences in arousal predispose people to be extraverted or introverted. He suggests that, to produce an optimal level of arousal, extraverts seek out stimulation, whereas introverts seek out a nonchanging environment to keep stimulation at tolerable levels. According to Gray, emotions are primarily determined by the behavioral inhibition system.

According to Barlow, there is a bidirectional effect between arousal and attention. The net result is that arousal not only narrows attention but also reorganizes attention, so that anxious individuals tend to worry all the time. Since worry is highly aversive, anxious individuals are inclined to engage in avoidant behavior. It has been suggested that, when people are anxious, they are prepared to make certain types of associations rather than others and, as a result, are more inclined to develop certain types of disorders, including panic, phobias, and obsessive disorders.

A key feature of anxiety is the tendency to be constantly vigilant for potential dangers or threats. According to Beck, the negative affect associated with anxiety leads people to process the environment in a distorted way. The negative schemata that result from such processing then determine how they are likely to process information in the future. Social learning theorists account for this effect in terms of such principles as imitation and modeling.

Many theorists have argued that our experience of anxiety depends on how we appraise the world. Differences in appraisal, according to these theories, are associated with differences in personality. Cognitive judgments about predictability and controllability are also important in determining how much anxiety we experience.

A major problem for anxious individuals is their tendency to react to everything as danger or threat. One way for them to change that perception is to develop a more positive view of the world. In addition, they need to see themselves as competent individuals capable of coping with the problems they encounter. Finally, they need to accept the idea that high arousal is a necessary condition for peak performance.

We now turn to state arousal, which, as we have seen, results basically from a person-situation interaction. We will consider three basic types of state arousal.

State Arousal: Sensory Overload

Arousal is constantly changing, in response to biological rhythms and also to incoming environmental stimulation. In this section, we will consider the effect of environmental stimulation on attention and, hence, on peak performance.

Note that one consequence of sensory overload, especially when prolonged, is stress, which is highly debilitating physically and emotionally. Thus, managing environmental stimulation is critical for peak performance.

Aircraft controllers must often deal with sensory overload, also called information overload.

The Biological Component

Sources of Arousal

First of all, let's review the two factors responsible for fluctuations of arousal.

1. **Rhythmic activity of the nervous system.** As we know, arousal—especially cortical arousal—is under the control of certain biological rhythms. Michel Jouvet's (1967) work suggests that the alternating activity of the raphe nuclei, which secrete the neurotransmitter serotonin, and the locus coeruleus, which secretes the neurotransmitter norepinephrine, governs arousal and alertness in humans. Jouvet found that serotonin is associated with reduced cortical activity (reduced arousal), while norepinephrine is associated with in-

creased cortical activity (increased arousal). All of us are more alert at some times than at others. Not only do all normal people experience these involuntary changes in arousal (alertness), but they often experience them at certain predictable times of the day. So-called morning people, for example, experience greater alertness in the mornings; night people experience greater alertness at night. Still others have a mixed pattern—a period of alertness in the morning, followed at midday by a drop in alertness, which is followed, in turn, by another period of increased alertness. Not surprisingly, people with this pattern are likely to take a nap.

2. **Stimulation of the sensory systems.** Stimulation of any of the sensory systems—visual, auditory, olfactory, or tactile—is accompanied by an increase in arousal.

The increase in arousal allows humans to maximize the input of incoming information. There is considerable evidence, however, that humans have a limited capacity to process incoming information. In other words, even when the brain is fully activated, we are unable to process all of the incoming data. As a result, we begin to experience confusion and distraction, which can be interpreted as anxiety.

The Concept of Sensory Overload

It is important to remember that our ability to process information is linked, at least in part, to the cognitive structures (schemas) that we have developed. It has been suggested that as the result of developing schemas we increase our ability to process information because we have developed a rule or type of organization that allows us to summarize information. G. A. Miller (1956) suggested that we refer to these units of information as "chunks." On the basis of his research he argued that we are limited to dealing with a maximum of perhaps seven chunks at a time, a relatively limited amount of information. As a result, we often experience sensory overload in a complex environment. One of the interesting and important things to keep in mind is that humans tend to experience sensory overload as highly aversive and stressful, perhaps because it represents a loss of predictability and control. From our perspective, we are interested in sensory overload because it produces fundamental shifts in attention that can interfere with peak performance.

Mechanisms to Reduce Sensory Overload

Lacey and Lacey's attention/rejection model.   Research indicates that a couple of systems are designed to help humans deal with sensory overload. One appears to be linked to increases in heart rate. Acceleration of the heart produces pressure on receptors in the carotid sinus and aortic arch, and this pressure has been shown to reduce RAS activity (Bonvallet & Allen, 1963). Accordingly, Lacey and Lacey (1970, 1978) have suggested that changes in heart rate determine reticular activity, at least in part. Most arousal theorists take the opposite position—that the RAS controls heart rate.

Lacey and Lacey have suggested that such a feedback system has important psychological significance. According to their model, the reduced RAS activity resulting from heart-rate acceleration would block a certain portion of the incoming stimulation and thereby reduce cognitive overload. Similarly, when the person was not working to capacity, deceleration of the heart would signal the RAS to increase activity and thereby allow the individual to process more information.

In one test of Lacey and Lacey's model, subjects had to do three tasks (Lacey, Kagan, Lacey, & Moss, 1963). The first task required the subjects to pay close attention to external stimulation; the second involved mental problem-solving, which presumably would be disturbed by external stimulation; the third task involved both internal and external stimulation. The results showed that the heart decelerated when the task called for careful attention to external stimulation, and accelerated when the task called for the momentary rejection of external stimulation. In the combined task, there was no change. The Laceys and their colleagues argued that the task in which the subject had to concentrate simultaneously on external and internal information produced a conflict, which explains why there was no change.

The GABA system.   GABA (gamma-aminobutyric acid) is a naturally occurring inhibitory neurotransmitter (Cooper, Bloom, & Roth, 1982; Tallman, Paul, Skolnick, & Gallager, 1980). That means that GABA somehow reduces the flow of neural transmission.

Since we will consider GABA in detail in Chapter 7, we will simply note here that the GABA system also appears to be designed to help protect us against sensory overload.

The Learned Component

Young children deal with sensory overload simply by covering their eyes or ears with their hands. As adults, we learn similar ways of dealing with sensory overload. We seek out a quiet place, or we listen to soothing music. Some businesses have instituted brief periods of relaxation at the beginning of the day, to ensure that employees are not so highly aroused that they cannot work efficiently. Coffee breaks often serve a similar function.

In Chapter 9, we will deal with a variety of procedures that are very effective in reducing arousal, including biofeedback, relaxation, and meditation. One such technique is restricted environmental stimulation technique (REST). REST is an effective treatment for excessive environmental stimulation, which, if chronic, can produce physical as well as psychological disorders (Suedfeld, 1975; Suedfeld & Kristeller, 1982).

Two basic methods have been used in the REST research. One involves secluded bed rest in a completely dark, soundproof room for 24 hours. A second method is to have the individual float for approximately an hour in a shallow tank filled with a solution of Epsom salts and water.

The REST technique has been found to increase the power of more standard stress-management techniques, such as biofeedback (Plotkin, 1978). When REST was used as a component in the treatment of essential hypertension, clinically significant drops in systolic and diastolic blood pressure were found (Suedfeld & Kristeller, 1982). REST has also been successfully used to help people stop smoking, lose weight, and reduce drug dependency.

Why does REST work? Studies have shown that REST has not only an immediate but a long-term effect. Peter Suedfeld and Jean Kristeller (1982) have suggested that REST may help people to shift their attention away from external cues to internal cues. High arousal, as we'll see shortly, often directs attention to survival-related cues, which are usually external because threats to our survival are typically external. It follows that people exposed to excessive environmental stimulation may learn to habitually attend to the external environment. REST may help such people to shift their attention to internal cues. As a result, they tend not only to monitor those cues more closely but to deal with them before they produce serious health problems.

Another interpretation of the REST research is that, during these sessions, people learn how to account for their arousal. As a result, unexplained arousal becomes explained and is no longer seen as a threat.

The Cognitive Component

Whenever we interpret an event as threatening or potentially exciting, we are likely to experience an increase in arousal, both cortical and autonomic. When we are threatened, the body must be prepared to deal with that threat, both mentally and physically. Similarly, when we select some challenging activity, our body must be prepared for it. If we are going scuba diving, for example, we need to be both physically and mentally prepared for it. An increase in arousal, in other words, is associated with a wide variety of forthcoming activities.

The important point to remember about this kind of arousal is that it is anticipatory; it occurs prior to some anticipated event (Spinks, Blowers, & Shek, 1985). Because it is based on our cognitive interpretation, it may be inappropriate. I may anticipate that I am going to be fired, for example, when nothing of the sort is about to happen. Sometimes the magnitude of the arousal we experience is not appropriate. I may have good reason to experience a very high level of arousal if I am asked to address a large audience, but it would be inappropriate to experience the same level of arousal if I were asked to introduce a friend to someone else I know.

The magnitude of our arousal is generally proportional to the importance of the forthcoming event. If we have a number of important things to do, we are likely to experience substantial anticipatory arousal. Like environmental arousal, anticipatory arousal is thought to be additive. If, on a particular day, we realize that we have too much to accomplish and too little time, for example, we may experience anticipatory arousal that exceeds some optimal level.

Dealing with Sensory Overload

Setting Priorities

One way of reducing sensory overload is to make lists of what we are going to do and what tasks are most important. Further, we need to promise ourselves that we are only going to focus on one task at a time. In this way, we avoid the tendency to think about everything at once. Unless I make a list when I have a lot of things to do, I tend to jump from one thing to the next. While much of our attention is outside of our control, research on goal setting (Locke & Latham, 1990) indicates that we can take charge of certain things. When we decide something is important, that becomes the focus of our attention. Only when we have not decided what is important is our attention governed by the arousal system.

We must be very careful about what we decide is important, because that will become the focus of our attention. Deciding not to fail, for example, may have serious consequences. We may become so obsessed with not failing that we became paralyzed. We will return to this topic shortly.

Managing Information

In the long run, the best way to manage a complex environment is to become completely familiar with it. When we are familiar with something, we have processed all the information contained in it (Berlyne, 1960). When we process information, we typically also develop schemata, categories, and rules that summarize that information. Those schemata are useful when we are placed in a new situation.

Very often, when we attempt to become familiar with something, we become overwhelmed. To avoid becoming overwhelmed, we need to break it down into manageable units (Horowitz, 1979). When I am writing, I can become overwhelmed and stressed if I attempt to do too much. If I keep my focus narrow, however, I find I can master a block of information and write about it. One way of knowing whether or not something is manageable is to monitor my feelings. If I feel stressed, I've tried to tackle something that is too big.

Sensory Overload and Performance

Arousal caused by sensory overload can lead to the narrowing of attention (Easterbrook, 1959). One problem associated with the narrowing of attention is the failure to perform at optimum levels. Moreover, there is evidence that sensory overload not only causes increases in arousal but may cause a stress reaction. Stress typically produces marked performance losses, especially if the immediate task demands sustained attention. Prolonged stress may trigger the reorganization of attention (Easterbrook, 1959). It may direct attention toward survival cues in the environment rather than to the immediate task. Under these conditions, individuals rarely learn anything new, apparently because they are focusing their attention on threat and survival cues. (We will return to this topic in Chapter 12.) The overall picture that emerges is that, when people are experiencing sensory overload, their performance on tasks suffers.

The main focus of techniques to deal with sensory overload is to reduce how much information must be processed in a given period. Sometimes people use drugs to deal with sensory overload, but this approach is counterproductive, because it further reduces our ability to process information. The best way to deal with sensory overload is to become familiar, over time, with that information. The way we become familiar with something is simply to interact with it. Our brain has been built to create schemata that will enable us to summarize very complex sources of information. Once those structures are in place, we will have the capacity to deal with vast amounts of information. Under those conditions, arousal will be lowered and attention will be broad and inclusive.

Summary

Sensory overload can result not only in high arousal but in stress. There are biological mechanisms to help control arousal. One of these systems appears to be linked to increased heart rate; another involves the GABA system.

Considerable evidence suggests that we can learn to control our arousal. The most obvious—and perhaps most efficient—way is to restrict incoming stimulation. We can also learn to focus our attention in ways that restrict incoming stimulation. An interesting side effect of our ability to anticipate events is that we sometimes experience high levels of anticipatory arousal.

To manage sensory overload, we need to decide what is important rather than simply allowing ourselves to be bombarded with information. Also, we need to break information down into manageable units.

Sensory overload has been linked to performance deficits. These deficits may be mediated by increases in arousal that accompany sensory overload.

State Arousal: Cognitive Dissonance

When we encounter new information that is inconsistent with our existing ways of thinking about the world, a state of cognitive dissonance typically arises. It has been postulated that cognitive dissonance creates a motivational state within us that disposes us to look for ways of reducing it (Festinger, 1957). To do this, we can add new cognitions or change existing ones, seek information that is consistent with existing cognitions, or simply avoid information that is inconsistent with existing cognitions.

The Biological Component

Festinger (1957) conceptualized cognitive dissonance in two distinguishable ways. He suggested that it leads to psychological discomfort and alluded to dissonance as a bodily condition analogous to a tension or drive state. Many early researchers who examined the motivational properties of cognitive dissonance focused on its drive-like properties. They conceptualized cognitive dissonance as arousal, and conducted studies that were designed to see if cognitive dissonance did in fact produce physiological arousal. A number of studies suggested that cognitive dissonance leads to increases in arousal (Croyle & Cooper, 1983), but one of the first definitive studies used the counterattitudinal essay induction technique (Elkin & Leippe, 1986). In this technique, typically, individuals are asked to write an essay that is inconsistent with some belief or attitude. Students may be asked, for example, to write an essay on why their tuition should increase, despite their opinion to the contrary. Elkin and Leippe (1986) found in two different studies that the galvanic skin response (GSR) was elevated following a freely written counterattitudinal essay. This finding has been replicated in other studies (e.g., Losch & Cacioppo, 1990).

It is not surprising that arousal has been closely linked to cognitive dissonance. When people need to process information, to think about some issue, or to resolve some conflict, the brain typically becomes active. However, when the brain is highly aroused in one task, it is able to perform other tasks less well. In a later section, we will consider the implications of this phenomenon.

The Learned Component

Festinger (1957) suggested that perceptions of an inconsistency among an individual's cognitions generates psychological discomfort—intrapersonal tension—and that this aversive state motivates individuals to take re-

medial action. Recently, in an experiment designed to examine this idea, participants were induced to write a counterattitudinal or proattitudinal essay about a 10% tuition increase the next term. Subsequently, they were asked to indicate how uncomfortable, uneasy, and bothered they were. The results provided data consistent with Festinger's motivational hypothesis (Elliot & Devine, 1994). When participants wrote counterattitudinal essays they indeed experienced psychological discomfort. However, when an attitudinal shift occurred, their psychological discomfort returned to baseline.

What is interesting from a learning perspective is that the strategies used to reduce dissonance are reinforced. When these strategies are employed, psychological discomfort decreases, and therefore individuals are inclined to use those strategies again when they experience cognitive dissonance. This explains why people can be presented repeatedly with certain information and yet never accept it—such as why a cigarette smoker is able to discount evidence regarding the negative health effects of smoking.

The Cognitive Component

As we have seen, cognitive dissonance theory can explain why people are inclined to maintain their existing beliefs. Cognitive dissonance theory also suggests that it is possible to change other people's attitudes. For one reason or another, people sometimes engage in behaviors that are not consistent with their underlying beliefs and attitudes. When that happens, they will sometimes change their attitudes to match their behavior. Festinger (1957) argued that, since they cannot go back and change their behavior, the only thing they can do to reduce cognitive dissonance is to change their beliefs. The counterattitudinal essay is one way of producing this effect in the laboratory.

Volunteer organizations often make use of this phenomenon. They ask people to perform seemingly innocuous tasks, such as stuffing envelopes with information about a political organization. Eventually, people need to rationalize to themselves why they are working for a political party. Often they come to the conclusion that the organization is not only worthwhile but needed to address a particular problem in society.

This strategy will only work if people freely engage in the behaviors. If they are coerced or paid, they may rationalize that they did it for those reasons. Bem (1967) suggests that people infer attitudes on the basis of observations of their own behavior. If they are paid for writing a counterattitudinal essay, for example, they might be inclined to attribute their behavior to being paid. As a result, they would experience no cognitive dissonance and no pressure to change their attitudes.

Cognitive Dissonance and Performance

Considerable research indicates cognitive dissonance can lead to performance decrements. Among other things, it has been shown that, while cognitive dissonance can facilitate performance on subsequent overlearned tasks, cognitive dissonance often interferes with performance on subsequent difficult or complex tasks (e.g., Pallak & Pittman, 1972). The basic interpretation of these and other findings is that cognitive dissonance increases arousal and it is the increased arousal that mediates these effects. According to an attentional model, increases in arousal narrow attention. While narrowed attention can facilitate performance on an existing highly practiced skill, high arousal would interfere with learning that required broad as opposed to narrow attention. Further, if high arousal tends to focus attention on survival-related cues, it would be difficult for the individual to integrate new information that did not pertain to survival.

Since cognitive dissonance can make it difficult for people to focus or concentrate, they sometimes attempt to control this type of arousal by managing information input. Actors, for example, may decide to put off reading their reviews until they have a block of time to think about them and put them in perspective. In the course of a sporting competition, an opponent may attempt to use cognitive dissonance to distract an individual—by saying, for instance, "My grandmother can run faster than you" or "Your team always folds under playoff pressure."

Summary

Festinger conceptualized cognitive dissonance in two ways. He suggested that it leads to psychological dis-comfort, on the one hand, and to a drive-like state, on the other. He contended that the psychological discomfort motivates individuals to implement remedial strategies. Researchers have interpreted the drive-like state as arousal. Several studies have provided convincing evidence that cognitive dissonance does produce physiological arousal. Not only that, these increases in arousal have been shown to facilitate performance on overlearned tasks but to interfere with performance on difficult or complex tasks. The results of such studies suggest that the arousal produced by cognitive dissonance is more or less the same as that responsible for narrowing of attention and ultimately reorganization of attention.

State Arousal: Evaluation Arousal

Peak performance is closely linked to evaluation arousal. Many people find that, when they are being evaluated, their performance deteriorates. In this section, we will examine why evaluation can lead to deterioration in performance, in the context of two lines of research—test anxiety and dislike of competitive situations.

Test Anxiety

For some time now, we have had evidence that tests are often perceived as a threat and this perception produces a high level of arousal. If the arousal is prolonged—for instance, when students have to take several tests—it can cause a stress reaction. The high level of arousal associated with tests has been linked to a deterioration in performance. Note that not everybody responds to tests as a threat; some people respond to tests as a challenge.

The Biological Component

Various physiological changes occur when students prepare for and take an examination. For example, glucose levels rise before an exam and decline significantly during the exam. Lactic acid, too, is elevated before an exam but, unlike glucose, continues to increase during the exam (Hall & Brown, 1979); both of these responses are indicative of the stress level. It has also been shown that norepinephrine levels rise, while levels of immunoglobin A (a compound in the blood that indicates the activity level of the immune system) decline, especially in people with a strong power motive (McClelland, Ross, & Patel, 1985). McClelland has argued that the power motive reflects, among other things, the need to control. People with a strong power motive tend to be most highly aroused by situations in which they fear loss of control, such as examinations. This research suggests that, following an examination (or loss of control), an individual might be more susceptible to infection.

The Learned Component

Sarason (1984) has argued that test anxiety is very largely a problem of *self-preoccupying intrusive thinking* (p. 929). A preoccupation with our own thoughts interferes with task-focused thinking. What kinds of thoughts? They seem generally to be responses that arise from a self-assessment of personal deficits in the face of certain situational demands. Neurotic individuals are particularly prone to such thinking. A study by Bolger (1990) found that neuroticism increases pre-examination anxiety and that neurotics are prone to engage in wishful thinking and self-blame, among other things.

   Can we learn to reduce the interference that comes from such thinking? Sarason has shown that self-preoccupying intrusive thinking is reduced when we focus on the task. He argues that helping people to focus on the task is a much better way of helping them to deal with test-induced stress than simply attempting to reassure them. Once again, note that, while attention is sometimes governed by arousal, humans can often redirect their attention. Simply learning that it is important to focus on the task seems to be a highly effective procedure for dealing with test-induced high arousal.

The Cognitive Component

There are large individual differences in the amount of stress induced by an examination. This is not surprising, because the outcome of the exam will have different implications for different individuals. Students who need a certain grade to get into graduate school, for example, may perceive the stakes as very high in-

Exams are often a source of anxiety and stress.

deed. Individuals also differ in the amount of control they feel as they prepare for the exam, wait for the day to arrive, and finally take the exam. Their perceptions of the exam's difficulty vary as well. We will look at the effects of perceived difficulty later.

   When students see the exam as a threat, how do they respond? Typically, they use a combination of problem-focused and emotion-focused coping strategies. (We will discuss this distinction in more detail in Chapter 9.) In the anticipatory stage, they tend to prepare for the examination. During such problem-focused coping, they experience positive emotions, such as hopefulness. Just before the exam, during the final waiting stage, their emotions begin to turn negative. Having reviewed the material to be covered by the exam, they are no longer as actively preparing, and they have time to appraise the adequacy of their efforts (Folkman & Lazarus, 1985).

Test Anxiety and Performance

There is considerable evidence that test anxiety causes poorer performance on tests. The poor performance of test-anxious individuals appears to be linked to their tendency to focus attention on the intrusive thoughts. Armed with this hypothesis, Sarason (1984) set out to help text-anxious individuals by teaching them to focus on the test and not their thoughts. His research provides data consistent with the view that the performance deficits are mediated by attention and are not due to any loss of memory or intellectual capacity.

Summary

While there are wide individual differences, test taking tends to produce a number of physiological changes, including increases in autonomic arousal. Attentional shifts have been found to be directly linked to these changes in arousal. In particular, people experience self-preoccupying intrusive thinking. The effect seems to depend on what is at stake for the individual. This finding indicates that cognitive processes play an important role.

Competition Arousal

A second form of evaluative arousal is the arousal associated with competition. Competition arousal and test arousal may be regarded as separate sources of evaluative arousal, because they are not significantly correlated (Franken & Prpich, 1996).

Research from various sources indicates that a competitive orientation often leads to a deterioration in performance. Some of the best work comes from Spence and Helmreich (1983), who hypothesized that three factors are linked to achievement: mastery, work, and competitiveness (Table 5-2). Research with their Achievement scale indicated that, contrary to their initial hypothesis, work and mastery predict achievement in various situations, but competitiveness does not. In fact, having a competitive orientation seems to undermine achievement. Let's look at three studies that showed this effect.

Predicting GPA. To see if their scale could predict academic achievement, as measured by a student's cumulative grade-point average (GPA), Spence and Helmreich (1983) administered their scale to more than 1300 students. The results pointed to an interaction of GPA with the three subscales. To determine how the students with higher GPAs differed from those with lower GPAs, the investigators divided the students by gender and then, within each gender, formed a group with GPAs above the median (the high-GPA group) and another group with GPAs below the median (the low-GPA group). Thus, they now had four groups. The results (Figure 5-10) indicate that the students with the highest GPAs were high in work and mastery and low in competitiveness. If competitiveness contributes to achievement, as Spence and Helmreich initially thought, why didn't students who were high in work and mastery and high in competitiveness get the highest GPAs? It appears from these results that being high in competitiveness tends to undermine the performance of those who are also high in work and mastery.

Predicting annual income. Annual income is often taken as an indication of achievement in the business world. To explore the possibility that competitiveness is detrimental to performance in the business world (at least as measured by income), a group of businesspeople were given the Achievement scale (Saunders, 1978). Businesspeople tend to score relatively high on competitiveness, which is consistent with the idea that a competitiveness orientation is necessary in order to survive in the business world. If we look at who makes the most money (Figure 5-11), however, we see that competitiveness has a detrimental effect. The people who make the most money are high in work and mastery and low in competitiveness.

Predicting scientific productivity. One way of measuring the worth of a scientific contribution is to count the number of times a scientific article has been cited by other scientists in their publications; this is called a citation index. A study of the citation indices of male academic psychologists suggests that the Achievement scale can also predict scientific attainment (Helmreich, Beane, Lucker, & Spence, 1978; Spence, Beane, Lucker, & Matthews, 1980). The people who make the most

Table 5-2. Items from the first part of the Achievement scale. The items are to be answered using a four-point scale that goes from *Not at all like me* to *Very much like me*. The items that measure competitiveness, mastery, and work are labeled with the letters C, M, and W. Items that are to be reverse-scored are marked with an asterisk (*).

1. I would rather do something at which I feel confident and relaxed than something which is challenging and difficult. (M)*
2. It is important to me to do my work as well as I can even if it isn't popular with co-workers. (W)
3. I enjoy working in situations involving competition with others. (C)
4. When a group I belong to plans an activity, I would rather direct it myself than just help out and have someone else organize it. (M)
5. I would rather learn easy fun games than difficult thought games. (M)*
6. I find satisfaction in working as well as I can. (W)
7. It is important to me to perform better than others on a task. (C)
8. If I am not good at something, I would rather keep struggling to master it than move on to something I may be good at. (M)
9. There is satisfaction in a job well done. (M)
10. I feel that winning is important in both work and games. (C)
11. Once I undertake a task, I persist. (W)
12. I find satisfaction in exceeding my previous performance even if I don't outperform others. (M)
13. It annoys me when other people perform better than I do. (C)
14. I prefer to work in situations that require a high level of skill. (M)
15. I like to work hard. (W)
16. I try harder when I'm in competition with other people. (C)
17. I more often attempt tasks that I am not sure I can do than tasks that I believe I can do. (M)
18. Part of my enjoyment in doing things is improving my past performance. (M)
19. I like to be busy at all times. (W)

Source: J. T. Spence and R. L. Helmreich, "Achievement-Related Motives and Behavior." In J. T. Spence (Ed.), *Achievement and Achievement Motivations*, 1983. W. H. Freeman. Reprinted with permission.

contributions are high in work and mastery and low in competitiveness (Figure 5-12). The consistency between the findings for students, businesspeople, and academics is particularly striking.

As usual, we'll now review the biological, learned, and cognitive components of competition arousal.

The Biological Component

There is considerable evidence that competition creates high autonomic arousal not only in physical sports but in interpersonal activities such as discussions and debates. While there is some question about how much of the arousal in sports is due to physical activity and how much to interpersonal rivalry, there is no doubt that interpersonal rivalry can lead to increases in arousal (Cratty, 1989). Note also that interpersonal conflict has been linked to arousal and stress (Lazarus & Folkman, 1984). According to another study, informing people that their performance outcome is very important increases their arousal levels and impairs their ability to make difficult judgments (Pelham & Neter, 1995). The need to perform at high levels and the need to win appear to be major sources not only of arousal but of stress.

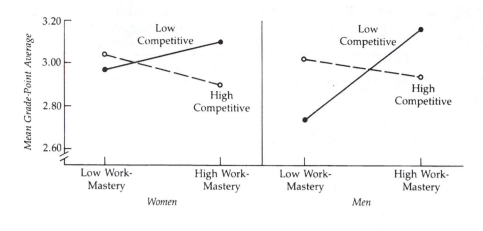

Figure 5-10.   Mean grade-point average in the four achievement-motive groups of male and female undergraduates. (From "Achievement-Related Motives and Behavior," by J. T. Spence & R. L. Helmreich. In J. T. Spence (Ed.), *Achievement and Achievement Motivations.* Copyright © 1983 by W. H. Freeman and Company. Used with permission.)

The Learned Component

In *No Contest: The Case Against Competition*, Alfie Kohn (1986) makes the case that competition is largely learned. As he points out, there are no data to support the idea that competitiveness is part of human nature. Kohn provides numerous examples of cultures where cooperation is the norm and reviews extensive research findings that children will adopt a cooperative model, rather than a competitive model, if appropriate reward contingencies are arranged (Johnson & Johnson, 1985). Finally, he discusses evidence that competing is often not the best way to achieve happiness.

"Winning isn't everything; it is the only thing." That famous line has been attributed to Vince Lombardi, former coach of the Greenbay Packers football team. As it turns out, Vince Lombardi never said that. What he said (at a speech in Milwaukee in 1968) was, "Winning isn't everything. Trying to win is." According to biographer Michael O'Brien (1987), Vince Lombardi later commented, "I wished to hell that I had never said that damned thing. I meant the effort. . . . I meant having a goal. . . . I sure as hell didn't mean for people to crush human values and morality."

Virtually all the evidence suggests that interpersonal rivalry tends to undermine rather than enhance personal performance (Kohn, 1986). For people to perform at their personal best, they cannot afford to divert their attention from the task at hand. Interpersonal rivalry can lead to the reorganization of attention; that is,

people can become more focused on undermining the competition than on performing at their personal best. There is some evidence that, when people have a highly developed skill, competition can motivate them to put forth more effort (Franken & Brown, 1995). Most likely, however, what is important is the arousal and not the interpersonal rivalry. In short, if competition only leads to arousal, it may facilitate performance by narrowing attention; however, if competition diverts or reorganizes attention (as in interpersonal rivalry), it can and often does undermine performance.

The Cognitive Component

Highly competitive people have a strong need to win. In an extension of Spence and Helmreich's work, a colleague and I developed three factors that correlated highly with their factors. We renamed the competitiveness scale the need-to-win scale, since our factor contained mainly items that pertained to winning (Franken & Brown, 1995). Note, however, that not all people who like competitive situations have a high need to win; some highly skilled (mastery-oriented) people appreciate a competitive situation because it motivates them to perform at a high level (Franken & Brown, 1995).

In order to better understand those competitive individuals characterized by a high need to win, we studied a group of university students. They were asked to fill out a variety of personality assessment

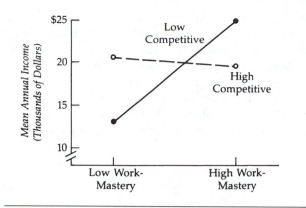

Figure 5-11. Income in four achievement-motive groups of businesspeople, corrected for years of experience. (From "Achievement-Related Motives and Behavior," by J. T. Spence & R. L. Helmreich. In J. T. Spence (Ed.), *Achievement and Achievement Motivations.* Copyright © 1983 by W. H. Freeman. Reprinted with permission of the editor.)

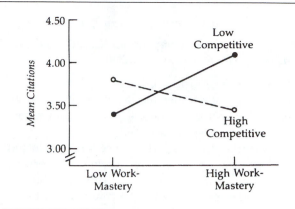

Figure 5-12. Citations to published research in four achievement-motive groups of male academic scientists. (From "Achievement Motivation and Scientific Attainment," by R. L. Helmreich, W. E. Beane, G. W. Lucker and J. T. Spence. *Personality & Social Psychology Bulletin,* 1978, 4(2), 222–226. Copyright © 1978 by Sage Publications, Inc. Reprinted with permission.)

measures, including the need-to-win scale and a couple of questionnaires designed to assess their reactions and attitudes (Franken & Brown, 1996). One questionnaire we administered was the COPE scale, which was designed to identify those personal and behavioral qualities that have been shown to make people resistant to the effects of stress (Carver, Scheier, & Weintraub, 1989). We found that people with a strong need to win have very poor coping strategies relative to people with a low need to win and people with a mastery orientation (Chapter 13). Among other things, people with a high need to win have poor active coping skills, tend to have poor social support systems, tend to face stress with denial and behavioral and mental disengagement, and tend to be low in acceptance, positive reinterpretation, and growth. In short, they tend to possess virtually none of the qualities that help people to resist the effects of stress (Carver, Scheier, & Weintraub, 1989).

The students' responses to a second questionnaire, designed to assess their implicit theories of the world, implicit theories of themselves, and theories of success, suggested that people with a strong need to win tend to lack those positive behavioral attributes that have

been linked to success. For example, people with a strong need to win tended to endorse such statements as: "It is a dog-eat-dog world," "Some people are winners and some are losers," "I take as much as I can get," and "I am inclined to hoard information."

How do they view themselves? Compared to people with a mastery orientation, they are low in hope, optimism, and self-esteem. Further, they tend to see abilities as fixed, whereas people with a mastery orientation generally perceive that they can improve their skills and abilities through effort. People with a need to win also see themselves as "aggressive" and "forceful" (Franken & Brown, 1995). Finally, they see the route to success as modeling others. They endorsed such statements as "Modeling others is a good way to get ahead" and "Appearance plays an important role in success."

The overall picture that emerges is fairly dismal: People with a strong need to win have a fairly negative view of themselves and a negative view of the world. Moreover, they lack the fundamental skills necessary to deal with the daily stresses of life. Since optimism and hope have been linked to health and stress has a negative impact on health, their future does not look good.

Competition Motivation and Performance

Many people dislike competition. Research indicates there are two main reasons (Franken and Prpich, 1996):

1. Competition arouses self-image concerns (ego concerns)—about not meeting the expectations of others, being seen as a loser, receiving negative comments from others, and so on.
2. Competition arouses performance concerns, including self-consciousness, apprehension, and nervousness. To determine if being evaluated might be one of the reasons people dislike competition, Prpich and I constructed 20 questions designed to assess various reasons why people might dislike being evaluated. Factor analysis of those items resulted in a single factor, which we called distraction of attention. The participants in our study indicated that, when they are being evaluated, they become distracted from what they are doing, lose their ability to concentrate, become self-conscious, and think about their faults and weaknesses. At a more global level, these results indicate that people dislike competition because it interferes with their ability to perform at their maximum. We also found that the personality traits of positive self-esteem and hope tend to mitigate these deleterious effects of competition (Franken & Prpich, 1996).

These results suggest that performance decrements are likely to result from self-image concerns and performance concerns. Research on self-focused attention has shown that, when attention is directed at the self—by having the subject work on a task in the presence of mirrors, for example—performance often deteriorates in low self-esteem individuals (Shrauger, 1972). Taken as a whole, the research on competitiveness suggests that having a competitive orientation is counterproductive for high levels of performance. It appears that having a competitive orientation diverts attention away from the task.

Coping with Evaluation Arousal

Research from a variety of sources indicates that, in the long run, the best way to prepare for evaluation is by developing skills and knowledge to their fullest (Dweck & Leggett, 1988). Moreover, when people are prepared, they are less likely to experience anxiety (e.g., Folkman & Lazarus, 1985) and less likely to experience distraction of attention (Franken & Prpich, 1996). Despite being well prepared, some people still experience evaluation anxiety. In that case, they need to learn how to bring down arousal levels through relaxation. In Chapter 9 we will examine more fully when to use problem-focused versus emotional-focused coping.

Summary

Several experimental studies have provided evidence that a competitive orientation (high need to win) interferes with the individual's ability to attain peak levels of performance. While the effect might be due in part to the high levels of arousal that characterize competition, there is reason to believe that learning and cognition play a key role. Evidence from a number of sources indicates that a competitive orientation is largely learned. Further, there is evidence that individuals with a competitive orientation see the world in more negative terms and see themselves as lacking in the ability to effect change. A particularly interesting finding is that people with a competitive orientation have poor skills for coping with stress.

Many people dislike competition, because it arouses performance concerns and self-image concerns. Self-report data suggest that being evaluated not only affects attention (individuals lose their ability to concentrate or become distracted) but causes self-doubt (they begin to think about their strengths and weaknesses). Procedures that create self-focused attention have confirmed that it produces performance decrements. In Practical Application 5-1, I discuss why athletes and others often make use of guided imagery to help them maintain their focus.

State Arousal and Performance: Some Concluding Comments

Arousal and Performance on an Immediate Task

As we have seen, arousal often arises out of a person-situation interaction. When trying to deal with a complex environment, for example, people often experience sensory overload; the result is high arousal. Cognitive dissonance also increases arousal. Finally, when people are being evaluated, there are increases in arousal. In all these cases, it has been shown that increases in arousal lead to a narrowing of attention. If arousal reaches high levels, there is typically a reorganization of attention: Attention shifts to threat cues. In the case of evaluation, for example, there is considerable evidence that attention shifts to self-image concerns; people become worried about being seen in a negative way.

Narrowing of attention can be highly adaptive. In sensory overload, it helps to reduce the amount of incoming information. In cognitive dissonance, it helps the individual to focus on the cognitive inconsistency. In the case of evaluation, it can help the individual to focus on the task.

What is the adaptive function of the reorganization of attention? Generally, the reorganization of attention involves a shift of attention to survival-related cues or to self-image concerns. It appears that both humans and animals have been designed to err on the side of caution when arousal exceeds some optimal level; they

shift their attention at once to survival-related cues. This has important implications for performance. In general, when attention shifts to survival-related cues or to self-image concerns, performance on a specific task will deteriorate.

Arousal and Performance on a Subsequent Task

Research indicates that, once arousal is elevated to meet the demands of a given task, it often persists after the challenge of the task has been met. This persistence has been demonstrated for sensory overload, for example. Sensory overload may even trigger a stress reaction; in order to manage that stress, the individual needs to learn how to relax. The work on REST supports this idea. Also, even after an attitude shift has been induced by cognitive dissonance, arousal persists for a time (Elkin & Leippe, 1986). Finally, there is evidence that arousal persists for a time following evaluation.

If arousal persists, then it can affect performance on a subsequent task. There have been only a few controlled studies to test this hypothesis (e.g., Zillman,

Practical Application 5-1

Using Guided Imagery to Overcome Distraction

Since evaluation arousal often results in such things as distraction, intrusive thinking, and self-image concerns, it has been suggested that one way to keep attention focused on the task is to master what has been called guided imagery. In guided imagery one creates a mental picture or image of how a response should look and then rehearses this over and over until it forms a clear image in the mind, much like a color video. The image is then synchronized with the actual performance of the response so that the image and the response become one. Once this has been well practiced, the person will feel as if they are executing the response even when they are only running the mental image in their mind. As a result of having mental images, people do not depend on having a certain level of arousal in order to execute a response. The beauty of mental images is that they tend to block out all other stimulation, thereby eliminating the distracting effects that often come from such stim-

ulation. Greg Louganis, the 1988 Olympic diving champion, used mental images to win the gold medal in diving. According to his account of the process, he rehearses a given dive in his mind several times before ever climbing to the high board. When it is time to execute the dive, he simply begins to run the mental image and lets it take him through the dive. Jack Nicklaus uses mental imagery in golf. As he gets ready to swing, he begins to visualize the ball flying through the air and landing at a specific location on the fairway or on the green. Like Greg Louganis, he typically rehearses the drive before actually stepping up to the ball to take his swing.

Performers also make extensive use of mental images to achieve the precision of performance that is currently demanded of professionals. The idea of using visual images in other fields has yet to be fully explored or exploited.

Katcher, & Milavsky, 1972), but the idea that arousal transfers from one activity to another is very prevalent in the psychological literature. It is also a common theme in sports psychology. Athletes are often encouraged to prepare for a forthcoming competition by isolating themselves from activities or information that might lead to increases in arousal. Even actors, politicians, and business executives often operate on that principle and will find a quiet place to help prepare them for a forthcoming challenge.

Pooled Arousal

There is considerable evidence for the idea of *pooled arousal*—the idea that arousal from different sources is additive. We know, for example, that trait-anxious people are often more reactive to sensory overload or to evaluation. In fact, one way researchers determine individual differences in trait anxiety is to see how reactive subjects are to situations that produce state arousal. If arousal is pooled, as many theorists believe, all of the arousal systems will affect each other (Neiss, 1988).

One implication of this idea is that, in order to achieve peak performance, people need to learn to identify and then manage each of these different sources of arousal. Let's look at some ways in which this might be done.

Self-Regulation of Arousal and Attention

Some theorists have argued that the best way to attain peak performance is to learn how to manage arousal—in other words, how to relax. Their position is that, by learning to manage arousal, we can learn to manage attention. Other theorists advocate managing attention more directly. They start from the position that high arousal is often necessary to achieve peak performance. Thus, trying to manage—usually, to reduce—arousal may be counterproductive, because we may reduce the arousal necessary to perform a certain task. Most practitioners, including sports psychologists, believe that both positions have merit. The following is a brief summary of the thinking that comes from sports psychology.

In order to perform at a high level, it is important to minimize residual arousal—dispositional trait anxiety, prior sensory overload, arousal due to cognitive dissonance, and so on. However, no attempt should be made to reduce or eliminate the arousal that comes from a person-task interaction. When focused on a task, the brain needs to become aroused in order to maximize its ability to process information.

It appears that intrusive thoughts—about how others may be thinking about them, for instance—and a tendency to focus on threat cues are more or less universal. In our evolutionary history, such thoughts developed for their survival value. However, they can be a source of annoyance when we attempt to achieve peak performance on a certain task. Skilled performers must learn to manage those thoughts. We will return to this subject later. For the moment, note that there is growing evidence that we can come to control such thoughts. If they are not controlled, they tend to become the focus of our attention, and performance deteriorates, often radically.

Main Points

1. Peak performance means doing the very best that we are capable of.
2. Arousal is the activation or energization of the brain (the cortex) and the body.
3. Arousal is produced by two primary mechanisms: the reticular activating system (RAS) and the autonomic nervous system.
4. Epinephrine and norepinephrine, which are secreted by the adrenal glands, provide the long-term backup for the more immediate action of the sympathetic nervous system.
5. Cortical arousal and autonomic arousal appears to be linked but functionally independent.
6. The relationship between arousal and affect appears to be best described as an inverted U-shaped function. Studies of anxiety and sensory deprivation provide evidence for this hypothesis.
7. Apter's theory assumes that, rather than always preferring some moderate level of arousal, people sometimes prefer high arousal and at other times prefer low arousal.
8. According to Apter's theory, people are sometimes motivated by a desire for achievement (by telic goals) and at other times by a desire to experience pleasure in the here and now (by paratelic goals).

9. According to Easterbrook, our attention is broad and inclusive at low levels of arousal and becomes narrow and exclusive at high levels.

10. Under high arousal, our attention is reorganized to focus on survival-related cues.

11. It has been proposed that performance and arousal can be described by an inverted U-shaped function.

12. It has been shown that trait arousal is inherited. Eysenck's theory describes how trait arousal interacts with environmental arousal to produce optimal hedonic states (affect).

13. It has been proposed that humans are prepared to acquire such things as phobias.

14. Whether we experience anxiety has been linked to how we are inclined to appraise situations.

15. Since trait arousal can undermine performance, people need to develop world theories that will enable them to reduce that source of arousal.

16. State arousal comes from environmental stimulation.

17. At least two biological systems have emerged to deal with sensory overload.

18. According to Lacey and Lacey's attention/rejection model of sensory overload, the heart provides feedback that affects activity in the reticular activating system (RAS).

19. GABA, a naturally occurring neurotransmitter, aids in the management of sensory overload.

20. Restricted environmental stimulation technique (REST) is useful in helping people deal with excessive environmental stimulation. It appears to work by helping people to focus their attention on internal rather than external cues.

21. Because humans can anticipate events, they often experience anticipatory arousal.

22. Two ways to manage sensory overload are to decide what is important and to break information down into manageable units.

23. Sensory overload can lead to increases in arousal that lead to narrowing and reorganization of attention.

24. Cognitive dissonance creates both psychological discomfort and arousal.

25. Psychological discomfort—also called intrapersonal tension—motivates individuals to implement strategies that will alleviate that state.

26. Cognitive dissonance is one reason people change their attitudes.

27. Evidence suggests that cognitive dissonance produces narrowing of attention.

28. Tests and competitions are sources of evaluation arousal.

29. Test anxiety not only increases arousal but causes self-preoccupying intrusive thinking.

30. Sarason has indicated that people can control intrusive thinking by focusing on the task.

31. Several laboratory studies have shown that a competitive orientation (high need to win) tends to undermine performance.

32. Evidence from a number of sources indicates that competitive orientation is learned.

33. Studies suggest that people with a strong need to win not only see the world as threatening but see themselves as lacking the skills to successfully cope with the world. Among other things, they have poor skills for coping with stress.

34. Many people dislike competition. It appears that competition raises not only performance concerns but also self-image concerns.

35. Evaluation appears to lead to distraction of attention. People report that evaluation makes them self-conscious, induces them to lose concentration, and leads them to think about their faults and weaknesses.

36. The best way to prepare for evaluation is to develop skills and knowledge to the fullest.

37. There is considerable evidence that, regardless of its source, arousal tends to alter attentional processes.

38. The narrowing of attention is often highly adaptive; in most instances, however, the reorganization of attention is not.

39. Arousal on one task often affects arousal on an immediately succeeding task.

40 There is considerable evidence that arousal from various sources is pooled.

41. There is evidence that arousal and attention can be managed independently of each other.

Chapter Six

Wakefulness, Alertness, Sleep, and Dreams

- Why do we fall asleep?
- Why do we wake up?
- Why can't we fall asleep any time we want to?
- How much sleep do we need?
- How should we deal with jet lag?

- Why can't we learn to do without sleep?
- Why do we dream?
- What is the significance of dreams?
- What causes insomnia?

Why do we feel tired and drowsy at some times but rested and alert at others? We all know from experience that these states are related, at least in part, to how long ago and how well we slept. Typically, as our normal sleep time approaches, we feel somewhat tired. Shortly after waking, we usually feel rested and alert—sometimes with the aid of a cup of coffee—unless, of course, we did not sleep well. We also know from experience, however, that feelings of drowsiness and alertness can be somewhat independent of how long and how well we slept. We sometimes feel drowsy even though we have slept recently, or alert even though it is well past our normal sleep time. We also know that it is difficult to shift our normal sleep pattern. As anyone who has tried to get up earlier than usual can attest, such a shift requires more than just going to bed earlier. Moreover, people who cross several time zones in their travels often have difficulty adjusting to a new clock time. Such experiences seem to suggest that humans have an internal clock that can only be reset with some difficulty. There is also the question of dreams. What is the function of dreams? Are they important for mental health, processing information, or what?

Years of controlled laboratory research have begun to provide answers to these and other fascinating questions about wakefulness and sleep. As we'll see, wakefulness and sleep involve physiological and psychological mechanisms that work together in a complex manner. While the states of wakefulness and sleep are not so distinct as we might think, we cross a very important line when we pass from one to the other; we lose consciousness—awareness of the external environment. Typically, loss of consciousness is fairly abrupt, although at times we seem to enter a detached intermediate state that may reflect what Gerald Vogel (1978) calls *sleep-onset mentation.*

Wakefulness, Sleep, and EEG Activity

Correlates of Sleep and Wakefulness

The best index of wakefulness, drowsiness, and sleep in humans is cortical activity (Webb, 1975). Figure 6-1 shows the types of EEG activity during the various stages of sleep. A typical night of sleep consists of gradual progress from stage 0 (wakefulness) through stages 1, 2, 3, and 4 and then backward through stages 3, 2, and 1 into what is called stage 1-REM. This cycle, which takes about 90–120 minutes, then repeats itself. In the course of 7–8 hours of sleep, we go through this cycle about five times. Individuals tend to show minor variations from this pattern. Figure 6-2 shows the EEG chart of a typical individual over the course of a night. Note that, while an individual may bypass certain stages from time to time, a rhythm (pattern) can nevertheless clearly be observed.

REM is an acronym for rapid eye movement. In studying electrical recordings of eye movements, Aserinsky and Kleitman (1953) found that rapid eye movements occurred in conjunction with low-voltage mixed brain-wave frequencies, and that when people were awakened on such occasions they regularly reported vivid dreams. Four years later, Dement (1972) found that dreams and REM were, indeed, related. Since then it has been common to refer to this pattern as REM sleep and to all other patterns as NREM (non-REM) sleep. Periods of REM sleep are identified in Figure 6-2. Although it was initially thought that REM sleep was synonymous with dreaming, it has since been shown that humans dream during other stages of sleep as well and sometimes fail to experience dream content during REM.

Periods of REM typically occur in conjunction with stage 1 sleep. REM bursts, as they are sometimes called, occur about 90 minutes after we go to sleep and then recur every 90 minutes, on average (the time varies between 70 and 110 minutes). Interestingly, REM sleep tends to lengthen as the night progresses until it lasts as much as an hour at a time. As a result, an adult who sleeps 7.5 hours generally experiences 1.5–2 hours of REM sleep (Dement, 1972). It has been found that, during REM, blood flow goes up by 40%; metabolism increases; spontaneous firing of nerve cells increases beyond the waking level; and the kidneys produce less urine, but it is higher in concentration.

Paralysis during REM

We know that the brain and the entire central nervous system tend to become very active during REM, so why don't people walk, talk, and engage in other

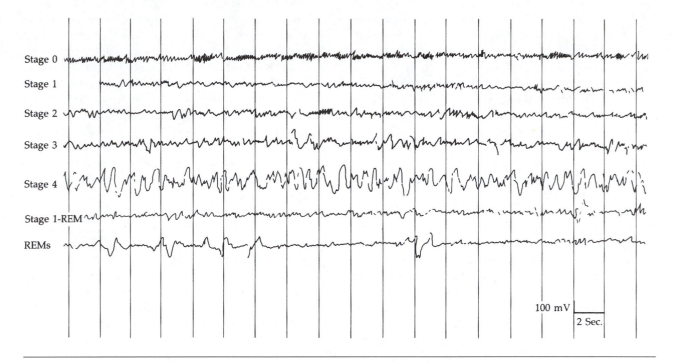

Figure 6-1.   EEG tracings of the sleep stages. State 0 is wakefulness. (From *Sleep: The Gentle Tyrant,* by W. B. Webb. Copyright © 1975 by Prentice-Hall, Inc. Reprinted by permission of the author and the University of Florida Sleep Laboratories.)

motor responses when they begin to dream? The answer is very simple. In each period of REM sleep, the action of the motor neurons of the spinal cord that cause skeletal muscles to contract is inhibited. As a result, the muscles are atonic (without tone); they are paralyzed. The mechanisms that control this inhibition and the release from it are located in the reticular formation (Morrison, 1983). One reason for research interest in these mechanisms is that some people experience a condition called narcolepsy, which causes them suddenly and unexpectedly to pass from wakefulness to REM sleep without losing consciousness. As a result, they experience paralysis but can do nothing to control it. If they are sitting, they may find they can do nothing to stop themselves from falling. Consequently, narcolepsy may be not only stressful but dangerous.

Sleep and Attention

It has been suggested that sleep can be considered a state of extremely low attention (Glaubman et al.,

1979). When we are asleep, our threshold for detecting incoming stimulation is very high and, as a result, information input is low. It has also been suggested that some type of filter allows only intense or specific forms of stimulation (such as a baby's cry) to reach the brain. This filter may be very important for maintaining the sleep state; without it, we might tend to awaken periodically.

Since learning new material involves the ability to process information, it is not surprising that people show little if any new learning when they are asleep (Aarons, 1976). However, during sleep, people can engage in important cognitive activities that involve information processed when they were awake, as we'll see later in the chapter.

Jouvet's Model of Sleep

Why do EEG patterns fluctuate during sleep? Probably the most widely held view is that EEG activity during sleep is governed by the reticular activating system

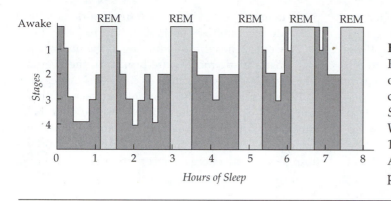

Figure 6-2.   A plot showing the pattern of REM sleep, NREM sleep, and the four stages of NREM sleep for an individual over the course of one entire night of sleep. (From *Some Must Watch While Others Must Sleep*, by William C. Dement. Copyright © 1972, 1974, 1976 by William C. Dement and the Stanford Alumni Association. Reprinted with permission.)

(RAS). Michel Jouvet (1967) has shown that changes in EEG activity during sleep are due to the alternating activity of two sites in the RAS. The raphe nuclei, which secrete serotonin when active, have been shown to increase NREM sleep in cats. Jouvet has suggested that the onset of sleep is due to the increased activity of the raphe nuclei. The locus coeruleus, which secretes norepinephrine when active, has been shown to increase REM sleep. Since increased EEG activity during REM sleep is typically associated with dreaming in humans, Jouvet has suggested that the onset of dreams is due to increased activity of the locus coeruleus. Because the activity of these two sites tends to alternate, Jouvet's model can readily account for the rhythmic nature of sleep—its fluctuation between deep and light sleep. Exactly why these two sites alternate in activity is not clear. One good possibility is that, after a time, activity in one center stimulates activity in the other center (J. M. Siegel, 1979). Morgane and Stern (1975) agree that serotonin and norepinephrine play a role in the generation and maintenance of sleep. They suggest, however, that these biogenic amines only trigger the processes that control the onset of waking or the onset of sleeping. That is, other chemical circuits triggered by the amines may actually induce sleep or waking.

Note that the biogenic amines mediate and/or regulate biological activity; an amine is simply a compound with hydrogenated nitrogen as its chemical signature. Mood, level of arousal, and the rate of metabolism are governed, at least in part, by biogenic amines. Many substances interact with biogenic amines and, in so doing, disrupt or sometimes enhance their normal regulatory action. The drug LSD (lysergic acid diethylamide), for example, can block serotonin

and cause hallucinations, whereas amphetamines can increase the sympathetic arousal normally caused by the presence of norepinephrine. We will talk more about how drugs interact with biogenic amines in Chapter 7.

Jouvet's model can account for fluctuations in EEG activity at night (and possibly during the day). It is not altogether clear, however, why a given center should become active at a particular time. Specifically, why do people wake up at a given hour, and why is it difficult to shift periods of wakefulness and sleep?

Why We Fall Asleep and Why We Wake Up

At least three sets of factors determine when we fall asleep and when we wake up. As we'll see, each set of factors interacts with the others.

Circadian Rhythm

One of the prime factors that determines when we fall asleep is our circadian rhythm. The word *circadian* comes from the Latin *circa diem*, "about a day." People who have been left to establish their own routines in caves, bunkers, or specially designed laboratories tend to adopt a 25-hour cycle, as opposed to the 24-hour circadian rhythm (Aschoff, 1965). It appears that the tendency to follow a 24-hour cycle is due largely to the synchronizing effects of events in our environment. Because we generally have regular times for eating, watching TV, going to bed, and so on, we tend to constantly reset our biological clocks so that they are attuned to the 24-hour day. When we free ourselves from the normal synchronizing effects of the environment—for instance, on a weekend or vacation or any time that we stay up late, sleep in, and eat when we like—we often experience great difficulty getting back into our normal routine. The Monday-morning blues may be a direct result of letting ourselves shift to our natural 25-hour biological rhythm. If we follow our internal biological clock on the weekends, by going to bed one hour later each night, we might find that, when Monday morning comes around, we are sleep-deprived when the alarm wakes us, and we don't become alert until two hours later than normal. Webb and Agnew (1975a) have argued that our society may produce a state of chronic sleep deprivation because we sleep according to clock time rather than our need for sleep. They found that subjects who were allowed to awaken spontaneously after three nights of controlled sleep (11 P.M. to 7 A.M.) slept an additional 126 minutes, on the average.

What produces this rhythm? There is evidence that not only the time we fall asleep but the soundness of our sleep and the length of time we sleep are linked to the output of epinephrine (adrenaline) by the adrenal glands. When the epinephrine level declines, we tend to fall asleep; when it rises, we tend to wake up (Nishihara, Mori, Endo, Ohta, & Kenshiro, 1985). Going back one step further, researchers have suggested that the rhythm of the adrenal glands is controlled by the hypothalamus. Ultimately, in other words, the circadian rhythm is due to some rhythmical activity of the hypothalamus.

Note that there is a correlation between body temperature and sleep. Our temperature tends to fluctuate 1–2° in the course of a day. When we fall asleep, our temperature drops rather suddenly. This lowering of body temperature may help not only to induce sleep but also to maintain it. If we try to stay up late to study or work on a project, we will often experience unexpected feelings of coldness. During the night, our temperature tends to rise gradually. It has been suggested that the rise in temperature (which is linked to our daily arousal rhythm) may signal us to wake up (Gillberg & Åkerstedt, 1982). The reason for our inability to maintain sleep during the day may simply be that our underlying arousal level (presumably governed by the adrenal glands) maintains our temperature at a level inconsistent with sleep. Several studies have confirmed a positive relation not only between temperature and wakefulness but between temperature and

performance on a vigilance (attention-demanding) task (Moses, Lubin, Naitoh, & Johnson, 1978; Taub, 1977). Consistent with this finding is the observation that most athletic records are broken in the evening, when our body temperature is highest. Parmeggiani (1977) has suggested that the link between temperature and sleep is governed directly by the hypothalamus. His reasoning is based largely on evidence that the hypothalamus governs the link between temperature, sleep, and energy conservation in hibernating animals.

Environmental Arousal

When we are under stress, our body moves into a state of high arousal. Under these conditions, we often find that we cannot go to sleep or that we have trouble staying asleep. Drugs that increase arousal, such as stimulants, also disturb sleep onset and interfere with the ability to stay asleep. An exciting event often produces increases in arousal and also tends to interfere with sleep onset and good sleep. Since environmental arousal is situational, the sleep disturbance usually disappears when the stimulating event is over.

Sleep Deprivation

One of the important factors that determines if and when we go to sleep is the length of time that has passed since we last slept. When people are deprived of a night's sleep, they tend to go to sleep sooner and to stay asleep longer, regardless of environmentally induced arousal. We'll return to this topic shortly.

Individual Differences in Sleep Cycles

There is evidence that personality variables may predict the rhythm of daily patterns. Extraversion and introversion measures, for example, may predict fluctuations not only in body temperature but in performance on vigilance tasks (Taub, Hawkins, & Van de Castle, 1978). Extraversion is associated with higher body temperature and better performance in the evening, and introversion with higher body temperature and better performance in the morning. It has been suggested that these two personality types grow out of biological differences. In other words, the underlying biology is ultimately responsible for this effect.

Other Sleep Rhythms

The Half-Day Rhythm

Studies have shown that when subjects are first deprived of sleep and then allowed to sleep for an extended period of time, there is a significant return of slow-wave sleep (SWS) after 12.5 hours of sleep (Gagnon, De Koninck, & Broughton, 1985). These findings are consistent with the observation that people tend to become not only less alert but sleepy around noon (Richardson, Carskadon, Orav, & Dement, 1982). In many cultures, it is the norm to take an afternoon siesta. The phenomenon of afternoon napping, according to Pierre Gagnon and his colleagues, "may reflect a biological propensity to re-enter the psychological state that accompanies SWS" (Gagnon, De Koninck, & Broughton, 1985, p. 127). SWS refers to stage 3 and 4 sleep.

The Basic Rest/Activity Cycle

There is a basic rest/activity cycle (BRAC) that lasts about 90–120 minutes. This cycle has been found in such waking activities as performance on various sensory tasks, vigilance tasks, and fantasy tasks. The ability to fall asleep during the day is determined by this cycle. That is, it is easier to fall asleep when we are in the rest part of the cycle.

The regularity of REM sleep every 90 minutes raises the interesting possibility that REM is somehow controlled by BRAC. It has been shown, for example, that people tend to dream at the same time every night (McPartland & Kupfer, 1978). Some researchers have supplied evidence that seems to contradict this conclusion. They have shown, for example, that REM tends to occur 90 minutes after sleep onset (McPartland & Kupfer, 1978; Moses, Naitoh, & Johnson, 1978). If REM is controlled by sleep onset, then it cannot be controlled by some natural BRAC rhythm that is independent of sleep onset. This apparent inconsistency disappears when we recognize that people often don't go to sleep until they are in a certain phase of their BRAC. In other words, not only our overall circadian rhythm but our BRAC rhythm affects our inclination to go to sleep.

The Left Brain/Right Brain Cycle

The brain has two hemispheres, each of which performs slightly different functions. The right hemisphere tends to be involved in fantasy and intuitive thought, while the left hemisphere tends to be involved in verbal and intellectual thought. What is fascinating is that each hemisphere has a cycle lasting 90–100 minutes that is 180° out of phase with the other hemisphere. Thus, we tend to swing back and forth between fantasy/intuitive thought and verbal/intellectual thought (Klein & Armitage, 1979). REM dreams tend to be more fantasy/intuitive in character, whereas NREM dreams tend to be more verbal and intellectual. It may well be that, before I can have REM dreams or NREM dreams, I need to be in the right mental state; that state is determined by my BRAC.

How Much Sleep Do We Need?

The fact that some people seem to need very little sleep has intrigued both the layperson who would like to get along on less sleep and the scientist who is interested in the function of sleep. In a study of long and short sleepers, it was observed that short sleepers tended, on the whole, to deny personal or interpersonal problems, to have a greater need to be accepted, and to be more socially skilled and more socially dominant. Long sleepers tended to be more shy, more depressed or anxious, and more inhibited sexually and in expressing aggression (Hartmann, Baekeland, & Zwilling, 1972). In a similar study, Webb and Friel (1971) found no differences. These results may be due to differences in sampling techniques. A more recent approach to the question of whether length of sleep is related to personality functioning has been to expose people to gradual sleep reduction to see what, if any, effects are observed.

It has been found that voluntary sleep reduction to 4.5–5.5 hours a night does not produce significant personality changes or reduce performance on certain types of tasks, but it tends to produce persistent feelings of fatigue (Friedmann et al., 1977). As we'll discuss shortly, sleep reduction produces a number of performance deficits, especially when the task is complex or demands sustained attention. It appears, however, that people can rise to the challenge for short periods of time on tasks that are more familiar or practiced.

As sleep time is reduced, the pattern of sleep undergoes several changes. Although there is no reduction in the amount of stage 3 and stage 4 sleep

(Figure 6-1), there is a significant reduction in REM and stage 2 sleep (Mullaney, Johnson, Naitoh, Friedmann, & Globus, 1977; Webb & Agnew, 1975a). When the regimen of partial sleep deprivation is maintained, REM sleep begins to occur earlier in the sleep period, thereby attenuating the REM deficit. However, it rarely replaces stage 4 in order of appearance, and it never achieves normal levels.

This tendency to make up for certain types of sleep when sleep time is curtailed is probably one of the important reasons that lack of sleep does not have a greater impact on our normal functioning. As we shall discuss in more detail shortly, stage 4 sleep and REM sleep seem to help maintain physiological and psychological integrity. Thus, it makes sense that such sleep would be prioritized. As a result, humans are able to function—albeit less than optimally—when sleep is shortened. Since shortened sleep regimens tend to lead to persistent fatigue, it appears that some mechanism tells us to return to more normal sleep patterns.

Interestingly, none of the subjects who voluntarily reduced their total sleep time for experimental purposes ever went below 4.5 hours of sleep per night; this suggests that there may be biological limits to sleep reduction (Mullaney et al., 1977).

Altering Sleep/Wakefulness Cycles

Accepting that adults need about 7–8 hours of sleep in each 24-hour period, we might wonder whether we can redistribute our sleeping time across the day. Studies indicate that adjustment to new sleep schedules is possible but difficult. Since the best predictor of sleep onset is elapsed time since last sleep, and since the best predictor of sleep termination is how long we have slept, it is not surprising that people in new schedules tend to lose sleep because they have difficulty getting to sleep or they wake up too soon. Finally, circadian rhythms make it difficult to adapt to schedules that do not follow the approximately 24- to 25-hour cycle (Webb & Agnew, 1975b).

The Effects of Sleep Reduction

Feelings of Sleepiness and Fatigue

Lack of sleep typically produces feelings of sleepiness and fatigue. The term *sleepiness* refers to a craving or desire for sleep, while *fatigue* refers to a general lack of motivation or energy. Sleepiness is generally viewed as the converse of alertness (Dement & Carskadon, 1982). The widespread belief that sleepiness will impair per-

Practical Application 6-1

Adjusting to Jet Lag

Let's say you left New York on a plane bound for Paris at 6 P.M. Eastern Standard Time. Flight time is about 8 hours. Therefore, when you arrive in Paris it's 10 A.M. Paris time, but your circadian clock is telling you it's 2 A.M. (two hours past your bedtime). What should you do—take a nap or stay up till midnight Paris time? The answer depends on whether you want to see Paris nightlife or be a regular tourist. If you go to your hotel and sleep, you're likely to sleep for 7–8 hours, so you'll wake up at 6 P.M. That will give you plenty of time to have a leisurely dinner, close down the last nightclub, and sip a brandy with or after breakfast, before retiring for 8 hours. But, if you want to be a regular tourist, then you should stay up until midnight. By midnight you will be experiencing the effects of sleep deprivation and you should have little or no difficulty getting to sleep and sleeping most of the night, even though you are not synchronized with your circadian rhythm. A night's sleep will help to reset your circadian rhythm. Remember that one of the factors that determines when you will next be sleepy is the time elapsed since you last slept. Even a short nap is not a good idea, because it will reduce some of the effects normally associated with sleep deprivation, and as a result you will not be able to sleep as long when you do go to sleep.

formance has not been convincingly documented in the laboratory by means of psychomotor and intellectual tests (Dement & Carskadon, 1982). There is also little evidence that sleepiness resulting from a reduced sleep regimen produces any physiological abnormalities (Hartse, Roth, & Zorick, 1982). Most people subjected to several days of sleep reduction show full recovery after a single night of sleep (Carskadon & Dement, 1981). It appears that REM sleep is more important than NREM as far as reversing sleepiness is concerned (Carskadon & Dement, 1977).

Deterioration in Performance

Despite the fact that lack of sleep does not seem to do any harm, people report difficulty in performing when they feel sleepy. Field studies have shown that people who work at night not only complain of sleepiness but perform less well than they do during the day (Åkerstedt, Torsvall, & Gillberg, 1982). Interestingly, older subjects seem more affected by sleep loss than are younger ones (Webb & Levy, 1982).

Here are some of the basic changes that occur as a result of sleep loss (Dinges, 1989; Dinges & Kribbs, 1991).

1. **Lapsing.** Lapsing refers to the unevenness in performance with sleep deprivation. Whereas people typically respond immediately to a signal or a crisis, sleep-deprived people may respond quite slowly at times, but normally at other times. As people become more sleep-deprived, lapsing becomes more of a problem, and performance gradually deteriorates. In situations where people need to react quickly, lapsing is a major safety concern (Dinges & Kribbs, 1991).

2. **Cognitive slowing.** When people are sleep deprived, there is a reduction in the number (speed) of their cognitive responses in a self-paced task. This cognitive slowing, originally attributed to lapses, is now thought to be due to *microsleeps*—very short sleep episodes interjected into an otherwise wakeful state. Microsleeps appear to increase in number as sleep deprivation increases. As a result, people tend to show greater cognitive slowing as sleep deprivation increases (Dinges & Kribbs, 1991).

3. **Memory problems.** Sleeplessness is often accompanied by reduction in immediate recall, which may be due to a combination of factors, including lapses and

failure to encode information properly. In many studies, memory loss is not significant until wakefulness has exceeded 30 hours (Dinges & Kribbs, 1991).

4. **Vigilance decrements and habituation.** As a general rule, the impact of sleep deprivation on performance will increase with increase in task duration. In other words, performance decrements due to sleep loss may not be apparent at the start of the work day, but will surface as the shift proceeds (Dinges & Kribbs, 1991). This has important implications for people who must monitor devices and make periodic adjustments at nuclear reactors and gas plants, for instance.

5. **Optimum response shifts.** In many situations, there is a limited time period in which people must respond with sustained attention to prevent some adverse consequence. It was thought for some time that sleep-deprived people could rise to these occasions, but more recent data suggest they may not (Dinges & Kribbs, 1991). This has important implications for pilots, doctors, and others who experience sleep loss on the job.

The extent to which any of these changes will be observed depends to some degree on feedback and the complexity of the task. There is evidence that feedback may improve performance, but it is unlikely to totally override the effects of sleep loss. Feedback that reports on whether the subject is succeeding or failing is better than feedback that merely provides information about speed and accuracy (Dinges & Kribbs, 1991).

There is considerable data that performance on complex tasks is most affected by sleep loss; however, performance on simple tasks that involve sustained attention also seems to deteriorate.

Sleep Loss and the Circadian Rhythm

To complicate matters, sleep loss interacts with circadian rhythm. Night shift workers are often chronically sleep-deprived and, since many of them have not completely adjusted their circadian rhythms to coincide with their new schedule, they are very likely to show performance decrements. These decrements tend to arise from about 3 A.M. to 5 A.M.

As already noted, field studies confirm impairments in night workers' performance (Åkerstedt, Torsvall, & Gillberg, 1982). The reason why researchers have had difficulty in linking sleepiness to poor performance in the laboratory is probably that humans are capable of rising to the occasion for short periods. The implication is that, while we may perform less well following sleep deprivation, probably because of lack of motivation, we can nevertheless perform well if we have to.

The Effects of Fragmented Sleep

Recently it was shown that, when people were repeatedly awakened in the course of a night's sleep (after every minute of sleep), the severe reduction in SWS (stages 3 and 4) and REM led to a decline in performance and indexes of sleepiness equivalent to those found after a loss of 40–64 hours of sleep, even though the subjects had been sleeping a great deal of the time (Bonnet, 1985). Later, we'll see why the loss of SWS and REM is so devastating. As already noted, when people

go on reduced sleep regimens, they typically compensate for the loss of sleep by increasing REM and SWS at the expense of other states of sleep.

Sleep Deprivation and Mood

Roth and his colleagues (Roth, Kramer, & Lutz, 1976) found that sleep deprivation adversely affects certain moods (friendliness and aggression) but not others. In a carefully controlled study, Cohen (1979) tried to determine whether REM deprivation was particularly important in the control of mood. All he could find was that, when people are awakened during either REM or NREM, they experience increases in aggression and decreases in friendliness.

Studies conducted in clinical laboratories suggest that mild to moderate antidepressant effects can follow

Practical Application 6-2

Shift Work, Sleepiness, and Catnaps

Shift work is a major problem in our society. The problem is worst for people who work night shifts (somewhere from 11 P.M. to 7 A.M.). Catastrophes such as those at Three Mile Island and Chernobyl took place in the early hours of the morning. Later afternoon shifts (4 P.M. to 12 P.M.) are also a problem, but to a lesser degree.

There are two basic problems. First, people who work night shifts and later afternoon shifts are often out of phase with their normal circadian rhythms. As a result, even though they are awake, they are not alert. As we know, temperature and alertness are correlated. People who work night shifts often show a drop in temperature in the early hours of the morning (3 A.M. to 5 A.M.), a time when many accidents occur (Dinges, 1984).

People often learn to shift their circadian rhythms, but that can take a considerable time. It's still not clear why some people can shift to a new circadian rhythm relatively quickly, but others cannot. When people cannot adjust, they experience feelings of sleepiness. This leads us to the second problem, which is sleep deprivation. There is considerable evidence that people who work night shifts are also experiencing chronic sleep loss, which also leads to

feelings of sleepiness. Many find it difficult to sleep during the day and, as a result, they are chronically sleep-deprived.

Pilots may find themselves in a particularly difficult situation, because they often must make a return after as little as 8–12 hours of rest. Many find they cannot sleep. As a result, when they make their return flight, they are experiencing sleep loss.

What Is the Best Way to Deal with Shift Work?

People who work later afternoon and night shifts often perform poorly and are accident-prone. This is particularly worrying in such occupations as pilot, train engineer, doctor, or nuclear plant operator, because it raises questions of public safety. Accordingly, much research has addressed the best ways for people to deal with shift work or with jobs that require them to perform at times when they are not normally at their peak.

The question is how best to help people who work later afternoon and night shifts to get the amount of sleep they need. One of the reasons these people are chronically sleep-deprived is that they attempt to maintain their social relations and family obligations, although they are out just one night of sleep deprivation in 30–60% of endogenously depressed individuals—that is, individuals whose depression cannot be linked to a specific life event (Gerner, Post, Gillin, & Bunney, 1979). It has been suggested that the neurophysiological effects of sleep deprivation are similar to those produced by antidepressant medication (Buchsbaum, Gerner, & Post, 1981).

Summary

EEG activity has a rhythmic pattern during sleep; Jouvet has suggested that these rhythms are controlled by the RAS. When we fall asleep and when we wake up are influenced by various biological rhythms (the circadian rhythm, the 12.5-hour cycle, and the BRAC). Our sleepiness also depends on the time elapsed since we last slept and our level of arousal. Rhythmic increases in temperature and arousal seem to be the main reason why we wake up.

Reduced sleep produces feelings of sleepiness and fatigue and impairs performance on tasks that require sustained interest and attention. While people can learn to get along with as little as 4.5–5 hours of sleep per day, their bodies need to maintain a certain minimal level of SWS and REM.

This research emphasizes what sleep consultants have said for some time: In order to go to sleep, maintain sleep, and have quality sleep, it is important to have a routine. Routines not only synchronize our biological rhythms with our daily performance demands of sync with other people. Interestingly, people who work late afternoon shifts and night shifts are often not aware that they are sleep-deprived (Dinges, 1989). Thus, it is important to educate people about their sleep needs and help them plan a sleep schedule that will enable them to get enough sleep as well as to satisfy their other needs. Even when people know they should get more sleep, they sometimes find it difficult to do so, because their circadian rhythms tell them it is time to be awake.

How can people adjust their circadian rhythms to the demands of the task? That topic has been addressed by researchers in chronobiology, which is the scientific study of rhythms of life that are an outgrowth of biology. There are several important considerations.

First, because it takes time to adjust circadian rhythms, a general rule of thumb is that people should not be required to change their shifts too often. As they settle into a shift, they can synchronize their biological rhythms with the demands of the task (Coleman, 1986). How long this takes varies greatly from individual to individual. Sleep deprivation is a good way to speed up this process (as we saw in discussing jet lag). Coleman (1986) has suggested that, under certain conditions, sleep deprivation combined with sleeping pills might be justified as a means of speeding up the adjustment time.

Second, when workers' shifts are changed, they should be moved from morning to afternoon to night and not in the reverse direction. Studies have found that people find it much easier to move in this direction (Coleman, 1986), because there is a natural tendency for the circadian rhythm to drift to a later time. That is, we are inclined to go to bed later and get up earlier because our circadian rhythm is around 25 hours.

Third, it might be advisable for shift workers to take catnaps.

Making Up for Loss of Sleep with Catnaps

There is a great deal of evidence that people should make use of catnaps to make up for loss of sleep. Most people can go without one night of sleep without much loss in performance, but attempts to go beyond that typically result in significant performance drops. Research has shown that, young or old, people can achieve complete or virtually complete recovery after one full night of sleep (Bonnet & Rosa, 1987). A catnap of any length is highly effective in helping to restore full functioning after a shortened sleep time. If we know ahead of time that we will need to forego

(continued on next page)

but allow us to have reasonably continuous sleep. Even when sleep must be reduced, a routine enables the body to schedule SWS and REM soon after we fall asleep, thereby ensuring that we get enough of them.

One very good way to make up for lost sleep is with catnaps. People who do not get adequate sleep because of their occupations or because of situational demands—such as the need to complete an important task—often use catnaps to compensate for lost sleep.

The Psychological Functions of Sleep

Experimental Procedures for Determining the Function of Sleep

Both animals and humans have been studied to determine the function of sleep. To date, the majority of studies have focused on REM sleep deprivation; how-ever, there is a growing interest in other types of sleep deprivation (Webb, 1979). Let's begin by considering REM sleep deprivation.

REM Deprivation in Animals

All mammalian species that have been studied have REM sleep. In addition, a sizable percentage of avian predators (such as hawks and eagles) have REM. Only a negligible amount of REM occurs in other birds, and reptilian species show no REM (Ellman & Weinstein, 1991).

The main technique for REM sleep deprivation of small mammals, such as rats, is to place them on a small elevated platform above a tank of water. The rat will become paralyzed when it goes into REM sleep and will fall off the platform into the water. The experience of falling into the water and climbing back onto the platform appears to provide powerful motivation for rats to learn to avoid REM sleep. Not surprisingly, there has been some controversy about whether this technique produces stress in addition to depriving rats of REM.

Practical Application 6-2 (continued)

sleep for a long period—for instance, for an entire night—we can prepare ourselves for it with a catnap (the longer the better, but any length will help) (Dinges, as reported in Saltus, 1990).

People who need to complete a lot of work over a short period might consider changing their sleep reg-imen so that they break up what sleep they can get into short naps. During his creative period, Leonardo da Vinci would reduce his sleep regimen to six cat-naps of 15 minutes each. Many famous people, in-cluding Winston Churchill, Napoleon, and Thomas Edison, are reported to have survived on catnaps. Laboratory studies have shown that it is indeed pos-sible for people to survive for up to two weeks on such a schedule. In the animal world, catnapping is widespread and may even be more normal than the sleep/wakefulness cycle that modern humans at-tempt to maintain. It has been suggested that the in-dustrial revolution forced us into a sleep cycle that is not consistent with our history as humans. In many cultures, the afternoon siesta is common; it allows people to get up early, on the one hand, and party late, on the other.

People who cannot get adequate sleep because of jet lag (for instance, pilots), interrupted sleep (for in-stance, combat soldiers or doctors), or the need to be on alert (for instance, combat pilots) might learn to use catnaps as a means of making up for the losses they experience because of their jobs. It has been shown that older people who find it difficult to sleep for 8 hours straight can benefit greatly from catnaps. Since many researchers believe that most people in North America—if not the industrialized world—do not get enough sleep, all of us should consider cat-naps as a way of getting more sleep. There is consid-erable evidence that people who have good sleep regimens are not only healthier but live longer (Hoth et al., 1989).

While there are strong arguments for catnaps, they can also contribute to sleep disturbances such as in-somnia if they begin to replace normal sleep. I dis-cuss this problem in Practical Application 6-4.

REM Deprivation in Humans

Researchers can selectively deprive subjects of a particular type of sleep—say, REM—by continuously monitoring their EEG and waking them whenever that sleep pattern appears. In that way, it is possible to study the effects of REM or other types of sleep deprivation on various activities. In these studies, one group of subjects is typically awakened after they enter REM, while a control group of subjects is awakened during NREM. Using such a procedure, we can be assured that the effects are not simply due to being awakened.

REM Deprivation and Motivation

Research with animals has shown that the thresholds for sexual aggressive behaviors and eating are lowered after REM deprivation. In other words, these behaviors are easier to arouse with appropriate stimuli. Dement (1969) has suggested that REM sleep provides a type of periodic drive discharge. If we are REM-deprived, there will be less discharge and, therefore, greater motivation, which implies lower thresholds for eating and aggression, for instance. Ellman and Steiner (1969a,b) have put forth a similar hypothesis; they postulate that, during REM sleep, some elements of the network for positive reinforcement (the reward pathways in the brain) are activated. This activation, they suggest, primes the brain for motivated behaviors. Obviously, if the brain is ready for motivated behaviors, the threshold for motivated behaviors will be lowered.

Ellman's Motivation Theory of REM

The essence of Ellman's theory is that, during both sleep and wakefulness, the positive reward system—also called the intracranial self-stimulation (ICSS) system—needs to be periodically fired. (We discussed this system in Chapter 2.) The ICSS system is assumed to maintain motivation when we are not involved in behaviors such as eating, drinking, sex, and aggression and is turned off when we are involved in these behaviors. During sleep, according to the theory, the REM state is responsible for periodically firing the ICSS system.

How can this be related to the content of REM dreams? Implicit in Ellman's theory is the idea that the environment is a rich source of stimulation that will periodically fire the ICSS (although it may also be fired in part by the BRAC or another rhythm). In sleep, the body needs to generate similar stimulation that will fire the ICSS. If the ICSS is to be activated, this stimulation needs to be as vivid and compelling as the environment. In order to produce such vivid and compelling stimulation, Ellman further argues, we need to momentarily set aside self-reflection. The net result is that REM dreams have a vivid and compelling quality, like that of the external environment, but may also have some strange organizational characteristics (bizarre qualities) when we reflect on them in a waking state (Ellman & Weinstein, 1991).

One fascinating feature of Ellman's theory is that it can explain why infants spend so much time in REM. In the absence of external stimulation, they need to generate stimulation that will keep the ICSS in a state of motivated readiness. If organisms were not in a state of readiness, their threshold for motivated behavior would increase, a highly nonadaptive state much like that observed in depressive individuals. Ellman and Weinstein (1991) go so far as to argue that the lack of REM in infancy may slow down the maturational process. In other words, REM in infancy is critical to maturation.

The REM Rebound Effect

Early studies of REM deprivation showed that people deprived of REM sleep for one or more nights show an *REM rebound*; that is, if allowed to sleep without interruption for a whole night, they spend more time in REM sleep than usual. This observation led researchers to conclude that REM must indeed be important for normal functioning. Consistent findings were obtained in a study of sleep patterns in subjects who were permitted to sleep for 30-minute periods separated by 60 minutes of forced wakefulness (Carskadon & Dement, 1977). Sleep-onset REM periods occurred frequently during the 30 minutes of sleep, although REM sleep normally begins 90 minutes after sleep onset. This indicates that the lack of REM for any significant period will trigger some mechanism to override the normal sleep schedule in order to insure that the body gets adequate REM sleep.

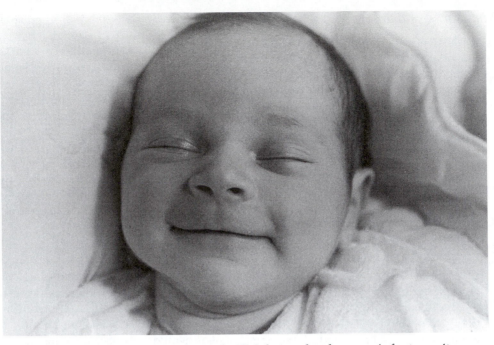

This infant seems to be having a good REM dream, but because infants can't verbalize their mental processes, we cannot assess the content of their REM dreams.

REM Sleep Deprivation and Psychological Health

Interest in REM sleep deprivation grew out of work by Dement (1960). He noted that people who were awakened from REM sleep reported vivid dream content and that interruptions of REM sleep (REM deprivation) produced anxiety, irritability, and difficulty in concentrating. People had for some time been interested in the function or purpose of dreams, and Dement's findings suggested that the REM deprivation technique might uncover their function. As we have noted, later research showed that dreams also occur in other stages of sleep (Foulkes, 1962; Foulkes & Vogel, 1965), but the impetus for REM deprivation studies had been well established by that time.

Following Dement's initial reports, researchers freely speculated on the relation between the absence of REM sleep and psychological health. It was suggested that absence of REM sleep could produce such disturbances as schizophrenia and depression (Fisher & Dement, 1962; Snyder, Scott, Karacan, & Anderson, 1968). These speculations, it turns out, were not well founded. Vogel (1975) has deprived people of REM sleep for up to three weeks without serious side effects. In fact, he has shown that REM deprivation can be beneficial in depressives. He has offered a motivational theory of REM deprivation that not only can account for this effect but has some important implications for understanding the function of REM sleep.

Vogel's Motivation Theory of REM

Vogel (1979) has suggested that neural activity is heightened during REM sleep and prevented or inhibited by REM deprivation. As a result, REM deprivation leads to greater neural activity or excitability during the waking state. (Neural excitability is a hypothetical state of neural readiness necessary for efficient and effective response to events in the environment. It is generally assumed to be due to some chemical process that readies the cells to fire.) Because there is evidence that greater neural excitability increases such drive-motivated behaviors as sex, aggression, pleasure seeking, food seeking, and grooming, Vogel argues that, under certain conditions, REM sleep can have a detrimental effect on certain waking behaviors. It is possible, he argues, that depression results from excessive neural disinhibition during REM sleep. That is, REM sleep dissipates too much accumulated neural excitability. As a result, depressives lose interest in, or fail to engage in, those activities that tend to provide positive rewards. According to this view, it is easy to understand why REM deprivation would lead to improved mood in depressed persons. Since such deprivation would prevent the discharge of neural excitability, depressed persons would again become more sensitive to their drive states and would engage in behaviors that produced rewards associated with these drive states. In short, they would experience the positive affect that typically flows from adaptive behaviors.

Note that Vogel's theory is concerned with endogenous depression, which occurs for unknown reasons, rather than with reactive depression, which is typically precipitated by some traumatic event—for example, the loss of a spouse, a child, or a job. According to Vogel's theory, endogenous depression occurs when, for still-unknown reasons, there is excessive neural disinhibition during REM sleep. Normally, he argues, neural activity is not allowed to dissipate completely. He believes that some inhibitory mechanism exists to prevent complete discharge and serves an important survival function by ensuring that the person is in a stage of readiness to respond to drive stimuli.

Vogel (1975) has reviewed some of the research showing that drugs can frequently alleviate symptoms of depression. The most effective drugs, he notes, are those that produce a dramatic and sustained reduction of REM sleep—the major antidepressants (monoamine oxidase inhibitors and the tricyclics). In other words, he maintains, these drugs work because they block REM sleep, which is assumed to be responsible for the dissipation of neural excitability.

Ellman's theory is essentially an extension of Vogel's theory. Ellman suggests that REM deprivation is able to alleviate depression because it ensures that motivation remains high (Ellman, Spielman, Luck, Steiner, & Halperin, 1991).

REM Sleep, Learning, and Adaptation

REM Sleep and the Consolidation of Memory

One of the most actively pursued hypotheses concerning sleep is that REM sleep is important for the consolidation of memory. According to the consolidation theory, it takes time for recently learned material to be transferred from immediate or short-term memory to long-term memory. There is very good evidence that the REM state facilitates this transfer (McGrath & Cohen, 1978; Grosvenor & Lack, 1984). There is further evidence that REM may be involved not simply in the consolidation of memory but in the active integration of complex information with previously learned information (Scrima, 1982).

REM Deprivation and Learning in Animals

Considerable data from animal studies indicate REM deprivation interferes with learning and retention (Ellman et al., 1991). Shuttle box avoidance learning, for example, depends on REM sleep (Smith & Young, 1980; Smith & Butler, 1982). Shuttle box avoidance learning involves putting an animal in a rectangular box that is designed to deliver shock to 1/2 of the box via a grid floor (the side on which the animal is standing). Prior to the shock being delivered, the animal is given a signal (often a tone or light) that indicates shock is forthcoming in a few seconds. By going to the other side of the box when the signal is presented (the side that is not electrified), the animal can learn to avoid the shock altogether. The word *shuttle* refers to the fact that the animals must learn in this apparatus to go back and forth on successive trials since there is always a safe area in this type of apparatus. It typically takes several days of training before an animal such as a rat will perform flawlessly.

Other studies have shown that whether REM deprivation disrupts learning depends on whether animals are in an emotional state. Emotionality in animals is typically determined by such behavioral indicators as amount of defecation and urination, which have been shown to be linked to autonomic arousal. If the animals are emotional when training takes place, REM deprivation disrupts learning; if not, REM deprivation has no effect (Koridze & Nemsadze, 1983; Oniani, 1984).

REM Deprivation and Learning in Humans

REM sleep and retention.   While REM sleep seems to facilitate most kinds of learning, it is particularly beneficial for certain kinds of tasks. In general, the REM deprivation literature shows consistent benefits from REM sleep on the learning and retention of more complex and/or emotionally loaded tasks. In one study that demonstrated beneficial effects of REM sleep (Cartwright et al., 1975), subjects were required to Q-sort adjectives as descriptive of themselves and of their ideal selves and were then tested for immediate and delayed (by 7 hours) recall of the words. In a Q-sort task, the subject places cards bearing descriptive words into stacks according to how well they describe some particular item—in this case, their actual and ideal selves. Subjects were divided into four groups, which were treated in different ways during the retention interval: the subjects in group 1 were maintained awake day and night; those in group 2 were allowed undisturbed sleep; those in group 3 were allowed to sleep but were REM-deprived; and those in group 4 had their REM sleep reduced by 25%. After the retention intervals, subjects were asked to recall as many of the adjectives as they could. For our purposes, the most important finding is that the REM-deprived subjects tended to recall more self-affirming items, whereas the normal-sleep subjects tended to recall more items indicating personal dissatisfaction; that is, REM sleep facilitated memory for items related to personal dissatisfaction. In contrast, studies in which subjects learned to associate two neutral words (paired-associate learning) have consistently failed to show that one or two nights of REM deprivation affect the retention of paired associates (e.g., Castaldo, Krynicki, & Goldstein, 1974).

Timing of REM.   Note that the benefits of REM sleep are directly proportional to its proximity to learning; that is, deprivation of early REM (soon after sleep onset) disrupts retention of the target material more than does deprivation of later REM (Hockey, Davies, & Gray, 1972). Finally, the research on REM deprivation does not show that REM sleep is necessary for good processing or storage of information; it only shows that, if a person must sleep, REM is the best form of sleep. Whether it is better to sleep or stay awake during the retention interval is another question (McGrath & Cohen, 1978). Studies suggest that it is better to stay asleep, presumably because, when awake, we learn new material that interferes with our ability to recall the target material. These findings are consistent with the consolidated hypothesis mentioned earlier.

REM Sleep and Stress

That REM sleep can increase adaptation to a stressful or noxious stimulus has been clearly demonstrated by Greenberg, Pillard, and Pearlman (1972). After watching a stressful movie, subjects were allowed (1) undisturbed sleep, (2) REM-deprived sleep, or (3) NREM-deprived sleep. After sleeping, the subjects were shown the movie again and their reactions to it were assessed. REM-deprived subjects showed the greatest anxiety, suggesting that the opportunity to experience REM sleep had produced some adaptation to the stressful events in the movie. This finding is consistent with the animal study already noted in which REM deprivation interfered with learning if the animals were emotional.

REM Sleep and Divergent (Creative) Thinking

If REM sleep facilitates the processing of information, especially information that must be integrated with existing information, the mental activity of REM sleep should be consistent with such a task. Indeed, there is evidence for such a position. Lewin and Glaubman (1975) have found that REM sleep is characterized by mental activity that is extremely flexible and divergent, rather than integrative and consolidating. However, it has been argued that the flexible and divergent aspects of REM mental activity would facilitate the integration of new, complex, emotional, or unusual information. A replication of Lewin and Glaubman's original study with somewhat different procedures again found that REM sleep facilitates divergent thinking (Glaubman et al., 1978). Subjects were assigned a divergent-thinking task in the evening and told they would have to perform the task in the morning. The task required them to tell what the consequences would be if gravity disappeared, for example, or if all people went blind. During the night, subjects were deprived of either REM or NREM sleep. NREM-deprived subjects gave not only more original responses but numerically more responses (both are indexes of degree of divergent thinking). Interestingly, the NREM-deprived subjects gave more positive consequences than did the REM-deprived subjects. For example, asked what would happen if all people went blind, they were more likely to say that wars would be abolished than that all people would die.

Individual Differences in the Need for REM Sleep

Research has established a clear pattern of variation in the amount of REM sleep across the life cycle. Infants have twice as much REM sleep as adults. As adults age, the percentage of REM sleep remains the same, but the absolute amount of REM is less in older adults (Table 6-1). Given this overall pattern, we might ask whether there are individual differences in the need for REM sleep.

If the amount of REM sleep under nondeprivation conditions is used as a measure, the evidence that different people have different needs is meager. Most studies have found equivocal results. While it has been shown that retardates with lower IQ scores need less REM sleep (e.g., Castaldo & Krynicki, 1973) and that older people with lower IQ scores also need less (Feinberg, Koresko, Heller, & Steinberg, 1973), these results must be treated with caution. Individuals with schizophrenia appear to show little or no increase in REM sleep following REM deprivation (e.g., Gillin & Wyatt, 1975) but, because of the complexity of the topic and various questions raised regarding these studies (Vogel, 1975), the significance of this finding remains unclear.

There is good evidence for individual differences, however, if increased REM sleep following REM deprivation (REM rebound) is used as a measure of need. Let's consider some of the evidence.

Field Dependence and REM Rebound

It has been shown that field-independent people exhibit greater REM rebound than field-dependent people (Cartwright, Monroe, & Palmer, 1967). Field dependence or independence is an aspect of cognitive style. Field-independent people tend to use an internal frame of reference in organizing incoming information; they generally relate information to the self, and so this style represents a very active form of information pro-

Table 6-1. Change in sleep patterns.

	Sleep	REM	Absolute
Infancy (3 months)	14.0	40%	5.6
Maturity	7.5	20%	1.5
Old age (70s)	6.0	20%	1.2

cessing. Field-dependent people, in contrast, tend to use external frames of reference; they are not likely to involve the self and thus take a more passive approach to information processing (Goodenough, 1978).*

According to the consolidation hypothesis of learning, it takes some time to transfer information from a temporary memory system into a more long-term storage system. On that hypothesis, dealing actively with information—organizing it with reference to the self—would not only be a more complex task, but would take more time and, consequently, field-independent subjects would tend to need more REM sleep. The data on REM rebound are consistent with this reasoning.

REM Sleep and Ego Threat

Greiser, Greenberg, and Harrison (1972) showed that ego-threatening manipulations affect memory. In their study, subjects were given anagrams preselected to ensure that about half could be solved in the allotted time. To threaten the subjects' self-concept (ego), they were told that the task was a measure of intelligence. The subjects were then exposed to sleep manipulation. The results showed that, as compared with NREM sleep deprivation, REM sleep deprivation disrupted recall of failed anagrams but did not affect recall of solved anagrams. These results suggest that REM sleep facilitates the processing of material that draws the individual's self-concept into question or is inconsistent with that self-concept.

*This distinction derives from studies on visual perception. Some people, it was found, would use themselves (their bodies) as reference points when making judgments about the direction in which a light is moving, for example (field-independent people), while other people would use some feature of the environment as a reference point (field-dependent people).

What would explain better recall of material inconsistent with or threatening to the individual's self-concept? One obvious explanation is that the person is motivated to resolve the discrepancy. We know from other work that this form of cognitive dissonance tends to produce arousal and that people are motivated to reduce such dissonance (Kiesler & Pallak, 1976). If a person fails to reduce the dissonance before sleep onset, REM sleep may offer an opportunity to accomplish this task.

Other researchers have threatened subjects' egos by giving them a difficult test that could not be completed in the allotted time and intimating that the test measured intelligence. Control subjects were given an easier version of the test that they could complete in the time allowed. The study found that ego threat did produce stress and that one night of uninterrupted sleep resulted in significant adaptation to the stress (Koulack, Prevost, & De Koninck, 1985). Further, subjects who recalled more of the stressful event in their dreams showed less adaptation upon awakening. These findings suggest that the adaptive value of sleep is the resolution or partial resolution of the stressful event (ego threat). Subjects who did not resolve the stressful event—that is, who showed less adaptation on awakening—continued to have elements of the stressful event represented in their REM-state dreams.

Neuroticism and REM Rebound

People who score high on neuroticism (sensitizers) show less REM rebound following deprivation than do low-neuroticism people (repressors) (e.g., Nakazawa, Kotorii, Kotorii, Tachibana, & Nakano, 1975). In neuroticism research, a *repressor* is defined as someone who tries to deny or minimize a threat or avoids thinking about its consequences, whereas a *sensitizer* tries to control the danger by dwelling on its potential consequences (Bell & Byrne, 1978). In one study, subjects were deprived of either REM or NREM sleep early in the sleep period to determine the effects on REM episodes later in the period (Pivik & Foulkes, 1966). Repressors showed increased dreamlike fantasy during these later REM periods; sensitizers did not. Finally, Cohen (1977) showed that repressors have a greater need for REM sleep.

Why do repressors need more REM sleep? We know that a repressor tends to deal with threat by denying it. Considerable cognitive activity will be required to resolve the dissonance associated with such a strategy; a good or adequate solution may involve the generation of a series of hypotheses. In that sense, the repressor may be behaving like Greiser's subjects who were subjected to ego-threatening manipulations (Greiser et al., 1972).

The REM rebound data considered in this section are consistent with the suggestion that REM sleep is necessary for the consolidation of learning that involves the "assimilation of unusual information" (Greenberg & Pearlman, 1974, p. 516).

Other Types of Sleep Deprivation

As already noted, reduction of total sleep produces a proportional increase in stage 4 sleep but not in REM sleep. Studies combining total sleep deprivation with selective deprivation of stage 4 and REM indicate that deprivation of stage 4 produces stage 4 rebound, just as REM deprivation produces REM rebound. Further, it appears that stage 4 sleep takes precedence over REM sleep; that is, any lack of stage 4 sleep will always be satisfied before a lack of REM sleep is made up (Moses, Johnson, Naitoh, & Lubin, 1975). It has also been shown that, when sleep regimens are varied in length, stage 4 and REM are maintained (Webb & Agnew, 1977). In a review of the research on sleep requirements and stages, Hartmann (1974) has concluded that there are two separate requirements for sleep—for SWS (such as stage 3 and 4) and desynchronized sleep (such as REM)—and that the need for SWS is more constant than the need for desynchronized sleep. Tilley (1985) has suggested that "obtaining a daily stage 4 quota acts as the primary drive mechanism of the sleep system" (p. 129).

Summary

All mammalian species that have been studied and many avian predators (such as hawks and eagles) have REM. In research with animals, it has been established, under controlled laboratory conditions, that REM is linked to lowering of the threshold for motivated behaviors such as sex and eating. According to Ellman's theory, REM sleep is important for periodically firing

The physical and emotional demands of dealing with emergencies often cause stress and fatigue that can typically be reversed by a single night of sleep.

the ICSS system. The function of REM dreams is to create the stimulation that can fire this system. According to Ellman, the explanation for infants' high level of REM is that, in the absence of external stimulation, the brain creates the stimulation needed for its own development. Early findings that deprivation of REM sleep produced anxiety, irritability, and difficulty in concentrating have not been replicated in more recent studies. In fact, Vogel has found that REM deprivation often alleviates the related symptoms of endogenous depression. Lack of REM sleep frequently leads to feelings of sleepiness and affects certain moods, such as friendliness and aggression. Considerable evidence indicates that REM sleep facilitates learning, especially learning that is complex or emotionally loaded. Consistent with the consolidation hypothesis, the timing of REM has been found to be important. There is also evidence that REM sleep increases adaptation to stressful and noxious events and enhances divergent thinking. Greenberg and Pearlman (1974) have argued that REM sleep is necessary for the consolidation of learning that involves the "assimilation of unusual information" (p. 576).

Not all people have the same need for REM sleep. Field-independent people, people who are ego-threatened, and repressors tend to need more. These findings are consistent with the hypothesis that certain cognitive styles or certain habitual ways of dealing with problems or events require a divergent approach that can be augmented through REM sleep.

Dreaming

Hobson's Activation/Synthesis Theory

In Hobson's activation-synthesis theory, activation is provided by the brainstem, while synthesis is provided by the forebrain (a part of the brain that is concerned with such things as thinking and planning). One interesting feature of activation phase is the shutting down of a group of neurons in the brainstem called the *aminergic cells*, which are linked to attention and memory. Unlike most brain cells, the aminergic cells rest during sleep, especially during REM sleep. The modulatory or inhibitory activity of the aminergic cells makes it possible for humans to focus their attention, process information, and systematically retrieve memories. When these cells shut down, other brain cells spontaneously become active. In this state, the brain operates free of external stimulation and internal inhibition. We are free to dream. Because the motor system is disabled during REM, the activity of the brain does not result in motor responses. This helps explain, in part, the unusual nature of the dream state.

Hobson suggests the REM state makes possible but does not determine the content of dreams. In order to make sense out of dreams, it is necessary to link the various elements of information in some logical and coherent manner. To accomplish this, the brain changes the way it normally processes information. Among other things, it sets aside both external and self-reference systems. This allows the brain to link together pieces of information that normally have not been linked or cannot be linked. For example, it allows me to incorporate images of my deceased brother into a current part of my life. According to Hobson, synthesis is story telling. He argues that we are born with the tendency to make sense out of nonsense by creating stories (themes) that link unrelated pieces of information. Together, these two parts of the dream state can account for five important features of dreams.

1. **Dreams as hallucination.** While external sensory input and motor output produce our sensory experiences, the mental activity we experience in sleep arises out of a special excitatory signal that activates the higher neurons in the visual system. The net effect is that the visual system responds to memories as though the signal came from the outside world, and we see memories as though they were produced from external sensory input and motor output. Fantasy, in contrast, does not involve this excitatory process and, as a result, fantasies lack the vivid and compelling quality of dreams.

2. **Dreams as delusions.** What makes these hallucinations so fascinating is that we tend to accept them as reality. Hobson argues that the internally generated signals grow out of memories that are synthesized into extraordinary stories. These stories, which link the vivid and compelling sensory experiences (the hallucinations), allow the past to be experienced as present. Like Ellman, Hobson believes that the extraordinary

stories can occur because the synthesis system bypasses or momentarily sets aside the self-reference system.

3. **Distortions in time, place, and person.** In REM sleep, multiple sensory channels are simultaneously activated by multiple memories. This is very unlike the waking stage, in which attention is focused sequentially on different sensory inputs. Hobson argues that, despite the great difference from the waking state, the brain still attempts to synthesize this information. To accomplish this feat, it must allow for distortions affecting the time, place, and characters of the dream. In other words, it sets aside certain fundamental rules that would govern perceptions in the waking state. If it did not do so, it would not be able to create a unifying story or theme to tie the elements of the dream together. Hobson has referred to this tendency of the forebrain to synthesize information differently in dreaming and waking as *mode switching*.

4. **Intensification of emotion.** Hobson argues that the activation produced by the brain stem is responsible for physiological changes such as increased heart rate or increased activity in some part of the limbic system, which is linked to emotions. In attempting to account for this physiological activity, the brain ascribes each physiological response to an emotion such as anxiety, surprise, fear, or elation. In other words, the brain creates an emotion that accounts for the increased physiological activity of the body and, at the same time, helps link the various memories into a unified theme or story.

5. **The failure of memory.** Hobson accounts for the failure of memory as follows:

> In dreaming, the brain-mind follows the instructions: "Integrate all signals received into the most meaningful story possible; however farcical the results, believe it; and then forget it." The "forget" instruction is most simply explained as the absence of a "remember" instruction. (Hobson, 1988, p. 214).

According to this interpretation, we can train our mind to remember our dreams. Many dream researchers have done so, by keeping a journal of their dreams.

The Meaning of Dreams

From the layperson's point of view, probably the most interesting question is: "Do my dreams have any meaning?" Over the years, some theorists have argued they do and others that they don't, while still others suggest that the content of dreams needs to be viewed in terms of the larger question of the neurophysiology of the brain.

Let's review some of the more important dream theories.

Freud: Symbolic and Disguised Dreams

Freud (1900–1953) conceptualized dreams as growing out of unfulfilled needs. He believed that the purpose of dreams is to act as a safety valve that would allow these unfulfilled needs to be filled; dreams serve to drain off energy that otherwise might build and lead to actions provoking interpersonal conflicts, guilt, or anxiety.

Freud argued that dreams can be important in understanding unconscious motivation. In his view, the unfulfilled needs underlying our dreams express themselves as wishes, often sexual, which were assumed to be a product of the id (the more biological part of the personality) and buried deep in the unconscious. Many of these motives are in direct conflict with the conscience or the superego (the social and moral part of the personality), which therefore exerts a strong counterforce to push them back into the unconscious. According to Freud's theory, these wishes will continue to grow in strength and eventually force their way into the conscious, where they find expression. Freud hypothesized that, in order to avoid this conflict, the ego transforms the unacceptable images that arise from needs into more acceptable images—specifically into universal symbols. Thus, if the individual were motivated to view a penis, the ego might transform the image of a penis into a pencil or a telephone pole (presumably depending on how large a penis the individual might be motivated to see). Similarly, someone who was motivated to have sex might instead have an image of being engaged in an up and down motion—for example, being in an elevator or riding a horse. The idea that there are universal images for things meant that anyone who knew the symbols that the unconscious used could understand the contents of his or her dreams.

Freud did not believe that universal symbols existed for all manifest dream content, however. He often asked patients to free-associate to the manifest content of their dreams in order to identify the underlying or

Dreams are often characterized by bizarreness.

latent content. Unlike some more recent theorists, Freud believed that dreams are highly meaningful and that it is possible to analyze even the most minute detail of a dream to find its meaning.

Hobson: Transparent and Unedited Dreams

Hobson (1988) starts from the position that dreams are caused by a neuronal state (REM state) and that the content of dreams emerges after the individual enters this REM state. The sensory experiences or hallucinations initially arise out of memories, and then the brain attempts to make sense of them with a story or narrative. These narratives are viewed as creative story telling. While the stories may resemble other stories used in the past, they are typically unique, even though the underlying theme of different stories may be the same.

According to Hobson, dreams are transparent and unedited. He suggests that they are also meaningful, undisguised, and often rich in conflictual impulses. This contrasts with Freud's view that dreams are obscure and disguised. Hobson believes that dreams are a mirror of our inner stories. In order to understand dreams, we need to look at the narrative that holds the diverse content together. He also believes that dreams are creative. During sleep, new ideas and new solutions are derived consciously or unconsciously from our inner mental world. Finally, Hobson believes that dreams are there to entertain us. We therefore need to accept them and enjoy them.

Crick and Mitchison: Meaningless Dreams

According to Crick and Mitchison, the content of dreams has little or no meaning. They maintain that dreams are simply the utilization of stored memories to make sense of random activation. They argue that the random activation accounts for the bizarreness, discontinuity, and incoherence of dreaming. While the content of dreams is assumed not to be important, they believe that REM sleep is, nevertheless, an important process that is "designed to make storage in an associative net more efficient" (Crick & Mitchison, 1983, p. 112). They proposed that the function of sleep

> is to remove certain undesirable modes of interactions in network of cells in the central cortex. We postulate that this is done in REM sleep by a reverse learning mechanism, so that the trace in the brain of the unconscious dream is weakened, rather than strengthened. (Crick & Mitchison, 1983, p. 111)

In a second paper, they suggested that dreams were important to reduce fantasy and obsession in the waking state (Crick & Mitchison, 1986). In other words, while they do not think that the content of dreams is important, they do believe that dreams serve a very important function in preparing the brain for optimal functioning in the waking state.

Cartwright: Dreams as Information Processing

Studies of dream content indicate that dreams are regular and orderly (Kramer, 1982). Dream content exhibits consistent patterns from night to night and within a single night. Cartwright (1990) has shown that this regular and orderly nature of dreams tends to be linked to the dreamer's affective state. She argues that these affective states trigger a network of memories and thus, over the course of a night, the content of different dreams will reflect a common theme. The implication is that, by sampling a night of dreams, we will be able to identify that theme.

Cartwright found that latencies for REM are shorter when an individual is in a highly emotional or affective state. This implies that there is some urgency for us to enter REM sleep when we are in a highly emotional state—for example, when our self-concept is threatened. Note that these findings are consistent with the research reviewed earlier on the role of REM sleep when the ego is threatened (Greiser et al., 1972).

The essence of Cartwright's theory is that dreams—REM states, in particular—serve a very important function: they review, rehearse, and reorganize conceptions of who we are and how we are doing. She contends that dreams can be viewed as information processing, in which we attempt to integrate information from our daily experiences into our conceptions about ourselves and the world. Dreams that are triggered by highly affective states are the most valuable for self-analysis, because they contain the most personal meaning. Less affective dreams simply reflect the normal assimilation of information.

Kramer: The Meaning of Nightmares

Nightmares are fairly common in children of ages 3–5. By the age of 5, most children outgrow them. Nonetheless, adults experience nightmares from time to time. Kramer (1990) has studied nightmares in males diagnosed with posttraumatic stress disorder as a result of their combat experience in Vietnam. The dreams of this group had a high proportion of military content. On the basis of comparison with a control population, Kramer has argued that the veterans' dreams reflected a common attempt to assimilate their military experience, which they perceived as profoundly threatening to their self-concept. One factor hindering resolution—and thus prolonging the nightmares—was that many of the veterans had engaged in violent acts in Vietnam and needed to come to terms with that after returning to a society where violence is not condoned.

Kramer (1990) has argued that dreams often involve more than just assimilating information; they also involve the process of accommodation. In accommodation, we develop new cognitive structures to deal with the complexity of the information in our lives. For many of the soldiers, the underlying theme of the dreams was how to move ahead and get on with life. Kramer views this as a metaphor for all dreams. In dreams, we attempt to come to terms with experiences and, in doing so, are able to move forward.

Lucid Dreaming

Although we are typically passive observers in our dreams, there is evidence that we can learn to actively participate in the dream state as though we were awake and aware; we seem to be fully conscious in the sensory world that characterizes dreams. In this state—called *lucid dreaming*—we can make decisions about what we want to do with the hallucinations we are experiencing. If we are walking down a hall, for example, we can decide to turn right or left or to open a door and see what is inside. We can talk to people and ask them to do things; we can leave if we don't like what is happening; we can do battle with a threatening figure (Gackenbach & Bosveld, 1989a,b; LaBerge, 1985).

In lucid dreaming, we can engage in extraordinary physical and psychological feats, because we are not bound by the laws of physics. We can fly, jump over skyscrapers, throw trucks through the air, or jump from one continent to another with no loss of time. People who have learned to become lucid dreamers often look forward to going to sleep, so that they can enter a world where they are in complete control.

Studies of lucid dreaming reveal not only its entertainment value but also its role in self-discovery and self-mastery.

Lucid Dreaming as Empowerment

In lucid dreaming, people, situations, and things seem less threatening. As a result, we can confront threatening people, situations, and things, and learn how to deal with them. For example, individuals who are unable to confront their parents in normal waking life can use lucidity to deal with them. It appears that, having learned to deal with their parents in their dreams, they can transfer that learning to the waking state.

Because it is possible to manipulate dream content, dreamers can actively get in touch with places, times, situations, or persons that are a source of anxiety or conflict. They can then use lucidity to resolve the anxiety or the conflict. It is even possible for people to get a new perspective on a situation by occupying an-

other person's body. There are clinical reports of people detaching themselves from their own body in dreams, floating over to another person's body, and occupying it (Gackenbach & Bosveld, 1989a).

Lucid Dreaming and Health

Lucid dreaming appears to have great potential as a vehicle to improved health. It has been linked to improved self-confidence, feelings of control, and optimism, all of which have been linked to good health (LaBerge, 1985). The evidence, which is mainly anecdotal, needs to be confirmed by controlled laboratory studies.

REM, NREM, and Sleep-Onset Dreams

As we have already noted, we experience several types of dreams, although most research has focused on REM dreams. Let's examine the differences between REM and non-REM dreams.

REM and NREM Dreams

While there are fewer NREM dreams, in many ways REM and NREM dreams are the same. They tend to be of similar length, to occur throughout the sleep period, and to be equally identified as having dreamlike qualities (Cohen, 1979; Foulkes, 1966). Nevertheless, they differ in some basic ways. First, NREM dreams tend to reflect greater conceptual thinking; their content is often a recreation of some recent psychologically important event. In contrast, REM dreams are more perceptual and emotional. Unrelated scenes and people are frequently brought together, and the dreams involve strong feelings—of anxiety and hostility, for instance (Foulkes, 1966). In Freudian terms, REM dreams are more like primary-process thinking, which is frequently unrealistic and emotional, whereas NREM dreams are more like secondary-process thinking, which is more realistic (Vogel, 1978).

REM dreams tend to become more intense throughout the sleep period (Czaya, Kramer, & Roth, 1973; Kramer, Czaya, Arand, & Roth, 1974), whereas NREM dreams apparently do not (Tracy & Tracy, 1974). In Czaya's study, according to subjects' ratings on a five-point scale, the emotion, recall, anxiety, and pleasantness of their dreams showed a significant linear increase throughout the sleep period. What does this mean? In Freudian terms, it might mean that the subjects were giving greater expression to primary-process thinking in later stages of sleep. It may be, for example, that some kind of inhibitory mechanism, such as that proposed by Vogel, is more operative in the early stages of the sleep period, and that, as the inhibition on this type of mental activity declines, the length and intensity of REM sleep increases. This idea is consistent with the finding that, as a person is deprived of REM sleep, attempts to compensate for it increase. Presumably, as the need for REM grows, the mechanism that inhibits this type of activity proves increasingly ineffective.

Sleep-Onset Dreams

Some people are more inclined to dream at sleep onset than are others (Vogel, 1978). The dreams of these people, sleep-onset (SO) dreamers, tend to resemble waking fantasy. To understand why certain people are more likely to dream at sleep onset, Foulkes, Spear, and Symonds (1966) gave a variety of psychological tests to SO dreamers and SO nondreamers. They found that SO dreamers were more self-accepting, less rigidly conforming to social standards, and more socially poised. SO nondreamers were more rigid, intolerant, and conformist. Since some people tend not to dream at sleep onset, it is not surprising that studies have found no correlation between REM dreams and SO dreams (Foulkes et al., 1966). For this reason, Vogel (1978) has argued that the mechanisms responsible for REM dreams and for SO dreams differ. In effect, this means that the two kinds of dreams have different functions. According to Vogel's psychoanalytic interpretation, REM dreams reflect the operation of the sub-

Practical Application 6-3

How to Become a Lucid Dreamer

If you are willing to persist and to exercise a bit of patience, you can probably become a lucid dreamer. Sampling my students, I find that about 15–20% of them have experienced lucid dreams without trying to do so. We do not fully understand the nature of lucid dreams, but the following five rules may help you to experience them.

1. **Practice dream recall.** As soon as you awake, you should record your dreams in a dream journal. The act of recording your dreams instructs the brain that you want it to store your dreams in memory. The natural tendency of the brain is to *not* store dreams in memory. When you start recording your dreams, you will find that you remember more and more of them. Learning to remember your dreams is the first step toward recognizing that you are dreaming. It is the ability to recognize that you are dreaming that will make you a lucid dreamer.

When you get up in the morning, you should ask yourself, "What did I dream?" Even if the answer does not come immediately, don't give up. After a short time, you will likely find that you can recall some fragments. As time passes, these fragments will evolve into complete dreams. It takes time for the

brain to clearly understand that you want to be able to record your dreams in some detail, as opposed to simply having some indication that you did dream.

Often your feelings and thoughts first thing in the morning are linked to the dreams you had during the night. By focusing your attention on these thoughts and feelings, you may be able to trigger your dream memories.

Make sure that you do not let other things interfere with recording your dreams. If you don't record them immediately, you won't remember them in as much detail, and you will tend to record them in a more wakinglike form. These dream records are important not only because they teach you to remember, but because they will provide you with the information you need to recognize that you are dreaming.

2. **Teach yourself to recognize that you are in a dream.** Start by asking yourself 5–10 times a day "Am I dreaming?" This will help you ask the question at night. Before going to bed, make it your intention to recognize dreams. If you wake up in the night, use LaBerge's (1985) MILD (mnemonic induction of lucid dreams) technique. Say to yourself, "Next time I am dreaming, I want to remember to recognize I am dreaming." LaBerge suggests that you

conscious as directed by the id, whereas SO dreams reflect the operation of more volitional processes as directed by the ego. According to this explanation, SO dreams are more controllable than REM dreams.

REM Dreams, NREM Dreams, and Waking Mentation

Different kinds of dreams probably satisfy different needs. This conclusion is based on the fact that depriving people of one type of dream (such as that associated with REM sleep) does not increase the frequency or length of other types, nor does it change the nature of dream mentation (Arkin, Antrobus, Ellman, & Farbar, 1978). There is some evidence, however, that depriving people of REM sleep does affect waking mentation. The extent of this effect appears to be related to

individual differences. Cartwright and her associates initially found that REM-deprived subjects, when given the opportunity for REM rebound, show one of three basic response patterns: disruption, compensation, or substitution. In subjects showing the disruption pattern, stage 2 intrusions occur during REM sleep. In the compensation pattern, REM time increases, and the first REM period after REM deprivation begins sooner after sleep onset than usual. In the substitution pattern, subjects do not show the normal REM rebound effect that characterizes the compensation pattern (Cartwright, Monroe, & Palmer, 1967). In a later study, Cartwright and Ratzel (1972) found that substituters were more likely than compensators to have dreamlike fantasies while awake. They interpret this finding to mean that, for substituters, dreamlike fantasy can take the place of a dream during sleep and

should generate this intention either immediately after waking from a REM period or following full wakefulness. In his research, he has found this technique particularly effective in triggering the recognition of dreams.

Learn to ask, "Am I dreaming?" whenever you experience a strong emotion or when something seems strange, bizarre, or has any of the other characteristics associated with dreams. Leaning to ask this question whenever you detect something similar to a dream in the waking state will increase the probability that you will ask this question when you are dreaming.

Read your dream journal so that you will become familiar with the characteristics of your dreams. This will help train your brain to recognize when you are in a dream. Identify any unique characteristic about your dreams, so that you will be able to more readily recognize that you are in a dream. Actively practice linking these and other characteristics of dreams to the idea that you are dreaming. Say to yourself, for example, "When two people from two different parts of the country are talking as old friends, it means I am probably dreaming." The more you become aware of the characteristics that differentiate dreams and the waking state, the better you will be at recognizing that you are dreaming.

3. **Learn to confirm to yourself that you are dreaming.** One of the easiest tests to determine whether you are dreaming is to see if you can violate the laws of gravity by floating, flying, or jumping 6 feet in the air. Sometimes people suspect they are dreaming but, in the absence of direct evidence, they fail to fully acknowledge the fact. In short, they fail to become fully lucid when they are on the threshold of lucidity.

4. **Plan ahead of time what you intend to do when you become lucid.** There are two reasons why this is a good practice. First, when you make plans, you give your brain the message that you want to know when you are in a dream, so that you can carry out some goal. Second, while lucid dreams can be highly entertaining, they may also be used to deal with specific problems or to achieve goals. In order to make sure you will fully exploit lucidity, you need to make plans in advance.

5. **Practice the necessary skills as often as possible.** As with any learned skill, the more you practice, the better you will become. Whether or not you acquire this skill will be largely determined by your motivation.

thus remove the need to make up for REM deprivation. Unable to employ this mechanism, the compensator has to make up for lost REM sleep through increased REM sleep (REM rebound). Responses to tests both before and after REM deprivation were consistent with the idea that REM deprivation affects mental activity during the waking state.

These studies suggest that some people can get along with less sleep because they are able to somehow substitute dreamlike waking activity for the REM activity lost when their sleep is restricted. To test this explanation, it is necessary to analyze waking activity and assess its relation to sleeping mental activity (Hoyt & Singer, 1978). Data on deprivation of stage 4 sleep suggest that a similar substitution of waking mentation is not possible in this case; further research is required.

Hartmann's Theory of Sleep

The Function of REM and NREM Sleep

Ernest Hartmann (1973) has suggested that REM sleep and NREM sleep serve two distinct and important functions: NREM sleep serves a general physiological restorative function, whereas REM sleep serves a more specialized reprogramming function. Because of the complexity of our daily lives, he argues, we have much unfinished business, such as stress, conflict, and unorganized information. REM not only helps deal with this unfinished business but plays a general role in maintaining the systems that underpin the processes of alertness and attention.

Electrical Activity during REM and SWS

In a study involving patients with implanted electrodes that monitored the activity of 13 deep subcortical structures, it was found that changes in electrical activity in the various areas were asynchronous (not related to activity in other areas) during SWS (NREM) sleep but were highly synchronous during REM (Moiseeva, 1979). This finding is consistent with Hartmann's theory that, during SWS, each of the various areas of the brain is undergoing repair, whereas, during REM, the various areas work together to reprogram the individual so that the individual will be prepared for the following day.

REM Sleep and Catecholamines

Hartmann has specifically argued that information processing depletes catecholamines and that REM sleep serves to replenish them. According to his theory, when we are awake, we are able to maintain our attention because of subtle feedback systems that allow us to block out irrelevant information or focus on relations that make the situation meaningful. These feedback-modulated guidance systems weaken with extended use (because of catecholamine depletion), and REM sleep restores these systems to their proper level. In effect, Hartmann argues that these systems are bypassed while they are under repair. From this perspective, he suggests, we can understand the nature of dreams. During dreams, he notes, we are often unable to focus attention; we simply experience a pattern of environmental events. Sometimes these events may even violate laws of time and space. We may put two things together that normally don't go together, or perceive two events occurring simultaneously when in fact they occurred at different times. For example, we may dream that two persons who have never met, although we know them both, are talking to each other as though they were old acquaintances. This can happen because the feedback systems are not operative.

In a test of this theory, Hartmann and Stern (1972) deprived rats of REM sleep, thus producing a decrement in acquisition of an avoidance task. When the rats were then injected with a drug that increased the availability of catecholamines, this deficit was reversed; that is, the rats learned normally when the catecholamine level was raised.

Summary

According to Freud, dreams are the result of unfulfilled wishes. In order to avoid a conflict with the conscious, the ego transforms unacceptable images into more acceptable symbols. Dreams, therefore, are both disguised and symbolic. Crick and Mitchison have argued that the content of dreams is random and, therefore, they have no meaning. According to their theory, REM sleep serves to reverse learning and prepare the individual for optimal functioning. According to Hobson, dreams are meaningful, undisguised and often rich in conflictual impulses. Hobson suggests that the brain has a natural tendency to synthesize the images produced when the inhibiting action of the aminergic cells is interrupted. It synthesizes the images by creating a story. The meaning of dreams is to be found in the story that our brain creates. According to Cartwright's theory, dreams that have been triggered by a strong affect have the most meaning as far as the self is concerned. She argues that dreams reflect normal information processing. Kramer's work on nightmares also suggests that dreams reflect an attempt to assimilate information. Nightmares may reflect the need not only to assimilate but to accommodate.

In lucid dreaming, individuals participate in the dream as though awake and aware. Some researchers view lucid dreaming as a potential means of attaining empowerment and health.

Most dreaming occurs during REM sleep, but dreams also occur during NREM sleep. Although REM and NREM dreams have many similarities (length, dreamlike qualities, periodic occurrence), their contents differ. NREM dreams tend to reflect greater conceptual thinking, whereas REM dreams are more perceptual and emotional. Further, REM dreams become more vivid as the sleep period goes on; NREM dreams do not. A separate class of dreams, called sleep-onset (SO) dreams, have been found to occur more for some people (SO dreamers) than others (SO nondreamers). Vogel has suggested that REM dreams reflect the operation of the id, whereas SO dreams reflect the operation of the ego. Research on the equivalence of REM dreams, NREM dreams, and waking mentation has led to the conclusion that lack of REM sleep affects waking mentation. The extent of this effect depends on individual differences, however. Hartmann has proposed that REM and NREM sleep serve two distinct functions: a reprogramming function and a restorative function.

Sleep Disorders

The best way to determine the exact nature of a sleep disorder is to take EEG measures during one or more nights of sleep in a sleep clinic. Often people who complain of a sleep disorder are unable to explain its exact nature, or they perceive a problem that in fact doesn't exist. With objective data, it is possible to chart a course of action that may alleviate the problem (Dement, 1972).

Insomnia

One of the most common categories of sleep disorders is insomnia. Insomnia is any failure of sleep. It may involve inability to get to sleep, inability to stay asleep, periodic awakenings, or light sleep, a condition in which the person has difficulty staying asleep and tends to have a high proportion of stage 1 sleep and a low proportion of stage 4 sleep (Webb & Agnew, 1975b). Large-scale surveys have found that about 14% of the population feel they have some difficulty with sleep. These studies indicate that difficulties with sleep are independent of racial origin, socioeconomic status, and nationality (Webb & Agnew, 1975b). Age, however, has been found to be a major predictor. Up to half of the older people questioned indicated they experienced troubled sleep from time to time.

Drug-Related Insomnias

Insomnia has commonly been treated with barbiturates. Barbiturates will increase sleep time at first, but larger and larger doses are typically required to maintain this pattern. Eventually, most people who use barbiturates develop a very disturbed sleep pattern. They can initially go to sleep with the aid of the barbiturates, but they have difficulty staying asleep. The reason has become clear. Initially, barbiturates suppress REM sleep. In larger and larger doses, barbiturates suppress not only REM sleep but also stages 3 and 4. Because the absence of REM and stage 4 sleep produces deficits that need to be made up, people who take barbiturates are in a state of continuous REM and stage 4 sleep deprivation. The many bursts of cortical arousal observed among barbiturate users during sleep can be interpreted as attempts to enter stage 3, 4, or REM sleep (Dement & Villablanca, 1974).

The effects of alcohol on sleep are similar in many respects to those of barbiturates. In single doses, alcohol reduces REM sleep, while sometimes slightly increasing slow-wave sleep. Chronic alcohol use typically produces fragmented sleep characterized by a reduction of REM and SWS. Withdrawal of alcohol following chronic use often results in hallucinations. It has been suggested that delirium tremens (the DTs) may result when REM sleep breaks into the waking state (Webb & Agnew, 1975b).

Mild stimulants such as caffeine—found, for example, in coffee, tea, some soft drinks, and NoDoz—produce a mild disruption of sleep. The equivalent of 3–4 cups of coffee before retiring lengthens the time it takes to get to sleep, produces more awakenings, and generally leads to the subjective evaluation of poor sleep. Strong stimulants such as amphetamines have a much more pronounced effect. They not only increase

the time it takes to get to sleep and the number of awakenings, but also reduce REM and SWS. Withdrawal from chronic use results in REM rebound and associated nightmares.

Antidepressants and some tranquilizers also decrease REM sleep, as do some nonprescription sleeping pills. The ultimate benefit of these drugs as far as sleep is concerned is therefore questionable.

Non–Drug-Related Insomnias

Webb and Agnew (1975b) have suggested that there are basically five categories of non–drug-related insomnias: situational, benign, and arrhythmic insomnias, sleep anomalies, and secondary sleep disorders.

Practical Application 6-4

Some Common Reasons for Insomnia

Many of us suffer from insomnia from time to time. There are at least four common reasons for difficulty in going to sleep.

Sleeping In

If we have stayed up late or if we have not been getting enough sleep, we are often inclined to sleep in. According to Kleitman, the grandfather of sleep research, one of the best predictors of the time we will go to sleep is the length of time we have been awake, because the body tends to alternate between sleep and wakefulness in a very orderly fashion. Because our circadian rhythm lasts 25 hours, the body will quickly adjust to any new pattern that puts us to bed later and gets us up later. In order to maintain a 24-hour rhythm, then, we must constantly reset the cycle by getting up at the same time each day. When we interrupt the pattern by sleeping in, our body adopts a new arousal (alertness) pattern that finds us staying alert longer in the evening and being less alert in the morning. Alertness (arousal) in the evening makes it very difficult to get to sleep. The Monday-morning blues that many people experience may simply be the result of having let their bodies get out of synchrony with the 24-hour world in which they live. On Sun-

day night, they discover that they cannot readily fall asleep. When they finally do fall asleep, they simply do not have time to get enough REM and stage 4 sleep, and they haven't reset their alertness cycle to match the working day.

Engaging in High-Arousal Activities before Sleep

I find that if I lecture for three hours in the evening—say, from 7 to 10 P.M.—I have great difficulty getting to sleep. The reason is fairly simple. Certain activities—in my case, lecturing for three hours—tend to produce a high level of arousal, which takes time to diminish, and even moderately high levels of arousal are incompatible with sleep. That is why people who win lotteries or suffer the death of a loved one typically cannot sleep. Students who must take an exam the following day often have difficulty sleeping. When we think about some forthcoming activity, especially if it is challenging, we often experience fairly high levels of arousal.

Irregular Bedtime

People who do not go to bed at the same time each night often experience insomnia, especially on a night when

Situational insomnias. These insomnias are produced by a response to some event in the waking world, such as excitement about a new business opportunity or a new love, the death of a loved one, guilt, or failure. The passage of time will often resolve a situationally induced sleep disorder.

Benign insomnias. In this case, people perceive they have poor sleep although in fact their sleep patterns are well within normal limits. It may be that the person simply doesn't need to sleep as long as he or she imagines. Such a person may simply need to be made aware that there are great variations not only in the length of sleep but in its timing.

Arrhythmic insomnias. These problems are caused by irregular sleep patterns. Going to bed or getting up at irregular hours eliminates some of the cues that normally control sleep. As a consequence, a person may have difficulty going to sleep or may not get enough sleep because of the tendency to wake up early. Following a regular sleep pattern will usually control if not eliminate such forms of insomnia.

Sleep anomalies. One kind of sleep anomaly involves the intrusion of sleep into the waking state (narcolepsy and hypersomnia). These disorders are frequently disruptive but can be treated by sleep clinics. A second kind involves the presence of wakelike behaviors

they try to go to bed early. The reason is that we thrive on regularity; our body attempts to synchronize itself with the demands or expectations that we place on it. When we tend to stay up late, our body attempts to accommodate that demand. Then, if one night we go to bed early, we find that our body is still operating at a higher level of arousal than is compatible with sleep. The net effect is that we lie awake waiting for our body to shut down.

While our body tends to respond to internal clocks (rhythms), we can reset those clocks by adopting a new pattern of waking and sleeping. Some people can adjust their rhythms quickly, but others find the task difficult. Most researchers agree that the best way to produce a good internal rhythm is to adopt a set schedule. When you do not stick to a schedule, the body fails to develop a consistent rhythm. As a result, you are likely to have occasional difficulty getting to sleep.

Napping

Since the ability to fall asleep is determined to a very large degree by the time that has passed since you last slept, a relatively long afternoon nap—as distinct from a catnap, of no more than 30 minutes—can make it very difficult for you to fall asleep at your regular bedtime. People who are inclined to nap in the evening can also suffer a form of in-

somnia. Sometimes the body treats such naps as part of the sleep cycle. Since awakening is very largely determined by the length of time we have slept, people who nap in the evening tend to wake up very early. Not surprisingly, they then have difficulty getting back to sleep. The best way to cure this problem is to discontinue the evening naps. This is often very difficult because people in the habit of taking such naps tend to fall asleep involuntarily while reading or watching TV. A nap serves to maintain the pattern they have established: early to sleep and much too early to wake. Not all people have trouble with naps; the body can learn to accommodate naps in the daily waking/ sleeping cycle. This indicates that, to some degree, the sleep/wakefulness pattern can be trained.

during sleep (sleepwalking, night terrors, nightmares, enuresis). These sleep disorders are age-related and typically disappear by mid-childhood.

Secondary sleep disorders.   Some sleep disruptions occur because of some form of pathology. Treatment requires an attack on the primary cause. Once the primary pathology has been removed, sleep typically returns to normal. For example, a person who has difficulty sleeping because of guilt feelings must deal with the guilt before normal sleep can be achieved.

Sleep Apnea

To be classified as suffering from sleep apnea, a person must stop breathing for an interval of about 10 seconds on 30 or more occasions during the night. In some cases, people will stop as often as 500 times a night. While this condition is reasonably rare (Bixler et al., 1982), it is considered life-threatening, because it can cause severe hypoxia (oxygen deficiency in the body tissues) and cardiac arrhythmias (irregular heartbeat). Sleep apnea was once considered a common cause of insomnia in adults, but controlled laboratory studies have not confirmed this belief (Kales et al., 1982). Cessation of breathing typically awakens the sleeper, who experiences fragmented sleep (which we have already discussed). Daytime sleepiness is a common consequence (Stepanski, Lamphere, Badia, Zorick, & Roth, 1984). The mechanism by which this disorder is produced is not completely understood. The condition has been successfully eliminated by surgery that increases the ability to take in air. Consumption of alcohol before bedtime can increase sleep apnea (Scrima, Broudy, Nay, & Cohn, 1982).

Summary

Insomnia is one of the most common sleep disorders. It may be caused by a wide variety of chemicals, including barbiturates, alcohol, and caffeine. Insomnia can also be produced by environmental conditions. Benign insomnia is a condition in which a person complains of sleep disruption but has sleep patterns within the normal range. There are several kinds of sleep anomaly, such as intrusion of sleep into waking state or the presence of wakelike behaviors during sleep. Though disruptive, many of these disorders can be treated. Sleep apnea, characterized by cessation of breathing for 10 seconds on 30 or more occasions during the night, is a life-threatening disorder.

Main Points

1. The best index of wakefulness, drowsiness, sleep, and dreams is cortical EEG activity.
2. In the course of a night (7–8 hours), an individual goes through approximately five sleep cycles; each cycle consists of four stages of sleep plus stage 1-REM.
3. Sleep has been divided into two general categories: REM and NREM.
4. Dreaming is typically associated with REM sleep.
5. REM sleep episodes lengthen as the sleep period continues; the total is about 1.5–2.0 hours of REM sleep per night.
6. Paralysis experienced during REM sleep is controlled by mechanisms in the RAS.
7. Sleep can be considered a state of extremely low attention in which the individual's threshold for detecting stimulation is high.
8. According to Jouvet's model of sleep, serotonin controls the onset of sleep and norepinephrine produces REM sleep.
9. If people are left to establish their own sleep/ wakefulness cycles (circadian rhythm), they tend to adopt a 25-hour cycle.
10. We tend to have more difficulty going to sleep when we have been aroused by some environmental event.
11. One of the factors that most strongly determines the time we go to sleep is the length of time that has elapsed since we last slept.
12. It has been shown that we have a 12.5-hour rhythm, which explains why many people like to nap in the afternoon.
13. The basic rest/activity cycle (BRAC) lasts 90–120 minutes.
14. The tendency to shift from fantasy and intuitive thought to verbal and intellectual thought and back again follows a 90- to 100-minute cycle.

15. People who reduce the total time they sleep to 4.5–5.5 hours experience less REM and stage 2 sleep than normal but the same amount of stage 4.

16. People typically experience difficulty in altering their sleep/wakefulness cycles.

17. Although reduced sleep may lead to feelings of sleepiness and fatigue, it does not seem to produce any serious psychological disturbances.

18. Typically, people recover completely from sleep deprivation after a full night of sleep.

19. Sleep reduction tends to reduce performance in tasks that demand persistence and attention but not in tasks that demand precision and cognitive functioning.

20. Fragmented sleep, defined as sleep from which the individual is awakened repeatedly, can produce deficits similar to those that accompany total deprivation of sleep.

21. Loss of sleep reduces friendliness and increases aggression.

22. A good way to make up for lost sleep is to learn to take catnaps.

23. Infants have about twice as much REM as adults.

24. All mammalian species that have been studied and many avian predators (such as hawks and eagles) have REM.

25. According to Ellman's theory, REM sleep is important for periodically firing the ICSS system.

26. Lack of REM sleep typically leads to REM rebound.

27. There has been some controversy as to whether lack of REM sleep produces serious psychological disturbances.

28. Vogel has provided evidence that REM deprivation may in fact benefit people experiencing endogenous depression.

29. Vogel's theory is that too much REM sleep leads to too much dissipation of neural energy.

30. There is convincing evidence that REM sleep is involved in the consolidation of memory.

31. Further, REM may be involved in the integration of recently learned material with previously learned material.

32. There is evidence that REM facilitates the learning not only of complex tasks but of emotionally loaded ones.

33. REM sleep appears to play a particularly important role in dealing with material that is threatening to the ego.

34. Field-independent people and repressors have a greater need for REM sleep.

35. REM sleep has been characterized as a form of divergent thinking.

36. Deprivation of stage 4 sleep reliably produces stage 4 rebound.

37. It appears that people need a daily quota of stage 4 sleep.

38. According to Freud, dreams are both disguised and symbolic.

39. Crick and Mitchison have argued that dreams have no meaning.

40. According to Hobson's theory, dreams are meaningful, undisguised, and often rich in conflictual impulses.

41. Cartwright suggests that dreams triggered by a highly affective state are the most meaningful as far as the self is concerned.

42. Kramer suggests that all dreams, including nightmares, reflect the need to assimilate information.

43. In lucid dreaming, individuals participate in the dream as though awake and aware.

44. People dream during several stages of sleep, but the nature of the dreams is different in the various stages.

45. NREM dreams tend to be conceptual and logical, whereas REM dreams tend to be perceptual and emotional.

46. Sleep-onset (SO) dreams are similar to waking fantasy.

47. Because REM dreams and NREM dreams differ somewhat in content, it has been suggested that they have different functions.

48. Hartmann has suggested that NREM sleep has a restorative function and that REM sleep has a reprogramming function.

49. Up to 14% of the population suffers from insomnia.

50. One major cause of insomnia is the use of drugs, including sleeping pills.

51. There are three categories of insomnia in addition to the kind related to drugs: situational, benign, and arrhythmic insomnia.

52. Sleep apnea is characterized by the cessation of breathing.

Chapter Seven

Drug Use and Drug Addiction

- *What is drug addiction?*
- *Is there an addictive personality? Why do some people fail to become addicted?*
- *What is the difference between drug abuse and drug addiction?*
- *What are some of the biochemical explanations of the effects of drugs?*
- *What role does learning play in the addictive process? What role do cognitive processes play in addiction? Do our expectations about what drugs do have any effect?*

- *Is abstinence the only cure for alcohol addiction, or can people who have become addicted learn to use alcohol responsibly?*
- *Does alcohol increase sexual arousal?*
- *Is having a couple of drinks a good way to relax?*
- *How do people quit addictions?*

When we speak of addiction, we typically mean the use and abuse of drugs—alcohol, barbiturates, stimulants, heroin, marijuana, nicotine, or even caffeine. However, there is a growing tendency to extend the term to such activities or behaviors as meditation, running, and work (Glasser, 1976).

In this chapter, I will focus my attention on the use and abuse of drugs. I will try to answer a number of basic questions: Why are people more likely to become addicted to some drugs than to others? Why is it that some people become addicted and others do not? Can the addiction process be reversed? If so, how? As we shall see, the answers to these questions are complex. There is no single determinant of drug addiction, nor is there a single route to drug addiction. Nevertheless, certain principles appear to describe the process, at least in part.

Some Basic Terms and Concepts

Drug Addiction: The World Health Organization Definition

The World Health Organization has defined *drug addiction* as "a state of periodic or chronic intoxication produced by repeated consumption of a drug" (Swinson & Eaves, 1978, p. 56). Characteristics of drug addiction described by the World Health Organization are presented in Figure 7-1.

The World Health Organization has recognized that there are many problems with this definition and, as a result, has suggested that the term may be counterproductive and should be dropped (Worick & Schaller, 1977). Because of its wide currency, however, it is unlikely to fade from use.

The main problem with this definition is that it identifies only the final stages of addiction. Often by the final stages—for instance, in confirmed alcoholism—serious health problems have set in and it is virtually impossible to reverse the process. There may also be serious psychological dependency on the drug. Prolonged use can dramatically alter a person's ability to cope with the real world. Years of failing to exercise normal coping responses can leave the person without any. In short, the drug may have changed the person both physically and psychologically. To understand

drug addiction, we need to know the motivation for drug use, not just its effects. What we need to know is why people initially take drugs and, further, why they continue to take drugs. What roles are played by biological factors, the environment, and personality?

Substance Abuse

The one common factor in most, if not all, instances of drug addiction is drug abuse or what has come to be called substance abuse (Worick & Schaller, 1977). Substance abuse refers to the tendency to use a substance to excess—either more than was prescribed by a doctor or more than the person can handle without physical and psychological ill effects. It also refers to any tendency to use substances indiscriminately without regard for our need to function as a member of society. The question that we need to answer, therefore, is why some people are able to use a drug or substance in moderation, so that it does not markedly affect their health, their performance, or their interpersonal relationships, while other people use the drug or substance to excess, so that it causes problems in these areas of their lives.

Psychoactive Drugs

A *psychoactive drug* affects mood and/or consciousness. It may be a prescription drug such as Valium, or it may be a nonprescription drug such as marijuana. This concept is generally viewed as important in the drug abuse literature, because people tend to abuse psychoactive drugs but not nonpsychoactive drugs. In short, it is because a drug can alter psychological functioning that people tend to use and abuse it.

Dependency

It can readily be shown that most drugs produce a variety of physiological and chemical changes in the body. A drug that produces addiction has altered normal body functions to such a degree that further doses of the drug are required to maintain a state of normal well-being. This state of drug *dependency* is generally assumed to be physiological, even though the main symptoms associated with the absence of the drug are often psychological. For example, a drug may produce

---

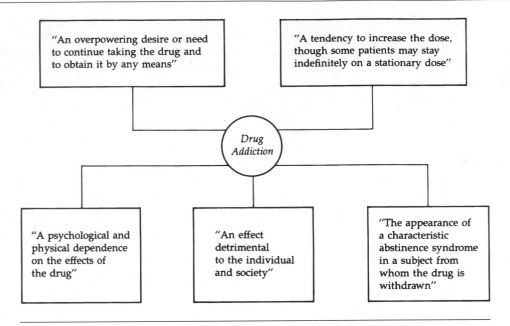

Figure 7-1. Characteristics of drug addiction as defined by the World Health Organization. (Based on R. P. Swinson and D. Eaves, *Alcoholism and Addiction.* Copyright © 1978 by Macdonald and Evans, Ltd., Estover, Plymouth.)

a very pronounced feeling of euphoria or general well-being. Once a dose of the drug has run its course, the person may suffer intense depression or anxiety. Because more of the drug is required to return the person to a normal psychological state—let alone a state of euphoria—the person is regarded as having a physical dependency on the drug, even though the main indicator is psychological.

Tolerance

People often need to use increasing amounts of a particular drug in order to obtain the same psychological effects. In the drug literature, this process is generally referred to as *tolerance.* There is evidence that tolerance to many—if not all—drugs is due to the physiological changes they produce. The fact that people tend to develop a tolerance has been taken as clear evidence that drug addiction is due to physiological changes that result from repeated use of a drug. We now consider an interesting model of tolerance.

Solomon's Opponent Process Model of Tolerance

Solomon has noted that a person who experiences an increase in positive affect is likely to experience a sharp increase in negative affect a short time afterward (Solomon & Corbit, 1974; Solomon, 1980). Similarly, an increase in negative affect is likely to be followed by a sharp increase in positive affect. He argues that the human is designed so that, whenever affect departs from a baseline, an *opponent process* is triggered to return the person to baseline. He suggests that the opponent process is rather sluggish and requires time to exert its full effect. When it does exert its effect, it produces for a time the affective state opposite to the one that triggered it. This sequence is illustrated in Figure 7-2.

Solomon holds that the opponent process is strengthened by use and weakened by disuse. He suggests that, because the opponent process tends to increase in strength each time it is triggered, the initial affective reaction will be shortened and the opponent affective reaction will grow stronger. Thus, in order for people to experience the same effect of the drug, they need to take larger amounts. According to Solomon, this mechanism accounts for the tolerance effects observed when people use opiates, barbiturates, amphetamines, and a number of other drugs.

Summary

Addiction typically involves abuse of such drugs as alcohol, barbiturates, stimulants, heroin, marijuana, nicotine, and even caffeine. In recent years, research has focused on attempts to determine what motivates people to use drugs rather than on the effects of drugs. This shift in emphasis grows out of the perception that it makes more sense to prevent addiction than to devise methods for treating it.

Drug dependency is generally thought to be physiological, even though the main symptoms associated with the absence of the drug are often psychological. People often need to use increasing amounts of a particular drug in order to obtain the same psychological effects; this process is usually called tolerance in the drug literature. Solomon's theory can account not only for the dependency and tolerance in connection with drug use but also for the observation that a marked mood shift—either very positive or very negative—is likely to be followed by the opposite mood. According to Solomon, an opponent process is triggered whenever there is a marked shift in mood. The opponent process is sluggish but, when it does exert its effect, it can be powerful, depending on past experience, and can push the mood not only back to baseline but in the opposite direction.

Why People Become Addicted

Approach and Avoidant Motivation

Who uses drugs and who becomes addicted are separate but related questions. Many people use drugs for years and do not become addicted; however, some people become addicted after only a short period. There is no simple explanation for this difference if you assume that it is the drug that causes addiction.

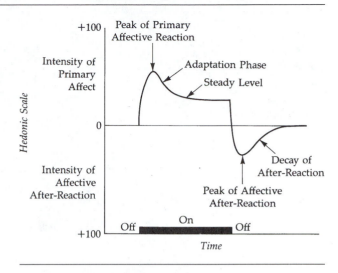

Figure 7-2. The standard pattern of affective dynamics, showing the five distinctive features: the peak of the primary affective reaction, the adaptation phase, the steady level, the peak of the affective after-reaction, and finally the decay of the after-reaction. The heavy black bar represents the time during which the affect-arousing stimulus is present. The ordinate represents two hedonic scales, each departing from neutrality, one for the primary affect, the other for the affective after-reaction. (From "The Opponent-Process Theory of Acquired Motivation," by R. L. Solomon, *American Psychologist*, 1980, *35*, 691–712. Copyright © 1980 by the American Psychological Association. Reprinted with permission of the author.)

It appears that people are more likely to become addicted if they use drugs to escape a noxious or aversive mood state, such as anxiety and depression, than if they use drugs to enhance an already positive mood state—that is, if they are seeking excitement. This general principle has its origins in the work of Kolb (1962), who noted that two more or less distinct types of people take drugs. On the one hand, the hedonist takes drugs to obtain a euphoric effect; on the other hand, the psychoneurotic takes drugs to obtain relief from anxiety.

As we have seen, avoidant motivation is more compelling than approach motivation. The reason for

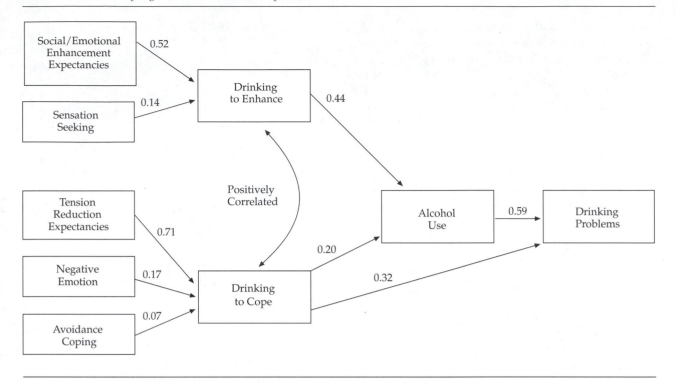

Figure 7-3.   People drink for two distinct reasons: drinking to enhance and drinking to cope. The above model shows the correlations for an adolescent sample. (From "Drinking to Regulate Positive and Negative Emotions: A Motivational Model of Alcohol Use," by M. L. Cooper, M. R. Frone, M. Russell and P. Mudar, *Journal of Personality and Social Psychology*, 1995, *69*, 990–1005. Copyright © 1995 by the American Psychological Association. Reprinted by permission of the author.)

this, it has been suggested, is that avoidant motivation often signals a threat to our survival. As a result, we are designed to learn quickly those reactions that will take us out of the threatening state. This general principle is used to explain why painkillers and antianxiety drugs are so addictive.

A Motivational Model

A recent study clearly illustrates that people often use drugs for different reasons and that the underlying reasons for their drug use determine whether they are likely to abuse that drug (Cooper, Frone, Russell, & Mudar, 1995). This study focused on alcohol use, but its findings are thought to provide a good model for thinking about other drugs.

The study grew out of a model of alcohol use suggesting that people are inclined to use drugs to regu-

late moods and that people drink for two distinct reasons: to enhance positive emotional experiences—for example, to feel more friendly or caring; and to reduce a negative mood, such as anxiety. According to the model, people who use drugs to cope with negative experiences are more likely to have drinking problems.

To test the model, various measures were taken to assess factors such as mood, expectations, and sensation seeking, for adolescent and adult samples. The results for the adolescent sample are presented in Figure 7-3.

The results confirmed that there are two distinct reasons why people drink: drinking to enhance and drinking to cope. Note that there is a positive relationship between drinking to enhance and drinking to cope; that is, people who drink to enhance are also likely to drink to cope. Such people simply drink more in all conditions. The overall finding is that drinking for any reason tends to lead to drinking problems. But note the direct path from drinking to cope to drinking problems. This is consistent with the general finding that people who drink for avoidant reasons are more likely to abuse alcohol and to become addicted.

The relatively small correlations found in this model between negative mood and drinking to cope indicate that negative moods themselves do not trigger drinking. Expectations were found to have a far greater predictive value. It appears that people are inclined to drink because of both social and emotional enhancement expectations and tension reduction expectations. Expectations come not only from our past experiences but also from what we have heard from other people or from the media—for example, that sex is more fun if you use alcohol or that alcohol reduces stress. There are strong indications that the reason adolescents first use drugs is to experience those expectations that have been handed down to them. Even if those expectations are not confirmed through the adolescents' own experiences, they may still play a significant role in their lives for some time. One possible reason for the maturing-out process—people's tendency to use fewer drugs or quit as they get older (Peele, 1989)—could be that drugs gradually lose their motivational impact when they fail to fulfill users' expectations.

The Initial Motivation to Use Drugs

It follows from the model just considered that, if we use drugs on a regular basis, we are more likely to abuse drugs or become addicted. From this perspective, it follows that, the earlier we start using drugs the more likely it is that we will begin to abuse drugs and perhaps become addicted. The key question, therefore, is why people use drugs in the first place. Let's consider the biological, learned, and cognitive components of this question.

The Biological Component

Children in urban areas in the United States often begin to experiment with drugs (tobacco and alcohol) at about 12 years of age (Kandel & Yamaguchi, 1985; Robins & Przybeck, 1985; Wills, DuHamel, & Vaccaro, 1995). To assess whether this initial tendency to use drugs is linked to our biology, researchers have exam-

ined the correlations between drug use and temperament—in particular, mood temperament, activity temperament, and novelty-seeking temperament.

Mood Temperament

Mood is generally conceptualized in terms of a continuum that ranges from negative affect to positive affect. Anxious or neurotic people are grouped at the negative end of the continuum. The individuals at the positive end of the continuum, according to Lerner and Lerner (1986), laugh and smile frequently, are generally cheerful, and enjoy life. We discussed the genetic basis for anxiety in Chapter 5.

There is considerable evidence that cigarette smokers and alcoholics tend to be more anxious and neurotic (e.g., Barnes, 1979; Sher, Walitzer, Wood, & Brent, 1991). These results are consistent with the hypothesis that people use drugs to manage moods. We'd expect that, if people are already in a positive mood state, they will be less inclined to use drugs (Tarter, 1988).

Activity Temperament

Activity temperament is conceptualized as a continuum from low activity—represented by individuals who pursue more sedentary pursuits—to high activity—represented by individuals who tend to be restless and who frequently move around and can't sit still, such as hyperactive individuals. According to optimal arousal theory, hyperactivity can be conceptualized as resulting from a chronic state of underarousal (Zentall & Zentall, 1983). In order to experience optimal arousal, hyperactive children engage in activities that will increase momentary arousal. Motor activity is a very good way of increasing momentary arousal; feedback from the muscles stimulates the RAS, which in turn activates the cortex. The impulsivity and short attention span that characterize hyperactive children are also believed to result from the tendency of such children to seek out new and different experiences. When we are confronted by new stimuli or new information, the brain automatically becomes aroused in order to process it. Once the new information has been processed, the brain relaxes. Thus, in order to maintain momentary arousal at an optimal level, the hyperactive child must continually seek out new stimulation.

Most drugs that people use for recreation tend to increase arousal. It is not surprising, therefore, that

Experimenting with drugs, such as nicotine, often begins in adolescence.

hyperactive children are more likely to use drugs than normal children (Wills, DuHammel, & Vaccaro, 1995) and that impulsivity has been linked to drug use (Cloninger, Sigvardsson, & Bohman, 1988). Note that Ritalin, the main drug used to treat hyperactivity (also called attention deficit disorder), is a central nervous system stimulant. Thus, these individuals' drug use might be considered a form of self-medication.

Novelty-Seeking Temperament

Considerable evidence links drug use to the trait called novelty seeking (Wills, Vaccaro, & McNamara, 1994). Novelty seeking is one aspect of sensation seeking. Zuckerman (1979) has defined sensation seeking as "a trait defined by the need for varied, novel and complex sensations and experiences and the willingness to take physical and social risks for the sake of such experiences" (p. 10). According to Zuckerman (1979), one reason sensation seekers find drug use so reinforcing is that their low levels of the enzyme monoamine oxidase

allows them to experience greater affect than people with high levels of monoamine oxidase (Chapter 12). It has been suggested that many hyperactive children become sensation seekers in order to increase their arousal (Tarter, Moss, & Vanyukov, 1995).

The Learned Component

Various researchers have suggested that the learned pattern of coping plays an important role in drug use (e.g., Tarter, 1988; Rothbart & Ahadi, 1994). The general line of argument is that children with certain temperaments, such as high activity, may experience greater anger and helplessness in problem-solving situations and therefore be more inclined to use drugs as a method of dealing with these emotions. If these children would learn to better cope with their problems, they might be less prone to use drugs as a way of managing their avoidant motivation (Wills, DuHamel, & Vaccaro, 1995).

Several lines of research support this argument. First, there is considerable evidence that, as children get older, individual differences tend to increase; that is, some children show a greater disposition to use drugs, while others show less. One reason that some children are less inclined to use drugs may be that they have learned to cope better with their environment. As a result, they experience fewer feelings of anger and helplessness. What about those who tend to show an increase in drug use? It has been suggested that, as a result of their temperament, some children tend to gravitate towards a social network of nonnormative peers, which not only provides initial access to drugs such as alcohol and tobacco but also provides social reinforcement for their use (Patterson, DeBaryshe, & Ramsey, 1989).

Second, research indicates that children with difficult temperaments often feel they have less family support (Wills, Vaccaro, & McNamara, 1992). Family support is important because it helps children get through difficult times. Children with active and negative temperaments may in part be responsible for their lack of support. If parents find that their actions have little effect on the child—at least as compared with other children—they find it less rewarding to deal with such children (Rothbart & Ahadi, 1994). In this scenario, a split grows between the child and the parents.

It follows that, as their parents become less supportive, children are more likely to turn to their peers for support. If those peers are nonnormative, the children would drift into a culture that rewards them for drug use.

The Cognitive Component

Self-control (or generalized self-regulation ability), which is an important predictor of success, is also related to drug use. The general finding is that drug abuse tends to be linked to undercontrol or lack of control. One study identified self-control as one of the main factors involved in drug use. Children with poor self-control also lacked coping skills and consequently experienced more anger and helplessness (Wills, DuHamel, & Vaccaro, 1995).

People are not born with self-control. Self-control is a developmental construct; it results, at least in

part, from our own self-analysis. As a result of self-monitoring, people come to realize that they can and do have control over many situations in their lives. This process is obviously much more difficult for children with an active or negative temperament. Because they are often at odds with their parents and society, they are more likely to entertain the belief that they are out of control. Their drug use may reinforce that belief. Indeed, it has been shown that perceptions of self-control is negatively related to temperaments such as activity and negative mood (Wills, DuHamel, & Vaccaro, 1995).

Summary

It appears that people who use drugs to escape a noxious or aversive situation are more likely to become addicted than are those who use drugs for entertainment. According to one model of addiction, people use drugs to regulate moods. They are more likely to become addicted, however, if they use drugs to cope.

There is considerable evidence that mood temperament, activity temperament, and novelty-seeking temperament are responsible for initial drug use. Learned and cognitive factors can reduce or increase this tendency.

Why Drugs Are Addictive

The general theories about the addictive process are useful in helping to conceptualize some of the factors involved in the addictive process but, in order to understand why people become addicted to a specific drug, we need to understand something about the nature of that drug and how that drug interacts with situational and personality variables. Some people do become addicted to several different drugs simultaneously but, as far as we can tell, becoming addicted to one drug does not automatically make a person addicted to all drugs or even a wide variety of drugs. To become addicted to a certain drug, the individual needs to use that drug within a certain context.

In the remainder of this chapter, we will look at some of the more common drugs to which people become addicted. Some are prescription drugs, and some are so-called recreational drugs, both legal—such as alcohol and tobacco—and illegal—such as marijuana and cocaine. Some of the prescription drugs can be bought on the street and are sold by the same people who sell illegal drugs.

To begin, we'll look at heroin and morphine. Because alcohol is a complex drug that affects several different systems, including some of those involved in such drugs as heroin and cocaine, we'll leave that until last.

Heroin and Morphine

The Biological Component

Heroin rapidly breaks down to morphine in the body. The most common mood change associated with heroin is euphoria, although panic and anxiety are not uncommon. The maximum effect is reached in about 2 hours, and the effect begins to wear off in 5 hours. One of the main medical reasons for administering mor-

Practical Application 7-1

Endorphins and Motivation

Many of the things we like to do trigger the release of endorphins. The release of endorphins is often linked to a defensive reaction of our body. It has been suggested that the release of endorphins is nature's way of rewarding us for doing things that are important for our survival. Lionel Tiger (1979), for example, has suggested that the release of endorphins played an important role in sustaining our ancestors' hunting behavior. The fact that people often learn to do things that will trigger the release of endorphins suggests that humans can learn to tap into this system. What this means, among other things, is that we may learn to do things which are sometimes neither healthy nor adaptive. In other words, by learning to tap into this system we can gain immediate self gratification which may or may not be healthy for us in the long term. One thing is clear: endorphins play an important role in a wide variety of behaviors in which we engage.

1. **Relief of pain.** Dennis Hough had three of his vertebral discs ruptured by a patient while he was working in a psychiatric unit of a hospital. Bed-ridden, suffering constant pain, with little hope after two failed operations, Hough was depressed to the point of suicide. In response to the intense pain that the patient was experiencing, doctors decided to implant electrodes in a tiny area in the brain known to release endorphins, called periaqueductal gray (PAG). After the operation Hough could, by using a radio transmitter, stimulate the PAG to release endorphins. His recovery was dramatic. He not only returned to

work, taking an office job, but he became engaged to be married (Hopson, 1988). Most scientists now agree that acupuncture (a treatment often used to reduce pain or induce relaxation) works by triggering the release of endorphins (Hopson, 1988).

2. **Self-Injury.** Pain, even self-inflicted pain, can release endorphins. It has been suggested that one reason autistic children bang their heads may be to produce an endorphin release. While this is hardly adaptive it may be one way that autistic children have learned to gain pleasure from an otherwise painful life.

In the pursuit of the sometimes elusive *runner's high,* runners may push themselves too hard. Basking in the glow of an endorphin high and reduced sensitivity to pain that comes with that high, runners may fail to draw back and continue to push themselves when the body needs to rest. One reason athletes may push themselves to the point of pain in a wide variety of endeavors may be to trigger an endorphin release.

3. **Self-Deprivation.** It has been shown that food deprivation in anorexics enhances the release of opiates in the brain. It has been suggested that like the autistic self-injury, the anorexic's self-starvation may be rewarding (Hopson, 1988).

4. **Exercise.** The positive mood that often accompanies exercise (such as running) can be blocked with naloxone, providing evidence that the exercise mood link is due to the release of endorphins (Hopson, 1988). It should be noted in this context that running has been linked to two very different moods, a *high* and a *calm.* While some

phine is to reduce pain. Secondary uses of morphine are for the treatment of diarrhea and the relief of cough. It appears that morphine does not reduce pain (the sensation) so much as it reduces the aversive qualities associated with a painful stimulus (Julien, 1975).

Opioids, such as heroin and morphine, are thought to produce their effects through a number of neurotransmitter systems, including norepinephrine, serotonin, and substance P (Jaffe & Martin, 1990; Dykstra, 1992). Substance P is important in the transmis-

sion of pain, whereas norepinephrine and serotonin have been implicated in elevated mood.

Endorphins: Natural Opiates of the Brain

In 1973, it was discovered that the brain has specific receptors for opiates (Snyder, 1977a,b). Subsequent research revealed that the body manufactures its own opiates, which are called *endorphins* (from *endogenous morphine*). Not only do endorphins kill pain, but they alter mood and remove symptoms of stress. Their

people talk about running to get high, others talk about running to relax. It may well be that running does produce these two distinct moods and that they come from different chemical processes (e.g., endorphins and norepinephrine). The question that needs to be answered is, if that is the case, what are the exact conditions that lead to a *high* emotional state and what leads to a *calm* emotional state? Perhaps the answer will be found in whether people focus on pushing themselves (to get high) or on the repetitious nature of running (to calm themselves). It may even be that people can learn to trigger both these chemical process simultaneously, thereby producing an emotional state that is an interaction of these two chemical processes, something that might be described as *relaxed awareness*. (This term has been used to describe how people feel when they take amphetamines.)

5. **Health.** One of the byproducts of exercise is better health. This might be due in part to the fact that the release of endorphins has been linked to an increase in the activity of the immune system.

6. **Risk-taking.** There is considerable evidence that endorphins are released when we experience fear. One reason people may take physical and psychological risks is to trigger an endorphin release (Bolles & Fanselow, 1982). Rock climbers, parachutists, hang gliders all talk about the *high* they get when they engage in these sports.

7. **Eating.** It has been argued that the presence of opioids tends to facilitate eating. Drugs that increase levels of opioids (e.g., butorphanol tartrate) lead to increased food intake, whereas drugs that block opioids (e.g., naloxone) lead

to decreased food intake (Fava et al., 1989). Evidence from animal research indicates that injections of small amounts of beta endorphin will trigger the eating of fats, proteins or sweets in satiated rats. It has been suggested that opiates increase the hedonic pleasures linked to food, and this would account for why naloxone decreases food intake in the obese (Hopson, 1988).

8. **Alcohol.** It has been shown that alcohol releases endorphins. It has been suggested that one reason people drink is to get the high that comes from alcohol consumption (Volpicelli, 1987).

9. **Music.** People who get a spine-tingling thrill from their favorite music get less of a thrill when they are given naloxone versus a placebo (Hopson, 1988).

10. **Laughter.** There is a great deal of circumstantial evidence that laughter triggers an endorphin release which, it has been hypothesized, somehow enhances the immune system. However, confirmation of this link is still lacking.

11. **Love and Attachment.** Panksepp (1986) has suggested that when humans fall in love their body secretes endorphins and therefore they literally become *addicted to love*. When separated, he argues, they go through withdrawal that people often characterize as being a painful experience. This link between attachment and the secretion of endorphins would account for the fact that separation, not just between lovers but with any close relationship, often leads to stress and disease. As I pointed out above, endorphins have been linked to activity of the immune system.

more subtle effects are to slow respiration, induce constipation, constrict the pupils, lower body temperature, and alter the functioning of the pituitary (Fincher, 1979). The fact that humans and animals show a marked tolerance to morphine suggests that an opposing metabolic process or antagonist is at work to counteract the effects of morphine.

The discovery of opiate receptor sites and of endorphins has provided us with a much clearer idea of why people become addicted to opiates such as morphine, heroin, and methadone. The existence of natural opiates (endorphins) suggests that somehow it was necessary for vertebrates to evolve these chemicals—that they were important for survival. (Endorphins are found only in vertebrates and the ancient hagfish.) Practical Application 7-1 summarizes some of the findings that suggest endorphins play a central role in motivation.

Psychological and Social Needs and the Power of Opioids

Although animals are sometimes used to study addiction, Vincent Dole (1980) states that "most animals cannot be made into addicts" (p. 142). This suggests that it is not the drug itself that is the cause of addiction. Indeed, special conditions must often be met in order to produce addiction in animals. Specifically, animals need to be deprived of the opportunity to express basic needs or drives.

For instance, a comprehensive research program at Simon Fraser University has shown that it is necessary to house rats under very restricted conditions (very little space, no social interaction, virtually nothing to explore) in order to produce morphine addiction (Alexander et al., 1985). Nichols (1965) devised a technique to produce withdrawal symptoms, one of the conditions that has been hypothesized to motivate drug use. As expected, this technique did produce increased morphine consumption but, interestingly, the effect was much greater in the animals housed under restricted conditions than in those housed under more natural conditions (more space, opportunity for social interaction, and availability of objects to explore). In other words, even under conditions of withdrawal, the tendency to select morphine is modified by housing conditions. One interesting finding was that female rats tended more than male rats to prefer morphine un-

der restricted conditions. This effect was magnified after the rats were trained with Nichols' procedure. As we'll see, this may have something to do with the female rat's greater need for social contact and/or opportunity for activity. Subsequent studies have shown that it is the combination of space and social contact rather than either space or social contact alone that produces the addictive results.

How can we account for these effects? It has been suggested that morphine interferes with complex rodent activity. If we assume that these activities are rewarding for rodents, it makes sense that rats in an environment that provided those rewards might tend to avoid morphine.

Expectations and the Power of Opioids

It has been repeatedly demonstrated that placebos can be just as effective as an active drug. In one study, a placebo killed pain as effectively as morphine (Lasagna, Mosteller, Von Felsinger, & Beecher, 1954). It has also been shown that the withdrawal symptoms people experience depend to a very large extent on their knowledge that heroin can produce withdrawal symptoms and on knowing what these symptoms are (Peele, 1985). Note that, often, these expectations are not based on direct experience, but rather on knowledge acquired through reading and talking. It appears that, from a biological perspective, opioids are not as powerful as we have been led to believe. It is not necessarily the case that they will produce strong and uncontrollable withdrawal symptoms and that, as a consequence, once we use heroin, we will be under its power.

The Learned Component

Conditioning of the Heroin Response

Individuals who inject opiates intravenously—sometimes called mainliners—report a rush (intense pleasure) shortly after an injection. According to the principles of classical and instrumental conditioning, if a drug that produces reinforcing effects is used in the presence of certain stimuli, those stimuli will come, over time, to be associated with the internal state that those drugs produce and will come to control drug-taking behavior (S. Siegel, 1979; Wikler, 1980). It is known that some addicts can get a high simply by inserting a needle into their arm (in the absence of any drug effect), presumably because they associate the insertion of a needle with the euphoric feeling that typically follows an injection of heroin.

The Power of Reinforcement: Short-Circuiting of Biological Drives

Because heroin will effectively reduce a variety of discomforts—including hunger, fatigue, anxiety, and pain (Martindale, 1977)—the heroin addict may fortuitously learn to use heroin to reduce such discomforts. For example, a person who used heroin at one point to eliminate withdrawal symptoms might learn, through continued use, that heroin is an effective way of coping with anxiety. Nichols (1965) originally suggested this possibility when he pointed out that morphine can short-circuit many biological drives, such as hunger, thirst, and sex. Note that the relapse rate for heroin addicts has been reported to be as high as 90% (Dole, 1980). This finding is consistent with Nichols' suggestion that heroin use becomes a habit that is probably triggered by a wide variety of stimuli in the environment.

The Vietnam War Study

Until the Vietnam war, the only data we had on human addiction to morphine (heroin) came from studies of street users. However, data from street users are problematic because these individuals do not represent a cross section of society. Many are on the street because they are disturbed; they have been abused as children; they lack basic skills that would allow them to be employed; they are constantly having to deal with lack of shelter; they are often subjected to threats from other street people, as well as from the police; they are not eating properly, they are exposed to disease and do not have access to proper medical treatment; they are stressed; and so forth. In other words, it's hard to know if data on street users reflect the effects of the drug or the effects of all the other circumstances of their existence. Attempts to locate other users failed because of people's fears about losing their jobs, being harassed by the police, and so forth. Would you admit that you were using heroin if a researcher came to your door and asked you?

When it became apparent that soldiers in the Vietnam war were using heroin, the conditions necessary

for obtaining good data seemed possible. Since they were a captive group who could be tested at will by the army, it proved relatively easy to identify a group of heroin addicts. The army was alarmed that the group of users was so large. Given the expected readdiction rate of around 90%, there was concern about turning loose such a large group of potential addicts into the population. To the surprise of both the army and researchers, only 15% of the heroin users readdicted themselves. On careful analysis of the results it was discovered that the 15% who readdicted themselves had all used drugs prior to going to Vietnam. The 85% who did not readdict themselves returned to environments (their homes, for example) where drug use was not accepted or not the norm (Siegel, 1983).

The basic interpretation of this finding is that the context controlled drug use. The 15% who readdicted themselves returned to environments where drug use was accepted or the norm. However, most theorists have argued that much more is involved (e.g., Davis, Goodwin, & Robins, 1975; Robins, Davis, & Goodwin, 1974; Peele, 1989). The model of drug addiction outlined in this chapter provides a good vehicle for coming to a broader understanding of what happened. Let's take a look.

The Vietnam war was very unpopular. Many of those serving were not fully committed to the official goal of the war—to stop the spread of communism in Asia—and were critical of the way the war was being waged. They felt there was too much dependence on ground forces and not enough emphasis on air strikes. Troops suspected that they were not there to win but rather to force a stalemate. As a result, many felt it was a stupid and pointless war. The ability of the Viet Cong to infiltrate and selectively kill US soldiers was a source of constant stress. While the war was technically between North and South Vietnam, it was virtually impossible to distinguish the enemy from allies. Away from family and friends, young soldiers were lonely. In short, the conditions for becoming addicted were ideal, at least according to the model in which an avoidant state is a precondition of addiction.

We know that social disapproval is one of the factors that inhibits drug use. However, in the late 1960s, the use of marijuana and other drugs by young people, especially university students, was the norm rather than the exception. In other words, the prohibitions

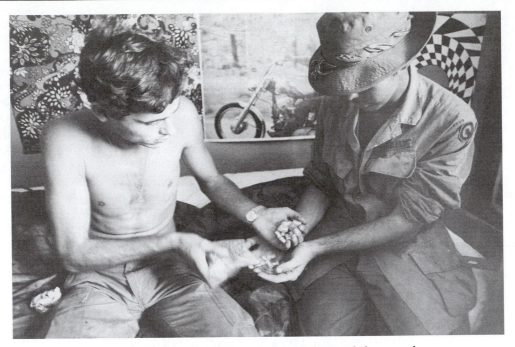

Drug use was common during the Vietnam war and paved the way for many soldiers to become heroin addicts.

against using drugs—at least certain drugs—were more or less absent for this group of soldiers. Further, heroin was readily available, and availability has repeatedly been shown to be a factor in drug use.

The model outlined in this chapter suggests that drug use does not necessarily lead to drug addiction. Even if drugs are used to avoid or cope with negative emotions. We can assume from the Vietnam study that the GIs used drugs to manage their emotions. If these same emotions were not present when they returned, however, the internal conditions that would cue them to use the drugs would also not be present.

Those who did readdict themselves had all previously used drugs. It they had used drugs in the past to manage their emotions, returning to the same environment would be likely to arouse the same emotions, and, with them, the risk of addition.

Finally, the model suggests that whether people use drugs will depend in part on their expectations. Soldiers from environments where drugs were viewed as a route to happiness would be inclined to use drugs

once they returned to that environment. In contrast, soldiers from environments where other activities were seen as a route to happiness would be more inclined to engage in those other activities.

Thus, on the basis of our model, it makes sense that only a certain portion of soldiers would become addicted again on returning home.

The Cognitive Component

Giving Up an Addiction

How do people give up a heroin addiction? Several circumstances are relevant here.

First, because many people use drugs to manage emotions—in particular, powerful aversive feelings—addicts need to learn other ways to manage those emotions.

Second, as is clear from Alexander's work with rats (Alexander et al., 1985), addicts must make efforts to identify activities that will fulfill their psychological needs, because drug abuse "depends on what behavior opportunities are available in life's situations, and whether the individual is prepared to exploit those opportunities" (Falk, 1983, p. 390). The Vietnam veterans who returned to lives they found satisfying and rewarding found no need to use drugs. If our only happiness has come from using drugs, then we will continue to use drugs.

Those who depend heavily on drugs to make them happy must find new activities that will provide them with happiness and satisfaction. A problem here is that new activities often depend on developing new skills. Nonetheless, the only true route to giving up drugs is to find such activities.

Interestingly, many people voluntarily give up drugs when they realize that their drug use is interfering with other positive and rewarding activities in their life, such as their job or their relationships (e.g., Peele, 1989). With many people, a good starting point is to ask them to assess whether the drug they are using is living up to their expectations. Is it providing happiness or interfering with their happiness? People often conclude that the drug is not helping. For many people, the benefits of drug use are more of an illusion than a reality.

There is a growing consensus that the best way to help people deal with drugs is to get them involved early in life in activities that are rewarding and satisfying. Out of those experiences, they find activities that make them immune to drugs. In other words, telling people to just say no is not enough. Drugs will be attractive to those who don't have meaningful alternatives.

Beliefs about Self-Control

A growing body of data suggests that people are most likely to give up an addiction when they make a clear decision to do so (Peele, 1985; Peele & Brodsky, 1991); that is, when they say to themselves that they can control their behavior, they change. The success rate is typically much higher for self-initiated change than for other-initiated change. When people are placed in programs designed to educate and train them, without making a commitment to themselves that they will change, they often fail. Success in beating addictions seems to start with the belief that we can control our behavior and the decision that we want to change our behavior. Unless we believe that we can change our behavior, we can't; if we don't want to change our behavior, we won't. The Vietnam veterans' experience indicates that, once we're addicted to a drug, we don't have to stay addicted. We have a choice.

Summary

Heroin and morphine, which are opioids, typically produce feelings of euphoria and suppress the aversive qualities of pain (analgesic properties). Opioids are thought to produce their effects through a number of neurotransmitter systems, as well as through substance P, which transmits pain signals. The discovery of receptor sites for morphine led scientists to conclude that the body produces its own morphine (endorphins).

Rats can be induced to become addicted to morphine if they are subjected to very restricted living conditions. The reason, it has been suggested, is that, under restricted living conditions, the rats are unable to experience natural rewards. One implication of this research is that people will have a tendency to become addicted in an environment that prevents them from experiencing natural rewards.

Many habits that humans acquire come to be controlled by internal or external stimuli. As a consequence, certain behaviors are performed in the absence of the motivating state that originally established the habit. Nichols' research shows that even animals will learn to use a drug out of habit. Because morphine can short-circuit various biological drives, people sometimes use morphine when they should be eating, drinking, and establishing social relationships.

The Vietnam war provided an excellent opportunity to determine some of the conditions that lead to addiction. The fact that only 15% of users readdicted themselves after the war attests to the importance of psychological variables in the addiction process. This finding has been explained in terms of learning principles.

Addictions can be viewed as attempts to manage moods or to provide personal satisfaction. Individuals with a psychologically rewarding life are unlikely to become addicted. Correspondingly, if people are to give up an addiction, they will typically need something to replace it. Beliefs about self-control have also been found to play an important role in determining whether people can give up an addiction.

Stimulants: Cocaine and Amphetamines

Although heroin and cannabis have been reported to induce euphoria, controlled studies comparing heroin and cannabis with amphetamines and cocaine have shown that amphetamines and cocaine produce euphoria more reliably and that the euphoria is far more intense (Grinspoon & Hedblom, 1975).

Cocaine and the amphetamines are two of the best known stimulants (euphoria-producing drugs). They work in a very similar way.

The Biological Component

Cocaine is a naturally occurring chemical found in significant quantities in the leaves of two species of the coca shrub. It reliably produces positive feelings in most people. Researchers have found that people have difficulty discriminating small doses (less than 10 mg) of cocaine from a placebo. At moderate to high levels (25–100 mg), people who take cocaine intranasally reliably report euphoria within 15–30 seconds. Some people may experience anxiety, depression, fatigue, and a desire for more cocaine 45–60 minutes after taking a 100-mg dose. There is often a crash period of extreme discomfort after a large amount of cocaine is smoked or injected. This effect is less common when cocaine is taken intranasally. As with many other drugs, the adverse effects (discomfort or disturbing thoughts) appear to be associated with higher doses (Van Dyke & Byck, 1982).

Under the influence of amphetamines, people tend to experience feelings of reduced fatigue and of increased efficiency, endurance, and perseverance. Note, however, that individuals' behavior may not be consistent with those feelings; they may, in fact, behave very inefficiently and exhibit little energy. Under certain conditions, though, amphetamines can lead to more energetic and efficient behavior. For example, they have been shown to improve performance in swimming, running, and cognitive problem-solving tasks.

Faster conditioning and decreases in reaction time have also been reported (Barr, 1969; Grinspoon & Hedblom, 1975; Kalant, 1973; Swinson & Eaves, 1978).

There is considerable evidence that cocaine and amphetamines produce their effect by stimulating the output of dopamine.

The Dopamine System

Cocaine appears to produce at least some of its effect by blocking the reuptake of dopamine and other monoamine transmitters such as norepinephrine and serotonin (Spealman, Madras, & Bergman, 1989). Figure 7-4 conceptualizes what happens when cocaine blocks the reuptake pump; concentrations of monoamines such as norepinephrine and dopamine increase at the synapses. We have evidence that an increase in norepinephrine or dopamine at the synapses is associated with feelings of euphoria, while a decrease is associated with feelings of depression. Note that tricyclic antidepressants also appear to work by blocking the reuptake of norepinephrine, dopamine, and serotonin.

Dopamine and the Self-Reward Systems

Research has shown that drugs that elevate catecholamines facilitate self-stimulation and drugs that block catecholamines block self-stimulation (Routtenberg, 1978; Wise & Stein, 1969). The direct link between the presence of certain catecholamines and the operation of the self-reward systems suggests that the experience of certain pleasurable moods, such as euphoria, may be due to the activation of one or more of these systems by the catecholamines.

Many natural activities affect catecholamine level. For example, the work of Davis (1973) and Howley (1976) clearly shows that running increases the level of norepinephrine. Zuckerman's work indicates that all forms of sensation-seeking behavior may increase norepinephrine levels (Zuckerman, 1978a; Zuckerman, Buchsbaum, & Murphy, 1980).

The Learned Component

There is experimental evidence that dopaminergic activity can be conditioned (Schiff, 1982). In a series of studies, rats were administered amphetamine or apomorphine, which are known to affect dopamine metab-

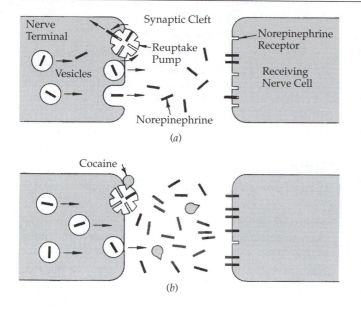

Figure 7-4. Cocaine blocks the reuptake of neurotransmitters such as norepinephrine at synapses of the sympathetic nervous system. (The sympathetic nervous system controls heart rate, blood pressure, and other functions.) When the neurotransmitter molecules are released from vesicles in the nerve terminal (*a*) they cross the synaptic cleft and stimulate the succeeding nerve cell. Ordinarily, some of the neurotransmitter molecules in the cleft are pumped back into the nerve that released them. In the presence of cocaine, the action of the reuptake pump is blocked (*b*), and the stimulation by the neurotransmitter molecules increases as their concentration in the synaptic cleft builds up. (From "Cocaine," by C. Van Dyke and R. I. Byck. *Scientific American*, March 1982, *246*, 128–141. Copyright © 1982 by Scientific American, Inc. All rights reserved.)

olism, and placed in a novel environment. These drugs produced certain predictable behavioral changes in head bobbing, sniffing, activity levels, amount of rearing, and so forth. After ten training trials, rats were given a test trial in which a placebo was administered. It was found that when the animals given the placebo were placed in the novel environment (the CS), they showed the distinctive pattern of behaviors that tend to be produced by injections of amphetamine or apomorphine, while the controls, which were given drug treatment but not placed in the novel environment, did not. To determine if this pattern of responses was mediated by changes in dopamine metabolism, the animals were sacrificed, so that certain chemicals in the brains could be carefully analyzed. The results of this analysis provided support for the idea that the conditioned responses to cues previously associated with amphetamine and apomorphine (the novel environment) were mediated by increased dopamine turnover.

The results have important implications. An abundance of data shows that medically cured addicts—people who have gone through a drying-out period and have received drug counseling—will often become addicted again on returning to an environment in which they previously used drugs. This may be due to conditioning. If the environment stimulates dopamin-

ergic activity, this may be sufficient to reinstate the habit of taking a drug (Schiff, 1982). Research has shown that rats will reinitiate drug administration following self-induced abstinence if they are given a small dose of the drug (Pickens, 1968). Note in this context that a basic tenet of incentive motivational theory is that reinforcers have response-instigating as well as response-reinforcing effects (Bindra, 1974).

The tendency for people to renew their addiction in response to a particular mood—such as stress, anxiety, or depression—can also be understood in terms of conditioning. If that mood has been linked to the habit of drug taking, then there will be a tendency for the habit to be evoked whenever that particular mood arises.

The Cognitive Component

Expectations

Different people report different effects from taking amphetamines or cocaine, including a wonderful sense of euphoria, a sense of control, a sense of power, improved sexual performance, increased creativity, and no effect at all. The most common reaction reported is a sense of euphoria. The feelings and thoughts that people experience when they take drugs such as amphetamines or cocaine depend very largely on their expectations (Peele, 1985). If individuals expect some effect before they take the drug, they usually experience that effect, whatever it is. While there is little evidence of withdrawal symptoms for cocaine, some people do report negative withdrawal symptoms. Some people show tolerance effects, even though the research demonstrates that cocaine sensitizes rather than desensitizes the dopamine system (Vezina, Kalivas, & Stewart, 1987). Some data even show that the magnitude of the reported reaction increases with increase in the cost of the drug.

Relapse

One of the central issues in all drug research is the problem of relapse. It appears that relapse is linked to our memory of the drug's effects. When we remember the experience we had with a drug, we may develop a craving for it (Wise, 1988). According to this interpretation, we are not compelled to take the drug; rather, we have some control over the process. For example, we may be able to recognize the consequences of indulging our craving. Alternatively, we may learn to substitute other memories of good experiences in activities unrelated to drugs.

Summary

Both cocaine and amphetamines are known for their ability to produce feelings of euphoria, their ability to reduce feelings of fatigue, and their ability to increase feelings of efficiency. They are sometimes used to enhance both physical and mental performance. Cocaine and amphetamines appear to work by increasing the concentration of neurotransmitters such as norepinephrine and dopamine at the synapses. The general consensus is that the dopamine system activates the self-reward system in the brain, which produces the euphoria linked to cocaine and amphetamines. While cocaine and amphetamines do not produce a tolerance effect and do not produce withdrawal symptoms, they are habit-forming.

There is evidence that the dopaminergic system can be conditioned. One implication of this is that a particular mood, if elicited, may prime the dopaminergic system and lead to readdiction.

The wide range of reactions to cocaine and amphetamines appears to be largely the result of particular users' expectations. The main explanation proposed for relapse is that users' pleasant memories of the drug's effects prompt them to try it again.

Relaxants: The New Antianxiety Drugs

Estimates indicate that 7% of the U.S. population experience anxiety to the degree that it becomes debilitating (Katz, 1990). Anxiety is a common emotion and is thought to be normal as long as it does not become completely debilitating. It becomes a disorder when it has no known cause and when it is completely out of proportion to the danger.

The prevalence of debilitating anxiety has prompted considerable interest in producing antianxiety drugs. The two most common antianxiety drugs, chlordiazepoxide (Librium) and diazepam (Valium), have proven highly effective but also highly addictive. Statistics indicate that about 15% of the US population is addicted to Valium (Ledwidge, 1980), although this drug was supposed to be nonaddictive and vastly superior to the barbiturates. The reason so many people are addicted is that these drugs have been prescribed not only for debilitating anxiety but also for a wide variety of complaints including inability to sleep, inability to relax, inability to cope, and both short-term and chronic stress. They have even become a popular street drug.

The Biological Component

Alprazolam, Librium, and Valium belong to a class of drugs called benzodiazepines, which act on the central nervous system. The main effects are decreased anxiety, sedation, muscle relaxation, and anticonvulsant - activity. While they initially produce drowsiness, the effect tends to wear off in a couple of days. When combined with alcohol, however, sedation is a serious problem. In addition, the benzodiazepines produce substantial memory impairment, motor incoordination, ataxia, and confusion in some people. Despite the substantial rate of addiction, it appears that most patients who use benzodiazepines do not abuse them (Woods, Katz, & Winger, 1987).

The general consensus is that the effect of the benzodiazepines is due to the actions of the gamma-aminobutyric acid (GABA), a naturally occurring inhibitory neurotransmitter (Cooper, Bloom, & Roth, 1982; Tallman et al., 1980). When GABA binds to receptor sites, GABA reduces the flow of neural transmission. The ability of GABA to bind, however, appears to depend on the presence of benzodiazepines. Benzodiazepines themselves have receptor sites and, when they bind to these sites, they increase the ability of GABA to bind. The net effect is that the potency of GABA is momentarily enhanced. The existence of receptors for alprazolam, Librium, and Valium suggests that the body probably produces its own benzodiazepines, though naturally produced benzodiazepines have not yet been isolated. When Valium binds with its receptor site, like a key in a lock, it changes the shape of the GABA site, as we see in Figure 7-5, and thus allows the GABA to bind. In other words, benzodiazepines must be present if GABA is to be effective.

The next step in this chain of events, it is thought, is that GABA receptors trigger the opening of chloride channels. These chloride channels lead to a decreased firing rate of critical neurons in many parts of the central nervous system (Dykstra, 1992).

One of the main antagonists for GABA is biculline. Such antagonists completely block the effects of benzodiazepines and thus allow researchers to establish whether a benzodiazepine is mediating a particular behavior.

The Learned Component

Benzodiazepines and Avoidant Motivation

Benzodiazepines are typically prescribed to help people deal with a wide range of aversive or noxious situations, including anxiety, death of a friend or relative, and all types of stress. As already noted, when people use a drug that will allow them to escape a noxious or aversive situation (a negative reinforcer), they become very susceptible to the reinforcing effects of that drug. Thus, it is not surprising that addiction to the benzodiazepines is relatively high in the general population. Even though the benzodiazepines may not produce physical symptoms of withdrawal, that does not mean people are not addicted. Similarly, the fact that people do not abuse benzodiazepines does not mean that they are not addicted (Woods et al., 1987).

The Persistence of Negative Emotions

Anxiety and stress are not only aversive and noxious, but tend, once triggered, to be very persistent and pervasive. It is very hard to ignore them; they tend to take complete charge of our attention. While recreational drug users might be able to distract themselves from cues for cocaine consumption, it is very difficult for anxious individuals to distract themselves from the fact that their heart is pounding. As a result, if people have learned to associate the reduction of anxiety or stress with the self-administration of benzodiazepines, the probability of their doing so again will be very high. Further, if people have no alternative means of dealing with these emotions—which is often why they have been prescribed the drug in the first place—the likelihood of their using benzodiazepines will be high.

Becoming Benzodiazepine-Free

To wean themselves off the benzodiazepines, people must either learn how to better cope with the events that elicit anxiety and stress or learn how to reduce the emotions. Learning how to cope, unfortunately, is not that easy, because people must do so without the support of the drug that enables them to function. Teaching people how to reduce anxiety and stress by means of relaxation techniques, although possible, is not the best long-term strategy. In the long run, they need to be in control of those events that elicit their emotions.

The Cognitive Component

It appears that some people are more inclined than others to view the world as threatening (Franken, Gibson, & Rowland, 1992) and are more likely to experience high anxiety. There is growing evidence that we can

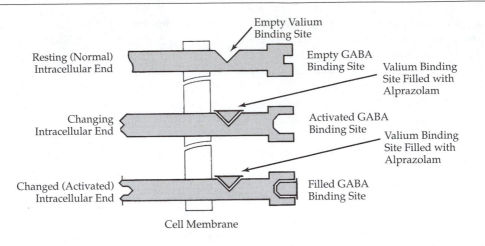

Empty Valium
Binding Site

Resting (Normal)
Intracellular End

Empty GABA
Binding Site

Valium Binding
Site Filled with
Alprazolam

Changing
Intracellular End

Activated GABA
Binding Site

Valium Binding
Site Filled with
Alprazolam

Changed (Activated)
Intracellular End

Filled GABA
Binding Site

Cell Membrane

Figure 7-5. Valium/GABA receptor. This simplified schematic drawing shows three stages in the activation of the receptor complex: (1) The receptor, lodged in a cell membrane, has unfilled binding sites for GABA and a benzodiazepine (Valium, alprazolam, etc.) molecule. (2) When alprazolam binds to its site, like a key in a lock, it may open (activate) the GABA site, allowing it to bind a GABA molecule. (3) Once both alprazolam and GABA are bound and active, the intracellular end of the receptor may change its shape, setting off a chemical domino effect that can transmit a message inside the cell. (From "Valium/GABA Receptor," by S. M. Fishman and D. V. Sheehan, *Psychology Today*. Reprinted from Psychology Today Magazine. Copyright © 1985 by the American Psychological Association. Reprinted with permission.)

teach these people to be habitually more relaxed or to habitually view the world as less threatening. The work of Benson suggests that, when people become habitually more relaxed, they tend to see the world as offering more alternatives and opportunities (Benson, 1987). We know that, when people learn to think about the world in more positive terms, they are less anxious and more in control of their emotions, and they tend to accomplish more (Seligman, 1990). In the final analysis, being in control depends on our beliefs about our ability to deal effectively with the world.

Thus, addiction to benzodiazepines must be viewed in the larger context of how people think about themselves. People use benzodiazepines because they are experiencing powerful negative emotions. Those negative emotions are intimately linked to their view of themselves and of their ability to cope with the world in which they live. We will examine ways in which people can change the ways they think about the world and about their ability to deal with it in Chapters 11 and 14.

Summary

Two of the most well-known antianxiety drugs are Librium and Valium. They exert their influence by making it possible for GABA to bind at the receptors. GABA reduces anxiety by reducing the flow of neural transmission; it seems to trigger the opening of chloride channels, which lead to decreased firing of critical neurons in many parts of the central nervous system.

Benzodiazepines have the power to reduce a number of noxious or aversive psychological states. As avoidant drugs, they are believed to be highly addictive. Since negative emotions are highly aversive, the occurrence of a negative emotion is often sufficient to trigger a relapse.

Because people who are anxious tend to view the world as threatening, their dependence on the benzodiazepines may be reduced if they can be trained to see the world as less threatening and to see themselves as having more positive alternatives.

The Hallucinogenics: Cannabis and LSD

The Biological Component

Cannabis (Marijuana, Hashish)

Cannabis produces a number of rather mild physical symptoms, including increased pulse rate, rise in blood pressure, dilation of the pupils, redness of the eyes (due to dilation of the conjunctival blood vessels), and occasionally breathlessness, choking, and some neurological changes reflected in unsteadiness, muscular twitches, tremors of the tongue, and changes in the deep reflexes (Swinson & Eaves, 1978).

Psychologically, cannabis produces a wide variety of reactions. Naive subjects often experience anxiety and apprehension. These reactions, however, may not reflect the action of the drug so much as fear of the unknown. Generally, the effects of the drug are agreeable: a general feeling of euphoria, distortions of time and space, illusions, and even hallucinations. Often there are changes in body image, together with a feeling of depersonalization (Joyce, 1970; Paton & Crown, 1972; Swinson & Eaves, 1978).

LSD (Lysergic Acid Diethylamide)

LSD produces a number of changes, including a rise in blood pressure, sweating, dilation of the pupils, increase in muscle tension (sometimes accompanied by nausea), headaches, and lightheadedness (Swinson & Eaves, 1978). These changes are due to the stimulant action of the drug on the reticular activating system (RAS). In addition, LSD often produces changes in perceptual processes associated with all sense modalities. The most dramatic changes typically occur in connection with visual perception. Objects appear to change in color, shape, and size. Two-dimensional objects may suddenly appear to be three-dimensional. Under certain conditions, people will experience fully formed hallucinations of objects, events, or even people. There are typically alterations in perception of time or the ability to gauge time. The ability to reason is often disturbed, as is the ability to plan ahead.

There is evidence that LSD depresses the activity of the serotonin-containing neurons in the raphe nuclei. Because serotonin normally inhibits certain kinds of visual and other activities of the brain, the net effect is that LSD disinhibits activity of the neurons in the visual system, the limbic system (the area of the brain linked to emotions), and other brain areas (Jacobs & Trulson, 1979; Jacobs, 1987). Drugs that increase the level of serotonin in the human brain have been found to reduce the effects of LSD, while drugs that block serotonin magnify its effects. Note that psilocybin (the active component of what recreational drug users call magic mushrooms) seems to work by the same mechanism.

The Learned Component

Addiction to cannabis and LSD does not appear to be a major problem. In reviews of addiction to drugs, cannabis and LSD often receive only passing attention (e.g., "Models of addiction," 1988). That is not to say that people cannot become addicted. However, in our society, relatively few people have become dysfunctional because of cannabis or LSD addiction in comparison with alcohol, heroin, and cocaine addiction.

In general, people rarely become addicted to drugs they use infrequently. LSD tends to be used infrequently, in part because it renders users virtually incapable of doing anything else for a period of many hours and so its use requires some forethought. Cannabis, in contrast, can be used more casually as part of daily life and tends to be used more frequently, with a correspondingly larger risk of addiction.

The Cognitive Component

Altered Perceptions

Cannabis and LSD are mainly known for their ability to alter perception, especially visual perception. Psychedelic designs produced in the 1960s represented the visual experiences of cannabis and LSD users; some were made while under the influence of the drugs. Auditory, tactile, and other sensory systems are also altered. Since the 1960s, some artists and musicians have used cannabis and LSD in order to see the world differently—for instance, to increase their comprehension of music, heighten their perception of color and form, and help them focus on artistic endeavors (Grinspoon & Bakalar, 1993).

Euphoria and Pain Relief

While the use of LSD is not very prevalent today, cannabis is the most widely used recreational drug after alcohol and nicotine. It is used by people of virtually all ages and all economic levels, for a wide variety of reasons. It is often used to reduce awareness of current problems and to create feelings of well-being (Grinspoon & Bakalar, 1993). Recently media attention has focused on its medical properties. It helps to relieve the chronic pain associated with cancer and other diseases and has been found useful by individuals with for example, glaucoma, epilepsy, multiple sclerosis, paraplegia and quadriplegia, AIDS, migraines, menstrual cramps, and labor pains. Many people use it to self-medicate for depression and various mood disorders (Grinspoon & Bakalar, 1993).

Summary

Cannabis and LSD have stimulant or euphoric properties and distort perceptions of time and space. LSD also produces powerful distortions of the sense modalities, especially vision. While there is some evidence that cannabis and LSD are addictive, they are not generally regarded as a major concern. Cannabis is often used to create feelings of well-being and to treat a wide range of physical and psychological symptoms.

Nicotine

The Biological Component

In a carefully controlled study, Stanley Schachter (1977) showed that, when nicotine levels are varied, smokers tend to adjust the number of cigarettes they smoke in order to maintain a constant (preferred) nicotine level. This suggests that, while smoking may have many social functions, it is primarily a form of drug use.

Nicotine produces a number of physiological changes. One of the primary effects is arousal (Eysenck, 1973). In small doses, nicotine increases arousal; in larger doses, paradoxically, it decreases arousal (Armitage, Hall, & Sellers, 1969; Gilbert, 1979). The arousal elicited by nicotine appears to be very similar to that elicited by amphetamines, caffeine, LSD, and other stimulants (Eysenck, 1973). Unlike other stimulants, however, nicotine produces arousal that is of short duration and is followed by three distinct phases: "a period of EEG alternations between sedation and excitation, a period of behavioral and EEG sedation and sleep, and, finally, a frequent occurrence of paradoxical or activated sleep" (Eysenck, 1973, p. 123). In other words, the effect of cigarettes varies with time after intake.

Wise and Bozarth (1987) have argued that nicotine, like caffeine, barbiturates, alcohol, benzodiazepines, cannabis, phencyclidine, and other drugs, activates the dopaminergic system. Recent research by Susan Wonnacott (1992) indicates that nicotine improves learning and memory. It does so, she argues, by mimicking one of the brain's natural signaling molecules: acetylcholine.

Urinary Acidity and Smoking

People smoke more when they are stressed and tend to smoke more at parties (Silverstein, Kozlowski, & Schachter, 1977). If people smoke for nicotine, then why would they be inclined to smoke more in those circumstances? The reason, it turns out, has to do with urinary acidity.

When people are put under stress or even when they attend a party, their urinary acidity levels increase, apparently as a result of increases in metabolism. The interesting thing is that smoking tends to increase at higher urinary acidity levels. Why is that? It appears that, when acidity levels are high, nicotine is excreted in the urine at a high rate, thereby lowering nicotine levels in the body (Silverstein et al., 1977). An interesting study shows that the increased smoking correlates primarily with urinary acidity levels, rather than levels of stress.

Students were studied on days when the class was divided into two: a group that was required to make class reports and a group that would simply listen. Since giving reports has been found to be a reliable source of stress, it was expected that the students required to give reports would show high urinary acidity levels, while the listeners would show low urinary acidity (high alkaline levels). This is what was found (Figure 7-6). When these same students were tested on a day when there were no class reports, they had almost identical acidity levels. The levels were relatively high because class participation would normally be expected on such a day, with an associated stress response (Schachter, Silverstein, & Perlick, 1977). To separate out the effects due to stress and acidity, some of the students were given bicarbonate of soda in order to reduce acidity levels. As predicted, subjects given the bicarbonate of soda smoked less, even though they had been stressed.

The bottom line is that people smoke to maintain nicotine levels in the blood. Events that deplete nicotine levels increase smoking. What is interesting is that a wide range of activities can lead to the depletion of nicotine levels.

The Learned Component

There is considerable evidence that smoking behavior is controlled to a very large degree by cues in the environment, both external and internal. Interestingly, heavy smokers appear to respond primarily to internal cues (nicotine levels), and light smokers to external cues. Light smokers can be made to smoke as much as heavy smokers if the external cues for smoking are made more prominent (Herman, 1974).

It is fascinating that people will often report that they didn't enjoy the cigarette they just smoked or will put out a cigarette shortly after lighting it. In other words, people often smoke even without experiencing a craving. Conversely, when people do experience a craving, they will go to great lengths to have a cigarette. Now that entire buildings have been designated as nonsmoking in many cities, it's common to see a crowd of people smoking outside an office building on a winter's day, as snow falls around them. We can conclude that, while often the result of a habit, smoking also has a biological basis.

For most smokers, many cues elicit smoking. This creates problems when people attempt to quit. Even after smokers have successfully weaned themselves from their nicotine dependence, the urge to smoke may

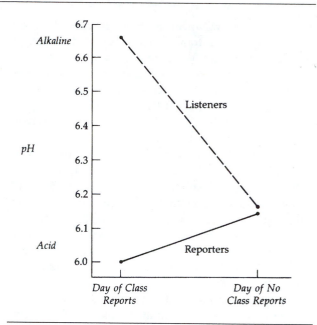

Figure 7-6.   Urinary pH among students assigned to give class reports (reporters) and among their classmates (listeners). (From "Effects of Stress on Cigarette Smoking and Urinary pH," by S. Schachter, B. Silverstein, L. T. Kozlowski, C. P. Herman, and B. Leibling, *Journal of Experimental Psychology: General,* 1977, *106,* 24–30. Copyright © 1977 by the American Psychological Association. Reprinted with permission.)

be triggered by one of those cues. This abundance of cues, which partly reflects the wide social acceptance of smoking until recently, helps to explain the very high relapse rate for smokers. A single cigarette is often enough to reestablish the smoking habit in ex-smokers.

People report that, even after months or even years of not smoking, they will suddenly get the urge to smoke in a situation with some prior link to smoking. Such situations elicit memories of the pleasure of smoking (Wise, 1988). Thus, even in the absence of a biological need, the urge to smoke can be triggered.

The Cognitive Component

People who enter a smoking program are often asked to keep track of when they smoke, so that they can become aware of the cues that control their smoking. By their nature, habits are automatic; we don't need to make a conscious decision each time we smoke a cigarette. However, if people are forced to make a conscious decision each time they take a cigarette, perhaps they will gain control over the habit (Langer, 1989). In the process, people can then replace old behaviors with new behaviors. For example, if my habit is to have a cigarette each time I drink a cup of coffee, I might decide to instead have a piece of gum after each cup of coffee. Unfortunately, such substitution procedures often lead to new habits: I may learn to chew gum after drinking coffee. Indeed, I have a friend who successfully quit smoking but is now a habitual gum chewer. Eventually gum chewing should disappear, because gum does not have the same reinforcing properties of nicotine (at least as far as we know).

It is important for people to learn to deal with the wide range of cues that elicit their behavior. Then, even if they relapse, they will have acquired an important set of skills related to a particular aspect of their addiction; those skills will eventually help them deal with their total addiction. In other words, relapse, which is so common in drug addiction (Niaura et al., 1988), can be regarded as part of a process of acquiring the skills that are necessary for eventual success; after each relapse, the individual is not starting from scratch, but is already farther along the path.

Many smokers who are also drinkers tend to relapse when drinking alcohol, probably because of alcohol's disinhibition effect. Eventual success, therefore, demands that they learn how to deal with this situation.

Summary

In small to moderate doses, nicotine typically acts as a stimulant; in larger doses, it can have a calming effect. Smoking often increases in stressful situations. It has been suggested that nicotine, like many other drugs, works by activating the dopaminergic system. There is also good evidence that urinary acidity mediates the tendency to smoke. When urinary acidity levels go up, nicotine is excreted more rapidly from the body, and so smoking increases. Stress leads to increases in urinary acidity levels, which may trigger the desire to smoke.

Smoking appears to be triggered by cues in the environment—usually to a diverse and extensive set of environmental cues. Teaching people to become aware of the cues that trigger their smoking habit and encouraging them to learn other ways of responding to these cues has been suggested as an important method of capitalizing on the power of cognition.

Alcohol

Without question, the drug that has received the most attention by researchers is alcohol. Alcohol is not only widely used but widely abused in our society and in many parts of the world. People often find it very difficult to quit drinking, and numerous programs have been developed to help people control their drinking or stop drinking altogether.

The Biological Component

In low doses, alcohol stimulates the central nervous system. In moderate doses, however, it depresses brain activity. This leads to a disinhibition effect, which will be discussed shortly. The heart rate rises with moderate doses, and the mechanical efficiency of the heart as a pump is reduced. In large doses, alcohol temporarily increases the level of blood glucose. Later, the blood glucose level falls, often to disastrously low levels. Alcohol tends to decrease the formation of glucose in the liver and accelerate the deposition of fat in the liver; this gives rise to cirrhosis. Large amounts of alcohol affect the cerebellum, which results in motor impairment (Swinson & Eaves, 1978).

Wise (1988) has argued that alcohol, like many other drugs, produces its pleasurable effect largely through the activation of the dopaminergic system and its effect on the brain's positive reward systems. To understand alcohol, however, it is necessary to understand some of its other effects.

Endorphin Hypothesis of Alcohol Addiction

There is considerable evidence that alcohol increases endorphin activity (Blum, Hamilton, & Wallace, 1977; Davis & Walsh, 1970; Vereby & Blum, 1979). This can provide a ready explanation for the sense of euphoria that drinkers often experience. This finding also offers an explanation of why people become addicted to alcohol. If alcohol can stimulate endorphin output, it could eventually produce a marked reduction in the concentration of endorphins circulating in the body. When this happens, a person experiences a negative mood state together with other symptoms of withdrawal. Through the learning process, a person would learn to drink alcohol in order to further stimulate endorphin activity. In other words, the person would become addicted to alcohol.

What is not clear from this explanation is how alcohol can stimulate endorphin activity if the stores of endorphins are depleted or markedly reduced. It may be that alcohol produces metabolites that can stimulate the receptors directly, thereby acting as a substitute for endorphins; that alcohol somehow increases the opiate receptors' sensitivity to endorphins; or that, when the stores are reduced, alcohol is still capable of triggering the output of still more endorphins. The evidence relating to these hypotheses has been reviewed by Volpicelli (1987).

Expectations and the Effects of Alcohol

It appears that how people behave after drinking alcohol depends, in part, on their expectations about its effects. People given a placebo in place of alcohol often experience a wide range of volitional behaviors, which they are willing and able to control, and nonvolitional behaviors, which they are unwilling or unable to control (Kirsch, 1985). For example, sober people become more aggressive and sexually aroused when they believe that they have been drinking alcohol (Wilson, 1981). Alcoholics even lose control when misinformed that they have been drinking alcohol (Engle & Williams, 1972). This suggests that it is alcoholics' belief about what alcohol does rather than the alcohol itself that leads to loss of control. After reviewing studies on the role of expectancy, Hull and Bond (1986) concluded: "Expectancy increases the incidence of illicit social behaviors and has few effects on nonsocial acts. Such a pattern of behavior is consistent with the hypothesis that expectancy provides an attributional excuse to engage in desired but socially prohibited acts" (p. 358).

Note that alcohol has been implicated in 70% of fatal automobile accidents, 65% of murders, 88% of knif-ings, 65% of spouse batterings, 55% of violent child abuse, and 60% of burglaries (National Commission on the Causes and Prevention of Violence, 1970).

Depression and Alcoholism

Researchers have repeatedly found a link between alcohol abuse and depression. Until recently, it was thought that people drink to reduce their depression. In other words, depression somehow leads to drinking. There is now good evidence that the reverse is true. Vaillant (1983) started tracking a group of 600 adolescents before any drinking problems had arisen. He concluded, among other things, that a difficult life was rarely a major reason for developing alcohol dependence. In a *Nova* segment broadcast on public television, Vaillant said, "I found to my surprise that alcoholics are depressed because they drink; they don't drink because they are depressed." This finding, of course, is consistent with the observation that alcohol leads to the depletion of dopamine and norepinephrine.

Alcohol and the Disinhibition Effect

Because one of the main functions of the cortex is to inhibit behavior (Eysenck, 1973), the depressant action of alcohol on the cortex (and the reticular activating system) produces a state of disinhibition. That is, behaviors that are normally inhibited are freely expressed under the influence of alcohol. This phenomenon was first shown by Masserman and Yum (1946). Cats that showed no inclination to drink alcohol were trained to obtain food from a closed feeding box. Once this habit was well learned, the cats were given an air blast when they opened the box. This noxious stimulus not only disrupted the cats' normal feeding pattern but produced a number of emotional responses that Masserman and Yum labeled experimental neurosis. When the cats were given alcohol, they approached the food box and persisted in spite of the noxious air blast. Many of these cats came to prefer a milk-alcohol mixture over plain milk. Other work has confirmed that alcohol tends to reduce anxiety in the type of situation that Masserman and Yum created (Smart, 1965).

Since Masserman and Yum's situation is a classic approach/avoidance conflict, Conger (1956) decided to determine whether alcohol was increasing the tendency to approach or decreasing the tendency to avoid. Conger first taught rats to eat at a particular

Alcohol is readily available in our society and is often used in a social context. Whether or not people become addicted depends to a large degree on whether or not they use alcohol to avoid an aversive or negative state.

location and then introduced shock at the feeding site. After measuring the rats' tendency to approach the food site under normal and alcoholic states, Conger concluded that alcohol reduced the avoidance gradient. His findings can be summarized in the form of a general model that includes approach and avoidance gradients (Figure 7-7). It has not always been possible to confirm these findings (e.g., Weiss, 1958), but there is considerable evidence that alcohol does reduce emotional reactivity in frustrating situations and leads to a greater persistence of goal-directed behavior in such situations (Barry, Wagner, & Miller, 1962).

Alcohol is frequently used in connection with sex. In small amounts, alcohol seems to facilitate sexual interest and performance, presumably because it reduces sexual inhibitions. In large amounts, alcohol lowers testosterone output in males, thereby interfering with sexual interest and performance (Farkas & Rosen, 1976).

The Learned Component

Situational Factors

Studies have shown that not only the tendency to use a drug but the amount of a drug that we use and where we use it are governed by situational factors—that is, by our perceptions of the appropriateness or social desirability of a behavior in a specific situation. Our tendency to develop a drinking problem can be predicted from the amount our companions drink and the extent to which our life revolves around drinking (Cahalan & Room, 1974).

Multiple Determinants of Alcohol Use

According to the principles of learning, any time a behavior occurs in the presence of a stimulus, the behavior will tend to come under the control of that stimulus. In other words, an association tends to develop

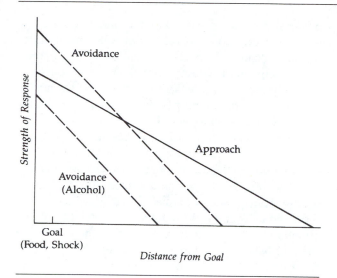

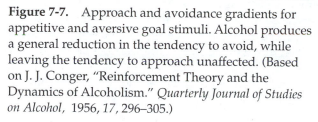

Figure 7-7.   Approach and avoidance gradients for appetitive and aversive goal stimuli. Alcohol produces a general reduction in the tendency to avoid, while leaving the tendency to approach unaffected. (Based on J. J. Conger, "Reinforcement Theory and the Dynamics of Alcoholism." *Quarterly Journal of Studies on Alcohol,* 1956, *17,* 296–305.)

between a stimulus and a behavior. In this way, a given behavior can come to be controlled by a wide variety of stimuli. A person who tends to drink alcohol when anxious, for example, will develop the habit of drinking alcohol at the onset of anxiety. Similarly, a person who tends to drink with dinner will come to develop a habit of drinking with dinner.

Alcoholism in France and Italy

France has a good climate for grapes and a thriving wine industry. It has been customary in many households to drink wine throughout the day—with breakfast, lunch, and dinner and between meals—either to quench thirst or to lubricate social occasions (Swinson & Eaves, 1978). Thus, the average French citizen has ample opportunity to experience the wide range of reinforcing effects that alcohol produces in various situations, and so to form multiple associations of alcohol intake with internal and external cues.

Italy also has a good climate for grapes and an extensive wine industry, but its rate of alcoholism is rela-

tively low (Swinson & Eaves, 1978). The reason for this difference is that most Italians drink wine only with the evening meal and drunkenness is not condoned. Accordingly, for Italians, drinking is restricted to a particular time and a particular setting, and they tend to drink moderately (Swinson & Eaves, 1978). Thus, Italians have less opportunity than the French to learn to associate alcohol with a wide variety of internal and external cues.

Cultural Factors

Stanton Peele (1984, 1985) has reviewed some of the data on the role of cultural factors in drug use. He points out that the Zuñi and Hopi Indians used alcohol in a ritualistic and regulated manner until the coming of the Spanish, after which they used it in a destructive and generally addictive manner. Peele further points out that the use of alcohol leads to antisocial aggressive behaviors in certain cultures (including Native American, Inuit, Scandinavian, Eastern European, and Anglo-American) but fails to do so in other cultures (including Greek, Italian, American Jewish, Chinese, and Japanese). These and other differences appear to relate to the beliefs people hold about what drugs do—not personal beliefs but cultural and societal beliefs.

Treating Alcoholism

There has been growing interest in using learning principles to treat addicts, especially alcoholics (Miller & Muñoz, 1976). The basic aim is to teach individuals to restrict their drinking to particular situations and then to limit the amount they drink in those situations. If they associate with people who drink excessively, they are encouraged to find new friends; if they go to a place where alcohol is readily available, they are encouraged to seek out places where it is more restricted. In essence, the goal of such programs is to put drinking under external control, as it is difficult for alcoholics to learn internal control.

The Cognitive Component

Alcohol and Myopia

While expectation seems to play an important role in the effects people experience, Steele and Josephs (1990) have argued that expectations alone do not explain the effects. They point out that, under the influence of alcohol, the same person can be aggressive and belligerent one night, amiable and generous another night, and morose and withdrawn a third night. If expectation alone were responsible, we would expect greater consistency.

They argue that alcohol causes *myopia*. Myopia is characterized by short-sighted information processing, in which people come to ignore certain pieces of information that would normally inhibit their behavior. Instead of attending to all the relevant cues, they attend to only the most salient. Suppose we meet our boss at a cocktail party on the same day as a negative encounter with the boss. Still reeling from this encounter, we are very aware of our feelings of injustice and anger. Normally, we would decide not to chew out the boss, because this could result in embarrassment, another unpleasant encounter, and even the loss of our job. In other words, normally we are able to deal with the complexity of the situation and act appropriately. Under alcohol, however, as Steele and Josephs argue, we are limited in our ability to deal with the complexity or the amount of information. As a result, we focus only on what is most salient—our feelings of anger. We do not consider the possible consequences.

What makes their theory so appealing is that it can explain why alcohol sometimes leads not only to increased aggression but also to a self-inflated ego (conceit). For most of us, the realization that we do not always measure up to our ideal teaches us modesty. Under the influence of alcohol, however, people often show an inflated ego; they brag about themselves. According to Steele and Josephs, when we drink, we are inclined to focus only on the more salient cues, one of which is our ideal self. In a study by Banaji and Steele (1989), subjects rated the importance of 35 traits pertaining to their real and ideal selves before and after they drank alcohol or a placebo. Since the differences between the real and the ideal self could be minimal or very large, Banaji and Steele distinguished between two groups: individuals with large differences that they viewed as important (individuals with high inhibition conflict); and individuals with small differences that they viewed as not important (individuals with low inhibition conflict). It was found that alcohol had a very significant effect on self-ratings in the case of high inhibition conflict; specifically, it greatly increased the self-ratings (Figure 7-8). On the basis of these results,

Banaji and Steele concluded that alcohol has a myopic effect that can result in a form of self-conceit. After drinking alcohol, the participants in this study ignored the relevant information about their limitations and saw only their strengths. In short, they lost the ability to temper or inhibit their positive self-image on the basis of a realistic assessment of their weaknesses.

To summarize, according to Steele and Joseph's model, the pharmacological effects of alcohol restrict our attention to the most salient cues. Increase in alcohol consumption is associated with greater restriction of attention (greater myopia). What is salient is determined by cognitions linked to our current thinking, attention, and motivation. Whether there will be marked behavioral change is assumed to depend on the amount of conflict in our cognitions. The greater the conflict, the greater the tendency for people to see those qualities that are central to their thinking, attention, and motivation. Since people seem to be motivated to see themselves in the best possible light, it is not surprising, for example, that they are inclined to see only their good qualities and ignore their limitations when intoxicated.

Beliefs about Control

People often have a great deal of information, correct and incorrect, about drug addiction. Much of this information comes from conversation, newspapers, and TV. You may have read, for example, that alcoholics lose control once they start drinking, or have a drink every day, or show a tendency to become aggressive when they drink, or find it impossible to quit, or drink progressively more as time goes on. These pieces of information then provide the basis for your belief system. There are two important things to note here. First, few people share precisely the same belief system. Second, two people may have basically the same drinking pattern, yet one may fit the criteria of addiction, while the other does not.

If belief controls behavior, then individuals who come to the conclusion that they are alcoholics will begin to behave in a manner consistent with that label: they will tend to lose control when they drink, find it virtually impossible to quit, and exhibit all the other behaviors that they associate with alcoholism. Individuals who do not label themselves as alcoholics, on the other hand, may drink just as much but manage not to

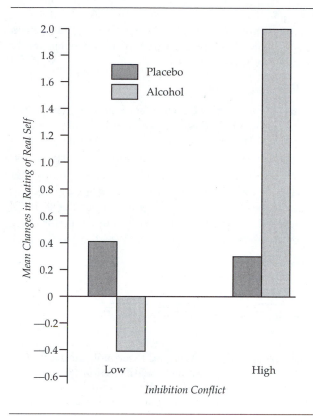

Figure 7-8. Changes in self-rating under the influence of alcohol for individuals characterized by low and high inhibition conflict. (From "Alcohol Myopia: Its Prized and Dangerous Effects," by C. M. Steele and R. A. Joseph, *American Psychologist*, 1990, *45*, 921–933 (Figure 3). Copyright © 1990 by the American Psychological Association. Reprinted with permission of the author.)

lose control and find it less difficult to quit. Indeed, data suggest that those who do not perceive themselves as alcoholics (or who perceive themselves as having at least some control) respond much better to rehabilitation programs that involve control of alcohol rather than total abstinence (e.g., Skinner, Glaser, & Annis, 1982). Conversely, individuals who perceive themselves as alcoholics (or as having no control) do not fare well in such programs but do benefit from programs that focus on abstinence (Miller, 1983). That makes sense; if you think you can't control your drinking, then the best solution is to not drink.

Note that the program of Alcoholics Anonymous (AA) is based on the principle that certain people can never learn to control their drinking and must recognize that fact if they are ever to live a normal life. AA members are required to openly identify themselves as alcoholics. This makes them admit to themselves that they have lost control and further reinforces the idea that they can never drink again. The message that they have lost control could be very damaging if AA members were to generalize it to other parts of their lives. However, the tendency to generalize is held in check by AA members' belief that alcoholism is a disease. Belief that it is a disease means, however, that you can never be cured. Scientific evidence for the disease theory of alcohol remains generally negative.

Finally, individuals who label themselves alcoholics run the risk of relapse. If alcoholics are unable to control their drinking, then individuals who accept an alcoholic identity will expect to lose control when they drink (Heather, Winton, & Rollnick, 1982; Peele, 1985). It is interesting to note that abstinence programs have success rates of only 5–10% (Emrick & Hansen, 1983).

Taking Control by Cutting Down

Can people who are abusing alcohol (drinking too much) learn to cut down on the amount they drink? Recent research (e.g., Miller & Muñoz, 1976; Sobell & Sobell, 1976), although it has come under vigorous attack, has found evidence that some people who have been classified as alcoholics—that is, uncontrolled drinkers—can learn to drink in moderation. In fact, Miller (1983) has reported that 23 of 24 studies on this question have found the reduced drinking technique superior to other treatment techniques for a range of alcohol abuse problems, and that no study has shown that abstinence is more effective overall than moderation. Note that we still do not know what determines whether a person can return to a pattern of moderate drinking. Values, beliefs about control, and stress are just some of the factors that need to be explored further in this context.

It has been suggested that perhaps not everybody can learn to control their drinking. In a 10-year follow-up of the subjects treated by Sobell and Sobell (1976), a group of researchers found that, of the 20 subjects treated, only one was drinking without problems, eight were drinking excessively, six were abstinent, four were dead for reasons related to alcohol consumption, and one could not be located (Pendery, Maltzman, & West, 1982). Faced with criticism that they were promoting a life-threatening procedure, the Sobells pointed out that the follow-up did not include the initial control group. When the Sobells did that follow-up, they found that the mortality rate for the control group was 30%, as against 20% for the controlled drinking subjects. The long and the short of this is that, while controlled drinking does not work for some, there is no evidence that people are worse off for having tried the procedure. One reason for the low success rate in the Sobells' study may be that they were attempting to treat people who had been abusing alcohol for some time. Studies in which people have been treated earlier in their pattern of abuse consistently find higher rates of success.

Beliefs about Self-Change

There are numerous accounts of people who, after drinking heavily for years, have suddenly altered their drinking patterns. A father who one day notices that his son is modeling his drinking suddenly stops drinking; a mother who realizes that she is slurring her speech at the dinner table abruptly stops having her usual three or four cocktails before dinner. Peele (1983) has noted that people frequently alter their drinking pattern when it begins to interfere with things they

Practical Application 7-2

Factors That Influence Drug Use

Commitment to other activities. In *The Meaning of Addiction*, Peele (1985) argues that, while there is very little evidence for an addictive personality per se, there is considerable evidence that the addiction process is linked to social, cultural, and parental influences, together with a desire to satisfy certain needs. He has argued that lack of commitment to nondrug activities often plays an important role in the process. If drugs interfere with activities that people value, they will limit their drug use or abstain, in order to maximize the rewards of the nondrug activity. In their therapy program, Cox and Klinger (1988) attempt to help people develop nonchemical goals as a means of developing a satisfying way of life.

Social class. A strong relationship has been found between socioeconomic level and alcohol addiction. Subjects of lower socioeconomic backgrounds are three times more likely to be addicted to alcohol than middle-class subjects (Vaillant, 1983). As we'll see, these differences may be due not to socioeconomic class per se but rather to other characteristics associated with the various classes. Personal values, for example, may be the important factor.

Peer and parental influences. Peers have consistently been found to play an important role in initiating drug use. Research studies have shown that the effect of peer pressure is greatest in regard to marijuana, somewhat less in regard to alcohol, and least in regard to hard drugs (Kandel, Kessler, & Margulies, 1978). While peers may be influential in the initial experimentation with drugs, it is questionable whether peer pressure can account for the tendency of a given individual to abuse drugs. In fact, peers may provide role models for moderation. For example, groups that encourage controlled use of heroin tend to limit the use of drugs to certain specific occasions, while simultaneously encouraging the maintenance of social, scholastic, and professional interests (Jacobson & Zinberg, 1975).

Culture and ethnicity. Membership in a particular ethnic group seems to exert an influence on the likelihood of drug abuse. Several studies indicate that cultures or ethnic groups vary widely in the attitudes they foster and that these attitudes influence drinking patterns. There are wide cultural and ethnic differences in regard to the acceptability of drunkenness, the tolerance of aggression in a drunken person, the idea of drinking as an expression of masculinity, and so forth. Jews as a group tend to be moderate drinkers, whereas the Irish tend to drink to excess (Vaillant, 1983). It has been suggested that this difference is linked to the Jewish tradition of high regard for rationality and self-control (Keller, 1970) and an Irish ethos that alcohol is both magical and tragic (Bales, 1946). The Irish, that is, treat drinking not as something that we may choose to do or not do, but rather as something that can bring magic value. While some individuals may indeed be unable to control their drinking, it is obvious that many can. George Vaillant (1983) has presented evidence that alcohol problems regularly reverse themselves without medical intervention. In other words, it is incorrect to speak of an inevitable progression affecting all alcoholics and drug users.

Summary

Alcohol is a stimulant in small to moderate amounts. The euphoric effect may be due to its ability to stimulate the dopaminergic system and the endorphin system.

Researchers believe that alcohol creates depression and is not the result of depression; this is consistent with the idea that alcohol stimulates the release and eventual depletion of dopamine and the endorphins, which seem to be the source of positive feelings. The disinhibition effect of moderate to high levels of alcohol consumption is well known. In an approach/ avoidance conflict, this effect is associated with a reduced tendency to avoid; the tendency to approach is not affected.

According to the learning model, if a drug is used in the presence of many different stimuli, all those stimuli will come to control that behavior. A comparison of the addiction rates for the French and Italians illustrates this principle.

into our life. The Japanese and Chinese tend to be moderate drinkers, whereas Native Americans and Inuits tend to be excessive drinkers (Klausner, Foulkes, & Moore, 1980). The incompatibility between excessive drinking and commitment to achievement may be responsible for the moderate drinking of the Japanese and Chinese (Peele, 1983).

Moderation as a life value. It has been suggested that drug abuse reflects a tendency to excessive behavior (Gilbert, 1981) and, conversely, that people for whom moderation is the central organizing principle will be less inclined to develop drug dependence (Peele, 1983). Individuals may be more likely to endorse moderation if they place a high value on health, which may be learned from parents or social peers (Becker, 1974).

Achievement motivation and fear of failure. There is evidence from a variety of sources that people characterized by strong achievement motivation are less likely to become addicted than people who lack such motivation. People with strong achievement motivation tend to work hard and generally have good opinions of their abilities. People with a strong fear of failure tend to have a low opinion of their abilities, and so tend to avoid situations that may demonstrate their ineptitude. In order to avoid looking bad, they look for easy problems or problems that are so difficult that no one would reasonably expect them to succeed. In short, their lives revolve around attempts to escape the need to perform (to test their skills). One

means of escape is to take drugs, often a highly ritualized activity that requires little skill and therefore offers no threat to low self-esteem. Birney, Burdick and Teevan (1969) have suggested that the rise in drug use in the 1960s grew out of this learned fear of failure. Peele (1982) has included this kind of drug use among the coping strategies he calls *magical solutions*. While such a coping strategy enables the individual to escape the immediate problem, it has no long-term survival value, since it keeps the individual from facing reality.

Alienation from society. When people become alienated from their society, they have an increased tendency to become addicted. It has been found, for example, that the use of marijuana is associated with alienation from social institutions (Kandel, 1984). When people become alienated from their society, they no longer feel bound by its rules. As a consequence, they see no value in the principle of moderation or the standards by which other people judge the appropriateness of behavior. The lack of activities designed to lead to achievement or other rewards valued by the society makes these people susceptible to the drug experience (Jessor, 1979). It makes sense that, when people experience no rewards from the society in which they live, they might look elsewhere for a rewarding experience.

Cognitive factors play an important role in alcohol use and abuse. Expectations about the effects of a drug seem to play a large part in determining how individuals respond. According to Steele and Josephs, however, expectation alone cannot account for many of the effects observed with alcohol. They argue in their interaction model that the pharmacological effects of alcohol produce restricted attention, in which people under the influence of alcohol attend to only the most salient cues. As a result, people react to a situation without considering certain important pieces

of information; they demonstrate what Steele and Josephs call a myopic approach to the world. Situational factors—for instance, whether a behavior is perceived to be appropriate—also determine to a very large degree the way people behave when they use drugs. It is not surprising that differences in cultural beliefs regarding the effects of drugs and appropriate behaviors are reflected in differences in the effects of drugs. The disease model of alcoholism links loss of control directly to the disease of alcoholism, not to cognitive variables.

Practical Application 7-3

How People Quit Addictions

Data from people who quit addictions indicate that most people do it on their own. The success rate from formal treatment programs tends to be very poor. Survey data about smoking, for example, indicates that millions of people quit smoking and most of these (as many as 95%) do so on their own (Cohen et al., 1989). In fact, 30% of adult Americans are now ex-smokers (Peele, 1989). Abstinence rates from formal treatment programs tend to cluster around 20% (Cohen et al., 1989). The same patterns have been found for alcohol. George Vaillant (1983) found (*The Natural History of Alcoholism*) that most alcohol abusers overcame their alcohol problem by either cutting back or quitting altogether. Very few of those who licked their drinking problem had sought formal treatment. Of those who chose to abstain, 60% had no contact with AA. Those who simply cut back did not contact AA, an organization which is based on the concept that the only way to deal with alcohol abuse is through abstinence. It is interesting to note that abstinence programs have success rates of only 5% to 10% (Emrick & Hansen, 1983). Even when it comes to losing weight, doing it on your own is more likely to work than if you join a formal program. Schachter and Rodin (1974) found in a study of two different populations that 62% of those who had tried to lose weight had succeeded. Not only had they succeeded in losing weight (the average weight loss was 34.7 pounds) but they had kept it off (11.2 years).

What data there are with heroin and cocaine suggest again that doing it on your own works best (Steele, 1989).

How do people do it? They seem to do it by designing their own programs. But before you can design your own program you need to believe that you can quit and you need to have a reason to quit. After that, it is often a trial-and-error procedure that eventually results in success. It has been described as a dynamic process, not a discrete event (Cohen, et al., 1989).

1. **Belief that one can quit.** Believing you can quit on your own is one of the most important factors. If you believe that you can only quit through a formal program, you give responsibility to an external agent. Should you fail, it is the program's fault and not yours. The formal programs that work best seem to be those that convince the individual they can succeed, and then put the responsibility on the individual (Peele, 1989).

2. **Developing self-efficacy.** When people take responsibility for designing their own program and succeed, their self-efficacy improves. Even small successes can improve feelings of self-efficacy. If someone tells you what to do and you succeed, you cannot take responsibility and, as a result, your self-efficacy will not improve. When people's self-efficacy improves it reinforces their initial belief that they can quit (Bandura, 1991).

3. **Learning how to interpret failure.** Since it is common for people to relapse, one might expect that self-efficacy would be undermined following failure. Whether or not it

Factors influencing drug use include commitment to other activities, social class, peer and parental influences, culture and ethnicity, a respect for the value of moderation, the need to achieve, the fear of failure, and the degree of alienation from society.

It appears that the best way to give up an addiction is to do it on your own. At least six factors have been linked to self-quitting: believing that it is possible to quit, developing feelings of self-efficacy, learning how to interpret failure, valuing health, developing interest in new activities, and maturing out.

Main Points

1. The World Health Organization has defined drug addiction as "a state of periodic or chronic intoxication produced by repeated consumption of a drug."
2. Because drug addiction is usually preceded by drug abuse, the current strategy for studying addiction is to identify the factors that lead to drug abuse.
3. Dependency refers to the need to take drugs to maintain normal feelings of well-being.

is undermined depends on how people interpret failure. If they interpret failure as a flaw in the design they have created, and not in themselves or their ability to quit, they learn how to focus on the design and improve it. For example, if they find they are inclined to drink too much, they might set a limit beforehand and then resolve to quit when they reach that self-imposed limit. Some people learn to drink one beer and then fill the bottle with water and drink that before having a second beer. When you begin to ask people how they have learned to succeed, you get literally hundreds of different answers. Different things work for different people. Each person needs to find out what works for him or her. It is important to note in this context that the number of previous unsuccessful attempts is unrelated to future success in quitting (Cohen et al., 1989).

4. **Valuing health.** When people value health they are less inclined to use drugs such as alcohol and nicotine because of the negative health implications. As people get older they often come to realize that if they are going to live a long productive life they need to take care of their health. There are many examples of people who drank heavily or used drugs in their younger years and then suddenly cut down or quit altogether (Peele, 1989).

5. **Developing interests in new activities or coming to value activities.** When people value their work, their family, the various activities they do, they often refrain from drinking or taking drugs in order to better appreciate those things. It is common to hear someone say that they

have had enough to drink or they are not going to take drugs tonight because tomorrow they want to get up early to engage in a cherished activity. It is when people have no other reason for living they fill their lives with drugs. One reason for the high addiction rate in the slums has been linked to the fact that many of these people do not have positive things on which they can focus their attention. One of the primary reasons athletes abstain from drugs is that virtually all drugs interfere with high-level athletic performance. It is only those athletes who do not value doing their very best who will typically fall prey to drugs. When people's lives are filled with activities they cherish, they have little reason for taking drugs (Cox & Klinger, 1988; Peele, 1985).

6. **Maturing out.** As a general rule, people tend to cut down or quit using drugs altogether as they get older (Peele, 1989). This reduction in drug use or quitting has been explained in many ways, ranging from the loss of reinforcing powers that drugs have on people as they get older (a biological explanation) to conscious control that results from such things as health concerns (a more cognitive explanation). Whatever the explanation, the idea that the longer you use drugs the more likely it is that you will become addicted is not the general rule. Quite the contrary, the general rule is that people seem to give up drugs after years of use. Quitting, in other words, is very natural.

4. Tolerance refers to the fact that people need to take increasing amounts of a drug to achieve the same feelings of well-being.

5. Solomon's opponent-process theory suggests that tolerance is due, at least in part, to the strengthening of an opponent process. People need to increase drug intake to overcome the opposing reaction.

6. There is good evidence that people who use drugs for avoidant purposes are more likely to abuse drugs.

7. Mood temperament, activity temperament, and novelty-seeking temperament have been linked to drug use.

8. Learned and cognitive factors can interact with temperament and result in either an increased or a decreased tendency to use drugs.

9. The discovery of opiate receptors in the brain has led researchers to suggest that the use of opiates is a means of tapping into certain naturally occurring reward and survival mechanisms.

10. Nichols has argued that morphine can short-circuit many biological drives.

11. It has been shown that placebos can be effective painkillers for a person who believes they are indeed painkillers.

12. Considerable evidence points to the idea that humans, as well as animals, only become addicted to drugs such as heroin if basic psychological and social needs are not being met.

13. It has been argued that social acceptability often plays an important role in the addiction process, especially to such drugs as heroin.

14. Beliefs about control play an important role in one's ability to recover from an addiction such as heroin.

15. Current evidence suggests that cocaine's main effect is by way of the dopamine system.

16. The fact that such drugs as amphetamines activate the self-reward systems of the brain suggests that one reason people take drugs is to experience the positive affect that occurs when such centers are activated.

17. While amphetamines do not produce tolerance or withdrawal, they can become habit-forming.

18. The reaction that people get from amphetamines depends to some extent on their expectations.

19. Antianxiety drugs such as Librium and Valium belong to a class of drugs called benzodiazepines. The general consensus is that the effect of the benzodiazepines is due to the actions of Gamma-aminobutyric acid (GABA) system.

20. It is generally thought that antianxiety drugs work by regulating neural transmission.

21. Benzodiazepines are very addictive because this class of drugs is a powerful negative reinforcer (reduces negative affect).

22. There is considerable evidence that people who are anxious tend to view the world as threatening.

23. In order to get people off benzodiazepines it is necessary for them to develop the confidence that they can effectively cope with the world in which they live.

24. Research indicates that LSD works via the serotonin-containing neurons in the raphe nuclei.

25. Hallucinogenics produce what people have referred to as an altered state of consciousness.

26. Cannabis is often used to create feelings of well-being and to treat a wide range of physical and psychological symptoms.

27. Adolescents who have experimented with marijuana but who have not become users tend to be well-adjusted.

28. Nicotine appears to produce its effect by activating the dopaminergic system.

29. There is considerable evidence that smoking behavior is controlled to a very large degree by cues in the environment, both external and internal.

30. In low doses, alcohol stimulates the central nervous system. In moderate doses, it depresses activity of the brain by direct action on the brain. This leads to a disinhibition effect.

31. Evidence points to the idea that alcohol produces its pleasurable effect largely through the activation of the dopaminergic system.

32. There is also evidence that alcohol produces its pleasurable effect by increasing endorphin activity.

33. The link between alcohol and depression can be explained by the tendency of alcohol to produce depression through the depletion of dopamine/norepinephrine stores.

34. It has been shown that alcohol reduces the avoidance gradient in an approach/avoidance conflict.

35. The different rates of alcohol addiction in France and Italy illustrate the idea that drinking can be conditioned to a wide range of stimuli.

36. It has been suggested that the effects of alcohol can be explained to a very large degree by people's expectations.

37. According to Steele and Josephs, alcohol produces restricted attention which, in turn, leads to a myopic view of the world.

38. The fact that people's reactions to drugs vary with the situation and with the drug taker's culture raises serious questions about the disease model of addiction.

39. There are considerable cultural differences in how people respond under the influence of alcohol.

40. Beliefs about control and ability to change play an important role in determining whether a person becomes addicted.

41. According to the interaction model of addiction, the extent of a drug's reinforcing properties depends on environmental conditions. An environment that is the source of positive reward tends to reduce the reinforcing properties of the drug.

42. Factors influencing drug use include commitment to other activities, social class, peer and parental influences, culture and ethnicity, attitudes toward moderation, degree of achievement motivation and fear of failure, and commitment to the values of society.

43. There is considerable evidence that when people quit on their own they are more likely to succeed.

Chapter Eight

Aggression, Coercive Action, and Anger

■ *Are there different kinds of aggression?*

■ *Is aggression in our genes?*

■ *How does our body respond when we become angry?*

■ *Does testosterone make males aggressive? What about females?*

■ *To what degree is aggression learned?*

■ *Can we learn to control our aggression?*

■ *Does viewing aggression on television and in movies lead to aggressive behavior?*

■ *What is coercive action?*

■ *Can people learn to control their anger?*

■ *Does anger have implications for our health?*

Kinds of Aggression

Aggression includes a wide range of behaviors. Moyer (1976) has identified at least eight different kinds of aggression in animals; all of them can be found, in one form or another, in human behavior. Moyer has argued that these types of aggression are distinct, although there is some overlap. Among other things, each type involves somewhat different brain structures. Here are Moyer's eight types:

1. **Predatory aggression:** Attack behavior that an animal directs against its natural prey. Many of our human ancestors hunted to feed themselves. More recently, we have domesticated a variety of animals to feed us. Nonetheless, even today, many recreational hunters like to track and kill animals, including deer, elk, moose, bear, pheasants, ducks, and geese. Others fish for food or sport.

2. **Intermale aggression:** Threat, attack, or submissive behavior by a male in response to a strange male. In the United States, 87% of those arrested for murder and aggravated assault were males (Tedeschi & Felson, 1994).

3. **Fear-induced aggression:** Aggressive behavior that occurs when an animal is confined. Attack behavior is usually preceded by an attempt to escape. Like animals, humans do not like to be confined. To prevent attempts at escape, convicted criminals and prisoners of war are typically held within highly fortified structures and guarded at all times. Attacks upon guards sometimes occur, despite the threat of reprisals. It seems that we are biologically programmed to resist any type of confinement. Infants who are physically restrained (by holding their wrist) show anger (Stenberg & Campos, 1990). At three months, they show signs of distress; at four months, they look angrily at the hand holding the wrist; and, at seven months, they look angrily at the face of the person holding the wrist.

4. **Territorial aggression:** Threat or attack behavior when an intruder is discovered on home-range territory or submissive and retreat behavior when an animal is confronted while intruding. Homes, offices, yards, and private land are all territories that humans tend to protect. The most valued and protected territory is our homes. Any uninvited intrusion by friends or strangers into our homes is viewed as very serious. Our laws recognize our right to protect our territory: An owner who shoots and kills an intruder is very unlikely to be charged.

Businesspeople often prefer to make deals on their own territory—at their office—because they feel at an advantage there. Negotiations between hostile parties are typically conducted on neutral territory. When US President Reagan and Soviet Premier Gorbachov decided to have discussions during the Cold War, they flew to Iceland, a country regarded as neutral by both parties.

5. **Maternal aggression:** Attack or threat directed by the female toward an intruder when her young are present. Human mothers are known for their tendency to protect their offspring. Should someone attempt to harm her children in any way, the mother will do whatever is in her power to protect them.

6. **Irritable aggression:** Attack or destructive behavior directed toward any object as the result of frustration, pain, deprivation, or any other stressor. For humans, frustrations only lead to aggression when they are large and unexpected. We have learned to expect certain frustrations, such as having to wait in line or to sit in a traffic jam. Should your new $30,000 car break down on the way home from the dealer, however, you will probably become angry and even aggressive. Pain and deprivation are highly compelling motivational states. Berkowitz (1993) has argued that, when negative feelings are evoked, they often lead to aggression and even rage in humans. Since aggression is typically not an appropriate response to such events, humans often need to learn more adaptive reactions.

7. **Sex-related aggression:** Aggressive behavior elicited by the same stimuli that elicit sexual behavior. A person who sexually excites us can also make us feel jealous and aggressive if, for example, we see that person flirting with someone else. Evolutionary psychologists argue that jealousy is linked to our desire to preserve our genes in future generations (Buss, 1994). When a person whom we regard as a potential sexual partner shows interest in a third party, the potential for us to reproduce with that person is threatened. Since the survival of our genes is a very primary motive, we are highly alert to cues that inspire jealousy. Verbal and even physical aggression may accompany such feelings.

8. **Instrumental aggression:** Aggressive behavior that has previously resulted in some kind of reward. Much of human aggression is instrumental aggression. We will look at how humans use coercive action to help them achieve their goals when we discuss the cognitive component of aggression. As we'll see, aggression is very common in everyday human behavior.

It is well beyond the scope of this chapter to deal in detail with all these forms of aggression. Instead, we will focus on a few areas of research. Historical evidence indicates that humans have an enormous capacity for violence. Despite incidents of genocide and mass warfare, however, we often live in remarkable harmony, because of our capacity to inhibit our aggression. Our natural tendency to act aggressively in a wide variety of situations can be socialized and, given the right set of conditions, we can live in peace with one another.

The Traditional Definition of Aggression

Traditionally, psychologists have defined aggression as behavior against another person with the intention of committing harm (Geen, 1990). Note that this definition refers to socially unacceptable behavior. In our everyday speech, aggression is used more broadly to refer not only to socially unacceptable behavior but also to certain forms of socially acceptable behavior. A person who works long and hard to win a business contract, a person who competes with others to become the executive of a large company, or an athlete who manages to become the top scorer on the team is often viewed in our society as aggressive in an acceptable and desirable way. By contrast, drivers who honk their horn at slower cars or individuals who challenge others to a fight in order to settle an argument are typically regarded as aggressive in a socially unacceptable or undesirable way.

In addition, aggression is not defined by harm but by the coming together of intention and harm. Unintentional harm may occur in a variety of situations. A driver might accidentally hit another car; a clerk might inadvertently short-change a customer; or a professor might err in grading a student's essay. The fact that these acts were unintentional means that they were not acts of aggression. In contrast, drivers who honk their horn at a slower car intend to goad another person to precipitate action, which could conceivably have fatal consequences.

Research on Aggression

Early Laboratory Research

The initial focus of laboratory research was to test the idea that aggression arises from an intent to harm. The main question was how to operationalize harm: Was it sufficient to simply observe a negative verbal exchange, or was it necessary to actually show that subjects will inflict physical harm on another person? In the end, many researchers felt that, in order to be sure that subjects were motivated by the intent to harm, it was necessary to show that they would in fact inflict physical harm. To this end, researchers decided to operationalize intent to harm in terms of whether participants would deliver a painful shock to another person (Baron, 1977).

These studies demonstrated that indeed individuals will deliver a painful shock to others. In most of the studies, the task was disguised. Individuals were told, for example, that they were part of a scientific study to determine whether giving people electrical shocks when they made mistakes would help them to learn. In these studies it was found that participants would deliver shocks even when they thought the shocks would be extremely painful (Milgram, 1963, 1974).

In a number of studies, participants were provoked by means of a negative evaluation (an unearned F for an essay they were asked to write) or insulted by the research assistant in the course of the experiment. They were then allowed to retaliate by delivering one or more shocks (often up to ten) to the research assistant who had been the source of the poor evaluation or the insult. They were typically told that delivering shocks was a way of evaluating the performance of the research assistant. Participants were not only willing to deliver shocks to the research assistant but were inclined to deliver more shocks to those research assistants who had been more severe in their evaluation or who had been more insulting (Baron, 1977). One of the main conclusions of these studies is that individuals

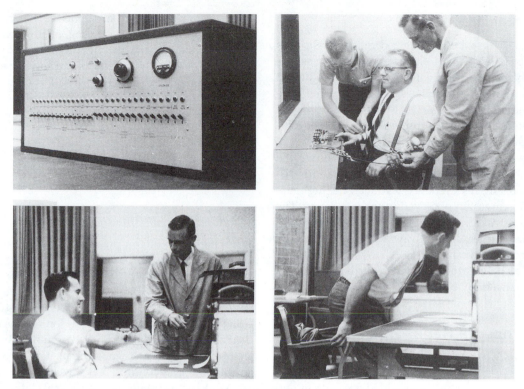

Scenes from Stanley Milgram's study of obedience to authority: the "shock genera-tor" (top left), the "learner" being strapped to his chair (top right), a subject being told to administer a severe shock (bottom left), and the subject refusing to continue (bottom right). Despite some objections, most subjects obeyed the experimenter.

usually need to be provoked in some way before they will retaliate.

Other studies found that, if they have been physically harmed—by a series of unprovoked shocks, for example—individuals normally retaliate in kind; that is, a recipient given a certain number of shocks is likely to return the same number (e.g., Borden, Bowen, & Taylor, 1971; Dengerink & Bertilson, 1974; Dengerink & Myers, 1977; Taylor, 1967). There is also evidence that, when subjects believe that they will not experience future retaliation (perhaps because they are anonymous in the study), they tend to inflict more shocks than they received (Zimbardo, 1969, 1972).

On certain occasions, people are inclined to engage in massive retaliation. Patterson (1976) has observed that, within the family setting, one family mem-

ber will often use aggressive behavior to stop the attacks of another. He has further observed that, when one family member suddenly increases the intensity of the aggressive exchange, the other is likely to terminate his or her attack; that is, whereas gradual escalation of the attack may increase an aggressive exchange, a sharp increase (massive retaliation) may decrease or end it. Evidence from other sources is consistent with this observation. For example, when the threat of retaliation for aggressive behavior is high, the tendency to initiate an attack is reduced (Baron, 1973; Dengerink & Levendusky, 1972; Shortell, Epstein, & Taylor, 1970). There is one important exception. When the person is very angry the threat of retaliation—even severe retaliation—does not reduce the tendency to initiate an attack (Baron, 1973).

Aggression in the Real World

These studies have been criticized on the basis that participants knew they were in a laboratory as opposed to the real world. Even then, the studies had to be disguised. In many instances, the participants were told that the immediate pain that they inflicted would have long-term benefits for humankind. Another criticism was that, when provoked, participants were normally only allowed to use physical aggression. In the real world, we often have other alternatives at our disposal. As a result, researchers questioned the high rate of physical aggression observed in the laboratory. The current focus is to examine aggression in the real world. Such studies don't always provide the level of control necessary to establish cause and effect, but they are essential if we are to understand the aggression that occurs on a daily basis.

New Concepts Regarding Aggression

While the laboratory studies provided a wealth of empirical data concerning the conditions under which individuals will and will not engage in physical acts of aggression, they largely failed to address the question of motivation. Obviously, the intent to harm must come from something more basic than a need to retaliate. It must come, researchers have argued, from our need to survive and adapt.

The Need to Control

Various researchers have suggested that the underlying motivation for acts of aggression is the human need for control. The need to exert control over events or people seems to be a fundamental human characteristic (Rotter, 1972). Many religious wars have been justified on the basis that, if people can be forced to behave in certain ways and to hold certain beliefs and attitudes, it will be a better world for all of us. It is not surprising, therefore, that humans have developed a wide range of strategies for exerting such control. Aggressive behaviors can be viewed as a subclass of control behaviors that are often but not always activated by anger.

Hans Toch (1969, 1992) has pointed out that violent criminals often lack the basic social skills neces-

sary to control people and events in the environment and tend to use force as a means of compensating for this deficiency. Young children often use physical violence but eventually develop more socially acceptable methods of control (Patterson, 1976). If individuals fail to develop such skills, physical aggression is the only method of control available to them. Toch believes that teaching physically aggressive criminals appropriate social skills for controlling events in the environment would reduce their tendency to initiate physical attacks on others.

A Working Definition of Aggression

If we start from the proposition that aggression grows out of a need to control others, and we assume that people differ in the strength of this need, we can define aggression as the willingness to engage in physical and psychological acts of harm in order to control the actions of other people. This definition retains all the essential features of the traditional definition but extends it in three important ways. First, it incorporates the idea that aggression involves psychological as well as physical harm. While the traditional definition of aggression does not exclude the idea of psychological harm, experiments that grew out of this definition typically operationalized aggression as physical harm. Second, it specifies that the motivation underlying aggression is to gain control over the behavior or other people. Third, it defines aggression as a disposition. If aggression is a disposition, learning and cognitive factors must play an important role in its expression. As we'll see, the tendency to act aggressively is frequently inhibited.

Note that this definition fails to explain unprovoked aggression, random acts of violence, and vandalism. It can be argued that such behaviors have their roots in anger, as we'll see when we look at Berkowitz's concept of generalized anger and rage.

Anger and Aggression

According to our working definition, aggression is an instrumental behavior that grows out of an underlying need to control. It is not to be confused with anger, which is typically conceptualized as an emotion. As an emotion, anger can and often does interact with instrumental aggression. Among other things, anger lowers the threshold for instrumental aggression. While there is a strong positive correlation between anger and aggression, people often feel angry without becoming aggressive and often become aggressive without feeling angry. For example, people may feel anger when they become sick, when they are frustrated in their attempts to achieve a goal, or when a relationship fails, but they do not strike out at someone else. Similarly, without feeling angry, people will act aggressively to achieve a desired goal—for instance, to win a sporting competition, to gain advantage in a political contest, or to exercise power. In the Milgram (1963) study, the participants who administered high levels of shock did so without experiencing anger.

Thus, it is useful to distinguish instrumental aggression, which is goal-directed and not associated with anger, from angry or affective aggression.

Summary

Moyer has identified eight kinds of aggression in animals; most of these can be found in humans. In psychology, aggression has traditionally been defined as behavior intended to harm another person. It does not apply to accidental harm, out of negligence or in the normal course of competitive behavior (for example, in an athletic contest).

The initial focus of laboratory research was to verify that aggression arises out of an intent to harm. In experiments, whose purpose was often disguised, it was repeatedly demonstrated that people will deliver a painful shock to another human being. Studies of retaliation suggest that people are normally inclined to retaliate in kind but will increase the level of retaliation if they perceive that they are protected against any future consequences such as when anonymous. Massive retaliation is often a message to the opponent to cease the aggressive exchange.

According to our working definition, aggression is the willingness to engage in physical and psychological acts of harm in order to control the actions of other people. This definition incorporates the essential features of the traditional definition and specifies the underlying motivation for aggressive behavior.

While there is a strong positive correlation between anger and aggression, people often feel angry without becoming aggressive and often become ag-

gressive without feeling angry. Accordingly, it is useful to distinguish between instrumental aggression, which does not involve anger, and affective aggression, which is characterized by anger.

Measuring Human Aggression

Casual observation of human behavior suggests that humans differ in their tendency to act aggressively. To determine whether some individuals tend to engage in more acts of aggression or have greater feelings of anger and hostility, researchers have constructed and validated self-report inventories. The frequently used Hostility Inventory developed by Buss and Darkee (1957) has been shown to predict a wide range of aggressive behaviors. Recently, Buss and Perry (1992) constructed a new inventory. Factor analysis of the items in this inventory has identified four factors or components: physical aggression, verbal aggression, anger, and hostility. Physical aggression and verbal aggression, which involve hurting other people, represent the instrumental component. Anger, which involves physiological arousal, represents the emotional or affective component. Hostility, which involves feelings of ill will and injustice, represents the cognitive component of aggression (Buss & Perry, 1992).

Now let's examine the biological, learned, and cognitive aspects of aggression.

The Biological Component of Aggression

Genetic Processes

Several studies have compared monozygotic and dizygotic twins on the basis of self-reported inventories of aggression. While some have found a genetic factor for aggression, others have not (Tedeschi & Felson, 1994). One study of 573 twin pairs, found a correlation of 0.40 for monozygotic twins and no correlation for dizygotic twins, results that indicate there is a strong genetic effect (Rushton, Fulker, Neale, Nias, & Eysenck, 1986). A shortcoming of these twin studies is that they fail to control for the environment. In order to address this problem, it is necessary to study twins reared in separate environments. In one such study, monozygotic twins were found to be more similar than dizygotic twins, on the basis not only of measures of aggression but also of other measures of personality (Tellegen et al., 1988), evidence consistent with the idea that genetics plays a central role.

Studies have also shown that the temperamental trait of impulsivity is related to aggressive and antisocial behavior (Coccaro, Bergeman, & McClearn, 1993; Karli, 1991). This tendency may be mediated by serotonin levels in the brain. Increased serotonin has been shown to produce response inhibition, while decreased serotonin has been shown to produce hyperactivity in associated brain structures. Researchers have been particularly interested in linking temperament to aggression as a step toward tracking developmental progression that leads to full-blown delinquent or criminal behavior. Remember that an individual with a temperamental disposition to act aggressively will not necessarily become a delinquent or a criminal. Perhaps the reason for the link between impulsivity and aggression is that we appear to inhibit the majority of our aggressive impulses. Impulsive people, who are unable to do so, would, therefore, be more inclined to act aggressively.

Hormones and Aggression

Hormones and Male Aggression

One of the main hormones linked to aggression is testosterone. While numerous studies have found a positive correlation between aggression and testosterone levels, we cannot be certain from those studies whether testosterone caused the aggression or the aggression caused the testosterone. It may be that testosterone is a chemical backup that maintains an aggressive behavior. Two research designs have been used to determine whether testosterone causes aggression: In one, testosterone levels are increased, and aggression is monitored; in the other, testosterone levels are decreased, and aggression is monitored.

Because it would be unethical to administer testosterone for experimental purposes, researchers have tried to identify individuals who self-administer drugs —such as steroids—that lead to increases in testosterone levels. A comparison of weight lifters who use steroids with nonsteroid users on the basis of the Buss-Durkee Hostility Inventory found that steroid users had higher levels of hostility (Yates, Perry, & Murray,

1992). This study doesn't rule out the possibility that being aggressive caused the steroid use. Note, however, that animal studies involving random assignment have shown that steroids increase aggressive behavior (Haug, Brain, & Kamis, 1985).

Studies on the effects of castration provide further evidence that testosterone plays an important role in aggression. Follow-up studies of castrated sex offenders have indicated that castration not only reduces the sex drive but reduces hostility and aggressive tendencies (Bremer, 1959; Hawke, 1950; Sturup, 1960). Injections of testosterone in castrated males have been shown to restore the previous aggressive tendencies (Hawke, 1950). Therefore, the reduction of aggression was probably due to a decrease in testosterone level and not simply a by-product of the trauma of castration or the accompanying therapy. Testosterone antagonists have also been used to treat sexual offenders. The findings are generally consistent with the idea that decreases in testosterone result in decreased aggression (e.g., Sturup, 1968; Money, 1980).

A recent study based on the Aggression Inventory, a self-report instrument that measures both physical and verbal aggression, found that high levels of testosterone and estradiol in blood samples were positively linked to indices of aggression in men (physical, verbal, and impulsive) but negatively linked to various indices in women (physical, verbal, and impatience) (Gladue, 1991). Animal work has shown that aggressive behavior can be established and induced by estrogen as well as androgens, presumably because testosterone can be metabolized into estradiol (Simon & Whalen, 1986).

Hormones and Female Aggression

Attempts to link female aggression to high levels of testosterone or estradiol have generally been inconclusive (Gladue, 1991). One line of research suggests that female aggression may come from an imbalance of progesterone and estrogen.

Just before menstruation and during the initial stage of menstruation, some women experience increased irritability and hostility, as part of *premenstrual syndrome* (PMS) (e.g., Ivey & Bardwick, 1968; Shainess, 1961). There is evidence that they tend to act out their feelings and so get into trouble. For example, one study found that schoolgirls tend to break more rules —and, as a consequence, receive more punishment—

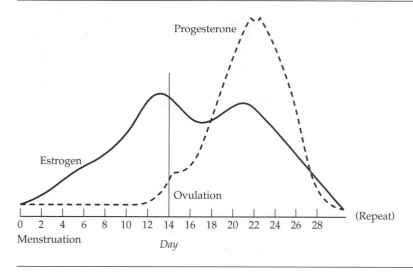

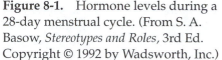

Figure 8-1. Hormone levels during a 28-day menstrual cycle. (From S. A. Basow, *Stereotypes and Roles*, 3rd Ed. Copyright © 1992 by Wadsworth, Inc.)

during menstruation, while older girls who are responsible for discipline are likely to mete out more punishment during menstruation (Dalton, 1960). Women prisoners are also more likely to get into trouble during early menstruation (Dalton, 1961). Aware of this tendency, many ask to be isolated during that phase (Dalton, 1964). In addition, there is evidence that women are more likely to commit crimes at that stage of their cycle (Dalton, 1961; Morton, Addition, Addison, Hunt, & Sullivan, 1953). Dalton suggests that these symptoms are linked with the fall in progesterone level in this phase, together with the increase in the ratio of estrogen to progesterone. The levels of estrogen and progesterone during a 28-day menstrual cycle are shown in Figure 8-1.

Several studies indicate that the administration of progesterone will alleviate not only irritability and hostility (e.g., Dalton, 1964, 1977; Greene & Dalton, 1953; Lloyd, 1964) but also a number of other symptoms that tend to increase during this part of the menstrual cycle, including asthma, herpes, tonsillitis, baby battering, epileptic seizures, and alcoholic bouts (Dalton, 1977).

The work of Dalton and others has been criticized on both methodological and conceptual grounds (Parlee, 1973; Fausto-Sterling, 1985). Methodological shortcomings include: lack of adequate controls in many cases; a failure to use double-blind testing procedures, which are critical in this type of study; small sample sizes; poor or nonexistent methods of measuring moods; and often a failure to check for testosterone levels. It is important to check for testosterone levels because of considerable evidence that both estrogen and progesterone tend to mask the effects of testosterone. If estrogen and progesterone levels are low, any increase in aggression could be due to testosterone. According to Figure 8-1, if aggression were linked to low estrogen and progesterone levels, the highest aggression would be expected at the beginning of the cycle.

A conceptual criticism of this work is that PMS may be due to a variety of other factors, including Vitamin A and Vitamin B deficiency, hypoglycemia, and disturbances in prolactin metabolism (Abplanalp, 1983; Reid & Yen, 1983). Finally, note that women in North America and western countries tend to believe that they should experience negative moods and feelings of aggressiveness during menstruation (McFarland, Ross, & DeCourville, 1989). Future studies will need to control for this factor if they are to show convincingly that aggression in females is due to imbalances in estrogen and progesterone, as Dalton and others believe.

Androstenedione and Aggression in the Female Hyena

Female spotted hyenas not only look and act like males, but they force their dominance over males through their size and aggression. Researchers have found, for example, that a single female will dominate the dominance hierarchy (the so-called pecking order). Studies have shown that levels of testosterone and related androgens are higher in this dominant female than in the average male and six times higher than in the average female.

What has particularly intrigued scientists about the female spotted hyena is the enlarged clitoris, which looks strikingly like the male penis. It turns out that this large clitoris is linked to a prehormone called androstenedione, which is produced in the gonads and adrenal glands of all mammals. Androstenedione is the last chemical in the chain of chemical reactions before it splits into the production of either male hormones or female hormones. As a result, this chemical may have the capacity to determine gender. It has been shown, for example, to induce bisexuality in male rats. When male rats were castrated, to remove their normal source of testosterone, and then injected with androstenedione, they displayed both female posturing and male mounting. When pregnant female rats were injected with androstenedione their offspring, whether genetically female, were born with a phallus and exhibited male-type sexual activity.

Researchers have suggested that the pattern of aggressive behavior evolved to give the female hyena and her offspring an evolutionary advantage. They suggest that masculinized genitals may have been an accidental by-product of this evolutionary process (Hopson, 1987).

Studies with humans have found that higher levels of androstenedione in both male and female adolescents is related to a variety of problem behaviors, including lying, disobedience, tendency to explode, talking back to parents and teachers (in boys), and taking an angry and dominating attitude towards parents (in girls) (Hopson, 1987).

How important is it for us to understand the role of hormones? It has been estimated that 20–25% of aggression may be due to endocrine factors (Gladue, 1991). While this is a significant proportion, we obviously need to look also at the role of learned and cognitive factors.

Sex Differences in Males and Females

In view of the positive correlation between testosterone and male aggression, it might be concluded that males are more aggressive than females. While crime statistics clearly show that males commit most crimes, research studies find little difference between male and female aggression.

After reviewing studies using different measures of aggression it was concluded that, while males, on the average, are more aggressive than females, the difference is quite small (Eagly & Steffen, 1986). In a meta-analysis of 143 studies, Hyde (1986) found that the difference between males and females was about one-half of a standard deviation ($d = 0.50$). This means that 63% of the males were above average in aggression and 38% of the females were above average. Her meta-analysis indicated that gender accounted for only 5% of the difference. A recent comparison of males and females using the Aggression Questionnaire found that men scored slightly higher on verbal aggression and hostility, much higher on physical aggression, and were equal on anger (Buss & Perry, 1992).

A fundamental problem when using averages to determine whether males or females are more aggressive is that a preponderance of one type of measure of aggression—physical or psychological, for example—can skew the data. In the studies reviewed by Eagly and Steffen (1986), a preponderance used the teacher-learner paradigm, which is more likely to elicit aggression in men than in women and tends to elicit greater aggression towards men than women. Eagly and Steffen point out that the magnitude of the difference between males and females is related to their tendency to use physical harm. It appears that women are much more cautious than males about using any form of physical aggression, largely because they seem to be more aware of the consequences. Further, it appears that women experience more guilt and anxiety in connection with the decision to retaliate. Finally, there is considerable evidence that females may be more motivated to turn off or deescalate aggression, especially in aggressive exchanges with males.

Neuromechanisms

Temporal Lobe Pathology

While there are numerous studies on brain structures and aggression in animals, there are very few studies of humans. An often-reported case involves Charles Whitman, an introspective young man with no previous history of violence, who one night killed his wife and his mother. The next morning he went to the University of Texas administration building, where he killed the receptionist and barricaded himself in the tower. From the top of the tower, he used his high-powered rifle to shoot anyone he saw through the telescopic lens. During the next 90 minutes, he killed 14 persons and injured another 24. His shooting spree ended only when the police were able to kill him. The autopsy showed a brain tumor, whose exact location was difficult to pinpoint because of the wounds inflicted by police bullets. The evidence seemed to indicate, however, that it was located on the medial part of the temporal lobe (Moyer, 1976).

Whitman's case is particularly interesting because he kept notes on his feelings and had consulted with a psychiatrist several months earlier. He revealed to the psychiatrist that he sometimes became so angry that he would like to go to the top of the university tower and start shooting people. The letter he wrote just before he killed his wife and mother provides some insight into his tortured mental state.*

I don't quite understand what it is that compels me to type this letter. Perhaps it is to leave some vague reason for the actions I have recently performed.

I don't really understand myself these days. I am supposed to be an average, reasonable and intelligent young man. However, lately (I can't recall when it started) I have been a victim of many unusual and irrational thoughts. These thoughts constantly recur, and it requires a tremendous mental effort to concentrate on useful and progressive tasks. In March when my parents made a physical break I noticed a great deal of stress. I consulted a Dr. Cochrum at the University Health Center and asked him to recommend someone that I could consult with about some psychiatric disorders I felt I had. I talked with a doctor once for about two hours and tried to convey to him my fears that I felt overcome (sick) by overwhelming violent impulses. After one session I never saw the doctor again and since then I have been fighting my mental turmoil alone, and seemingly to no avail. After my death I wish that an autopsy would be performed on me to see if there is any visible physical disorder. I have had some tremendous headaches in the past and have consumed two large bottles of Excedrin in the past three months.

It was after much thought that I decided to kill my wife Kathy, tonight after I pick her up from work. . . . I love her dearly, and she has been as fine a wife to me as any man could ever hope to have. I cannot rationally pin-point any specific reason for doing this. I don't know whether it is selfishness or if I don't want her to have to face the embarrassment my actions would surely cause her. At this time though, the prominent reason in my mind is that I truly do not consider this world worth living in, and am prepared to die, and I do not want to leave her to suffer alone in it. I intend to kill her as painlessly as possible. (Moyer, 1976, p. 26)

After he had killed his mother and wife, he wrote:

I imagine it appears that I brutally killed both of my loved ones. I was only trying to do a good and thorough job.

If my life insurance policy is valid please see that all the worthless checks I wrote this weekend are made good. Please pay off all my debts. I am 25 years old and have never been financially independent. Donate the rest anonymously to a mental health foundation. Maybe research can prevent further tragedies of this type. (Moyer, 1976, p. 26)

Amygdala

There is considerable evidence from animal work that lesions or ablations of the amygdala produce a calming effect (Grossman, 1967; Pribram, 1976). While psychosurgery is a radical treatment, it has been used with humans who experience outbursts of violence and aggression. Using animal research as a model, surgeons have cut away part of the temporal lobes and the amygdala. The results of such surgery have shown that it is partially effective in reducing aggression and violence (Brain, 1984; Moyer, 1987). The amygdala and the temporal lobe are show in Figure 8-2.

The amygdala has been implicated in a wide range of emotional behaviors. It triggers the body's fight-or-flight hormones, mobilizes the center for movement, activates the cardiovascular system, triggers the release of norepinephrine, and generally makes us more alert (LeDoux, 1986, 1992, 1993, 1996). LeDoux has suggested that the amygdala plays a pivotal role in governing our behavior, because it can initiate actions before our thinking (rational) brain has been fully able to comprehend an incoming signal. The essence of his argument is that a sensory signal first goes to the thalamus and then is routed to two different locations: the amygdala and the neocortex. Since it takes longer to reach the cortex, the amygdala is free to act—at least for a few milliseconds—before the cortex can evaluate and confirm the nature of the incoming signal. He suggests,

*Excerpts from *The Psychobiology of Aggression*, by K. E. Moyer. Copyright © 1976 by K. E. Moyer. Reprinted with permission of Harper & Row, Publishers, Inc.

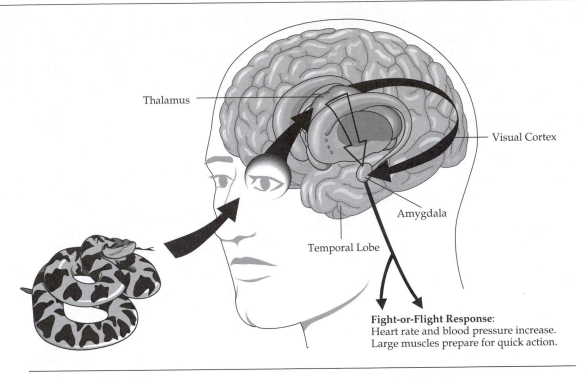

Thalamus

Visual Cortex

Amygdala

Temporal Lobe

Fight-or-Flight Response:
Heart rate and blood pressure increase.
Large muscles prepare for quick action.

Figure 8-2.   Some important brain structures involved in aggressive behavior.

as other theorists have, that humans are prepared to treat a novel stimulus as a potential threat to our survival. He goes on to argue that, because of this delay, some emotional reactions and memories can be formed without any conscious or cognitive participation. What we have, in short, is two memory systems: one for ordinary events and one for emotionally charged events.

The problem is that memories in the amygdala may be faulty guides to the present. They may prime us to perceive harmless stimuli as threatening and therefore to act aggressively. LeDoux also points out that this emotional system sustains its own activity once activated. As a result, we will be primed—at least for some period—to see things as threatening. When we perceive that we are threatened, we are more dispositionally inclined to act aggressively.

The essence of impulsivity is acting without complete information. LeDoux's findings not only explain the initial tendency to act impulsively but also indicate why this tendency is very resistant to change. His findings also help us to understand why impulsivity is

likely to lead to antisocial behavior and even violence. Unless this system is somehow retrained, it tends to push people towards more aggressive and antisocial behavior.

Summary

Using self-report inventories, individuals can be differentiated with respect to dispositional aggression. While some studies of monozygotic and dizygotic twins have shown there is a genetic component to aggression, others have not. Studies of temperament have shown that impulsivity is linked to aggressive and antisocial behavior. This tendency may be mediated by serotonin levels in the brain. While a large body of data links male aggression to testosterone, data linking female aggression to testosterone or to changes in the ratio of estrogen and progesterone are inconclusive. Research with hyenas suggests that testosterone may be an important source of aggression in females as well as males. However, there is no support for the idea that testosterone governs aggression in human females. We don't know why human aggression is organized so differently in males and females.

Using a variety of measures of aggression, persistent differences between men and women have been found. Males tend to be slightly higher on verbal aggression and hostility and much higher on measures of physical aggression. It appears that the expression of aggression—especially physical aggression—is more inhibited in females, who also experience more guilt and anxiety about aggression.

Considerable evidence links animal aggression to various brain structures, but human data do not permit solid inferences as yet. Results from psychosurgery indicate that removing the temporal lobes and the amygdala has a marked calming effect. LeDoux has argued that the amygdala plays a central role in aggression. It not only triggers the fight-or-flight response, but also initiates defensive actions without the full involvement of the neocortex. His model provides an explanation for the link between impulsivity and antisocial behavior.

The Learned Component of Aggression

Frustration

Frustration has long been regarded as a major cause of aggression. According to the frustration hypothesis, the tendency to become aggressive increases when goal-directed behavior is blocked (Berkowitz, 1962, 1969; Miller, 1941). Thus, such everyday events as finding that a favorite restaurant is closed, having to wait in line to see a movie, or not getting a good grade on a test might produce frustration, which, in turn, would increase the tendency to engage in aggressive behavior.

Frustration and the Energization of Behavior

Frustration is comparable to nonreward, which appears to energize behavior (Amsel, 1958); any behavior that follows nonreward will be executed with more vigor. While behaviors that follow nonreward are often directed at removing the source of the frustration, not all frustrated behaviors lead to aggression.

While many studies have produced results consistent with the frustration hypothesis (e.g., Berkowitz & Geen, 1966; Burnstein & Worchel, 1962; Geen, 1968), others have not (e.g., Buss, 1963; Kuhn, Madsen, & Becker, 1967; Taylor & Pisano, 1971). After a careful examination of the conflicting results, Baron (1977) has concluded that "frustration can indeed facilitate later aggression" (p. 91) but is likely to do so only when frustration is (1) "quite intense" and (2) "unexpected or arbitrary in nature" (p. 91). Thus, having to wait in line may fail to facilitate aggression, because the accompanying frustration is not intense enough. In fact, most of us learn that at times we will have to wait and, as a result, we tend to experience little or no frustration in that situation. Whether a student's failure to receive the expected grade will facilitate aggression might be affected by the student's perception of whether the grading was fair.

Frustration and the Direction of Behavior

Despite what we might expect, frustrated people often do not attack the source of the frustration, for several reasons; attack may result in retaliation, for example. When frustrated, however, people will engage in a range of behaviors. Because frustration is a negative motivational state, the reduction of frustration should be highly rewarding, and any behavior that has that effect is likely to occur more often in the future.

In a recent reexamination of research on the frustration hypothesis, Berkowitz (1989) suggested that frustration generates aggressive inclinations to the degree that it arouses negative affect. Situations in which people do not act aggressively when frustrated fail to arouse negative affect, according to Berkowitz. Whether a situation arouses negative affect depends, in part, on our cognitive processes—for example, on whether we perceive that we have been blocked deliberately or accidentally. If we perceive that someone else deliberately blocked us from reaching our goal, we are more likely to react with anger and aggression.

The Concept of Displacement

If we are frustrated by something, it makes sense to attack the cause. However, it's not always possible to attack the source of the problem. If I have to wait in line at a bank, the source of the problem is often the manager, who has failed to assign enough tellers to handle the volume of people; however, that may not stop me from snapping at the teller. When I was a graduate student, I saw how rats responded to nonreward. In an experiment, rats were rewarded on a full reinforcement schedule for a time and then switched to a partial reinforcement schedule. When nonrewarded trials were introduced, the rats would bite the food dish or attack some other nearby portion of the cage. When I removed the rat from the apparatus, it would often try to bite me as well. I was obviously the source of the problem, but the frustration was initially displaced towards other things, because I wasn't available. Sometimes we aren't even sure what is the source of the problem; in that case, we might strike out indiscriminately (Tedeschi & Felson, 1994).

Generalization and Inhibition

Following intense frustration, humans typically do not strike out indiscriminately. Both animal and human data indicate that we are equipped with inhibitory mechanisms that enable us to use aggression selectively or to suppress it altogether, when it is in our interest to do so (Lore & Schultz, 1993). The principle of *generalization* has been invoked to explain why we strike out selectively. According to this principle, stimuli can be ranked along a continuum in terms of their similarity to one another. In regard to aggression, the principle of generalization says that, if the target of our frustration is unavailable, we will direct our actions towards those stimuli that are most similar to the target. Thus, if we are forced to stand in line and the bank manager is unavailable, the next best target is the teller. In a job setting, we may find it very difficult to strike out at anybody. As a result, we may strike out at other people who somehow symbolize our frustrated state. A spouse is often the first available target after a frustrating day at work. Some people take out their frustrations by cutting off people in traffic.

Our actions are also governed by the principle of *inhibition*. Early in life, we discover that, when we engage in certain behaviors—such as physically attacking another person who has frustrated us—we will be punished. If frustrated children bite, hit, or kick their parents, such acts usually incur quick and often painful consequences; as a result, children learn to inhibit such behaviors. Acceptable responses to frustra-

tion depend on culture, economic status, gender, and other factors. Males are often taught to channel their aggressive energy into sports; females are often taught to deal with aggression by sharing their feelings with someone else. As a result of these early experiences, we learn to do certain things and not others.

By understanding the principles of generalization and inhibition, we can better understand why frustration leads to different behaviors in different people.

Blind Rage: Generalized Anger and Aggression

With no apparent provocation, certain individuals commonly respond to negative situations with anger and aggression; they lash out at anything and everything in sight. Berkowitz (1990) explains this phenomenon in terms of generalization.

Berkowitz starts with the observation that anger and aggression may be provoked by a range of unpleasant experiences, including foul odors, high temperatures, exposure to pain, cold water, getting sick, and getting caught in a traffic jam. Sometimes people become angry when they are sad—when a close friend dies, for example—or when they are depressed—after losing their job, for instance. Berkowitz suggests that the tendency to become angry and aggressive in response to a wide range of stimuli is largely learned. Once people learn to associate a wide range of negative feelings with anger and aggression, they become angry and may become aggressive whenever they experience those feelings. Specifically, he suggests that negative affect activates ideas, memories, and actions associated with anger and aggression. As a result, when we begin to experience negative affect, we are put in a state of readiness to experience anger and to engage in a variety of aggressive acts.

Cognitive theorists maintain that certain kinds of beliefs are necessary before the emotion of anger can arise, but Berkowitz disagrees. Consider the example of a person who develops a toothache, asks, "Why me?" and angrily kicks a door. To explain such incidents, Berkowitz argues that pain elicits memories of previous negative feelings, such as anger, and the associated actions, such as aggression. As a result, people come to express their anger and engage in aggression whenever they experience pain, even from a toothache. Note that, in this theory, the negative affect is the common mediator of the two distinct emotions. Clearly, in this way, a wide range of negative emotions might, over time, come to elicit aggression.

Berkowitz does acknowledge the role of cognitions; in fact, he calls his theory a cognitive-neoassociationistic approach. Most people, he argues, have a rudimentary idea (prototype) of the primary emotions and what factors are involved in these emotions (sensation, thoughts, memories, and so on). As a result, there is a limit on the degree to which negative emotions can become linked to anger and aggression. According to his theory, as we learn to differentiate emotions—that is, to define our prototypes more clearly. As a result, we are less inclined to generalize. As a result, while one person may respond to pain with anger and aggression, someone else may not.

The strength of Berkowitz's theory lies in its ability to account for two things: (1) why certain negative emotions can come to elicit anger and aggression even though these responses are not adaptive, at least from a biological perspective; and (2) why people who have learned to differentiate their emotions do not show this maladaptive tendency.

According to this theory, teaching people how to better differentiate their emotions should reduce generalized aggression in our society. Biologists maintain that emotions evolved to make us adaptive. In order to maximize our adaptiveness as humans, we must learn to differentiate our emotions, so that we respond appropriately to each of the emotions we experience.

Social Learning Theory

According to social learning theory, the environment often plays an important role in the acquisition, expression, and maintenance of aggressive behavior (Bandura, 1973).

Modeling and Imitation

One of the main ways children learn aggression is through observation and imitation. We know, for example, that how people discipline their children is often very similar to how they were disciplined as children (Patterson, 1980). Those raised with strict discipline tend to employ strict discipline with their children; those raised more leniently tend to be lenient. We also know that physical and sexual abuse is often

passed on from generation to generation; this has been called the cycle of violence.

The Cycle of Violence

Parents who abuse their children often know that it is wrong by the standards of society but continue anyway. It is as if they have a habit that they cannot break. The consensus among experts in the field is that, unless it can be broken, this pattern will continue into succeeding generations. This is a powerful example of the role learning plays in the acquisition and maintenance of an aggressive behavior pattern.

A recent review of research on the cycle of violence indicates that not all children who grow up in homes characterized by violence and neglect become violent or abuse their children (Widom, 1989a,b). Unfortunately, at this point we do not know why the cycle is broken in some cases but not in others. As DiLalla and Gottesman (1991) point out, important biological and genetic factors have been implicated in the transmission of violence from generation to generation. It may be that the individual must possess a certain biological temperament, for example, before such learning takes place.

Aggression and TV Violence

Does watching violent TV shows promote violent behavior? Despite extensive research, the answer is still not clear. It seems that, once exposed to violence on TV, some individuals may be more inclined to engage in aggressive behaviors if they are provoked. This does not mean, however, that exposure to TV violence causes aggressive behavior in the absence of provocation. It may be that TV violence acts indirectly to increase aggressiveness (e.g., Fenigstein, 1979). At least four explanations have been offered: (1) modeling and imitation of aggression; (2) release—or disinhibition—of aggressive impulses; (3) elicitation of aggressive actions that have been previously learned; and (4) an increase in arousal produced by watching aggressive activities (Bandura, 1973; Geen, 1976).

A large proportion of the children who watch violence on television do not show increased aggressiveness. Why is that? One important factor is how the parents view violence. If the parents do not endorse violence as a means of settling disputes, achieving goals, and so on, children who watch violence on television

Children frequently model aggression they see from watching television.

utor to aggression, at least for a short time, when a person is angry (Doob & Climie, 1972). This finding suggests that TV violence has a general arousal effect that facilitates aggressiveness, as opposed to a specific modeling effect.

In a study comparing American cities that had television and those that did not, no effect was found for the presence or absence of television (Hennigan et al., 1982). Further, when cities without television obtained it, violent crimes did not increase. Thus, there is no evidence for the idea that viewing television leads to aggressive behavior.

Pornography and Aggression

Does aggression in pornographic films lead to increasing violence toward women, especially rape? The extensive research on this topic (Donnerstein & Linz, 1986; Malamuth & Donnerstein, 1984) has focused on the distinction between erotica that involves no violence or force and pornography that does portray violence and force. A film showing a woman being raped or tortured, for example, differs substantially from a film depicting sexual activity between two lovers. The research has shown that erotic images do not seem to lead to an increase in male aggression toward women, but violent pornography with scenes of rape may lead to an increase in the tendency to rape. These studies have not shown that the male volunteers have actually raped as a result of watching scenes of rape; however, they have shown rather that the men tended to see rape as having little or no serious or harmful effect on women, possibly because, in pornographic films, the woman typically offers only token resistance to rape before she is swept away by passion for her attacker. Men who fail to understand that rape is a terrifying and traumatic experience for a woman may be misled by these portrayals. As a result of viewing films in which women are represented as enjoying rape, men may come to view rape not as the infliction of harm on another person but as the delivery of pleasure. As a result, their inhibitions around rape are lowered.

If men's inhibitions about rape are reduced as a result of the way women are portrayed in pornographic films, rather than by the depiction of sexual activity, we might conclude that it is important to consider how the media in general portray women. It has been suggested that violence toward women is endemic in TV shows, films, and advertising. At this point, very little

tend not to be affected by it (Dominick & Greenberg, 1971). Another relevant factor is whether a given child prefers violence. Not all children, it appears, like to watch violence. Those who do prefer violence on TV tend to be more innately aggressive (Eron, Huesmann, Lefkowitz, & Walder, 1972; Fenigstein, 1979; Bushman, 1995). Consequently, the correlation found between watching violence on TV and aggressive behavior may simply reflect a greater preexisting inclination to aggression in children who enjoy TV violence. Figure 8-3 shows that, as the trait of aggressiveness becomes stronger, so does preference for violent films. Parental attitudes may again play an important role in facilitating or inhibiting this tendency. Finally, it appears that TV violence can be a very powerful contrib-

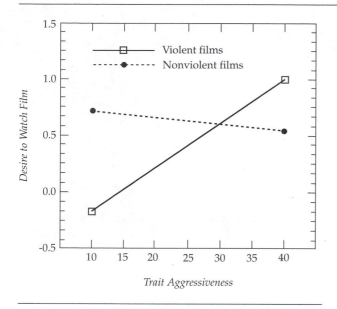

Figure 8-3.   The moderating role of trait aggressiveness on desire to watch the violent and nonviolent films.

work has been done to evaluate the effects of these violent images.

In 1987, the Attorney General's Commission on Pornography concluded that there is a causal relationship between exposure to pornography and several antisocial behaviors, including violence towards women (Linz, Donnerstein, & Penrod, 1987), and called for more stringent law enforcement. Some scientists whose work was used by the commission have argued that some of the extrapolations made by the commission are unwarranted and that some of the findings are inconsistent with research data. These critics argue that we should be concerned with violent images throughout the media, not just in pornography, and design educational programs to mitigate against all forms of violence, including sexual violence (Linz, Donnerstein, & Penrod, 1987).

Summary

According to the frustration hypothesis, the tendency to become aggressive increases when goal-directed behavior is blocked. If frustration is to cause aggression, it must be quite intense, unexpected, or arbitrary. Frustration does not give direction to aggressive behavior; rather, it gives rise to a negative motivational state that, when reduced, will reinforce behavior. Much of the aggression that occurs as a result of frustrations is displaced, because humans have learned to inhibit aggressive attacks towards certain targets. Berkowitz has suggested that negative affect is one of the main sources of anger and aggression. He argues that negative affect activates ideas, memories, and actions associated with anger and aggression. As a result, when we begin to experience such negative feelings, we are in a state of readiness to experience anger and engage in aggressive acts. Berkowitz points out that people who learn to better differentiate their emotions are less likely to engage in this maladaptive tendency to respond to all negative affect with anger and aggression.

Social learning theory suggests that the environment plays an important role in the acquisition, expression, and maintenance of aggressive behavior, through the mechanisms of modeling and imitation. The cycle of violence is thought to be an example of learned behavior. After many studies, there is little evidence of a causal link between TV violence and aggression. However, TV violence may send the message that violence is an acceptable way of settling conflicts. Researchers have also been unable to establish a clear causal link between pornography and violence against women, but argue that any portrayal of violence towards women is a source of concern. Research on this topic should not be limited to studies of pornography.

The Cognitive Component of Aggression

Tedeschi and Felson (1994) have proposed a theory of coercive action that focuses on the social functions of harm-doing. Their theory is concerned not only with physical harm but also with psychological harm. They start from the perspective that people use threats and punishment to achieve certain goals or to preserve certain values they hold. In other words, coercive behavior is not simply reactive, but is intentional. They define a *coercive action* as an action taken with the intention of imposing harm on another person or forcing compliance.

Coercive action takes many forms. It is designed to get another person to comply. It often involves the use of threats and punishments. In a parent-child relationship, where the parent is most likely to use coercive action, it might involve such things as scolding the child, withdrawing of privileges (such as watching television), or physical punishment. At work, where the boss is most likely to use coercion, it might involve giving a suggestion, berating, or withholding a promotion. In a romantic relationship, where either party might use coercive actions, it might involve insults, withholding of affection, or even physical abuse.

A Model of Coercive Action

Let's begin with three of the important concepts within the theory of coercive action. First, the *actor* is the person who evaluates information and makes decisions about what to do under a variety of different circumstances. Second, the *targets* are people who are threatened by the actor or do not fall in line with the actor's desires. Finally, the *terminal goal* represents the motives and values that causes the actor to think in certain ways and decide on certain courses of action (Figure 8-4).

There is no need for coercive action when the behavior of the target is consistent with the motives and values of the actor (solid line). Coercive action only arises when the behavior of others is not in line with the wishes of the actor (dashed line). The point of the coercive action is to bring that behavior back into alignment with the desired behavior (the solid line). When parents look at the behavior of their child—how tidy the child's room is, for example—they decide whether it matches their expectations. If it does, there is no need for coercive action. If not, the parents will engage in some form of coercive action—perhaps a simple scolding.

The Costs of Coercive Action

The theory of coercive action is designed to account for a wide range of behavior. For example, consider the behavior of bank robbers during a holdup. As long as the bank employees and the hostages follow the robbers' instructions (the solid line), there would be no need to engage in coercive action. Should someone not follow their instructions (the dashed line), they would have to consider some kind of coercive action; they might threaten to hit or even kill the noncomplying individ-

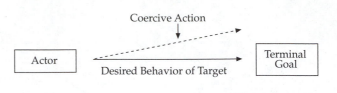

Figure 8-4. Model of coercive action.

ual. The terminal goal, of course, is to get the money from the bank vault. They can only achieve that goal if others comply.

The nature of the coercive action chosen by an actor is determined to a large degree by costs. In the theory, there are at least four types of costs:

1. *Opportunity costs.* Actors ask themselves whether it is worth the time, effort, and energy to engage in coercive behaviors.
2. Potential *retaliation costs.* Actors evaluate, perhaps on the basis of previous experiences with the target, whether the target is likely to retaliate or to comply. If the retaliation costs are too high, the actor may decide against coercive behavior. On the other hand if the target is likely to comply, the costs would be minimal.
3. *Costs of noncoercion.* Sometimes the target is faced with a no-win or least-of-evils choice. An employee faced with unacceptable conditions may decide it would be better to quit than to comply. The employer must then weigh how important is it to keep this person against how important is it to make the employee comply.
4. *Third-party costs.* For example, what if a parent disciplines a child and the neighbors or the police intervene? If there are substantial third-party costs, the actor may decide not to engage in coercive behavior.

There is evidence that, as people get older, they perceive that the costs associated with criminal activity increase. This would account for the negative correlation between age and criminal activity.

The Relationship between Skills and Costs

According to the model, actors who see themselves as highly skilled are inclined to feel that the costs of securing compliance are relatively low. An actor who has mastered the art of telling people what they want to hear or giving them what they want may feel confident about securing the target's compliance by means of those skills. The underlying theme of the actor's presentation in that case might be: "If you do that for me, I can get this for you." An actor who knows that the most important thing for me is my children might do something for my children and attempt to use the leverage of indebtedness to gain compliance. In all these cases, the actor's strategy is highly calculated from the outset.

Irrational Coercive Action

As we see, the theory of coercive action proposes that people make rational decisions about how to get what they want by means of coercive action. Like other rational models, this theory assumes complete information processing. That means that the actor is inclined to analyze all aspects of the situation and consider all the possible alternatives. In reality, people are rarely completely rational. Tedeschi and Felson acknowledge that people often take coercive actions without complete information processing. They recognize that we often engage in mindless repetitive behaviors or simply behaviors copied from others. They argue that one of the main reasons for incomplete information processing is that, as humans, we have a limited ability to process information. Because we are preoccupied with other things, we fail to fully appreciate what is necessary and appropriate.

Alcohol and Coercive Action

There is a strong correlation between alcohol and criminal behavior. One study, for example, found that, in 64% of the criminal homicides studied, one of the parties was drinking alcohol (Wolfgang & Strohm, 1956). As we saw in Chapter 7, one of the most significant effects of alcohol consumption is disinhibition. After several drinks, people's behavior becomes less constrained.

The general interpretation of disinhibition is that our ability to process information is impaired under the influence of alcohol. For example, our attention is narrowed. As a result, we fail to consider certain important information when making decisions. We may fail to consider how others will evaluate us, for example.

Steele and his colleagues (Steele and Josephs, 1990; Banji and Steele, 1989) have suggested that alcohol pro-

duces a kind of myopia in which people tend to ignore, disregard, or downgrade certain pieces of relevant negative information when making judgments, especially judgments about the self (Chapter 7). As a result, people tend to see themselves in a more positive light (more like their ideal self). This is analogous to what happens in the approach/avoidance conflict when people use alcohol; while approach motivation is left more or less unchanged under the influence of alcohol, avoidant motivation is markedly reduced. The net effect is that people are more willing to act on the basis of their positive motives or feelings. Often, the consequences of ignoring negative motives are not fully understood until some later time. A person who insults a co-worker at an office party, for example, may not realize the likely consequences until the next day.

Using this line of argument, Tedeschi and Felson argue that people are more coercive under the influence of alcohol because they fail to fully consider the costs of engaging in a coercive act, which, in turn, is because of their alcohol-induced myopia leads them to ignore or disregard negative information. As the apparent costs decline, the tendency to engage in coercive action increases.

Justice

The decision to take coercive action often involves considerations of justice. Justice is a value that we acquire early in life from our interactions with parents, teachers, and other role models. We are taught that, if we do something now, we can expect something else to happen later—for example, that, if we do our chores, we can expect an allowance at the end of the week. In a longer time frame, we are told that, if we get good grades in school, we can expect a job when we graduate from high school. Lerner (1977) has suggested that, if certain promises are kept when we are young, we will come to believe in a just world. In such a world, we can live without undue anxiety about our future. When the time comes, there will be a job and money to live.

In a just world, we need to follow certain rules of conduct. One of the simple but important rules of conduct is that we need to wait our turn. The fundamental idea is that, if everybody abides by this rule, then we will all get what we deserve. Waiting in line is a good example. If even one person is allowed to go to the head of the line, others may do the same. If that happens, I can no longer be assured that I will get what I deserve.

The rules of conduct can be understood as norms. Take borrowing, for example. Should I refuse to return a borrowed book, I would be in violation of a norm. However, if I violate one norm, I prompt the suspicion that I will violate others. If I don't return a book, can I be trusted to return a borrowed car? In the end, I will be deprived of the privilege of borrowing.

The rules of justice involve not only obeying norms, but also taking responsibility for our actions. If we all take responsibility for our actions, we can be assured that we will not be harmed, for example, or that others will not take more than their fair share. We make allowances within our implicit theories of justice for mental and physical disability, age, and even gender. Again, norms come into play. Even though I may think that certain people should not receive welfare, the larger group of which I am a part may not operate on this norm. As a result, I am obliged to go along with the norm.

Different groups of people often hold different norms. While some believe that women have a right to decide whether to abort an unwanted child, others fiercely disagree. Political parties are often based on beliefs regarding which norms are good and which are bad and will sometimes attempt to force one norm on all people. The current debate about welfare involves norms: To what degree should people be required to take responsibility for their own well-being?

Retributive Justice

Retributive justice refers to the belief that blameworthy behavior should be punished. According to retributive justice, people whose behavior deviates from the norm (norm violation) need to be punished in order to bring compliance with the norm (Figure 8-5). Figure 8-5 resembles Figure 8-4, except that the terminal goal is labeled as a norm. Conceptually, norms and terminal goals are very similar. They both represent what we want for ourselves or what we think is right.

Three Types of Norm Violation

Interestingly, all the various types of norm violations can be summarized under three types.

Figure 8-5.   Model of retributive justice.

1. **Distributive justice** refers to the fair allocation of resources, the fair distribution of duties, and recognition of the amount of effort and level of performance. Children often fight over the division and use of property: Who gets the best room? Who gets to use the car? They also fight over duties that they must perform: Are two sets of chores equivalent in terms of time, effort, and skill required? Distributive justice plays an important role in employee satisfaction. If workers perceive that resources are not be distributed fairly, there is likely to be resentment and even retaliation.

2. **Procedural justice** refers to the means or procedures that are used to resolve conflicts of interest. We typically try to resolve such differences by having the two aggrieved parties tell their respective stories to a neutral party. Within the legal system, we have a highly formalized set of rules that govern this process.

3. **Interactional justice** involves conformity to norms about demeanor, respect, and politeness towards other people. The more common forms of perceived interactional injustice include lack of loyalty, lack of regard for the feelings of others, selfishness, hostility, and failure to keep agreements (Mikula, Petri, & Tanzer, 1989). Research indicates that this is by far the most important category of unjust events, because it intimately linked to our self-identities.

Justice as Self-Worth

Folger (1991) has suggested that all three aspects of justice are important because they reflect on our perceived self-worth. Violations of our sense of justice are perceived as a direct attack on our value as a person. It is very important for businesses, schools, and governments to insure that standards of justice are met, since our willingness to work and cooperate is linked to feelings of self-worth.

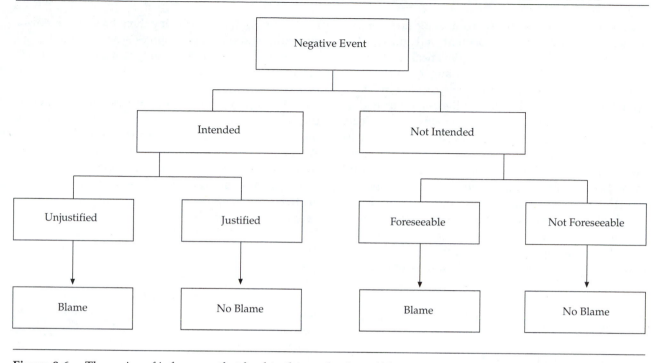

Figure 8-6.   The series of inferences that lead to the attribution of blame.

Attribution of Blame

How do we decide that some behavior is blameworthy? It has been suggested that, whenever we observe unwanted or unexpected behaviors, we search for an explanation (Wong & Weiner, 1981). As we see in Figure 8-6, the attribution of blame can be viewed as a series of steps at which inferences are made (Rule & Nesdale, 1976).

According to Figure 8-6, the observer initially makes a judgment about whether or not some external actor caused the negative outcome. If the decision is made that the actor caused the outcome, the observer then considers whether the outcome was intended or unintended. If the wrong was intended, the observer then decides whether or not the actor's intention was justified or unjustified. If the action was justified, no blame is assigned; however, if the action was not justified, blame is assigned. Being reprimanded for not doing something they were never instructed to do (such as making sure a certain setting was used before starting a machine) would be considered an unjustified act and therefore worthy of blame. Had they been told

ahead of time to use a certain setting, the reprimand would not be viewed as justified and therefore no blame would be assigned. Note that according to this decision tree, even if an act is not intended but some consequence is foreseeable, there is justification for assigning blame. Knowing that a certain lever setting should be used before starting a machine and allowing someone to proceed would be blameworthy. According to this framework, what leads people to consider an act as aggressive is linked to whether or not some type of injustice occurred.

Anger and Injustice

Anger commonly accompanies the attribution of blame (Averill, 1983). Because unjust treatment is perceived as a direct attack on our self-worth, it is not surprising that we respond as though our survival is being threatened (Klein & Bierhoff, 1992).

Angry people are characterized by energized behavior (loud voice, slamming doors) and impaired information processing. Instead of making a clear and coherent presentation of their grievance, they will often loudly attack the other person. Typically, their behavior is impulsive and incoherent and violates the very norms that underlie their grievance. As a result, they elicit feelings of injustice and anger in the target. This often begins a cycle of escalating conflict, in which both parties work hard to protect their self-worth.

This pattern of behavior is probably due, at least in part, to the high level of arousal that characterizes the angry person. Under high levels of arousal, attention narrows and shifts to threat cues in the environment. Instead of thinking and acting rationally, people resort to behaviors that are designed to forestall unexpected and arbitrary attacks. Anger frequently culminates in physical aggression. Perceived injustices would likely result in more physical acts of violence if it were not for the strong prohibition in our society against physical aggression.

Interpersonal Violence

The Link between Control and Power

Controlling other people is highly instrumental in achieving our goals and preserving our values. Feminist, multicultural, and gay and lesbian scholars have suggested that attempts to control others through violent means can often be understood in terms of the link between power and control (e.g., Walker, 1989). A common theme in that literature is that people who have power or perceive that they have power will be inclined not only to exercise it on their own behalf but also to maintain their power base because they have come to believe that they have the right to control others, even to the extent of using violent means.

What triggers acts of violence? According to psychological control theory, it is the threat of loss of power (control). Parents who abuse their children do so because they want to retain power. Lacking the skills to control their children's behavior through more socially accepted means, they resort to physical violence. Similarly, individuals who engage in spousal abuse are motivated by the desire for power; again, lacking the skills to maintain control, they resort to physical abuse.

Some theorists have suggested that violence against people of color, gay men, and lesbians reflects a struggle for power. As oppressed groups try to free themselves from the control of those in power and to take charge of their lives, they threaten existing power structures and the way resources are distributed. Consequently, their attempts at empowerment trigger acts of violence against them (Staub, 1996). According to this analysis, one approach to reducing such violence would be a public education campaign to explain that the empowerment of one group does not necessarily mean that other groups will lose their power.

Politics has to do with gaining and maintaining power. Through the political system, people attempt to insure that resources are distributed fairly and that they are treated in a fair and just way. It is not surprising that people who do not see themselves as having fair access to resources or being treated fairly will often reject the government and its laws and resort to violence.

Violence as the Last Resort

According to the coercive action model, aggression must be understood within the larger context of how people attempt to gain control of others. For most of us, physical acts of aggression are the last in a chain of strategies designed to gain compliance. However, people who lack other means of control are inclined to become aggressive and violent. Anger and alcohol are among the factors that can short-circuit the normal constructive ways that people use to gain control.

Summary

Tedeschi and Felson have proposed a theory of coercive action on the basis that individuals use threats and punishment to achieve certain goals or preserve certain values. According to their theory, there is no need for coercive action when the target complies with our wishes. However, when the target fails to comply, we engage in coercive action to bring the target's behavior in line with what we want. They have identified four costs associated with coercive action: opportunity costs; potential retaliation costs; noncoercion costs; and third-party costs.

Their model is basically a rational model of how people should act if they process all the available information. However, people sometimes fail to process all the information and do not act in a completely rational manner. Alcohol provides an interesting example of how people behave when they fail to consider certain important pieces of information.

Many coercive actions are motivated by the value of justice. Retributive justice refers to the belief that blameworthy behavior—behavior that departs from some norm—should be punished. Three other important aspects of justice are distributive justice, procedural justice, and interactional justice. It has been suggested that the attribution of blame involves a series of inferential steps that result in judgments of blame or no blame. Anger commonly accompanies the attribution of blame. There is good reason to argue that the high arousal that comes with blame is responsible, at least in part, for the poor decisions and the escalation of aggression that often accompanies a sense of injustice.

It has been suggested that violence against women, people of color, and gay men and lesbians can be understood in terms of the link between power and control. People who believe that they have the right to control another person will often resort to acts of coercion, including physical aggression. It appears that people often resort to physical aggression when verbal means of control fail.

Youth Violence

Youth violence in the United States has increased significantly in the past decade (Eron, Gentry, & Schlegel, 1994). For example, the homicide rate for young men in the United States is 7 times that of Canada and 18 times that of the United Kingdom (Tedeschi & Felson, 1994). There are several possible explanations for this. Some researchers have pointed out that poverty increased in this period and suggest that poverty is the best predictor of violence, including homicide (Hill, Soriano, Chen, & LaFromboise, 1994). Many children who grow up in poverty, however, do not become violent. San Francisco's Chinatown is one of the poorest areas of the city and yet the murder rate there remains extremely low (Staub, 1996). It has also been suggested that those abused in childhood will be more inclined toward violence and aggression, especially against their own children, but only about 30% show this trend (Staub, 1996). Although abused children often display other forms of aggression in their teens and later life, the pattern is not universal. As a result of such findings, researchers have concluded that early experiences of abuse only create a disposition towards violence. High rates of violence on TV and elsewhere in

the media have been cited as a possible cause of youth violence; however, many children who watch such violence do not themselves become violent.

It appears that many factors promote and inhibit violence. The model in Figure 8-7 summarizes some of the research findings on the development of violence. It includes two paths: One leads to antisocial and criminal behavior, while the other leads to noncriminal behavior. Starting at the same point, these paths diverge more and more as children have different experiences. The model is based on the idea that biological, learned, and cognitive factors interact. In the model, they move broadly from the biological on the left to the cognitive on the right.

The lower path consists of risk factors for antisocial, criminal behavior. Individuals with more risk factors will be more likely to engage in criminal behaviors. The upper path consists of factors that give rise to more conventional participant behavior.

The Biological Component

According to Berkowitz (1993, 1994), frustration and other negative affects give rise to aggression. This proposal has its roots in the idea that humans are motivated to survive and that they come into the world with general mechanisms and systems to help them survive. One of those is the tendency to take what we need and to use force if necessary. The noxious cry of babies when their biological needs are not met serves to insure that we attend to their needs. Staub (1996) has argued that, when basic needs are frustrated, a very powerful force is set loose. When such frustration is combined with difficult life conditions, the stage is set for the development of aggressive behaviors.

In the model in Figure 8-7, frustration does not lead immediately to aggression; it leads to hostile feelings. Feelings of hostility are very basic; they do not have to be learned. Hostility and anxiety are part of the fight-or-flight response, which is triggered by the amygdala in response to a perceived threat. As we've seen, this process often does not involve the brain's rational systems.

If, as the model in Figure 8-7 suggests, frustrated needs are the first step toward criminal behavior, does it make sense that youth violence is much higher in the United States? Remember that frustration is relative to what is possible. If everyone is poor, there should be

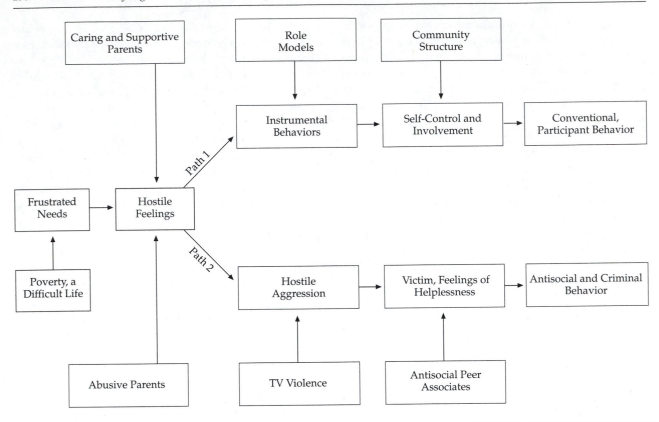

Figure 8-7. Two paths that follow from hostile feelings. One path is adaptive, while the other is maladaptive.

little frustration, because the discrepancy between individuals is small. Frustration will be greater where there is a large discrepancy between rich and poor. In some societies, individuals are born into a certain class and stay there. In that case, the frustration for a poor person should be low. In the United States, however, everyone is encouraged to realize the American Dream—to become enormously wealthy. For the poor, the discrepancy between their circumstances and what is possible is very large.

Considerable research indicates that hostile feelings can be modified by other experiences. On the one hand, adults who have grown up in caring homes with a great deal of nurturance do not show the same level of aggression as those who experienced little nurturance (Staub, 1996). On the other hand, children who

were abused tend to be more aggressive, other things being equal (Dodge, 1993; Widom, 1989a, b). It makes sense that, if counteracting forces—such as love, understanding, and acceptance—are at work, perceptions of threat will be reduced. Conversely, individuals whose needs are not being met and who are also being physically beaten and psychologically rejected will experience greater feelings of hostility.

The Learned Component

Responses to Threat

On different occasions, animals use very different methods of dealing with threats and pain. Sometimes, they physically attack the source of threat; at other times they engage in instrumental behaviors that put distance between themselves and the object of threat. Humans show a similar pattern (Pinel, 1993).

In the model in Figure 8-7, hostile feelings can take two different directions. On the one hand, they motivate the individual to engage in instrumental behaviors to escape the threat. Children from abusive families may run away from home, for example. On the other hand, hostile feelings can motivate an individual to attack the threat. Some children attempt to fight back when they are abused by their parents, for example.

Not all instrumental behaviors are equally effective. Research indicates that children who have good guidance, good role models, and good education are more likely to escape from their plight. For example, by engaging in certain adaptive instrumental behaviors, they are able to fulfill their basic needs and remove themselves from an environment that is harsh and difficult.

Many children, however, fall into a pattern involving helplessness and hostile aggression. They watch violence on television, which confirms their belief that it is a bad world. They join gangs, which reinforce the view that the only way to get what we want is to act in a violent and aggressive manner (Hammond & Yung, 1993). Many male youth assume a macho role characterized by insensitivity, dominance, and hostility to women (Sanday, 1981). Typically, gang members regard the world as hostile and threatening. It perhaps is not surprising that gangs often confine themselves to a very limited territory. For many, it is too frightening to venture outside those self-imposed boundaries.

Empathy

People who tend to be more empathetic, as indicated by self-report, are less inclined to be aggressive (Miller & Eisenberg, 1988). As might be expected, abusive parents tend to score lower than other parents on measures of empathy (Feshbach, 1987). Further, children who were abused tend to exhibit less empathy than nonabused children. In fact, there is considerable evidence that abusive parents' lack of empathy has long-term negative implications for the socioemotional development of these children. This lack of empathy and generally poor emotional development may account for the cycle of violence. Miller & Eisenberg (1988) have suggested empathy training as a way of helping to break this cycle of violence.

The Cognitive Component

The model in Figure 8-7 suggests that, if people have nurturing parents, good guidance, and good role models, they are more likely to develop a positive self-concept characterized by self-control. Alternatively, individuals exposed to violence from their parents and deviant role models will come to see themselves as victims.

Many theorists have argued that, ultimately, people need to develop a sense of control, which often has its roots in beliefs about competence and justice. A sense of control allows people to believe that they can deal with their unfulfilled needs.

These perceptions tend to grow out of a strong, well-functioning community. When there is structure, there are rules. Participants within such a system can expect certain things to happen should they do certain things. It has been suggested that a good way to help children who might otherwise fall into criminal behavior is to get them to participate in their community. In the process of participating, they will come to see that they can have an effect (control) and that the route to that control is learning the rules. In other words, they learn that there is justice, provided they respect certain norms.

People come to see themselves as victims when they have no sense of real control and they attribute this and their misfortunes to their past history. A consistent finding in the aggression research literature is that individuals tend to be highly influenced by those with whom they associate and from whom they seek approval (Staub, 1996). Individuals who live in the larger world composed of communities and nations will be sensitive to all the diverse needs of other people. However, those whose only world is their antisocial friends will allow their antisocial friends to define their values.

Summary

Violence in youth can be understood in terms of two paths: one that leads to more conventional, participant behavior; and another that leads to antisocial and criminal behavior. According to the model, frustrated needs lead to hostile feelings. Whether these hostile feelings are channeled into more instrumental and

Positive role models can help youth channel hostile feelings into more instrumental and adaptive behaviors.

adaptive behaviors or into hostile aggression behaviors depends largely on how the parents treat the child. Further, role models, both positive and negative, serve to reinforce those initial differences in direction. If the disposition to act in an adaptive way is reinforced in schools and the community, youth can come to develop a sense of self-control and involvement. This is the basis for conventional and participatory behavior. If the disposition to act in a more hostile way is supported by antisocial peers, youth can develop a sense of being helpless victims. This is the basis for antisocial and criminal behavior.

Aggression and Health Issues

The Type A Personality and Coronary Heart Disease

Because physiological indicators are only moderately good predictors of coronary heart disease (CHD) and,

further, because people who experience coronary heart disease tend to have a distinct personality style, Friedman and Rosenman (1974) attempted to measure that personality style and to see if it was a predictor of heart disease. In their landmark studies, they established that there is indeed a distinct personality style that leads to coronary heart disease, which they labeled the *Type A personality.* This pattern has subsequently come to be called the coronary-prone behavior pattern or Type A behavior pattern (TABP). The Type A person, as originally described by Friedman and Rosenman, is characterized by three qualities: a competitive striving for achievement; an exaggerated sense of urgency; and a tendency towards aggressiveness and hostility in interpersonal behaviors. The Type B person, in contrast, is less competitive and more easygoing but not necessarily less effective. The Western Collaborative Group Study, a study of men in the San Francisco area, found that the Type A person was three times as likely to have a heart attack as the Type B person (Rosenman et al., 1966, 1970, 1975).

Hostility and Heart Disease

Since the early work of Rosenman and Friedman, it has been shown repeatedly that the component of the TABP most clearly related to coronary heart disease is hostility (e.g., Dembroski & Costa, 1987). Some researchers refer to this quality as the *potential for hostility* (e.g., Matthews, Glass, Rosenman, & Bortner, 1977). Dembroski and Costa (1987) point out that potential for hostility is a multidimensional construct. In order to better identify the nature of this construct, they did ratings using established dimensions of personality (McCrae & Costa, 1987). Their research led them to conclude that potential for hostility is highly related to low agreeableness or antagonism. In terms of style of social interaction, they found that high potential for hostility identifies individuals who are uncooperative, antagonistic, rude, disagreeable, unsympathetic, and callous.

Hostility and Anger in Hypertension and Coronary Heart Disease

When fear is induced in a laboratory setting, it produces a physiological reaction similar to that elicited by epinephrine; when anger is induced, it produces a physiological reaction similar to a mixed epinephrine-norepinephrine response (Ax, 1953; Schachter, 1957). Whether the individual expresses anger (anger-out) or holds it in (anger-in) plays an important role in this process (Figure 8-8). While anger-out subjects show increased diastolic blood pressure with little change in heart rate, anger-in subjects show increased systolic blood pressure and increased heart rate (Funkenstein, King, & Drolette, 1974). Since this early work, it has been shown that repressed anger (anger-in) is linked to hypertension and cardiovascular problems (Dembrowski & Costa, 1987). In other words, compared to those who do not express anger (anger-in), those who do (anger-out) seem to be less at risk for cardiovascular problems, with lower systolic blood pressure (in some studies) and diastolic blood pressure (in some studies) and lower heart rate. Coping style plays an important role in reducing risk. People who let their anger out, both in their jobs and in everyday life, show less hypertension (Gentry, 1985).

It has also been found that men are at greater risk for cardiovascular problems than women, that African

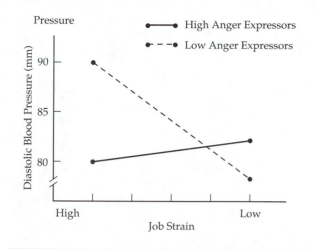

Figure 8-8.   Effects of anger expression on relation of job strain to blood pressure. (From "Relationship of Anger-Coping Style and Blood Pressure Among Black Americans," by W. D. Gentry. In M. A. Chesney and R. H. Rosenman (Eds.), *Anger and Hostility in Cardiovascular and Behavioral Disorders*, 1985, pp. 139–147. Copyright © 1985 Hemisphere Publishing. Reprinted with permission.)

Americans are at a greater risk than whites, and that people living in high-stress neighborhoods are at greater risk than those in low-stress neighborhoods (Gentry, Chesney, Gary, Hall, & Harburg, 1982; Johnson, Spielberger, Worden, & Jacobs, 1987).

People with a personality style characterized by hostility are also at risk for hypertension and coronary heart disease (Dembrowski & Costa, 1987). It has been suggested that a hostile orientation is rooted in a tendency to be suspicious and mistrustful of others. When this orientation is combined with highly competitive behavior (the Type A personality), the risk for coronary heart disease becomes even greater (Weidner, Sexton, McLellarn, Connor, & Matarazzo, 1987). Figure 8-9 shows the relationship between potential for hostility and number of occluded vessels. As can be seen from Figure 8-9, increase in the potential for hostility is accompanied by increase in the number of occluded vessels for high anger-in but not for low anger-in.

It seems that the best way to deal with interpersonal anger is neither to express it (anger-out) nor to

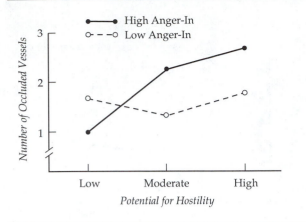

Figure 8-9. Relationship between anger expression, potential for hostility, and prevalence of coronary artery disease. From "Components of Type A, Hostility, and Anger-In: Relationship to Angiographic Findings," by T. M. Dembroski, J. M. MacDougall, R. B. Williams, T. L. Haney, and J. A. Blumenthal. *Psychosomatic Medicine*, 1985, *47*, 219–233. Copyright © 1985 by Williams & Wilkins. Reprinted with permission.)

hold it in (anger-in). Expressing anger before we calm down may make the situation worse because we may say something that we later regret. On the other hand, letting anger smolder within us also takes its toll because as we dwell on it, our blood pressure remains elevated. The best way to deal with anger, it appears, is to calm down or engage in anger control (Spielberger, Krasner, & Solomon, 1988) and then to try to reason with the other person (Tavris, 1989). Anger often involves a conflict that needs to be resolved. Unless we work at resolving the conflict, we will be prone to reexperience our anger. We need to learn to reflect on our anger (Harburg, Blakelock, & Roeper, 1979), so that we can understand what prompts it. Once we do this, we are in a better position to change the way we think and respond.

Cynical Hostility

Cynical hostility has been proposed as an important predictor of heart disease (Smith & Frohm, 1985; Fisch-

man, 1987). A person who is cynically hostile carries around a great deal of anger and resentment, often over little daily problems, but possesses poor adaptive skills or adjustive mechanisms. The anger, therefore, tends to become expressed in hostile and irritating ways that alienate other people and lead to social rejection and lack of support. Aversive social feedback simply reinforces the bleak expectations of the cynical person and helps to maintain his or her hostile behavior (Geen, 1990).

Redford Williams (1989) has argued that the Type A pattern characterized by cynical hostility has grown out of a disturbed thinking process. He argues that these people must learn to reduce their cynical mistrust of others. He takes an optimistic view of their ability to change, although he admits that it can be difficult. He suggests that they should start by monitoring their thinking, so that they can identify these cynical and hostile thoughts. Then, to change their thinking, they need to learn to listen, to see the world from the other person's point of view, to trust, to be assertive, to laugh at themselves, and to forgive.

Hostility, TABP, and Plasma Lipids

When hostility and TABP are high, levels of plasma lipids (cholesterol and triglycerides) are also elevated, but neither high hostility nor high TABP alone reliably leads to elevated plasma lipids (Weidner et al., 1987). It seems that the combination of high hostility and high TABP puts people into a psychological state of constant vigilance, which, in turn, produces a chronic stress reaction. The general consensus is that chronic stress triggers the release of high levels of catecholamines (such as epinephrine and norepinephrine), which are physical risk factors. The high catecholamine levels, in turn, mobilize the plasma lipids, which have been implicated in blood platelet aggregation, another risk factor for CHD (Carruthers, 1974; Simpson et al., 1974).

Summary

The Type A personality—more recently referred to as the Type A behavior pattern (TABP) is characterized by a competitive striving for achievement, an exaggerated sense of urgency, and a tendency toward aggressiveness and hostility. The Type A person is inclined to rise to a challenge, to experience annoyance and impatience when interrupted, and to retaliate when provoked. The strong link found in early studies between the Type A personality and coronary heart disease has not been confirmed by some recent studies. However, suppressed anger and cynical hostility have been clearly linked to coronary heart disease.

People who score high in TABP and hostility tend to have high plasma lipids, which have been impli-

cated in coronary heart disease. It has also been shown that cortisol and testosterone levels tend to be higher in certain Type A individuals.

Anger-out subjects show increased diastolic blood pressure with little change in heart rate, while anger-in subjects show increased systolic blood pressure and increased heart rate. Further, individuals with a high anger-in pattern generally have more occluded vessels than do those with a low anger-in pattern. These findings are important because anger suppressors are at

Practical Application 8-1

Learning to Manage Anger

Anger is the bridge both to physical and verbal aggression and to hostility (Buss & Perry, 1992). Accordingly, we need to learn how to manage anger if we are to reduce our aggression and hostility.

Much has been written on how to deal with anxiety and with depression, but there is little material on dealing with anger, because we often think of anger as something that we cannot or should not control (Tavris, 1989).

However, anger can be a very powerful source of positive energy if it is properly channeled. The civil rights movement and the feminist movement both grew out of a strong sense of injustice fueled by feelings of anger. While some people in both movements allowed their anger to turn to aggression and violence, most directed their anger towards changing the system. As Martin Luther King reported, "When I am angry I can write, pray, and preach well, for then my whole temperament is quickened, my understanding sharpened, and all mundane vexations and temptations gone." In your own experience, a critical comment from a professor on a paper you wrote may have angered you but also stirred you to think more clearly and argue more precisely. That has been true for me.

When not properly directed or managed, however, anger can be a very destructive emotion. If we allow it to fester inside us, it can lead to physical problems such as hypertension. On the other hand, if we ventilate it—if we strike out at the source of our

anger—we often make matters worse. There is little evidence to support the idea that ventilation is a good way of draining off hostile energy. Many people who ventilate experience shame and loss of control. In the heat of an angry exchange, they do things that they later regret. In addition, yelling or shouting escalates the negative bodily reactions; anger turns to rage and we are left in a state of heightened negative emotion. If we learn to control our anger—to cool down—we are less likely to fall prey to this problem.

However, learning to cool down—by counting to ten, for example—may not be the best long-term solution, especially for people who are chronically angry. Many chronically angry people interpret the actions of others as motivated by anger and aggression. As a result, they feel constantly provoked. When a person on a bus rings the bell twice, for example, a chronically angry bus driver might interpret the response as a deliberate act of provocation. It may be, however, that the person who rang twice is merely anxious about missing the next stop.

How do we learn to change our perceptual habits without becoming totally passive and helpless? Here are some suggestions. (For more on this topic, see Tavris, 1989.)

1. **Look for another explanation.** When people are critical or act in ways that violate our norms or expectations, they may be distracted or under stress. On one occasion, a car ran a stop sign and forced me to

(continued on next page)

greater risk for cardiovascular disorders than anger expressors.

It has been suggested that people with a lot of anger need to identify the source of their anger, so that they can learn to reduce it.

Main Points

1. Moyer has identified at least eight types of aggression in animals, all of which can also be found in humans.

2. Human aggression is traditionally defined as behavior against another person with the intention of committing harm.

3. Early laboratory studies operationalized aggression as physical harm.

4. One consistent finding from those studies is that most acts of aggression are provoked.

5. Another is that humans are inclined to retaliate in kind to an aggressive act.

6. Massive retaliation, according to Patterson, is designed to inform the attacker that the aggressive exchange should stop.

Practical Application 8-1 (continued)

slam on my brake. In the process it sliced off my front license plate. Not surprisingly, I felt angry. However, when the driver apologized and explained that his wife had just been diagnosed with cancer, my anger quickly subsided.

2. **Distract yourself.** One of the best ways to reduce anger is to get involved in some absorbing activity. Some people find exercise works; others read or watch TV; still others become involved in their favorite hobby.

3. **Look for the humor.** Humor is a way of recasting a situation to find the incongruity or the absurdity in it. When we can do that, our anger will subside, because humor is incompatible with anger. Learning to laugh at our reactions not only helps relieve our anger but also communicates to others that we understand our reactions were inappropriate.

4. **Determine what triggers your anger.** Keep a diary of your anger, so that you can discover what types of situations make you angry. Some people, for example, find that criticism makes them angry; others find that certain behaviors of others make them angry; and so forth. Once you understand what triggers your anger, you can develop plans to deal with such situations (Novaco, 1985).

5. **Create an inner dialogue that reduces anger.** Most people carry on inner dialogues with themselves. While some people have dialogues that reduce anger, others have dialogues that escalate or maintain their anger (Jacobs, cited in Tavris, 1989). After a divorce, couples may stay angry with each other for years. They may, for example, dwell on one thing, such as an affair their spouse had, and still be trying to extract the kind of apology they thought they deserved. By becoming aware of our inner dialogue, we can begin to change it.

6. **Learn to recognize that life is not always fair.** Unless we accept that the world is less than perfect, we will become angry at anything and everything—being treated impolitely, breaking a leg because we tripped on a broken sidewalk, finding we weren't invited to a party, having a flat tire on our way to work, and so on. Whether to become angry or not can be a decision. It is a decision that we can learn to make both consciously and unconsciously. We can develop the habit of accepting the fact that life is unfair.

7. **Learn to talk it out and negotiate.** Anger often accompanies conflict. One way to decrease anger is to engage in a dialogue that will enable us to see how the other party views the situation. While we may not always agree, talking provides the basis for negotiating some kind of solution or compromise. Most of us do not like to compromise but, once we learn that compromise is better than prolonging anger, we can appreciate the fine art of compromise as a means for living a happier and more stress-free life.

7. It seems that much aggression has it roots in our need to control the actions of others.

8. According to our working definition, aggression is the willingness to engage in physical and psychological acts of harm in order to control the actions of other people.

9. An aggressive act motivated by the desire to achieve a desired goal, and not by the desire to harm another person, is called instrumental aggression.

10. Aggression linked to anger is called affective or angry aggression.

11. The temperamental trait of impulsivity has been linked to aggressive and antisocial behavior.

12. Testosterone has been linked to male aggression.

13. In women, the fall in progesterone level just before menstruation, together with the relative rise in estrogen level, has been associated with aggression.

14. While various indices of self-reported aggression in human males have been linked to testosterone and estradiol, other indices of self-reported aggression in human females have been negatively linked to high levels of testosterone and estradiol.

15. The prehormone androstenedione has been linked to female aggression.

16. About 20–25% of aggression can be linked to endocrine factors.

17. Research using a number of different measures indicates that, while males tend to be more aggressive than females, the differences are usually small.

18. The temporal lobes and the amygdala have been implicated in human aggression.

19. Frustration tends to energize most—if not all—subsequent behaviors; however, the frustration must be intense and unexpected.

20. Frustration does not appear to provide the direction for subsequent behavior.

21. It has been suggested that frustration is a negative emotional state that, when reduced, can reinforce behavior.

22. While frustration may motivate people to strike out at the source of the frustration, often behavior is displaced to a safer goal object. The principles of generalization and inhibition can account for this phenomenon.

23. It has been suggested that blind rage is due to a tendency to associate a wide range of negative feelings with anger and aggression.

24. One of the main ways children learn aggression is through observation and imitation.

25. Modeling and imitation are thought to account for the cycle of violence.

26. There is evidence that watching TV violence is correlated with increased aggression. However, children who are already aggressive are more likely to watch violence on TV.

27. Pornography that portrays violence toward women can give rise to attitudes or beliefs that may lead to increases in aggression by men against women.

28. According to the theory of coercive action, people are inclined to use threats and punishment to achieve certain terminal goals.

29. People assess the costs associated with coercive actions and decide, on the basis of this analysis, whether to engage in such actions.

30. It appears that people are more inclined to engage in coercive actions after consuming alcohol because they fail to fully process all the important information—in particular, the costs.

31. Many coercive actions are motivated by the value of justice.

32. Retributive justice refers to the belief that blameworthy behavior should be punished.

33. People decide whether a behavior is blameworthy by engaging in a series of steps that involve inferences. They ask whether the behavior was intended and was justified.

34. Three aspects of justice may be distinguished: distributive justice, procedural justice, and interactional justice.

35. It has been suggested that anger often impairs our ability to determine blame, because it impairs information processing.

36. Beliefs about power and control have been linked to violence against women, people of color, and gay men and lesbians.

37. It appears that people who are chronically unable to get what they want through verbal means will sometimes resort to violence.

38. It has been suggested that youth violence has its roots in frustrated needs that give rise to hostile feelings.

39. Whether these hostile feelings lead to instrumental and adaptive behaviors depends on parental attitudes and the available role models.

40. Children who have abusive parents and are exposed to a great deal of violence are more likely to engage in hostile aggressive acts.

41. Associating with antisocial peers is a risk factor for criminal and antisocial behavior.

42. Empathy is a mediator of violence; empathy training may help to reduce violence.

43. The Type A behavior pattern is characterized by a competitive striving for achievement, an exaggerated sense of urgency, and a tendency towards aggressiveness and hostility in interpersonal behaviors.

44. The hostility component of the Type A pattern has been found to be a good predictor of coronary heart disease.

45. Suppressed anger and cynical hostility have also been linked to coronary heart disease.

46. The interaction of hostility and TABP has been shown to increase plasma lipids, which have been implicated in coronary heart disease.

47. Compared to anger expressors, anger suppressors are at greater risk for hypertension and cardiovascular disorders and tend to have more occluded blood vessels.

48. Learning to control anger is not only possible but desirable.

Chapter Nine

Emotions, Stress, and Health

- Do we have any control over our emotions?

- Why is stress regarded as an emotion?

- Why is stress often linked to health?

- Why is stress often referred to as the fight-or-flight response?

- What chemicals are released when we are under stress, and what do these chemicals do?

- Why is stress often linked to diseases such as cancer?

- Do certain personality types experience more stress?

- How can people make themselves more resistant to stress and disease?

Emotions and Motivation

Recently, researchers have argued that you cannot think about emotions without considering motivation and that you cannot think about motivation without considering emotion (Frijda, 1988; Lazarus, 1991). This has not always been the case. In the 1930s and 1940s, motivation was conceptualized in terms of needs. Needs were thought to provide the impetus (energy), the direction, and the persistence of behavior. Little was said about the role of emotions. In the 1950s and 1960s, motivation was conceptualized as due to the existence of drives. In these early theories, drives provided the energy or impetus for behavior, while learning provided the direction (Hull, 1943). According to the drive theorists, emotions were thought to be mainly a by-product of motivation but not integral to motivation. Berlyne (1960), for example, conceptualized motivation as the drive for optimal arousal and regarded affect as a by-product of satisfying that drive. Within drive theory, persistence was conceptualized as largely learned. According to Amsel's (1958, 1972) theory, for example, persistence was largely due to the counterconditioning of stimuli linked with frustration, and frustration represented a very limited concept of emotion—an emotion that grew out of failure to receive a reward.

In the later 1960s and early 1970s, psychologists began to talk about motivation in terms of action. Motives and needs were central in this conceptualization, but needs were conceptualized very differently than in the 1930s and 1940s. Psychologists began to view needs not as causing action, but merely as dispositions to action. What created actions were goals and threats; goals were conceptualized as positive incentives and threats as negative incentives (Atkinson & Birch, 1978; de Rivera, 1982; Raynor, 1974; Weiner, 1974).

Conceptualizing motivation in terms of goals proved to be a powerful theory (Locke & Latham, 1990; Pervin, 1989; Snyder et al., 1991), but it became apparent to a number of theorists that goals and threats, although perhaps the impetus to immediate action, often failed to account for long-term action. While some people persisted in their goal-directed behavior, others did not. What seemed to differentiate people in terms of their persistence was their emotions. Those who could remain optimistic in the face of threats and difficulties persisted, whereas those who developed feelings of pessimism and self-doubt often abandoned

their goals (Seligman, 1990). Despite differences of emphasis, most contemporary theorists agree that emotions play a critical role in motivation.

This observation led some psychologists to stress the self-regulation of emotions. As Albert Bandura (1991) pointed out, "Talent is only as good as its execution." In order to achieve their goals, he argued, people need to learn how to manage their emotions, especially self-doubt.

In this chapter, we will discuss some of the basic emotions that have been implicated in goal-directed behavior. The major focus is on how people can learn to develop emotions that sustain goal-directed behavior and to neutralize or deflect emotions that tend to undermine goal-directed behavior.

The Definition of Emotions

Probably because emotions are so complex, many different definitions have been proposed over the years. Paul Kleinginna and Anne Kleinginna (1981a) have proposed a definition that incorporates the key elements of previous definitions. According to this consensual definition, emotions occur as a result of an interaction between subjective factors, environmental factors, and neural and hormonal processes. In support of this definition, they make the following points:

1. Emotions give rise to affective experiences, such as pleasure or displeasure.
2. Emotions stimulate us to generate cognitive explanations—to attribute the cause to ourselves or to the environment, for example.
3. Emotions trigger a variety of internal adjustments, such as increased heart rate.
4. Emotions elicit behaviors that are often, but not always, expressive (laughing or crying), goal-directed (helping or avoiding), and adaptive (removal of a potential threat to our survival).

As we see, this definition acknowledges that emotions result from the interaction of biological, learned, and cognitive processes.

Another very important function of emotions is to reward and punish behavior. When people experience a very positive emotion, they are likely to engage in behaviors that will produce that emotion again. Similarly, when people experience a very negative emotion, they will avoid behaviors that will cause them to feel that emotion again. In other words, emotions act as re-inforcers of behavior (Thorndike's law of effect; Thorndike, 1913).

The Universal Nature of Emotions

Core Relational Themes

Various theorists argue that emotions result from our attempts to adapt to the environment. Evidence suggests that all humans experience a common set of emotions. Lazarus (1991) has suggested that these emotions can be described by their *core relational themes* (Table 9-1). By adopting this term, Lazarus emphasizes that our emotional responses grow out of our interactions with the environment (are relational); are highly cognitive; and are often complex, frequently involving two or more emotions operating simultaneously. Identifying the various core themes in an emotional response would obviously help us to reduce its complexity.

Summing up his approach, Lazarus (1991) states:

> The fundamental premise is that in order to survive and flourish, animals (humans in particular) are constructed biologically to be constantly evaluating (appraising) their relationships with the environment with respect to significance for well-being. (p. 825)

Facial Expressions

Studies of facial expressions reveal that certain basic emotions, such as happiness, anger, distress, and disgust, can be identified in a wide range of cultures. This supports the idea that there are core relational themes underlying emotions. On the basis of data on facial expressions, some researchers have even argued that most—if not all—emotions are a product of heredity. Whether this is true is still being hotly debated, since other researchers view emotions as largely the product of learning and culture (Ekman, 1994; Russell, 1995).

What seems quite clear is that, when people experience an emotion, they are inclined to wear that emotion on their face. Further, there is evidence that, when people deliberately put on a happy or a sad face, they tend to trigger the emotion that corresponds to the facial expression (e.g., Izard, 1990). Noting the close link between emotions and facial expression, Izard has suggested that people can learn to regulate their subjective feelings by learning to control their facial expressions

Table 9-1. Core relational themes for various emotions.

Emotion	Core Relational Theme
Anger	A demeaning offense against me and mine.
Anxiety	Facing uncertain, existential threat.
Fright	Facing immediate, concrete, and overwhelming physical danger.
Guilt	Having transgressed a moral imperative.
Shame	Having failed to live up to an ego-ideal.
Sadness	Having experienced an irrevocable loss.
Envy	Wanting what someone else has.
Jealousy	Resenting a third party for loss of or threat to another's affection.
Disgust	Taking in or being too close to an indigestible object or idea (metaphorically speaking).
Happiness	Making reasonable progress towards the realization of a goal.
Pride	Enhancement of one's ego-identity by taking credit for a valued object or achievement.
Relief	A distressing goal-incongruent condition that has changed for the better or gone away.
Hope	Fearing the worst but yearning for better.
Love	Desiring or participating in affection, usually but not necessarily reciprocated.
Compassion	Being moved by another's suffering and wanting to help.

Source: Adapted from *Emotion and Adaptation,* by R. S. Lazarus, p. 122. Copyright © 1991 by Oxford University Press, Inc. Reprinted with permission.

(Izard, 1990). The bottom line is that, if you want to be happy, you put on a happy face.

The Role of Appraisal in Emotions

According to Lazarus (1991) whether we experience a certain emotion depends on how we appraise a situation. For example, we might ask ourselves, "What emotion is appropriate for this situation, given my goals, my motives, and my concerns?" The idea that appraisal plays an important role in our emotions suggests, of course, that cognitions are central to emotions. If cognitions (ways of thinking) are important, then the implicit theories that people hold are also important. For example, people who tend to be optimistic and those who tend to pessimism will experience very different patterns of emotions; people are happier if they think optimistically. As we will see, how much stress people experience depends very largely on whether they appraise a situation as a threat or a challenge. Because people are inclined to appraise situations differently, large individual differences in emotion often occur.

Summary

While early theorists conceptualized motivation in terms of drives, current theorists conceptualize motivation in terms of needs, which are viewed as disposi-

Practical Application 9-1

Using Emotions to Identify Goals, Motives, and Concerns

We can use our emotions to help identify our goals, motives, and concerns (Frijda, 1988). At first, this may sound like an odd exercise. Most people believe they have a good knowledge of what they want and what is important to them. However, as humans, we have goals, motives, and concerns of which we are largely unaware (Epstein, 1991)—in particular, those that our parents gave us early in life. If we systematically keep track of our emotional responses in a variety of situations and analyze them, we can discover the meaning structures that explain them. I like to analyze situations in which my reactions were inappropriate, exaggerated, or inhibited. In other words, I like to analyze reactions that do not fit with my perceptions of my ideal self.

Consider the case of Jane. On hearing that her brother had won a scholarship, she immediately called her mother to find out more details. As she talked with her mother, she felt hurt that her mother expressed such admiration for her brother's achievement. Jane began to denigrate his accomplishment by saying that a lot of people got that award. She further suggested that he had buttered up the right people to win it. After hanging up, she felt guilty. She loved her brother and wished him the best. Why had she been so mean? She would be mortified if her brother ever found out what she had said. She began to experience shame.

Analyzing her response, Jane realized that she had done the same thing before. She became aware that she often felt hurt when she was not the center of her mother's attention. As she reflected, she recognized the emotion she was experiencing as envy or perhaps jealousy (Table 9-7). She had always been envious of her brother, even though her mother often praised her for her accomplishments. Some time later, Jane heard about conditional love—the concept that some parents give love only when their children have done something they value. Then she understood why she was envious of her brother. Because he had accomplished so much, he was the recipient of more love. She felt left out and, like any child who senses a scarcity of something he or she wants, she tried to convince her mother that he didn't really deserve the praise, in the hope that she could get some of that same praise for herself.

As an exercise, identify an emotional response to a situation, either positive or negative, and see if you can explain it. Why did you feel so proud or so mortified? One reason why people experience rage is that they have failed to clearly differentiate their emotions. You may not be able to totally explain your reactions the first time, but you will improve with practice. When you can explain why, then you have discovered the meaning structure for that emotion in that situation. Because emotions are situation-specific, you need to keep track of the situation in order to discover your meaning structure for a certain emotion.

tions. Whereas goals are often the impetus for action, sustained action appears to depend on positive emotions such as optimism. It seems that people can learn to regulate their emotions and thus sustain goal-directed behavior.

According to the definition proposed by Kleinginna and Kleinginna, emotions give rise to affective experiences, stimulate the individual to generate cognitive explanations, trigger a variety of internal adjustments, and elicit expressive, goal-directed, and adaptive behaviors.

Evidence from a variety of sources suggests that humans share a common set of emotions, which can be described in terms of their core relational themes. This idea is consistent with the work on facial expression. Whether we experience a certain emotion depends on how we appraise a situation.

What Is Stress?

The Definition of Stress

Stress has to do with adapting to threat, or, to use a more positive word, adapting to challenge (Friedman, 1992). In our daily lives, we speak of stress in connection with, for instance, taking examinations, the breakup of a marriage or relationship, struggling to pay our bills, commuting on congested roads, and dealing with people we dislike. Notice that stress has come to describe a diverse set of negative feelings. Failing an examination produces feelings of humiliation and shame; the breakup of a relationship may lead to a deep sense of loss and remorse; not being able to pay our bills can be frustrating and irritating; driving on a crowded road may produce both frustration and anger; conflicts in interpersonal relationships may lead to contempt and disgust.

While laypeople generally use the term *stress* to refer to various negative feelings, the scientist thinks of stress somewhat differently—as a set of neurological and physiological reactions that serve some ultimate adaptive purpose. How the individual responds to those reactions determines whether they produce feelings of *distress* (a negative feeling) or *eustress* (a positive feeling). In general, when people view an event as threatening, they experience distress; when they view it as challenging, they experience eustress.

Current research indicates that, when people interpret an event as challenging their health is not adversely affected; however, when they interpret it as threatening, their health can be adversely affected. In general, people who interpret an event as challenging engage in coping responses, which may be responsible for the different health outcomes of the two interpretations. This implies that simply learning appropriate coping responses will lead to improved health (Cohen & Williamson, 1991; Friedman, 1991). We will consider the links between stress and health later in the chapter.

Stress as a Fight-or-Flight Response

When people talk about the stress reaction, they frequently refer to it as the fight-or-flight response. This label grows out of an evolutionary analysis. Animals have two basic ways of dealing with threats: they fight or they flee. A rabbit depends on its ability to flee in order to stay alive. A lion, in contrast, depends on its ability to fight to stay alive and to obtain the food supply that it requires. Whether we fight or flee, certain basic requirements must be met. First, we need to expend a great deal of energy. Second, we have to keep our head. Third, we frequently have to deal with injury. The stress reaction clearly meets these requirements (Figure 9-1). To maximize energy needs, blood rushes to the sites where it is needed (the muscles and brain); fats are released into the bloodstream; we perspire to cool ourselves; and so forth. To keep our head, the high level of arousal that we experience helps us to focus our attention on survival cues. To help us deal with injury, our blood thickens, and chemicals are released to enable our body to deal with injury, should it occur.

In our lives today, we do not have to expend as much physical energy as our foraging ancestors did, nor are we normally threatened with injury when we experience stress. We no longer need to have so much fat released in our blood; we do not need to perspire; our blood pressure need not skyrocket; our blood need not thicken to guard against an injury; we do not need chemicals circulating in our blood to attack some foreign body that might enter our system. Nevertheless, each time we experience stress, our body prepares itself as though we were still living as our ancestors lived.

Let's consider the biological, learned, and cognitive components of stress.

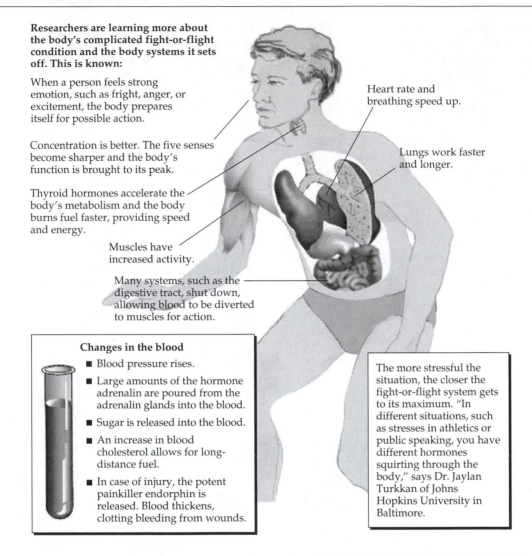

Researchers are learning more about the body's complicated fight-or-flight condition and the body systems it sets off. This is known:

When a person feels strong emotion, such as fright, anger, or excitement, the body prepares itself for possible action.

Concentration is better. The five senses become sharper and the body's function is brought to its peak.

Thyroid hormones accelerate the body's metabolism and the body burns fuel faster, providing speed and energy.

Muscles have increased activity.

Many systems, such as the digestive tract, shut down, allowing blood to be diverted to muscles for action.

Heart rate and breathing speed up.

Lungs work faster and longer.

Changes in the blood
- Blood pressure rises.
- Large amounts of the hormone adrenalin are poured from the adrenalin glands into the blood.
- Sugar is released into the blood.
- An increase in blood cholesterol allows for long-distance fuel.
- In case of injury, the potent painkiller endorphin is released. Blood thickens, clotting bleeding from wounds.

The more stressful the situation, the closer the fight-or-flight system gets to its maximum. "In different situations, such as stresses in athletics or public speaking, you have different hormones squirting through the body," says Dr. Jaylan Turkkan of Johns Hopkins University in Baltimore.

Figure 9-1. Stress can be viewed as a fight-or-flight response. It is defined by psychologists as a set of neurological and physiological reactions that are ultimately adaptive. (Adapted from "Stress Reaction," by Rob Struthers. Copyright © *The Calgary Herald*. Reprinted with permission.)

The Biological Component of Stress

The Sympathetic/Adrenal and Pituitary/Adrenal Responses

When people are challenged, they tend to mobilize a great deal of effort in order to deal with that event.

Similarly, when people lose control, they may try to reassert control. Under these conditions, the body makes a sympathetic/adrenal response. The sympathetic system allows us to respond to the immediate demands of the situation by activating the body: our heart rate accelerates, our blood pressure rises, and we become more alert. In short, we become aroused (Chapter 5).

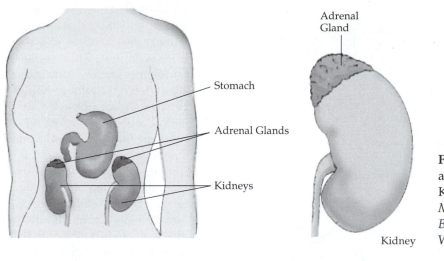

Figure 9-2.   The location of the adrenal glands in the body. (From K. B. Hoyenga and K. T. Hoyenga, *Motivational Explanations of Behavior.* Copyright © 1984 by Wadsworth, Inc.)

To provide a longer-term chemical backup to the immediate action of the sympathetic system, the adrenal glands (Figure 9-2)—specifically, the adrenal medulla (the inner part of the gland; Figure 9-3)—release epinephrine and norepinephrine.*

Whereas the sympathetic/adrenal system takes care of arousal, the pituitary/adrenal system is more closely associated with what is traditionally called the stress reaction—our fight-or-flight responses. The adrenal cortex (the outer part of the gland) secretes two main types of hormones: the mineralocorticoids and the glucocorticoids (including cortisol and corticosterone). The release of these hormones is linked to the release of other chemicals, as we'll see shortly. Note that, under stress, the sympathetic/adrenal and the pituitary/adrenal responses typically occur together. However, these two systems operate separately in some circumstances—generally when we attempt to gain control over stress by engaging in some kind of adaptive behavior. As we gain control, the cortisol level frequently drops, while the epinephrine level remains high (Frankenhaeuser, Lundberg, & Forsman, 1980). Cortisol is frequently used as a measure of the action of the pituitary/adrenal system, whereas urinary epinephrine is a measure of the activity of the

sympathetic/adrenal system. The endocrine glands and hormones associated with stress responses are summarized in Table 9-2. We explored the sympathetic/adrenal system in Chapter 5. Let's now turn to the pituitary/adrenal system.

The Pituitary/Adrenal Response

The hypothalamus initiates activity in the pituitary/adrenal system (Figure 9-3) by secreting corticotropin-releasing factor (CRF), which stimulates the pituitary. The pituitary, in turn, secretes adrenocorticotropic hormone (ACTH).

Experimental findings suggest that ACTH plays a central role in our ability to respond to threatening stimuli. Curiously, ACTH stimulates another hormonal reaction that is responsible for terminating further ACTH secretion. Specifically, ACTH stimulates the adrenal cortex, which then secretes glucocorticoids. When the glucocorticoid level is elevated, the central nervous system shuts down the processes that lead to ACTH secretion (de Wied, 1967, 1980; Vernikos-Danellis & Heybach, 1980).

Animal research indicates that ACTH is released approximately 10 seconds after a stressful event. The slowness of this reaction—relative to the central nervous system, which acts immediately—suggests that the endocrine system is probably involved in longer-term survival reactions, rather than the immediate survival responses of fight-or-flight. For example, ACTH

*Epinephrine and norepinephrine are also referred to as adrenaline and noradrenaline, respectively, especially when they are released to the periphery of the system rather than to the brain. This distinction is often ignored, however.

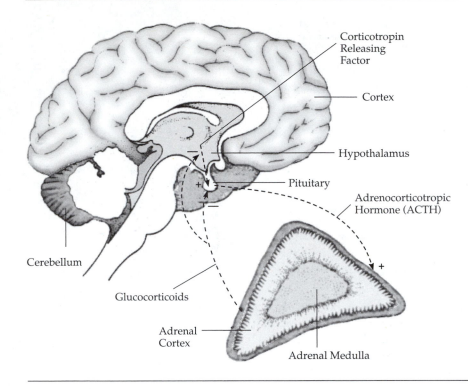

Figure 9-3. The interaction of the pituitary, hypothalamic, and adrenal cortical hormones. The brain is illustrated in a so-called midsagittal section—that is, as if sliced down the middle, halfway between the ears, from front to back. Corticotropin-releasing hormone from the hypothalamus stimulates secretion of ACTH from the pituitary. ACTH stimulates the secretion of the corticosteroids from the adrenal cortex into the bloodstream. In turn, the glucocorticoids inhibit both the hypothalamic and pituitary secretion of hormones. This is an example of a negative feedback loop. (From K. B. Hoyenga and K. T. Hoyenga, *Motivational Explanations of Behavior.* Copyright © 1984 by Wadsworth, Inc.)

stimulates fatty acid release and glucose utilization, thereby providing the energy to deal with a threat (White, Handler, & Smith, 1964). It takes between 15 minutes and 1 hour for the glucocorticoids to reach a level sufficient to terminate ACTH secretion (Vernikos-Danellis & Heybach, 1980). Thus, once set in motion, the stress reaction continues for a time. The glucocorticoids remain active much longer than ACTH. The continued presence of glucocorticoids in the blood may account for some poststress reactions, such as weight loss, changes in body temperature, and increased secretion of stomach acid (Weiss, 1968).

It appears that prolonged stress results in a breakdown of the adrenal system, accompanied by susceptibility to a wide variety of diseases. We'll return to this topic shortly.

Endorphins and Stress

Beta-endorphin is mobilized from the pituitary during stress in approximately the same quantities as ACTH (Rossier, Bloom, & Guillemin, 1980). This may explain why stress tends to induce analgesia (Akil, Madden,

Patrick, & Barchas, 1976). In addition, endorphins produce feelings of euphoria, apparently by altering the concentrations of neurotransmitters that activate the reward pathways in the brain (Smith, Freeman, Sands, & Lane, 1980).

Laboratory studies of endorphins indicate that the endorphin response can be triggered not only by physical stressors, such as shock, but by fear (Bolles & Fanselow, 1982). This may explain why people expose themselves to situations that elicit fear, such as parachuting and mountain climbing.

Stress and the Immune System

Over the past 30 years, numerous studies have demonstrated how stressors cause changes in the immune system (Maier, Watkins, & Fleshner, 1994). Specifically, stressors seem to turn off the immune response. For example, it has been demonstrated that stress makes us more susceptible to infections and common colds (Cohen, Tyrrell, & Smith, 1991). There is still some question about the role of stress in cancer, but a number of

Table 9-2.   Endocrine glands involved in stress, distress, and coping.

Gland	Hormone	Action/Function
Hypothalamus	Corticotropin-releasing hormone	Stimulates the pituitary to release ACTH. The hypothalamus is initially triggered by the thalamus, but that action can be inhibited by the cortex.
Pituitary	ACTH (adrenocorticotropic hormone)	Stimulates the adrenal cortex to release glucocorticoids.
Adrenal Cortex	Glucocorticoids:	The glucocorticoids are also important in energy metabolism.
	Cortisol	Antiinflammatory, antiallergy (important in the fight-or-flight response).
	Corticosterone	Suppresses the immune system (important for keeping the immune response in check).
Adrenal Medulla	Epinephrine	Released following environmental extremes (for example, cold), physical exertion, fear. Increases heart rate, oxygen consumption, and glycogen mobilization.
	Norepinephrine	Released during coping, especially when coping response is vigorous. Increases blood pressure and constricts blood vessels.

researchers assert, mainly on the basis of correlational studies, that there is a link. These findings need to be replicated using designs that can establish a causal link (Andersen, Kiecolt-Glaser, & Glaser, 1994).

This research has wide-ranging implications for our health. Why would the immune system not work at maximum efficiency when we need it most? To answer that question, let's look at how the immune system operates.

Two Immune Systems

The immune system is very complex. In fact, it is divided into two systems: nonspecific (innate) and specific (acquired). The nonspecific immune system is present from birth and, as its name suggests, operates in a nonspecific way, without regard to particular pathogens (for example, bacteria). The specific immune system is an acquired system; it learns to recognize foreign substances. T and B lymphocytes play a critical role in this system, which is involved in fighting such things as cancer and AIDS. The specific sys-

tem has evolved more recently and involves some of the same mechanisms as the nonspecific system.

Let's begin by examining the bidirectional effects between stress and nonspecific immunity and nonspecific immunity on stress. Understanding bidirectional effects allows us to understand such things as how and why such coping serves to not only improve our mental health but our physical health as well. Following that discussion I will discuss some of the current thinking on how and why stress affects the specific system. My purpose is to show that there is, indeed, good reason to argue that if we want to be physically healthy, we need to develop certain health enabling behaviors, including coping.

Stress and the Nonspecific Immune System

Links between the central nervous system and the immune system. To illustrate that immunity cannot be explained simply in physical terms, consider an experiment done with rats (Fleshner, Laudenslager, Simons,

& Maier, 1989). When male rats are housed in groups, one—called the alpha rat—will become dominant. If a stranger is introduced, the alpha rat will attack the intruder. The intruder typically engages in defensive behaviors but, in the end, makes submissive responses (defeat postures). In this experiment, the intruder was administered an antigen before being introduced. Measurements of antibody activity indicated that being introduced into an established territory—even for brief periods of time—markedly reduced antibody activity. The reduction in antibody levels lasted as much as three weeks. To meet the objection that being bitten or attacked could explain the change in antibody activity, the experimenters measured the time spent in defeat postures and attacks. The results clearly showed that defeat postures were linked to antibody activity ($r = -0.80$). A small number of animals did not submit and received numerous bites; antibody activity in these animals was unaffected.

In humans, both *acute stressors*, such as final examinations, battle task vigilance and sleep deprivation, and *chronic stressors*, such as divorce and bereavement, have been shown to affect the immune response. Additionally, it has been shown that depression, anger, and anxiety affect the immune system (Maier et al., 1994). Note, however, that different stressors cause different mixes of autonomic activation and hormone activity. Thus, it is necessary to study each stressor to determine how it affects us. As we'll see shortly, many things moderate the effects of stressors.

Links between the immune system and the central nervous system.   In order for the brain to participate in the immune response, it must receive information that an immune response is occurring. Indeed, there is considerable evidence that both electrical and chemical activity does change when the immune response is activated. For example, it has been shown that the level of the neurotransmitter norepinephrine changes in the hypothalamus (Carlson, Felten, Livnat, & Felten, 1987). There is also evidence that the immune response activates the pituitary/adrenal response by triggering the release of CRF in the hypothalamus (Maier et al., 1994). In other words, there is considerable evidence that the central nervous system somehow monitors what is happening in the periphery of the body and then participates in the process.

It appears that an activated immune response triggers circuitry in the central nervous system to increase our sensitivity to pain. Sensitivity to pain is thought to have adaptive value during the recuperative process; for example, it helps us to avoid reinjuring ourselves. Further research is needed to determine how mood, emotional reactivity, and attention are affected by the immune response.

Functional significance of the bidirectional effects.   Perhaps the best way to understand the functional significance of this bidirectional system involving stress and our immune responses is to consider inflammation, which is one of the most important aspects of the nonspecific immune response. Inflammation is a highly localized reaction that is designed to limit the damage resulting from tissue injury to one location and to prevent the invasion of infection and other irritants. In the inflammation process, agents are called to the site to remove pathogens and repairs are initiated. Inflammation lasts 1–2 hours and is followed in 8–12 hours by the acute phase response.

The acute phase response involves processes such as the production of agents to fight pathogens; the removal of the nutrients necessary for pathogens to grow; the synthesis of proteins involved in scavenging and removing cellular debris; and fever. Fever is highly adaptive. Elevated body temperature enhances a number of enzymatic reactions important for repairs and the proliferation of immune cells but suppresses the replication of unwanted microbes (Maier et al., 1994). The acute phase also involves reduced activity; being lethargic has benefits for recuperation. Since the hypothalamus is responsible for the regulation of temperature, the involvement of the central nervous system is important in the acute phase response.

Stress, Energy, and Immunity

Under stress, the body's energy is redistributed. When we perceive that we are threatened, cardiac output is increased, blood from the digestive tract is shunted to the muscles, the muscles become more receptive to blood, the brain becomes active, pupils dilate for better distance vision, and so forth. It is highly adaptive to put on hold those things that do not immediately threaten our survival and to shift our energy resources to survival-related behavior.

Similarly, wouldn't it be productive to take the considerable energy going to the immune response and shift that to survival-related functions? Moreover, when dealing with a threat, we don't want to experience enhanced pain, fever, and reduced activity. In fact, it would be useful to experience analgesic effects, which is what happens under stress.

If energy is the key to maximizing survival, we would expect that the systems responsible for energy production will be mobilized. The glucocorticoids have been implicated not only in shutting down—or regulating—the inflammation process but in the mobilization of energy. The inflammation system appears to be very old, in evolutionary terms. The fight-or-flight response emerged much later, when organisms had developed the capacity to detect predators or other dangers, the motor capacity to take necessary action, and the ability to integrate these two functions. Since that evolution often works by using old systems for new purposes, theorists have suggested that, when the fight-or-flight response emerged, it simply made use of the inflammation system (Maier et al., 1994). All that was required was to insure that the system reacted immediately, and not 8–12 hours later when the acute phase of the inflammatory process normally begins.

What this means is that our immune response is now under the control of the stress response. While this may be viewed as an unfortunate byproduct of our evolutionary history, there is good reason to be optimistic. Because there are links between not only behaviors and the immune system but thinking and the immune system, we can compensate for this loss. The answer lies in learning how to think and act when stressed. If we learn such responses, our immune system will continue to do what it was designed to do.

Brief Stress and Disease

Researchers often distinguish between acute stress, such as taking final examinations, and chronic stress, such as bereavement and divorce. In both cases, the stress response occurs over a period of time—hours, days, months, or even years—and seems to take its toll on health. What about brief periods of stress, such as an encounter with a hostile person or a visit to the dentist? There is little evidence that such events play a major role in health. The stress response and its associated health problems are provoked by stressors that last many hours or days. As we'll see in the next section, many people learn to deal successfully with brief stressors on a regular basis and show no long-term effects.

Summary

A physical or psychological threat provokes a characteristic pattern of responses called the stress response. A series of chemical reactions set in motion by the hypothalamus alters, in a predictable way, our response to events in the environment. Most researchers have conceptualized the stress response as a fight-or-flight response, in which the body and brain are mobilized to deal with a threat. The stress response is thought to be due to the action of the pituitary/adrenal system. This system causes the release of endorphins and the glucocorticoids, the hormones that have been implicated in the downgrading of the immune system.

Research has shown a bidirectional effect between the central nervous system and the immune system. This bidirectional action is important for regulating such things as the inflammation response. The impact of stress on the immune response has been explained in terms of the evolutionary advantage of shutting down the immune response when threatened, in order to shunt the associated energy to the fight-or-flight response. The net result is that our immune system has come under the control of the stress response.

The Learned Component of Stress

In this section, we focus on how people deal with brief periods of stress. Brief stresses are often associated with threats to our survival and/or sensory overload. In many respects, this form of stress is hard to distinguish from anxiety. Anxiety, however, is typically defined in more existential terms; it has more to do with our perceptions about the future. Stress is here and now; it has to do with what is impacting us at the moment.

Unpredictability and Stress

Whether we experience stress depends on a number of psychological factors. In particular, it has been shown repeatedly that exposure to aversive events is much more likely to produce stress and disease if the events are unpredictable than if they can be foreseen. In comparison with predictable stress, unpredictable stress produces higher levels of corticosterone (Weiss, 1970, 1971a), more severe stomach ulceration (Caul, Buchanan, & Hays, 1972; Weiss, 1971a), greater weight loss (Weiss, 1970), alterations in the levels of glucose and free fatty acids (Quirce, Odio, & Solano, 1981), and myocardial dysfunction (Miller, Grossman, Richardson, Wistow, & Thomas, 1978).

In exploring the role of unpredictability, researchers have examined three main factors that influence whether an aversive event will lead to stress: discrimination of stress cues; availability of a coping response; and repeated experience with the aversive stimulus. Let's look at these factors.

Discrimination of Stress Cues

Research has shown that, if an organism experiences intermittent stress, knowing when that stress will come helps the organism to prepare for the stress just before onset and to relax after the stress has ended. The problem for the organism, therefore, is to learn to discriminate the cues that predict the onset of stress. Laboratory research has confirmed that this is an important factor. In one study (Weiss, 1970), rats were given a warning signal that they were about to receive a tail shock. A yoked control group received the same duration and pattern of shocks but without a warning signal. Intermittent shocks produce not only a reliable stress reaction but also lesions in the stomach (thought to be a precursor to ulcers). The question was whether signaled or unsignaled shock would produce more lesions. As we see in Figure 9-4, unsignaled shocks are more stressful than signaled shocks. The analogy with humans is obvious. For instance, scheduled tests are difficult enough; unscheduled tests are even more stressful, because they do not allow the student to relax. In the office, knowing when the boss is scheduled to arrive or when things normally go wrong can have important implications for learning to deal with stress.

Several studies have failed to show that signaled shock leads to less stress (Averill, 1973). Commenting on these studies, Averill notes that signaled shock seems to work only if the signal tells the subject not only when the shock will come but also when the subject can relax. The key, in other words, is knowing when to relax.

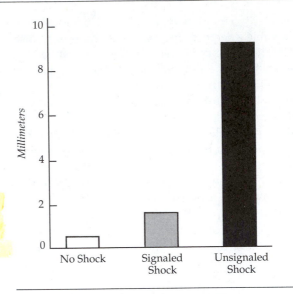

Figure 9-4. Total length of stomach lesions produced by shocks that are signaled, so that rats can learn a discrimination, and shocks that are unsignaled, so that no discrimination is possible. (From "Somatic Effects of Predictable and Unpredictable Shock," by J. M. Weiss, *Psychosomatic Medicine*, 1970, *32(4)*, 397–408. Copyright © 1970 by Elsevier North-Holland, Inc. Reprinted with permission.)

Availability of a Coping Response

Monkeys in a shock-avoidance situation show somewhat different patterns of catecholamine output when they can and cannot avoid shock (Brady, 1975). Weiss (1968, 1971a) found that animals that learn an avoidance response not only experience less lesioning of the stomach but show less stress (as measured by level of plasma corticosterone) than do yoked control subjects with no opportunity to make an avoidance response. Exactly why coping responses reduce stress is not altogether clear. Studies have ruled out the possibility that their effectiveness is due to the greater activity (exercise) that accompanies active avoidance (Weiss, Glazer, & Pohorecky, 1976). As we'll see in the next section, there is good evidence that the effect is cognitively mediated, at least in part.

If it is to be effective, the coping response must be fairly easy, as well as free of conflict. In one study, rats had to perform either an easy coping response (a single

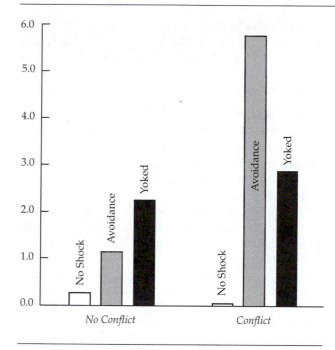

Figure 9-5. Total length of stomach lesions produced by an avoidance task when the avoidance response involves conflict and when it does not. The rat that learned the avoidance (coping) response suffered fewer stomach lesions than did yoked control subjects when the task was simple and clear-cut but considerably more when the task involved conflict. (From "Effects of Punishing the Coping Response (Conflict) on Stress Pathology in Rats," by J. M. Weiss, *Journal of Comparative and Physiological Psychology,* 1971, 77, 14–21. Copyright © 1971 by the American Psychological Association. Reprinted with permission of the author.)

bar press) or a more difficult response (several bar presses) to avoid shock. Animals with an easy response had fewer stomach lesions than did their yoked partners (Tsuda & Hirai, 1975). In another experiment, rats had to experience a brief shock while making an avoidance response that prevented a longer train of shocks. In this situation, the coping group developed more stomach lesions than did the yoked control subjects, as we see in Figure 9-5 (Weiss, 1971b).

In everyday life, we learn to experience less stress if we know what to do. Say, for example, that your job is to deal with customer complaints. How can you learn to deal with constant exposure to customers' anger? Many training programs have been designed to deal with such situations. After training, most people experience very little stress. What these programs teach is how to diffuse the anger and solve the problem. This involves two steps. First, they need to accept that the customer has been inconvenienced and so has a right to be angry, but that such anger is not directed at them personally. In accepting the anger, they communicate to the customer that they understand how the customer feels and are sympathetic. Second, they need to turn their attention to solving the problem. Once people see that someone is willing to help them, their anger often subsides and they too become involved in helping to solve the problem. People who learn this technique well can often turn a bad situation into a positive one for both themselves and the customer.

We'll return to the role of coping when we discuss moderators of stress.

Repeated Experience with the Aversive Stimulus

Studies have shown that an acute stress reaction depletes norepinephrine (Miller, 1980). Animals are slow to learn after an acute stress reaction, and it has been suggested that the failure to learn is due to the norepinephrine depletion.

In a study to determine if the stress response can be habituated, rats were exposed to acute stress for 15 consecutive days. Control rats were exposed to acute stress on only one day, with no prior exposure. After exposure, indices of norepinephrine metabolism in the rats' brains were examined. The prior-exposure animals had higher levels of enzymes involved in norepinephrine synthesis than did the no-exposure animals (Weiss, Glazer, Pohorecky, Brick, & Miller, 1975).

Marianne Frankenhaeuser (1980) has argued that repeated exposure to a stressor will reduce the stress reaction (particularly the activity of the adrenal medulla) only if there is a decrease in psychological involvement. For example, she notes that parachute jumping never becomes routine. Catecholamine secretion during jump periods tends to remain high even after several jumps (Bloom, von Euler, & Frankenhaeuser, 1963). Probably the reason is that parachute jumping demands constant attention and concentration. In other words, when a high degree of psychological readiness is required, the stress reaction remains high.

Prior exposure is often used as a training procedure to help people in a variety of situations deal more effectively with stressful stimulation. Training soldiers for combat duty typically involves exposing them to acute stress over a period of time. Mountain climbers train extensively, by exposing themselves to the conditions that they may expect to encounter in an important climb, such as cold, rain, wind, and prolonged physical exertion. Pilots are trained in simulators to react to a wide range of emergencies. In all these situations, the goal is not only to train the stress reaction but to teach the person to correctly evaluate the nature of the stimulus that is a potential stressor. Certain patterns of stimulation should elicit the stress reaction and others should not.

Learning How to Respond to Stress

As a general rule of thumb, it is not a good idea to make decisions or engage in a wide variety of behaviors when under stress. Here are two suggestions for functioning under stress.

1. **Learn a prescribed set of rules for making decisions under stress.** Why do people tend to make bad decisions under stress? Research indicates that it is largely due to their failure to fulfill an elementary requirement of the decision-making process, which is to systematically consider all the relevant alternatives (Keinan, 1987). To ensure sound decision making—for example, when controllers are guiding planes into an airport for a landing—people are carefully trained to make sure they follow a prescribed set of rules. Sometimes, they are required to actually check off each function as they complete it.

2. **Learn not to react.** It is not just poor decision making that leads to poor performance under stress. Stress has been shown to disrupt behavior that we consider automatic or habitual. After being told that his wife has cancer, a man drives through a stop sign on his way home; after being refused a loan by her banker, a woman forgets to pick up her purse. The reasoning behind learning not to react immediately is that humans tend to process information with two systems: one a quick and dirty system that does not fully process all the information and another more thorough system that involves rational thought processes (LeDoux, 1993). If an individual feels pressured to

respond quickly, such as when threatened, they are inclined to make use of the quick and dirty system, a system that evolved to help us deal with emergencies, however, a system that is based on incomplete information processing.

One way to help people deal with emergencies is to teach them a pattern of response that they can automatically use in an emergency situation. Airplane pilots are given special training in simulators to insure that in the event of an emergency, they will know what to do without having to think. Astronauts are trained not to respond personally and consult ground control. Because of the complexity of a spaceship, it is necessary to use a computer to analyze all the implications of a particular response before it is executed. In our daily lives we would do well to resist the temptation to respond to stress with a hasty action and instead allow our more thorough information processing system to help us decide a proper course of action.

Social Factors and Stress: The Workplace Example

The stress reaction is elicited by a wide variety of psychosocial stimuli—stimuli associated with our jobs, our residences, our social interactions, and the activities we engage in. Because they are part of our daily lives, they can elicit a prolonged stress reaction, which may precipitate a variety of adaptive diseases. To illustrate social factors, let's look at stress in the workplace.

Conflict-Prone and Conflict-Resistant Organizations

Stokols (1992a) suggests that the physical arrangements and the social conditions of an organization can predispose their members towards chronic conflict and resultant health problems. Table 9-3 presents the qualities of conflict-prone and conflict-resistant organizations, under three general categories: (1) the social-psychological qualities of groups; (2) organizational structure; and (3) environmental conditions. Stokols argues that the conflict-prone organization is often a major source of stress and illness in people.

The Individual-Environment Interaction

In his work on organizations, Stokols (1992a) argues that more attention needs to be paid to the physical

Table 9-3. Qualities of conflict-prone and conflict-resistant organizations.

Levels of Organizational Analysis	Tendencies toward Conflict or Cohesion	
	Conflict-Prone Organizations	Conflict-Resistant Organizations
Social-psychological qualities *(norms, goals, and role expectations)*	Absence of shared goals among group members.	Presence of and commitment to shared goals among group members.
	Incompatible styles and role assignments among group members.	Compatible style and role assignments among group members.
	Presence of rigid ideologies; low tolerance for diverse points of view.	Absence of rigid ideologies; high tolerance for diverse points of view.
Organizational structure *(interrelations among roles and resources)*	Existence of competitive coalitions.	Absence of competitive coalitions.
	Nonparticipatory organizational processes.	Participatory organizational processes.
	Overstaffed organization.	Adequately staffed organization.
	Pervasive competition among members for scarce roles and resources.	Minimal competition among members for roles and resources.
	Ambiguous organization of space and territory among group members.	Clear-cut territorial organization and use of space among group members.
	Relatively unstable role structure and membership.	Relatively stable role structure and membership.
	Absence of formal and informal dispute-resolution mechanisms.	Availability of formal and informal dispute-resolution mechanisms.
Environmental conditions	Local and remote environmental resources for meeting organizational goals are inadequate.	Ample environmental resources for meeting organizational goals are available.
	Environment external to the organization is anomic and turbulent.	Environment external to the organization is cohesive and nonturbulent.

Source: From "Conflict-Prone and Conflict-Resistant Organizations," by D. Stokols. In H. S. Friedman (Ed.), *Hostility, Coping and Health* (Table 5-1). Copyright © 1992 by the American Psychological Association. Reprinted with permission of the author.

environment and the sociocultural environment. In the past, researchers have focused on the individual's ability to adapt as the main source of difficulty and have put the blame more or less on the individual for his or her stress. While an individual with a disposition towards optimism, hardiness, and high self-esteem, for example, will tend to be less affected by stress, these factors alone may not be sufficient to eliminate work-related stress. If the environment plays havoc with people who have relatively positive dispositions, then how much more impact will it have on people with more negative dispositions (towards hos-

tility, anger, and low self-esteem). As yet, we do not have any direct estimates, but indirect evidence gives cause for concern. Indeed, some people's jobs are killing them, and it is worse for those who have more negative dispositions.

Note that people who have a competitive orientation tend to react poorly to stress. Among other things, they tend to engage in denial and to behaviorally and mentally disengage; show poor active coping skills; do not seek out social support, which is important in dealing with stress); and tend not to accept or interpret events in an adaptive manner (Franken & Brown,

1996). Since all of these characteristics have negative health implications, it is not surprising that organizations that promote a competitive atmosphere are typically characterized by poor employee health. By contrast, people who hold an exchange orientation (the general expectation of reciprocity) and a communal orientation (a positive regard for the needs and feelings of others) tend to experience less stress in organizational settings (Buunk, Doosje, Jans, & Hopstaken, 1993).

These principles apply not only to the workplace but to marital relationships, family functioning, interactions with friends, and casual interactions. It would be a useful exercise to analyze such everyday situations in terms of the principles in Table 9-3.

Summary

Both the nature of the stress reaction and the way a person or animal tends to respond under stress can be modified by learning. Learning to predict when a stressor will come allows the individual to relax when the stressor is absent. Short periods of relaxation appear to help ward off the effects of stress. In addition, learning a coping response seems to reduce some of the adverse effects of stress, such as ulcers. Habituating a response under stress seems to mobilize the body to provide the necessary physiological base for good performance. Evidence from a wide variety of sources indicates that, under stress, automatic and habitual responses deteriorate. The failure to make good decisions under stress is an example of how stress disrupts performance, probably by disrupting attention.

Social interactions—especially social conflicts—can be a significant source of stress. Studies of conflict-prone and conflict-resistant organizations indicate that stress tends to be higher in organizations characterized by a lack of shared goals, a rigid structure that is intolerant of diverse viewpoints, competitiveness, unstable roles and structure, and the absence of adequate resources. Correspondingly, stress tends to be less in organizations characterized by commitment to shared goals, a structure that tolerates and even encourages diversity, absence of competitiveness, and ample resources. One of the main dividends from working in a stress-resistant organization is good health.

The Cognitive Component of Stress

One of the most comprehensive theories about the role of cognitive factors in stress has been developed by Richard Lazarus and his colleagues (Coyne & Lazarus, 1980; Folkman, 1984; Folkman, Lazarus, Dunkel-Schetter, Delongis, & Gruen, 1986; Folkman, Schaefer, & Lazarus, 1979; Lazarus, 1981, 1991; Lazarus & Launier, 1978). According to this theory, how an individual appraises an event plays a fundamental role in determining not only the magnitude of the stress response but the kind of coping strategies that the individual may employ to deal with the stress. Appraisal occurs in two stages.

1. **Primary appraisal.** At this stage, we determine whether a stressful event represents harm/loss, threat, or challenge. *Harm/loss* refers to injury or damage that has already taken place, such as loss of a limb, loss of a job, or simply loss of self-esteem. *Threat* refers to something that could produce harm or loss. *Challenge* refers to the potential for growth, mastery, or some form of gain. As we'll see, numerous factors, both personal and situational, are involved in an individual's appraisal of a situation. From this perspective, the origins of stress cannot be assessed by looking solely at the nature of the environmental event that precipitates it. Rather, stress involves the interaction of the individual with the environment.

2. **Secondary appraisal.** After determining whether a stressful event represents harm/loss, threat, or challenge, we evaluate our coping resources and options; we ask what we can do. Generally, we have access to physical, social, psychological, and material coping resources. Physical resources include health and energy; social resources include family and friends; psychological resources include self-esteem and problem-solving abilities; and material resources include money and equipment.

Problem-Focused and Emotion-Focused Coping

According to Lazarus's theory, *coping* refers to cognitive and behavioral efforts to master, reduce, or tolerate the internal and/or external demands created by the stressful transaction (Folkman, 1984). Note that, by this definition, coping refers to efforts to manage rather than to the outcome of those efforts. In other words, having or developing a positive attitude is a form of coping, even if that positive attitude ultimately fails to resolve the situation.

The theory makes an important distinction between two ways of reducing stress. In *problem-focused coping,* we engage in some kind of problem-solving behavior designed to resolve the stressful transaction. If I'm experiencing stress on the job because of another person, for example, I may be able to reduce that stress by asking to be transferred to another department, arranging for the other person to be transferred, or devising some strategy to change the other person's behavior. In *emotion-focused coping,* by contrast, we focus on controlling the symptoms of stress. If it is impossible to avoid the other person, for example, I might deliberately take time out after every encounter to relax and think about the positive aspects of the job or to talk with some other person who might provide sympathy.

Situational Factors and Personal Control

Whether an individual tends to focus on the problem or on the emotion in dealing with stress depends very largely on whether the individual appraises the situation as controllable and on whether the situation is, in fact, controllable. Some stressful situations are basically uncontrollable, such as living near a nuclear reactor, perhaps, or working as a police officer, or having a friend who is dying of cancer. Other situations are subject to control (controllable), such as having an examination scheduled next week, perhaps, or having a tire on your car that has a slow leak, or having no money but having a job that permits you to work overtime. Note that circumstances may make what appears to be an uncontrollable situation controllable and vice versa. More importantly, people sometimes appraise as uncontrollable a situation that is really under their control and, conversely, may perceive themselves to have control when they do not.

Potentially Controllable Situations

When people are faced with a forthcoming examination, they tend to appraise that event as both challenging and threatening (Folkman & Lazarus, 1985). When people appraise an event as challenging, two things typically happen. First, they engage in problem-solving

behavior. Second, they develop a positive emotion (excitement, eagerness, hopefulness) that acts as a motivational support for their problem solving. In other words, two complementary processes lead to effort. When people appraise an event as threatening, however, something quite different happens; they experience a negative emotion. Negative emotions are indicators that something is wrong—at least that is our traditional way of viewing negative emotions. Whatever the exact reason, humans experiencing a negative emotion tend to focus on that emotion, and the time and effort devoted to coping with it distract the individual from activities better calculated to solve the problem. Note that people tend to appraise a situation as threatening when they perceive that it may not be altogether controllable.

Getting a promotion or simply having a high-level job can be perceived as both challenging and threatening. What makes a promotion threatening is the possibility that we may not succeed in the job. As long as the job is perceived as challenging, we are likely to handle it effectively. When feelings of threat arise, however, we will tend to waste time and effort in coping with those feelings. Management systems that use threats to motivate people obviously undermine the employees' motivation.

Situations Unlikely to Be Controllable

Faced with events over which we are unlikely to gain much control, we may do best to accept this fact, rather than to treat the situation as potentially controllable. This may seem like bad advice, because we know that viewing a situation as a challenge leads to a positive psychological state. But what happens when people make repeated attempts to control a situation that, in fact, is not controllable? A study of residents of Three Mile Island, the site of a major nuclear accident (Collins, Baum, & Singer, 1983), suggests that people who engage in problem-focused coping to deal with such an uncontrollable situation develop more psychological symptoms than do people who rely on more emotion-focused coping. When we are faced with a problem that is truly beyond our control, it seems to make more sense simply to deal with our emotions.

Controllability and Longevity

Apparently, perceived controllability even promotes longevity. In a long-term study, two groups of older people in institutions with different levels of opportunity for control and responsibility were compared. Those given more control not only became more active but reported being happier. Their reduced levels of corticosteroids suggested that these subjects were experiencing less stress. After two years, this group was significantly healthier than the comparison group. Moreover, in that period, half as many people died in this group as in the comparison group (Rodin & Langer, 1977).

Summary

Primary appraisal, according to Lazarus's theory, involves classifying or labeling a stressful event as representing either harm/loss, threat, or challenge. Secondary appraisal involves the evaluation of the relevant coping resources and options that are available. In general, coping strategies are either problem-focused or emotion-focused. According to Lazarus's theory, whether an individual tends to use problem-focused or emotion-focused coping depends on two additional factors: whether the threat is potentially controllable and, if it is, whether the individual perceives that he or she has the skills to deal with it.

Moderators of Stress

A moderator of stress tends to reduce the stress response. Stress moderators can be broken down roughly into biological, learned, and cognitive factors. While the fit is not perfect, these categories emphasize the idea that moderators work in different ways to achieve their final common goal, which is to reduce stress.

Practical Application 9-2

Pet Ownership and Health

As people get older, their health often deteriorates, and they seek out doctors to help them. This puts a great burden on the medical system. A great deal of anecdotal lore suggests that pets can improve the psychological outlook of patients and can even help sustain life in times of physical and psychological stress. Research by Judith Siegel (1990) confirms these benefits. In a prospective study of 938 Medicare enrollees in a health maintenance organization over the span of one year, she found not only that people with pets visited their physicians less, but that pets helped them to deal better with stressful events. People with pets, for example, experienced less stress associated with the loss of companionship. In this sample, 26% experienced the death of a close friend. Over 75% of the pet owners mentioned that their pet provided them with companionship and comfort, while 25% indicated that they felt more secure with their pets and 21% said they felt loved by the pet. In other words, owning a pet seems to help meet people's companionship needs. Siegel suggests that one reason people go to see their doctor is to satisfy their need for companionship.

Which is the best pet to own? The results indicated that only a dog is a stress buffer. Finer analysis of the data indicated that dog owners spent more time outdoors with their pet and talked more with their pet. Once again, this provides evidence that the pet is a source of companionship. Since Siegel controlled for health status in all of her data analyses, it appears that pet ownership influences social and psychological processes rather than physical health. Nonetheless, we know that psychological health is often a good predictor of physical health. Two studies of older individuals found that those who felt more attached to their pets were in better physical health (Garrity, Stallones, Marx, & Johnson, 1989; Ory & Goldberg, 1983); this indicates that there is a positive relationship between psychological and physical variables.

The Biological Component

Social Support and Stress

Social support has consistently emerged as a moderator of life stress (Vaux, 1992: Veiel & Baumann, 1992). Three dimensions of social support have been identified (Schwarzer, Dunkel-Schetter, & Kemeny, 1994; Vaux, 1992):

1. Emotional support (intimacy and reassurance), which can come from family, friends, spouses or partners, volunteers, and community groups such as churches.
2. Tangible support (the provision of aid and service), which involves receiving such necessities as clothing, food, and shelter, as well as help with daily chores such as cleaning, shoveling snow, raking leaves, and banking.
3. Informational support (advice and feedback), which involves receiving information and advice on how to take care of ourselves, on the one hand, and having someone who will listen in an empathetic manner, on the other.

Whether social contacts are beneficial depends on whether they are discretionary or obligatory (Bolger & Eckenrode, 1991). If it is apparent that someone is only helping out of a sense of duty, we are not likely to experience a reduction in stress.

The Repressive Personality Type and Social Support

It appears that certain people who resist seeking out social support are susceptible to a number of physical diseases, particularly cancer (Eysenck, 1988). These people, who are said to have a *repressive* personality, are characterized by their tendency to chronically defend themselves against negative affects, particularly anger and anxiety, and to deny that they are distressed (Emmons, 1992). Of particular interest is evidence that repressors tend to experience difficulties in interpersonal functioning. They seem to be preoccupied with issues of relatedness and are troubled by feelings of dependency and ambivalence in their relations with others (Bonanno & Singer, 1990).

Several mechanisms have been offered to explain why repressive individuals are more susceptible to disease (Weingberger, 1990). The bottom line, it appears, is

that people tend to be healthier when they have good social support systems and feel connected.

Social Support and Bereavement

Can social support help us to cope with the considerable stress associated with the death of a loved one? Some theorists contend that bereavement can be compensated by a strong social support network (e.g., Stroebe & Stroebe, 1987), but attachment theory suggests that no amount of social support can make up for such losses (Bowlby, 1979). Tests of these two opposing views indicate that attachment theory is a better explanation of the research findings (Stroebe, Stroebe, Abakoumkin, & Schut, 1996). When a loved one dies, we experience emotional loneliness, which cannot readily be compensated by reducing social loneliness.

The Learned Component

Managing Stressful Information

One of the main theoretical explanations of stress due to serious life events is based on the idea that we need to be in control of events in our lives (Geer, Davison, & Gatchel, 1970; Krantz & Schulz, 1980). Horowitz (1979) argues that, in order to deal with life stressors, we must avoid becoming overwhelmed. To do this, we engage in a variety of control operations that allow us to keep the stress within bounds. For example, we might use denial in order to regain composure or we might focus on only one aspect of the event. Horowitz speaks of breaking the stressful information down into a series of micro-intervals, so that it is within our ability to deal with it. In this way, we master a stressful event by sequentially attacking each of its units. Failure to put the stressful information under tight control, Horowitz says, might lead to information overload, which could precipitate a total breakdown. In computer language, we might say that the system would crash.

Epstein's Theory

Epstein's theory is largely cognitive, but the way people think is habitual. As we'll see in this section, it's because we learn to think about things in certain ways that we experience stress. By learning to think differently, we gain control over stress.

The search for universal coping strategies.   For some time, coping has been regarded as one of the main moderators of stress. Despite a great deal of anecdotal evidence linking individual coping strategies to reduction in stress, psychologists have had difficulty identifying universal coping principles or styles of coping that underlie these diverse individual strategies. Along with the work of Folkman and Lazarus (1985), which we have already discussed, the work of Seymour Epstein and his associates at the University of Massachusetts has moved us closer to identifying such universal strategies. In a nutshell, Epstein's theory is that people who are effective in dealing with stress tend to think more *constructively* when faced with problems, whereas those who tend to experience stress think more *destructively* (Epstein & Meier, 1989).

Intelligence and adjustment.   Epstein's theory grew out of his work on practical intelligence. Like others before him, he has observed that academic intelligence does not predict adjustment. Specifically, academic intelligence does not predict mental health, physical health, good family relations, good social relations, satisfactory romantic relations, or success at work. According to Epstein's cognitive-experiential self-theory (CEST), people have three semiindependent systems that help them deal with daily life: a rational system, roughly corresponding to academic intelligence; an experiential system, which we will consider shortly; and an associationistic system, observed in altered states of consciousness. Epstein believes that the experiential system gives rise to good mental and physical health, good relationships, and success at work. Note that, while academic intelligence predicts grades and is therefore indirectly related to success at work, many people who are successful at work do not have high academic intelligence. Academic intelligence does not predict who makes the most money, who gets promoted, and other indicators of success at work (Epstein, 1990).

To test this theory, Epstein and Meier (1989) created an inventory to measure experiential abilities—the Constructive Thinking Inventory (CTI). This inventory provides an index of the degree to which people tend to be constructive thinkers rather than destructive thinkers when dealing with daily problems. It contains a global measure of coping, plus six specific measures

or scales: emotional coping, behavioral coping, categorical thinking, superstitious thinking, naive optimism, and negative thinking. The first two scales—emotional coping and behavior coping—are not only the best predictors of coping but correspond to Lazarus's emotion-focused coping and problem-focused coping. Often, the best way to understand what a scale measures is to examine some of the items (Table 9-4). Scales such as this typically contain positively and negatively worded items, and subjects are asked to indicate, using a five-point scale, the degree to which they think the item is like them or not like them. A minus sign (–) beside the item indicates that the item is reverse-scored; that is, if a person scores the item as 1, it will be recorded as 5 when computing the final score.

The four remaining scales—categorical thinking, superstitious thinking, naive optimism, and negative thinking—all measure nonadaptive thinking. The underlying finding of Epstein and others is that, in order to act adaptively, we need to think accurately. None of these four types of thinking gives us a realistic view of the world. *Categorical thinking* is a type of black-and-white thinking that has been linked to rigid and intolerant people. In reality, most things are neither black nor white. The ability to recognize gray is useful in seeing the world as it is. *Superstitious thinking* is irrational thinking in which doing or saying certain things is believed to produce certain outcomes. It can sometimes be seen in children's play—for instance, the game in which children avoid cracks in the sidewalk as they say: "If you step on a crack it will break your mother's back." *Naive optimism*—also called Pollyanna thinking—is another kind of irrational thinking, rooted in the idea that all you have to do to succeed is think positively. *Negative thinking* is a tendency to expect the worst. For many people, negative thinking becomes a self-fulfilling prophecy.

Differences between constructive and destructive thinkers. Work with the CTI scales (especially the global scale) has provided some indication of how people who are good constructive thinkers differ from poor constructive thinkers. The main difference, it appears, relates to dealing with negative outcomes. While both good and poor constructive thinkers tend to respond favorably to good outcomes (they remain positive and optimistic about future performance), poor constructive thinkers

Table 9-4. Examples of items from constructive thinking inventory scales.

Emotional Coping

I worry a great deal about what other people think of me. (–)
I don't let little things bother me.
I tend to take things personally. (–)

Behavioral Coping

I am the kind of person who takes action rather than just thinks or complains about a situation.
I avoid challenges because it hurts too much when I fail. (–)
When faced with upcoming unpleasant events, I usually carefully think through how I will deal with them.

Categorical Thinking

There are basically two kinds of people in this world, good and bad.
I think there are many wrong ways, but only one right way, to do almost anything.
I tend to classify people as either for me or against me.

Superstitious Thinking

I have found that talking about successes that I am looking forward to can keep them from happening.
I do not believe in any superstitions. (–)
When something good happens to me, I believe it is likely to be balanced by something bad.

Naive Optimism

If I do well on an important test, I feel like a total success and that I will go very far in life.
I believe that people can accomplish anything they want to if they have enough willpower.

Negative Thinking

When I am faced with a new situation, I tend to think the worst possible outcome will happen.
I tend to dwell more on pleasant than unpleasant incidents from the past. (–)
I get so distressed when I notice that I am doing poorly in something that it makes me do worse.

Source: "Constructive Thinking: A Broad Coping Variable with Specific Components," by S. Epstein & P. Meier, *Journal of Personality and Social Psychology,* 1989, *57,* 332–350. Copyright © 1989 by the American Psychological Association. Reprinted with permission.

tend to overgeneralize about the self after negative outcomes. Among other things, their self-esteem plummets, they feel depressed, and they assume a helpless attitude about future performance. Interestingly, these are some of the symptoms that characterize depressed individuals.

Origins of destructive thinking. Why do some people develop such a profound negative self-view following poor performance, while others do not? Epstein (1992) speculates that this may be linked to self-schemata within the implicit self theory that we developed as children. Like many others before him, he suggests that, when love is withdrawn for poor performance or

when love is made conditional on good performance, we tend to develop, as part of our implicit self theory, the idea or belief that making mistakes or performing poorly will result in the withdrawal of love. Since the withdrawal of love is one of the most profound and devastating experiences that a child can experience, making mistakes or performing poorly takes on much greater significance than it should. Even though, as adults, we may come to the conclusion that our reactions are inappropriate, we often have difficulty learning how to respond more appropriately. Why we have difficulty unlearning this belief and replacing it with a more rational or reasonable one is not altogether clear. Among other things, it has been suggested that the experiential system does not work by rules of reason or logic and, therefore, to change requires something more than just understanding the source of our problem (Epstein & Meier, 1989).

Poor constructive thinking and stress. In laboratory studies where stress was induced by having subjects subtract 7s from 300 or engage in mirror-tracing and constantly telling them of their errors, poor constructive thinkers reported more negative thoughts—both related and unrelated to the experiment—and experienced more negative affect (Katz & Epstein, 1991). Physiological measures of poor constructive thinkers also indicated that they experienced greater stress than did good constructive thinkers. It was concluded that poor constructive thinkers contribute to the stress they experience by spontaneously generating negative

thoughts in the absence of external stressors and that they appraise external stressors as more threatening.

Constructive thinking and success in life. Epstein's theory is relevant not only to managing stress but to achieving success. In Chapter 13, we will discuss the importance of developing the kind of thinking that has been used by successful people.

Emotion-Focused Coping Strategies

Strategies that have been advocated to deal with stress include exercise, relaxation, meditation, and even biofeedback training. Let's review some of the research assessing the effectiveness of these techniques.

Meditation. Transcendental meditation (TM) was introduced to North America by Maharishi Mahesh Yogi

Practical Application 9-3

Becoming a Constructive Thinker

From the work of Epstein, it appears that those who think destructively focus their negative thinking not only on the self but also on the outside world. As a result, they see themselves as inadequate and the world as threatening. Research suggests these two tendencies are different but highly related and probably have a common origin in the implicit theories that people have constructed about their ability to deal with the external world. All behavior involves, at least to some degree, an attempt to interact with the environment. To interact successfully involves an assessment of our abilities (the self) and the challenge offered by the environment.

How do we learn to deal successfully with the external world? First, we need to believe that we can succeed and then we need to learn the skills that will enable us to succeed. Many people never make the effort to develop the skills they need, because they don't believe they can succeed. The first step, therefore, is to develop a more positive attitude about our ability to deal with the environment. The second

thing, of course, is to see the world in terms of opportunity—as a source of pleasure as opposed to pain. We will consider the specifics of developing such thinking in Chapters 9 and 14. For the moment, note that many psychologists are coming to regard thinking styles as habits that we have developed. If they are habits, we can learn to change them through the principles of reinforcement. In other words, we have reason to be optimistic that we can all become constructive thinkers.

The idea that our thinking consists of habits helps me understand why I often have difficulty changing the way I think. Even when I know, at a rational level, that I need to think differently, I find myself falling back into my previous mode of thinking. It seems easier and more natural—more me. Eventually, however, I feel very comfortable with my new way of thinking.

It has been my experience that, when I do change the way I think—often after repeated attempts—the world looks very different to me; it is a better world.

in the 1960s. More than half a million people have already been trained, and their numbers continue to grow. Countless books and articles advocate the use of meditation to overcome stress and increase inner energy (e.g., Bloomfield, Cain, Jaffe, & Kory, 1975; Schwartz, 1974).

The various techniques for meditation seem to be equally effective in lowering anxiety and countering the effects of stress. Each of these techniques retrains attention in some way, according to Daniel Goleman (1976), who has offered the following simple procedure for meditation:

> Find a quiet place with a straight-back chair. Sit in any comfortable position with your back straight. Close your eyes. Bring your full attention to the movement of your breath as it enters and leaves your nostrils. Don't follow the breath into your lungs or out into the air. Keep your focus at the nostrils, noting the full passage of each in- and out-breath, from its beginning to its end. Each time your mind wanders to other thoughts, or is caught by background noises, bring your attention back to the easy, natural rhythm of your breathing. Don't try to control the breath; simply be aware of it. Fast or slow, shallow or deep, the nature of the breath does not matter; your total attention to it is what counts. If you have trouble keeping your mind on your breath, count each inhalation and exhalation up to 10, then start over again. Meditate for 20 minutes; set a timer, or peek at your watch occasionally. Doing so won't break your concentration. For the best results, meditate regularly, twice a day, in the same time and place (p. 84).

The evidence showing that meditation does reduce the stress reaction is fairly impressive. It has been shown, for example, that meditation will reduce high blood pressure (Benson & Wallace, 1972) and the frequency of headaches, colds, and insomnia (Wallace, Benson, & Wilson, 1971). One series of studies showed that transcendental meditation practiced by volunteer subjects produced a decrease in oxygen consumption (Wallace & Benson, 1972). These results (Figure 9-6) are particularly impressive because oxygen consumption reflects metabolic rate, a physiological response that cannot be altered through voluntary efforts. We might ask whether meditators can reduce the activity of the adrenal cortex. It appears that meditation does reduce adrenocortical activity, as indicated by reduced cortisol levels (Jevning, Wilson, & Davidson, 1978).

Goleman (1976) has noted that meditators typically recover rapidly from stress and suggests that fact is the key to understanding why meditators successfully resist the effects of stress. If a person can relax after each stressful event, the aversive effects associated with stress are kept to a minimum, and the person has greater reserves of energy to deal with future stressful events. Rather than letting each stressful event add to the previous one, the person treats each event more or less separately. As we have noted, stress seems to have a damaging effect only if it is prolonged. It appears that, because meditators recovery so rapidly, they do not experience prolonged stress.

Relaxation.   If the beneficial effects of meditation are due to the increased relaxation that it produces, then other forms of relaxation might be just as effective. Indeed, several lines of research have shown that to be the case (Beary, Benson, & Klemchuk, 1974; Cauthen & Prymak, 1977; Fenwick et al., 1977; Holmes, 1984; Morse, Martin, Furst, & Dubin, 1977). Relaxation is found to be effective in reducing both systolic and diastolic blood pressure (e.g., Fey & Lindholm, 1978; Mount, Walters, Rowland, Barnes, & Payton, 1978). In *The Relaxation Response*, Herbert Benson (1975) tells how relaxation can be readily learned and used.

Exercise.   Research data on exercise relate mainly to anxiety, which is often associated with stress. A study comparing the effects of exercise and meditation found that, although exercise reduced certain somatic aspects of anxiety, it did not necessarily reduce the cognitive aspects (Schwartz, Davidson, & Goleman, 1978). These researchers argue that exercise, if combined with relaxation, could enhance the beneficial effects of relaxation, but exercise cannot be substituted for relaxation. Nonetheless, there is considerable evidence that physical fitness does moderate the negative health effects of life stress (Brown, 1991).

Biofeedback.   Since the discovery that involuntary responses mediated by the autonomic nervous system can be altered through operant conditioning procedures, there has been considerable interest in using these procedures to reduce the stress reaction. After reviewing the relevant research, Tarler-Benlolo (1978) found no evidence that biofeedback is better than

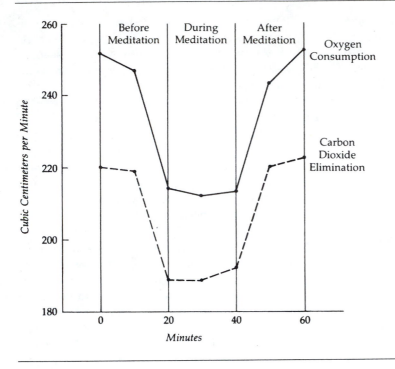

Figure 9-6. Effect of meditation on subjects' oxygen consumption (solid line) and carbon dioxide elimination (dashed line), recorded in 20 and 15 cases, respectively. After the subjects were invited to meditate, both rates decreased markedly. Consumption and elimination returned to the pre-meditation level soon after the subjects stopped meditating. (From "The Physiology of Meditation," by R. K. Wallace and H. Benson, *Scientific American*, February 1972, 84–90. Copyright © 1972 by Scientific American, Inc. All rights reserved.)

relaxation for dealing with a variety of stress-induced disorders, including migraine headaches and elevated blood pressure. Each technique may be particularly suited to certain people or certain disorders, but more data are required before specific conclusions can be drawn. There may be reason to use both techniques at once (Cuthbert, Kristeller, Simons, Hodes, & Lang, 1981; Fey & Lindholm, 1978).

The Cognitive Component

Inhibition and Trauma

Individuals who have suffered from a variety of traumas in childhood are far more likely to become ill if they never talk about the traumas (Pennebaker, 1992). Several studies have confirmed that talking or writing about a trauma leads to health benefits. Among other things, people who wrote about their traumas visited the doctor less and had an improved immune response (Pennebaker, 1990). Pennebaker argues that while inhibition is normally highly adaptive, because inhibition allow us to control our thinking and behavior (as in goal-directed behavior), inhibition of traumatic events

is very harmful. Over time, he argues, the constant injunction to not think about the trauma creates stress. In order for people to reduce this stress, they need to deal with the trauma and put it to rest. Various theorists have argued that, when people actually translate an experience into language, they can *assimilate* it (Horowitz, 1976). Whatever the actual process, talking and writing seem to reduce the tension associated with constantly repressing something that affected us deeply.

The Hardy Personality

People who remain healthy after experiencing high degrees of life stress often exhibit a distinctive personality profile—the *hardy personality,* with three main characteristics (Kobasa, 1979a, b, 1982; Kobasa, Maddi, & Kahn, 1982):

1. *Control*—the belief that it is possible to influence the course of life events.
2. *Commitment*—the belief that life is meaningful and has a purpose.
3. *Challenge*—the attitude that difficult or onerous events are normal and can provide an opportunity for mastery and development.

The concept of hardiness may account for other moderators of stress, such as the locus of control and sensation seeking, which we will discuss shortly (Kobasa & Puccetti, 1983). Suzanne Kobasa has shown that people with a hardy personality profile are less likely to become ill after experiencing stress. The work of Hull, Van Treuren, and Virnelli (1987) suggests that hardiness should be treated as three separate phenomena: They found that only commitment and control were significantly related to health outcome.

The concept of a hardy personality has generated a great deal of interest. A number of studies have been designed to determine exactly how and why the hardy personality leads to lower rates of illness. The bulk of the evidence seems to indicate that hardy people not only see the world as less threatening but see themselves as more capable of dealing with stressful events by means of problem-solving and support-seeking strategies (Florian, Mikulincer, & Taubman, 1995). When confronted with stress, hardy people show less frustration (Wiebe, 1989) and offer more positive self-statements and fewer negative self-statements (Allred & Smith, 1989), as illustrated in Figure 9-7.

Internal and External Locus of Control

According to the locus-of-control theory, as we know, some individuals (internals) believe that the ultimate source of control is within themselves, whereas others (externals) believe that control rests outside themselves, in the environment. Internals' belief that the environment is essentially controllable makes an important contribution to stress reduction (Lefcourt, Miller, Ware, & Sherk, 1981). But what happens in a situation that is not controllable? Lundberg and Frankenhaeuser (1978) have shown that internals give evidence of greater stress in such situations than in situations that are controllable, whereas externals show less stress when the situation is uncontrollable than when it is controllable. Thus, in both cases, the stress was greater when their cognitive orientation was inconsistent with the outcome of their efforts to control the stressor.

One particularly interesting finding is that, compared to externals, internals derive greater benefits from social support (Lefcourt, Martin, & Saleh, 1984). This may help to explain the variability in research data on internal orientation and stress. Apparently, the internal orientation interacts with variables such as so-

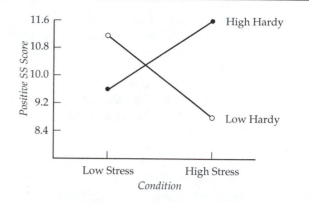

Figure 9-7. Effects of stress and hardiness on positive self-statements (SS). (From "The Hardy Personality: Cognitive and Physiological Responses to Evaluative Threat," by K. D. Alfred and T. W. Smith, *Journal of Personality and Social Psychology,* 1989, *56,* 257–266. Copyright © 1989 by the American Psychological Association. Reprinted with permission of the author.)

cial support and cognitive appraisal. One study demonstrated that internals appraise situations in a more adaptive fashion than do externals (Parkes, 1984).

Optimism and Health

There is considerable evidence that optimists—people who adopt a positive and hopeful outlook—are healthier than pessimists. Shelly Taylor (1989) makes the case that people who see the world from an optimistic point of view tend to show better recovery from a wide range of illnesses, including cancer. The current evidence suggests that, when pessimists are under stress, their catecholamines become depleted; this triggers the endorphin response, which, in turn, shuts down the immune system (Seligman, 1990).

We'll return to the role of optimism in Chapter 11.

Instrumentality and Stress

Both cross-sectional and longitudinal studies show that instrumentality is a significant stress buffer (Shaw, 1982; Roos & Cohen, 1987). Instrumentality is a measure, among other things, of problem-solving behavior, which has been implicated in adjustment. Confirming previous work, Roos and Cohen (1987) found that instrumentality was negatively related to psychological distress. Interestingly, androgynous individuals—those who scored high on both instrumentality and expressiveness on Spence and Helmreich's (1978) scale—showed the greatest resilience to recent life stress.

The positive link between instrumentality and health is consistent with the idea that active coping is important for good health. When people take charge of their lives, they are less likely to fall prey to the debilitating effects of stress.

Sensation Seeking and Stress

Sensation seeking has also been found to be a moderator of stress (Cohen, 1982; Smith, Ptacek, & Smoll, 1992). Like hardy individuals, sensation seekers tend to view the world as less threatening (Franken, Gibson, & Rowland, 1992) and to engage in more active coping

(Smith, Ptacek & Smoll, 1992). Like optimists, they tend to view the world in positive terms, and they tend to be highly instrumental (Franken, 1992).

As we'll discuss in Chapter 14, sensation seekers see the world as benevolent. They take the view that life is to be embraced and enjoyed and are ready to disclose their feelings to others (Franken, Gibson, & Mohan, 1990). They are able to accept imperfection, and they like people and have a great deal of tolerance for different values and points of view. They also have a good sense of humor. In short, they have many qualities that make them resistant to the effects of stress.

Humor and Stress

Initial work on humor showed that humor helps to reduce stress (Martin & Lefcourt, 1983). In a follow-up

Practical Application 9-4

Some Rules for Dealing with Stress

A wide variety of organizations and educational institutions are offering courses designed to help people deal with unwanted stress. Some teach methods for reducing the magnitude of the stress reaction, including meditation, relaxation, exercise, and biofeedback. Others help people plan their lives so that they encounter fewer stressors or the stressors come at times when they are physically and psychologically prepared to deal with them. Here are seven rules for dealing with unwanted stress.

1. **Plan activities to reduce or eliminate stressors.** Our daily routine exposes many of us to a wide variety of stressful events, such as traffic snarls on the way to and from work, periodic interruptions, noise, the need to make quick decisions, requests for assistance in areas that are not our responsibility, criticisms of the quality or quantity of our work, and involvement in hostile exchanges. Although some of these events are unavoidable, it is often possible to reduce the number or magnitude of such stressors. For example, arranging to go to work earlier and leaving earlier could allow us to avoid traffic jams, to work at least for a time without interruptions, and to experience less noise and would also limit the opportunity

for people to make unwarranted requests, and reduce hostile exchanges. If we can do at least part of our job before the other employees arrive, we may have more time to make decisions and to respond tactfully to criticisms and requests. The resulting reduction in stress may decrease irritability and arousal and thus make us less sensitive to other potential stressors. It could also lead to improved performance, with further reduction in criticisms and the possibility of rewards and promotions.

2. **Plan activities so that stressors come at times when they are easier to handle or tolerate.** The same event may induce a more intense stress reaction at certain times than at others. For example, a common source of stress results from interruptions that occur when we are trying to complete a task—a ringing telephone, a person dropping by to ask questions or simply to chat, or certain distracting noises. It is often possible to reduce or eliminate this source of stress by systematic planning. Turning off the telephone ringer, telling the secretary to hold all calls, putting up a "Do Not Disturb" sign, or moving to a location where such interruptions are unlikely are some possible solutions. People often find that after an important task is completed, distracting events are less stressful or not stressful at all. Alternatively, we might take care of

study, it was shown that humor reduces stress but only for depressed individuals and not for individuals with anxiety symptomology (Nezu, Nezu, & Blissett, 1988). Why does humor reduce stress? One possible interpretation is that people with a sense of humor appraise stressful situations differently than do humorless people. Another possibility is that a sense of humor leads to responses that are incompatible with the stress reaction. It has been shown, for example, that putting on a happy face is sufficient to produce the changes in heart rate and other physiological reactions associated with happiness. Ekman, Levenson, and Friesen (1983) established that even thinking about an emotion produces the reactions that generally accompany the emotion and concluded that some sort of feedback mechanism helps to reduce stress.

Whatever the exact mechanism, we would expect intuitively that humor would reduce stress. It remains to be seen why humor fails to reduce feelings of anxiety.

Summary

One of the most fundamental moderators of life stress is social support. It seems that certain people who resist seeking out social support—repressive types—are susceptible to a number of physical diseases, particularly cancer. Interestingly, owning a pet—especially a dog—has significant health benefits. However, social support does not appear to mitigate the stress associated with bereavement.

details early in the day, so that a block of time is available later in the day to work at certain tasks.

3. **Learn to relax between activities.** Some people tend to experience less stress than others do in the course of a demanding or rigorous schedule. Although constitutional differences may play a role here, another contributory factor is the way people pace themselves. Shutting down the stress reaction periodically by relaxing appears to keep stress under control. Research from a variety of sources suggests that stress becomes distressful when it is allowed to become intense. Unless we shut down the stress reaction periodically, the stress of one activity tends to add to the stress of another. At some point, stress becomes our enemy. It is likely to have an adverse affect not only on our health but on our performance. We can reduce these effects by learning to relax between activities. It may also be easier to reduce low stress than high stress. When the stress reaction becomes very intense, it frequently provokes a psychological state of helplessness; we feel that we no longer have control over events. Such a feeling can, of course, act as a primary source of stress. Because stress can interfere with our ability to cope, we are caught in a vicious circle, in which the experience of stress becomes a stimulus for further stress.

4. **Learn to recognize the early signs of stress.** Because humans are dynamic, their reactions to events are always affected by previous activities. This means that at certain times an event may cause only mild stress, while at other times it may cause intense stress. If we are to gain control of the stress reaction before it becomes too intense, we must be able to recognize when stress is starting to exceed some *safe limit*. This is not an easy task for many people, who can recognize stress only when it has reached a high intensity. Biofeedback training can help such people understand the stress reaction and teach them how to intervene when it starts to exceed some safe limit.

5. **Learn to treat stress as a challenge.** Stressful events often demand that we react. We can react with fear and helplessness, or we can rise to the challenge. If we treat a stressor as a challenge, we will trigger a norepinephrine response, which not only helps supply us with energy but provides us with positive affect. In other words, it appears that norepinephrine has evolved to help us cope with stress. To tap that adaptive chemical, we must rise to the challenge. We must view stress as an opportunity to exercise our adaptive responses or to develop such responses.

(continued on next page)

Coping appears to be a major moderator of stress. According to Epstein's theory, people who are effective in dealing with stress tend to think more constructively when faced with problems, whereas those who tend to experience stress think more destructively. The Constructive Thinking Inventory (CTI) contains a global measure of coping, plus six specific measures or scales: emotional coping, behavioral coping, categorical thinking, superstitious thinking, naive optimism, and negative thinking. Work with the CTI indicates that constructive thinkers tend to deal effectively with negative outcomes. They score high on emotional and behavioral coping measures. It has been suggested that the destructive thinking style emerges early in life and may result from the withdrawal of parental love fol-

lowing poor performance. People can become constructive thinkers by learning to change how they think about themselves and the world.

Among the emotion-focused coping strategies, transcendental meditation has been shown to be effective. Researchers such as Goleman have concluded that all forms of meditation are equally effective. It appears that meditation teaches people to relax following a stressful event and thus allows them to reduce the adverse effects of a prolonged stress reaction. Some researchers have suggested that relaxation can be taught directly, without meditation. Exercise has also been advocated as a way of reducing stress. Although exercise reduces certain somatic components, it does not appear to be a substitute for relaxation. Biofeedback is ef-

Practical Application 9-4 *(continued)*

Failure to rise to the challenge will only undermine our self-concept and our natural tendency to control stressful events in our environment.

6. **Learn to prevail by becoming problem-focused.** Considerable research emphasizes that people need to learn how to manage self-doubt because it is an important aspect of learning to prevail. As Bandura (1991) points out, everybody experiences self-doubt from time to time, especially when faced with a negative life event. What differentiates those who prevail from those who give up is how they deal with such self-doubt. People who fail typically ruminate on their self-doubts, rehearse all their past failures, and count all their inadequacies. Those who succeed, in contrast, learn to rehearse their past successes and to enumerate their strengths.

The key to managing self-doubt is learning to become problem-focused. When attention is focused on the problem, some change may happen; that is the basis for hope and optimism. When people become self-focused, by contrast, they tend to focus on the negative and to accept that nothing can change because the source of their difficulty lies in their personal inadequacies. The more they ruminate, the more distressed they become, and the harder it is for

them to think about a solution to their problem (e.g., Wood, Saltzberg, Neale, Stone, & Rachmiel, 1990).

In order to become more problem-focused, start by thinking of how you succeeded in the past under similar circumstances. In other words, give yourself a pep talk. Next, look for ways that other people succeeded under similar circumstances. This will get your thinking off yourself. Finally, ask people to help you find a solution. This is a good way to establish social relations and make use of the considerable skills that other people have.

7. **Actively develop those personality characteristics that will ward off stress.** Your personality is largely a matter of your attitude towards the world and yourself. People who are healthy are positive and optimistic, accept themselves, take charge of their lives, have a sense of humor, and have good social relations. Most people cannot change their personality overnight. But people do change; personality is not carved in stone (Chapter 14). One of the most powerful reasons I can think of for wanting to change is to be physically healthier and as a result live longer. Stress is not inevitable. We can keep it to a minimum if we are willing to create an environment that is conducive to harmony, cooperation, and support.

fective, but it appears to be no better than relaxation. Exactly why relaxation is so effective is not clear. Research is needed to determine whether relaxation affects only bodily reactions or both bodily and cognitive reactions.

Another moderator of life stress is the hardy personality, characterized by control, commitment, and challenge. Most research on hardiness suggests that the effects are due to the way hardy people appraise their interactions with the environment: Specifically, they not only see the world as less threatening but see themselves as more capable of coping. In terms of locus of control, internals are more stressed by uncontrollable situations, whereas externals are more stressed by situations they feel they can control. Optimism—taking a positive and hopeful outlook—has been found to be a major moderator of stressful life events. Instrumentality has also been implicated. People who are more instrumental seem to be more resilient. Sensation seeking has also been implicated in stress reduction. This is not surprising, in that sensation seekers tend to view the world as less threatening, tend to be optimistic, and tend to be highly instrumental.

Finally, it has been demonstrated that a sense of humor can reduce stress. Even putting on a happy face can be an effective way of reducing stress.

Stress and Health

Hans Selye, a pioneer of stress research, was initially interested in understanding the adaptive role of stress in the repair of injuries and the ability of the body to resist disease. Within a fairly short period, he discovered that the stress response can be provoked by a wide range of events, including psychological events such as the loss of a job or the death of a family member. He conceptualized the stress response as involving three stages: the alarm reaction, the stage of resistance, and the stage of exhaustion (characterized by collapse of the adrenal system and death). He came to believe that diseases of adaptation take place in the stage of resistance. Diseases of adaptation include insomnia, headaches, sinus attacks, high blood pressure, gastric and duodenal ulcers, certain somatic or allergic afflictions, and cardiovascular and kidney diseases (Selye, 1974).

Since these early studies, a great deal of research on the role of stress in disease has indicated that there is a bidirectional effect. While disease typically causes stress, the progression of a disease is largely governed by the magnitude of the stress response. Since stress can be controlled by a wide range of behaviors, we ultimately can learn to control the progression of a disease (Andersen, Kiecolt-Glaser, & Glaser, 1994). This has broad implications not only for quality of life and life expectancy following disease onset but for our ability to remain immune from a wide range of diseases.

The Cancer Model

Cancer is a major health problem. It accounts for 23% of all deaths in the United States. While death rates due to heart disease, strokes, and other conditions have been decreasing, deaths due to cancer have risen by 20% in the last 30 years (American Cancer Society, 1994). Extensive research into the nature of this disease suggests that we may be able to control the progression of cancer, at least to some degree, by developing a range of behaviors that ultimately strengthen the immune system.

Current research indicates that cancer tends to develop, at least in part, from the failure of the immune system. Specifically, the development of cancer is linked to lower natural killer (NK) cell activity and to B- and T-cell activity. Knowing this has allowed researchers to determine how a range of variables may affect the progression of cancer. For example, if it can be shown that certain behaviors cause an increase in NK activity, then we can conclude that those behaviors affect cancer via the immune system.

The immune system is affected both directly and indirectly by a number of systems and behaviors. Note that indirect effects are not necessarily less important. Often we have more control over things that indirectly affect cancer and thus, by identifying those indirect routes, we can develop behaviors that will impede the development of cancer.

The following behavioral model is directed towards insuring that people engage in behaviors that will strengthen the immune system. Once again, we will consider the biological, learned, and cognitive components in turn.

The Biological Component

Direct Effects

Both the central nervous system and the neuro-endocrine system have direct effects on the immune system. As we saw earlier in this chapter, there is considerable evidence that the central nervous system monitors what is happening in the periphery of the body and then participates in the process—in particular, by activating the stress response. Unfortunately, as we have also seen, the suppressed immune response appears to be due directly to the activation of the stress response—specifically to the release of one of the glucocorticoids, corticosterone. Nevertheless, the existence of direct effects suggests that humans can learn to influence the immune system by engaging in behaviors that will lead to decreased stress.

Indirect Effects

Diet, exercise, quality of sleep, alcohol consumption, and other factors have an indirect effect on our health. Individuals who are being treated for cancer tend not to eat properly. This is not surprising in that distressed individuals often have appetite disturbances and correspondingly eat meals of less nutritional value (Andersen et al., 1994). Getting cancer patients to eat properly is important for many reasons. Since their body is in a highly distressed state, they need enormous energy to fight the disease. Further, they need vitamins and minerals as the building blocks for a properly functioning immune system. It is especially important to eat fruits and vegetables since they have been found to decrease the likelihood of developing various types of cancer. Moreover, poor nutrition has been associated with a variety of immunological impairments (Chandra & Newberne, 1977). Thus, the hope is that, through proper education, people can learn to eat foods that will strengthen their immune system.

Substantial research indicates that exercise is positively related to mental and physical health, good sleep, and positive mood and negatively related to anxiety and depression (Dubbert, 1992). All of these factors have been linked in one way or another to the immune system and/or cancer. It appears that exercise lowers the overall stress response and in one study has been shown to assist breast cancer patients (MacVicar, Winningham, & Nickel, 1989). Exercise has also been implicated in sound sleep, most likely because it reduces stress.

Drugs such as alcohol and nicotine have been negatively implicated in cancer. The mechanisms by which they act are still not completely understood. Alcohol may exert its effect by such routes as disturbing sleep, altering metabolism, and depleting certain catecholamines.

The Learned Component

Direct Effects

The relaxation response is a learned response; however, once acquired, it can be effectively used in a wide variety of situations. For some time, psychologists have used relaxation to help people reduce stress. In a study to determine if relaxation training would affect the immune system, older adults (with a mean age of 74 years) were randomly assigned to a relaxation group, a contact group, and a no-contact group. Analysis of psychological measures indicated that relaxation treatment improved affect and sleep. Moreover, it produced a significant increase—about 30%—in NK cell activity (Kiecolt-Glaser & Glaser, 1992). Such data indicate the importance of managing the stress response in cancer.

Indirect Effects

Let's look at three indirect effects that have been examined in the research literature.

Social support.   Social support has long been linked to improved mental and physical health. The exact mechanism is not altogether clear. One suggestion is that social support helps us to address fears and anxieties. When we do so, we often experience reduced stress. If perceived threat determines the magnitude of the stress response, anything that alters our perceptions of threat might be viewed as a direct effect. Research suggests that this is a highly effective tool for people dealing with cancer (e.g., Cain, Kohorn, Quinlan, Latimer, & Schwartz, 1986). Although we have previously used the term *direct effect* to refer only to behaviors that reduce the stress response once it has been triggered, there is no reason to exclude variables that reduce the initial magnitude of the stress response. We will return to this question when we consider the cognitive component.

Coping skills.   Teaching people behavioral and emotional coping skills has been proposed as an important component of any treatment program (Andersen et al., 1994). We have already discussed coping skills at length. Again, as we'll see shortly, they might be regarded as direct effects.

Compliance.   It is important to induce cancer patients to comply with the treatment program. Failure of cancer patients to take their medication as scheduled or to show up for treatments as scheduled is a very significant problem for cancer treatment. The patient's willingness to comply is critical to the effectiveness of any treatment program and hence to the recovery of the patient's immune system (Andersen et al., 1994). Many cancer patients fail to comply because of negative moods or because they believe treatment is futile. Compliance is more likely within a larger context of social support and education about the disease and the importance of good health and exercise (Andersen et al., 1994).

The Cognitive Component

Distinguishing between Direct and Indirect Effects

Do cognitions have a direct effect on health? To answer that question, researchers must control for the indirect effects of certain cognitions. There is considerable evidence, for example, that perceived control has positive health implications; however, people who believe they can control something also tend to engage in positive coping behaviors. One way of thinking about this question is to ask if these people would engage in the same behaviors if they did not hold the same beliefs. In other words, would the same effect be obtained if people were simply conditioned to engage in the same behaviors, or is it necessary for people to believe in what they are doing?

We have already discussed indirect effects. As we saw, the process of education shows that there are many indirect effects. We will now review the evidence—from cancer research and beyond—that there may be direct links between cognition and the immune system.

The Evidence for Direct Effects

It has been assumed for some time that stress is the cause of a diminished immune response, but there is now good reason to challenge that assumption. It may well be that the diminished immune response is due to negative cognitions. In studying depression, Seligman (1990) noted that depletion of the catecholamines triggers an endorphin response, which then shuts down the immune system. While stress often depletes the catecholamines, it is important to note that the immune system often shuts down in the absence of stress. If negative cognitions are the cause of a diminished immune response, this would explain why researchers have not been able to consistently predict poor health on the basis of stress markers, such as high blood pressure, and why indicators of negative cognitions often predict poor health.

Another piece of evidence relates to interaction of implicit theories and stress. It appears that people who have a malevolent implicit theory of the world tend to experience more stress than do people who have a benign or benevolent implicit theory of the world (e.g., Epstein, 1990). Likewise, a recent study found that individuals who believe in a just world had a more benign cognitive appraisal of stress tasks, rated experimental tasks as less stressful, and had autonomic reactions more consistent with challenge than threat (Tomaka & Blascovish, 1994). According to Lazarus, there are two distinct steps in the appraisal process: primary appraisal which assess threat and harm and secondary appraisal, which assesses coping skills. Numerous studies have found that primary appraisal and secondary appraisal account for different portions of the variance (e.g., Florian, Mikulincer, and Taubman, 1995). According to Lazarus's theory, primary and secondary appraisal are distinct processes. Primary appraisal occurs first and produces the initial stress reaction to threat or harm, while secondary appraisal follows and modulates that initial reaction. If we perceive that our coping skills are good, the stress reaction should go down; if not, it should remain the same. This is consistent with the idea proposed by LeDoux (1996)—and discussed in Chapter 8—that incoming threat information is relayed from the thalamus to two different locations, the amygdala and the neocortex. The amygdala produces the stress reaction (the fight-or-flight response), while the neocortex provides an inhibitory function (regulating the fight-or-flight response). In other words, our perception of the threat activates the stress response, but our cognitive assessment of the threat—in relation to our coping skills, in particular—determines whether the stress response continues.

According to Lazarus's theory, we do not actually have to engage in coping responses in order to reduce stress. Simply knowing that we have coping responses seems to be sufficient. Again, this suggests that the effect is highly cognitive. Since these people typically do have coping responses, it could be argued that this is merely a conditioned effect. That is, because stress was reduced in the past when people used their coping responses, the thought of coping in the past (memory, if you like) is sufficient to trigger a lowered stress response.

In order to determine which interpretation is correct, we need to find people who believe they can cope even before they have acquired or used coping responses. Considerable research has shown that beliefs about control—beliefs about being able to cope or to develop coping skills—tend to reduce stress. People often experience less stress when they simply decide to see a therapist, for example. Because they believe the therapist is going to help them, there is a so-called placebo effect. Further, substantial research indicates that people will talk themselves into believing they can control things even before they have developed the necessary coping skills. This line of research—known variously as research on need for control, desire for control, or illusion of control (e.g., Friedland, Keinan, & Regev, 1992; Law, Logan, & Baron, 1994; Taylor, 1989)—shows that such beliefs exert a powerful positive influence on health.

Hope, optimism, and constructive thinking have repeatedly been linked to health. It appears that people with a positive view of the world and of themselves tend to bounce back relatively easily from adversity. They typically engage in behaviors that will get them out of their present predicament. A study of HIV-positive men found that those characterized by dispositional optimism engaged in more positive health-related coping behaviors and experienced less distress, even though the virus they were carrying would almost certainly kill them in due course (Taylor et al., 1992). The ability to think positively not only reduces the magnitude of the stress response but leads to the development of coping skills. Both are important for strengthening the immune response. In this example, as in many of the others, we cannot rule out indirect effects. Nonetheless, we cannot rule out the idea there may be direct effects. Obviously, further research is needed.

A long-term study comparing optimists and pessimists on various health measures found that, while they did not show any differences in health at the age of 25, health differences began to emerge after about the age of 45 (Peterson, Seligman, & Vaillant, 1988). People who were more pessimistic began to show more health disorders, while people who remained optimistic often showed little deterioration. In other words, people who are more negative may ultimately pay the price for their pessimism.

We know positive thinking is important, but we still don't completely understand why. Perhaps it is because positive thinking leads to coping. In other words, the key to good health may boil down to doing the right things, something that seems to come naturally to optimistic people. Another possibility is raised by the work of Ellen Langer (1989), who has suggested, on the basis of her research, that the effects of physical and psychological aging are moderated by remaining mindful—staying in touch with the world as an active decision maker and an active learner. In the past, many researchers viewed such activities as stressful. Perhaps all this shows is that we need to experience optimal stress for good health.

Herbert Benson (1987), who for many years has advocated learning the relaxation response as a means of reducing stress, has recently suggested a bidirectional effect between relaxation and cognition. For example, he has found that, as a result of learning to relax, people often come to perceive the world as less threatening and perceive themselves as more in control. Obviously, a life that is relatively free of threat is very important if we are to reduce stress and remain healthy. In recent years, there have been many reports that meditation can improve individuals' view of the world and can play a significant role in helping them to give up their addiction to drugs.

The question that remains to be answered is whether these research findings represent direct effects of cognitive patterns on health, or simply indirect effects.

Summary

The first studies of the stress response focused on the role of stress in adapting to disease. However, Selye discovered that stress is not only involved in adapting to injury and diseases but has other health implications, which he referred to as diseases of adaptation.

There is considerable evidence that there are bidirectional effects between stress and disease. For example, cancer triggers stress, and stress itself plays a central role in the progression of cancer. One implication of this is that anything we can do to reduce stress will slow the progression of a disease such as cancer.

The immune system is affected both directly and indirectly by a number of systems and behaviors. Stress has a direct effect. Thus, lowering stress through relaxation, for example, can have a direct effect. Diet, exercise, and alcohol seem to have a more indirect effect.

There is some evidence of a direct effect between certain patterns of thought—for example, optimism—and the immune system, but more research is needed on this topic. However, even if there is no direct effect, it is clear that optimistic thinking has positive health benefits.

Main Points

1. While early motivation theorists conceptualized motivation in terms of drives or needs that lead directly to action, current theorists conceptualize motivation in terms of dispositions. Whether these dispositions will result in action often depends on emotions, which can undermine or sustain goal-directed behavior.
2. Emotions arise out of our interactions with the environment and represent our attempts to adapt to the environment.
3. According to the Kleinginnas' definition, emotions give rise to affective experiences, stimulate us to generate cognitive explanations, trigger a variety of internal responses, and elicit behaviors that are expressive, goal-directed, and adaptive.
4. It has been suggested that emotions are universal in nature and can be described by certain core relational themes.
5. Evidence for the universal nature of emotions comes from the study of facial expressions.
6. Lazarus has suggested that appraisal plays a critical role in determining the emotions we experience.
7. Stress is frequently conceptualized as the fight-or-flight response.
8. Stress can be elicited by a variety of physical and psychological stimuli called stressors.
9. Two separate systems—the sympathetic/adrenal and the pituitary/adrenal—are involved in the stress response.
10. The sympathetic system acts quickly and produces, among other things, a general increase in arousal.
11. In the case of the pituitary/adrenal response, the hypothalamus initiates activity in the endocrine system by stimulating the pituitary, which secretes ACTH (adrenocorticotropic hormone).
12. Endorphins are mobilized from the pituitary and are important for their analgesic and euphoric properties. The stress response triggers the release of endorphins.
13. Considerable research indicates that the stress response changes certain aspects of the immune response.
14. There are two immune systems—the innate (nonspecific) and acquired (specific) systems.
15. There is clear evidence that immunity cannot be explained simply in physical terms.
16. The brain participates in the immune response, which originates in the periphery of the body, by activating the stress response.
17. It has been argued that the existence of bidirectional effects between stress and the immune system is highly functional.
18. It seems that one of the main reasons immunity is downgraded during stress is to free up energy for the flight-or-fight response.
19. It has been suggested that the suppressed immune response came to be controlled by the stress response at some point in our evolutionary past.
20. Generally, the stress response is more likely to be triggered by unpredictable events than by predictable events.

21. Being able to discriminate (predict) the onset of stress can reduce the magnitude of the stress response.

22. Coping responses can reduce stress.

23. Under certain conditions, it is possible to habituate the stress response.

24. We can learn to respond appropriately under stress by learning a prescribed set of rules. Sometimes it is important to learn not to respond.

25. It has been suggested that some organizations are more conflict-prone than others and that more conflict-prone organizations are likely to lead to health problems.

26. In primary appraisal, we assess three categories: harm/loss, threat, and challenge.

27. Secondary appraisal involves the evaluation of coping resources and options and may be either problem-focused or emotion-focused.

28. Whether we use a problem-focused or an emotion-focused approach depends on whether we perceive the situation to be controllable and on whether we perceive that we have the ability to control it.

29. Perhaps the most important biological moderator of stress is social support. People with a repressive temperament who are resistant to biological support, tend to experience more stress.

30. One good way to manage stress is to break information down into manageable units.

31. Epstein has identified constructive thinking as one of the universal coping styles that can lead to a reduction in the stress reaction.

32. Emotion-focused strategies for coping with stress include meditation, relaxation, exercise, and biofeedback.

33. Studies have confirmed that talking or writing about a trauma can lead to health benefits.

34. The personality profile of people who remain healthy after experiencing high degrees of life stress—known as the hardy personality—is distinguished by three main characteristics: control, commitment, and challenge.

35. Other moderators of stress include optimism, instrumentality, sensation seeking, and a sense of humor.

36. The immune system is affected both directly and indirectly by various behaviors.

37. Since stress has been found to control the immune system, relaxation can directly affect the immune system.

38. Diet, exercise, drugs, social support, coping strategies, and compliance are thought to have an indirect effect on the immune system.

39. There is considerable evidence that thinking may have a direct effect on the immune system.

40. It may well be that how we think about the world—in particular, whether we view it positively or negatively—has a direct effect on the magnitude of the stress response.

Chapter Ten

Goal-Incongruent (Negative) Emotions:
Fear and Anxiety; Pessimism and Depression; Guilt and Shame

- *What are goal-incongruent emotions?*
- *What is the difference between fear and anxiety?*
- *Can people learn to become less fearful and less anxious?*
- *What is the relationship between pessimism and depression?*
- *Do antidepressants cure depression, or do they simply remove the symptoms?*

- *When people become depressed, why do they often feel helpless?*
- *Can people get rid of depressed feelings by changing the way they think?*
- *What is the difference between guilt and shame?*
- *Why do some people experience more guilt and shame than others?*
- *Is it adaptive to experience no guilt or shame?*

Lazarus (1991) has suggested a distinction between goal-incongruent emotions, which thwart the attainment of personal goals, and goal-congruent emotions, which facilitate the attainment of personal goals; goal-incongruent emotions are generally negative (associated with negative affect), whereas goal-congruent emotions are generally positive. This way of classifying emotions is consistent with recent approaches to motivation in which goals are central (Locke & Latham, 1990). Within this framework, emotions that are involved in goal-directed behaviors are of most interest, from a motivational perspective.

Emotion theorists generally analyze emotions in terms of how they help humans to adapt. Adaptation here refers not only to survival but also to the attainment of positive psychological states such as happiness. As we'll see in this chapter and the next, emotions can sustain or thwart goal-directed behavior. At the end of each chapter, we'll look at some emotions that are important in social interactions. Humans are social beings and they need to maintain and sometimes repair these interactions.

Fear and Anxiety

Is there a distinction between fear and anxiety? Some theorists have suggested that the two are basically the same (Izard & Tomkins, 1966); others have suggested that the goal object of fear is fairly specific, while the goal object of anxiety is more vague or ambiguous (Miller, 1951). For example, whereas we may fear snakes or high places or failing a test, we might experience anxiety in connection with the prospect of giving a speech. While we have no good reason to think that anything will go wrong, but we still have a feeling that something terrible may happen.

Some theorists have suggested that anxiety is a more powerful emotion than fear. When we are afraid, we know what is causing our emotion. When we are anxious, however, the emotion is so unfocused that we have difficulty dealing with it (Epstein, 1972).

Anxiety has been defined in many ways by different theorists. Most theorists suggest its origins come from a future orientation in which the individual is apprehensive about the future (Barlow, 1988). Many the-

orists also incorporate the idea that anxiety comes from concerns about choice, freedom, the meaning of life, and other issues that have their roots in existential philosophy.

Rollo May (1983) has proposed the following comprehensive definition of anxiety:

> Anxiety is the apprehension cued off by a threat to some value that the individual holds essential to his existence as a personality. The threat may be physical (the threat of death), or to psychological existence (the loss of freedom, meaninglessness). Or, the threat may be to some other value that one identifies with one's existence: patriotism, the love of another person, "success," etc. (p. 205)

The Biological Component

As we saw in Chapter 5, there is considerable evidence for the heritability of trait anxiety. According to Gray's model, what is inherited is a tendency or disposition for a certain area of the brain to be highly active (Gray, 1982; Gray & McNaughton, 1996). Gray has argued that anxiety is due to the activation of the behavioral inhibition system (BIS). The BIS consists of the septo-hippocampal system and the closely related Papez loop. The Papez loop includes the ascending adrenergic (from the locus coeruleus) and serotonergic (from the raphe nuclei) pathways that innervate the septo-hippocampal system and neocortical structures. When this system is activated, there is an increase in nonspecific arousal, and the organism directs its attention to environmental stimuli. It appears that the BIS evolved to protect organisms from potential threats that would lead to injury and perhaps death.

This survival system is activated by both unconditioned and conditioned stimuli. At the unconditioned level, it is activated by innate fears, as we might expect, and also by novelty. Why should novelty activate this system? It has been argued that organisms need complete knowledge about their immediate environment in order to survive. A rabbit, for example, will explore all the available escape routes, in case it meets a coyote. Any change in that environment constitutes a potential threat and, therefore, the rabbit will attend to that new source of information. In Gray's terms, the rabbit will stop, look, and listen when it encounters a novel stimulus.

Gray makes a fundamental distinction between the BIS and the fight-or-flight system (Chapter 9). He points out that antianxiety drugs affect the BIS system but not the fight-or-flight system. This finding is central to his argument that anxiety is mediated by the BIS and not the fight-or-flight system. Gray notes that all antianxiety drugs exert their influence by deactivating the BIS. The net result is that when under the influence of antianxiety drugs, people are less inclined to stop, look, and listen, and more inclined to carry on with task-related behaviors.

According to Gray, the fight-or-flight system is activated by pain. It is an unconditioned reaction as opposed to a conditioned one. Gray feels that a wide range of responses currently ascribed to stress should more accurately be called anxiety.

The Learned Component

Conditioned Stimuli and Gray's Model

Gray argues that the BIS can be conditioned to two general classes of stimuli (Gray, 1982; Gray & McNaughton, 1996): cues that signal punishment is forthcoming; or cues that signal rewards will be withheld (frustrative nonreward). According to Gray, a child who has been punished in the past for touching an expensive vase will learn to feel anxiety at the idea of touching that vase again.

Gray's model is summarized in Figure 10-1. Like others, Gray has argued that anxiety is essentially an anticipatory response to the possibility of an aversive outcome. Because aversive outcomes are a threat to our survival, it is important to deal with them immediately. However, while it is important to be vigilant about threats, being too vigilant means that we fail to get on with other goal-directed activities.

Phobias and Panic Attacks

A long line of research has linked anxiety to impaired performance. If anxiety is an adaptive emotion, how does it become maladaptive? For example, in what circumstances does it interfere with goal-directed activities? To answer this question, we need to examine some clinical disorders of anxiety. Within this literature we can find the conditions that not only give rise to maladaptive anxiety but the conditions that will enable people to manage maladaptive anxiety.

The development of phobias. According to Mineka (1985), phobia is a persistent and recognizable irrational fear of an object or situation and is characterized by distress and a compelling desire to avoid that object or situation. The thing that differentiates phobias from fear is the irrational aspect of phobias. People often come to fear such things as spiders or snakes even when they know they are harmless.

Phobias may be viewed as the product of classical conditioning. However, classical conditioning alone does not explain why people are inclined to become fearful of certain things but not others (Mineka, 1985). It may be that, because we needed to avoid spiders and snakes in our evolutionary past, we are biologically prepared to make certain associations more readily than others (Seligman, 1970). Research has shown that, even if a phobic reaction is not elicited when spiders and snakes are initially presented, it is very easy to condition a fear reaction to these stimuli (Seligman, 1970).

Gray has argued that we have evolved a "quick and dirty system" to help us deal with threats to our survival. As he points out, "Failing to respond to danger is more costly than responding inappropriately to a benign stimulus" (Gray & McNaughton, 1996, p. 104). Thus, we are biologically prepared to develop phobias even though they can be maladaptive. Within this context, it is not too hard to understand why people might develop a wide variety of phobias such as *claustrophobia* (fear of enclosed places) or *acrophobia* (fear of heights).

Treating phobias with systematic desensitization. Systematic desensitization is a very effective procedure for eliminating fears. It is possible to rank-order stimuli along a continuum ranging from those that elicit only mild fear (usually symbolic stimuli) to those that elicit extreme fear (usually concrete stimuli). People who are afraid of spiders, for example, usually respond with only mild fear to the word *spider,* with greater fear to pictures of spiders, and with intense fear to an actual spider. Typically, before systematic desensitization training begins, the therapist teaches the patient how to become fully relaxed. Then the therapist presents a stimulus that normally elicits mild fear. Presented when the patient is relaxed, the mild stimulus often loses its ability to elicit the fear reaction. The therapist then moves to a stronger stimulus and repeats the

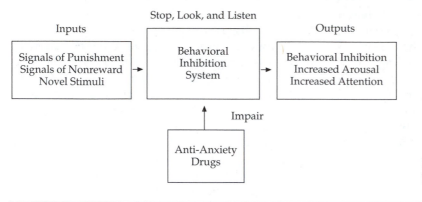

Figure 10-1. Gray's model of the behavioral inhibition system.

procedure. Eventually, the therapist moves to the strongest stimulus. This procedure is based on the idea of counterconditioning; that is, the client is being conditioned to experience a feeling of relaxation and a sense of control to the stimuli that originally elicited fear.

An important feature of this procedure is that the subject is not allowed to make an avoidance response. If the subject is able to make an avoidance response, the procedure is not nearly as effective. It appears that the persistence of the avoidance response is linked to the anxiety reduction that accompanies it. From learning theory, we know that, if a response is continuously rewarded, it will be maintained at a very high level. To get rid of the response, we need to eliminate the ongoing reward.

The development of panic attacks.   Panic attacks (traditionally considered an anxiety disorder) are characterized by somatic symptoms, fear of dying, and fear of losing control. Like Gray, Barlow has argued that panic attacks can be understood as a conditioned flight-or-flight response (Barlow, 1988; Barlow, Chorpita, & Turovsky, 1996). Barlow distinguishes between two types of anxiety: anxious apprehension and fear. Fear, according to Barlow, is governed by the *alarm reaction—* the first stage of the fight-or-flight response, which involves the activation of the sympathetic nervous system. Anxious apprehension, by contrast, is governed by the BIS system, or something like it. Anxious apprehension prepares the individual to cope with challenges of everyday life. It involves high arousal, negative affect, perceptions of helplessness and loss of control over future events, and something called worry. Barlow has identified four risk factors for anx-

ious apprehension: (1) a high level of biologically based stress reactivity of genetic origin; (2) the perception that negative events are neither predictable or controllable; (3) an absence of good coping skills; and (4) inadequate social support. As we see in Figure 10-2, anxious apprehension plays a mediating role in panic-related disorders.

The alarm reaction is normally triggered in life-threatening situations (when it is considered a *true alarm*) but can also occur spontaneously (when it is considered a *false alarm*). Subjectively, the two responses are the same—somatic symptoms, fear of dying, fear of losing control—but, in the case of false alarms, we cannot identify what triggered the response. Barlow argues that the alarm reaction can be conditioned. In other words, we come to develop *learned alarm reactions.* Going into our office, for example, could trigger the alarm reaction if it has been a source of stress in the past.

Research indicates that there are no obvious external cues for panic attacks. They occur under a wide variety of conditions—at home, at work, or on a bus, for example. Given the human propensity to look for causes of their behavior, it may be that, in the absence of external cues, they will be inclined to look for internal ones. This hypothesis is consistent with the finding that panic patients are more sensitive to internal cues (Barlow, 1988).

If panic attacks are truly false alarms, they should occur for virtually everyone. Why, then, do only a few people become disabled by panic attacks? Why do a certain portion of the population decide to stay home and avoid going out? Research shows that people who experience panic attacks find it more stressful to experience the panic attack in situations where they feel

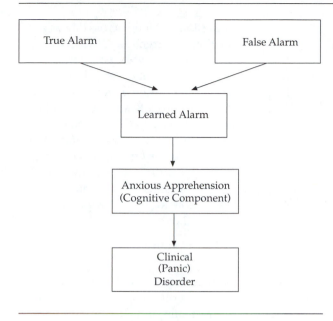

Figure 10-2.   Origins of panic-related disorders.

trapped or where they would be embarrassed. Their focus, in other words, shifts from the panic attack to being embarrassed. The fear of having a panic attack in public is often sufficient to imprison such individuals in their own homes (Chambless & Gracely, 1989).

Treating panic attacks with information.   People who experience panic attacks are typically perplexed and troubled by them and come to believe that they might die or lose control in an attack. Thus, one way to help such people is to provide them with some basic information about the nature of panic attacks. Research has shown that three things are useful. First, convincing people that they are not going to die or experience a major medical problem as a result of a panic attack is often sufficient to stop them from having a full-blown attack (Salkovskis, Clark, & Hackmann, 1991). Second, convincing them that the attacks are no more likely to occur in public than at home tends to reduce their need to stay at home. Third, convincing them that they will not lose control or embarrass themselves if they have a panic attack in public lessens the anxiety associated with leaving their homes.

These findings are consistent with the idea that people's emotional reactions can be understood, in

part, through a *normative approach*—that is, in terms of what is perceived as normal or expected. The fact that normative arguments can affect anticipated emotions, such as a panic attack, indicates that people are inclined to bring their emotional response in line with what they believe to be appropriate or normal (Baron, 1992).

It is important for all of us to understand that some of the anxiety we experience has been learned. When we realize that our reactions are inappropriate or irrational, we might decide to design a program—perhaps with professional help—that will help us bring our behavior in line with what is useful and appropriate.

The Cognitive Component

Cognitive factors play an important role in the arousal of fear and anxiety. Let's look at a few of these.

Viewing the World as Threatening

Several lines of research indicate that anxious people have a bias towards viewing the world as threatening.

1. **Negative affectivity.** Negative affectivity is a mood or dispositional tendency. People high in this quality: (a) are more likely to experience stress and dissatisfaction as they interact with the environment; (b) tend to dwell on their failures more; (c) tend to see the world in negative terms; and (d) have a poor self-concept, characterized by dissatisfaction with themselves and their lives (Watson & Clark, 1984).

As we see in Figure 10-3, people high in negative affectivity experience more stress, often at the beginning of a day, and are also more reactive to increases in stress—that is, they show greater cumulative effects of the many stressful events encountered in the course of a day (Marco & Suls, 1993). It is also found that people high in negative affectivity tend to have slower recovery rates to stress. These results demonstrate that it is not the environment alone that causes stress. How much stress we experience depends on how we interpret the environment. These results are consistent with the idea that cognitions play a key role in understanding negative moods and emotions such as anxiety. If stress were due solely to environmental stressors, there would be no differences between people with different cognitions. Remember that most theories of stress are based on the premise that stress results from seeing the

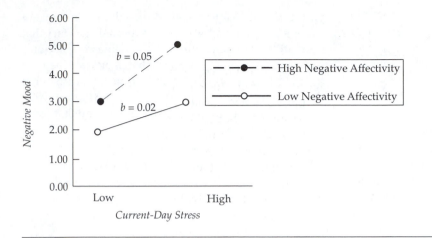

Figure 10-3. Mood across day as a function of current-day stress and negative affectivity, while holding all other variables constant at zero. (From "Daily Stress and the Trajectory of Mood: Spillover, Response Assimilation, Contrast, and Chronic Negative Affectivity," by C. A. Marco and J. Suls, *Journal of Personality and Social Psychology*, 1993, *64*, 1053–1063. Copyright © 1993 by the American Psychological Association. Reprinted by permission of the author.)

world as a potential source of threat to the individual's well-being.

2. **Bias in interpreting ambiguous stimuli.** There is considerable evidence of a positive relationship between anxiety and the tendency to see the world as threatening, but what does that mean? Does our interpretation of the world give rise to anxiety, or does anxiety make us see the world as threatening? To answer this question, McNally (1996) has undertaken some laboratory experiments with clinically anxious individuals. He has concluded that anxious people have an interpretive bias; they are inclined to interpret ambiguous stimuli as threatening. It is important to remember that if the situation were not ambiguous, you would not expect differences to emerge, and they don't.

3. **Attentional bias to process threat cues.** A person who holds an implicit theory that the world is a source of constant threat is likely to develop a mental set to identify those threats. This follows directly from the assumption of evolutionary psychologists that humans are programmed at birth to attend to their survival needs first. Using a variety of paradigms, various researchers have provided evidence that "patients with anxiety disorders exhibit an attentional bias favoring the processing of threat cues" (McNally, 1996, p. 223).

Note that the research on cognitive bias indicates that healthy control subjects are often characterized by biases in the opposite direction to those exhibited by anxious patients. These people tend to see the world as benevolent (Chapter 12).

One obvious implication that follows from this line of research is that anxious people must learn to see the world as less threatening if their symptoms are to abate. While antianxiety drugs can create the perception that the world is less threatening, that perception seems to be almost completely drug-dependent.

Unwanted or Intrusive Thoughts

Unwanted or intrusive thoughts—also known as automaticity—are typically associated with anxiety. Intrusive thoughts are not only a problem for clinical populations, but are also commonly found in nonclinical populations (Kelly & Kahn, 1994). The content of intrusive thoughts is different in a panic state, an obsessive-compulsive state, or merely a generalized anxiety state. Panic patients experience thoughts about imminent insanity, death, and loss of control in the midst of their attacks. Obsessive-compulsive patients experience intrusive thoughts about violence, contamination, and other upsetting themes. People with a generalized anxiety disorder often ruminate about possible misfortunes (McNally, 1996).

A number of researchers have examined whether people can learn to suppress intrusive thoughts using techniques such as distraction. In some studies, people have successfully learned to suppress intrusive thoughts (e.g., Kelly & Kahn, 1994), but in others attempts to suppress have resulted in a rebound effect (e.g., Wegner, 1989). Evidence from various sources suggests that people can learn to reduce and even eliminate unwanted thoughts—for example, by undergoing therapy (McNally, 1996). Perhaps the answer lies in getting people to think in new ways about important events in their lives. We will return to this topic when we discuss depression.

Loss of Control

Losing control, or simply the fear of losing control, often leads to feelings of anxiety. Seligman (1975) has suggested that, when events are unpredictable, we develop feelings of helplessness, which are sufficient to produce not only anxiety but depression. For example, if we need to give a talk in public, our anxiety derives partly from the fear that we may lose control. The uncertainty and unpredictability associated with the task are what makes us anxious.

Inability to Make a Coping Response

Lazarus (1991) has argued that the inability (or the perceived inability) to make an adaptive response to a threatening event or the fact (or perception) that no such response is available will lead to feelings of anxiety. Lazarus points out that ambiguity is the key consideration here, because it prevents the elaboration of clear action patterns (coping strategies) that would allow the individual to deal with the threat.

Lazarus suggests that transforming anxiety into fear might be a useful way of getting people to cope with a threat. Once they know what is threatening them, they can devise a pattern of action to deal with it. When they don't know what the threat is, they are left in limbo; they experience anxiety but don't know what to do about it.

Top-Down and Bottom-Up Theories of Subjective Well-Being

It has been suggested that the opposite of anxiety is subjective well-being. Theories of subjective well-being adopt two very different perspectives.

■ *Bottom-up theories* start with the assumption that happiness comes from a summation of pleasurable and unpleasurable experiences. According to this line of thinking, if you have more pleasurable than unpleasurable experiences during the day, you will be happy.

■ *Top-down theories* assume that individuals are happy because they tend to see the world and themselves in a positive way.

There is evidence for both theories. A study designed to examine the relative contributions of bottom-up and top-down variables found that both make an important contribution (Brief, Butcher, George, & Link, 1993). On the one hand, if individuals think about the world and themselves in negative terms, they will become anxious but, if they think of the world in positive terms, they will experience subjective well-being. On the other hand, if individuals have bad experiences, such as poor health, they will experience anxiety but, if they have good experiences, such as good grades, they will experience subjective well-being. The results of this experiment are consistent with the model in Figure 10-4.

The implication of this research is that individuals need to develop:

1. Beliefs and attitudes that will engender a positive mental set about the world and themselves, so that they see the world as a place where goals can be attained and they can grow and experience satisfaction and meaning.
2. Habits that will insure their daily lives are filled with good experiences—that is, habits that will give them good health, minimal stress, and reduced conflict.
3. Friends and social support networks to which they can turn when things look bleak.

Summary

The general consensus is that the goal object of fear is fairly specific, while the goal object of anxiety is more vague or ambiguous. Gray has argued that anxiety is due to the activation of the behavioral inhibition system (BIS). The system is activated by both unconditioned stimuli—innate fears and novelty—and conditioned stimuli—signals indicating punishment or nonreward. Gray makes a fundamental distinction between the BIS and the fight-or-flight system (Chapter 9). He points out that antianxiety drugs affect the BIS system but not the fight-or-flight system. Gray argues

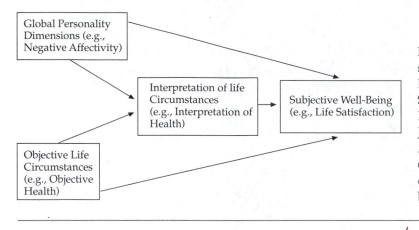

Figure 10-4.   An integrated approach to subjective well-being. (From "Integrating Bottom-up and Top-down theories of Subjective Well-being: The Case of Health," by A. P. Brief, A. H. Butcher, J. M. George, and K. E. Link, *Journal of Personality and Social Psychology*, 1993, *64*, 646–653. Copyright © 1993 by the American Psychological Association. Reprinted by permission of the author.)

that phobias are learned and have their roots in the BIS, while panic has its roots in the fight-or-flight response. Barlow has made a distinction between true and false alarms as ways of thinking about panic. Desensitization has been found to be highly effective in helping people to deal with phobias. While it is difficult to eliminate panic attacks, giving people information about the origins of panic attacks has proven effective in helping them to deal with their attacks.

Anxious individuals tend to view the world as threatening. They have a bias to interpret ambiguous stimuli as threatening and to attend to threatening stimuli first. Unwanted or intrusive thoughts are a major problem for anxious people, because they perpetuate feelings of threat and negative emotion. Perceived absence of a coping response also tends to perpetuate feelings of anxiety. Research indicates that subjective well-being, the opposite of anxiety, comes from two classes of variables: a positive mental attitude towards the world; and a set of well-developed habits that insure good physical and mental health.

Pessimism and Depression

The concepts of pessimism and depression are closely linked. The study of depressed individuals shows that most tend to use a *pessimistic explanatory style*, and considerable data indicate that people who use a pessimistic explanatory style are more likely to become depressed (Seligman, 1991). Nevertheless, it is impor-

tant to note that there is a difference. While people who are depressed are characterized by loss of motivation (loss of interest in food, sex, work, social relationships, achievement, and so on) and loss of interest in life (they are often suicidal), pessimistic people generally remain motivated, despite their limited tendency to embrace and interact with the outside world.

The overlap between anxiety and depression has been estimated at 20–70% (Petersen, et al., 1993). It is not surprising, therefore, that many of the same psychological antecedents that underlie anxiety also underlie depression. For example, both anxious individuals and depressed individuals are characterized by negative implicit theories of the world (e.g., Brief, Butcher, George, & Link, 1993) and by a tendency to be self-critical (Blatt, 1995). One important thing that differentiates depression from both anxiety and pessimism is that depressed people tend to entertain thoughts of suicide.

How prevalent is depression?   Some years ago, in a survey to determine the prevalence of depression among university students, 78% of the students reported that they had experienced depression at some time during the academic year, and 46% of those indicated that their symptoms had been severe enough to warrant psychiatric help (Beck & Young, 1978). As already noted, when people are depressed, they frequently entertain thoughts of suicide; of the 9–10 million people in the United States and Canada who experience depression in any given year, upwards of 150,000 (about 1.5%) eventually commit suicide (Rosenfeld, 1985).

Beck and Young (1978) reported that depression is generally twice as high among university students as in a comparable group of nonstudents. Women are 2–5 times more prone to depression than men. In the past, depression tended to occur more frequently at midlife (the 40s or 50s), but recently it has also been occurring earlier; many people in their 30s, 20s, and even teens are experiencing depression. Between 1960 and 1988, for example, adolescent suicides increased from 3.6 to 11.3 per 100,000 population. This represents a 200% increase, as compared with a general population increase of 17%. While not all these suicides could be linked to depression, depression was clearly the most direct psychiatric antecedent. Completed suicides were typically precipitated by a shameful or humiliating experience such as an arrest, a perceived failure at school or work, or rejection or conflict in an interpersonal or romantic relationship (Garland & Zigler, 1993).

Let's examine the biological, learned, and cognitive components of depression.

The Biological Component of Depression

The Heritability of Depression

There is a long line of evidence that depression runs in families (Weissman, Lear, Holzer, Meyers, & Tischler, 1984). Perhaps the best data come from twin studies. Identical twins are 4–5 times more likely to show concordances for major depressive disorder than are fraternal twins (Kendler, Heath, Martin, & Eaves, 1986; Wender et al., 1986). The genetic loading for childhood and adolescent depression may be greater than that for depression that occurs in adulthood, and earlier onset appears to be predictive of more frequent and severe episodes (Petersen et al., 1993). Note, however, that most family studies have failed to disentangle genetic and environmental influences. As a result, it is still not clear what role learning and cognition play; the only thing we really know is that there is a significant genetic component.

Researchers have found that depressed individuals show relatively more electrical activity in the right hemisphere of the brain. It's possible that chronic activation of the right hemisphere predisposes individuals to depressive or anxiety disorders as well as other types of illness (National Advisory Mental Health Council, 1995).

The Catecholamine Hypothesis

After analyzing the relationship between affective disorders and catecholamines, Schildkraut and Kety (1967) formulated the catecholamine hypothesis of affective disorders. Because drugs that deplete or block norepinephrine and also, to some extent, dopamine produce sedation and depression, whereas drugs that increase norepinephrine relieve depression and produce elation and euphoria, they concluded that norepinephrine and dopamine are the chemicals primarily involved in the mood changes that characterize various affective disorders. According to their hypothesis, excessive amounts of norepinephrine and dopamine produce the manic state—the high end of the manic-depressive continuum—and a deficiency of norepinephrine and dopamine produces the depressive state at the low end.

The Serotonin Hypothesis

Glassman (1969) noted that while the catecholamines have received a lot of attention, there is evidence that the indolamines—especially serotonin (also called 5-HT)—are also implicated in depression. Resperine is known to deplete stores of norepinephrine and serotonin and, thus, to lead to depression, while monoamine oxidase inhibitors (MAOI) are known to prevent this action of resperine and, thus, to reduce depression. Which theory is correct? To get some idea, we need to examine the research literature which shows how various antidepressant drugs affect depression.

Using Drugs to Treat Depression

Depression is often initially treated with drugs. Research indicates that 60–80% of patients treated with drugs experience significant short-term improvement. In the long term, however, people often fall back into a negative mood state, together with negative thinking unless cognitive therapy is combined with drug therapy (Hollon, DeRubeis, & Evans, 1990).

Traditionally, tricyclic antidepressants, such as Tofranil and Elavil, were preferred for the initial treatment of symptoms of depression. They take about two weeks to take effect and can have some unpleasant side effects. The tricyclics work in the same way that cocaine works; they help to block the reuptake of norepinephrine and serotonin at the receptors, thereby increasing the concentration of norepinephrine and serotonin at the receptor sites. Monoamine oxidase inhibitors, such as Narplan, Nardil, and Parnate, are also used as antidepressants, especially if the tricyclics fail to work or have severe side effects. Monoamine oxidase (MAO) is an enzyme important in the regulation of catecholamines such as norepinephrine and serotonin. When the monoamine oxidase level is high, it somehow reduces the levels of norepinephrine and

serotonin. As the MAOI inhibits monoamine oxidase, the norepinephrine and serotonin levels rise.

Prozac, which blocks the reuptake of serotonin, has now become the preferred drug to begin treatment of depression mainly because it has fewer side effects. The effectiveness of Prozac, although less than that of the tricyclics in some cases, has led some researchers to speculate that serotonin is a key regulator of mood and

Practical Application 10-1

Modern Individualism and the Rise of Depression

The rate of depression has increased 10 times in the United States over the last two generations, but there has been no increase in depression among the Amish, a closely knit religious community of 10,000 farmers, who use no electricity, shun modern technology, and use no drugs or alcohol. Research indicates that depression is prevalent mainly in technologically advanced countries. In a study of one primitive tribe, the Kaluli of New Guinea, scientists were unable to find any signs of depression at all (Seligman, 1988).

Martin Seligman has suggested that this prevalence of depression in technologically advanced countries is the result of a new form of individualism that is highly susceptible to depression. Individualism has deep roots in North American history (de Tocqueville, 1835/1969; Bellah, Madsen, Sullivan, Swidler, & Tipton, 1985) and has had many positive consequences. However, Seligman and others have suggested that, in modern society, some people have pursued individualism at the expense of obligation (for example, to the family), commitment (for example, to marriage), and involvement (for example, in the community). The two basic characteristics of modern individualism are autonomy and self-reliance.

The modern individual has also been encouraged to embrace consumerism. We have been told that we can find happiness by owning objects, which can provide pleasure but do not demand commitment, obligation, or feeling; they do not threaten autonomy and self-reliance. Drugs and sex have also been marketed as part of this new consumerism. To be happy, you simply need more and better drugs and sex.

If the complete focus on the self is causing problems, why don't we return to a more traditional lifestyle? One reason may be a reluctance to give up our autonomy and self-reliance, two attributes that we have come to value (Bellah et al., 1985). However, many writers have concluded that, to dispel depression, we must acknowledge a fact of human nature—that we are social animals. We need other humans to experience certain basic emotions (Izard, 1977)—to experience love and worth, for example. Unless these emotions are satisfied, we will experience a lack of meaning. Trying a new drug, buying a new car, or trying another diet can never provide the same sense of well-being as belonging to a group. While belonging to a group entails certain obligations, the group is the source of love and worth. If we attempt to bypass the group, we feel empty. Here lies the paradox: To find the self, we must become part of a group (or groups); we must learn cooperation and trust.

This does not mean that we have to give up individualism altogether. Deci and Ryan (1991) distinguish between self-reliance and self-determination. Self-reliance means that we do not need other people. Self-determination, by contrast, means making choices, developing competencies, and adapting to our social environment, so as to take charge of our life (Deci & Ryan, 1985). Deci and Ryan (1991) suggest that people have three needs: the need for autonomy, the need for competence, and the need for relatedness. Satisfying these needs is what brings happiness.

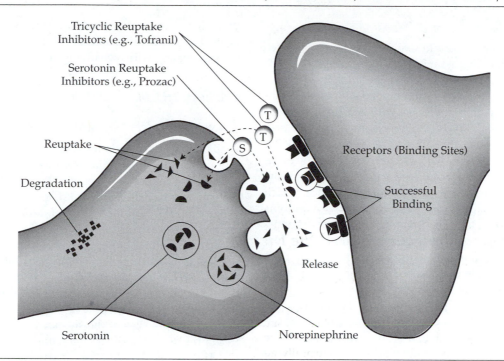

Figure 10-5.   Serotonin and norepinephrine are neurotransmitters that carry messages across the synapses from one nerve cell to another. After carrying a message across a synapse, a process that involves binding, they are reabsorbed through a process called reuptake. It has been suggested that some antidepressants plug the reuptake pump, which is responsible for the reabsorption. While tricyclics appear to block the reuptake of both norepinephrine and serotonin, serotonin reuptake inhibitors (such as Prozac) simply block the reuptake of serotonin. The net result is that concentrations of norepinephrine and serotonin are high at the synaptic gap, a phenomenon that has been linked to elevated mood. The monoamine oxidase inhibitors (MAOI) work in a very different way. They block the action of monoamine oxidase (MAO), an enzyme involved in the regulation of these neurotransmitters. It has been found that, when MAO is high, norepinephrine and serotonin are low. Blocking the action of MAO allows levels of norepinephrine and serotonin to rise, and mood is elevated. Note that this diagram ignores the role of dopamine, which may also be involved in depression.

that depression represents a shortage of serotonin. It may well turn out that more than one neurotransmitter is involved in depression (Figure 10-5).

Stress and Depression

Numerous studies have found a link between stress and depression. One laboratory technique for inducing stress is to expose humans or animals to uncontrollable shock. When animals are exposed to uncontrollable shock, norepinephrine is released at a high rate from the locus coeruleus, an area in the brainstem that we discussed in connection with sleep and dreams (Chapter 6). Apparently, the receptors in the brainstem do not use all of the available norepinephrine, and the unused norepinephrine is reabsorbed by the neuron and destroyed. The store of norepinephrine is then depleted. Once the body cannot synthesize norepinephrine as quickly as it is being released, the norepinephrine level in the locus coeruleus is lowered. This lowered level of norepinephrine is believed to result in feelings of depression (Weiss, 1982, cited in Turkington, 1982).

Depression as an Adaptive Mood

Because so many people experience depression, we might wonder whether it is adaptive (Costello, 1976). If depression is adaptive, what function does it serve?

We know that depression often disappears spontaneously—in fact, sometimes with startling suddenness. One possibility is that depression may be a protective mechanism that allows the body to rebuild or reprogram itself after we have been exposed to conditions that prevent us from exercising control. Once the rebuilding or reprogramming has taken place, which may take quite a long time, the depressive symptoms disappear. The lack of motivation or initiative that accompanies the mood disorder prevents the individual from engaging in new activities, so that the rebuilding or reprogramming can proceed without interruption.

Another possibility is that depression helps the individual to abandon goals that are unattainable (Klinger, 1975). When people find that events are uncontrollable, they tend to become depressed. When they become depressed, they tend to disengage themselves from ongoing activities. Having abandoned activities that are not adaptive, they can eventually switch to new activities.

What these explanations don't tell us is why people develop self-destructive feelings. Thoughts of suicide hardly seem adaptive.

Summary

Studies of twins indicate that depression can be inherited. There is strong evidence that depression is linked to the catecholamines, especially to norepinephrine. We tend to experience depression when the norepinephrine level is low, and euphoria when it is high. This hypothesis is consistent with the finding that antidepressant drugs elevate the norepinephrine level at the synapses, with an accompanying mood change from negative to positive. Serotonin has also been implicated in depression. Drugs that elevate serotonin levels alleviate feelings of depression. Further evidence for the link between neurotransmitters and depression comes from work done with monoamine oxidase inhibitors (MAOI). Monoamine oxidase (MAO) is an enzyme that regulates neurotransmitters in the brain.

Various people have argued that depression should be viewed as an adaptive mechanism that can be of value to us in dealing with a changing environment.

The Learned Component of Depression

Seligman's Model of Learned Helplessness

While doing research on the relation between fear conditioning and instrumental learning, Martin Seligman and two colleagues discovered a striking phenomenon that came to be called *learned helplessness* (Overmier & Seligman, 1967; Seligman & Maier, 1967). Initially, they restrained dogs in a harness in order to administer moderately painful but not physically damaging shock (Figure 10-6). Although their original intent had not been to study inescapable shock, that is in fact what they had fortuitously arranged for the dogs. Nothing the dogs did could affect the onset, the offset, the duration, or the intensity of the shocks. From the perspective of the dogs, the shocks were uncontrollable.

The second phase of the experiment was designed to study how these dogs behaved in a shuttle box (Figure 10-7). Normally, when naive (untrained) dogs are placed in the shuttle box and the shock is turned on, they frantically jump about the box and accidentally scramble over the barrier to the safe (no-shock) side. In a very few trials, these dogs learn to jump as soon as the shock begins, thereby drastically limiting the amount of shock they experience at any given trial. Typically, it takes several more trials before the dogs will begin to avoid the shock by jumping at the onset of the signal rather than the onset of the shock. They eventually learn this very important adaptive response, which enables them to avoid the painful stimulus altogether.

Much to the surprise of Seligman and his colleagues, the dogs given the inescapable-shock training showed a markedly different pattern of responses. Initially, they behaved like naive dogs; they frantically ran around the shuttle box when the shock was turned on. After 30 seconds, however, their behavior suddenly changed. They stopped jumping and running, lay down on the shock grid, and whined. When the animals failed to make any further responses for 60 seconds, the shock was turned off. They had, of course, failed to make an escape response. The same pattern of behavior occurred in the next trial. The ani-

Figure 10-6. Experimental apparatus used to study the effects of inescapable and uncontrollable shock in dogs. (From *Discovering Psychology,* by N. Carlson. Copyright © 1988 by Allyn and Bacon. Reprinted by permission.)

Shocker

mal struggled at first and then gave up, passively accepting the shock. On succeeding trials, the behavior followed a similar pattern, with increasing passivity toward the shock. On none of the trials did the animal attempt to escape.

To make sure the effects observed were due to lack of control over the shock, Seligman and his colleagues designed an experiment to isolate the effects of controllability from the effects of the shock itself. The design involved three groups.

The first group of dogs received pretreatment shock that they could control by some response. In one study the dog was able to limit the duration of the shock by pressing a panel with its nose (Seligman & Maier, 1967) and in another study by not moving (Maier, 1970). A second group consisted of yoked controls. These dogs received the same pattern of shock but had no way of controlling it. Thus, the second group experienced exactly the same amount of shock as the first, but without the critical factor of control. In both conditions, the animals were restrained by a hammock to prevent them from jumping or running. A third group was given no pretreatment.

After 24 hours, the dogs were given escape-avoidance training in a shuttle box. The no-pretreatment group and the group allowed to control the shock during pretreatment readily learned the task. They jumped over the barrier at the onset of shock and then learned to avoid the shock. The group given un-

controllable shock performed much more poorly. Most of the dogs failed to jump the barrier at the onset of shock. These results clearly show that the deficit was due not to the shock itself but to the inability to control the shock. Maier's (1970) study makes it impossible to argue that the animals were simply learning to be active; in Maier's study, the animals were learning to be inactive.

Learned Helplessness in Humans

The phenomenon of learned helplessness is by no means restricted to dogs. Learned helplessness has been demonstrated in cats (e.g., Thomas & Balter, cited in Seligman, 1975), in fish (e.g., Padilla, Padilla, Ketterer, & Giacolone, 1970), in rats (e.g., Maier, Seligman, & Solomon, 1969; Seligman, Maier, & Solomon, 1971), and in primates (e.g., Seligman, 1975). However, learned helplessness in humans has attracted most interest.

In one study using human subjects, Hiroto (1974) replicated almost exactly the findings obtained by Seligman and his colleagues. Subjects in his controllability group were exposed to a loud noise, which they could turn off by pushing a button. His no-control group received the same loud noise but could not control it. After this pretreatment, the subjects were tested in a finger-shuttle box that simply required them to move their hand from one side to the other to escape the noise. As in the dog experiments, the no-

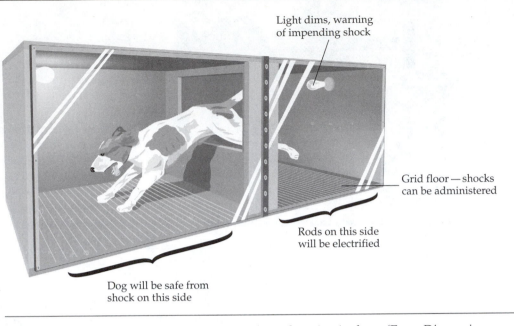

Light dims, warning
of impending shock

Grid floor — shocks
can be administered

Rods on this side
will be electrified

Dog will be safe from
shock on this side

Figure 10-7.   Shuttle box used to study avoidance learning in dogs. (From *Discovering Psychology*, by N. Carlson. Copyright © 1988 by Allyn and Bacon. Reprinted by permission.)

pretreatment and controllability groups quickly learned the escape problem, but the no-control group failed to learn it. Most of the subjects in the no-control condition sat passively and accepted the noxious noise.

Hiroto also studied the influence of two additional variables on the subjects' responses. First, half of the subjects in each of the three groups were told that their performance in the shuttle box was a test of skill; the others were told that their scores were governed by chance. As expected, subjects who received the chance instructions tended to respond more helplessly in all the conditions.

Hiroto also decided to examine personality differences. Using a personality inventory measure, he divided his subjects into two groups corresponding to externals and internals. As we have seen, externals believe that events in their lives are governed to a large degree by events over which they have little or no control, whereas internals believe that events can be controlled and that the application of skills can bring about positive outcomes (Rotter, 1966). As predicted, externals were more inclined to become helpless than internals.

The results of Hiroto's study not only confirm that humans react to lack of control in the same way as animals do, but emphasize the cognitive nature of helplessness in humans. This is consistent with Seligman's suggestion that helplessness reflects a belief about the effectiveness of responding. Helpless individuals do not believe that their responses will have any effect on aversive or noxious events, whereas those who have not learned to be helpless believe that their responses will be effective in terminating such events.

Deficits in Learned Helplessness

Seligman has concluded from these and other studies that learned helplessness is characterized by three deficits: (1) failure to initiate responses; (2) failure to learn; and (3) emotional disturbance. Let's examine these deficits.

Failure to initiate responses.   Adaptive behavior is generally characterized by repeated attempts to achieve a goal. The individual typically tries a wide range of responses. Sometimes these behaviors are highly systematic, and it seems that the individual may be systematically testing all possible alternatives in some hierarchy of adaptive responses. Aggressive behavior may fall within the hierarchy of adaptive responses. That is, aggressive responses may enable the individual to regain control of the environment (Chapter 8).

There is evidence that certain adaptive responses are inherited (unlearned) or, at least, that the predisposition to make these responses is inherited (Bolles, 1970). Other adaptive responses, however, are clearly learned. According to the principles of learning, a response will be repeated if it results in reinforcement. For example, a dog in a shuttle box learns the escape response because jumping over the barrier reduces the duration of a noxious event, and that is reinforcing. In human terms, we might say that termination of a noxious event produces relief. We feel relief when we turn off a noxious TV program or when the neighbor's dog stops barking after we yell at the dog or its owner. Studies of learning indicate that these responses are likely to be repeated because the responses produced a desired effect: relief from the noxious or aversive stimulus. Within learning theory, the presentation of an aversive or noxious stimulus is called a negative reinforcer.

In some circumstances, aversive events in our environment come and go, and we can do nothing about them. For example, our next-door neighbor may play the stereo into the early hours of the morning. We complain, but nothing happens, and then unexpectedly the person moves. A neighbor may have a dog that, despite our pleas, is allowed to bark throughout the night. One day, the neighbor sells the dog. In such cases, the relief we experience is independent of our responses. According to the principles of learning, there can be no learning, because there is no predictable association between a response and the occurrence of a reward. Seligman has argued, however, that we do in fact learn something. We learn that relief is sometimes independent of our responses. If this cognitive set, or belief, generalizes to other situations, we may fail to initiate responses in the presence of aversive or noxious stimuli.

Failure to initiate responses of any kind is very nonadaptive. Noxious stimulation not only is aversive but in some cases may threaten our very survival. It is critical, therefore, for us to try to remove or stop the noxious event. We can do so only if we initiate a response, no matter how poor or inappropriate that response may be. Even random behavior may result in termination of the aversive event. Given that most of us have some previous experience dealing with noxious events, we have at our disposal a hierarchy of responses that may help us deal with such events. Failure to initiate responses of any kind reflects, therefore, a loss of basic survival motivation.

Failure to learn.   Another striking characteristic of learned helplessness is inability to learn that we can control certain events in our environment. In an experiment very similar to that of Hiroto (1974), Miller and Seligman (1975) studied three groups of students who received escapable, inescapable, or no loud noise in the prelearning phase and were then confronted with a task involving skill and a task involving chance. The skill task required subjects to sort 15 cards into ten categories with a time limit of 15 seconds. The experimenter arranged to have them succeed or fail on a given sorting trial by saying the time was up either before or after they had finished. The subjects were unaware that the experimenter was ignoring clock time. At the end of each trial, subjects were asked to estimate their chances of succeeding on the next trial. Subjects who had previously been exposed to the inescapable noise (the helpless condition) showed little change in their expectancy after each new success or failure. The escape group and the no-pretreatment group, in contrast, showed large changes in their expectancy of success after each new success or failure. In other words, the helpless subjects did not perceive that the outcomes were related to their actions, while the escape and no-pretreatment groups did. When the three groups were exposed to a chance task, they showed no difference in expectancy change following success and failure. All three groups responded as though the outcome were independent of their actions—an appropriate way of responding to a chance event. Other studies have replicated this basic finding (e.g., Hiroto & Seligman, 1975).

As Seligman (1975) has pointed out, evidence from a variety of sources indicates that experiencing two events as independent (noncontingent) makes it very difficult, at some later time, to learn that they are dependent, or related, when they have been made contingent (e.g., Kemler & Shepp, 1971). To explain this fact, Seligman has argued that organisms acquire information about which events are mutually dependent in the environment. He suggests that once two things are perceived as independent, it is just as difficult to alter this perception as to alter the idea that two things are dependent. The confirmation that two things are related or unrelated seems to retard subsequent information processing. As a result, the helpless person fails to learn that two events have become dependent; and according to Hiroto (1974), the person has become an external. As we shall see, the internal, like the external, fails to respond to certain types of new information. Whereas externals fail to respond to information that their responses are producing changes in the environment, internals fail to respond to information that their responses are not producing changes in the environment.

Emotional disturbance.   Numerous studies have shown that lack of controllability produces various emotional responses. As we noted in Chapter 9, uncontrollable shocks are associated with high outputs of epinephrine (e.g., Brady, 1967), as well as ulceration (e.g., Weiss, 1968, 1971a,b,c). In contrast, being in control is associated with high outputs of norepinephrine (Brady, 1967, 1975) and the absence of ulcers (Weiss, 1968, 1971a,b,c). Higher blood pressure is also typical of people who are exposed to uncontrollable situations (e.g., Hokanson, DeGood, Forrest, & Brittain, 1971).

In addition to these and other physiological changes, there are at least two distinct psychological changes. Lack of controllability produces increases in anxiety and depression (Seligman, 1975). Both anxiety and depression have been shown to have a very debilitating effect on humans. It is clear that some very basic and important emotional changes are produced when aversive stimulation becomes uncontrollable.

Immunization

If exposure to uncontrollable events is sufficient to produce learned helplessness, then is it possible to immunize people against learned helplessness by teaching them that events are often controllable? Early successes (Maier & Seligman, 1976) has been confirmed by more recent findings that giving people a controllable experience produces a proactive interference against attempts to induce helplessness (Ramírez, Maldonado, & Martos, 1992).

Summary

According to Seligman's model, when animals or humans are presented with an aversive stimulus such as shock, and are unable to escape that stimulus, they develop a sense of helplessness. In contrast, when animals or humans are presented with an aversive stimulus that they can learn to escape, they do not develop a sense of helplessness. Individuals who develop a sense of helplessness fail to initiate behaviors that will allow them to learn how to escape an aversive situation. By contrast, those who fail to develop a sense of helplessness are inclined to initiate behaviors that will allow them to learn how to escape an aversive situation. As Seligman has pointed out, evidence from various sources indicates that experiencing two events as independent (noncontingent) makes it very difficult at some later time to learn that they are dependent, or related, when they have been made contingent. As a result, the individual who has experienced noncontingency will tend to behave as though there is no contingency.

From his studies of helplessness, Seligman suggested that learned helplessness is characterized by three deficits: failure to initiate responses, failure to learn, and emotional disturbance.

Although Seligman suggests that experiencing noncontingencies is the basis for learned helplessness, not all experiences of noncontingencies will necessarily lead to feelings of helplessness. If, for example, an individual has previously learned that two events are contingent, suddenly making them noncontingent will not result in feelings of helplessness. It appears that the previous contingency training is sufficient to immunize the individual against helplessness training.

The Cognitive Component of Depression

For a decade, Seligman's theory seemed to be a plausible explanation of why some people get depressed when placed in situations that they were unable to control. The major problem with the theory, as John Teasdale of Oxford pointed out, was that the helplessness training procedure that had been used to demonstrate the validity of the theory only seemed to work on two out of three people; a third of the people resisted the training procedure and showed no inclination to become helpless (Seligman, 1990). This observation, together with doubts expressed by two of his own graduate students, led Seligman and his critics to recast the theory in more cognitive terms.

The Reformulated Theory of Learned Helplessness

One of the main contributing forces behind the reformulation of the learned helplessness theory came from the work of Bernard Weiner (1972, 1974) of the University of California at Los Angeles, who had been studying people's explanatory styles (attributions) in achievement situations. Weiner found that whether people are inclined to persist at a task in the face of failure is linked, for example, to whether they have concluded that the failure is simply due to a lack of effort on their part or is due to something over which they have no control (Weiner et al., 1971). The reformulated theory expanded some of Weiner's ideas to help explain why some people become depressed and others never do (Abramson, Seligman, & Teasdale, 1978; Miller & Norman, 1979). The reformulated theory suggests that there are three basic reasons why some people fail to become depressed when they experience bad events (Peterson & Seligman, 1984).

According to the reformulated theory, individuals' propensity to become depressed is associated with their personal explanatory style. In other words, whether individuals become depressed in challenging situations depends on how they explain bad events and good events. There are three main patterns, which relate to evaluations of permanence, pervasiveness, and personal responsibility (personalization). Let's look at these three issues.

Permanence

Explaining bad events.   People who give up and become helpless believe that the causes of bad events that happen to them are permanent. People who do not give up, in contrast, believe that bad events are temporary. If we believe that something is temporary, then there is reason to persist. Here are some examples (based on Seligman, 1990).

Permanent (Pessimistic):	Temporary (Optimistic):
"I'm all washed up."	"I'm exhausted."
"Diets never work."	"Diets don't work when you eat out."
"The boss is a bastard."	"The boss is in a bad mood."

Failure tends to make almost everyone momentarily helpless. The people who succeed, however, are those who pick themselves up and try again. The finding that persistence is one of the major characteristics of success is so consistent that it might be called the law of success: People who persist will eventually succeed. Unless we persist in the face of difficulty, we will never learn how to do something correctly and thus attain a goal. As we persist, we alter our responses systematically so that we can discover how to reach a goal.

Explaining good events.   When good things happen to pessimists, they see that outcome as temporary. Optimists, by contrast, see that outcome as more or less permanent.

Permanent (Optimistic):	Temporary (Pessimistic):
"I'm always lucky."	"It's my lucky day."
"I'm talented."	"I try hard."
"My rival is no good."	"My rival got tired."

Note that people who believe that good events have permanent causes try harder after success, whereas people who believe good events are due to temporary causes tend to give up. If we believe good events are temporary, we will regard what happened as a fluke. We gambled and won, and now we'll take our earnings and quit.

Pervasiveness

Explaining bad events.   While permanence is about time, pervasiveness is about space. When pessimists experience a bad event, they allow it to affect all parts of their life; they view the bad event as universal. When a relationship breaks up, for example, they are inclined to stop eating, stop seeing their friends, stop working, and so forth. While all of us might be affected by such events for a few days, pessimists tend to wallow in their sadness and allow it to affect every other part of their life, until they are totally depressed. Optimists, in contrast, may initially feel that life is not worth living but, after a few days, they begin to bounce back; they see the bad event as specific and localized. Realizing that life has much else to offer, they may, for example, make special efforts to see their friends, throw themselves into their work, or decide to learn a new language. It is as though optimists see life as made up of many little boxes, each of which contains a little treasure they need to preserve. Pessimists, in contrast, seem to see life as one big box, where everything is mixed together. When one little treasure gets broken, all the other treasures in the box get broken as well.

As we've seen, pessimists allow themselves to wallow in their misery. One of the most exciting new ideas that has come out of therapy in some time is that people can learn to stop themselves from sinking deeper and deeper into depression. Optimists, it seems, have learned to do this on their own. We will examine how to become an optimist in the next chapter.

Here are some examples of how pessimists and optimists explain bad events.

Universal (Pessimistic):	Specific (Optimistic):
"All teachers are unfair."	"Professor Franken is unfair."
"I'm repulsive."	"I'm repulsive to him."
"Books are useless."	"This book is useless."

Explaining good events.   The way pessimists and optimists explain good events is just the opposite of how they explain bad events.

Specific (Pessimistic):	Universal (Optimistic):
"I'm smart at math."	"I'm smart."
"My broker knows oil stocks."	"My broker knows Wall Street."
"I was charming to her."	"I was charming."

While pessimists explain good events in terms of *transient* causes, such as mood and effort, optimists explain good events in terms of *permanent* causes, such as traits and abilities. While one says *sometimes*, the other says *always*.

The nature of hope and hopelessness.   Note that hope and hopelessness in Seligman's theory grow out of the two dimensions of pervasiveness and permanence. In order to be characterized as hopeful, people need to respond to bad events in terms of *specific* and *temporary* causes. People who are hopeless, in contrast, respond to bad events as *permanent* and *universal*.

Personalization: Internal versus External

Explaining bad events.   When bad things happen, people are inclined to either blame themselves (internal-ize) or blame someone else (externalize). One day, when I had left my sailboat in the driveway, my son backed our car into it and caused some minor damage. My son blamed me for not putting the boat away; I blamed him for not watching where he was going. Further, I argued, he should have remembered that I had gone sailing, to which he replied, "Why am I supposed to keep track of what you are doing?" Psychologists have established that people with low self-esteem blame themselves when something goes wrong, whereas people with good self-esteem tend to blame others. I guess my son and I are both on the right track for good self-esteem.

Here are some examples of how low self-esteem and high self-esteem people are inclined to respond to bad events.

Internal (Low self-esteem)	External (High self-esteem)
"I'm stupid."	"You're stupid."
"I have no talent at poker."	"I have no luck at poker."
"I'm insecure."	"I grew up in poverty."

Explaining good events.   Again, the style for explaining good events is the opposite to that of explaining bad events. Here are some examples.

External (Pessimistic):	Internal (Optimistic):
" A stroke of luck."	"I can take advantage of luck."
"My teammates' skill."	"My skill."

When people believe they cause good things to happen, they like themselves; when they believe that good things come from some circumstances over which they have no control, they are less inclined to like themselves.

A caveat about responsibility.   Seligman (1990) is careful to point out that, despite the clear benefits of an external belief system, he does not advocate that people should switch from being internals to externals, because individual responsibility is important. However, there are times when people assume too much responsibility. For example, if I blame the fact that my wife did not get a promotion on something I said, I may be taking too much responsibility. In the final analysis, people must learn to take responsibility for those things they can control and not to take responsibility for those things they can't control (Weiner, 1995).

Pessimism as a Cause of Depression

Types of depression.   Is depression the ultimate form of pessimism? Before we can answer that question, we need to look at the definitions of depression.

There are three kinds of depression: normal, unipolar, and bipolar. Bipolar depression has also been called a manic-depressive disorder, because it is characterized by both manic episodes and depressive episodes. Bipolar depression is much more heritable than unipolar depression and is very responsive to lithium carbonate. There is good reason to believe that bipolar depression is not the result of pessimistic thinking but rather due to a genetic disorder (Seligman, 1990).

The prevailing view is that normal depression is simply a passing demoralization, whereas unipolar depression is a chemical or clinical disorder and needs to be treated with drugs and/or psychotherapy. Taking exception to this view, Seligman (1990) points out that the two cannot be distinguished on the basis of their symptomatology. He argues that the reason those with normal depression are more likely to recover is that they are not as severely depressed.

According to the American Psychiatric Association's (1994) *Diagnostic and Statistical Manual of Mental Disorders* (DSM-IV), a major depressive episode is characterized by five of the following criteria, including depressed mood or loss of interest. They typically must occur on a daily basis.

1. Depressed mood most of the day.
2. Markedly diminished interest or pleasure in usual daily activities.
3. Significant weight loss when not dieting, or weight gain, or decrease or increase in appetite.
4. Insomnia or hypersomnia.
5. Psychomotor agitation or retardation.
6. Fatigue or loss of energy.
7. Feelings of worthlessness or excessive or inappropriate guilt.
8. Diminished ability to think or concentrate or indecisiveness.
9. Recurrent thoughts of death and/or recurrent suicidal ideation (with or without plan).

Studies on pessimism and depression.   How can we demonstrate that pessimism is the cause of depression? One way is to take people who tend to think more pessimistically and see what happens when they experience bad events. Seligman has shown that people who think more pessimistically are more likely to become depressed. In a study of students who did not perform as well as they expected on an examination, he found that people with a more pessimistic thinking style were more likely to demonstrate the symptoms of depression. In another case, he studied prisoners. Prisons consistently produce depression in people who tended not to show depression before they were sentenced. Seligman found that pessimists sentenced to prison were inclined to develop deeper depression than did optimists (Abramson, Metalsky, & Alloy, 1989; Sweeney, Anderson, & Bailey, 1986; Seligman, 1990).

A second way to demonstrate a link between pessimism and depression is to change subjects' pessimistic thinking style to a more optimistic one and to observe whether their symptoms of depression then wane. A great deal of research shows that teaching people to think more optimistically does result in the lessening—and often the elimination—of their depression.

Is there any difference between people treated with antidepressant drugs and those who have learned to think more optimistically? The general finding is that drugs will often work for a period of time, but people who have been given only drug treatment tend to relapse, whereas people who have been given drugs and also taught how to think differently are much less inclined to relapse (Hollon et al., 1990).

Rumination

One of the main characteristics of depressed people is that they tend to engage in excessive analysis, or *rumination* (which also means chewing the cud). Because of their pessimistic thinking style, depressed people who ruminate tend to create a highly negative world for themselves. Optimists may also ruminate but, when they do so, they create a highly positive world for themselves.

Research shows that people who tend to be pessimists but not ruminators are less likely to become depressed. In other words, the combination of being pessimistic and being a ruminator is very likely to produce depression (Kuhl, 1981; Nolen-Hoeksema, 1990).

When people become depressed, they lose their motivation, they develop feelings of worthlessness and guilt, and frequently entertain thoughts of suicide.

Women, Depression, and the Rumination/Distraction Theory

Women tend to show depression in developed nations at about twice the rate of men. In the United States, women are at a higher risk for depression for a wide range of risk variables, including biological, learned, and cognitive factors. Depressed women, for example, tend to have poorer problem-solving skills and to possess cognitive styles that make them more susceptible to depression (Culberston, 1997). In addition, they tend to come from lower socioeconomic levels, are more likely to be married, and have often been subjected to sexual and physical abuse. Nolen-Hoeksema (1990), who has studied depression outside the United States, has suggested that cultural attitudes are a significant determinant of male-female differences in depression.

Various theories have been advanced to account for these differences. According to one theory, women have learned to be more helpless than men because of their gender roles (Culbertson, 1997). If this were the

case, women would be expected to be more pessimistic than men, but there is virtually no evidence to support this idea. Most studies find little difference between men and women in terms of pessimism. According to the *rumination/distraction theory,* women tend to be ruminators, whereas men tend to be distractors. When bad things happen to women, they are more likely to engage in excessive analysis; however, when bad things happen to men, they are more inclined to engage in some distracting activity, such as sports. As a result, women with a pessimistic thinking style are more likely to become depressed than are men with a pessimistic thinking style (Nolen-Hoeksema, 1987, 1990). Why men and women have different styles remains to be determined.

Beck's Theory of Depression

Aaron Beck (1967, 1976, 1991), a pioneer of cognitive approaches to depression, has proposed that the thinking patterns of depressed people play a critical role not only in initially producing depression but in maintaining it. He has pointed out that depressed people tend to view their current and future situations in negative terms. Such thinking is characterized by three tendencies. First, depressed people tend to view situations as negative even when a positive interpretation is possible. Second, they view interactions with the environment in terms of deprivation, disease, and defeat. Third, they tend to tailor facts to fit their negative conclusions. They may even ignore external input that is not consistent with their conclusion that life is essentially bad.

Beck argues that depressed people tend to develop an organized and stable *schema,* or representation of themselves, and they process information on the basis of this schema. They screen, differentiate, and code the environment in accordance with the representation they have formed of themselves.

Beck emphasizes that the thinking process of depressed people often leads to *cognitive distortions.* Because depressed people have a systematic bias against the self, so that they compare themselves unfavorably with other people, they develop feelings of deprivation, depreciation, and failure. These cognitive distortions can be viewed as errors in thinking. Beck identified four kinds of errors of thinking:

1. Exaggeration: exaggerating the negative aspects of our experiences. We might say, "I made a complete fool of myself," when we simply made a social error in an otherwise impeccable performance.
2. Dichotomous thinking: viewing a partial failure as complete failure. We might say, "My talk was a total bomb," when the only problem with our talk was the lack of a good ending.
3. Selective abstraction: seeing only the negative aspects of an experience and using that information to make an inference about our ability. We might say, "Nobody liked my performance," when one person raised an objection and most people voiced their approval.
4. Overgeneralization: using one outcome to make inferences about our ability. We might say, "I have no ability whatsoever to do that kind of thing," when we have a great deal of ability but we didn't do so well in one particular situation.

Beck (1983, 1991) has distinguished between two types of individuals who are prone to become depressed after a negative experience. The *autonomous* individual, who is motivated by the need for independent achievement, mobility, and solitary pleasures, is prone to become depressed after an autonomous stressor such as failure, immobilization, or enforced conformity. The *sociotropic* individual is motivated by acceptance and attention from others and is prone to become depressed by sociotropic traumas such as social deprivation or rejection.

According to this distinction, the lack of good social relationships would not affect the autonomous type but would affect the sociotropic type. Indeed, this is what has been found (Hokanson & Butler, 1992).

Perfectionism, Depression, and the Chemical Imbalance Theory

Humiliating events, failures, and rejection are common antecedents of suicide. However, a significant number of talented and successful people commit suicide each year. One of the underlying characteristics of these people is an intense perfectionism (Blatt, 1995). Perfectionism—satisfaction from attaining a very high standard of excellence—is an admirable quality but, when people set unrealistically high standards for themselves, they may find it impossible to find satisfaction in a job well done and instead experience humiliation and defeat.

Research on goal setting indicates that people should set difficult goals for themselves in order to motivate themselves. However, they obviously need to set goals that will not lead to self-destruction. In Chapter 14, we will consider how to set appropriate goals.

The research on intense perfectionism illustrates the role of personal belief systems in depression, in contrast to the popular view that depression results from a chemical imbalance that can be treated with drugs. While there is no question that depression is linked to a chemical imbalance, treating the symptoms will not cure perfectionists of their potentially self-destructive belief system. That can only be addressed with some type of cognitive therapy or, perhaps, through learning how to interpret failure so that it does not undermine our sense of self.

Summary

Some people get depressed when exposed to helplessness training procedures, while others do not. According to the reformulated theory of learned helplessness, these differences are linked to differences in individuals' explanatory style. People who are inclined to see bad events as temporary, specific, and external are less inclined to become helpless and depressed. Considerable evidence supports the idea that depression is the result of a pessimistic explanatory style. In particular, it has been shown that people who are more pessimistic

Practical Application 10-2

Cognitive Therapy and Depression: Learning the Art of Constructive Thinking

Cognitive therapy can be summarized in terms of six tactics that we can use to take charge of our thinking (Beck, 1983; Seligman, 1990). These tactics should prove helpful to anyone who is prone to pessimism and depression.

1. **Learn to recognize destructive automatic thoughts.** When things go bad, people often hear themselves repeat short phrases or sentences. A mother who has lost her temper, for example, may hear herself say, "I'm a terrible mother." A student who has done poorly on an exam might hear himself say, "I should be shot, I'm such an idiot." A teenager who feels embarrassed after a social blunder may hear herself say, "I wish I were dead." The curious thing about such fleeting thoughts is that they seem to come from somewhere inside us and yet we know that we haven't consciously created them. They are therefore called *automatic thoughts.*

2. **Learn to dispute destructive automatic thoughts.** Most people fail to challenge their automatic thoughts. They accept them as coming from somewhere deep inside themselves and therefore as fair and valid commentary. At the same time, most people find these thoughts to be disturbing and are perplexed by their occurrence. Why they arise is not clear.

Most cognitive therapists argue that these thoughts are not fair commentary and that it is critical that we learn to dispute them. The best way to dispute them is to marshal contrary evidence. A mother who has lost her temper is not necessarily a bad mother; she likely does a number of good things. To deal with such disturbing thoughts, she needs to enumerate her good qualities. Similarly, the student who has performed poorly needs to say to himself, "I didn't do as well as I expected, but they don't shoot people for doing poorly." In addition, he needs to recount the number of times he performed admirably.

3. **Learn to avoid using destructive explanations.** Many of the fleeting comments that people experience are characterized by permanence and pervasiveness. People need to learn to find an explanation that is more temporary and situation-specific. The mother might learn to say, "I'm a good mother most of the time but, later in the afternoon when it gets hot or I'm tired, I tend to become irritable. And that little rascal is not in such a great mood when it gets hot either." The student might say, "I had a bad day. The exam was different than I expected, and I guess I ended up studying the wrong thing." The teenager who made a social blunder might say, "I was thinking about something else and I slipped up. If someone had videotaped that one, it would get a lot of laughs on TV."

4. **Learn to distract yourself from depressive thoughts.** Becoming involved in an activity is a very good way of distracting yourself from depressive thoughts. As we have seen, men are more inclined than women to adopt this strategy. Among the numerous activities that will work are reading a book, going for coffee with a friend, becoming involved in a hobby, going to a movie, or simply imagining yourself in some activity that you might like.

5. **Learn to create less self-limiting happiness self-statements.** Many people put limits on what will allow them to be happy. They say such things as:

"I won't be happy until I have a new car."

are more likely to become depressed, and that people given antidepressant drugs plus cognitive therapy are more likely to recover from depression than are people given only drugs.

People who engage in excessive analysis (rumination) are more likely to become depressed. Interest-ingly, women are more likely to ruminate and also more likely to become depressed. Men, in contrast, are more likely to distract themselves in the aftermath of bad events.

Beck has noted that depressed people tend to view the present and future in negative terms. This negative

---

"I'll be happy when I fall in love."

"I can't be happy unless I know that everybody likes me."

"I'll be happy when I retire."

Each of these statements puts severe limits on when or how we can be happy. As a result, they are inclined to set us up for depression. There is nothing wrong with wanting a new car or wanting to be in love or looking forward to retirement. The problem lies in saying that we can't be happy until those conditions have been met.

When people engage in this form of inner dialogue, the statements they make to themselves become rules or principles. As a result, they find themselves unable to experience happiness until these self-imposed conditions have been met. Unfortunately, when the conditions are met, people often experience only momentary happiness, because happiness is rarely found in reaching a goal. Rather, it tends to be found in the process of working toward a goal.

To become less susceptible to depression, you will need to assess and redesign your inner dialogue. First, take some time to analyze your inner dialogue to see if you are setting limits on your happiness. Give yourself time to become aware of your automatic thoughts. Whenever you become aware of one, write it down, so that you can analyze it rationally.

Having recognized these negative self-statements, you will need to replace them with more positive versions. Here is how you might redesign the statements noted earlier so as to preserve the goals but to permit happiness in the interim.

"This is a good car for now but my goal is to buy a new one eventually."

"I am enjoying dating and look forward to falling in love."

"I'd like to be viewed as a sensitive and considerate person but, because my values are different from other people's, I need to learn that others may not always understand or appreciate where I am coming from."

"It is great to be healthy and earning a good living, both of which are going to make retirement rewarding."

6. **Learn to make your inner dialogue process-oriented.** You might go one step further and turn each of your happiness statements into a process goal, which focuses more on the process and less on the end goal. Most people seem to get their happiness out of the process, perhaps because humans are inclined to become habituated to static emotions very quickly (Frijda, 1988). Here are some examples of how to turn the original happiness statements into process statements.

"I get a great deal of enjoyment out of cars, and I hope to own several fine cars in my lifetime."

"Love and being loved is a skill. I am going to work hard at making love a central focus of my life."

"My goal is to gain the respect and admiration of many people in my life. It is a skill that others before me have nurtured and developed, and I am determined to see if I can emulate them."

"To be truly happy in retirement takes a great deal of work and planning. I am going to study people who are happy in retirement so that, when I retire, I can be truly happy."

style of thinking grows out of a stable internal representation, or schema. Depressed people, Beck argues, have a bias against the self that leads to errors in thinking, such as the tendency to overgeneralize and to make inferences without consideration of alternative points of view.

Beck has distinguished between two types of people who are prone to become depressed—the sociotropic and the autonomous. Among other things, his theory predicts that good social relationships are important for the sociotropic type but less so for the autonomous type. The link between perfectionism and suicide indicates the role of cognitive variables in depression and suicide.

To take charge of our thinking, we need to: (1) learn to recognize automatic thoughts; (2) learn to dispute destructive automatic thoughts; (3) learn to avoid using destructive explanations; (4) learn the art of distracting ourselves; (5) learn to create less self-limiting happiness self-statements; and (6) learn to make our inner dialogue process-oriented.

Guilt and Shame

Guilt and shame are usually treated as overlapping emotions. Until recently, there was little empirical information on the nature and origins of these emotions (Zahn-Waxler & Kochanska, 1990). As more data accumulate, the consensus is that these emotions are implicated in a wide range of human motivated behaviors. There are at least five important points about guilt and shame.

1. Guilt and shame are uniquely human emotions, although some have argued that canines are capable of guilt.
2. Guilt and shame play a role in a wide variety of behaviors, including sexual abuse, rape, eating disorders, stress-related physical disorders, alcoholism, divorce, and emotional illness. As research continues, further links between these emotions and motivated behaviors are expected to emerge.
3. Shame and, in particular, guilt have been linked to pessimism and depression. People who are more depressed experience more guilt and shame. Some researchers believe that guilt and shame cause depression (Zahn-Waxler & Kochanska, 1990).
4. It is widely held that the capacity for these emotions is innate, but that their mode of expression is learned (Zahn-Waxler & Kochanska, 1990). Among other things, this means that individuals differ greatly in the expression of these emotions as a result of their developmental experiences. Moreover, if the mode of expression is learned, it can be redirected more adaptively.
5. Like virtually all other negative emotions, guilt and shame tend to disrupt adaptive behavior when they become excessive. Hence, if people wish to achieve goals they must learn how to manage these emotions. Many researchers now feel that this is a distinct possibility (Thompson, 1990).

Guilt and shame can elicit and sustain certain behaviors (such as achievement and cooperation), while inhibiting others (such as anger and aggression). From an adaptive perspective, this is very important. The proper execution of any response typically demands the excitation and inhibition of various emotions. Businesspeople who are negotiating a contract, for example, may need to inhibit expressions of anger or dislike.

It is also important to distinguish between acts of commission (such as becoming angry and aggressive, belittling someone's achievements, or criticizing) and acts of omission (failure to achieve a goal, failure to provide for our family, failure to live up to a family value). Recognizing this distinction, Lazarus (1991) has suggested that the core relational theme for guilt is having transgressed a moral imperative, while the core relational theme for shame is having failed to live up to an ego-ideal. Note that Beck's view of depression is consistent with this definition of shame. Beck suggests that depressed people tend to view their interactions with the environment in terms of failure, an explanatory style that leads to depression.

It has been suggested that the opposite of guilt is empathy (Zahn-Waxler & Kochanska, 1990). Whereas we often feel guilt after being insensitive to the feelings or needs of others (acting in our own self-interest), empathy involves being sensitive to the feelings and needs of others. In the next chapter, we will deal not only with empathy but with worth, two important

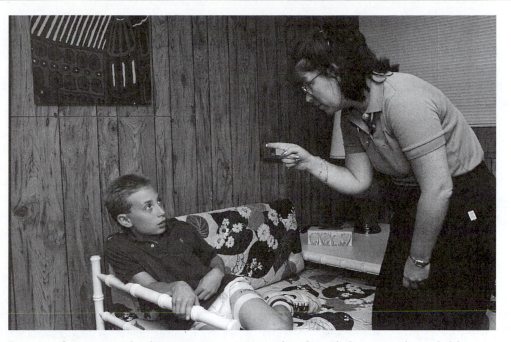

Parents play a central role in creating a sense of guilt and shame in their children.

emotions that seem to play a fundamental role in helping and acts of altruism.

Both guilt and shame are clearly involved in goal-directed behavior. In our desire to achieve our goals, we may do various things that cause us to feel guilty. For instance, we may take short-cuts, hoard information to prevent others from finding the solution, take the ideas of others and pass them off as our own, or undermine the attempts of others. Similarly, we may experience shame for not having achieved the level we think we should have, for not having worked as hard as we might have, for not having won the praise that we thought we should have, and so forth.

While it has been suggested from time to time that shame and guilt are similar and overlapping emotions, a recent study indicates differences (Tangney, Miller, Flicker, & Barlow, 1996). The most substantial difference is that shame is more intense and aversive and involves more physiological change. Young people who experienced shame felt more isolated, diminished, and inferior to others and were more compelled to hide

and less inclined to admit what they had done. Contrary to the suggestion that shame is more public than guilt, research indicates that both emotions are experienced in public and in private.

The Biological Component

Guilt and Shame as Adaptive Emotions

Numerous writers agree that guilt and shame are basically adaptive emotions; they serve to ensure good social relationships (Kagan, 1984). The maintenance of good social relationships is important from an evolutionary perspective, because the survival of the individual often depends on conditions in the larger group to which the individual belongs.

It has been suggested that maintaining good social relations depends on two complementary processes: being sensitive to the needs of others; and being motivated to make amends or make reparations when a transgression does occur. In short, it depends on the capacity for guilt. Hoffman (1982), who has focused on the guilt that comes from harming others, suggests that the motivational basis for this guilt is empathetic distress. Empathetic distress occurs when people realize their actions had caused harm or pain to another person. Motivated by feelings of guilt, they are inclined to make amends for their actions. Making amends serves to repair damaged social relations and restore group harmony.

Discrete Emotions Theory

In Izard's (1977) theory, guilt is viewed as a discrete emotion—that is, as one of the primary constituents or components of motivation. According to Izard, discrete emotions involve three basic elements: a neural substrate; a characteristic facial pattern (or neuromuscular expressive pattern); and a distinct subjective feeling. The cardiovascular, endocrine, respiratory, and other systems are also involved and are presumably governed by the neural substrate. According to the theory, emotions evolved to serve an adaptive function, and the communication of emotions take place via the recognition of facial expression.

The main adaptive function of guilt, according to Izard, is to prevent waste and exploitation. Taking responsibility and making amends for wrongdoing have survival value for individuals and relationships and ultimately ensures the survival of societies and civilization. Guilt serves to inhibit aggression and to encourage people to make reparations—a key method of restoring harmony. Note that this evolutionary view emphasizes the survival of the group, rather than the survival of the individual.

Psychoanalytic Theory

In Freudian theory, guilt was thought to emerge as a result of restraints that parents imposed on expression of sexual and aggressive impulses. In attempting to express these impulses, it was argued, children often found that they were in conflict with their parents and hence felt anger and hostility towards the parents. Because they feared punishment or the withdrawal of their parents' love, children learned to inhibit their impulses and to eventually internalize proper standards of conduct.

Anxiety is central to the Freudian analysis of guilt. It is argued that, whenever children are confronted with the possibility of losing the love of their parents, their intense feelings of anxiety serve to suppress—at least at the conscious level—feelings of anger and hatred towards their parents. More specifically, whenever the children felt the urge to indulge their impulses, they would experience a complex set of emotions that anticipated how they would feel if they actually did indulge these impulses. These anticipatory feelings, therefore, were thought to act as a powerful source of motivation for inhibiting sexual and aggressive impulses.

The Learned Component

The social learning theorists avoid using such mentalistic terms as guilt and shame to explain social conduct and good social relations. They prefer concepts such as rewards, punishment, extinction, discrimination, and generalization. According to the social learning theorists, good social behavior—including the appropriate expression of aggression—has its origins in our social interactions, especially those with our parents. They argue that, when our parents show disappointment and disapproval, we experience a negative emotion (a punishment), which we come to associate with the initiating event. Whenever we find ourselves engaging in the same behaviors, these negative feelings are automatically elicited. Engaging in these behaviors may even trigger memories and images of our parents. When we feel guilty for some transgression, for example, we see our mother frowning in disapproval. When we experience shame for not having lived up to some ideal, we may see our father's face bathed in disappointment. Guilt, in this analysis, does not involve any mentalistic or cognitive elements; it is simply a conditioned negative feeling (Zahn-Waxler & Kochanska, 1990).

The learning theorists have focused mainly on affectively driven guilt (empathetic guilt and anxiety- or fear-based guilt). In their approach, they have examined factors such as the timing and severity of punishment, the specific techniques used, and the quality of the affective relationship between parent and child (Zahn-Waxler & Kochanska, 1990). Let's review the portion of their research that focuses on discipline and parental love.

Discipline Techniques

Three types of discipline techniques may be distinguished (Hoffman, 1970b, 1982):

1. Power assertion—physical punishment, threats, deprivation of privileges or objects, and direct control.
2. Love withdrawal—nonphysical expressions of dislike and anger, in which the parent shows disapproval by techniques such as turning away, refusing to communicate, and threatening separation.
3. Induction—providing explanations so that the child can understand why his or her behavior is a cause for concern (for instance, "It makes Sally unhappy when you tease her").

Naturalistic studies of children have shown that power assertion leads to low levels of moral development, as measured by, for example, ability to resist temptation, feelings of guilt, or confession. Induction, in contrast, has been linked to high levels of moral development. Love withdrawal has been found to be related to moral development but less consistently than has induction (Hoffman, 1970b).

Love Withdrawal and Induction

Some studies have shown that love withdrawal and induction lead to different kinds of guilt. Hoffman (1970a), for example, distinguished between two types of children, representing two types of guilt: *humanistic-flexible* children, who were concerned about the harm they had done to others; and *conventional-rigid* children, who were more concerned with whether or not they had violated institutionalized norms. Hoffman suggests that the humanistic-flexible children are motivated by feelings of empathy, whereas the conventional-rigid are motivated more by their lack of impulse control. Note that the conventional-rigid type corresponds closely to the psychoanalytic concept of guilt. When Hoffman examined the socialization of these two types, he found that humanistic-flexible children had been socialized more by induction, while conventional-rigid children had been socialized more by love withdrawal.

Quality of the Affective Relationship between Parent and Child

In general, it has been found that there is a positive relationship between parental warmth and the development of conscience and guilt in children. One reason for the inconsistent effects of love withdrawal on guilt may be linked to whether the parents tend to be warm and affectionate. There is some evidence that love withdrawal will only be effective if the parent tends to be warm and affectionate in general.

The Cognitive Component

According to the cognitive theorists, guilt is a conscious process that involves a well-developed self-structure. Feelings of guilt occur when the process of self-reflection (also called self-judgment) leads us to conclude that our behavior failed to meet some internal standard of conduct. As we have seen, Lazarus (1991) clearly views shame as growing out of the self-concept (the ego-ideal).

Where do internal standards of conduct come from? Most cognitive theorists take the position that they are due, in part, to learning or role taking (for example, we accept the beliefs and values of our parents, or we accept norms) and, in part, to rational construction that grows out of self-reflection—a process that involves an analysis of a body of facts about the external world and our belief about those facts. For example, we may decide, after reading several articles on the state of the environment, that proper conduct includes the recycling of waste. We may decide on this conduct even though our parents and friends do not share our view.

It is important to keep in mind the distinction between acts of commission (for which we feel guilt) and acts of omission (for which we feel shame). While acts of commission often grow out of transgressions against others, acts of omission grow more out of our failure to work towards our goals, whether given to us by our parents ("You should become an engineer") or selected for ourselves ("I don't want to become an engineer because I hate math" or "I think I should become a doctor because I like the life sciences and I like helping people"). In everyday language, we tend to speak of guilt in relation to both acts of commission and acts of omission. As psychologists, however, we need to be aware of the distinction between guilt and shame.

Cognitive theorists hold the view that we not only construct standards but also change them through a process of self-reflection. We may, for example, decide to alter our goals when we acknowledge that our talents do not match our goals. I have a friend who entered a university with the ultimate goal of becoming an engineer, like his uncle. When he realized that he was not particularly interested in engineering but found economics fascinating, he decided to abandon his previous goal, which had largely been given to him by his parents, and set a new goal for himself. In due course, his parents came to terms with his new goal and gave him their wholehearted support.

Practical Application 10-3

Managing Excessive Guilt and Shame

Many people experience excessive guilt and shame—that is, guilt and shame that are totally out of proportion to the situation. For example, a woman may feel guilty when two members of her family get into an argument. Because she knew that they are prone to conflict, she blames herself for not having intervened. Children sometimes feel guilty when their parents break up and divorce. They reason that something they did provoked the split. A man may feel guilty when his wife is fired. He reasons that if he had been more friendly towards his wife's boss, even though he disliked the man, his wife would not have been fired.

A similar thing happens in the case of shame. When a student receives a B+ instead of the A she expected, she reasons that she has failed not only herself but her family. A father who takes great care to teach his children honesty experiences sharp pangs of shame each time he remembers the day he was called into the principal's office because his son had copied someone else's work. The head of a company feels a sense of despair as the company she heads loses money in the middle of a recession. She reasons that she should have been better prepared to deal with the recession.

Often, people realize that the guilt and shame they experience are unwarranted but still find they are unable to do anything about their feelings. They feel trapped. Frijda (1988) explains this by proposing the law of conservation of emotional momentum as a restriction on the law of habituation: He suggests that, under certain conditions, "emotional events retain their power to elicit emotions indefinitely, unless counteracted by repetitive exposures that permit extinction or habituation, to the extent these are possible" (p. 354).

Various writers have suggested that two parallel systems control our behavior. The conscious system is generally conceptualized as more abstract and rational; it involves logical explanations, for instance. The unconscious system, by contrast, is generally conceptualized as more sensory-based—operating by way of images, memories, and the principles of associative learning, such as classical conditioning (e.g., Lazarus, 1991)—or more experientially based, operating by way of concrete images, metaphors, and narratives (e.g., Epstein, 1990). In the more sensory-based system described by Lazarus, images and memories are thought to become linked to feelings, so that certain images, when elicited, automatically trigger certain feelings. In the sensory-based system, guilt might be elicited by something as simple as a frown. If my mother frowned in the past when she disapproved of some transgression, I might feel pangs of guilt at the sight of a frown on anyone's face. Presumably, the precise feeling would depend on the feeling that I experienced when caught in a transgression. That feeling could be loss of love, pain that comes from punishment, or simply the negative emotion associated with conflict. The feeling component may be somewhat different for different people.

What about the feelings that come from the more rational system? Some theorists contend that they may be very different from those appearing in the sensory-based system. Hoffman (1982) suggests, for example, that the rational system is more likely to be based on empathetic distress. Rather than reexperiencing our own pain, we learn to experience the pain or distress of others.

If we can construct new and different standards of conduct for ourselves, it may be possible for us to manage our guilt and shame by modifying our standards (Practical Application 10-3).

The Link between Guilt and Depression

Guilt and depression have been explicitly linked in the theories of Beck and Seligman. In Beck's (1967)

model, depressives are likely to assume personal responsibility for events with negative outcomes that result in feelings of guilt, self-blame, self-deprecation, and dejection. In Seligman's reformulated model (Seligman, 1990), the self is also held responsible for negative outcomes and these self-attributions of responsibility are permanent, pervasive, and consistently internal. One obvious conclusion is that guilt

In general, most theorists seem to believe that the feelings that come from the sensory- or narrative-based system are much more difficult to alter than those from the rational system (e.g., Epstein, Lipson, Holstein, & Huh, 1992; Epstein, 1990). In theory, it should be possible to extinguish (habituate) these feelings by repeatedly exposing an individual to the stimuli that cause them. However, we often do things that in some way remove the stimuli that caused our guilt feelings. When a person frowns, for example, we may stop what we were doing, so that the frown disappears. As a result, the guilt feelings never become full-blown, and therefore cannot extinguish or habituate (Frijda, 1988). Most theorists seem to agree that, in order for habituation to occur, a response must be allowed to run its course; it must be allowed to wear out, so to speak. Also, acts of reparation are positively reinforcing, because they reduce or remove the negative feeling of guilt. As a result of this repeated positive reinforcement, we are inclined to perpetuate acts of reparation and thus never put ourselves in a situation that would allow the emotions to habituate. Because we work hard to ensure that our parents are not upset, we continue to feel guilt in their presence. Only by allowing our parents to become upset can we allow habituation to take place. It is apparent from this example that guilt serves to minimize conflict, even though it may cause a great deal of internal stress. The question of excess might best be conceptualized as a problem of rumination. People who experience guilt or shame often ruminate about their feelings; and in the course of ruminating, they become debilitated.

Note that feelings of guilt and shame are often reinforced in our society. We tell people how important it is for them to be considerate of the feelings and wishes of

other people, especially their parents, even when it undermines their own ability to deal with important events in their lives. We also praise people for taking full responsibility for their actions.

Is there any hope for the person who is experiencing too much guilt? Probably the best solution is to tackle the problem at the rational (thinking) level. Epstein argues that when we operate out of the experiential system we tend to overgeneralize. Often we need to learn that our reactions to other people, such as our parents, have not been thought through rationally but have been learned through our experiential system.

We can better manage feelings of guilt and shame if we adopt a new explanatory style that is relatively free of permanence and pervasiveness. Instead of attempting to get rid of guilt and shame (to habituate them), we need to make them more situation- and time-specific, as both Beck and Seligman suggest. Most people experience pangs of guilt from time to time, and there is nothing wrong with being sensitive to social conflict and wanting to make amends for our acts of transgression (sins of commission) or lapses in sensitivity or empathy (sins of omission). Those who lack a desire to maintain good social relations or to experience feelings of empathy are often psychopaths. We need to view feelings of guilt and shame as simple reminders that we are social beings. Making quick and simple corrections or reparations has always been the mark of socially sophisticated people. The key is not to expect perfection in ourselves or to think that we can please everybody.

comes from taking far too much responsibility for negative outcomes.

Negative Emotions and Goal-Directed Behavior

All of the negative emotions discussed in this chapter tend to undermine goal-directed behavior. When people see the world as threatening—when they are troubled by fear and anxiety, for example—they are less inclined to initiate goal-directed behaviors. Rather, they tend to pull back and focus their energies on protecting themselves from a world that they perceive as hostile to their intentions. In contrast, as we'll see in the next chapter, people who view the world as more benign or benevolent are more willing to explore the world and to master and shape the environment so that it can provide them with pleasure.

Similarly, when people interpret any failure in their attempts to master and shape the world as evidence that they are helpless victims—as in the case of pessimists and depressives—they are inclined to discontinue their goal-directed efforts. In contrast, as we'll see in the next chapter, optimists are not debilitated by failure and are inclined to carry on in the face of obstacles.

Finally, people who set excessively high standards for themselves can feel overwhelmed by guilt or shame. In contrast, as we'll see in the next chapter, people with a strong sense of self-worth take joy in their encounters and can forgive themselves for their shortcomings.

Summary

According to Lazarus, guilt is defined as having transgressed a moral imperative, while shame is defined as having failed to live up to an ego-ideal. The biological theorists have argued that guilt is innate and universal and that its modes of expression are learned. Working from an adaptive framework, they argue that guilt is designed to maintain good social relations. According to Izard, the main adaptive function of guilt is to prevent waste and exploitation. This has survival value not only for the individual but for the larger group. Psychoanalytic theorists contend that guilt grows out of a conflict between the biological and social parts of the personality and serves to protect children from engaging in behaviors that would result in punishment or loss of love.

The learning theorists have focused on affectively driven guilt (empathetic guilt and anxiety- or fear-based guilt). The study of discipline techniques has shown that the highest level of moral development comes from a technique called induction, while the worst comes from power assertion. Love withdrawal has been found to be inconsistently related to moral development. The work of Hoffman suggests that love withdrawal leads to two different kinds of guilt—humanistic-flexible and conventional-rigid—each of which has been linked to different socialization processes.

Cognitive theorists have focused on symbolic and representational skills such as roletaking and self-reflection in their analyses of guilt. They have argued that guilt and shame come from the internal representation of norms (often through roletaking) and through rational construction of standards (through self-reflection). Through self-reflection, people can change their standards.

Guilt and shame have been explicitly linked to depression in the theories of Beck and Seligman. Learning to deal with excessive guilt and shame plays an important role in reducing depression.

Main Points

1. It has been suggested that the goal object of fear is fairly specific, while the goal object of anxiety is more vague or ambiguous.
2. Gray has proposed that anxiety is due to the activation of the behavioral inhibition system (BIS).
3. The BIS can be activated by both conditioned and unconditioned stimuli.
4. Antianxiety drugs work by deactivating the BIS.
5. The BIS can be conditioned to two classes of stimuli: those that signal punishment is forthcoming; and those that signal rewards will be withheld (frustrative nonreward).
6. It has been suggested that phobias are the product of classical conditioning.
7. Gray believes that panic attacks are conditioned fight-or-flight responses.
8. When panic attacks occur in life-threatening situations, they are referred to as true alarms; when

they occur spontaneously, they are referred to as false alarms.

9. Converging research indicates that people who view the world as threatening tend to be more prone to debilitating anxiety.

10. Unwanted or intrusive thoughts have been linked to anxiety.

11. Loss of control and inability to make a coping response have been linked to feelings of anxiety.

12. Research evidence lends support to both a top-down and bottom-up theory of subjective well-being.

13. Depression is very prevalent in our society and is characterized by a lack of motivation.

14. When depression is very severe it leads to thoughts about self-destruction (suicide).

15. Modern individualism has been linked to increases in depression.

16. The solution to modern individualism may be relearning the importance of the group and the importance of cooperation.

17. It has been suggested that all depression involves a reduction in certain catecholamines, especially norepinephrine.

18. More recently, it has been suggested that depletion of serotonin is a major cause of depression. One of the newest antidepressants is Prozac, which blocks the reuptake of serotonin.

19. Various drugs used in the treatment of depression work by elevating norepinephrine levels or serotonin levels.

20. Stress appears to cause depression by lowering norepinephrine levels.

21. It has been suggested that depression is an adaptive mood. Depression may play a role in reprogramming; for example, it may help people abandon goals that are unattainable.

22. Seligman has suggested that depression is learned helplessness, defined as a psychological state that frequently results when events are uncontrollable.

23. Experiments with both animals and humans have shown that exposure to an aversive stimulus event that is both inescapable and uncontrollable is often sufficient to produce learned helplessness.

24. According to Seligman, learned helplessness is characterized by three deficits: (1) failure to initiate responses; (2) failure to learn; and (3) emotional disturbance.

25. The reformulated model of learned helplessness suggests that people are inclined to become depressed if they use an explanatory style characterized by permanence, pervasiveness, and personalization.

26. Hope and hopelessness grow out of two dimensions: pervasiveness and permanence.

27. The idea that pessimism causes depression is supported by the research finding that people who tend to use a pessimistic explanatory style are more likely to become depressed when they experience bad events.

28. Rumination is excessive analysis. When pessimists ruminate, they create a negative world for themselves; when optimists ruminate, they create a positive world for themselves.

29. Whereas women tend to be ruminators, men tend to be distractors.

30. According to Beck's theory, depression results from a negative thinking style that alters the way people screen, differentiate, and code the environment. Their bias against the self leads to cognitive distortions or errors in thinking.

31. Beck has distinguished between two subtypes of depression and their associated personality types. Sociotropic individuals are motivated by acceptance and attention from others, while autonomous individuals are motivated by the need for achievement, control, and the avoidance of interpersonal impediments.

32. We can change our thinking by learning: (1) to recognize destructive automatic thoughts; (2) to dispute destructive automatic thoughts; (3) to avoid using destructive explanations; (4) to distract ourselves from depressive thoughts; and (5) to create happiness self-statements that are less self-limiting.

33. Guilt and shame are involved in a wide range of adaptive and maladaptive behaviors.

34. Guilt and shame can sustain certain adaptive behaviors (such as achievement and cooperation), while inhibiting others (such as anger and aggression).

35. Guilt is associated with acts of commission and shame with acts of omission.

36. According to the Izard's theory of discrete emotions, guilt evolved to prevent waste and exploitation.

37. According to Freudian theory, guilt emerges as a result of restraints that parents impose on their children.

38. According to social learning theorists, guilt is simply a conditioned negative feeling.

39. Parents are inclined to employ one of three discipline techniques: power assertion, love withdrawal, and induction.

40. Induction tends to produce a humanistic-flexible type of personality, whereas love withdrawal tends to produce a conventional-rigid type.

41. Cognitive approaches to guilt and shame emphasize the role of self and link guilt to self-reflection.

42. Getting rid of guilt and shame may not be altogether desirable.

43. However, because excessive guilt and shame tend to undermine goal-directed behavior, people often need to learn how to manage these emotions.

44. It has been suggested that the best way to manage excessive guilt and shame is to develop a new explanatory style that is relatively free of permanence and pervasiveness.

Chapter Eleven

Goal-Congruent (Positive) Emotions:
Happiness, Hope and Optimism, Attachment and Belongingness

■ *What are goal-congruent emotions?*

■ *Is happiness a state of mind or simply a sensory or chemical experience?*

■ *Can people learn to create happiness?*

■ *Are people who take risks striving to experience elation and euphoria, or do they have a death wish?*

■ *What role do cognitions play in happiness?*

■ *What is the difference between optimism and hope?*

■ *Are some people born optimists, or can anybody learn to be an optimist?*

■ *Does hope come from inside us, or is it triggered in us by our environment?*

■ *Have any particular chemicals been linked to optimism and hope?*

■ *How do the emotions of belonging and attachment affect our physical and psychological health?*

■ *What role do cognitions play in belonging and attachment?*

Goal-congruent emotions are those that facilitate and sustain the attainment of personal goals (Lazarus, 1991). In this chapter, we'll briefly survey some of these emotions, to get an idea of their power in our daily lives. In Chapter 13, we will examine another goal-congruent emotion, pride.

Hedonism and Happiness

Happiness is a prime example of a positive emotion. But what exactly is happiness? Let's begin by distinguishing between the approaches of the hedonists and of cognitive theorists.

Hedonism

According to the principles of hedonism, organisms are motivated to seek pleasure and avoid pain. Hedonism is typically conceptualized in terms of those feelings that result from stimulation of the different sensory systems (vision, hearing, taste, smell, and touch) or from being bombarded with stimulation (arousal). According to the principles of hedonism, our feelings can be represented by a continuum ranging from positive affect at one end to negative affect at the other. Happiness involves maximizing positive affect.

One of the best-known hedonists is Paul Young (1975), who did extensive research on food preferences. His work, together with that of Carl Pfaffman (1960), showed that organisms are motivated to avoid certain substances (for instance, those that are bitter) and to approach others (for instance, those that are sweet). Their work indicates that organisms select foods on the basis of their sensory qualities rather than their nutrition or energy values (as with artificial sweeteners or various seasonings, for example). Harry Harlow and Margaret Harlow (1969) demonstrated the importance of tactile stimulation in infant-mother bonding. Infant monkeys, they showed, prefer mothers that can provide tactile stimulation over mothers that just provide food. Mothering, in short, is more than just providing for their offspring's nutritional requirements. Daniel Berlyne (1960) demonstrated that organisms are motivated to seek out and obtain optimal levels of arousal. When stimulation is very low, they increase stimula-

tion, often by engaging in exploratory behavior; when it is high, they decrease stimulation, often by seeking out familiar and predictable stimulation. According to Berlyne's theory, when levels of stimulation are optimal, people experience positive affect, whereas low or very high stimulation is experienced as aversive.

In popular speech, we often describe pleasure-seeking motivation in terms of *getting high*. This term is used in connection with a variety of activities—sometimes called thrill-seeking activities (Farley, 1986) or sensation-seeking activities (Zuckerman, 1979)—that seem to have little or no short-term or long-term survival value. They include hang gliding, bungee jumping, parachuting, downhill skiing, high-speed driving, and rock climbing.

With the discovery of reward pathways in the brain, many people felt that the concept of hedonism had a sound scientific basis. More than 30 years ago, James Olds discovered that rats would learn to press a bar in order to receive electrical stimulation from electrodes implanted in certain areas of the brain (Olds, 1956; Olds & Milner, 1954). Those particular brain areas appeared to be reward centers. Note that self-reward systems have also been found in humans (Heath, 1963). The reward systems of the human brain are illustrated in Figure 11-1.

Can people activate the reward pathway without engaging in any goal-directed behavior? One way of doing so is to take certain drugs. It appears that this pathway becomes active when certain neurotransmitter levels are elevated. Aryeh Routtenberg (1978) has demonstrated, for example, that the amphetamines facilitate self-stimulation, whereas chlorpromazine reduces self-stimulation. Note that amphetamines do not themselves activate the reward centers but rather stimulate the output of two brain chemicals, dopamine and norepinephrine, that activate the reward pathways (Stein, 1980).

Is the reward pathway activated when we engage in goal-directed behavior? There is good evidence that norepinephrine is released when people engage in a variety of coping behaviors as well as thrill-seeking behaviors. For example, work with race-car drivers indicates that norepinephrine is released in the course of competing (Taggart & Carruthers, 1971). It is also elevated in the course of parachuting (Hansen, Støa, Blix, & Ursin, 1978).

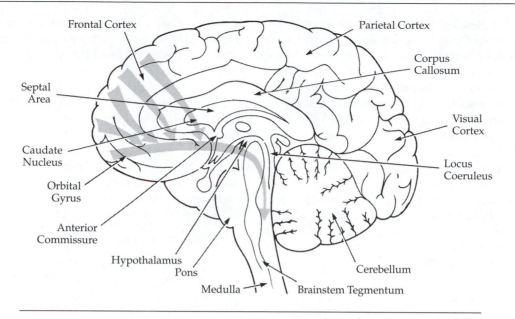

Figure 11-1. The reward system of the human brain has been roughly localized in the shaded regions. These areas correspond to the parts of the rat brain that support self-stimulation behavior (From "The Reward System of the Brain," by A. Routtenberg. *Scientific American*, November 1978, p. 160. Copyright © 1978 by Scientific American, Inc. All rights reserved.)

Cognitive Theories of Happiness

In theories of hedonism, the affect is viewed as an emotion. However, cognitive theorists argue that, in order to be called an emotion, an affect must have a core relational theme. Core relational themes result from our appraisal of our interactions with the environment. In the case of happiness, the core relational theme is defined as making reasonable progress towards the realization of a goal (Lazarus, 1991, p. 121). Thus, it is a person-environment interaction that denotes the existence of an emotion.

If the affect referred to in theories of hedonism and the affect referred to by the cognitive theorists arise out of distinct processes or systems, are they the same affect or are they different? We will assume that these are two distinct forms of affect but that they often merge, to produce a new emotion. Lazarus (1991) has noted that the simultaneous arousal of two or more core relational themes produces a new emotion that reflects

their combination. Unlike Lazarus, however, we will consider emotions that reflect the merging of sensory affect and core relational themes.

Hedonic Enjoyment and Hedonic Happiness

The idea that there are different forms of happiness was proposed by Tefler (1980), who argued that some activities are characterized only by their ability to produce hedonistic feelings (*hedonic enjoyment*), while others—called *personally expressive activities* (Waterman, 1993)—are characterized by their ability to produce both hedonic feelings and feelings of self-satisfaction that come from realizing our potential. Kraut (1979) has defined *hedonic happiness*—the outcome of these personally expressive activities—as "the belief that one is getting the important things one wants, as well as certain pleasant affects that normally go along with this belief" (p. 178).

Data collected by Waterman (1993) support the idea that activities involving self-realization are sufficient to produce happiness but that people can experience happiness without realizing their potential. As expected, Waterman found that hedonic happiness was more strongly associated with a feeling of being challenged, experiencing competence, putting forth effort, concentration, feeling assertive, and having clear goals, whereas hedonic enjoyment was more strongly associated with feeling relaxed, excited, content, happy, losing track of time, and forgetting personal problems.

As we have seen, the discovery of reward pathways in the brain, together with the demonstration that organisms are motivated to seek out sensory stimulation, has provided compelling data for the existence of hedonic enjoyment. This work suggests that we can experience positive affect without achieving a goal, overcoming obstacles, or satisfying a basic drive (such as hunger). That idea is also supported by the finding that various drugs can stimulate the release of chemicals that activate the reward pathways.

Lazarus, by contrast, assumes that positive emotions such as happiness exist to facilitate or sustain goal-directed behavior. In other words, some goal other than pleasure is involved. For the cognitive theorists, happiness (hedonic happiness) is something that you experience on the way to a goal.

Later in the chapter, we will examine why people engage in various thrill-seeking activities. While many of these activities—for example, rock climbing—are goal-directed and demand coping skills, others—for example, bungee jumping—involve no clearly defined goals and require no clearly defined set of skills. Yet, in both cases, the motivation is to get high. I am going to argue that, while they both are motivated by the same end state (to get high), they represent different means to that end. Some people have learned to make use of goals as a means of getting high (hedonic happiness), while others have learned to tap into their sensory systems in order to get high (hedonic enjoyment).

Happiness and Coping Behavior

If happiness comes from making reasonable progress towards the realization of a goal (or the realization of potential), how do we know if we are making reasonable progress? A number of researchers have suggested that coping with the demands of the immediate task provides the basis for such a judgment (e.g., Bandura, 1991; Lazarus, 1991). Note that coping does not imply that people have attained the goal, have solved the problem, or are performing without error. Rather, it means that they are dealing with it as effectively as can be expected, given their present state of competency. Implicit in many theories of coping is the idea that people believe that, by improving their competencies, they will be able to deal with their situation more effectively as time goes by. Let's look at the biological, learned, and cognitive components of coping.

The Biological Component

There is considerable evidence that, when people make a coping response, various chemical changes take place in the brain and body. For example, Joseph Brady (1967, 1975) has shown that norepinephrine is released when animals learn an avoidance response (see also Mason, 1975; Mason, Brady, & Tolson, 1966). Recall that norepinephrine plays a very primary role in determining our emotions. When concentrations of norepinephrine are high at the synapses, we tend to feel optimistic or euphoric. This accounts for the stimulant effect of cocaine, as we saw in Chapter 7. When concentrations of norepinephrine are low, conversely, we tend to feel depressed (Chapter 10).

Brady and his colleagues measured epinephrine and norepinephrine output in monkeys during a shock-avoidance task. In such a task, the monkey is presented with a signal (for example, by sounding a horn), which is followed several seconds later by a shock. The point of the task is for the monkey to learn to avoid the shock by making some adaptive response, such as pressing a lever. Being fairly intelligent animals, monkeys quickly learn what they must do to avoid the shock. The investigators measured the levels of epinephrine and norepinephrine both before and after the monkeys had learned to avoid the shock. Before learning had occurred, as the first two panels in Figure 11-2 illustrate, the levels of both catecholamines were quite low when either the horn or the shock was presented alone. After learning, however, norepinephrine levels rose quite dramatically when the horn was sounded. In other words, making a coping response triggers the release of norepinephrine.

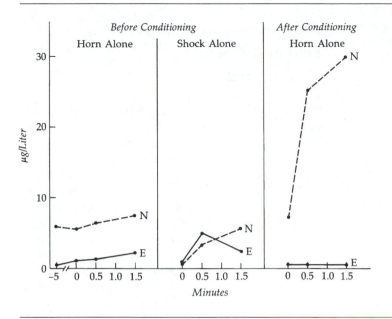

Figure 11-2. Plasma norepinephrine (N) and epinephrine (E) responses in monkeys before and after shock-avoidance conditioning. (From "Behavioral Adaptations and Endocrine Activity," by J. W. Mason, J. V. Brady, and W. W. Tolson. In R. Levine (Ed.), *Endocrines and the Central Nervous System: Proceedings of the Association for Research in Nervous and Mental Diseases*, 1966, *43*, 227–248. Copyright © 1966 by the Association of Research in Nervous and Mental Diseases. Reprinted with permission.)

The Learned Component

Evidence from a wide variety of sources indicates that, when people make a coping response, they experience a wide range of emotions. They may, for example, feel gratified, pleased, elated, euphoric, or triumphant (Lazarus, 1991). If they had to acquire a new skill in the process of exercising control, they may even experience a sense of pride or self-efficacy (a sense of being able to deal effectively with the demands of the task). In addition, when people engage in behavioral coping, norepinephrine levels typically increase.

In the case of dealing with a feared object, people often experience a sense of *relief*. This emotion has not received a great deal of attention in the research literature but is potentially important for understanding behavior (Lazarus, 1991). In Brady's studies, the level of plasma 17-OH-CS (17-hydroxycorticosteroids) declined after the monkeys had acquired an avoidance response—that is, had exercised a well-practiced coping response. Because 17-OH-CS has been associated with anxiety, the decline in 17-OH-CS suggests that the ability to make a coping response reduces anxiety (Brady, 1967, 1975). This finding, of course, is consistent with our general impression that anxiety is less-

ened when we gain control over events in our lives. Further evidence in support of Brady's position comes from the work of Jay Weiss and his colleagues (Weiss, Stone, & Harrell, 1970), who subjected rats to shock under conditions in which they could escape and avoid the shock and under conditions in which they could not. Animals that could escape showed a significant elevation in brain norepinephrine, whereas animals in the inescapable condition showed a significant decrease in brain norepinephrine. This and other studies show that norepinephrine levels are elevated when the situation is predictable and controllable.

The Cognitive Component

The work of Albert Bandura (1991) suggests that, when people develop the skills they need to cope with a given situation, they develop strong feelings of self-efficacy. Thus, when they approach a similar task, they will likely have strong feelings of self-efficacy in that new task as well. Within Bandura's theory, self-efficacy is a powerful cognitive and emotional state that determines whether people will decide to put forth energy. Moreover, when people do put forth the energy and achieve a goal, they experience self-satisfaction. Goal attainment often brings rising personal standards and increased social expectations. Therefore, in order to maintain self-satisfaction, people find they need to set higher goals for themselves.

Summary

According to the principle of hedonism, organisms are motivated to seek pleasure and avoid pain. Over the years, hedonism has been concerned with the relationship between our sensory systems and the feelings we experience. Not only do our senses produce qualitatively different feelings, but the amount of stimulation we experience is important. The discovery of reward pathways in the brain suggests that a structure in the brain produces the positive feelings that we experience in connection with a wide variety of behaviors. It has been shown that these reward pathways are activated by the release of dopamine and norepinephrine.

According to the cognitive theorists, happiness is defined as making reasonable progress towards the realization of a goal. Some activities are characterized only by their ability to produce hedonistic feelings (hedonic enjoyment), while others are characterized by their ability to produce both hedonic feelings and feelings of self-satisfaction that come from realizing our potential (hedonic happiness).

The work of Brady and his associates indicates that, when organisms make an adaptive response, norepinephrine is released. These studies suggest that we may be able to learn responses that lead to the release of norepinephrine, a chemical that has been implicated in positive feelings. Brady's work also indicates that, after learning has taken place, the release of norepinephrine is associated with a coping response. Since norepinephrine tends to produce positive affect, the reward that people experience as a result of a coping response is likely due to the release of this chemical.

According to self-efficacy theory, people develop strong feelings of self-efficacy when they make a coping response. Feelings of self-efficacy are one of the main factors that lead to action. When people have goals and strong feelings of self-efficacy, they are likely to engage in an activity and put forth effort. Goal attainment results in feelings of self-satisfaction.

Happiness from Confronting Fear and Uncertainty: Developing a Bias for Action

Often, we refrain from doing what we believe will bring us happiness because of the fear and uncertainty associated with taking action. Since fear alerts us to threats to our survival, it makes sense not to do what we fear. Uncertainty is a cognitive state in which we are unable to fully understand something or to fully know the outcome of an act. Not surprisingly, it has been found that uncertainty leads to high arousal (Berlyne, 1960), which can lead to the reorganization of attention (Chapter 5). In order to survive, we need to be fully informed about our environment. Uncertainty alerts us that we are not fully prepared to deal with our environment and typically elicits anxiety. Thus, it makes sense that uncertainty predisposes us to inaction.

In the previous chapter we noted that acts of omission and commission that pertain to moral transgressions trigger feelings of guilt and shame. Acts of omission and commission can also trigger other feelings such as embarrassment, sadness, and yearning. For example, we might experience embarrassment when we have failed to prepare for a speech (I made a fool of myself and will never be able to show myself in public again), or we might experience sadness if we failed to seize the moment and allowed a potential life partner to slip away (I wish I had answered that letter), or we might experience yearning if we failed to attend university and thus do not have the qualifications to practice medicine (I wish I could somehow help those people). Gilovich and Medvec (1995) suggest that acts of omission refer to not living up to our potential, whereas acts of commission refer to not being prepared. These feelings have collectively been referred to as feelings of regret. While acts of commission generally affect us immediately and can dominate our attention (not being prepared for a speech, for example), acts of omission tend to become important over time (not going to university, for example).

The most common regret is that of inaction (Erskine, 1973; Gilovich & Medvec, 1995). One of the common reasons people fail to take action is because they are anxious or afraid. When people do confront their fears, they are often rewarded handsomely. Once again

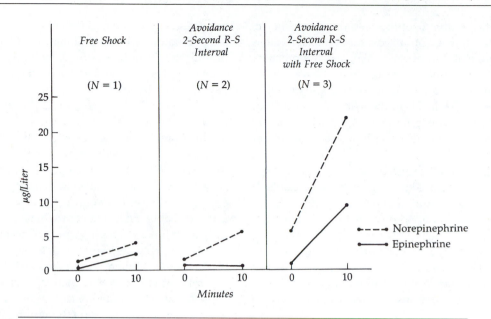

Figure 11-3.   Plasma epinephrine and norepinephrine responses to free shock alone, regular nondiscriminated avoidance, and avoidance with free shock. *N* is the number of animals in the sample. (From "Behavioral Adaptations and Endocrine Activity," by J. W. Mason, J. V. Brady, and W. W. Tolson. In R. Levine (Ed.), *Endocrines and the Central Nervous System: Proceedings of the Association for Research in Nervous and Mental Diseases,* 1966, *43,* 227–248. Copyright © 1966 by the Association of Research in Nervous and Mental Diseases. Reprinted with permission.)

let's look at the biological, learned, and cognitive aspects of taking action.

The Biological Component

What happens to the chemicals in our body when there is an element of uncertainty? To examine this question, Mason, Brady, & Tolson (1966) introduced random shocks in a shock-avoidance task, using monkeys as subjects. Introducing random shocks means introducing uncertainty. Introducing random shocks for the monkey can be viewed as analogous to introducing risk for the rock climber (increasing the chances of making a mistake). As a result of introducing uncertainty, both epinephrine and norepinephrine levels were elevated (Figure 11-3). These and other findings indicate that epinephrine may be elevated when the situation includes an uncontrollable element. Comparing Figures 11-2 and 11-3, we see that, whereas epinephrine remained fairly low in the highly predictable situation, it was relatively high in the unpredictable or uncertain situation.

After examining this and other experimental evidence, Schildkraut and Kety (1967) suggested that

> increased epinephrine excretion seems to occur in states of anxiety or in threatening situations of uncertain or unpredictable nature in which active coping may be required but has not been achieved. In contrast, norepinephrine excretion may occur in states of anger or aggression or in situations which are challenging but predictable and which allow active and appropriate behavioral responses to the challenge. Under various conditions, increase of either epinephrine or norepinephrine or of both of these catecholamines may represent specific adaptive responses. (p. 23)

Research indicates that people respond to, for instance, injections, the threat of an examination (Frankenhaeuser, Dunne, & Lundberg, 1976), and the prospect of jumping from a mock-training tower (Hansen et al., 1978) by releasing more norepinephrine and epinephrine, as measured by levels in the urine. It appears that these two chemicals are reliably released whenever we find ourselves in a situation with a certain degree of unpredictability.

To deal with unpredictability, we typically engage in behaviors that will make things more predictable. If we are faced with an imminent attack, for example, we may attempt to build defenses that will protect us. Psychologists call such acts *behavioral coping*. Note that, whenever we engage in behavioral coping, norepinephrine is released in large amounts and our mood improves. As a general rule, when we engage in behavioral coping, our emotions change from anxiety to hope.

These data have often been analyzed in terms of the theory of Schachter and Singer (1962), according to which it is important to consider two things: the emotion itself and the arousal that accompanies the emotion. When confronting uncertainty, we typically experience fear or anxiety, which has been linked to high levels of epinephrine. When we engage in behavioral coping, our emotion shifts from fear or anxiety to hope, which has been linked to high levels of norepinephrine. In other words, the shift in emotions may be viewed as linked, at least in part, to changes in the levels of epinephrine and norepinephrine. This is not to say that our cognitive interpretation is not important. Indeed, it appears that our cognitive interpretation produces the changes in the catecholamine levels. The catecholamines, however, produce the feelings.

The Learned Component

There is a great deal of evidence that people get significantly more self-satisfaction from exercising a coping response when the task is difficult than when it is easy (Bandura, 1991a; Locke & Latham, 1990). In learning terminology, the reward value of being able to control the outcome in a very demanding situation is greater than that of being able to control the outcome in a less demanding situation. Personal control over threatening events appears to be a powerful source of motiva-

tion for humans, and inability to control such events is often a source of stress (Bandura, Cioffi, Taylor, & Brouillard, 1988). It is perhaps not surprising that we experience less stress when we perceive our coping behavior to be high in effectiveness.

Note that there is generally a positive relationship between the difficulty of coping and the magnitude of the norepinephrine response (Frankenhaeuser & Johansson, 1976), perhaps because people must put forth more effort when the response is more difficult. As extensive research has shown, organisms are inclined to redouble their efforts when situations become uncontrollable. Efforts to control a situation have typically been linked to high outputs of norepinephrine, as long as the response is potentially adaptive (Chapter 9). As humans, when we get feedback that we cannot control a situation, we are inclined to redouble our efforts in order to regain control. Similarly, it can be argued that the reason for the high norepinephrine output in the shock-avoidance study is that the monkeys were attempting to gain control of a situation that was only partially controllable.

The Cognitive Component

It appears that people can reframe or reinterpret a negative situation by adopting a positive perspective (Lazarus & Launier, 1978). A rock climber, for example, may decide to focus on the self-satisfaction associated with successfully executing a climb, as opposed to the potential dangers. If individuals view a situation from a positive perspective, they typically experience a positive emotion. Such findings attest to the role of cognitions in motivation and emotion.

What remains to be determined is the amount of control that people have over their perceptions. We will return to the question shortly.

Before we move on to our next topic, we should note one last point. The research that we have just reviewed tells us that deciding to take action triggers a number of mechanisms that will reinforce our behavior. What this research doesn't tell us is why people are inclined to take action in the first place. Why should anyone struggle to overcome fear and uncertainty? Gilovich and Medvec (1995) have suggested that, as humans, unless we learn to seize the moment, we may end up at some point in our lives with a list of regrets.

We need to understand that, while making mistakes may produce momentary pain, in the long haul regrets tend to outweigh any memory of failure. In short, we need to develop a bias for action.

The Motivation for Thrill Seeking

Thrill-seeking or risk-taking behaviors have captured the attention of psychologists because they seem to represent a form of irrational behavior. It is easy to understand why people should learn to overcome fear of public speaking or fear of failure, but why should someone learn to overcome a fear that seems to serve a clear adaptive function, such as reducing the likelihood of death? It is interesting that many businesses are sending their employees to leadership programs that include thrill-seeking activities. Is there anything to be learned from such activities?

In this section, we will consider an interpretation of thrill seeking based on the interaction of biological, learned, and cognitive factors.

The Interaction of Biological, Learned, and Cognitive Variables

We know from studies of sky diving, hang gliding, mountain climbing, and other thrill-seeking activities that norepinephrine and epinephrine are commonly released in the course of such activities (Zuckerman, 1979). We also know from self-reports that risk-takers experience a psychological high when they take risks (e.g., Fenz & Epstein, 1969). These results can be understood in terms of Schachter and Singer's (1962) theory of emotions.

Most thrill-seeking activities involve the acquisition of a set of skills. Rock climbers, for example, need to acquire a number of appropriate hand and foot movements. Psychologists typically view these as behavioral coping skills. The idea is consistent with the finding that engaging in thrill-seeking behaviors triggers the release of norepinephrine, a chemical that has been linked to positive mood.

This explains why people might develop and execute a set of skills. However, it doesn't explain why people take risks to engage in these behaviors. To understand that, we should first take note that many risk

activities involve speed and/or height, which typically trigger an innate fear or anxiety response and thus give rise to a dramatic increase in arousal. According to the Schachter and Singer theory, increases in arousal can increase the intensity of an emotion. Thus, it could be argued that thrill seekers learn—perhaps through trial and error—to use fear as a means of increasing their arousal level, in order to experience a psychological high.

Thus, in this interpretation, people make use of fear or uncertainty to trigger arousal, which ultimately gives them their psychological high. Because they have good coping skills, they do not in fact experience much fear. Instead, they experience the self-satisfaction associated with exercising a highly developed coping skill in the face of uncertainty. As we have seen, this type of self-satisfaction should lead to hedonic happiness, which involves both a hedonic component and a personal expressive component.

One problem with this interpretation is the idea that, more or less at will, people can get rid of the cognitive component of fear and anxiety—the negative thoughts and feelings of apprehension. In practice, that may not be an easy task. Let's look at some means of controlling anxiety.

Self-Efficacy Theory and the Dual Route to Anxiety Control

We know that some people are more likely than others to confront their fears and anxieties. Why is that? Bandura (1989) suggests that one reason people initiate actions is because they have feelings of *self-efficacy*. According to Ozer and Bandura (1990), perceived self-efficacy is concerned with people's belief in their capabilities to mobilize the motivation, cognitive resources, and courses of action needed to exercise control over given events (p. 472). Self-efficacy determines what challenges people undertake, how much effort they will expend, how long they will persevere, and how much stress and despondency they will endure in the face of difficulties and failures (Bandura, 1991a). In terms of thrill seeking, people must ask themselves if they have the skills, the energy, and the ability to endure the fear and anxiety they will experience. A second reason people initiate a certain course of action is linked to *outcome efficacy*—that is, their beliefs about

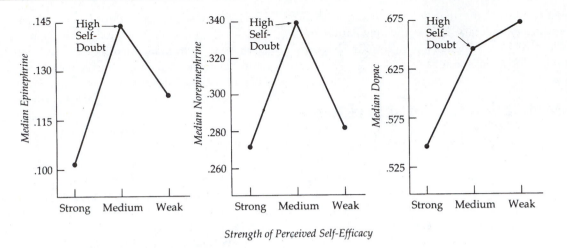

Strength of Perceived Self-Efficacy

Figure 11-4.   Median level of plasma catecholamine (epinephrine, norepinephrine, and dopamine) secretion as a function of perceived coping self-efficacy. (From "Catecholamine Secretion as a Function of Perceived Coping Self-Efficacy," by A. Bandura, C. B. Taylor, S. L. Williams, I. N. Mefford, & J. D. Barchas. *Journal of Consulting and Clinical Psychology,* 1985, *53,* 406–414. Copyright © 1985 by the American Psychological Association. Reprinted with permission.)

how satisfying it will be to achieve a certain goal. The thrill seeker might ask whether engaging in a particular risk-taking activity will produce the desired emotional outcome. According to self-efficacy theory, people carefully weigh the various elements—personal and situational—that are involved in taking action.

Bandura (1991a) has suggested that, when people avoid potentially threatening situations, it is not because they experience anxiety and arousal, but rather because they fear that they will be unable to cope, either behaviorally or cognitively. In behavioral coping, people engage in behaviors that will prevent or at least curtail the threat; while in cognitive coping, people operate under the belief that they can manage their thinking or cognitions. According to Bandura (1991a), one of the greatest sources of threat at the cognitive level is the inability to deal with perturbing thoughts that often arise in the face of fear and threat. One reason that people with agoraphobia are reluctant to leave their homes is that they are afraid they will have a panic attack in a new or strange situation. The possibility of not being in control terrifies them.

Thus, according to self-efficacy theory, whether we choose to engage in a particular activity depends on

whether we perceive that we have behavioral coping skills and that we can control our thinking. Evidence for this idea comes from a variety of sources but is perhaps best illustrated by a study of women who were fearful of being assaulted (Ozer & Bandura, 1990). In the study, women were taught how to fend off potential attackers (mastery training). The women were asked to indicate to what degree they felt their feelings of self-efficacy had changed as a result of the training. The results indicated that this training led women to perceive that they could better cope behaviorally with an assault, and that they were less fearful of going to places that previously aroused a great deal of anxiety. In short, they felt less constricted and less threatened as they went about their daily activities.

Note that there is a strong link between feelings of self-efficacy and catecholamines such as norepinephrine and epinephrine (Figure 11-4). When feelings of self-efficacy are strong, catecholamines are typically at a low level. As self-doubt begins to increase (at moderate levels of self-efficacy), the level of these two catecholamines increases markedly. When people refuse to participate in a potentially threatening activity (when self-efficacy is weak), the level of these two cate-

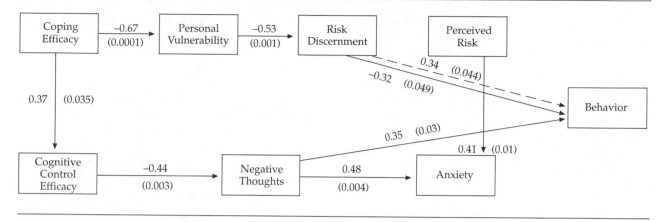

Figure 11-5. Path analysis of causal structures at the follow-up stage (after mastery training). The numbers on the paths are significant standardized path coefficients; the numbers in parentheses are the significance levels. The solid line to behavior represents avoidant behavior; the dashed line represents participant behavior. Path coefficients in the model that fell below the 0.10 significance level are not shown. (From "Mechanisms Governing Empowerment Effects: A Self-efficacy Approach," by E. M. Ozer and A. Bandura, *Journal of Personality and Social Psychology*, 1990, *58*, 472–486. Copyright © 1990 by the American Psychological Association. Reprinted by permission of the author.)

cholamines goes down (Bandura, Taylor, Williams, Mefford, & Barchas, 1985). It is important to note that Figure 11-4 reflects cognitive coping, as opposed to behavioral coping. Typically, behavioral coping leads to an increase in norepinephrine (Figure 11-3). Thus, as self-doubt increases, there are marked changes in catecholamine levels, which, as we know, are closely linked to feelings.

In order to identify the causal structure underlying the tendency to participate in various activities (approach motivation), even though there might be a potential threat to their safety (avoidant motivation), Ozer and Bandura (1990) undertook a path analysis of their results. The results of this path analysis for women who have received mastery training—that is, training to help them deal with a potential assault— are shown in Figure 11-5. Let's look at the top pathway. Following mastery training (called coping efficacy in Figure 11-5), the women felt less vulnerable and were better able to discern if a particular situation was risky. Because they felt less vulnerable and were better at discerning risk, the tendency to approach (get involved in activities) increased, and the tendency to avoid (not get involved) decreased. Note that some-

times people do not get involved in activities because of apathy, for example, and not simply because they are afraid. For this reason, Ozer and Bandura took separate measures to determine the degree to which people are likely to get involved (approach behavior) or not (avoidant behavior).

The lower pathway of Figure 11-5 links mastery training (coping efficacy) with increased cognitive control efficacy. Ozer and Bandura measured cognitive control efficacy by asking women to indicate how easy or difficult it was for them to turn off thoughts about sexual assault. It makes sense that mastery training would lead to increased cognitive control efficacy. If the women felt they could fend off an attack, there would be less reason to worry. Following the lower pathway, we see that, when cognitive control efficacy was high, negative thoughts were low and, when negative thoughts were low, the tendency to avoid was also low. A long line of research shows that negative thoughts tend to be closely linked to avoidant behaviors (Bandura, 1991). Note that in the path analysis, negative thoughts, not anxiety, caused women to avoid becoming engaged in activities. While the women did experience anxiety, that anxiety was the result of two things:

negative thought and perceived risk. The finding that anxiety did not by itself inhibit action is consistent with other research that shows that while anxiety often makes us apprehensive, it is often not the primary reason that we fail to act (Barlow, 1988). Remember that anxiety is a complex emotion that has both an arousal and cognitive component. What anxiety causes us to do is to be cautious—to stop, look, and listen before proceeding. What this model shows is that in order for us to gain control over our actions, as well as our anxiety, we need to gain control over our negative thoughts. One thing that can help us gain control over our negative thoughts is to become competent, what Ozer and Bandura refer to in their model as having or developing coping efficacy.

Self-Efficacy Theory and Thrill Seeking

Making Use of Arousal

The self-efficacy model provides a good framework for understanding thrill-seeking behavior.

We have already considered the possibility that thrill seekers attempt to use the arousal component of fear and anxiety to increase the intensity of their emotions. However, in order to do so, according to Ozer and Bandura's model (Figure 11-5), they would need to be able to discern risk and also to control their negative thoughts, since both of these factors lead to avoidant motivation. The self-efficacy model suggests that they can attain both of those goals by acquiring the skills necessary for the particular activity. In short, people come to control their fears and anxiety through mastery training.

I once told a student of mine, an avid hang glider, that, according to a newspaper article I'd read, hang gliding is, on a per capita basis, the sport most likely to result in death. He replied, "It's only dangerous if you are not careful." He went on to point out that he was skilled and had the best equipment that money can buy; for him, there was no risk. Previously, he had indicated to me that he loved to hang glide because it made him feel fully aware and fully conscious. This anecdote illustrates that fear is closely linked to our perceptions of our skills.

In many ways, the essence of being happy is to be highly aroused without being afraid. One reason that people take amphetamine, an arousal-producing drug, is that it produces a state of relaxed awareness—that is, an arousal high without feelings of anxiety.

Why are people attracted to bungee jumping, which doesn't involve a complex set of skills? It can be argued that what keeps people from bungee jumping is their negative thoughts. Should they be able to control those thoughts—and to feel reasonably confident in the equipment—they would be in a position to enjoy effects of high arousal without anxiety.

Increasing the Level of Risk

One of the characteristics of thrill-seeking behaviors is that people are inclined to increase the level of risk as their skills improve. This makes sense. A situation must include some uncertainty in order to elicit fear and anxiety, without which arousal would remain relatively low. Thus, in order to get the increased arousal, it is necessary to increase the level of risk. What this means is that thrill seekers appear to be constantly endangering their lives. From the thrill seekers' perspective, the level of risk may not be that high. Thrill seekers know there is some risk but accept that a certain level of risk is necessary in order to be happy (Rowland, Franken, & Harrison, 1986).

Some Concluding Remarks

The perspective adopted in this section integrates various approaches. Our starting point is that people take risks in order to trigger a variety of chemical reactions. In other words, people engage in certain behaviors with no apparent adaptive function for the sake of hedonic enjoyment. However, goals are also important. Setting and achieving goals gives rise to feelings of self-efficacy and self-satisfaction and also plays a role in triggering the release of certain chemicals. A shortcoming of cognitive interpretations is that they fail to recognize that we are biological creatures and that our feelings are linked to the release of chemicals in our brain. However, the hedonistic interpretation fails to address how we deal with our perturbing thoughts, which so often prevent us from doing things. Learning

There is a large sport industry devoted to helping people get high by taking risks under careful supervision.

interpretations, by contrast, fail to adequately acknowledge the importance of chemicals released in the brain and the role of cognitions in determining behavior.

Both research findings and anecdotal reports are consistent with the interpretation offered here. Note, however, that the large individual differences with respect to thrill seeking have not been considered. We'll take up that topic in the next chapter.

Does encouraging executives—or anybody, for that matter—to take risks help them to perform better at work? Despite the many claims by promoters of such trainings, that question has not been adequately tested. A valid study would include control groups who are taught the same things but not in a thrill-seeking context. Certainly, people can learn something in thrill-seeking tasks. But what do they learn? If the desire is to make people less fearful and anxious and thus better decision makers, perhaps a better route, as least according to Ozer and Bandura, would be to focus on mastery training. Through mastery training, people come to discern risk and reduce negative thoughts.

Summary

Research indicates that the most common regret is the regret of not taking action when the opportunity presented itself. One of the main reasons for inaction is the fear and uncertainty associated with taking action. Research has shown that, when we are confronted with uncertainty, epinephrine levels typically rise. Epinephrine has been linked not only to arousal but to anxiety and stress. Whether people experience anxiety and stress seems to be linked to whether they have developed a coping response that will enable them to deal with the aversive stimulus. The fact that people can reframe a negative situation in positive terms has important implications for understanding why some people are more likely to confront fear and uncertainty than are others.

Thrill-seeking behaviors can be understood as an interaction of biological, learned, and cognitive variables. According to Schachter and Singer's theory of emotions, one reason people may put themselves into situations that elicit fear is to intensify the positive emotion that results from successful coping. The main problem with this interpretation is that it ignores the complexity of emotions such as fear and anxiety; they have both an arousal component—which appears to be neutral as far as approach and avoidant behaviors are concerned—and a cognitive component—such as personal vulnerability, risk, and negative thoughts—which has been linked to avoidant behaviors. Research by Ozer and Bandura suggests that people can come to manage many of the cognitive aspects of anxiety. As a consequence, it may be possible for people to experience the high arousal that often comes with fear and uncertainty, without the accompanying negative motivation. This interpretation overcomes some of the major problems associated with wholly biological or wholly cognitive approaches.

Optimism and Hope

Introduction

When people see desired outcomes as attainable, they are inclined to continue to exert efforts to attain those outcomes; however, when they see outcomes as unattainable, whether it is due to something they lack or to external constraints, people reduce their efforts and eventually give up (Scheier & Carver, 1988). In other words, outcome expectancies play an important role in determining whether people are inclined to continue or give up.

Optimists and hopeful people tend to view all desired outcomes as attainable, even in the midst of failures and setbacks. They tend to persist, and even put forth more effort, when things are presently going against them. Some people have suggested that they tend to be very unrealistic (e.g., Alloy & Abramson, 1979) or that they live in an illusionary world (e.g., Taylor, 1986) because they fail to accept that things are not going well. They refuse to acknowledge that the best predictor of the future is how things are going right now. Why can't these people accept that and get on with their lives?

The paradox, of course, is that people who refuse to give up often end up accomplishing great things. Even though the idea of a light bulb was not new when Edison began his work, it took him and a staff of scientists nearly three years before they found the combination of features that would make the light bulb a viable commercial product.

When things are going well, there is not a great deal of difference between optimists and pessimists—hopeful and hopeless people. However, when things start to go badly, pessimistic and hopeless people tend to give up, whereas optimists and hopeful people tend to persist. In this section, we will examine why some people refuse to give up.

Note that giving up is not all that bad. Being too hopeful is both a blessing and a curse. As Tillich (1965) said, "Hope is easy for the foolish, but hard for the wise. Everybody can lose himself in foolish hope, but genuine hope is something rare and great" (p. 17).

Definitions

Conceptualizations of optimism and hope include definitions in terms of biological variables; learning approaches, adopted by Seligman and others, in which optimism is regarded as the result of a particular explanatory style; and more cognitive approaches (e.g., Synder et al., 1991), in which optimism is defined in terms of the self-concept that people have.

For a working definition of optimism, we will adopt that offered by Scheier and Carver (1985): Optimism is a generalized expectancy that good, as opposed to bad, outcomes will generally occur when confronted with problems across important life domains. Using their Life Orientation Scale (LOT), Scheier and Carver (1985) have been able to demonstrate a positive relationship between optimism, health, and recovery from surgery (Scheier et al., 1989).

We will discuss definitions of hope in more detail after we have reviewed some of the work on optimism. In general, optimism denotes a positive attitude or disposition that good things will happen, regardless of our ability, whereas hope is associated with goal-directed behavior. The concept of hope implies that we can find the path to our goal, often by using our skills or ability or perhaps by persisting (e.g., Snyder et al., 1991).

Optimism and Pessimism

Are optimism and pessimism two ends of the same continuum? If they were, then there would be little reason to have separate measures of these two constructs. Recent research indicates that they are not (Marshall, Wortman, Kusulas, Hervig, & Vickers, 1992). Pessimism seems to be principally associated with neuroticism and negative affect, whereas optimism is principally linked with extraversion and positive affect. Among other things, this seems to indicate that, while optimists tend to be open to new experiences or new stimulation, pessimists tend to be more withdrawn and inhibited in their interactions with the world.

The Biological Component

Lionel Tiger (1979) offers an evolutionary perspective on optimism. He argues that, when our ancestors left the forest and became plains animals, they were faced with the task of obtaining food by killing other animals. In the course of hunting, they doubtless experienced many adverse circumstances; many of them must have suffered a variety of injuries. Learning principles tell us that humans tend to abandon tasks that are associated with negative consequences. So why did hunters carry on in the face of such adverse conditions? Tiger argues that it was biologically adaptive for our ancestors to develop a sense of optimism. Optimism would carry them through adverse circumstances, even injury.

By what mechanisms did optimism develop? Tiger suggests that one of the mechanisms involved the endorphins. When we are injured, our bodies typically release endorphins. Endorphins have at least two important qualities (Chapter 7): They have analgesic properties (the ability to reduce pain); and they produce feelings of euphoria. Tiger contends that it was adaptive for our hunting ancestors to experience a positive emotion when they were injured, because that would reinforce their tendency to hunt in the future. It would have been disastrous, he argues, if our ancestors had abandoned the tendency to hunt.

Tiger emphasizes the utility of a sense of optimism. When things go wrong, it is important not to give up. He points out that optimism is not only a positive emotion but an active one as well. It makes us turn to our environment for the resources that we need. Such an attitude, he argues, was very important

for our ancestors' survival, especially in the face of hardships and setbacks.

The Learned Component

Optimism as an Acquired Thinking Style

A number of researchers are beginning to conceptualize thinking styles as habits. This has proven a very powerful way to conceptualize the behavior of optimists and hopeful people. If optimism and hope are merely ways that people have learned to think about the world and do not reflect deep underlying personality attributes, it should be relatively easy to change such thinking styles. Indeed, this is the premise on which Seligman's thinking program is based.

As we saw in Chapter 10, Seligman (1990) has taken the approach that optimism grows out of people's explanatory style. Optimists regard setbacks, failures, and adversity as temporary, as specific to a given situation, and as due to external causes. Similarly, hope involves an explanatory style in which problems are regarded as temporary and specific to a given situation. Thus, within Seligman's system, optimism is a more inclusive concept; it contains three elements, whereas hope contains only two. As we'll see later, other theorists view hope as the more global of these two concepts.

Evidence for Seligman's Theory

There is considerable support for Seligman's theory in the research literature. Let's review a few examples that illustrate the diverse areas in which the theory is applicable.

Success at sales. Selling life insurance is a very tough job, because salespeople are faced with repeated rejections. Typically, after a period of time, many salespeople quit. Over the years, insurance companies have developed a variety of tests to assess the suitability of applicants, because it is very expensive to train new salespeople. To determine whether measures of optimism might be good predictors of sales success, Seligman compared his test of optimism with the Career Profile tests developed by Metropolitan Life to select their sales staff. The salespeople in the control group (the regular group) were hired using the Career Profile. The salespeople in the special force group, as they were called, were hired using two criteria: they had to have high optimism scores (in the top half), and they had to have failed the Career Profile.

The salespeople in the regular group were also given Seligman's Attribution Style Questionnaire (ASQ),

Practical Application 11-1

How to Become an Optimist: The ABCDE Method

There is considerable evidence that people who are inclined towards depression—that is, who use an explanatory style characterized by permanence, pervasiveness, and personalization—can learn to change to a more optimistic style. The ABCDE method is designed to help people think more accurately when they are faced with adversity. This method, developed by Seligman (in conjunction with Dr. Steven Hollon of Vanderbilt University and Dr. Arthur Freeman of University of Medicine and Dentistry of New Jersey), is based on the ideas and work of Albert Ellis, an early pioneer in cognitive therapy.

To understand this method, we'll break it down into two parts: ABC and DE. Let's start with ABC.

Step 1: Identifying Adversity, Belief, and Consequences (ABC)

As we've seen, what differentiates optimists from pessimists is how they deal with adversity. The reason optimists are more successful is that they do not fall apart, as pessimists do, when they encounter adversity. Instead of giving up, they tend to persist. Thus, the focus of this method is to help people better deal with adversity by analyzing the accompanying inner dialogue.

Humans tend to engage in a perpetual dialogue that is often just below our level of awareness. Ellis, Beck, Seligman, and others have discovered that, by asking the right questions, we can become fully aware of our inner dialogues. They start by pointing out that it is common for people to encounter setbacks, failures, obstacles, and frustrations, which fall under the general heading of *adversity* (A). Next they point out that adversities tend to trigger interpretations or explanations that fall under the general heading of *belief* (B). Finally, our interpretations give rise to feelings, which fall under the heading of *consequences* (C). Let's look at some examples of adversity and the accompanying thinking process.

Example 1: Jeff

Jeff left his small hometown to attend a large university in the city. He missed his old friends and was feeling lonely as he began his studies. He suggested to Chris, a student he met in one of his classes, that they might go hiking on the weekend, and Chris seemed genuinely interested. They agreed to go on Saturday. When he stopped by to pick up Chris on Saturday morning, Chris's roommate told him that Chris had decided to go home for the weekend. As Jeff walked down the sidewalk towards his Jeep, he said to himself: "It's going to be a very lonely year for me. I'm never going to make any friends. I should never have decided to come to this university. I come from a small town and people probably think I'm a hick. Maybe I should pack my bags and go home." When Jeff was asked to analyze this adversity into the three components, he offered the following.

Adversity: "I want to develop some friendships but I haven't been able to do so."

Belief: "I lack the ability to make friends."

Consequence (feeling): "I am feeling more lonely than ever."

If we look carefully at his inner dialogue, we see that it contains all the elements typical of a pessimist. The failure has led to an explanatory style that is permanent (I can't make friends), pervasive (I will never make friends), and personal (I lack the ability to make friends).

Example 2: Mary

Mary was one of the top students in her high school and had no difficulty being admitted to a top university. She which measures optimism and pessimism, so that it would be possible to look at the role of optimism independently of the Career Profile. At the end of the first year, the optimists in the regular force outsold the pessimists by only 8%. At the end of the second year, however, the optimists had outsold the pessimists by 31%.

What about the special force group? They outsold the pessimists in the regular force by 21% in the first

expected to get As at university, as she had in the past but, when she got her first essay back, it was only a B+. As she returned to her room, she found herself thinking: "I really blew this one. I thought I was bright, but maybe I have been fooling myself. Now I'm in the big leagues, and that's what counts. Probably the reason I got the grades I did in high school was because I was one of those polite kind of people who teachers reward for being nice. With those grades I will never be able to get into Med school. I probably shouldn't even be here. All these people are much smarter than I am. Maybe I should quit at the end of this year."

When Mary was asked to analyze her adversity into the three components, she offered the following.

Adversity: "I want to go into medicine but I don't think I will be able to get into Med School."

Belief: "I am not as smart as I thought I was."

Consequence: "I feel awful and wish I could drop out of the university."

If we look carefully at her inner dialogue, we see that it too contains all the elements typical of a pessimist. The failure leads to an explanatory style that is permanent (I can't get the grades I think I need), pervasive (I will never get those grades), and personal (I lack the ability to get good grades).

Keeping a Record of Adversities

If you want to determine if you are prone to pessimistic thinking and might like to change your thinking style, you should collect at least five examples of adversity over a period of a few days. There are many possibilities: for example, someone not returning your phone call; someone not returning something you loaned them; discovering that you lost your parking stall because your check was misplaced; discovering that someone dented your car and did not leave a note or contact you; getting a

poor mark on a test; not being able to get a course that you need to graduate; finding your bicycle has been stolen; discovering that the dry cleaner damaged your favorite coat; or finding that your bank made a mistake and, as a result, one of your checks bounced.

Once you have collected your examples, write down your interpretation or explanation (beliefs), followed by your feelings (consequences). Analyze these examples to see if they reflect a pessimistic thinking style. You may discover that your style is not completely pessimistic but has elements of pessimism. Most people respond inconsistently—sometimes with pessimism, sometimes with optimism.

Step 2: Distraction and Disputation (D) and Energization (E)

Jeff's and Mary's stories are not that unusual. Having friends and doing well in college are important to people. As a result, they often respond dramatically to adversities when these domains of their lives are threatened.

Seligman identifies two ways of dealing with pessimistic thinking: *distraction* and *disputation* (D). If we don't distract ourselves or dispute our thinking, we are inclined to ruminate. As we saw in Chapter 10, one of the worst things that people can do is to allow themselves to ruminate about adversity.

Distraction means that you try to think of something else or simply get involved in something else. Some time ago, Ellis suggested that people should simply say "No" or "Stop" when they do not want to think about something. This has proven to be a fairly effective way of eliminating unwanted thoughts. You should feel free to say "No" or "Stop" out loud or to write these words in bold letters on a card and put it

(continued on next page)

year and 57% in the second year. They even outsold the average of the regular force over the two years by 27%. As a result of this study, Metropolitan Life began to use optimism scores as their main hiring criteria (Seligman, 1990; Seligman & Schulman, 1986).

Academic success. Although academic intelligence is a reasonably good predictor of success in school, educators have argued for some time that intelligence scores by themselves fail to account for the wide range of achievement that teachers observe daily. Clearly, many

Practical Application 11-1 (continued)

in front of yourself. After you have practiced saying "No" or "Stop," you will find that you can indeed stop some of this negative thinking.

Disputation involves learning how to argue with yourself. You need to ask yourself four questions.

1. What evidence do I have for my interpretation? When Jeff was asked what evidence he had that he couldn't make friends, he could only cite this one example. It was the same for Mary. This was a one-shot deal.
2. What alternative interpretations are there? As it turned out, the reason Chris was not there when Jeff arrived was that he left in a hurry, because his mother was ill. Chris's roommate failed to pass that information along, because he assumed that Jeff already knew that Chris's mother had been ill. Mary found out that the best mark for that particular paper was a B+. It was standard practice for this particular professor to give low grades on the first paper to chasten new students. Before you jump to a conclusion, you should investigate other possible explanations for what has happened.
3. What are the implications for me if I take this position? Even if my belief is correct, what does it mean? Is it really that important? When Jeff was asked to think about the implications, he began to realize that life was not over just yet. So what if Chris is irresponsible? Surely there were plenty of people at the college like those he knew in his hometown. When Mary was asked to consider the implications of her adversity, she too decided things weren't as bad as they initially looked. She knew she had worked as hard as she could have. Further, she had often thought that pursuing a career in arts would be far more exciting than medicine, even if she would likely be poor.

4. How useful is my belief? Life is not always fair, nor does it always work out as we plan. It would be nice if life worked out just as we had planned. But how realistic is that? Besides, much of the excitement in life comes from the unexpected.

Jeff began to realize as the year progressed that people were more competitive at the university than at his high school. They were also less tolerant of, or less interested in, some of his more rural ways of having fun. But others found him fresh and sincere. One person said "Jeff's a genuine article." The friends he developed turned out to be far more interesting and diverse than he had anticipated. Chris, he discovered, was a nice person but lacked imagination.

Mary learned that good grades were tougher to get than she had thought. "Everybody is smart here," she concluded. She began to discover that, by using her social skills, she could get the help and guidance she needed to rise to the top. By the end of the year, she was close to being a straight-A student. Because she asked so many questions, she was offered a summer job as a research assistant by one of her professors, who told her, "I like you because you aren't afraid to ask tough questions."

Energization (E)

Energization involves summarizing your thoughts and actions and planning where you will go next. It is important to gain some degree of closure, so that you can put this event behind you and move ahead. This will help to prevent further rumination and set the stage for further adaptive actions. You might like to view energization as an internal pep talk in which you are your own coach.

Let's return to Jeff and Mary and look at their finished ABCDE records after their first adversity. Their disputation is particularly important, because that is where their educators have argued, motivation plays a critical role. Those children who persist get the top marks. More recently, educators have observed that one reason performance in the classroom dives is because children get depressed.

In a study to examine their reactions to failure, two groups of schoolchildren with different explanatory styles—helpless children (pessimists) and mastery-oriented children—were given solvable and unsolvable problems. Before failure was introduced,

thinking changes. (Their use of the four questions is noted in the disputation sections.)

Jeff's ABCDE Record

Adversity: "I want to develop some friendships but I haven't been able to do so."

Belief: "I lack the ability to make friends."

Consequence (feeling): "I am feeling more lonely than ever."

Disputation: "I was disappointed when I found out that Chris had gone home and was upset that he hadn't called me [evidence]. He probably didn't realize how important it was for me [alternative]. The fact that he didn't call was inconsiderate of him, but there may be some explanation [alternative]. I really shouldn't let one event get me so upset [usefulness]. It's not as though this is the last person in the world [implications]. I think I have a pretty good record for making friends [implications]."

Energization: "There will undoubtedly be more opportunities for making friends this coming week. Who knows, I might be able to meet someone tonight if I go to the local coffee house or possibly the bar. I hate going by myself but maybe it's time to put aside my pride and admit that I'm lonely. I can't be the only person at this university who is feeling lonely tonight. Surely there is nothing wrong in admitting that you are lonely."

Mary's ABCDE Record

Adversity: "I want to go into medicine but I don't think I will be able to get into Med School."

Belief: "I am not as smart as I thought I was."

Consequence: "I feel awful and wish I could drop out."

Disputation: "It was a real shock for me to receive a B+ because I always did very well on papers in high school

[evidence]. I guess I thought that I could put forth the same effort I did in high school and get the same grades [implication]. I wonder if I really understood the assignment [alternative]. Perhaps the professor was looking for something different [alternative]. If worse comes to worse, I can pursue one of my other strengths [alternative/usefulness]. I really should stick it out a little longer before I decide I don't have the ability [implication]. I may be working myself into a snit over nothing [usefulness]."

Energization: "The first thing I must do is make an appointment with my professor, so I can get his honest appraisal. I've heard for years that it is much tougher to get As at the university than in high school. I know I can put forth more effort if that is what's required. I've always been good at asking questions, so now it is time to make use of those skills."

Catastrophizing and Decatastrophizing

These two examples illustrate how people often jump to conclusions or *catastrophize*. When we catastrophize, we see the worst-case scenario. Disputation serves, among other things, to *decatastrophize*. This is important because it allows us to think about other alternatives and eventually to think about positive ways of producing the results we want. The world is not always as we would like it to be. However, armed with a sense of openness and a willingness to learn, we can often succeed in ways that we had not expected or planned.

For a more detailed discussion of how to become an optimist, read Martin E. P. Seligman's (1990) book *Learned Optimism*.

the two groups showed no difference in their problem-solving skills. After failure, however, the problem-solving skills of the pessimistic children deteriorated to the first-grade level. When the mastery-oriented students failed, their problem-solving skills stayed at the fourth-grade level (Dweck & Licht, 1990).

In a longitudinal study to examine the role of optimism and pessimism on depression and intellectual achievement, it was found that there were two major risk factors for poor achievement: pessimism and bad life events (parents separating, family deaths, family job loss). Not only are these factors predictors of poor achievement, but they are predictors of depression in children (Seligman, 1990).

To assess whether optimism plays any role in success at a university, first-year students were given the ASQ. Since they had already submitted their Scholastic Aptitude Test (SAT) scores as part of the admission procedure, it was possible, at the end of the first semester, when the grades were submitted, to determine if optimism played any role in their performance. The results showed that students who did better than their SAT scores would predict were optimists. It appears that being optimists prepared them to deal with this new environment and the challenges it presented.

Optimism and Health

Numerous studies have shown that optimistic people are healthier than pessimistic people. For example, Peterson (1988) monitored the health of 150 students for a year. He found that, as compared to optimists, pessimists had twice as many infectious illnesses and made twice as many visits to their doctors. There is also evidence that optimists survive cancer longer than do pessimists (Seligman, 1990).

Over the years, the idea that an explanatory style can influence the progression of a disease such as cancer has provoked considerable skepticism. The assumption in our society has been that disease progression is independent of mental processes. If anything, a disease should undermine our mood, rather than the reverse.

To determine if a disease such as cancer can be affected by psychological states, Visintainer (1982) decided to produce helplessness in rats using the helplessness training procedure that Seligman had used with his dogs (see Chapter 11). The main difference in

her study was that she used rats that had been implanted with a few cells of sarcoma under each flank the day before she began her helplessness procedure. The tumor she selected was one that invariably leads to death if it grows and is not rejected by the animal's immune system.

At the end of a month, 50% of the rats not given helplessness training (not shocked) had died, while the other 50% had rejected the tumors. She had determined ahead of the experiment just how much of the cancer cells needed to be implanted to produce a 50% death rate. Of the rats given mastery training, 70% rejected the tumor compared to only 27% of those given helplessness training. What Visintainer showed conclusively in this well-controlled study is that helplessness training reduced the ability of the body to reject the cancer cells (Visintainer, Volpicelli, & Seligman, 1982). This finding is consistent with the idea that helplessness training produces a reduction in the immune response.

Preliminary results indicate that it is indeed possible to increase the immune activity of cancer patients using cognitive therapy (see Seligman, 1990). If these preliminary results can be replicated in other studies, the implications for health care delivery in humans may be dramatically altered.

The Cognitive Component

Although Seligman's theory is written in terms of thinking and cognition, we have discussed his ideas in the context of the learned component of optimism, because he believes that the individual's explanatory style is learned and becomes a habit with continued practice and, most importantly, that it is possible to learn a new explanatory style. In this section, we will look at the work of Snyder and his colleagues, who suggest that optimism contains a proactive component—planning.

Snyder's Definition of Hope

Snyder and his colleagues define hope in terms of two major elements (Snyder et al., 1991). First, they argue that hope is fueled by the perception of *agency* related to goals. That is, people have a sense that they can attain future goals—perhaps by means of good goal-setting procedures or perhaps through new learning—

because they were able to attain goals in the past using those means. This very generalized belief—a belief in oneself—may be summarized by the saying, "Where there's a will, there's a way." Second, they argue that hope is based on the perception that *pathways* to attain those goals are available. More specifically, people who are characterized by hope believe that they can generate those paths. They may believe in their own creativity, for example. (We will consider a motivational interpretation of creativity in Chapter 12.)

Snyder and his colleagues regard the relationship between agency and pathways as reciprocal. Hopeful people believe, on the one hand, that they can attain goals (agency) and, on the other, that they can generate the alternatives (pathways) needed to achieve those goals. In their theory, these two elements are interdependent.

They contrast their theory with that of Scheier and Carver (1985), who argue that outcome expectancies are the best predictors of behavior. According to Scheier and Carver, optimism is a generalized expectancy that good outcomes will generally occur across important life domains. Snyder argues that putting all the emphasis on outcomes fails to adequately account for behavior.

Empirical Support for Snyder's Model

Hope and negative feedback. According to Snyder's model, hope sustains people in the presence of a stressor, such as an obstacle to a goal. Yoshinobu (1989) conducted a study to test this prediction. Study participants were divided into groups characterized by high, medium, and low hope. Each group was divided into negative-feedback and no-feedback conditions. Those in the negative-feedback condition were asked to imagine the following scenario:

> Although you have set your goal of getting a B, when your first examination score—worth 30% of your final grade—is returned, you have received a D. It is now one week after you have learned about the D grade.

They were then asked to respond to five agency questions on a seven-point scale:

1. How much effort are you exerting to reach your goal (no effort to extreme effort)?

2. When you think about this goal, do you feel energized (not at all to extremely)?
3. How confident are you of reaching your goal (not at all to extremely)?
4. How important is receiving this grade goal to you (not at all to extremely)?
5. What is the probability of reaching this goal (0% to 100%)?

Subjects were also asked five pathways questions, which involved listing potential strategies for reaching the grade goal of B.

With respect to the agency measure, the results showed that, unlike the high-hope individuals, medium- and, especially, low-hope individuals reported less agency in the negative feedback condition than in the no-feedback condition. With respect to the pathways measure, the high-hope individuals reported more pathways than medium-hope individuals, who, in turn, reported more pathways than the low-hope individuals. To summarize, when confronted with a setback or an obstacle, high-hope individuals exhibited sustained agency and pathway behaviors, whereas low-hope individuals showed decreased agency and pathway behaviors.

Hope and number of goals. Snyder's model also predicts that people with enhanced goal agency and a sense of pathways to goals would pursue a greater number of goals in their lives. A study of people in their 20s, 30s, and 40s found that indeed people who are high in hope tend to have more goals (Langelle, 1989).

Hope and preferred difficulty of goals. Snyder's model also predicts that, because high-hope people have a stronger sense of agency and pathways, they should set more difficult goals. Two studies (Harris, 1988; Sigmon & Snyder, 1990) have provided clear evidence that high-hope people are more inclined to select difficult tasks. Scheier and Carver's LOT scale was not as good a predictor. This is consistent with the idea that goal-directed behavior is mediated by the interaction of agency and pathways.

Hope and goal attainment. Do high-hope people actually meet the more difficult goals they set for themselves? The results of a study in which students were asked to set a realistic goal for their final grade indicated that: (1) as compared to low-hope students, high-hope students said they would get higher grades; (2) they were more successful at attaining those higher grades even when early feedback suggested they might not; and (3) they actually did obtain the higher grades they set for themselves (Anderson, 1988).

Optimism and Competence

In Chapter 13, we will see that, as the cognitive theorists have argued, optimism must be accompanied by feelings of competency if individuals are to achieve their goals. Scheier and Carver (1985) have demonstrated the importance of seeing the world as positive. In the previous chapter, we saw that, when people see the world as threatening, they are inclined to become fearful and anxious. This interferes with their goal setting. As Scheier and Carver have shown, we are inclined to persist when we view the world in positive terms.

As we'll see in Chapter 13, when we view the world as positive and also view ourselves as competent, we have reason to be hopeful. Optimism is not enough; we need a sense of hope. That can only come from developing our competencies.

Summary

Scheier and Carver define optimism as a generalized expectancy that good outcomes will generally occur across important life domains. According to Tiger, optimism not only provides the motivation for acting (engaging in adaptive behavior) but rewards behaviors that have an adaptive function. According to the learning theorists, optimism can be viewed as an acquired thinking style. Seligman has suggested that optimists view (explain) setbacks, failures, and adversity, as temporary, specific to a given situation, and due to external causes. Evidence for Seligman's theory is extensive. Among other things, the theory has been successful in predicting the success of life insurance salespeople, academic success, and health. Together with Hollon and Freeman, Seligman has developed the ABCDE program, which is designed to change pessimistic thinking styles into more optimistic thinking styles. This program trains people to dispute their negative thinking by asking four questions: (1) What evidence

do I have for my interpretation? (2) What alternative interpretations are there? (3) What are the implications if I take this position? (4) How useful is my belief?

Cognitive theorists such as Snyder and his colleagues have argued that hope involves both a sense of agency and a sense of pathways. They have offered a series of convincing studies to show that, indeed, there is a reciprocal relationship between a sense of agency and a sense of pathways. They have shown that their measure of hope, which taps into both agency and pathways, predicts behavior in response to negative feedback, the number of goals that people set for themselves, the difficulty of the goals that they select for themselves, and the attainment of goals.

Belongingness, Attachment, and Community

Various writers have argued that the need to belong or the desire for interpersonal attachment is a fundamental human motivation (e.g., Maslow, 1970; Baumeister & Leary, 1995). It has been suggested that this need is characterized by the desire for frequent, nonaversive interactions within a relational bond (Baumeister & Leary, 1995). In recent years, some theorists have begun to speak of being attached and even of community; they argue that humans need to be part of a social support system to which they can reach out for help in times of difficulty. In some respects, community has come to replace the concept of family. When people lived close to their family, the family would help in times of difficulty. Now, as people move away to seek better jobs or a better climate, they look for support from a community, which may be a church, friends, neighbors, or some other organization (e.g., Peck, 1988).

There is considerable evidence that people with good social support systems are less prone to depression and tend to be healthier (Sarason, Pierce, & Sarason, 1990). It can be argued that the low depression rate among the Amish, for example, is due to the existence of a highly developed community, while the high depression rate in urban societies is due to the lack of community.

Community has also been linked to self-worth. Self-worth plays an important role not only in our health but in our achievement strivings. Having a

Feelings of attachment and belongingness typically give rise to happiness, self-confidence, and good health.

sense of worth seems to come largely from the effects of our efforts on the lives of other people. Mother Teresa, for example, has a strong sense of self-worth, which seems to come largely from her efforts to benefit others. Many retired people get a strong sense of self-worth through volunteering to help others. It has even been shown, as we saw in Chapter 9, that people who live with a pet tend to be healthy and to experience a strong sense of self-worth.

In this section, we will review some of the results relating to belonging, attachment, and community. As usual, we'll consider the biological, learned, and cognitive factors.

The Biological Component

Research on Belongingness and Attachment

The need to belong, to be attached, and to be loved appears to be as fundamental as the need to eat. People who do not experience a sense of belonging or being loved often fail to develop normally. Some time ago, Bettelheim (1950) described how children raised in orphanages without the opportunity for love or attachment would simply die, even though all their physical

needs had been met. Subsequently, researchers documented that children who have been cut off from one of their parents as the result of a divorce perceive the divorce as much more traumatic than children who continue to have free access to both parents (Rosen, 1979). A recent study found that students' sense of belonging to their university was correlated ($r = 0.65$) with their involvement in university activities. This indicates that daily interactions are important (Hoyle & Crawford, 1996). Such findings suggest that the need to belong is innate. From an evolutionary perspective, Barchas (1986) argued that "over the course of evolution, the small group became the basic survival strategy developed by the human species" (p. 212). Some research indicates that the tendency to form social bonds and the emotional effects of social loss (such as sadness or grief) are mediated by opioid peptides (endorphins and related peptides) (Panksepp, Siviy, & Normansell, 1985). It appears that, when social bonds are formed, they stimulate opioid production. When bonds are broken, opioid production is impeded. In other words, "social affect and social bonding are in some fundamental neurochemical sense opioid addictions" (Panksepp et al., 1985, p. 25).

One of the first theorists to make the case that belonging is a basic innate need was Abraham Maslow (1970), who suggested that needs are organized in a hierarchical fashion. Let's examine Maslow's theory of needs.

Maslow's Need-Fulfillment Model

Abraham Maslow (1970) posits that humans are born with a set of needs that not only energize but direct behavior. He argues that these needs are organized in a hierarchical fashion, and needs lowest in the hierarchy must be satisfied first. These needs dominate the person's attention until they are satisfied. When these basic needs have been satisfied, the next set of needs in the hierarchy comes to dominate the person's attention. And so the process continues. Eventually, if all the basic needs have been satisfied, the person will reach the top of the hierarchy. Thus, Maslow's need hierarchy is a pyramid in which the emergence of higher, more sophisticated needs rests on the base provided by the fulfillment of lower needs such as hunger and thirst. Let's begin at the bottom of the hierarchy.

Physiological needs. Humans must satisfy a number of basic physiological needs. For example, they must eat, drink, control their temperature, and ingest certain nutrients in order to live and function normally. Since failure to remedy an imbalance in any of these areas would disrupt normal functioning and eventually result in death, it is critical for the individual to attend to such states of imbalance at once. From an evolutionary viewpoint, therefore, it makes good sense that a person should become preoccupied with such need states. That humans do become preoccupied with such physiological need states has been well documented. For example, in Chapter 5, we discussed research in which men on semistarvation diets spent much of their waking and sleeping time thinking about food; they showed little interest even in such basic motives as sex (Keys et al., 1950).

Safety needs. Maslow says that, once these basic physiological needs have been satisfied, the person comes to focus on safety needs. While safety needs are important, in that failure to meet them could result in harm or even death, they are clearly secondary to our physiological needs: If safety needs took precedence, we might not venture forth to find the food and water necessary to our survival. For many animals, the satisfaction of physiological needs entails risks, such as venturing into unknown territory in pursuit of food or traveling to the watering hole.

For humans, safety comes from knowing our environment and making it as orderly, predictable, and lawful as possible. In such an environment, we can then pursue our other needs without constant fear for our safety. Children, Maslow argues, have a strong need for things to be orderly and predictable within their environment; within such an environment, they can explore and learn.

Neurotic people are in many ways like the fearful child. They are typically anxious, always afraid that something dreadful will happen to them. Consequently, they are preoccupied with making the world safe. Maslow argues that they adopt a strategy of using rigid and often stereotyped behaviors to assure themselves that the world is orderly and predictable and therefore safe. Because of their preoccupation with safety, they cannot respond to the new developments in their world. In psychoanalytic language, they are fixated at the level of satisfying safety needs.

Belongingness and love needs. When both the physiological and safety needs are fairly well gratified, Maslow says, needs for love, affection, and belonging will emerge. Although there is little scientific information about these needs, they are a common theme in books, poems, songs, and plays. In school or at work, we see how humans gather into groups at coffee breaks or at lunchtime. When people have been isolated for some time, they often have a strong need to engage in some type of social exchange. The family unit seems to be held together, in large part, by a need to belong. After a divorce, for example, all members of the family seem to suffer stress. Bouts of loneliness and depression are common not only for the spouses but for the children as well. Finally, Maslow theorizes that the tendency to join organizations is often motivated by the desire to belong.

Although our need to belong is not as fundamental as our safety and physiological needs, its strength cannot be doubted. People will risk their lives for those they love and even for complete strangers. People will give money or work hard to preserve organizations—such as universities, churches, and social clubs—that have provided them with help, support, or a sense of community. Attempts to maintain family relationships have characterized humans from the beginning of history. We find meaning in life in our relationships to other people.

Esteem needs. All people need to have a good opinion of themselves. Maslow distinguishes between two sets of esteem needs: (1) desires for strength, achievement, adequacy, mastery, and competence; and (2) the needs for reputation and prestige, status, fame, glory, dominance, recognition, attention, importance, dignity, or appreciation. Satisfaction of the esteem needs, Maslow argues, leads to feelings of self-confidence, worth, strength, and capacity, as well as the feeling of being useful. Failure to satisfy the esteem needs leads to feelings of inferiority, weakness, and helplessness.

Need for self-actualization. Even if all these needs have been satisfied, Maslow says, we will still experience discontent and restlessness. Each of us, he argues, is a unique person with unique skills and abilities. To be truly happy, we must do that for which we are uniquely suited. The artist must paint; the musician must make music. Although we may not all be artists, each of us can be creative in our own way. Therefore, Maslow contends, each of us must search for our uniqueness, so that what we may experience satisfaction in doing what we as individuals are specially equipped to do.

We will return to the need for self-actualization in Chapter 14.

The Learned Component

Belonging to a group helps to promote and sustain a number of important behaviors, including health and exploration. Many theorists argue, therefore, that people need to learn to develop friendships and to establish communities, in order to gain the most happiness they can from their lives. In this section, we will review two lines of research that show the importance of belonging and community. In Practical Application 11-2, we look at the links between belonging and the immune response.

Social Support Systems and Health

When things are going well, social support systems don't seem to be that important. However, in the face of adversity, people who have a strong social support system—family or community—tend to recover more quickly than those who do not (Cohen & McKay, 1984, Taylor, 1990).

Social support involves emotional support, informational support, tangible assistance, and appraisal support (feedback on the accuracy of our evaluations of the environment). It has been argued that different types of support are needed in different situations. Tightly knit communities, such as the Amish community, embody a comprehensive network system in which different people within the community provide different types of support when they are needed.

McClelland (1989) has found that affiliative trust (a willingness to cooperate with others), together with a sense of agency, is linked to a strong immune response and good health. This is consistent with a growing body of evidence that people with good social support systems tend to be healthier.

Providing social support to another person will not necessarily reduce stress in that person. Social support has been found not only to interact with various personality attributes but with constitutional difference. For example, it has been shown that the support of a spouse is more important than a friend (Schuster, Kessler, & Aseltine, 1990). It has also been shown that the stress-buffering effects of perceived support is higher in people with an internal locus of control (Lefcourt, Martin, & Saleh, 1984). Finally, it has been shown, using twins, that genetics plays a key role. It has been found, for example, that genetics can explain between 28% and 52% of the variance on certain support measures (Kessler, Kendler, Heath, Neale, & Eaves, 1992). One of the important conclusions that we can draw from this research is that social support is more in the eye of the beholder than the provider. That is, people who are open to receiving social support can benefit greatly from it; however, those who close themselves off, for whatever reason, are the losers. It is interesting to note in this context that women who have good social support from their husbands benefit most from social support (House, Landis, & Umberson, 1988).

Attachment Theory

Attachment theory suggests that the degree of security and confidence that we feel determines our willingness to explore, learn, and take on new challenges; when we develop secure attachments (mainly with our mother), we see the world as less threatening and hostile and, as a result, we are less vulnerable to adversity (Ainsworth, Blehar, Waters, & Wall, 1978; Bowlby, 1969, 1973, 1980).

Some adherents of attachment theory have suggested that we need someone to believe in us if we are to believe in ourselves—that our self-confidence depends not only on our accomplishments, but also on some form of external (social) validation.

Attachment theory emphasizes the role of parents in the development of traits such as self-confidence.

Practical Application 11-2

Belongingness and the Immune Response

Humans react to adversity by releasing several powerful neurohormones, including catecholamines, corticosteroids, and endorphins. These chemicals in turn alter the immune function. Corticosteroids exert a powerful immunosuppressive effect. In order to counteract this effect, steroids are often used—especially in connection with allergic reactions like asthma and hay fever and autoimmune disorders like rheumatoid arthritis and also to suppress the rejection of transplanted organs. Endorphins also have an immunosuppressive effect. In one study, it was shown that delivering brief electrical shocks to rats to trigger endorphin release reduced their tumor fighting ability. In another study, it was shown that exposure to uncontrollable shock suppressed the ability of the T-cells to multiply when they were later stimulated to do so (Maier, Laudenslager, & Ryan, 1985). How are the catecholamines involved? It appears that, when the catecholamines get depleted, endorphins are released. This means that, when people get depressed and their catecholamine levels go down, endorphin activity goes up, which in turn shuts down the immune system (Angell, 1985). This research suggests that anything leading to a reduction in the catecholamines, such as drugs, could make us susceptible to disease.

Several studies have linked the onset and course of virus infections to stress-altered immune function. The recurrence of oral herpes has been linked to increased stressful life events, daily hassles, and anxiety. It has also been shown that loneliness and midlife stress can trigger decreased immune cell activity (Ornstein & Sobel, 1987; O'Leary, 1990).

There is growing evidence that people can learn to improve their immune function and thereby prevent disease. It has been shown, for example that relaxation training can improve immune function. There is even some evidence that hypnosis together with imagery may help to increase immune function (Taylor, 1990).

Some of the most striking evidence, however, links immune function to belonging and community. There is considerable data which show that stressful life events, especially the death of a spouse, result in an impaired immune response and sometimes death. People who have good social support systems when they experience a stressful life event, however, often show fairly rapid recovery. Ornstein and Sobel (1987) note that the immune system shuts down when people perceive they are no longer a useful part of a social system, but that

> conversely, a solid and stable connection to a larger social group, or to humanity in general, may have the opposite result: improved resistance because the person is probably more valuable as a member of a group. From our speculative viewpoint this may be one reason why almost all societies have developed conventions emphasizing the same virtues and why there is such an emphasis in most religions upon caring for others, being generous to others and serving them. Perhaps one of the many reasons is that doing so is not only helpful to the entire community but also to the health of the donor. (p. 52)

Many of us who have been raised in a society that promotes individualism characterized by self-reliance need to become more aware of the value of belonging, not only for our psychological health but for our physical health.

However, it acknowledges that other attachments later in life can provide the basis for feelings of security. For example, in later childhood we may form a strong attachment to a teacher, or perhaps a coach, and develop a sense of security from that attachment. Mentors often provide security for individuals who are venturing out into the world. In times of difficulty, the mentor provides the emotional and informational support that they need to carry on.

The Cognitive Component

An extensive body of research shows that our beliefs, our attitudes, and our values play an important role in determining our physical and psychological health. In this section, we will briefly consider two lines of research that have helped to shape how we think about belongingness, attachment, and community.

Health and the Commitment to Family and Values

Suzanne Kobasa has identified and studied a personality type characterized by good health and resistance to stress—the *hardy personality*. It appears that the health benefits of this personality type are associated with the way hardy people appraise their interactions with the environment. Hardy people not only see the world as less threatening but see themselves as more capable of dealing with stressful events.

As we saw earlier, people with a hardy personality are characterized by control, commitment, and challenge (Kobasa, 1979a,b, 1982). When people refer to Kobasa's work, they often fail to emphasize that her definition of commitment encompasses commitment not only to self and work but also to family and values. We know that the family is often a source of social support that buffers stress (Taylor, 1990). Values provide people with a sense of belonging and community. They are at the heart of feeling part of something larger than ourselves, something with meaning and purpose.

Many health psychologists are beginning to recognize the importance of an environment in which people can experience a sense of community (e.g., Kaplan, 1990; Stokols, 1992a). While such psychologists acknowledge that an individual's attitude (for instance, being positive and optimistic) plays an important role in promoting good health, they also emphasize the role of community in creating a climate for health. In particular, they emphasize the importance of environments with strong *social cohesion* (Stokols, 1992).

Mindfulness and Health

Ellen Langer (1989) has done a great deal of work on health, especially health in older people. She has shown that, when people become more mindful, their psychological and physical health improves. Becoming mindful means becoming actively involved in making plans and making decisions. It means creating new distinctions, in order to think more clearly about what is happening. It means breaking out of old ways of thinking (stereotypes and traditions) and developing new ways of thinking (generating new alternatives). It means being open to new information and new experiences. It means becoming more aware of what we need to do in order to become happy and hopeful.

Many older people live their lives mindlessly. They do things out of habit, rather than considering what alternatives might exist. It is important for older people to be aware of what makes them happy and what they can do to make their lives more interesting and challenging. I know a woman in her 90s who is very mindful. Her philosophy is to savor every moment of life. She asks herself what she can do to make each day special. It may be going for a walk, talking with friends, reading a new book, savoring a poem, or writing a letter. Often she spends several days planning how to make a special day happen. It may be making plans to have a group of people over for tea or coffee; reading a book that she plans to discuss at her reading club; setting aside some time to attend her painting class; or calling to volunteer for a luncheon at her church. She does not wait for things to happen; she makes them happen.

A study of nursing home residents by Langer and Rodin (1976) bears directly on the relationship of mindfulness and health. Staff in nursing homes tend to make virtually all the decisions for the residents. They assume responsibility for routine tasks such as watering plants and cleaning rooms, and they tell the residents where to entertain their family and friends and what movies to watch. It occurred to Langer and Rodin that this would be an ideal place to study what happens when people are forced to become more mindful and responsible. They divided a population of residents into two groups: those in the experimental group were given responsibility for routine activities, while those in the control group remained subject to the decisions of the staff. An evaluation 18 months later found that residents forced to make decisions were more active, vigorous, and sociable. Moreover, the health of the experimental group improved, while the health of the control group worsened. The death rate of the experimental group was also half that of the control group. Clearly, making the residents more mindful had a powerful effect on their well-being.

Summary

Various researchers have argued the need to belong or the desire for interpersonal attachment is a fundamental human motivation. Evolutionary theorists have suggested that the tendency to establish and maintain small groups has survival value. According to one line of research, opioids produced by the body, such as endorphins, mediate the need for attachment. In Maslow's theory, the need to belong and to be loved is in the middle of a hierarchy of needs—above physiological and safety needs and below esteem and self-actualization needs.

There is substantial evidence that people with strong social support systems—from family or community—tend to get sick less often and recover more rapidly than people without such a support system. Social support involves emotional support, informational support, tangible assistance, and appraisal support. McClelland has found that affiliative trust, together with a sense of agency, is linked to a strong immune response and good health. Social support has been shown to interact with not only personality variables as locus of control but with constitutional differences.

Attachment research suggests that the degree of security and confidence that people feel determines their willingness to explore, learn, and take on new challenges. When we develop secure attachments (mainly with our mother), we see the world as less threatening and hostile and, as a result, we are less vulnerable to adversity. Attachment theory emphasizes the role of parents in the development of traits such as

self-confidence but acknowledges that other attachments later in life can also provide the basis for feelings of security. The theory suggests that people are particularly important to us in times of adversity.

Research has indicated that our beliefs, our attitudes, and our values play an important role in determining our physical and psychological health. Kobasa has emphasized the importance of commitment to work, to the self, and also to family and values. Health psychologists are beginning to recognize the importance of creating an environment in which people can experience a sense of community. Ellen Langer's work on health underlines the importance of becoming more mindful.

Main Points

1. Goal-congruent emotions facilitate and sustain the attainment of personal goals.
2. According to the principles of hedonism, organisms are motivated to seek pleasure and avoid pain. Hedonists define happiness as the maximization of pleasure.
3. With the discovery of reward pathways in the brain, many theorists felt that the concept of hedonism had a sound scientific basis.
4. Reward pathways are activated by the release of norepinephrine and (probably) dopamine.
5. Cognitive theorists argue that emotions are characterized by a core relational theme that results from our appraisal of our interactions with the world.
6. Lazarus suggests that the core relational theme of happiness is making reasonable progress towards the realization of a goal.
7. While cognitive theorists view happiness as a means to an end (goal), hedonists conceptualize happiness as an end (goal).
8. Some activities are characterized only by their ability to produce hedonistic feelings (hedonic enjoyment), while others are characterized by their ability to produce both hedonic feelings and feelings of self-satisfaction associated with realizing our potential (hedonic happiness).
9. Research indicates that norepinephrine is released when organisms make coping responses and that

making coping responses typically leads to a reduction in stress and anxiety.

10. When people develop the skills they need to cope with a given situation, they develop strong feelings of self-efficacy for that and similar tasks—that is, a sense that they can effectively deal with such tasks.

11. One cause of inaction is the fear and uncertainty associated with taking action.

12. Research indicates that both norepinephrine and epinephrine are released in a situation characterized by unpredictability or uncertainty.

13. Evidence suggests that people experience more self-satisfaction from making a coping response in a difficult task than in an easy task.

14. It has been shown that people can learn to reframe a negative situation in positive terms. When they do so, their emotions abruptly shift from negative to positive.

15. One reason that thrill seekers take risks may be to experience the arousal that comes from the fear and uncertainty associated with high-risk activities.

16. Bandura has argued that people do not avoid potentially threatening situations because they experience anxiety and arousal but rather because they fear they will not be able to cope either behaviorally or cognitively.

17. Our choices of activities depend, in part, on whether we perceive that we have behavioral coping skills and that we can control our thinking.

18. Ozer and Bandura have suggested that there is a dual route to the control of anxiety. Their research suggests that the main route to anxiety control comes from developing skills (mastery training).

19. Optimists and hopeful people tend to view all desired outcomes as potentially attainable.

20. Whereas pessimists and hopeless people tend to give up in the face of adversity, optimists and hopeful people tend to persist.

21. Tiger has argued that optimism not only provides the motivation to act but rewards adaptive behaviors. He has suggested that endorphins are the chemical basis of optimism, from which hope develops.

22. A number of researchers conceptualize thinking styles as habits that can be changed.

23. Seligman has taken the approach that optimism grows out of people's explanatory style. Optimists view (explain) setbacks, failures, and adversity as temporary, specific to a given situation, and due to external causes.

24. Within Seligman's system, hope involves an explanatory style in which factors that are temporary and specific to a given situation are emphasized.

25. Optimism is one of the best predictors of success for life insurance salespeople.

26. Two major risk factors for poor achievement are pessimism and bad life events (such as parental separation, family deaths, and family job loss).

27. One study showed that students who got better grades than expected on the basis of their SAT scores were optimists.

28. Helplessness training can impair the immune response.

29. Seligman has proposed the ABCDE method as a means of becoming an optimist. This method involves first identifying adversities, beliefs, and consequences. Next, people must learn to distract themselves and dispute their thinking and then to act, which will result in energization.

30. Snyder and his associates have defined hope as based on two reciprocal elements: a sense of agency and a sense of pathways.

31. Support for this theory comes from research findings that high-hope people sustained both agency and a sense of pathways when confronted with a setback or an obstacle, that high-hope people had more goals, that high-hope people set more difficult goals for themselves, and that high-hope people tended to actually meet the more difficult goals they set for themselves.

32. Various theorists have argued that the need to belong or the desire for attachment is a fundamental human motivation.

33. There is considerable evidence that people who have good social support systems are less prone to depression and tend to be healthier than people without such social support system.

34. Humans respond to adversity by releasing several powerful neurohormones, including catecholamines, corticosteroids, and endorphins, which have been linked to the immunosuppressive effect.

35. The need to belong and be loved is one of five groups of needs in Maslow's hierarchical model.

36. People who have a strong social support system—from family or community—tend to recover more quickly than those who do not.

37. Social support involves emotional support, informational support, tangible assistance, and appraisal support.

38. Attachment theory suggests that, when we develop secure attachments (mainly with our mother), we see the world as less threatening and hostile and, as a result, we are less vulnerable to adversity.

39. Many health psychologists have recognized the importance of creating an environment in which people can experience a sense of community or social cohesion.

Chapter Twelve

Curiosity, Exploratory Behavior, Sensation Seeking, and Creativity

- *What motivates people to explore a new city?*
- *Is this exploratory behavior learned or unlearned?*
- *Why do people believe that exploratory behavior is motivated by the curiosity drive?*
- *What activates the curiosity drive?*
- *What is sensation seeking?*
- *Is the trait of sensation seeking learned or acquired, or is it something we are born with?*

- *What motivates people to be creative?*
- *Why is it that people sometimes feel creative and at other times they do not?*
- *Do people have to be inspired in order to be creative or can people be creative at will?*
- *Are younger people more creative than older people?*

Prior to 1950, it was generally believed that much of what we learn results from being taught—that is, that learning is extrinsically motivated, rather than intrinsically motivated. In the 1950s, a group of researchers challenged that idea with a series of well-designed studies that clearly showed that much of what we learn and master is not only intrinsically motivated but has its roots in curiosity and exploratory behavior.

Those early studies provided, in many ways, the impetus for two lines of research. The first is work on sensation seeking. Sensation seekers are characterized not only by a strong curiosity drive but by a willingness to take risks to satisfy that curiosity drive. What makes sensation seekers so interesting is that they come to develop a distinct personality.

The second line of research that grew out of the early work on curiosity and exploratory behaviors was the study of competency. In order to become successful and happy, humans need to become competent in a variety of domains. Becoming competent, it turns out, involves taking the talents that we have and developing them to their fullest. To do that, people need to be free of anxiety and to develop mental attitudes that will support the development of competency. Because competency is so important, we will devote the next chapter to various facets of competency, including predictability and control, achievement mastery, and self-esteem.

In the last part of this chapter, we look at the motivation for creativity. Creative performance involves the generation of novel ideas and behaviors that meet a standard of quality or utility. Creative people, it turns out, not only need to have a base of knowledge (competency) but also need personality attributes that will allow them to generate novel ideas and behaviors. The creative process, in many ways, represents the coming together of competency with qualities that are possessed by the sensation seeker.

Exploratory Behavior

Children like to explore their environment. Young children might take the pots and pans out of the kitchen cupboard or rummage through a book of old photos that they found in a box in the basement. They might disassemble a watch and find that they can't put it back together.

As children grow up, they begin to explore other areas, such as the neighborhood in which they live. They develop friendships and learn to play games. All of this exploratory behavior seems to occur without very much encouragement from their parents. In fact, parents often try to discourage children from their interest in the contents of closets and cupboards and from wandering too far from home. What motivates children's behavior? We often say that such behaviors grow out of a strong curiosity drive.

Initially, psychologists conceptualized curiosity and exploratory behaviors as learned behaviors. However, learning could not account for certain important research findings. Let's look at some of those findings.

The Behaviorist Explanation

How do we come to learn about our environment? Before the 1950s, the behaviorists argued that primary drives, such as hunger, energized the organism to engage in random behavior. When the organism encountered the appropriate goal object in the course of such random movements, the drive would be reduced. As a result, the preceding behavior would be reinforced. Through learning, the organism would then become increasingly more efficient at finding the appropriate goal object when a given drive state had been activated.

Note that exploratory behavior was assumed to be random in the first instance. It became systematic only as a result of learning (reinforcement). Accordingly, a different pattern of exploratory behavior should occur for each drive state. When you are hungry, you engage in one pattern of responses; when you are thirsty, you engage in another pattern of responses; when you are sexually motivated, you engage in still another pattern of responses. In other words, according to the behaviorists, there was no such thing as a generalized curiosity drive. You did not learn for learning's sake; you learned only in order to help you satisfy a more basic (biological) motive system.

Challenges to Behaviorism

Alternation Behavior

In the 1950s, many studies challenged the behaviorists' explanation of exploratory behavior. One group of studies involved *alternation behavior.* If you place a rat

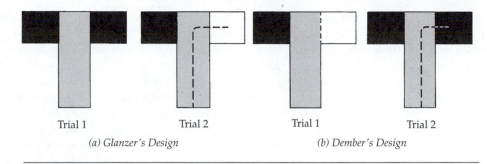

Trial 1   Trial 2   Trial 1   Trial 2

(a) Glanzer's Design   *(b) Dember's Design*

Figure 12-1.   (a) Glanzer's design to test his stimulus satiation hypothesis; (b) Dember's design to test his stimulus change hypothesis.

in a T-maze and allow it to select one arm of the maze, the probability of its selecting either arm is 50%. If you then remove the animal and immediately give it a second choice, you find that it tends to select the other arm of the maze. This has been referred to as alternation behavior.

A series of explanations have been proposed for alternation behavior.

The reactive inhibition model. Clark Hull, a behaviorist, attributed alternation behavior to reactive inhibition. Hull (1943) argued that, when organisms make a response, some kind of inhibition to that response builds up. For a time—until the inhibition wears off—the animal will be unlikely to repeat that response. Thus, if an animal made a right-turn response on trial 1, it would not be inclined to make that same response on trial 2. In a T-maze, with only two possible options, it would tend to make a left-turn response.

The stimulus satiation model. An alternative model suggested that, on trial 1, the animal became satiated for the stimulus to which it had just been exposed (Glanzer, 1953). Satiation is like inhibition, except that the inhibition is not limited to responses. You could become satiated visually or auditorially or olfactorily. When we're talking about humans, we tend to use the word *bored*. Murray Glanzer demonstrated that if the rat made, say, a right-turn response in trail 1 and then you changed the color of the walls in the right arm of the maze, the animal tended to repeat a right-turn response, as Figure 12-1a indicates. (The dashed line shows where the animal went on trial 2.)

The stimulus change model. Were the animals in Glanzer's experiment avoiding a stimulus for which they had become satiated or were they simply approaching a new stimulus? Dember and Earl (1957) suggested that animals are motivated by change or by novel stimulation. In order to determine whether this was the case, Dember (1956) designed an ingenious experiment. He made one of the arms of a T-maze white and the other black, and at the entry to each arm he put a glass panel that prevented the animal from entering. As it could turn neither right nor left, it could not develop reactive inhibition. As the animal saw one white arm and one black arm, it would be satiated equally for black and white at the termination of trial 1. As we shall see, this was an important manipulation. After 10 minutes in the maze, the animal was removed, the glass panels were removed, and one of the arms was changed so that both arms were now either black or white. On trial 2, Dember watched to see if the animal entered the changed arm or if its behavior was random. According to the reactive inhibition model, since the animal made no response on trial 1, the probability of entering one of the arms on trial 2 should be 50%. According to the satiation model, since the animal was equally satiated to black and white, the probability of entering one of the two arms should also be 50%. According to the stimulus change model, on the other hand, the animal should enter the changed arm. Dember found, as he had predicted, that his animals entered the changed arm (Figure 12-1b).

These studies, together with others that we will discuss shortly, changed forever the way that psychologists thought about curiosity and exploratory behaviors. Because the animals used in these studies were deprived of neither food nor water, their exploratory behavior had occurred without the activation of some more basic primary drive. The general conclusion, therefore, was that these animals explored because it is their nature to do so. In other words, a curiosity drive motivates organisms to investigate novel things in their environment.

Other Studies of the Curiosity Drive

Many studies have been conducted to investigate the curiosity drive. In a number of studies at the University of Wisconsin, Robert Butler and Harry Harlow showed that monkeys have a very strong exploratory drive that is motivated by the visual, auditory, and manipulatory properties of the objects they encounter. Harlow (1953) showed, for example, that monkeys will learn to solve various kinds of mechanical puzzles when no motivation is provided other than the presence of the puzzles. Moreover, the monkeys had a persistent tendency to carry out the solution in a flawless manner. Butler (1953) put monkeys in a room with four windows that they could open to see a toy train, various other objects, or other monkeys. These monkeys spent a great deal of time simply looking at things. The monkeys learned which window provided which kind of stimulation. Thus, Butler demonstrated that the curiosity drive could reinforce learning. This finding is not surprising now but represented, at that time, an important challenge to the behaviorists' view of the curiosity drive as weak, transient, and insignificant in the overall functioning of the individual.

Variety, Novelty, and Complexity

Children like to seek out new and varied stimulation. Presented with an object they have not previously encountered, for example, children in a familiar and secure environment will tend to approach the object, visually inspect it, and then begin to interact with it, by touching it, holding it, picking it up, tapping it, turning it over, and so on. The children will almost certainly discover any parts that can be moved or removed. Once they have thoroughly investigated the object, their interactions with it will begin to wane.

Corinne Hutt (1966) gave children a novel object in which a lever was connected to a set of counters and

the numbers on the counters changed as the lever was moved. In one condition, the children could see the counters move; in another, the counters were covered. As expected, when the counters were visible, the children spent more time pressing the lever. Also as expected, their interest in the counters diminished with repeated trials.

When a person stops interacting with a novel object, we say that he or she has become satiated. This implies that the person has had enough, that the object is no longer a source of motivation, and that the person has exhausted all the information or entertainment value of the object. Since children often return to objects previously abandoned, it appears that satiation dissipates with time. This finding needs to be explained by a theory of curiosity and exploratory behaviors. When children abandon an object, it is usually because they have shifted their interest and attention to other objects—usually objects that are new or that have not been encountered for a while. Thus, children have a natural tendency to interact constantly with more and more of the environment.

The Preference for Complexity

If animals are given a choice between two novel stimuli, one of which is more complex, they will choose the more complex stimulus (Earl, Franken, & May, 1967). Humans also show a preference for complexity. Robert Earl (1957) had children work on block-design puzzles of moderate complexity and then gave them the opportunity to select a new block-design puzzle. The children could choose either more complex or simpler designs. Most selected a design that was somewhat more complex than the design they had just been working on. They did not, for the most part, select either a design that was simpler or a design that was much more complex. This tendency to select a slightly more complex puzzle indicates that human exploratory behavior is highly systematic. Humans, it appears, do not explore their environment haphazardly.

Earl's findings have been duplicated by Richard May (1963), who had preschool children look at checkerboard designs of moderate complexity and then gave them the opportunity to look at a pile of simpler or more complex checkerboard designs. Like Earl, May found that most of the children selected the more complex designs.

The Effect of Anxiety

Many researchers who attempted to replicate the alternation phenomenon could not do so. It soon became apparent that, when animals are anxious or emotional, they will not approach a novel stimulus. Instead, they choose the familiar stimulus. In order to replicate the alternation phenomenon, the experimenter had to tame the animals and to familiarize them with the T-maze. It has repeatedly been shown that such taming not only reduces emotionality but produces increases in exploratory behavior (Denenberg, 1967).

Now that we have surveyed some of the earlier studies on curiosity and exploratory behavior, let's analyze this topic within our customary framework—in terms of the biological, learned, and cognitive components.

The Biological Component

Some time ago it was found that children vary in their tendency to approach novelty (Thomas, Chess, & Birch, 1970). Children with a relatively stable temperament are more receptive to new situations. Children who are less receptive to new experiences will eventually respond to these experiences, explore, and adapt to new situations, once they have become secure in their environment. There is a clear parallel here to the anxious person who becomes less anxious or the highly aroused person who becomes less aroused.

As we saw in Chapter 5, Kagan and Snidman (1991) have been doing research on timidity for over a decade. They have found that, while some children are inclined to approach unfamiliar (novel) people and objects, other are not. They have made a distinction between what they call inhibited and uninhibited children. Their research indicates that these two temperaments are inherited.

Extraversion has also been linked to the tendency to select variety, novelty, and complexity. Since it has been repeatedly shown that extraversion is inherited, at least to some degree, these results are consistent with the idea that preference for variety has a biological basis.

Research from these and other sources suggests that the tendency to explore must be viewed within a hierarchical motive system. It appears that the motive to explore is only fully aroused when fear and anxiety are at some minimal level (White, 1959). It has been suggested that, when anxiety and arousal are high, attention is focused on survival cues. Only when survival needs have been met do other motives become activated and only then does attention shift elsewhere.

Note that virtually all of the temperamental dispositions that have been linked to reduced curiosity and exploratory behavior in humans are characterized by higher than normal levels of anxiety and/or arousal. Thus, it can be argued that anxiety is probably responsible for the reduced tendency to explore.

The Learned Component

Age and Preference for Complexity

There is considerable evidence that experience plays a central role in the tendency to respond to variety, novelty, and complexity. In the literature on novelty and complexity, experience is typically described in information-processing terms. According to this model, organisms become familiar with something by processing information. Information processing is assumed to be more or less directly linked to attention. As we attend more closely to something, we process more of the information in that stimulus. The information-processing model, such as that proposed by Piaget (1970), also assumes that we tend to develop more highly differentiated or complex cognitive structures as the result of processing information. In other words, as we grow older, we are able to process more complex cognitive stimuli. If humans are motivated to process new information, it follows that older individuals will prefer more complex stimuli. To test this hypothesis, various experiments have used geometrical figures—such as those in Figure 12-2—that vary in complexity, as defined by the number of angles and sides. In these studies, people are asked what they prefer. In general, it is found that older people tend to prefer stimuli of greater complexity (Munsinger & Kessen, 1964; Thomas, 1966).

Experience and Preference for Complexity

According to the information-processing hypothesis, if individuals are repeatedly exposed to a stimulus, they will lose interest in it, because they will exhaust all the information that it contains. To test this hypothesis,

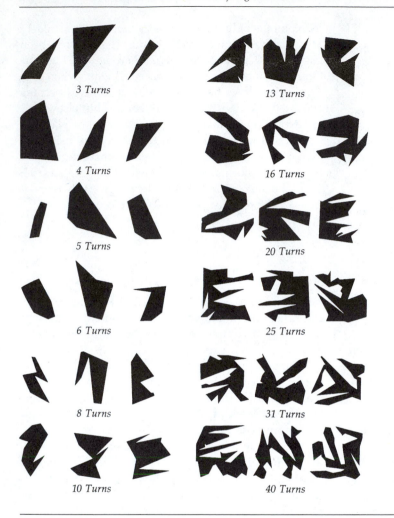

3 Turns

4 Turns

5 Turns

6 Turns

8 Turns

10 Turns

13 Turns

16 Turns

20 Turns

25 Turns

31 Turns

40 Turns

Figure 12-2.   Twelve sets of three asymmetrical shapes used in experiments to assess individual preferences for complex stimuli. (From by "Uncertainty, Structure, and Preference," by H. Munsinger and W. Kessen. *Psychological Monographs*, 1964, *78*, 1–23. Copyright © 1964 by the American Psychological Association. Reprinted with permission.)

Smith and Dorfman (1975) divided their study participants into three groups, who were to be exposed to low, medium, and high levels of complexity. The individuals in each of these complexity groups were further divided into four subgroups, which were shown a stimulus, respectively, 1, 5, 10, and 20 times. According to the information-processing hypothesis, it would take very little time to extract all the new information contained in a stimulus of low complexity, and therefore individuals would quickly lose interest in such a stimulus with repeated exposures. Since stimuli of medium complexity might require individuals to develop new cognitive structures, such stimuli might not be preferred initially but would come to be preferred

once the individuals had developed the cognitive structures necessary to process them. Having developed such structures, however, the individuals would then lose interest in those stimuli, just as they had lost interest in stimuli of low complexity. Since it would take even longer for individuals to develop the cognitive structures necessary to process the information contained in a stimulus of high complexity, it should take even more exposures before individuals come to prefer high-complexity stimuli. The results of this study (Figure 12-3) are consistent with the information-processing hypothesis.

Munsinger and Kessen (1964) argued that, since art students tend, on the average, to have had more experience with complex visual stimuli, they should already possess the cognitive structures to process complex visual stimuli and therefore they should, on the average, tend to prefer more complex visual stimuli. This is exactly what they found when they compared art students with nonart students.

Arkes and Boykin (1971) have further shown that children who participated in a Head Start program came to prefer more complex stimulation. There have been numerous demonstrations that animals also tend to select more complex stimulation after being exposed to moderate complexity. The fact that a wide variety of animals respond in the same way as humans provides evidence for the generality of this phenomenon.

The Cognitive Component

The main cognitive concepts formulated to account for curiosity and exploratory behavior is the information-processing hypothesis, which we have already encountered. Two theories that emerged in the 1950s and 1960s made direct or indirect use of this idea—Dember and Earl's theory and Berlyne's theory.

Dember and Earl's Theory

Dember and Earl (1957) assume that organisms are motivated to experience optimal complexity. One important feature of their theory is the concept of a *pacer range* (Figure 12-4). They suggest that an organism becomes accustomed, or habituated, to a certain level of complexity (called an *adaptation level*) and is motivated to explore stimuli that are slightly more complex than this adaptation level. This concept is intended to explain why exploratory, curiosity, and play behaviors tend to be systematically directed towards more complex levels of stimulation and also why individuals prefer certain stimuli to others. The appeal of the theory is its simplicity. It predicts that individuals will always select stimuli slightly more complex than those to which they have adapted and that, over time, individuals will come to prefer more and more complex stimulation.

The measure of any theory, however, is how well it can account for the research findings. Several tests of the theory have shown that, indeed, many forms of stimulation can be ordered in terms of their psycholog-

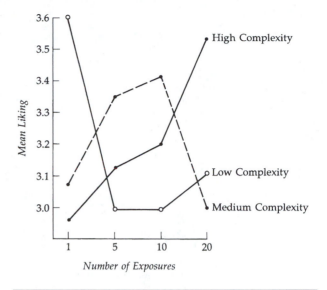

Figure 12-3.   Mean preference ratings at three levels of stimulus complexity as a function of number of exposures to the stimulus. (From "The Effect of Stimulus Uncertainty and the Relationship between Frequency and Exposure and Liking," by G. F. Smith and D. D. Dorfman. *Journal of Personality and Social Psychology*, 1975, *31*, 150–155. Copyright © 1975 by the American Psychological Association. Reprinted with permission.)

ical complexity and, further, that preferences are systematically related to psychological complexity. For example, preference for auditory stimuli appears to be determined by their complexity (Vitz, 1966a,b). As we have seen, the same is true of preference for visual stimuli (e.g., Munsinger & Kessen, 1964; Smith & Dorfman, 1975). In addition, a number of studies have shown that preference for complexity shifts upward as a result of experience with a certain kind of stimulation. For example, Vitz (1966b) found that subjects with greater musical experience rated complex auditory stimuli as more pleasant than other subjects did. Sackett (1965) found that rhesus monkeys raised in more complex environments preferred more complex stimuli. As already noted, Munsinger and Kessen (1964) found that art students preferred more complexity than did other students, and Arkes and Boykin

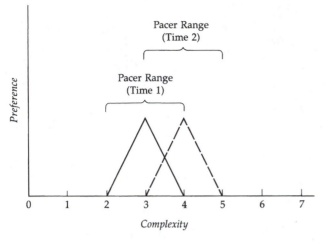

Figure 12-4. The pacer range. According to Dember and Earl's theory, an organism that has adapted to the level of complexity represented by point 2 on the complexity dimension will be inclined to respond only to stimuli enclosed by points 2 and 4; maximum attention will be directed toward stimuli at point 3. Interacting with stimuli at point 3 will lead to a new adaptation level corresponding to point 3. As a result, there will be a new pacer range, enclosed by points 3 and 5. Thus, as long as there are stimuli corresponding to those in the pacer range, over time the individual will systematically interact with all the stimuli in its environment.

(1971) found that children in a Head Start program significantly increased their preference for complexity.

Berlyne's Theory

Probably the most influential theory of exploration was proposed by Berlyne (1960, 1971). His fundamental assumption is that exploration and play are directed toward the processing of information. Through exploration and play, individuals become knowledgeable about their environment. Drawing on a large body of data, he concluded that such behaviors are highly systematic. Animals and humans respond systematically to events, especially novel events (Berlyne, 1958). Berlyne addressed himself to two questions:

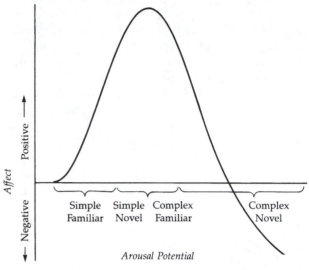

Figure 12-5. The relation between affect and the arousal potential of a stimulus, according to Berlyne's theory. Note that positive affect is greatest when a stimulus is moderately complex or moderately novel. (From "Novelty, Complexity and Hedonic Value," by D. E. Berlyne. *Perception and Psychophysics,* 1970, 283. Copyright © 1970 by the Psychonomic Society, Inc. Reprinted with permission.)

1. What motivates the tendency to process information?
2. What governs the tendency to respond systematically to certain stimuli and not to others?

Berlyne (1960) suggested that the basic mechanism underlying exploratory and play behaviors is the level of arousal. He proposed that the relation between arousal and hedonic tone can be described as an inverted U-shaped function, such that hedonic tone is greatest when arousal is moderate (Figure 12-5). He argued that either a very low level of stimulation or very complex stimulation produces low affect and that high complexity or novelty can even lead to negative affect. According to Berlyne's theory, organisms are motivated to seek out positive affect and avoid negative affect. Therefore, a person experiencing low arousal—in

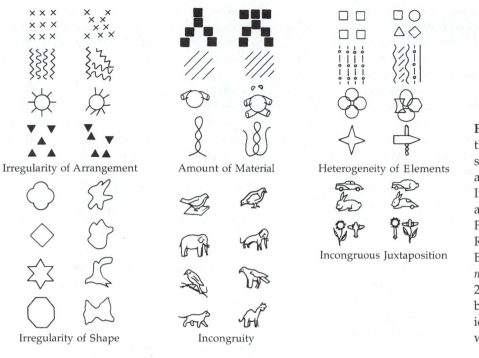

Irregularity of Arrangement

Amount of Material

Heterogeneity of Elements

Incongruous Juxtaposition

Irregularity of Shape

Incongruity

Figure 12-6.   Materials of the type used by Berlyne to study collative variables and arousal. (From "The Influence of Complexity and Novelty in Visual Figures on Orientating Responses," by D. E. Berlyne. *Journal of Experimental Psychology*, 1958, 55, 289–296. Copyright © 1958 by the American Psychological Association. Reprinted with permission.)

a situation that has low arousal potential—will seek out situations that will increase arousal, while a person experiencing high arousal—in a situation that has high arousal potential—will seek out situations that will lower arousal.

Berlyne assumes that arousal comes from interacting with external stimulation or from exercising internal processes, such as imagining, fantasizing, and thinking. Much of his research focused on identifying and classifying those characteristics of a stimulation that could produce arousal. After carefully analyzing a large body of research, he concluded that arousal is linked to what he called the *collative variables*: novelty, degree of change, suddenness of change, surprisingness, incongruity, conflict, complexity, and uncertainty. Figure 12-6 presents examples of stimulus materials used in Berlyne's research on collative variables.

Berlyne refers to these variables as collative because their ability to produce arousal is assumed to depend on our comparison of a given stimulus with some standard stimulus—some form of memory representation. He suggested that, when we attend to a

stimulus, we compare that stimulus with other stimuli represented in memory. If the stimulus departs in some way from other stimuli represented in memory, it should elicit arousal.

How does a standard develop? Berlyne suggested that we tend to process all the information contained in a stimulus. He argues that processing information is as natural as seeing. We do not simply store a detailed icon but tend rather to abstract essential features of the stimulus, which make up the standard. Once all the essential features have been abstracted, the stimulus loses its ability to elicit further attention. The standard then becomes the backdrop against which all new information is processed. When we attend to a new stimulus, we compare its essential features with those of the standard.

According to Berlyne, the tendency to process new information is governed by the ability of the new stimulus to elicit arousal. When we encounter a new stimulus that departs in some way from the standard, the discrepancy will elicit arousal. The greater the discrepancy, the greater the arousal. If the discrepancy is moderate, it will elicit moderate arousal, and since moderate arousal is pleasurable, the person will try to maintain contact with the stimulus. However, because organisms are inclined to process the information contained in a stimulus, it is simply a matter of time before the essential features of the new stimulus have been abstracted. As a result, a novel stimulus becomes familiar, a surprising stimulus loses its ability to elicit surprise, and an incongruous stimulus becomes ordinary and predictable. Because organisms are motivated to maintain moderate arousal, they will be inclined to seek out new stimuli that depart from the standard in order to experience moderate arousal once again. In this way, the organism tends, over time, to learn more and more about different parts of its environment.

According to Berlyne's theory, a stimulus could evoke too much arousal and thus become aversive. Rather than explore such a stimulus, the individual would tend to terminate contact with the stimulus in order to avoid or reduce negative hedonic tone. This motivational tendency, Berlyne argues, serves an important function. If the ability to process information depends on the existence of certain cognitive structures, then certain stimuli may exceed the individual's ability to abstract the information they contain. Therefore, until the individual has developed the appropriate structures (presumably as a result of interacting with stimuli that can be processed), there is no point in interacting with such stimuli. In short, it is a waste of the individual's time.

To summarize, Berlyne's theory predicts that people and animals are motivated to explore stimuli that contain a moderate amount of new information (novelty). Such stimuli are defined as having a moderate amount of arousal potential. If an individual attends to them, they will evoke a moderate amount of arousal, which is the optimal level for producing positive hedonic tone.

Berlyne recognized that organisms could, for a variety of reasons, experience a chronically high level of arousal. Anxiety, for example, is often characterized by high arousal. Such an individual, according to Berlyne's theory, would be less inclined—or not inclined at all—to seek out new and different stimulation. In fact, such an individual might be inclined to seek out very common and familiar stimuli to keep arousal from increasing further.

In one experiment designed to determine whether high levels of arousal will lead to decreased exploratory behavior, Franken and Strain (1974) used a large multi-unit maze that permitted certain sections to be changed from white to black or black to white between the two daily trials. Figure 12-7 shows the arrangement of the maze, together with the changes made between trials 1 and 2. If exploratory behavior is motivated by the tendency to seek out new stimulation, animals high in that tendency should select and respond to the changed parts of the maze. To determine whether this tendency might decrease when an animal is highly aroused, half of the animals (rats) were injected with methamphetamine (an arousal-producing drug) between the two daily trials, and the other half were injected with saline solution (an inert substance).

As expected, the animals injected with saline solution (low-arousal animals) responded to the changes in the maze. These animals entered somewhat more cul-de-sacs on trial 2 than on trial 1 even when the cul-de-sacs were not changed. When they were changed, the animals entered many more of them. The results for the methamphetamine-injected (highly aroused) animals are almost opposite to those of the saline animals but are exactly as predicted by Berlyne's theory. When the cul-de-sacs were changed, the animals tended to avoid them. They entered fewer cul-de-sacs on trial 2 than on trial 1. These results (Figure 12-8) clearly show that arousal mediates the tendency to respond to new stimulation. In similar experiments, Berlyne has manipulated arousal with drugs and has obtained results consistent with his theory (Berlyne, 1969; Berlyne, Koenig, & Hirota, 1966).

The fact that arousal mediates exploratory behavior means that arousal indirectly governs what and how much we come to know about our environment. Most developmental psychologists argue that, through the process of exploration, children come to be knowledgeable about their environment and competent in dealing with it (e.g., Piaget, 1952; White, 1959).

Anxiety, Arousal, and Exploratory Behavior

In Chapter 5, we saw that anxiety plays a key role in peak performance. When anxiety is high, attention is narrow and exclusive and tends to shift to survival cues. The research reported in this chapter is consistent with those results. If people are to learn new things,

No Change   Cul-de-sacs Changed

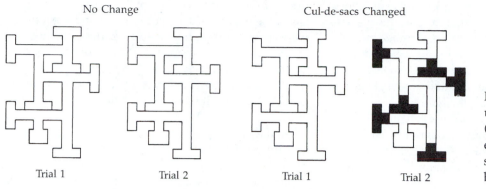

Trial 1   Trial 2   Trial 1   Trial 2

Figure 12-7.   The maze used by Franken & Strain (1974) in studies of exploratory behavior, showing the changes between trials 1 and 2.

they must be free of anxiety. An anxious environment will produce increases in arousal that interfere with learning. Good teachers are aware of this and work hard to create a relaxed atmosphere, characterized by arousal that is low but not too low.

Summary

Research with animals has indicated that the tendency to explore is motivated by novelty or stimulus change. In fact, it appears that animals are motivated by the opportunity to explore the visual, auditory, tactile, and olfactory properties of objects and that they will learn behaviors that allow them to experience the stimulation that comes from interacting with various objects. Like animals, humans are motivated by the variety and novelty of objects we encounter. There is considerable evidence that animals and humans are motivated by the complexity of objects. It has been shown that children tend to select increasingly complex objects. Apparently, as children's ability to handle more complex forms of stimulation increases, they have a natural preference for more complex stimuli.

The tendency to explore is often markedly reduced when organisms are anxious or fearful. Research with humans suggests that some individuals have a temperamental disposition that markedly reduces their tendency to explore. There is considerable evidence that the tendency to explore novel and complex stimuli increases as a result of exposure to certain kinds of stimuli.

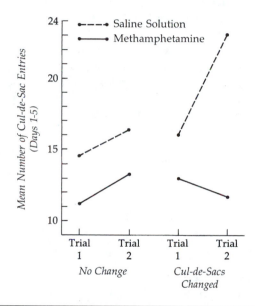

Figure 12-8.   Number of cul-de-sacs entered by rats injected with methamphetamine and rats injected with saline solution when cul-de-sacs were changed in color between trials and when they were not. Methamphetamine reduced exploration (number of cul-de-sacs entered) as well as the tendency to approach the changed cul-de-sacs on the second trial. (Reproduced with permission of the publisher from "Effect of Increased Arousal on Response to Stimulus Change in a Complex Maze," by R. E. Franken and A. Strain. *Perceptual and Motor Skills*, 1974, *39*, 1076–1078. Copyright © 1974 Perceptual and Motor Skills.)

The two main theories of curiosity and exploratory behavior grew out of the idea that humans have a natural tendency to process information. Dember and Earl argue that organisms are motivated to seek a level of complexity slightly above their current level. According to Dember and Earl, only a certain range of stimuli (the pacer range) will be acceptable.

Berlyne has suggested that the mechanism underlying exploratory and play behaviors is arousal. When arousal is low, organisms are motivated to increase arousal by interacting with novel stimuli in their environment; stimuli that can provide optimal arousal will become the objects of attention. According to Berlyne's theory, attention to an object is sufficient to produce information processing. Once all the information has been processed, the individual will be inclined to seek out new stimuli.

The tendency to explore is reduced by high levels of arousal, such as those produced by drugs, and also by fear. Because individuals often differ in terms of arousal levels and fear, it is not surprising that there are also great differences in their tendency to explore. Teachers and parents may be able to increase children's tendency to explore by creating an environment that is relaxed (low in arousal properties).

Extrinsic Motivation

Extrinsic Motivation and Exploration

Condry (1977) has concluded that, in certain contexts, extrinsic incentives undermine not only performance but also interest in the activity. Since then, a number of other articles have echoed that idea (e.g., Schwartz, 1990; Tegano, Moran, & Sawyers, 1991). Why do extrinsic incentives undermine performance and interest? Before we attempt to answer this question, let's look briefly at some of the research on this problem.

An obvious extrinsic incentive, or reward, is money. In a series of studies to examine whether money would increase or decrease subsequent interest in a task, Deci (1972) used a game called SOMA®. This game includes a number of blocks that can be arranged into different patterns. Participants in the study were asked to play the game and in different conditions were offered (1) nothing, (2) a monetary reward, or (3) a social reward (praise) for every configuration they pro-

duced. In the middle of each of three experimental sessions, the experimenter left the room and the subjects were viewed surreptitiously to determine whether they continued to play at the game. The amount of time they played with the blocks during these free sessions was used as a measure of interest, or intrinsic motivation. Deci found that intrinsic motivation was less when subjects were given an external reward but greater when they were given verbal praise. According to Deci and Ryan (1985), rewards reduce intrinsic motivation by undermining feelings of competence and self-determination. They argue that extrinsic rewards place the motivation for learning outside the individual and, as a result, the individual no longer experiences feelings of competency and self-determination.

The important point about these and other studies is that it is not the receipt of the reward itself that affects subsequent interest but whether the subject undertakes the task in order to receive a monetary reward. For example, if a subject unexpectedly receives a reward, it does not affect his or her performance (for example, Greene & Lepper, 1974; Lepper & Greene, 1975; Lepper, Greene, & Nisbett, 1973). It appears that the promise of a reward alters the person's approach to the task. Several sources (for example, Haddad, McCullers, & Moran, 1976; McGraw & McCullers, 1974, 1975; Miller & Estes, 1961; Spence, 1970) indicate that rewarded children learn less than nonrewarded children. Further, Condry and Chambers (1978) and Maehr and Stallings (1972) have found that rewarded children attempted easier problems and were more answer-oriented. Thus, as Condry (1977) points out, there is evidence that extrinsic motivation leads subjects to adopt different strategies in a learning or problem-solving situation—strategies that do not breed intrinsic motivation.

In a recent review of these studies, Eisenberger and Cameron (1996) have argued that the detrimental effects of external reward are very limited and easily avoidable. They point out, among other things, that praise often leads to increased interest, a finding that is inconsistent with the suggestion that all extrinsic rewards undermine motivation. Further, they note that extrinsic rewards in the form of money only lead to a decrement in performance when the money is not directly linked to performance. Someone who isn't told what the reward is for may believe it is simply for putting in time, for example. If the reward is clearly linked to some desired behavior or performance, motivation is unlikely to suffer. Otherwise, the reward may lead subjects to adopt a different—for instance, answer-oriented—strategy for learning.

Later in the chapter, we will examine the effect of extrinsic rewards on creativity.

Individual Differences and Extrinsic Motivation

Achievement motivation is typically regarded as an example of intrinsic motivation. It is found that subjects high in need for achievement are more likely to volunteer for difficult tasks when evaluation is internal and for easy tasks when evaluation is external (Maehr & Stallings, 1972). This clearly demonstrates that external factors modify the normal tendency of high achievers to select tasks of moderate difficulty. Switzky and Haywood (1974) have also shown that external factors tend to override intrinsically motivated behavior. Using a personality test to identify intrinsically and extrinsically motivated types (Haywood, 1971), Switzky and Haywood found that, under conditions of self-reward for performance, intrinsically motivated children maintained their performance longer than did extrinsically motivated types. When the rewards were externally administered, extrinsically motivated children maintained their performance longer than did intrinsically motivated children.

Summary

Considerable evidence shows that extrinsic motivation not only is the enemy of exploration but also leads to incomplete learning or, at least, to a different kind of learning. Extrinsic motivation may alter attentional processes, which in turn affect what is learned. Alternatively, extrinsic motivation may simply teach a series of responses that are not based on an understanding of the task. Intrinsic motivation seems to be tied to the motivation to process information. A person who is free from constraints is inclined to learn about relations between elements in a given situation. Such learning can not only facilitate later problem solving but also breed intrinsic motivation.

Critiques of the studies on extrinsic reward and learning have pointed out that rewards do not lead to decrements in performance if they are contingent on

the desired behavior. Individuals high in achievement motivation are more inclined to select difficult tasks if evaluation is internal and moderately difficult tasks when evaluation is external.

Sensation Seeking

According to Berlyne's (1960) model, as we have seen, humans are strongly motivated to process information in the environment, in order to maintain optimal arousal. If stimulation falls below some optimal level, the individual will experience negative affect. To explore the role of stimulation, various researchers have studied the effects of depriving people of all stimulation. As a graduate student, Marvin Zuckerman (1979) conducted various studies on sensory deprivation that required volunteers to stay for an extended period under conditions of minimal stimulation. He noticed that the people who volunteered for his experiments had certain common characteristics: they were very curious, liked to have new experiences, and were willing to take certain risks in order to have those experiences. Most of them had volunteered for his experiments because that was something they had never done before. He wondered if perhaps these people represented a personality type that could be measured. After talking with them, he created a questionnaire called the Sensation Seeking Scale (SSS). People who score high on this scale are typically referred to as high sensation seekers, while those who score low are referred to as low sensation seekers or sensation avoiders. To find out if you are a high, medium, or low sensation seeker, take the test in Practical Application 12-2.

According to Zuckerman (1979), sensation seeking "is a trait defined by the need for varied, novel and complex sensations and experiences and the willingness to take physical and social risks for the sake of such experiences" (p. 10). Note that one of the key elements of sensation seeking is the willingness to take risks. Work on exploratory behavior suggests that organisms tend to avoid exploration (the search for new sensations and new experiences) when it entails risks. Risks are thought to arouse fear, which is incompatible with exploratory behavior. Several theories of exploratory behavior assume that fear produces high levels of arousal. If organisms explore in order to increase arousal, it makes sense that organisms experiencing fear will not explore, because they are already at an optimal level of arousal. Alternatively, it has been suggested that high arousal tends to shift attention to more survival-related cues, which is incompatible with exploratory behavior. It is interesting, therefore, that Zuckerman has been able to identify people who are willing to take risks in order to explore.

Zuckerman's Sensation Seeking Scale is based on four related but independent factors that were derived through factor analytic procedures. These factors denote slightly different aspects of sensation seeking.

1. **Thrill and adventure seeking.** Some people are inclined to seek excitement through risky but socially acceptable activities such as parachuting or driving fast, even if they haven't engaged in such activities.

2. **Experience seeking.** Some people desire to seek sensation by engaging in activities outside a conventional lifestyle. They may travel, seek out unusual friends, engage in artistic endeavors, experiment with drugs, and in general lead less conventional lives.

3. **Disinhibition.** Those who choose to follow a conventional lifestyle may periodically escape by engaging in social drinking or gambling or by pursuing a variety of sexual partners. They drink to free themselves from the social inhibitions that are part of their conventional lifestyles.

Practical Application 12-1

Facilitating Intrinsic Motivation

What factors facilitate the development of intrinsic motivation? It appears that one of the main factors is freedom from constraints or external demands, such as having to finish a task quickly, to do it in a certain way, or to please someone else. For example, when goals are imposed by someone else, intrinsic motivation is found to decrease (Manderlink & Harackiewicz, 1984; Mossholder, 1980). Let's examine what happens in the presence of constraints.

In the presence of constraints—for instance, the need to finish a task quickly or to find a particular solution—behavior is often characterized as answer-oriented and shallow (Condry, 1977; Sylva, Bruner, & Genova, 1976). It appears that the person is not trying to discover the underlying structure or the relation between elements but is simply generating a series of more or less random responses, often to external cues from the environment or from other people, such as the experimenter. Why is that? There are two lines of argument.

1. Extrinsic demands increase anxiety or arousal level or simply increase drive level. Increases in anxiety, arousal, or drive, it is argued, alter the way a person processes information. They narrow attention (Bruner, Matter, & Papanek, 1955) or shift attention in some way that interferes with the learner's ability to deal with the more subtle aspects of the situation (Easterbrook, 1959). If learners cannot deal with all the information, they cannot generate a series of systematic responses. In short, they will be forced to respond with strategies that have worked before or to try to proceed on the basis of limited information.

2. Learning based on external demands teaches responses, rather than rules or understanding. The individual merely imitates another person's behavior or learns a sequence of responses that somehow works. Although such responding may work in certain situations, it won't work when the task demands are shifted.

When there is freedom and personal choice, something quite different happens. In that case, a person learns about relations between elements. Studies (e.g., Sylva et al., 1976) have shown that a person who has been able to interact freely with the materials to be used in a later problem can generate a wide variety of approaches. This suggests that the person is testing a series of hypotheses. Why should freedom from constraints facilitate intrinsic motivation? Several factors seem to be involved.

First, there is evidence that when people are free from anxiety, emotionality, or any form of excessive arousal, information processing not only is highly motivating but

4. **Boredom susceptibility.** Some people have a much lower tolerance for repetition and sameness. They tend to seek out stimulation and change in order to escape the monotony of everyday life. These people are inclined to engage in sensation-seeking activities.

The Biological Component

Monoamine Oxidase and Sensation Seeking

What is the origin of the sensation-seeking trait? It has been shown that sensation seeking is negatively correlated with monoamine oxidase levels (Zuckerman, 1979). That is, levels of monoamine oxidase are low in high sensation seekers and high in low sensation seekers. Monoamine oxidase (MAO) is an enzyme that is important in the regulation—and therefore the ultimate availability—of neurotransmitters such as norepinephrine. When the MAO level is high, little norepinephrine is available; however, when it is low, considerable norepinephrine is available. As we know, the level of norepinephrine in the brain is linked to whether or not the reward centers of the brain can be activated. Because sensation seekers are characterized by low MAO levels, their levels of norepinephrine tend to be high; and the brain's reward centers are available for activation. That means that high sensation seekers are likely to experience greater pleasure, or greater reward,

takes a much different form than when people are anxious, emotional, or highly aroused. People who are free from arousal are more inclined to explore systematically all the various elements of the situation and the relations between them and, thus, are more prepared to deal with problems based on that material.

Second, there is considerable evidence that the opportunity to process information is highly motivating for humans as well as animals. Humans, it appears, tend to abstract principles and laws from the information they encounter. This information then becomes the backdrop for the processing of other information. Humans are good at fitting together the pieces of a cognitive puzzle and find the activity pleasurable. As Festinger (1957) noted, reducing dissonance is rewarding.

If information processing is rewarding, it follows that activities offering this opportunity will be valued. Further, if exercising our skill at a task increases our ability, we will be inclined to practice, so as to have more opportunity to engage in this highly valued activity. Thus, the more we process information, the more likely we are to do so in the future. The key to learning, therefore, is to eliminate the constraints that block or interfere with the natural tendency to process information.

Deci and Ryan (1985) have offered a theory of intrinsic motivation based on the concept of *self-determination*, which has two components: (1) becoming aware of our needs, and (2) setting goals so that those needs can be satisfied. They argue that reaching a goal typically involves learning or mastery. By contrast, *automatic behaviors*—behaviors that are not self-determined—simply involve acting to terminate external forces, often without having mastered anything. In learning to set and achieve goals, people learn to become self-determined, which is the essence of what it means to be intrinsically motivated. Note that, when people set goals for themselves, they typically set relatively difficult goals, which means that they tend to learn more than those whose goals are set by others (Bandura, 1991a). When goals are set by others, the individual typically engages in a very different kind of learning, which is motivated by the need to terminate an external force—specifically, to please those who set the goals.

In a work setting, people often become intrinsically motivated when assigned difficult goals. Locke and Latham (1990) argue that workers often interpret such a goal assignment as confidence in their ability and, as a result, will typically adopt the goal as their own.

when they take drugs such as cocaine, which stimulate the reward centers. As a result, high sensation seekers are likely to use drugs again. Conversely, because of their different brain chemistry, low sensation seekers do not experience the same level of reward when they use those drugs and therefore are less likely to use them again.

The Heritability of Monoamine Oxidase Levels

Where do these differences in monoamine oxidase level come from? Zuckerman (1979, 1983) has argued that they are inherited. Twin studies have indeed supported the hypothesis that the monoamine level has a genetic component. Frank Farley (1986) has pointed out, however, that sensation seeking has also been linked to testosterone level. Whatever the exact mechanism, he also endorses the hypothesis that sensation seeking is inherited.

Animal research has shown that exploratory behavior is inherited. Since exploratory behavior has been linked to the need for variety and change, such data provide converging evidence that the sensation-

seeking need, or the need to experience novelty and change, may indeed be inherited.

Gender and Age Differences

For reasons that are not altogether clear, levels of sensation seeking tend to be higher in men than in women. It has also been found that the sensation-seeking trait tends to diminish with age. While biological factors may be at work here, these findings may also be related to the fact that one of the scales to measure sensation seeking contains a large number of sports interest items.

The Learned Component

Although the disposition for sensation seeking has a biological basis, learning and cognition must obviously play a key role in its development and expression.

Research indicates that, when they administer punishment, fathers do not suppress their children's sensation-seeking motive (Zuckerman, 1994), although

Practical Application 12-2

Are You a High or a Low Sensation Seeker?

To test your own sensation-seeking tendencies, try this shortened version of one of Marvin Zuckerman's earlier scales. For each of the 13 items, circle the choice, A or B, that best describes your likes or dislikes or the way you feel. Instructions for scoring appear at the end of the test.

1. A. I would like a job that requires a lot of traveling.
   B. I would prefer a job in one location.
2. A. I am invigorated by a brisk, cold day.
   B. I can't wait to get indoors on a cold day.
3. A. I get bored seeing the same old faces.
   B. I like the comfortable familiarity of everyday friends.
4. A. I would prefer living in an ideal society in which everyone is safe, secure, and happy.
   B. I would prefer living in the unsettled days of our history.

5. A. Sometimes I like to do things that are a little frightening.
   B. A sensible person avoids activities that are dangerous.
6. A. I would not like to be hypnotized.
   B. I would like to have the experience of being hypnotized.
7. A. The most important goal of life is to live it to the fullest and experience as much as possible.
   B. The most important goal in life is to find peace and happiness.
8. A. I would like to try parachute-jumping.
   B. I would never want to try jumping out of a plane, with or without a parachute.
9. A. I enter cold water gradually, giving myself time to get used to it.
   B. I like to dive or jump right into the ocean or a cold pool.

they may play a key role in giving direction to it. Peers play a key role not only in nurturing the motive but in giving direction to it (Farley, 1986; Zuckerman, 1994). In a more delinquent peer group, the motive may well be expressed in behaviors such as drug taking and law breaking. In a more conventional peer group, by contrast, it may be expressed in behaviors such as risky sports or even the arts.

The sensation-seeking motive can be satisfied in a variety of ways. Since high sensation seekers tend to be more unconventional and rebellious than low sensation seekers, their behavior may often appear foolish and even stupid to others. Let's briefly review some of the ways in which the sensation-seeking motive is satisfied.

Sports

Sensation seekers tend to get involved in sports, especially those regarded as risky. They climb mountains, hang glide, scuba dive, and go downhill skiing, for example. However, there is no evidence that they are attracted to danger for its own sake. It appears, rather, that sensation seekers do not let risk stand in the way of new experiences. Rowland, Franken, and Harrison (1986) found that high sensation seekers more quickly get bored with a given sport and try something new. Over a period of time, then, they tend to participate in more sports than do low sensation seekers. Sooner or later, they are likely to try high-risk activities. Since high sensation seekers are not put off by risk, it is not surprising that more high than low sensation seekers tend to get involved in risky sports.

Experience Seeking

Sensations seekers satisfy their need for new experiences in many ways—by traveling, making new friends, and becoming involved in new activities, for example (Zuckerman, 1994). They value variety. For instance, they are inclined to have a broad set of friends with diverse views about the world. They are also inclined to become involved in artistic activities. They seek out music that is new and different and take pleasure in poetry and humor (Zuckerman, 1994). High sensation seekers tend to be open to all new forms of artistic endeavor.

---

10. A. When I go on a vacation, I prefer the comfort of a good room and bed.
    B. When I go on vacation, I prefer the change of camping out.
11. A. I prefer people who are emotionally expressive even if they are a bit unstable.
    B. I prefer people who are calm and even-tempered.
12. A. A good painting should shock or jolt the senses.
    B. A good painting should give one a feeling of peace and security.
13. A. People who ride motorcycles must have some kind of unconscious need to hurt themselves.
    B. I would like to drive or ride a motorcycle.

Scoring. Count one point for each of the following items that you have circled: 1A, 2A, 3A, 4B, 5A, 6B, 7A, 8A, 9B, 10B, 11A, 12A, 13B. Add up your total and compare it with the following norms.

0–3	Very low on sensation seeking
4–5	Low
6–9	Average
10–11	High
12–13	Very high

Although the test gives some indication of a person's rating, it is not a highly reliable measure. One reason, of course, is that the test has been abbreviated. Another is that the norms are based largely on the scores of college students who have taken the test. As people get older, their scores on sensation seeking tend to go down.

Drug Use, Sexual Behavior, and Uninhibited Behaviors

There is abundant evidence that sensation seekers tend to use alcohol, marijuana, and cocaine (e.g., Huba, Newcomb, & Bentler, 1981). As we have seen, this has been attributed to their biological constitution—specifically, their brain chemistry. Research also shows that sensation seekers like to have sex frequently and with a variety of partners (Zuckerman, 1979). Finally, there is a great deal of evidence that sensation seekers like parties, especially parties characterized by uninhibited behavior. Parties provide a wealth of sensory stimulation. They typically include food (olfactory and gustatory stimulation), music (auditory stimulation), dancing (tactile and kinesthetic stimulation, arousal), conversation (social stimulation, arousal), sexual stimuli, and alcohol or other drugs.

The Cognitive Component

Sensation seekers possess a number of personality attributes that come to govern their behavior in a wide range of situations. In many ways, the distinctive characteristics of sensation seekers are associated with their cognitive attributes.

Let's begin with three important trait qualities that characterize sensation seekers: openness, unconventionality, and undependability.

We already know that sensation seekers are open to new experiences. If they are to explore those new experiences, they cannot be constrained by conventions—by what other people think or say. They are also unwilling to let previous decisions prevent them from taking advantage of new experiences. Sensation seekers are quite willing to break a commitment if they find something more interesting to do (Franken, 1987). They are undependable.

Sensation seeking can lead to delinquency, on the one hand, and creativity, on the other (Farley, 1986). In both cases, there is a tendency to be open to new ways of doing and seeing, a disdain for convention and tradition, and a lack of commitment to the ways other people think and act.

Thinking Styles and Creativity

It would be wrong to assume that sensation seekers are simply jocks or party animals. They often become entrepreneurs, artists, educators, entertainers, scientists, and adventurers. They can be found at the leading edge of many fields, because of their creativity, which grows out of their thinking style.

Creative people are able to view things in new ways or from a different perspective and to generate new possibilities or alternatives. Tests of creativity measure not only the number of alternatives that people can generate but the uniqueness of those alternatives. The ability to generate new alternatives or to see in new ways is linked to other, more fundamental qualities of thinking, such as flexibility, tolerance of ambiguity or unpredictability, and the enjoyment of novelty. Sensation seekers have all of these qualities (Farley, 1986; Franken, 1987).

Decision-Making Styles and Sensation Seeking

Peters and Waterman (1982) have studied the planning and decision-making styles of the top executives of the best-run companies in the United States. They point out that these executives like to make decisions, like to make them quickly, can make them without having complete information, and are willing to abandon plans that are not working. In short, the executives have the capacity to stay on the cutting edge of their fields by following their hunches. These characteristics are also typical of sensation seekers (Franken, 1988). Sensation seekers' personality style makes them adept at working in environments where change is a way of life.

Sensation Seeking and Commitment

Sensation seekers cannot afford to become committed to any one activity, because they need to be able to explore any new and more interesting opportunities that come along. To ensure that they can take advantage of change, they need to be vigilant about keeping their options open. A recent study found that sensation seekers are inclined to make decisions at the last minute; make only short-term commitments; do not feel guilty when they break commitments because something more interesting came up; do not make plans but rather let things happen; and do not carefully consider the consequences before they act (Franken, 1993). Sensation seekers even indicate that keeping their options open is more important than being viewed as dependable.

It is interesting to note in this context that while sensation seekers are inclined to self-disclose (a quality that has been linked to intimacy), they are not inclined to commit themselves to long-term relationships (Franken, Gibson, & Mohan, 1990). While there is evidence that high sensation seekers are inclined to marry high sensation seekers and that low sensation seekers are inclined to marry low sensation seekers, it has been found that sensation seeking has more of a negative impact on marital satisfaction in high-sensation seeking women (Gibson, Franken, & Rowland, 1989). One explanation of these results is that there is more pressure for high-sensation seeking women to conform to the traditional role of wife in a marital relationship than for high-sensation seeking men to conform to the traditional role of husband. As a result, high-sensation seeking women would experience less satisfaction with marriage than high-sensation seeking men.

Summary

Sensation seeking "is a trait defined by the need for varied novel and complex sensations and experiences and the willingness to take physical and social risks for the sake of such experiences" (Zuckerman, 1979, p. 10). High sensation seekers tend to be open and unconventional people. This trait can lead to creativity or, if it is not properly channeled, to delinquency.

Twin studies provide considerable evidence that the sensation-seeking trait may be inherited. Zuckerman has argued that sensation seeking is governed by monoamine oxidase levels. High sensation seekers have low monoamine oxidase levels, while low sensation seekers have high monoamine oxidase levels. Farley has suggested that testosterone may also play an important role in motivating sensation seeking. Consistent with this interpretation is the finding that men score higher than women on Zuckerman's Sensation Seeking Scale. The sensation-seeking trait, as measured by Zuckerman's scale, has been shown to decline with age. Factor analytic studies have identified four distinct factors that characterize the sensation-seeking motive: thrill and adventure seeking, experience seeking, disinhibition, and boredom susceptibility.

High sensation seekers are inclined to get involved in a variety of high-risk sports activities, apparently because of their interest in new experiences rather than because of any attraction to risk itself. High sensation seekers also tend to use drugs, have a variety of sex partners, and seek out situations—such as parties—where they can behave in an uninhibited manner.

High sensation seekers like to make decisions, like to make them quickly, and are willing to make them with incomplete information. In addition, they are willing to abandon plans that are not working. High sensation seekers tend to keep their options open. Among other things, they are unwilling to make long-term commitments. While sensation seekers are inclined to self-disclose, they are not inclined to commit to long-term relationships.

Creativity

Creativity is closely linked to curiosity and exploratory behavior. It is also closely linked to sensation seeking—the desire to be unconventional.

Why are people motivated to engage in creative acts? There are at least three reasons.

1. The need for novel, varied, and complex stimulation. One way to meet this need is to create or find new things that will stimulate our senses (for instance, new recipes, new art, or new cars) or challenge our intellect (for instance, books, computers, or movies). Berlyne (1960) has attributed the creation or appreciation of beauty to this need.
2. The need to communicate ideas and values. Concerned that children are dying of starvation, a photographer triggers our compassion with a picture of an emaciated child. A politician wanting to make a difference writes a book to challenge our beliefs and stimulate us to action.
3. The need to solve problems. As we encounter new diseases or our business begins to fail, we search for answers that can give us hope.

Definition.   A great deal of controversy surrounds the definition of creativity (Mumford & Gustafson, 1988). Some writers have argued that creativity should be defined in terms of problem-solving ability (Cattell, 1971). By that definition, some of the world's most famous paintings or novels are not creative products. Other writers have suggested that it is a personality trait (MacKinnon, 1962). Such a definition suggests that some people are creative and others are not. Some writers have suggested a definition in terms of the

Artists constantly strive to find new ways of expressing an idea or emotion.

production of ideas (Guilford, 1967), which would exclude people who, although not good at producing ideas themselves, can recognize a creative idea or product when they encounter it. Other writers have suggested that the definition should include the recognition of ideas (Tyler, 1978). In that case, a movie producer or publisher who makes truly creative products available to the public also plays a creative role.

All of these various definitions offer useful ways of thinking about creativity. For our purposes, creativity is defined as the tendency to generate or recognize ideas, alternatives, or possibilities that may be useful in solving problems, communicating with others, and entertaining ourselves and others. While I accept the idea that there are individual differences, I think that all people have the innate capacity to act creatively when the situation demands or when they are properly motivated. For me, creativity is more an expression of motivation than of talent.

The Biological Component

Adaptive Benefits of Creativity

Edward DeBono (e.g., 1970, 1987) has written extensively on the topic of creativity and has taken the position that the brain evolved to isolate predictability and consistency. In other words, like other theorists, he believes that the main function of curiosity and exploratory behavior is to ensure that we make sense out of the complex array of stimulation that falls on our receptors. As organisms explore their environment, they link together various elements of a stimulus. This enables them to form an image of the stimulus at some later time, even though they may have seen only one element. For example, a rabbit needs to see only the head of a dog and not the whole body before it engages in flight. Obviously, this is highly adaptive.

The problem, DeBono argues, is that, if we view elements only as parts of something larger, it is difficult for us to combine them in new and different ways. How, then, do people learn to recombine elements? DeBono has devoted much of his life to designing exercises that help people to do this.

Langer (1989) has used a similar line of reasoning to account for lack of creativity. She argues that many of our behaviors become habitual, automatic, and unconscious. As a result, we behave in a mindless (thoughtless) as opposed to a mindful (thoughtful) way. Like DeBono, she acknowledges that it is highly adaptive for us to perform routine tasks without actively thinking about them. Among other things, it frees our brain to focus on other things. The downside to having well-ingrained habits, however, is that they may come to control our behavior. As our environment changes, we continue to engage in the same responses, even though they are no longer adaptive. In order to break out of our routine behavior patterns, we need to become mindful, but how do we do that? Langer suggests that the first step is to become aware that we have the choice to behave differently. The next step is to become aware of what our alternatives are. That involves generating alternatives on the basis of our assessment of the situation.

Langer believes that people can become mindful at will. This parallels DeBono's conviction that people can learn to become creative. To do so, they need motivation and also a set of techniques for generating new possibilities. For Langer, that means learning to make new distinctions and create new categories. For DeBono, it means learning to recombine elements in new ways or to see them from a different perspective.

Origins of Creativity

Various theorists have suggested that the tendency to create has its roots in our need to adapt (e.g., Sulloway, 1996). Others have argued that the tendency to create is part of our need to self-actualize—that we are born with an urge to create. Maslow (1970), for example, suggests that creativity—more specifically, the need for self-actualization—is at the top of our hierarchy of needs. In other words, we must satisfy all of our more basic needs before we are inclined to express ourselves creatively. Zuckerman's (1979) finding that people high in the sensation-seeking motive tend to be more creative than people low in this motive suggests that creativity helps sensation seekers to satisfy their need for variety and change.

It seems that creativity has its roots both in our need to survive (adapt) and in our need for expression. Historically, creativity has been defined in terms of both problem-solving behaviors and expressive behaviors. It will be important to keep these two aspects in mind as we consider the learned and cognitive components of creativity.

The Learned Component

Creativity as Disinhibition

Convention and tradition. Researchers have suggested that people often have a tendency to act creatively but inhibit such tendencies for fear of rejection by society (Franken, 1990). Such people may be motivated more by the need to be accepted or to belong than by a need to experience variety and change. As a result, they become conventional and traditional in their views. In-

stead of questioning the values of society, as more creative people do, they go along. Research on creativity suggests that, in order to be creative, we need to be able to let go of conventional perspectives (Strickland, 1989)—in other words, to become disinhibited. We need to feel free to recombine things in new and different ways, even if those combinations may seem silly or even wrong.

Rigidity. Many people are afraid of change or motivated to avoid it. They may be anxious, fearful, or highly aroused. In order to manage those feelings, they look for consistency and predictability in their environment. People who are chronically anxious or aroused often develop a behavior pattern characterized by excessive rigidity. To become creative, these people need to throw off their rigidity, although that will not be easy for them (e.g., Berlyne, 1960).

Rigidity can also occur simply because we have allowed ourselves to become creatures of habit, as Langer (1989) pointed out. Of course, being rigid is inconsistent with creativity.

Psychological Climate and Creativity

It has been shown that otherwise uncreative people will suddenly demonstrate creativity in certain conditions (Mumford & Gustafson, 1988). For example, if people know that creativity is expected, they will perform better on divergent-thinking measures of creativity (Harrington, 1981; Torrence, 1965). In tests of divergent thinking, people are typically presented with a question or stimulus and asked to generate as many ideas and associations as possible, without reflecting on the usefulness or practicality of their responses. They might be asked, for example, to think of things to do with a piece of chalk. Their divergent thinking score increases with the number of ideas that they generate. Sometimes people are given a higher score if they generate more unusual ideas—throwing the chalk to get someone's attention, rather than using it to write, for instance.

Studies indicate that scientific productivity is enhanced when the organizational climate provides physical support for creative efforts and encourages independent action—that is, when a company is committed to creativity and innovation, rewards creative people, and attempts to provide whatever might assist people to become more creative (Taylor, 1972; Andrews, 1975). These data are consistent with that finding that support and recognition of creative effort, particularly in the early stages of a project, lead to innovation (e.g., Lind & Mumford, 1987). A wealth of research suggests that removing inhibitions on the expression of creativity—such as undue reliance on custom and tradition—and rewarding creativity can unleash creativity in virtually anyone. Again, it appears that creativity is actively inhibited in certain environments.

There is some evidence that people tend to be more creative when affect is positive. It appears that positive affect facilitates cognitive organization—specifically, it increases our tendency to combine things in new ways and to see relatedness among divergent stimuli (Isen, Daubman, & Nowicki, 1987).

Rewards and Creativity

As we discussed earlier, a number of researchers have suggested that extrinsic rewards inhibit the development of intrinsic motivation. Accordingly, it has also been suggested that extrinsic rewards inhibit creativity. Eisenberger and Cameron (1996) argue that this idea is largely a myth. When people are rewarded repeatedly for high creativity in one task, creativity in a subsequent task is enhanced (Eisenberger & Selbst, 1994). It appears that rewards only reduce creativity in a subsequent task if people are repeatedly rewarded for low creativity. Eisenberger and Cameron (1996) argue that, under these conditions, people are essentially being rewarded for being lazy or uncreative. The key to promoting creativity is to make rewards contingent on high creative output.

Personality Traits and Creativity

Barron and Harrington (1981) have linked creativity to a set of personality characteristics, including intellectual and artistic values, breadth of interests, attraction to complexity, high energy, a concern with work and achievement, independence of judgment, autonomy, intuition, self-confidence, ability to tolerate and resolve conflict, and creative self-image. More recently, openness to experience has been identified as a characteristic of creative people (McCrae, 1987). It remains to be determined whether people are born with these traits, or learn them—for instance, through modeling. If we admire someone, for example, we may adopt the

traits of that person. Another possibility is that the development of these traits is the outgrowth of the desire to be creative. In other words, because creativity is rewarding, we learn to adopt certain orientations to the world and ourselves—certain beliefs and attitudes—that will increase the likelihood of our being creative (Franken, 1987).

How does this work? If I value creativity, I might learn to become more tolerant of ambiguity in my life or I might become more inclined to keep an open mind, because I have learned that these are key elements of the creative process. Similarly, in order to be more creative, I might learn to see myself as autonomous, independent, and creative. In order to buffer myself or to make myself less sensitive to criticism, I might adopt a more unconventional attitude or even begin to question tradition. Because creativity demands that I become highly involved with my materials, I might develop an achievement orientation. According to this interpretation, the traits that characterize creative individuals emerge over time, as a result of their desire to maximize their creativity.

According to this model of creativity, two interdependent and opposing forces are at work: the reward that comes from acting creatively; and the punishment that acting creatively sometimes brings. Teenagers are often acutely aware of the punishment (criticism) that comes when they dress differently or when they invent a new vocabulary to communicate their experiences. Similarly, academics are acutely aware of the punishment (criticism) that they may experience when they attempt to put forth a new theory (e.g., Seligman, 1990). In order to become truly creative and enjoy the rewards that come with creativity, individuals need to learn how to reduce the punishment (criticism) they often experience. They do this by attaching less importance to others' opinions. An unconventional attitude will also help serve to buffer them from criticism.

Early Experiences and Creativity

The work on early experiences suggests that learning plays an important role in developing the kind of personality that makes people more prone to be creative as adults. First, it has been shown that the intellectual values that characterize creative individuals seem to come from their families. Families that foster intellectual development tend to produce more creative individuals (Mumford & Gustafson, 1988). Second, the autonomy and independence that characterize creative individuals also come from their early upbringing. It has been shown, for example, that scientists who are more creative were subjected to less structure and less discipline (Stein, 1968), that their parents were less controlling and more likely to encourage openness to experience (Getzels & Jackson, 1962), and that the family environment gave them a firm sense of self as a creative entity (Trollinger, 1979). All of this research is consistent with the idea that creativity is largely learned.

Later Experiences and Creativity

Considerable evidence indicates that creativity is often fostered later in life through mentors and teachers. This research suggests that, at least in the sciences, what teachers and mentors do is to help novices internalize exacting professional standards along with a sense of excellence, achievement, and self-confidence (Zuckerman, 1974). The themes of excellence, achievement, and self-confidence run through much of the research on later influences. Mentors seem to teach—often through their example—the conditions that are necessary for creativity to emerge.

Birth Order and Creativity

In a fascinating book on birth order and family dynamics, Sulloway (1996) provides considerable evidence that later-borns are more creative than first-borns. He sets forth the proposition that, because first-borns tend to be the initial recipients of parents' attention, they are highly motivated to preserve their special position when other siblings come into the family. They do this by complying with the wishes of the parents and carrying on the traditions of the family. In short, they try to maintain the status quo. Later-borns, he argues, feel excluded from the position of privilege occupied by the first-born and, as a result, are inclined to rebel against the repressive power of the first-born siblings and devise strategies that will provide them with recognition and privilege. Thus, the later-borns nurture not only their creative abilities but their tendency to rebel against conventions and traditions. This is consistent with Sulloway's finding that later-borns tend to be characterized by openness to experience, a personality trait associated with being unconventional, adventurous, and rebellious. Sulloway argues, in essence, that openness is an acquired personality trait that grows out of the perception of being treated as a downtrodden underdog.

He offers some interesting historical information in support of his theory. For example, later-borns were 9.7 times more likely that first-borns to endorse the theory of evolution before the publication of Darwin's books. During the Reformation, later-borns were 46 times more likely to be burned at the stake than first-borns. Left-wing revolutionaries are 18 times more likely than right-wing revolutionaries to be later-borns.

The Cognitive Component

In this section, we will see that it is possible to increase creativity. By understanding the conditions that lead to greater creativity, we can learn how to motivate people to become more creative.

The Process of Creativity

Let's look at some of the important components of creativity: delineating the problem, knowledge, the ability to construct images and/or categories, the ability to synthesize, and the willingness to withhold judgment.

Delineating the problem. Delineating or defining the problem gives direction to our thinking. When we know the problem, we can immediately recognize which of the various patterns that our brain generates are potentially important or useful. Movie producers, publishers, and CEOs of large companies often depend on others for the solutions they require. Unless they know what the problem is, they are unable to determine which of the solutions that are constantly being offered to them are worth considering. Generally spending time to define the problem speeds up the subsequent creative process. By delineating and defining, we tell the brain what is and is not important. Obviously, the brain can arrive at a solution more quickly when it has less to deal with.

Knowledge. In order to generate new alternatives or new ideas, we need a well-developed information or knowledge base. Ideas do not arise spontaneously; they are typically the result of synthesizing information (Langley, Simon, Bradshaw, & Zykow, 1986). Accordingly, creativity is moderately related to intelligence,

The process of creativity typically involves the application of existing knowledge to a carefully delineated problem.

because we need a certain basic level of intelligence in order to acquire a knowledge base. Given that basic level of intelligence, what differentiates those who are creative from those who are not is their motivation to gather that information or acquire the knowledge base they need.

Recently, there has been a trend to teach creativity without providing the necessary knowledge base. People will encourage children to write creative stories or will hire a facilitator to help them solve problems. However, it is a misconception that creativity is independent of knowledge. If there is no depth to our knowledge, our creativity will blossom and then die, just as a flower will die without soil to nourish it.

New ideas are frequently the elaboration, extension, or new application of an existing idea. For example, Steve Jobs and Steve Woznicak, the co-inventors of the Apple Computer, used ideas and technology from a variety of sources to create the first personal computer (Young, 1988). Jazz composer Dave Brubeck used basic themes from Chopin and Japanese music to create some of his most successful songs (Calgary, 1997). If

creativity is the extension of existing ideas, it makes a great deal of sense to go out and systematically research what has been done before. That knowledge base could well provide the ingredients to create something new and different. To invent a commercial light bulb, Thomas Edison brought together a group of engineers who systematically tested a variety of ideas and principles. The greatest ideas in the world typically come from people who are best educated. It is no coincidence that countries such as the United States, with some of the best universities in the world, has produced proportionally more Nobel prizes than any other country (Business Week, Special Issue, 1989). To compete with the United States, Japan has adopted a principle of making endless small improvements, a principle that has come to be adopted by many industrialized countries throughout the world (Business Week, Special Issue, 1989).

Constructing images and categories. Pieces of information can be regarded as involving groups of patterns or components. Thinking about the sky, for example, fires a group of cells that correspond to the sensory experience I get when I look at the sky. I can also ask my brain to activate several memories or patterns simultaneously and thereby create a new image. For example, I can superimpose some clouds, perhaps add an airplane, and even insert the funnel of a tornado into my image of the sky. In each step, my image of the sky abruptly changes. I can also create images that no one has seen by combining patterns. I can, for example, insert a flying elephant into my sky if I wish. Dreams, it has been suggested, are nothing more than several patterns of neurons firing in the brain simultaneously (Hobson, 1988).

A verbal category, such as dog or silverware, can also be viewed as a pattern, even if I don't get a visual image. Thinking about the word *dog*, fires a group of cells that correspond to the attributes that define the corresponding category. If I try to think simultaneously of several different animals, such as dogs, cats, bears, and wolves, I would probably activate the superordinate category of animals or perhaps mammals.

Synthesis. Synthesis involves putting together components in order to create a whole. How does this happen? It can happen spontaneously, through what we call insight or creativity, or it can be approached in a very logical way, at least according to Edward DeBono, a specialist in how to become more creative. DeBono conceptualizes the brain as a highly sophisticated problem solver that looks for redundancy. When it finds that redundancy, a new pattern emerges in the brain. This model is consistent with the way behavioral scientists regard the emergence of distinct images.

According to DeBono, we can speed up this process of finding redundancy by deliberately activating various patterns in the brain. DeBono calls this *lateral thinking* (1987). According to him, we do not have to learn how to see new patterns when they emerge. As soon as a new pattern emerges, it will be recognized immediately as something new and distinct. Patterns are the basis for categories. The only thing left for us to do when a pattern emerges is to assign a name to the new pattern, so that we can retrieve it at will. Note that the early writers described creativity as an "aha" or insight experience. It happened when people suddenly recognized that two disparate things were related, because they shared certain common features.

Redundancy is the basis for perception and meaning. For example, when we can see something—a chair, perhaps—as distinct from the background, we have a perception. Meaning typically involves intention. Thus, if I take another person by the arm and lead him or her across the street, we say the act has meaning; it was intended to help or assist.

Obviously, the idea that the brain is designed to search for redundancy among patterns is consistent with the finding that creativity is linked to the willingness to tolerate ambiguity—the willingness to simultaneously entertain various pieces of information that do not seem related. Likewise, this idea is consistent with the link between creativity and openness to information. The brain is always alert for new information to include in its search for redundancy.

We can use lateral thinking to generate alternatives when we are problem solving. Instead of waiting patiently for an idea to emerge, we actively generate possibilities, often using past experience. If I want to get a ball off a roof, I might think of various possibilities, the most obvious being a ladder. In the absence of a ladder, I might become more creative and entertain possibilities such as throwing rocks at it, using the force of the water from a garden hose to dislodge it, climbing a tree near the house and jumping over to the roof to get it, hiring a helicopter, and so forth. Obviously, some of these ideas are better than others, and I can simply select from among the alternatives. Another example of lateral thinking is to open the dictionary at random and start reading words, in the hope that one of the words will stimulate me to come up with an answer. The words are intended to activate various patterns in the brain.

Hobson (1988), whose ideas on dreaming we discussed in Chapter 6, has suggested that the brain has a natural tendency to link these different patterns by creating a story. Other theorists have suggested that the brain creates categories that allow us to summarize the essential features contained in a body of information (Langer, 1989). Still others have argued that some type of reorganization or reintegration allows us to make sense out of information or gain insight into it (Kaha, 1983). If you are in New Orleans, for example, you might wonder why there are costumed people in the street; realizing that it is Mardi Gras would make sense of that information. These various ideas—storytelling, the creation of categories, and reintegration—all imply some type of synthesis.

Suspension of judgment. Making judgments will stop the creative process—that is, stop synthesis (Strickland, 1989). People with strong opinions often have difficulty being creative, because they are inclined to short-circuit the creative process by making premature judgments. Langer (1989) has identified premature judgments as a cause or characteristic of mindlessness. Hobson (1988) has suggested that, in order to dream (which is a kind of creative storytelling), people need to set aside their self-referent or self-reflection systems. Some researchers have suggested that being introspective or self-focused can interfere with making good decisions. For example, Wilson & Schooler (1991) found that, when people were made aware of the reasons for their choices, they adopted nonoptimal strategies, presumably because their attention shifted away from the more global problem at hand. In order for categories to emerge spontaneously, we need to free the brain from constraints. We need to learn to suspend judgment long enough for the creative process to run its course.

Adopting a playful attitude is a good way of suspending judgment. The very nature of play is to have fun without the need to achieve a goal or find closure. Play allows us to deal with uncertainty and ambiguity and to incorporate fantasy. In its purest form, creativity involves the complete suspension of judgment.

Learning to Be Creative

If the brain is designed to synthesize, then it should be possible to promote creativity by simply juxtaposing certain pieces of information in our brain. Extensive data supports this idea.

Remote associations. An interesting study showed that giving people moderately remote word associations as opposed to highly remote associations produced greater creative achievements (MacKinnon, 1962;

Practical Application 12-3

Motivating Creativity by Asking, "What If?"

The brain tends to resist forming new ideas. When people try to think creatively, their brains only generate solutions that are consistent with socially accepted ideas of what is true or correct. As a result, people find that, when they attempt to be creative, their brain only offers them a rehash of everything they already know. The problem, therefore, is to get the brain to break out of existing patterns and entertain new ones.

At least three conditions are necessary to trigger the emergence of new patterns (DeBono, 1970). First, we need to juxtapose two seemingly unrelated ideas, so the brain will look for new ways of relating that information. While juxtaposing two pieces of unrelated information is not that difficult, the brain's initial tendency is to ignore the juxtaposition. If the pieces of information haven't been perceived as related in the past, the brain is inclined to make the judgment that they are unrelated and should remain so. Thus, the second thing we need to do is to induce the brain to withhold this kind of premature judgment. Sometimes, simply telling the brain to withhold judgment is sufficient to increase creativity. The third thing we must do is to allow the brain time to do its job. There is considerable evidence that, given enough time, the brain will find areas of similarity, no matter how remote those similarities might be. During this time of incubation, as it is often called, the brain appears to ruminate—to look at ideas from many perspectives. This process of rumination allows the brain to discover relationships. Sometimes people have access to this process via their inner dialogue. They will hear themselves say, for example, "If I did X, then maybe Y would occur and perhaps, if I did Y, then Z would happen." If rumination is to occur, we must learn to tolerate ambiguity and uncertainty. By demanding certainty and predictability at all times, we will certainly short-circuit the process.

In *Lateral Thinking*, DeBono (1970) suggests a number of techniques to facilitate the formulation of juxtapositions and to inhibit the brain's natural tendency to reject

Gough, 1976). A moderately remote association involves words with some overlap, whereas a highly remote association involves words with little overlap. In the context of designing a building, for example, the name of a shape, such as pyramid, would represent a moderately remote association, whereas the name of a fruit, such as pear, would represent a highly remote association. It is not hard to imagine the relevance of a pyramid to the design of a building; the relevance of a pear is much less clear.

According to DeBono (1987), exercises that encourage individuals to make remote associations can trigger their creativity. He has invented a number of such exercises (Practical Application 12-3). If the techniques used to solve these exercises become habitual, people may learn to be creative. This idea is consistent with the finding that the dreams of creative professionals were more implausible and unrealistic than the dreams of less creative professionals (Sladeczek & Domino, 1985). Perhaps, as DeBono has suggested, some people learn to make more remote associations, and that style of thinking is found in their dreams as well as their waking state.

Creativity across the lifespan. In various areas of endeavor, major contributions tend to be made by people in young adulthood, whereas minor contributions tend to peak at middle age (Lehman, 1966). There are at least three possibilities: creativity declines with age, motivation changes with age, or younger people are more likely to make remote associations.

Few psychologists believe that the capacity for creativity decreases with increasing age. Often, middle-aged people have an excellent knowledge base and, therefore, there is no reason why they shouldn't be able to make major contributions. Further, the fact that they often make good minor contributions suggests they have the capacity for dealing with complex material. Finally, there is considerable evidence that many older people remain highly creative throughout their lives.

such juxtapositions. One technique he suggests is the random-word method. If we get stuck on a problem, we can simply pick up a dictionary and randomly read out words. The goal of this technique is to stimulate the brain to activate patterns that were previously inactive, in the hope that they will provide the link between two seemingly remote ideas on our path to a solution. In addition, the random-word technique seems to elicit a playful attitude, which can help to inhibit the judgment process.

DeBono emphasizes that solutions to problems often involve a series of steps; this idea is contrary to the popular myth that the correct solutions to problems emerge suddenly and in their final form. He argues that the key to problem-solving and creativity is to induce the brain to do what it does naturally—find links between things that initially may seem unrelated.

By forcing the brain to look for these relationships and learning to tolerate ambiguity in the process, we should be able to become more creative. According to DeBono, we need to learn to withhold judgment, to accept as many divergent views as possible, and to feel comfortable with ambiguity. We need to learn to ask, "What if?"

By adopting this playful attitude, we free ourselves from the rules of convention, the rules of tradition, the rules of closure, the rules of consistency, the rules of logic, the rules of time, and the rules of place. In short, we put ourselves in a position to juxtapose anything we like, in any way we like. When we do this, we provide the brain with the ideal set of conditions for doing what it has been designed to do: to generate new possibilities, new alternatives, and new realities.

However, it appears that motivational concerns may shift from youth to middle age. For example, as people reach middle age, they come to value pragmatic achievements, perhaps because they are more concerned with career development than are younger people (e.g., Vaillant, 1977). There are also data to indicate that the generation of ideas is more important to younger individuals than to older individuals (Macon, 1987).

What about the ability to make remote associations? Again, this may simply be a matter of motivation. Although young adults often produce a number of highly creative solutions—for instance, to a problem requiring mechanical ingenuity—middle-aged adults produce more workable solutions. It may well be that, with experience, people learn which types of associations have a higher payoff (Owens, 1969). Alternatively, it may be that, with experience, people tend to rely more on tried and true procedures, which may inhibit reintegration by virtue of their stability, prior use, and automaticity (Barsalou, 1983).

Summary

There are at least three reasons why people engage in acts of creativity: to satisfy their need for novel and varied stimulation; to improve their ability to communicate ideas and values; and to help them to solve problems. The various definitions of creativity offered over the years have all been useful in helping us to understand the nature of creativity.

DeBono takes the position that the brain evolved to isolate predictability and consistency and, as a result, is highly resistant to forming new patterns. Similarly, Langer argues that many behaviors become automatic (habitual) and that, as a result, we tend to become mindless. Like DeBono, she argues that it is highly adaptive for us to be able to do things without thinking about them. Unfortunately, as our environment changes, we continue to do the same things, even though they are no longer adaptive. To break out of our habitual behavior patterns, we need to become mindful.

Maslow and other writers have argued that we have an urge to create that is not driven wholly by our need to adapt. In Maslow's theory, this urge to create is called the need for self-actualization. Zuckerman's research suggests that sensation seekers may partly satisfy their need for variety and change through acts of creativity.

Numerous researchers have suggested that many people, while potentially creative, inhibit creative behavior because it may conflict with conventional or traditional opinions. People characterized by rigidity may inhibit creativity because of their strong need for predictability. The idea that all people are potentially creative is consistent with the observation that, when the right conditions exist, generally uncreative people will suddenly demonstrate that they can be creative and also with the demonstration that creativity can be increased through rewards.

Personality characteristics that have been linked to creativity include intellectual and artistic values, breadth of interests, attraction to complexity, high energy, a concern with work and achievement, independence of judgment, autonomy, intuition, self-confidence, tolerance for ambiguity, a willingness to resolve conflict, creative self-image, and openness to new experiences and new ways of viewing things.

It can be argued that, because they find creativity so rewarding, people learn to adopt certain orientations to the world and themselves—certain beliefs and attitudes—that increase the likelihood of their being creative. Work on the effect of early and later experiences is consistent with this hypothesis.

Creativity involves at least five important steps: delineating or defining the problem; gathering information and knowledge; constructing images and/or categories; synthesizing; and withholding judgment. Many writers have suggested that we can learn to be more creative. An interesting study on this topic showed that people produced greater creative achievements when confronted with moderately remote word associations, rather than highly remote associations.

Major creative contributions tend to be made in young adulthood, whereas minor contributions tend to peak at middle age. The evidence suggests that motivation changes with age, so that younger people are more inclined to make remote associations. Research on birth order indicates that later-borns are more likely to be creative than first-borns.

According to DeBono, we can learn to be more creative (1) by learning to juxtapose information or ideas;

(2) by learning to withhold our natural tendency to reject the juxtaposition of two things because past experience suggests that they are unrelated; and (3) by giving ourselves time.

Main Points

1. The early behaviorists suggested that exploratory behavior was learned.

2. The tendency of animals to alternate in a T-maze has been shown to be motivated by the tendency to respond to change.

3. Research has shown that monkeys are motivated by the visual, auditory, and manipulatory properties of stimulus objects.

4. Humans are motivated to seek out variety and novelty.

5. Various studies have shown that animals and humans are motivated to seek out optimal complexity.

6. When animals are anxious or emotional, they tend not to seek out novelty or complexity.

7. There is considerable evidence that the tendency to explore has a genetic basis. Individuals with a temperamental disposition characterized by low curiosity and exploratory behavior are usually also characterized by high anxiety.

8. According to the information-processing model, the tendency to explore is linked to the need or tendency to process new and different information.

9. The preference for complexity increases with age and the degree of previous exposure to various levels of complexity.

10. Dember and Earl's theory suggests that stimulation of optimal complexity motivates exploration.

11. According to Berlyne's theory, arousal will increase when a person or animal processes new information. Therefore, the environment is always a source of potential arousal.

12. Berlyne has identified a class of variables associated with arousal—the collative variables. These include novelty, degree of change, suddenness of change, surprisingness, incongruity, conflict, complexity, and uncertainty.

13. Numerous studies have shown that, when arousal is too high, organisms are not inclined to explore novelty.

14. One implication of the research on arousal and exploration is that, to promote exploratory behavior, it is important to make people relaxed and free from anxiety.

15. Extrinsic motivation not only reduces the tendency to explore but undermines intrinsic motivation.

16. We can facilitate intrinsic motivation by giving people the freedom to organize tasks as they want and by reducing or eliminating competing motives.

17. High sensation seekers are motivated by a need for varied, novel, and complex sensations and experiences and are willing to take physical and social risks in order to get them.

18. High sensation seekers' tendency to be open and unconventional can result in delinquency; if properly channeled, it can lead to creativity and productivity.

19. High sensation seekers have low monoamine oxidase levels, while low sensation seekers have high monoamine oxidase levels.

20. High sensation seekers tend to be involved in a wide range of sports over a period of time.

21. High sensation seekers tend to use drugs, to have a variety of sex partners, and to like situations that allow them to behave in an uninhibited manner.

22. High sensation seekers tend to have a thinking style that is characterized by flexibility, tolerance of ambiguity, and unpredictability. These qualities probably make the sensation seeker more creative.

23. High sensation seekers like to make decisions, like to make them quickly, are willing to make them with incomplete information, and are inclined to abandon plans that aren't working.

24. Sensation seekers are inclined to keep their options open.

25. People are motivated to be creative by, in particular, the need for novel, varied and complex stimulation, the need to communicate, and the need to solve problems.

26. Creativity is defined as the tendency to generate or recognize ideas, alternatives, or possibilities that may be useful in solving problems, communicating with others, and entertaining ourselves and others.

27. DeBono has suggested that the tendency to create patterns in the brain tends to make our brains resistant to creativity.

28. Langer suggests that we have a natural tendency to become mindless, and that in order to act creatively we need to become more mindful.
29. It has been suggested that, as humans, we have a creative urge; despite our tendency to be motivated towards predictability and consistency.
30. Learning theories suggest that creativity can be viewed as disinhibition.
31. The tendency towards rigidity may be motivated by the desire to reduce anxiety or arousal.
32. Creativity can be increased by a psycholgical climate that encourages creativity. This idea is consistent with the demonstration that creativity can be increased with rewards.
33. Personality characteristics that can be linked to creativity include intellectual and artistic values, breadth of interests, attraction to complexity, high energy, a concern with work and achievement, independence of judgment, autonomy, intuition, self-confidence, ability to tolerate and resolve conflict, a creative self-image, and openness to new experiences and new ways of viewing things.
34. It has been suggested that, because creativity is rewarding, people learn to adopt certain beliefs and attitudes that increase their opportunity to act creatively.
35. People who are creative tend to come from families that value intellectual development and encourage autonomy and independence.
36. There are four important components of creativity: knowledge, the ability to construct images and/or categories, the ability to synthesize, and the willingness to withhold judgment.
37. Moderately remote associations are more likely to lead to creativity than highly remote associations.
38. Major creative contributions tend to be made by younger people, whereas minor creative contributions are more likely to be made by older people.
39. DeBono has offered a number of techniques that can help people overcome their natural tendency to be uncreative.

Chapter Thirteen

Competence: Predictability and Control, Achievement and Mastery, and Self-Esteem

■ *Does everybody have a need for predictability and control?*

■ *Is it a good thing to have a need to control?*

■ *Does the need for control make people more successful?*

■ *Do people vary in the need to achieve or master?*

■ *Can people develop the motivation to achieve?*

■ *How do success and failure experiences affect the tendency to achieve?*

■ *Why do some people set difficult goals, while others do not?*

■ *Where do our feelings of self-esteem and self-worth come from?*

■ *Is it good to take pride in our achievements, or does pride make us vulnerable?*

■ *Is it normal for people to experience self-doubt when they fail?*

■ *If we are to experience high self-esteem, what kind of self-concept do we need?*

To survive, succeed, and go where no person has gone before, organisms need to develop competence. Competence is more than simply having or developing a set of skills. It involves being able to successfully deal with threats, being able to successfully interact with the environment, being able to set goals, and being able to see oneself as capable of going where no other person has gone before. In this chapter we look at some basic human needs that pertain to the development of competence. First we look at the need to control. It has been suggested that the need to control grows out of our need for a predictable environment. This need insures that we can deal efficiently and effectively with the world in which we live. Research indicates that when we lose control we begin to experience negative emotions such as anxiety, depression, and stress. Conversely, when we have control, we experience a sense of well-being, together with good physical and psychological health. Next we discuss the need to achieve and the need to master. These needs or dispositions are fundamental to developing the knowledge and skills that allow us to interact successfully with the environment as well as get what we need and want from life. Much of human behavior, at least in the Western world, is devoted to going beyond satisfying survival needs. Humans have aspirations, they set goals, and they experience the satisfaction that comes from doing what no other person has done before. Finally, we will consider self-esteem. Because humans are self-reflective by nature, they can experience self-esteem. Research indicates that when people have a good opinion of their ability to deal with important things in their lives (good self-esteem), they are inclined to take charge of their lives, to set difficult goals for themselves, and aspire to do things that no other person has done before. Good self-esteem, in other words, is central to developing competence. Without it, people often fail to realize their potential.

The Need for Predictability and Control

The need to control may be one of the most fundamental of all human needs (Shapiro, Schwartz, & Astin, 1996). Individuals' ability to gain and maintain control

is essential for their survival (Averill, 1973). Furthermore, the need to control appears to be linked to our need for predictability.

At birth, the infant's focus is almost solely on survival. The baby is only interested in food, comfort, and safety, and attempts to make those elements predictable by crying whenever they are absent (Hoffman, 1982). Once these basic needs of survival are predictable, the infant turns to other things, such as exploring the environment. As we saw in Chapter 12, some theorists suggest that mastery is the outcome of such exploratory behavior. This implies that mastery only arises when the individual is free of anxiety, but it seems likely that mastery also takes place under conditions of anxiety. Sternberg (1991) has suggested that we need to recognize different kinds of competency that arise out of different situational demands.

Research indicates that personal control provides the cognitive basis for experiencing optimism and hope. More fundamentally, personal control is linked to health.

Control and Health

Psychological Health

Control appears to be one of the most critical variables involved in psychological health and well-being (e.g., Bandura, 1989; Seligman, 1990). In fact, feelings of loss or lack of control have been implicated in a wide range of disorders, including stress, depression, anxiety, drug addiction, and eating disorders (Shapiro et al., 1996). Note that comparisons of clinical and nonclinical populations have shown that nonclinical individuals "overestimate the amount of control they have in a situation, are more optimistic about their ability to control and believe they have more skills than they actually do" (Shapiro et al., 1996, p. 1214). Such results point to the importance of having a sense of control to function normally and successfully within our society. Without that sense of control, people lose their ability to cope effectively with even the smallest difficulties.

The stress literature also indicates the importance of control. Laboratory studies have shown that it is relatively easy to trigger the stress response, by first giving people control over an aversive stimulus, such as shock, and then removing that control. When the abil-

We attempt, to the best of our abilities, to make our lives relatively predictable.

ity to control is restored, the stress response typically subsides (e.g., Glass, 1977). The stress literature indicates that, when people are able to make coping responses, they are far less inclined to experience stress. Interestingly, they benefit even if the attempts to cope do not work. This suggests that the individuals' belief that they are in control is of primary importance.

Physical Health

People who have greater perceived control over their lives tend to live longer. In an oft-cited study by Rodin and Langer (1977), nursing home residents who were given control over such things as the time and nature of meals and the choice of movies were healthier, and lived longer, than a matched comparison group.

Studies of cancer patients have shown that low perceived control and a sense of helplessness are strong predictors not only of recurrence of the disease but of death. Similarly, low perceived control has been implicated in cardiovascular disease (Shapiro et al., 1996). While a sense of control often does not reverse the course of a disease, at least in its final stages, perceived control has been linked to individuals' adjustment to the disease and overall quality of life.

Laboratory studies suggest that low perceived control may suppress the immune function (Kamen, Rodin, Seligman, & Dwyer, 1991). Numerous studies have shown that both acute and chronic stress suppress the immune response (Kiecolt-Glaser & Glaser, 1992). It has been suggested that the link between stress and the immune system is mediated by feelings of loss of control (Hassenfeld, 1993).

Now that we have some preliminary understanding of the need for control, let's analyze its biological, learned, and cognitive components.

The Biological Component

Is there a genetic basis for individuals' sense of personal control? To answer this question we need a way of measuring personal control. One of the most widely used instruments, Rotter's Locus of Control Scale, provides a score indicating the degree to which individuals are internal—that is, believe the cause of behavior lies within themselves—or external—that is, believe the cause of behavior lies outside themselves. Twin studies using Rotter's scale have found that genetics accounts for about 30% of the variance associated not only with personal control but with how responsible people felt for misfortunes in their lives (Pedersen, Gatz, Plomin, Nesselroade, & McClearn, 1989). These results indicate that there is a genetic basis for feelings of personal control.

The Learned Component

Rotter's (1966) distinction between internal and external personality types has its roots in reinforcement theory. He suggests that people adopt an internal locus of control if they perceive, as a result of their past experiences, that taking control produces certain anticipated or desired results. Conversely, if they perceive that taking control does not produce certain anticipated or desired results, they will perceive that things that happen to them lie outside their control. While he recognizes that individuals may feel more control in certain situations than in others, he argues, nonetheless, that they come to develop a generalized belief that they are the cause of events in their life including their misfortunes (internal locus) or that the cause of such events lies outside themselves (external locus).

More recently, researchers have concluded that beliefs about cause and control are not determined solely by the individuals' past reinforcement history. In western cultures, we are inclined to think about *active control*—that is, about our ability to change the external environment. If we are experiencing stress, for example, we are inclined to engage in behaviors that will remove the stressors from our lives. If we cannot remove the stressors, we may decide to distance ourselves from them. In Asian cultures, people are more inclined to think in terms of *self-control*. Rather than actively trying to get rid of stressors, they would be inclined to reduce the impact of the stressors by engaging in self-control strategies (Shapiro et al., 1996).

These two approaches to control are very different. Moreover, they imply different approaches to helping those who are experiencing a loss of control. In western cultures, a therapist might encourage such people to become more assertive. This approach grows out of a philosophy of individualism that encourages self-determination. In Asian cultures, a therapist might be more inclined to train people to accept loss of control and to use self-control strategies such as meditation, relaxation, and cognitive modification to reduce the impact of the stressor. This approach grows out of a philosophy that emphasizes the collective or the community (the larger group) as opposed to the individual (Shapiro et al., 1996).

In more recent times, many western theorists have come to incorporate more Asian ideas into their theories. For example, Lazarus, whose work we considered in Chapter 9, has made a distinction between two forms of coping: one involves mastery or problem-solving (active coping), while the other involves controlling our autonomic responses by meditation, relaxation, or biofeedback (Lazarus, 1991). Similarly, when people from Asian cultures come to the United States,

they often find it necessary to become more assertive. In western society, assertiveness is viewed not only as adaptive but as essential.

The key point here is simply that our attitudes to control issues are shaped by how our parents thought and acted, by how they trained us to think and act, and by how our culture taught us to act.

The Cognitive Component

We live in a world in which we can control some things but not others. What if I find that I might miss an important appointment because traffic is particularly heavy. Should I attempt to see if I can make up time by cutting in and out and running a few red lights, or should I simply accept it? Alternatively, what if I discover that I lost some important points on a test that was returned. Should I simply ignore it, or should I point this out to my professor?

Researchers have established that individuals react very differently to situations involving issues of control (Evans, Shapiro, & Lewis, 1993). Some people realize that there are situations they can control and others they cannot control. Others react inappropriately, however: those with a high need to control may attempt to control the uncontrollable; those with a low need to control may make no attempt to control a situation that is in fact controllable.

When people try to control situations that are essentially uncontrollable, they are inclined to experience high levels of stress. Thus, suggesting that they need to take active control is bad advice in those situations. What they need to do is to accept that some things are beyond their control. Similarly, teaching people to accept a situation that could readily be changed may be bad advice; sometimes the only way to get what you want is to take active control. Research has shown that, when people who feel helpless fail to take control, they experience negative emotional states such as anxiety and depression. Like stress, these negative emotions can impair the immune response. It is obvious from all this that health is not linearly related to control. For optimum health, people should be encouraged to take control up to a point but to recognize the point at which further control is impossible.

It's important to note that the internal and external dimensions of Rotter's Locus of Control Scale are independent (Levenson, 1981). That means we can be high on both, low on both, or high on one and low on the other. Recall that, according to Seligman's theory, an internal orientation is more likely to result in depression, whereas an external orientation may be a defense against depression. As Seligman was careful to point out, he did not mean that people should give up their attempts to control; rather, they should come to understand that there are benefits from not taking too much control.

A famous prayer sums up this issue: "Please, God, give me the courage to change what can be changed, the serenity to accept what I cannot, and the wisdom to know the difference."

Control and Mastery

The research literature indicates that believing that we have control is essential if we are to engage in mastery and achievement behaviors. Without this generalized belief, we will not be inclined to initiate such behaviors.

Bandura's research indicates that not only behavioral control but also cognitive control is necessary in order to initiate new behaviors, something we discussed in detail in Chapter 11 (Ozer & Bandura, 1990). Bandura's concept of cognitive control corresponds to Rotter's internal orientation. That orientation is what allows people to initiate mastery behaviors. As we saw in Chapter 11, there is also considerable evidence that people only initiate new behaviors when they have optimism and hope. The bottom line is that people will not be motivated to work toward mastery and achievement unless they believe that their behavior will effect some desired outcome.

Summary

The need for control is fundamental. It has been implicated in psychological and physical health and in our ability to get what we want from life. Twin studies have been shown that about 30% of the variance associated with personal control is due to genetics. Cultural differences in attitudes to control have been noted: in western societies, the emphasis is on active control, whereas Asian societies value self-control. While both active control and self-control can be effective proce-

dures, we need to match our control strategy to the demands of the situation. Attempting to control an uncontrollable situation tends to produce stress, whereas making no attempt to take charge of a controllable situation has been linked to anxiety and depression.

Mastery and Achievement Motivation

Mastery involves acquiring knowledge and developing skills. It also denotes complete learning. To master something, you learn everything there is to know about it or you develop the skill to its highest possible level. *Achievement* involves attaining a goal such as a university degree. Mastery is usually implicated in high levels of achievement, but not always; some people achieve things without complete mastery.

Achievement often calls upon us not only to master a certain set of skills or acquire a certain body of knowledge but also to learn how to deal with our emotions, including self-doubt. In other words, while mastery may be important for achievement, it does not guarantee that you will achieve your goals. Being an optimist, for example, may be the most important factor in achieving goals.

The function of mastery is to insure that the individual develops competence in various areas. *Competence,* among other things, involves skill, ability, capacity, proficiency, or fitness. These are some of the qualities that we need in order to interact with the environment and to get what we want from life. Take social competency as an example. In order to be socially accepted or to work in certain social situations, we need a basic set of social skills and knowledge. Without social competency, we might be excluded from certain jobs or social events. It might even be difficult or impossible to marry and raise children unless we possess some basic level of social competency.

Mastery and achievement can be contrasted with a laissez-faire approach to life. Instead of searching for a job, the laissez-faire person simply waits for a job to come along. As we have seen, whether an individual initiates mastery and achievement behaviors will depend on his or her beliefs about control.

People with a mastery and achievement orientation have a sense of *agency* (Bandura, 1989). They take action so that they get what they want from life. Psychologists often characterize the person who is inclined to make things happen as *instrumental*. To make things happen, such individuals set goals and make plans to attain those goals. Moreover, as Bandura and others have pointed out, they are not undermined the first time they fail to attain their goal. Instead, they adjust their plan or simply make a new plan. In the final analysis, people who take control also take responsibility for their actions. They take responsibility not only for successes but for their failures.

Achievement Motivation

Henry Murray (1938), a pioneer in this field, defined the need to achieve as a desire or tendency to "overcome obstacles, to exercise power, to strive to do something difficult as well as and as quickly as possible" (pp. 80–81). As we see from this definition, Murray saw achievement as a generalized need. Like others, he believed that the pleasure of achievement is not in attaining the goal but rather in developing and exercising skills. In other words, it is the process that provides the motivation for achievement. As we'll see shortly, many other theorists have come to the same conclusion.

For over four decades, David McClelland has been doing research related to the achievement motive. His extensive contributions are summarized in his book *Human Motivation* (McClelland, 1985). In order to measure the achievement motive with more precision, McClelland and his colleagues adapted the Thematic Apperception Test (TAT) and developed a precise method for scoring the achievement motive (McClelland, Atkinson, Clark, & Lowell, 1953). A number of studies to assess the validity of the TAT measure that they devised show that a generalized motive or disposition does exist and that it can predict behavior in a wide variety of situations (e.g., Atkinson, 1953; French, 1956; Mischel, 1961).

The Biological Component

While researchers have not been able to identify an obvious biological link to a brain center or a neurotransmitter, McClelland and others have argued that achievement motive grows out of a more basic incentive to "do something better"—not to gain approval or any other kind of external reward, but "for its own sake" (McClelland, 1985, p. 228). McClelland points out that the development of this natural incentive is shaped by the environment. For example, parents play an important role, often by providing the kind of environment that allows the achievement motive to flourish. We'll return to this topic shortly.

White's Theory of Competence

One of the most influential articles on the nature of mastery and competence was published by Robert White (1959). Drawing heavily on the work conducted in the early 1950s, which showed that curiosity and exploratory behavior are not tied to primary drives such as hunger, thirst, and sex, he suggested that the tendency to explore is based on a more general motive, which he called *effectance motivation*. This motive, White suggested, is directed towards understanding the nature of the environment and the order inherent in it. Feelings of *efficacy* occur when the individual comes to understand or know that he or she is able to affect the environment. Such feelings, White argues, can act as a reward. An infant who discovers that, whenever she kicks her feet, the mobile hanging above her head moves, for example, will experience feelings of efficacy. She might smile, laugh, or show some other outward sign of her internal state. Most important, she will gain a sense of mastery.

White suggests that effectance motivation subsides when the situation has been so thoroughly explored that it no longer presents new possibilities. Thus, unlike primary (biological) rewards, which tend to produce a highly repetitive behavior, feelings of efficacy lead to the persistence of a behavior only so long as it can produce new stimulation or knowledge. This is very similar to Berlyne's idea that arousal potential subsides as the individual processes all the information contained in a stimulus and to Dember and Earl's idea that the motivational incentive of a stimulus wanes as the individual's complexity level shifts upward in the pacer range.

White notes that effectance motivation often fails to be aroused when the individual is anxious or when other motive systems are engaged. He suggests that this arrangement is biologically adaptive. It means that, when survival motives are engaged, the individual fully attends to the task at hand and that, when survival needs are not pressing, the individual can spend the time necessary to explore all the possibilities in the situation. Note that it takes time to exhaust the possibilities of a situation. The individual must not feel pressured or try to take shortcuts; doing so would result in incomplete knowledge.

Piaget's Theory of Competence

Another theorist who has had a profound impact on the understanding the competency is Jean Piaget, whose ideas we discussed in Chapter 2. Like White, Piaget believed that the need to interact with the environment forces the child to engage in the process of mastery (Piaget, 1970). Piaget conceptualized this in terms of two complementary processes. First, the child has to develop cognitive structures, a process called *accommodation*. Equipped with certain cognitive structures, the child then integrates information contained in his or her environment though a process called *assimilation*, which most psychologists now simply call information processing. Assimilation is always limited by existing cognitive structures, and consequently, when the child encounters new information that is inconsistent with existing structures, he or she will be unable to process that information adequately. This leads to the process of accommodation. Thus over a lifetime, the individual goes back and forth between assimilation and accommodation. The end result is the development of competence.

Some of the implications of these two theories for parents and teachers are considered in Practical Application 13-1.

Conclusions

While theorists have argued that an underlying biology governs mastery and competency, none have tried to single out certain brain structures or neurotransmitters. White and others have pointed out that anxiety plays an important role in the mastery process. Perhaps, rather than saying that anxiety eliminates the tendency to master, we should say that anxiety alters individuals' focus. When they are anxious, their focus tends to narrow and become restrictive; it is directed towards survival cues. When they are free of anxiety,

Practical Application 13-1

Competence: Lessons for Parents and Teachers

What lessons can parents and teachers draw from the research on competence? The theories of Berlyne, Dember and Earl (Chapter 12), White, and Piaget all suggest that children are biologically equipped to develop competence provided certain conditions are met.

1. A stimulating and varied environment must be available. Without such an environment, the motivation to develop competence will be lacking. It appears that stimulation at a level such as to create moderate incongruity will elicit the intrinsic motivation necessary for developing new cognitive structures, raising the adaptation level, or abstracting new principles.
2. The child must be freed from competing motives. Survival motives, such as hunger and thirst, take precedence over the motivation to develop competence; anxiety appears to be particularly debilitating (White, 1959; Dember & Earl, 1957).
3. The child must be free to respond as he or she sees fit. There is good reason to believe that a child left to his or her own ways will eventually exhaust all the possibilities. That children do this in different ways should not be surprising if we remember that the motivation for processing information comes from the environment, which is highly varied.
4. The child must not be pressured by time. The development of cognitive structures appears to be essentially an abstracting process, in which the child must differentiate relevant from irrelevant information. This can be a very time-consuming process, even for a computer.

by contrast, their focus tends to be broad and inclusive; it is directed more towards general learning.

As already noted, researchers are tending to turn their attention away from general mastery and instead are analyzing the factors that give rise to particular competencies. Using that strategy, researchers will be able to better incorporate the concept of talent. *Talent* is a capacity for doing or learning something. There is considerable evidence that people are born with different talents for music, athletics, and academics, for instance. Even within those broad areas, there appear to be differences in talent. Researchers need to examine how talent interacts with learned and cognitive variables to produce high levels of achievement.

The Learned Component

Social Learning Theory

According to social learning theory, children learn from their observation of adults that one way to get what they want from life is to gain knowledge and develop skills. They may notice, for example, that an athlete they admire receives not only a great deal of money but also approval from society. As a result, they may begin to model those whom they admire. They not only dress like their hero but they begin to imitate the behavior. In order to facilitate this process, they may buy books and magazines and they try to watch the athlete as often as they can, on television or at a sporting event. According to social learning theory, modeling and imitation are the processes by which individuals secure what they want from life. The motivation is provided by money, social approval, and other rewards.

Social learning theory provides a broad framework that allows us to understand not only why individuals in our society may be inclined to select particular goals but also how individuals acquire the skills they need. What it doesn't tell us is why people often develop a generalized need state called—by Murray and others—the need to achieve or the need to master. Why are some people inclined to engage in achievement and mastery behaviors for their own sake? According to McClelland, we come to internalize certain values, and this internalization process is what gives rise to the disposition to achieve. Let's look at some research that has its roots in McClelland's theory.

Independence and Mastery Parenting

Several studies in the experimental literature show that, when parents emphasized or encouraged early independence and mastery, children scored higher on need for achievement. In these studies, need for achievement was measured by asking children to produce imaginative stories and coding the stories by a procedure designed to assess the amount of achievement imagery. McClelland and his colleagues employed this procedure, which is rather time-consuming but essentially reliable and valid, because they were unable to construct questionnaires that were consistently valid (McClelland, 1985).

Other studies used different techniques to determine whether certain parenting methods resulted in high need achievement scores. One study established that children who scored high on need for achievement had parents who had encouraged them, for instance, to do well in school, to look after their possessions, and to try hard things by themselves (Winterbottom, 1958). In another study, children who were high and low in need for achievement were blindfolded and asked to stack blocks as high as they could with their left hand, while their parents watched. The parents were asked how well they thought their children would do. As predicted, children with a high need to achieve were more likely to have parents who had high expectations (Rosen & D'Andrade, 1959). One study showed that even putting children on a feeding schedule and requiring them to regulate their sphincters in a socially appropriate manner led to increased achievement motivation (McClelland & Pilon, 1983).

What these and other studies showed is that, when children are encouraged to be independent and to master, they tend to develop a higher need to achieve. To assess whether this motive tends to grow and develop over time and is the result of the cumulative number of demands, McClelland and his colleagues looked at the strength of the need to achieve motive at different ages. As Figure 13-1 shows, there is considerable evidence that the motive is linked to independence and mastery (McClelland et al., 1953).

The general theory that McClelland (1985) has offered for these findings is that children have an inborn capacity to experience satisfaction (reward) as a result of *progressive mastery*. If the individual repeatedly expe-

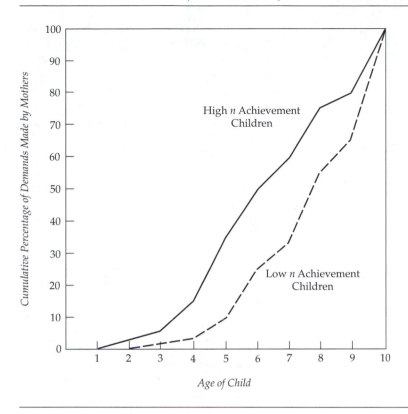

Figure 13-1. Cumulative curves showing the proportion of total demands made up to each age level as reported by mothers of children scoring high and low on *n* achievement (McClelland, Atkinson, Clark, & Lowell, 1953, after Winterbottom, 1958).

riences that satisfaction, the corresponding inborn motive state will be strengthened.

McClelland argues that the achievement motive can be aroused directly by challenging the individual or by presenting the individual with a situation that would offer the opportunity to master. What is aroused, presumably, are anticipatory feelings of satisfaction that could come from engaging in mastery behaviors.

Conclusions

Learning theorists have attempted to show that the tendency to achieve, master, or gain competence can be largely understood on the basis of principles of learning. While social learning theorists have focused on why people come to learn certain behaviors rather than others, theorists such as McClelland have focused on how the behavior expressing the motive for achievement is acquired through the principles of reinforcement. According to McClelland, we are not born with the motive to achieve and master. We come to discover the underlying rewards of mastery in the process of

achieving goals as children. When parents encourage us, they help us to discover that gaining mastery is rewarding. As a result, we continue to set goals throughout our lives in order to experience the rewards associated with mastery.

The Cognitive Component

Atkinson's Cognitive-Choice Theory

John Atkinson, who collaborated with David McClelland in some early work on the achievement motive, developed a distinctively cognitive theory of achievement motivation that retained the basic idea of McClelland's theory—that people select and work towards goals because they have an underlying need to achieve.

Atkinson (1957) made two important additions. First, he argued that the need to achieve is always tempered by another fundamental need, the need to avoid failure. He suggested that, if the need to achieve is stronger than the need to avoid failure, the individual will engage in approach behavior; however, if the need to avoid failure is stronger than the need to achieve, the individual will engage in avoidant behavior. Second, Atkinson suggested that these two fundamental needs interact with expectations and values in a multiplicative fashion. Accordingly, he represented hope of success, as he called it, by the formula

$$T_s = M_S \times P_s \times In_s$$

where T_s is the tendency to achieve success (hope of success); M_S is the motive to achieve success; P_s is the perceived probability of success; and In_s is the incentive value of success $(1 - P_s)$. Similarly, he represented fear of failure by the formula

$$T_{-f} = M_F \times P_f \times In_f$$

where T_{-f} is the tendency to avoid failure; MF is the motive to avoid failure; $P_f = (1 - P_s)$ is the probability of failure; and In_f is the negative incentive value of failure.

Atkinson suggested that these two motives are additive; they combine to produce resultant (total) motivation as follows

$$T_s + T_{-f} = (M_S \times P_s \times In_s) + (M_F \times P_f \times In_f)$$

There is no need to memorize these formulas; they simply illustrate the mathematical aspects of the theory. In the 1950s, psychologists were intrigued with the idea of using mathematical formulas to describe behavior. According to Atkinson's theory, expectancy (perceived probability of success and probability of failure) and value (incentive value of success and negative incentive value of failure) can be thought of as real numbers, and we should be able to actually make mathematical calculations. In fact, that is what Atkinson did.

According to the theory, people could be classified as $M_S > M_F$ (the motive to succeed is higher than the motive to avoid failure) or $M_F > M_S$ (the motive to avoid failure is higher than the motive to succeed). The theory predicts that individuals classified as $M_S > M_F$ will be inclined to select tasks of moderate difficulty—that is, tasks at which success and failure are equally likely. In contrast, individuals classified as $M_F > M_S$ will be most likely to select tasks that are either very easy or, perhaps surprisingly, very difficult. Atkinson has suggested that this can be understood if we re-

member that failing at a very difficult task produces little or no shame. For a person who has played tennis only a few times, losing to the current world champion would be no disgrace.

Despite numerous studies consistent with the theory, it has some problems. In particular, females tested in the laboratory did not conform to the predictions of the theory. For reasons that could not be fully explained, Atkinson's theory only describes male behavior.

Let's look at some of the theories that have come to replace Atkinson's.

Weiner's Explanatory Style Theory

Bernard Weiner's theory grows out of the observation that people have different explanations for success and failure (Weiner, 1972, 1991). He postulated that success and failure at achievement tasks may be attributed to any of four factors: ability, effort, task difficulty, and luck (see also Weiner et al., 1971). These four factors can be classified along two dimensions (Table 13-1): locus of control (internal or external) and stability (stable or unstable). Internals believe that their successes and failures result from their own actions. Whether they succeed or fail, they attribute the outcome to their ability or to the effort they expended. Externals, in contrast, tend to believe that success or failure is beyond their control. When they succeed, it is because they had an easy task or they were lucky. When they fail, it is because they had a difficult task or were unlucky.

Turning to the second dimension, we see that ability is relatively stable. It may change over the long run, but typically not in the short run. Abilities take time to develop. Effort, in contrast, is not at all stable. Some days we work very hard at a task; other days, we don't. Task difficulty is also stable over time, whereas luck is not. The best we can do with luck is to take advantage of it when it comes.

It is interesting to compare how people high in resultant achievement motivation ($M_S > M_F$) and low in resultant achievement motivation ($M_F > M_S$) perceive why they succeed and fail. This comparison might help to explain why, paradoxically, people high in resultant achievement motivation are motivated by failure, whereas people low in resultant achievement motivation are motivated by success (Weiner & Kukla, 1971a).

Table 13-1.   Attributions for success and failure.

| | Locus of Control | |
	Internal	External
Stable	Ability	Task difficulty
Unstable	Effort	Luck

Weiner and Kukla (1970) found that people high in resultant achievement motivation perceived success as due to ability and effort and perceived failure as due to lack of effort. People low in resultant achievement motivation perceived success as due to task difficulty or luck and perceived failure as due to lack of ability. These rather complicated findings can be readily understood, if we consider that people high in resultant achievement motivation see themselves as high in ability, whereas people low in resultant achievement motivation see themselves as low in ability (Weiner & Potepan, 1970). Weiner (1972) has suggested that, because people high in achievement motivation perceive themselves as high in ability, they tend to attribute variability in performance to effort. Thus, when they fail, they attribute it to lack of effort. Failure, therefore, motivates them to work harder. (Failure may also challenge their view that they are high in ability and may thereby motivate them to reaffirm this view by trying harder.) Curiously, success reduces their motivation. To explain this, Weiner suggests that, following success, they tend to relax.

Because people low in resultant achievement motivation perceive themselves as low in ability, they easily account for failure. It is simply due to lack of ability. Clearly, it is useless to work harder if they lack the basic ability. How do such individuals account for success? Obviously, if they lack ability, it would be illogical to attribute success to ability. Because effort is closely linked to ability, it would also be illogical to ascribe success to effort. If effort is the energy for an action, while ability provides the direction for that energy, they cannot succeed merely by increasing effort. Success, therefore, must have occurred because the task was easy or they were lucky.

Why should success motivate individuals low in resultant achievement motivation when they perceive that their performance is due to luck? It may simply be that such people want to take advantage of a run of good luck.

Practical Application 13-2 describes how it might be possible to motivate people who are reluctant to accept challenges.

Dweck's Theory of Competence Development

Dweck and her colleagues have suggested that we can understand differences in achievement and competency by understanding the implicit theories that people have about the origins of achievement and competency. She argues that some people view competency in terms of the skills and knowledge they now possess. They say to themselves, "This is what I am, and therefore this is what I can do." Other people, she argues, view competency in terms of their ability to acquire skills and knowledge. They say to themselves, "Look what I've accomplished so far. That's a good indication of what I can do in the future." Individuals of the first type subscribe to what she calls an *entity* theory; they see intelligence as fixed. Individuals of the second type subscribe to an *incremental* theory; they see intelligence as changeable (Dweck, 1991; Dweck & Leggett, 1988). For reasons that are still not completely clear, some people believe that learning stops at a certain age or that their capacity to learn is limited and that, therefore, no matter how hard they work, there is little hope for real change. Such people regard their possibilities as limited. People who hold the incremental theory, on the other hand, believe that the only thing that limits their ability to learn and develop new skills is their willingness to work. They regard their possibilities as virtually unlimited; how much they learn depends on how much they think they can learn. Our nervous system places limits on us, of course. Nonetheless, it has been shown that one of the major factors determining how far we go is how persistent we are, and how persistent we are is linked to our beliefs about whether we can learn and develop.

Research with people who perceive that they have ability indicates that, when given a choice among tasks of various levels of difficulty, people who hold an incremental theory tend to choose challenging tasks—tasks that call upon them to stretch themselves—whereas people who ascribe to an entity theory tend to choose tasks that are more in line with their abilities. People who perceive themselves to be low in ability and who hold an entity theory are inclined to choose relatively easy tasks, because they are likely to succeed in such tasks and, consequently, they can avoid judgments about their lack of competency. Should they fail, of course, it would be devastating to their already low self-image. The net result is that people with low perceived ability who hold to an entity theory are inclined to avoid challenges and to choose easy tasks.

Dweck and Leggett (1988) contend that avoiding a challenging activity is a maladaptive strategy, whereas the tendency to select challenging tasks is adaptive. Because most achievement involves overcoming obstacles, acquiring skills, and persisting in the face of setbacks, they argue, it is important to be dispositionally disposed to select challenging tasks. Dweck and Leggett's theory is summarized in Table 13-2. Note that

Practical Application 13-2

Inducing People to Accept Challenges

People with high resultant achievement motivation tend to accept challenges. They will take on difficult tasks and, once they have committed themselves to a course of action, they persist. How can we get people with low resultant achievement motivation also to accept challenges and take on difficult tasks. In short, how can we motivate people who are not now motivated? At least three approaches have been suggested.

Reducing the Negative Affect Associated with Failure

It has been found repeatedly that people who are high in resultant achievement motivation (success-oriented people) experience pride when they succeed but relatively little shame or guilt when they fail, whereas people low in resultant achievement motivation (fear-oriented people) experience guilt and shame when they fail but relatively little pride when they succeed (Sorrentino & Hewitt, 1984). Rather than pride, fear-oriented people seem to experience something akin to relief. Success means that they do not have to deal with the guilt and shame that come with failure.

At this point, we do not have a clear understanding of why the affect associated with success and fear is asymmetrical. There are several possibilities. It may simply be that the individual was punished for failure in the past, and therefore shame and guilt have become conditioned rejection or punishment responses. Another possibility grows out of Terrace's (1969) finding that pigeons taught to make discriminations without errors became very emotional when

they were transferred to a more difficult task at which they did make errors. It may be that people react to negative feedback (failure) with an unlearned emotional response when they have not previously been exposed to failure. In short, people may become hypersensitive to failure if they have previously known nothing but success.

How do you treat people who are hypersensitive to failure? One obvious procedure is to try to desensitize them. It has been suggested that people who are allowed to fail from time to time in the course of learning automatically become desensitized to failure, not only in that task but in general. People who are hypersensitive would have to be introduced to failure under very supportive conditions. They might then come to realize that they have nothing to fear when they fail. The idea here is that, if people no longer fear failure, they will be more inclined to try difficult or challenging tasks.

Motivating People with Difficult Tasks

A second approach is to require people to work at a difficult task (Locke & Latham, 1990)—in other words, to give them no choice. This approach is designed to capitalize on the attributional process that takes place in such situations. When people succeed at difficult tasks, they tend to take credit for their success (self-serving bias), whereas when they succeed at an easy task, they tend to attribute their success to the fact that the task was not difficult. When the task is difficult, they say to themselves, "Since I did that pretty well, I must be pretty good"; when the task is easy, they say to themselves, "Well, of course I did it well—any fool could have done that." As we have noted, people tend to put forth effort if they perceive themselves people with low perceived ability are prone to help-lessness (Chapter 10).

To end this discussion of Dweck's ideas, let's compare the consequences of believing in the entity theory or the incremental theory.

Consequences of believing in the entity theory. According to Dweck's model, people who believe in the entity

theory are motivated to select goals that will indicate they do have intelligence and to avoid goals that might provide evidence that they lack intelligence. Research indicates that, when these people experience failure, they tend to attribute it to lack of intelligence (e.g., Elliott & Dweck, 1985, cited in Dweck, 1986). If I believe I lack intelligence, why should I put forth effort? People who reason this way have to select their tasks

to have ability. It makes no sense for people to work hard at a task for which they think they have no ability.

The second reason for giving people a difficult task is that, if they fail, they will tend to attribute their failure to the difficulty of the task ("Of course I couldn't do that. I'm not Superman"). That response doesn't undermine their perceptions of their ability. When they fail at an easy task, though, they tend to blame their own lack of ability ("Any fool could have done that. I'm no good at this"). Perceiving that they lack ability, they are then reluctant to put forth effort.

One variant of this approach is to give people an easy task at which they are likely to succeed and tell them that this task will predict future performance. In that case, people treat that task as providing them with an estimate of their ability (e.g., Brickman, Linsenmeier, & McCareins, 1976; Feldman & Bernstein, 1978; Vreven & Nuttin, 1976).

Attributional Retraining

Sometimes, people expect to do poorly because of their gender, age, education, race, or whatever. In that case, they are not going to put forth effort. Providing examples may help to eliminate such stereotypes. If they see that someone else of the same gender or age or whatever has succeeded, their belief in the disabling effects of such factors may diminish.

It is also important to emphasize the role of effort and persistence (Ostrove, 1978). Sometimes people are simply unaware of the factors that differentiate successful and unsuccessful people. If they can be made aware of those factors, they are more likely to adopt a strategy that will help them succeed. Then, once they begin to experience

success, they will be more likely to repeat the behaviors that lead to success.

Another approach is to make people aware that performance is often unstable and not necessarily a good predictor of future performance. In one study, incoming college students were informed that the factors that lead to low grades in the first year are temporary. This led to improved performance on sample items of the Graduate Record Exam and to improved grades the following semester (Wilson & Linville, 1985). The effects were greater among women than among men. This finding is consistent with the idea that women have a greater tendency to adopt what Dweck (1991) calls the entity model of ability.

Note that providing children with continuous success by giving them relatively easy tasks is not an effective way of producing stable confidence, challenge seeking, and persistence (Relich, 1983). In fact, such procedures can backfire and lower children's confidence in their ability (Meyer, 1982). Young children who are always given easy tasks to ensure success may conclude that the parent or the teacher has no confidence in their ability. Further, children who notice that they are being protected from failure may come to the conclusion that it is bad to fail. What does this train of thought do for self-esteem? If children come to regard their ability as so limited that they can't be permitted to choose a challenging task, they're not likely to have much self-esteem left to protect. A major ingredient of self-esteem is the belief that we have ability.

Table 13-2.   Dweck and Leggett's theory of the relationship between implicit theories of intelligence and the behavior patterns of mastery and helpless types.

Theory of Intelligence	Goal Orientation	Perceived Present Ability	Behavior Pattern
Entity theory (intelligence is fixed)	Performance orientation; the goal is to gain positive judgments and to avoid negative judgments of competence.	High	Mastery; the individual seeks challenge and is high in persistence.
		Low	Helplessness; the individual avoids challenge and is low in persistence.
Incremental theory (intelligence is changeable)	Learning orientation; the goal is to increase competence.	High or low	Mastery; the individual seeks challenge that fosters learning and is high in persistence.

Source: From "A Social-Cognitive Approach to Motivation and Personality," by C. S. Dweck and E. L. Leggett, *Psychological Review*, 1988, *95*, 256–273. Copyright © 1988 by the American Psychological Association. Reprinted with permission.

very carefully, because any failure confirms their lack of intelligence. After reviewing the research literature on the way children react to success and failure, Dweck has suggested that even a single encounter with failure can make a person helpless.

Thus, failure can be devastating to people who hold to the entity theory. For this reason they learn to avoid challenges. These people may become low achievers in order to avoid the failure they fear.

Consequences of believing in the incremental theory. According to Dweck, people who believe in the incremental theory tend to select goals that will enable them to increase their competence (e.g., Nicholls, 1984). If intelligence is something that we can acquire, it is important to select goals that maximize learning. To maximize learning, we must be careful not to select goals on the basis of certainty of success. Sometimes we can learn a great deal in situations where failure is likely. For instance, we can't learn the skills needed to be good at the ring-toss task by simply standing next to the post and dropping the ring over it. This obvious observation is not always clear to the person obsessed with the need to avoid failure.

Since the development of competence at any task usually requires persistence, belief in the incremental theory of intelligence turns out to be very adaptive in the process of setting and attaining goals. Both rewards and failure simply provide feedback to the individual.

Note that Dweck's theory incorporates the idea that people with a generalized belief that they can control important things in their lives are inclined to engage in mastery behaviors.

Conclusions

Cognitive theorists suggests that people come to achieve, master, or gain competence because they have the capacity to anticipate the future—that is, because they have expectations about what might be. Various theories have suggested that, when people have positive expectations, they are inclined to put forth effort. Conversely, they are unlikely to put forth effort if they don't believe that the effort will pay off—for instance, if they perceive that they lack ability.

Summary

The initial impetus for work on achievement motivation came from Henry Murray, who recognized that people vary in their desire or tendency to "overcome obstacles, to exercise power, to strive to do something difficult as well as and as quickly as possible." In order to measure the achievement motive with more precision, McClelland and his colleagues adapted the TAT and developed a precise method of scoring the achievement motive.

White has proposed that competence grows out of curiosity and exploratory behaviors, which are based on a general motive he has called effectance motivation. This motive is directed towards understanding the nature of the environment and the order inherent in it. Feelings of efficacy occur, he suggests, when individuals come to understand that they are able to affect the environment. Piaget has argued that individuals are motivated to integrate the information contained in their environment. Integration occurs by a process called assimilation. When no structures exist to assimilate information, the person must develop new cognitive structures; this process is called accommodation.

David McClelland has shown that, when parents encourage independence and mastery, their children develop a stronger need to achieve. He argues that engaging in mastery behaviors results in feelings of satisfaction that strengthen the need to achieve.

One of Atkinson's important and fundamental contributions was his suggestion that the need to achieve is always tempered by another fundamental need, the need to avoid failure. According to Atkinson's theory, resultant achievement motivation is determined by two factors—hope of success and fear of failure. Hope of success is made up of three values: motive to succeed, probability of success, and the incentive value of success. Similarly, fear of failure is made up of three values: motive to avoid failure, probability of failure, and the incentive value of failure. According to the theory, people in whom the motive to succeed is greater than the motive to avoid failure ($M_S > M_F$) will choose tasks with an intermediate level of difficulty, while people in whom the motive to avoid failure is greater than the motive to succeed ($M_F > M_S$) will choose tasks that are either very easy or very difficult.

Weiner has suggested that there are four basic perceived causes of success and failure at achievement tasks: ability, effort, task difficulty, and luck. People who are high and low in resultant achievement motivation respond quite differently to success and failure. Weiner and Kukla found that people high in resultant achievement motivation perceived success as due to ability or effort and perceived failure as due to lack of effort, while people low in resultant achievement motivation perceived success as due to task difficulty or luck and perceived failure as due to lack of ability. The key to understanding these findings is that people high in resultant achievement motivation typically perceive themselves as high in ability, whereas people low in resultant achievement motivation typically see themselves as low in ability.

According to Dweck's model, people who believe in the entity theory are motivated to select goals that will indicate that they do have ability and to avoid goals that might provide evidence that they lack ability. People who believe in the incremental theory tend to select goals that will enable them to increase their competence. If ability (intelligence) can be acquired, it is important to select goals that can maximize learning.

What are the consequences of believing in the entity model or the incremental model? People who believe in the entity model of intelligence are motivated to select goals that will put them in a favorable light. Should they fail, they tend to attribute their failure to lack of ability (intelligence). This perception tends to undermine any future desire to put forth effort. People who hold to the incremental model of intelligence tend to set a goal that will increase their competence. When these people fail, they tend to interpret failure not as lack of ability but as feedback that tells them how well they are performing. They often interpret failure as an indication that they did not put forth the necessary effort, and so they are motivated to work harder.

Self-Esteem

Self-esteem has been positively linked to a wide range of behaviors, including mastery and achievement, subjective well-being, and health. Low self-esteem has been identified as a risk factor for aggression, delinquency, drug use, depression, poor school performance, spousal abuse, child abuse, and so forth. Recently, some politicians and school boards have suggested that schools and other social agencies should design programs to raise self-esteem, on the assumption that self-esteem is the cause, rather than the effect, of societal problems, that it exists independent of a specific situation and can be elevated by external interventions.

In this section, we will review some research findings on self-esteem and consider how feasible it is to raise self-esteem.

The Definition of Self-Esteem

There are many definitions of high self-esteem. All of them try to capture in one way or another the positive feelings/beliefs that people enjoy when they experience high self-esteem. Rarely can one find definitions of low self-esteem, even though it is low self-esteem that has been the main focus of therapists and the self-esteem movement. Let me define both high and low self-esteem.

High Self-Esteem

High self-esteem is "pride in oneself in which one becomes aware and accepting of one's imperfection while cherishing one's inherent strengths and positive qualities" (proposed by Andrea Parecki as quoted in Lazarus, 1991, p. 441).

A key element in this definition is pride. We feel pride when we can take responsibility for producing a socially valued outcome or for being a socially valued person (Mascolo & Fischer, 1995). Storm and Storm (1987) suggest that pride can be grouped with other positive emotions such as the feelings of being triumphant, victorious, accomplished, special, brave, and courageous. Lazarus (1991) suggests that the core relational theme for pride is enhancement of our ego-identity by taking credit for a valued object or achievement, either our own or that of some person or group with whom we identify. This emphasizes the important role of pride in the emergence of the self both as an individual and as a member of a group. Like Lazarus, others have suggested that pride is important for the emergence of traits linked with high self-esteem, such as confidence, independence, curiosity, and initiative (Harter, 1990). From being able to experience pride (to take credit) people gain a strong sense of their own power and agency; it provides them with the unshakable belief that they can effect change and thereby cope.

Pride can help sustain goal-directed behavior. People sustain themselves in the face of adversity because they are convinced that their actions will eventually make a difference. Persistence is learned; it is based on developing an unshakable belief that, over the long haul, our abilities will make a difference. People who have a sense of agency and pathways have hope (Snyder et al., 1991) and, as we saw earlier, it is people with hope who persist and succeed.

People who can believe in themselves can often accomplish the impossible.

Children need to experience pride because it gives them a sense of autonomy, power, and self-confidence (Deci & Ryan, 1985). Can anyone prevent them from experiencing pride? It appears so. Parents or teachers who take credit for things that children have done rob them of this powerful emotion. In addition, some children are raised in environments that prevent them from doing things on their own. It seems that pride is nurtured when people make their own choices and receive full credit for their accomplishments but are not blamed for their shortcomings.

Another key aspect of high self-esteem is that we must accept our imperfections. As we saw in Chapter 10, perfectionists set themselves up for depression by not allowing themselves to fail. People who can accept that they are less than perfect can better deal with adversity and setbacks.

It has been suggested that self-esteem is not a global attribute that cuts across all situations but rather is specific to certain situations (domains). To emphasize that feelings of self-worth come from competencies in different domains, Susan Harter (1990) prefers to speak of *global self-worth*. She has pointed out that feelings of self-worth are essential to a wide range of behaviors, including establishing and maintaining social relationships.

Low Self-Esteem

Low self-esteem may be defined as the shame that comes from appraising ourselves as lacking skills and abilities important to valued others.

A key element of this definition is shame. Low self-esteem is not simply the absence of pride; it is a highly negative emotional state. The emotion that most closely approximates that state is shame (Tangney, Burggraf, & Wagner, 1995). Mascolo & Fisher (1995) suggest that we feel shame when we have failed to live up to the standards of worth in valued others: "In shame the entire person seems to be experienced as unworthy" (p. 68).

Another key element of low self-esteem is that individuals believe they are lacking in important skills and abilities. As a result, they feel a persistent sense of hopelessness.

Although self-esteem often drops momentarily as the result of negative feedback, individuals' levels of self-esteem for each particular domain seem to be relatively stable over time. Most researchers emphasize the role of early experiences in establishing these relatively stable levels of self-esteem (Heatherton & Polivy, 1991).

In my view, low self-esteem is a highly overused term. It is frequently used to refer to people who lack high self-esteem or simply lack confidence; people who do not know if they can do something or have feelings of apprehension; and people who have self-doubt, which all of us experience from time to time when we set difficult goals (Bandura, 1991). However, some people truly suffer from low self-esteem. They are plagued with feelings of guilt and shame.

The Origins of Self-Esteem

We can identify three major sources of self-esteem.

1. **Self-evaluation.** The consensus is that feelings of self-esteem grow out of self-evaluation (e.g., Osborne,

1996; Swann, 1996). Self-evaluation is most likely to occur when individuals experience success or failure. Intuitively, we might expect that people would experience pride when they succeed and shame when they fail. Curiously, as we will discuss later, individuals with high self-esteem tend to experience feelings of pride when they succeed but fail to experience feelings of shame then they fail. The research indicates that they have developed effective ways of appraising failure that minimize its impact. Conversely, people with low self-esteem tend to experience feelings of shame when they fail but rarely experience feelings of pride when they succeed. They have developed ways of appraising success that prevent them from experiencing pride. As a result, they tend to maintain their low self-esteem.

2. **Successes in valued domains.** Different domains are important to different people. For some people, physical attributes are important; for others, athletic performance is important; for still others, academic success is important. As a result, individuals attach more importance to successes in certain domains than in others. If I value sports, for example, I will experience greater pride—and self-esteem—from winning at some sporting event than from getting a good grade on a test. Likewise, failing at something I value will produce greater shame than failing at something that I do not value.

At least three distinct domains have been identified: performance, social skills, and appearance (Heatherton & Polivy, 1991). Research using a scale designed to measure these domains showed that people's self-esteem for each of these domains often drops momentarily when they experience private failure on a task (performance self-esteem), when they experience public failure on a task (social self-esteem), and when they have concerns about their physical appearance (physical self-esteem). Other research suggests that there are many more domains and they change with age (Harter, 1990).

3. **Societal values.** What people value is often a reflection of societal values, parental values, and peer values. In our society, material success is valued. From the day we are born, we hear about the American Dream. As Swann (1996) has pointed out, we are told not simply that we can become wealthy but that we should. Thus, when we don't become rich, we may be inclined to develop lower self-esteem. If we don't buy into this

value, on the other hand, we will not experience lower self-esteem as a result of not becoming rich.

Parental values are also important, because children are likely to internalize their parents' values. If parents value education, for example, their children will be inclined to value education. As a result, their self-esteem will be more affected by their performance at school than by their performance in other domains.

Peers also shape our values. Part of the developmental process involves separating ourselves from our parents. This theme is particularly strong in adolescence. During that stage, adolescents often look to their peers to tell them how to behave. An adolescent who decides not to buy into the values of their peers—not to smoke, for example—might find it difficult to experience high self-esteem.

The important point is that our self-esteem results largely from our appraisal of our behavior relative to some standard or value. People who do not have the skills they need to achieve that standard will experience low self-esteem. One way for them to experience high self-esteem would be to rethink what is important. Do they need to be rich to be happy? Do they need to succeed at school to be successful? Do they need to be good at sports to experience pride? Sometimes when people follow their strengths, rather than some standard given to them by society, their parents, or their peers, they begin to develop high self-esteem. In our society, artistic skills are often not valued. As a result people who excel in the arts but not in other domains may experience lower self-esteem. For some of these people, discovering a group of artists who appreciate their skills can result in a rapid improvement in self-esteem.

The Perpetuation of Low Self-Esteem

People with low self-esteem engage in behaviors that perpetuate low self-esteem. First, although most theorists believe that humans are inherently motivated to experience positive self-regard or high self-esteem (e.g., Rogers, 1959), the research literature indicates that people with low self-esteem do not accept positive feedback but do accept negative feedback. Told that they have done something well, they will disregard that compliment as invalid. Told that they have done

poorly, however, they will accept and process that information as correct and fair. This makes no intuitive sense. It also means that they are doomed to experience low self-esteem for the rest of their lives.

Second, people with low self-esteem set low goals. According to Dweck (1991), one reason for this is to avoid disapproval due to failure. Third, they engage in *self-handicapping*; that is, they set up obstacles to successful performance—for example, by getting drunk the night before an exam or failing to prepare for a presentation at work.

Because self-esteem is linked to such behavior, theorists have argued that self-esteem involves an entire way of relating to the world. Among other things, it involves strategies for setting goals, strategies for reacting to challenges, and strategies for dealing with failures and setbacks (Swann, 1996). The curious thing is that these strategies seem designed to perpetuate low self-esteem. Why is that? At least three explanations have been proposed.

1. The need for predictability. It appears that the need for predictability, which we discussed at the beginning of this chapter, may take precedence over the principles of reinforcement. This may explain why the individual with low self-esteem ignores positive feedback and the individual with high self-esteem ignores negative feedback.
2. The need for self-verification. Self-verification is linked to the maintenance of the individual's self-concept. Research suggests that the self-concept emerges as early as the first year of life. At that time, individuals become aware of themselves as distinct and separate from the environment. Swann (1983) has suggested that the need for self-verification would enhance or maximize the need for predictability.
3. The need to avoid shame. Shame carries with it the possibility of exclusion from the group or collective. Because this has profound implications for the individual's survival, shame may take precedence over pride in human motivation. Thus, when people with low self-esteem set easy goals for themselves, they may be protecting themselves against the shame associated with failure.

Note that people who have a mastery orientation tend to be relatively high in self-esteem, whereas people with a performance orientation tend to be low in self-esteem (e.g., Franken & Prpich, 1996). This finding is consistent with the view that people with low self-esteem are motivated by the need or desire to avoid shame and that people with high self-esteem are motivated by the need or desire to experience pride.

Self-Esteem and Reactions to Success and Failure

Research has consistently shown that, whereas people with high self-esteem perform equally well following success and failure, people with low self-esteem perform significantly less well after failure. Research by Brockner (1979), however, indicates that this is only true under self-focusing stimulus conditions. That is, when subjects were encouraged to focus on their performance or simply tended to be self-conscious about their performance, subjects with low self-esteem tended to perform poorly after a previous failure. These findings are consistent with Carver's (1979) model, which suggests that fear or anxiety cues will disrupt performance if they become salient. According to Carver, when such cues become salient, the person is inclined to assess the likelihood of completing the task. Subjects whose expectations are positive—for instance, after a success—will be motivated to match their behavior against the standard. If they begin to think that they will not be able to complete the task, however, they will respond with passivity and withdrawal. Since subjects with low self-esteem tend to have a low opinion of their ability, they will be more inclined to respond to failure with reduced motivation. Tests of this model have shown that, in comparison with negative expectations, positive expectations do lead to greater persistence or performance, but only when there is self-focused attention (Carver, Blaney, & Scheier, 1979a,b).

The finding that individuals with high self-esteem and those with low self-esteem respond differently to failure is consistent with the idea that individuals with low self-esteem are more motivated by the need to avoid shame than are those with high self-esteem. In the next section, we will see why.

Interestingly, both individuals with high self-esteem and those with low self-esteem tend to experience self-doubt when they fail. An approach to managing self-doubt is outlined in Practical Application 13-3.

The Development of Self-Esteem

As we have seen, levels of self-esteem tend to be relatively stable over time and highly resistant to change. Moreover, a number of studies have shown that the individual's level of self-esteem develops relatively early in life. Let's examine the biological, learned, and cognitive aspects of that process.

The Biological Component

People with high self-esteem tend to be low in anxiety, whereas people with low self-esteem tend to be high in anxiety (e.g., Franken & Prpich, 1996). Because there is considerable evidence that anxiety has a strong genetic component (Chapter 5), there is reason to believe that anxiety may be partly responsible for low self-esteem. As we have seen, anxious people tend to be apprehensive about the future (Barlow, 1988). Among other things, they have a bias to process threat cues (Chapter 10) and tend to seek out the familiar and predictable (Chapter 12). In contrast, people who are low in anxiety tend to have a bias towards processing new stimuli (Chapter 12). Moreover, individuals with low anxiety are more inclined to engage in mastery behaviors. This pattern of behavior is very similar to that for individuals with low and high self-esteem, respectively (Osborne, 1996).

Though the two patterns of behavior are similar, most researchers recognize that self-esteem is a higher-order construct; it involves not only anxiety but also our conceptions about the world.

The Learned Component

The self-esteem movement has grown out of the assumption that individuals will have high self-esteem if their life experiences are mainly positive. To produce high self-esteem, then, the individual needs an environment in which successes are more likely than failures. One approach, of course, would be to lower the standards for success. The self-esteem movement also assumes that, if the balance between positive and negative experiences is shifted, individuals with low self-esteem will automatically begin to behave in the same way as those with high self-esteem; they will suddenly begin to select difficult tasks, and so forth. Such a transformation would be almost magical. That idea may be what made the self-esteem movement so appealing. It appears to bypass all the complicated stuff about teaching people to set goals, encouraging them to be independent, and encouraging them to persist.

The idea that self-esteem can be improved by a predominance of positive reinforcement is analogous to the bottom-up model of subject well-being. As we saw in Chapter 10, there is only weak evidence to support that model (Osborne, 1996). Research on high self-esteem strongly indicates that it grows out of a mastery orientation. Among other things, people with high self-esteem tend to select difficult tasks (e.g., Franken & Prpich, 1996). McClelland's (1985) work shows that people with a strong need to achieve also tend to have high self-esteem. While the self-esteem movement has generally argued that self-esteem causes achievement, McClelland's research suggests that achievement has

its roots in independence training. The same conclusion follows from a classic study by Coopersmith, which we will look at next.

Self-esteem and parental guidance. Stanley Coopersmith (1967) concluded that individuals with high self-esteem differ in a number of important ways from individuals with low self-esteem. They set more difficult goals; are less troubled by anxiety; experience less stress and fewer psychosomatic symptoms; are less sensitive to failure and criticism; experience greater feelings of control and fewer feelings of helplessness; tend to be more enterprising in approaching problems; and tend to explore more—show more curiosity toward themselves and their environment. They are intrinsically moti-

Practical Application 13-3

Managing Self-Doubt after Failure: Downward Comparison

One of the things most likely to undermine goal-directed behavior is failure. All individuals, whether high or low in self-esteem, experience self-doubt following failure and tend to reduce their efforts markedly as a result. Interestingly, while people with low self-esteem often give up following failure, those with high self-esteem bounce back as though nothing happened.

Why is that? It appears that, following a failure, people with high self-esteem lower their expectations, at least momentarily. Specifically, instead of comparing themselves to high performers—those who have already achieved difficult goals—they compare themselves to low performers—people whom they have already passed on the road to success. As a result, they feel much better about themselves. Instead of seeing themselves as in the bottom of the high group, they see themselves as in the top of the low group. In short, they see themselves as winners; they take pride in what they have already achieved.

Those with low self-esteem are not inclined to do this. They continue to compare themselves with people in the high-performance group and come to feel that they have not achieved much. As a result, they cannot take pride in their past accomplishments and they begin to see themselves as losers (e.g., Gibbons & McCoy, 1991; Wills, 1981, 1991).

We might ask why anyone would want to select the high-performance group as a standard of comparison in the first place? Why not select the low-performance group? Wouldn't that ensure good self-esteem?

In fact, that doesn't work for most people, for at least two reasons. First, people are normally well aware that they are part of a larger society and they know that, in the long run, they are going to be judged in terms of what the larger group has done. Second, certain people take a great deal of satisfaction in maximizing their skills and becoming the best. To know what it means to be the best, they look to others around them. Whether this inclination to excel is learned or innate remains unclear.

Research indicates that, after a failure, individuals with high self-esteem will eventually select the high performers as their standard of comparison once again, because high performers motivate them to develop their skills.

Note that some people never select the high-performance group as their standard. By selecting low performers as their standard of comparison, low achievers attempt to maintain their self-esteem. To select the high performers would be devastating for such people.

vated people who tend not only to be competent but to have a positive attitude toward themselves.

Coopersmith's research indicates that self-esteem can be nurtured and that parents play a primary role in that nurturing process. Parents of children with high self-esteem are characterized by total acceptance of, and respect for, the child; a tendency to set clearly understandable limits on what the child is permitted and not permitted to do; and a tendency to allow the child great latitude to explore and test within those limits. Coopersmith argues that parents of children with high self-esteem create a climate that frees the child from anxiety and doubt. Within such an environment, the child can explore freely and, in so doing, gain competence. Coopersmith notes that parents of children with high self-esteem not only encourage the children to become responsible and competent but accept the independence and diversity of expression that accompany the emergence of such behavior. In other words, the children learn from their parents—a significant source of acceptance and love—that they are important individuals, who can expect continued acceptance by their parents and by society at large even if they occasionally fail or if their behavior deviates somewhat from the norm. The children react to that signal, Coopersmith finds, by continuing to set high goals and working hard to attain them.

Coopersmith's work indicates that self-esteem may mediate, in part, the tendency to achieve. It also suggests that individual differences in self-esteem are acquired early in life. As we noted earlier, one of the reasons that changing achievement behavior is difficult is that it involves changing individuals' perceptions of their ability. If self-esteem affects their perception of their ability (competence), then their self-esteem must also be changed. The work on changing achievement motivation suggests that we need to focus on both self-esteem and perceptions of ability (control), because they influence each other.

Coopersmith's research suggests how to maximize feelings of pride in children and, in the process, to nurture high self-esteem. When children are viewed as independent, autonomous, and capable of making choices, they learn, in their own small way, that they can be victorious and triumphant. That gives them the confidence to accept challenges later in life.

Carl Rogers considered the parental role in the development of self-esteem within a somewhat different framework—in terms of conditional and unconditional love. Let's look at Rogers' approach.

Self-esteem and unconditional love. Rogers (1959) assumed that we are innately motivated to develop high self-esteem, which he calls positive self-regard. Whether we develop positive self-regard, Rogers suggested, is linked to whether we are raised with unconditional or conditional love. If we are raised with conditional love, we will have difficulty experiencing positive self-regard. Conditional love is dependent on our acting in an acceptable way. Instead of being loved for who we are or for what we believe, we are loved for what we do or what we accomplish. According to Rogers, conditional love often produces a negative self-image. When parents or other significant people in our lives emphasize the importance of achieving important goals or acting in a certain way, we develop unrealistic ideas about what we must do before we can think positively about ourselves. Rogers maintained that, if we are to be able to think positively about ourselves, we need to have a sense of worth that is not conditional on a specific behavior. All of us make mistakes; we all fail sometimes. Faced with this reality, we often develop a sense of conditional worth: "When I act in a certain way, I am worthy but, when I don't act in that way, I am not worthy." Conditional worth eventually leads to a negative self-concept. According to Rogers, the realization that we can never achieve certain goals—never live up to our ideals—leads to a sense of futility.

Unconditional love, in contrast, leads to positive self-regard. If love is not dependent on acting in prescribed ways, it doesn't matter if we sometimes fail or make mistakes. Rogers maintained that, when mistakes and failures are not linked directly to feelings of worth, they can be viewed in a more realistic and less destructive way. We can view our mistakes simply as part of the process of maturing or as feedback about our progress. When parents withdraw love in order to indicate their disapproval, it creates enormous anxiety in the child, because the parent is their primary means of survival. If, on the other hand, parents do not withdraw their love when they disapprove, the child is not overpowered with feelings of anxiety.

This argument recalls Dweck's (1991) suggestion that people who have learned to seek approval from others develop an other-directed performance orientation, rather than a learning orientation, in which the goal is to increase personal competence. It is also consistent with Coopersmith's findings that children with high self-esteem come from environments characterized by acceptance and that such environments tend to produce a mastery orientation.

The Cognitive Component

A number of recent studies have examined how people's ideas about themselves and their relationship to the world influence their self-esteem. Let's begin by considering the role of the individual's locus of control.

Locus of control. Weiner (1979, 1991) has suggested that an event will have little effect on our self-esteem unless we perceive the locus of control for that event as internal. He notes that people with an internal frame of reference are likely to experience feelings of pride and competence when they succeed and feelings of shame and incompetence when they fail. Weiner believes that these feelings have a great influence on a person's tendency to persist or not to persist. As we have seen, the main factor in changing achievement behavior is to change people's ability or their perceptions of their ability. Apparently, when people have a good opinion of their ability, they are inclined to put forth effort. Once they have put forth effort and succeeded, feelings of self-esteem emerge. Thus, esteem feelings become the factor that mediates persistence (Weiner, 1979). To the degree that persistence is a necessary requirement for developing competence, self-esteem plays an important role in producing competence.

What about individuals with an external frame of reference? Because they tend to view success and failure as due to luck, succeeding or failing will have little influence on their perceptions of their ability. As a result, they will not be inclined to have either a particularly good or particularly bad view of themselves, nor will they be inclined to persist at a task. To the degree that persistence is an important requirement for developing competence, such people will tend not to become highly competent. In summary, Weiner's position is that individuals who have a good opinion of their ability, and perceive the environment as essentially controllable, will be inclined to put forth effort. To the degree that effort is fundamental to developing skills, such individuals will become competent.

As we noted at the beginning of this chapter, whether a person has an internal or external locus of control is partly determined by genetics. Further, we have seen that parents and society play an important role in determining whether a person is inclined to take responsibility for their actions. Thus, in the final analysis, the individual's self-esteem depends on the interaction of biological, learned, and cognitive variables.

Self-concept and self-esteem. It appears that, as the result of certain early experiences, people construct a self-concept that is either good at enhancing and maintaining their self-esteem or is not. Let's look at some of the differences in self-concept between individuals with high and low self-esteem.

There is substantial evidence that people with high self-esteem have a clearly differentiated self-concept (Campbell, 1990; Markus & Nurius, 1986). Among other things, that means that they have a clear idea of the life domains that are important to them and of their strengths and weaknesses in these domains. As a result, they have a clear and stable view of themselves and so they can deal with both positive and negative feedback. Those with low self-esteem, in contrast, seem to have no clearly defined idea of the life domains that are important to them nor of their strengths and weaknesses in these domains. As a result, they are unable to deal with negative feedback.

Remember that high self-esteem involves learning to acknowledge and accept our weaknesses. This seems to lessen the impact of negative feedback. As Baumgardner (1990) has pointed out, "To know oneself is to like oneself" (p. 1062). When people know themselves, they can maximize outcomes because they know what they can and cannot do. For example, they can find ways of compensating for their weaknesses. In contrast, people who don't know their strengths and weaknesses are not in a position to take effective action. As a result, they experience a sense of insecurity.

One of the strategies of people with low self-esteem—or unstable self-esteem, that is, a view of themselves that is positive but fragile—is to resist or ward off evaluative feedback (Kernis, Grannemann, & Barclay, 1989). Although it may spare them some negative feedback, this strategy prevents them from forming a clear idea of who they are and robs them of valuable information that they need to improve their behavior.

When people come to know themselves, they are inclined to like themselves and the world in which they live.

People are more likely to learn and develop when they are willing to seek out evaluation and assistance.

Showers (1992) has found that some people compartmentalize their self-knowledge into positive and negative categories. If they activate one of these categories, access to the other is temporarily blocked. As a result, if people activate the positive category, they will feel good about themselves; if they activate the negative category, they will feel bad about themselves. In general, people high in self-esteem are more inclined to perceive their positive qualities or strengths, and so they tend to feel good about themselves most of the time. People low in self-esteem, in contrast, tend to perceive their negative qualities or weaknesses and tend to feel bad about themselves much of the time.

Showers (1992) also found that having a highly differentiated self-concept—that is, having many distinct categories—tends to reduce the impact of negative feedback.

Increasing Self-Esteem

As we have seen, research indicates that people with high self-esteem are characterized by optimism and

hope (Franken & Prpich, 1996). According to Seligman (1990), optimism allows individuals to take credit for their successes and to avoid shame when they fail. According to Snyder and his colleagues, hope gives people a sense of agency and of pathways (Snyder et al., 1991). Agency is a tendency to take the initiative, to engage in coping behaviors, or to take control. Deci and Ryan (1991) refer to this as self-determination. A sense of pathways is the awareness that there are many ways to get to a goal. If one path doesn't work, there is always another.

Conversely, people with low self-esteem are characterized by pessimism and despair (Franken and Prpich, 1996). How can we replace pessimism with optimism, and despair with hope? Most researchers (e.g., Osborne, 1996) argue that, if people are to achieve high self-esteem, they must identify their core strengths—strengths that can bring them a sense of pride and accomplishment. They need to develop a mastery orientation.

Individuals who are unable to experience love and acceptance at home often develop low self-esteem. Adolescents who do not experience self-worth at home often turn to their friends. Children with low self-esteem are at risk for drug use and crime (Chapter 8) because they will be attracted to any group, delinquent or not, that satisfies their craving for acceptance.

A persistent theme in the literature is that our self-esteem is linked to getting what we want from life. If people see themselves as possessing the skills and abilities that they need to get what they want, they are likely to be high in self-esteem. It is this anticipatory cognition, based on beliefs about control, that allows people to set goals and persist in the face of failure. It appears that one of the central reasons people are low in self-esteem is that they don't see themselves as having the skills and abilities to realize their goals (e.g., Osborne, 1996).

In order to increase individuals' self-esteem, it is necessary to change their self-concept. They need to perceive themselves as possessing the resources to get

the important things that they want from life. Much of what people want reflects the values of society, parents, and peers. If they have skills consistent with those values, they are more likely to experience high self-esteem (Harter, 1993). Should their strengths lie elsewhere, they might need to change their values, so that they can derive self-esteem from the skills that they have.

There is no quick fix for low self-esteem. Nonetheless, researchers feel that it is possible for people to change. Many of us can improve our self-esteem by becoming more optimistic, by becoming more hopeful, and by becoming aware of our strengths and weaknesses. Ultimately, perhaps, the best approach is to help people become more mastery-oriented.

Practical Application 13-4 summarizes some ways of counteracting the tendency to overgeneralize following failure, which is an important component of low self-esteem.

Practical Application 13-4

Learning Not to Overgeneralize after Failure

The tendency of people with low self-esteem to overgeneralize following failure results from lack of differentiation. Overgeneralization is the tendency of negative outcomes to trigger other feelings of personal inadequacy in domains that are unrelated to the initial negative outcome (Kernis, Brockner, & Frankel, 1989). What this means is that, when people experience a negative outcome at work, say, they are inclined to generalize that negative outcome to other domains in their life—for example, to their social relations, appearance, and intelligence. In other words, the criticism makes them question not only their ability to do the job but also their intelligence, their appearance, and their social skills. The process seems to involve rumination. As they think about what they did wrong, they begin looking for other instances where they failed in their life. They may come to the conclusion, based on the examples they dredge up while ruminating, that they are not worthy of positive self-regard. As a result, their self-worth plummets.

What happens to people with high self-esteem when they receive negative feedback? First, presumably because they have highly differentiated self-concepts, the negative feedback does not cross over into other domains of their lives; it remains highly compartmentalized. If the work domain itself is highly differentiated, they may be able to further compartmentalize the negative feedback into a subcategory of that domain. The net result is that people with high self-esteem simply reconfirm something they already knew about themselves before they received the negative feedback.

Note that negative feedback creates self-doubt in everyone. However, whereas those low in self-esteem overgeneralize when this happens, those high in self-esteem do not. The tendency to overgeneralize is the source of the problem. This is reminiscent of the antecedents of pessimism and depression.

Summary

According to Andrea Parecki, high self-esteem is "pride in oneself in which one becomes aware and accepting of one's imperfections while cherishing one's inherent strengths and positive qualities." The core relational theme for pride, according to Lazarus, is enhancement of our ego-identity by taking credit for a valued object or achievement, either our own or that of some person or group with whom we identify. When children experience pride, they gain a sense of autonomy, power, curiosity, and self-confidence. On that basis, they can see themselves as agents capable of initiating change. Lazarus has argued that children who are able to experience pride develop high self-esteem.

Low self-esteem is the "shame in oneself that comes from appraising oneself as lacking skills and abilities important to valued others." Research indicates that feelings of self-esteem come from self-evaluation. They come from succeeding and failing in important domains. Further, they come from internalizing the values of society.

A consistent research finding is that individuals with low self-esteem tend to perpetuate their low self-esteem. At least three explanations have been offered to account for this finding: that individuals are motivated by predictability, that individuals are motivated by self-verification, and that individuals are motivated to avoid shame.

Since individuals who experience low self-esteem tend to be anxious, and since anxiety has a genetic basis, it can be argued that low self-esteem has it roots in our biology. There is considerable evidence, however, that self-esteem can be increased with mastery training. Coopersmith's work suggests that parents who create an atmosphere that is characterized by acceptance and freedom from anxiety tend to promote the development of high self-esteem. Such an atmosphere, it appears, tends to encourage curiosity and exploratory behaviors. Rogers has argued that people who are raised with unconditional love tend to develop positive self-regard.

Weiner has examined the relationship between feelings of self-esteem and competence. He has observed that when people perceive the locus of control as internal, they are more likely to experience feelings of pride and competence when they succeed and to experience feelings of shame and incompetence when they fail. Having a highly differentiated or complex self-concept has also been linked to high self-esteem.

One of the consistent themes in the research literature is that to change self-esteem it is necessary to get people to go with their strengths so they can experience pride.

Finally, people with high self-esteem are more inclined to make a downward comparison, a strategy that serves to enhance their self-esteem.

Main Points

1. Humans have a fundamental need for predictability and control.
2. Control has been implicated in both physical and psychological health.
3. Twins studies have shown that about 30% of the variance associated with personal control (internality) is due to genetics.
4. Rotter has argued that reinforcement theory can explain, at least in part, why people tend to be internal or external.
5. We may distinguish between two styles of personal control: active control and self-control. Different cultures tend to favor different styles.
6. Good health has been linked to active control. However, the relationship is not linear.
7. Competence involves skill, ability, capacity, proficiency, or fitness.
8. Murray defined the need to achieve as the desire or tendency to "overcome obstacles, to exercise power, to strive to do something difficult as well as and as quickly as possible."
9. Through extensive research, McClelland has validated the TAT as a measure of the need to achieve.
10. McClelland has argued that the achievement motive grows out of a more basic incentive to "do something better"—not to gain approval or any other kind of external reward, but "for its own sake."
11. According to White's theory of competence, feelings of efficacy reward the development of competence.

12. Piaget argued that competence develops out of children's need to interact with their environment.

13. Social learning theory has suggested that achievement can be explained by the processes of modeling and imitation.

14. McClelland has shown that the need to achieve is nurtured by independence and mastery training.

15. According to Atkinson, resultant achievement motivation is a joint function of the need to achieve and the need to avoid failure.

16. Because the strengths of these two motives appear to vary independently, Atkinson says that the need or motive to achieve may be stronger than the need or motive to avoid failure ($M_S > M_F$), they may be equal ($M_S = M_F$), or the motive to avoid failure may be stronger than the motive to succeed ($M_F > M_S$).

17. According to Atkinson's theory, people in whom $MS > MF$ tend to select tasks of intermediate difficulty, whereas people in whom $M_F > M_S$ tend to select either very easy or very difficult tasks.

18. People attribute success and failure to four factors: ability, effort, task difficulty, and luck.

19. People high in resultant achievement motivation ($M_S > M_F$) attribute success to ability and effort and attribute failure to lack of effort; people low in resultant achievement motivation ($M_F > M_S$) attribute success to task difficulty and luck and attribute failure to lack of ability.

20. It is important for people to accept challenges. At least three strategies are useful in inducing them to do so: reducing the negative affect associated with failure; motivating people with difficult tasks; and giving people attributional retraining.

21. People have different implicit theories of intelligence. Some people see intelligence as fixed; this is called the entity model. Others see intelligence as changeable; this is the incremental model.

22. People who believe in the entity model of intelligence are motivated to select goals that will put them in a favorable light, whereas people who hold to the incremental model of intelligence tend to set a goal that will increase their competence.

23. Andrea Parecki has defined self-esteem as "pride in oneself in which one becomes aware and accepting of one's imperfections while cherishing one's inherent strengths and positive qualities."

24. Lazarus suggests that the core relational theme for pride is enhancement of our ego-identity by taking credit for a valued object or achievement, either our own or that of some person or group with whom we identify.

25. Low self-esteem may be defined as the shame that comes from appraising ourselves as lacking skills and abilities important to valued others.

26. Feelings of self-esteem come from the process of self-evaluation.

27. They also depend on successes and failures in valued domains such as performance, social skills, and appearance.

28. Finally, they have their roots in our societal values.

29. People with high self-esteem have a bias to perceive their positive qualities or strengths, whereas people with low self-esteem, in contrast, have a bias to perceive their negative qualities or weaknesses.

30. People high in self-esteem perform equally well following success and failure; people low in self-esteem perform significantly less well following failure, but only under self-focusing stimulus conditions.

31. Anxiety tends to characterize people with low self-esteem.

32. Three factors—acceptance by parents, having limits, and having the opportunity to explore—appear to be important in the development of self-esteem, which, Coopersmith suggests, influences a child's tendency to achieve.

33. Rogers has suggested that unconditional love is likely to result in high self-esteem.

34. Weiner has suggested that an event will have little influence on our self-esteem unless we perceive the locus of control for that event as internal.

35. People with high self-esteem typically have a clearly differentiated self-concept.

36. Baumgardner has suggested that "to know oneself is to like oneself."

37. Some people compartmentalize their self-knowledge into positive and negative categories.

38. High self-esteem has been linked to a mastery orientation.

39. Overgeneralization refers to the tendency of negative outcomes to trigger other feelings of personal inadequacy in domains that are unrelated to the initial negative outcome.

Chapter Fourteen

Self-Regulation of Motivation

- What does it mean to self-regulate?
- Are we really free to choose?
- Should we set long-term goals for ourselves?
- Is it important to have short-term goals?
- Is it normal to experience self-doubt?
- Is it important to have dreams?

- Which is more important for success—ability or motivation?
- How do we learn to maintain an optimistic outlook when things are not going well?
- Do we need a good self-concept in order to succeed?
- Can we change our self-concept?

Psychologists are coming to accept that humans self-regulate their behavior. They do so mainly by setting goals. Most goal theories are based on the idea that goals create a discrepancy between where the individual is and where the individual aspires to be, and the tension created by that discrepancy creates action. Some theories argue that individuals have the capacity to anticipate a goal state and thereby to anticipate the satisfaction of reaching that goal (Bandura, 1991). Thus, attainment of the goal state produces not only a reduction in the tension (avoidant motivation) but also satisfaction (approach motivation).

As we will see, goal-setting is governed by a set of principles (e.g., Locke and Latham, 1990); unless certain conditions are met, the process of goal setting does not work. Moreover, if we are to understand goal setting, we need to understand the nature of the self. The structure of the self gives goals their meaning and the ability to create action. In this chapter, we will examine how people can learn to set goals and also to persist in the face of self-doubt and even failure.

Let's begin with a basic question: What is the self-regulation of behavior?

The Self-Regulation of Behavior

Self-regulation theories have their roots in social-cognitive theories of behavior. Self-regulation involves three processes: (1) self-observation (self-monitoring); (2) self-evaluation, (self-judgment); and (3) self-reaction (self-incentive) (Bandura, 1991b).

1. **Self-observation (self-monitoring).** Before we can change a behavior, we need to become aware of it. This involves monitoring our behavior. The more systematically we monitor our behavior. The more quickly we will become aware of what we are doing. If we attend carefully to our performance, we will be inclined to set goals that lead to progressive improvement. If we want to improve our social skills, for example, we might start by making a list of things we do in social situations (for example, compliment, criticize, complain). Next, we might observe how often we do these things and under what conditions. Finally, we might set goals that will help us to become the person we want to be.

2. **Self-evaluation (self-judgment).** The next step is to decide if what we are doing is congruent with what we want or, more generally, our personal standards. Personal standards are developed from information that we gain from significant others. Note that we do not passively absorb standards from others; rather, we construct them by reflecting on those behaviors and the effects that they produce. We ask ourselves whether it makes sense to criticize those with whom we want to develop a friendship, for example.

Social-cognitive theory assumes that most of us possess a considerable knowledge about the best course of action to achieve a certain outcome but do not have a clear idea of what we are presently doing. That's why we need to begin by self-monitoring. Once aware of our behavior, we need to determine whether to change that behavior, by focusing on its consequences. Does it produce the effect we want? By focusing on the consequences of our behavior, we can determine, for example, whether we tend to be overly critical or unduly passive.

Having decided what we need to do, we set a goal and then attempt to match our behavior to that goal. By continuing self-evaluation, we can determine if we are on the right track.

3. **Self-reaction (self-incentive).** Self-judgments are typically accompanied by affective reactions. When we succeed or do well, we typically experience pleasure or satisfaction; however, when we fail or perform poorly, we typically experience a negative mood or dissatisfaction. These self-reactions may lead us to set higher goals, on the one hand, or to abandon a goal, on the other.

To achieve our goals, we need to pursue a course of action that produces positive self-reactions and avoid courses of action that produce self-censure. When we make self-satisfaction contingent upon certain accomplishments, we motivate ourselves to expend the energy needed to attain our goals. Those who succeed in regulating their motivation make effective use of self-incentives—for instance, by making self-satisfaction contingent on performing a certain prescribed set of actions, such as those necessary to achieve their goals (Bandura, 1991b).

Setting Goals

Under the right conditions, goals (1) arouse effort; (2) give rise to persistence; (3) provide direction; and (4) motivate strategy development (Bandura, 1991a; Locke & Latham, 1990). While the first three effects derive from traditional motivation theory, the fourth has its roots in cognitive motivation theory. Strategy development involves finding routes to our goals. According to cognitive motivation theory, we take an active role in determining the best route to a particular goal. To do so, we need to acquire knowledge, to generate alternatives, to make plans, and so forth. Cognitive motivation theorists maintain that goals create the motivation to engage in these activities.

Proximal and Distal Goals

It is important to distinguish between different kinds of goals. If a goal is to create action, it must be proximal rather than distal. Proximal goals relate to the immediate future. By meeting proximal goals, we will eventually achieve our distal goals. By achieving the proximal goal of writing a term paper, for example, I move toward my distal goal of obtaining a postsecondary degree. Distal goals are sometimes referred to as aspirations.

A general rule of thumb is that distal goals are useless without proximal goals, and proximal goals are useless without distal goals. Distal goals are typically associated with greater anticipatory emotion. Thinking about being a doctor, for example, produces greater feelings of satisfaction than thinking about finishing a term paper. As a result, distal goals have the capacity to sustain motivation even when we are pursuing a boring or time-consuming proximal goal. We often use distal goals to sustain motivation when the proximal goal is unable to do so. The image of being a doctor, for instance, will sustain a student in a difficult chemistry class.

Distal goals also keep us on course. Without them, we are inclined to drift off in other directions. We turn our attention to a more interesting proximal goal, for example. Extensive anecdotal evidence indicates that those without distal goals are inclined to change their

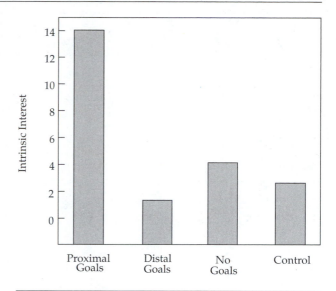

Figure 14-1.   Level of intrinsic interest in arithmetic activities shown by children in different goal conditions when given free choice of activities. (From "Cultivating Competence, Self-Efficacy and Intrinsic Interest through Proximal Self-Motivation," by A. Bandura & D. H. Schunk, *Journal of Personality and Social Psychology*, 1981, *41*, 586–598. Copyright © 1981 by the American Psychological Association. Reprinted by permission.)

direction often, whereas those with a clear distal goal are more inclined to stay the course.

Distal goals without proximal goals tend to result in no action. When we talk about doing something one day, we typically fail to get on with the task. It is the proximal goal that motivates us to action. A proximal goal is what we plan to do today or tomorrow. My experience is that, without a game plan for the immediate present, I tend to do very little. On days when I make a list, I get things done.

Evidence from a range of sources attests to the importance of having immediate goals. For example, the data in Figure 14-1 show the level of interest in arithmetic activities expressed by children with different types of goals, when given a free choice of activities (Bandura & Schunk, 1981). Bandura (1991a) argues that meeting proximal goals or subgoals generates

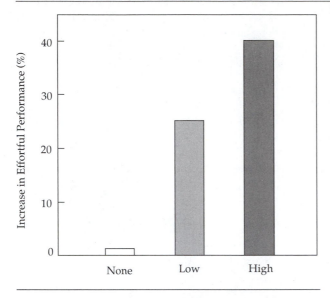

Figure 14-2. Mean increases in motivational level under conditions of performance feedback for people who continue to perform the activity without goals and those who spontaneously set low or high goals for themselves. (From "Self-Regulation of Motivation through Anticipatory and Self-Reactive Mechanisms," by A. Bandura. In R. A. Dienstbier (Ed.), *Perspectives of Motivation. Nebraska Symposium on Motivation,* 1991, 69–164 (Figure 6). Copyright © 1991 by University of Nebraska Press. Reprinted with permission.)

self-satisfaction. These immediate subgoals offer a continuing source of motivation, quite apart from the loftier superordinate goals.

People may be reluctant to set goals—difficult goals, in particular—because they fear the regret that will come if they do not achieve those goals. To put it another way, people do not set goals for themselves because they are motivated to protect their self-esteem. Research has shown that people with low self-esteem are inclined to minimize opportunities for regret (Josephs, Larrick, Steele, & Nisbett, 1992).

Setting Difficult but Attainable Goals

According to Locke and Latham (1990), we should set difficult but attainable goals for ourselves. Most of us have the capacity to determine whether we can or cannot do something. Research indicates that, once we

have decided that we can attain a particular goal, we are inclined to put forth effort and persist until we reach it. If the goal is not sufficiently difficult, it will fail to motivate. Alternatively, if the goal is perceived as unattainable, we will not put forth effort.

Bandura (1991a) has compared the effort expended, under the action of feedback, by people with no goals and those who spontaneously set low or high goals. It is evident from Figure 14-2 that goal difficulty plays a critical role in the amount of effort people are willing to put forth. (As we'll see shortly, feedback is a critical variable in performance.) Note that, when people are not given goals, they often spontaneously set goals for themselves (Locke & Latham, 1990). Many people have learned, it appears, that setting goals is a good way to motivate themselves.

Why do some people set easy goals for themselves, while others set difficult goals? As a general rule, people do not like to be viewed as lacking in competence. To avoid that possibility, some individuals select only easy tasks. By failing to stretch themselves, however, they impede the development of a sense of competence. Individuals with an entity theory of intelligence (Chapter 13) tend to select easy tasks, because failure would further undermine their already fragile sense of competence.

Feedback

Within Bandura's theory, feedback is essential if motivation is to be maintained at a high level (Bandura, 1991a). Bandura and Cervone (1983) found that motivation is highest in the presence of both goals and feedback (Figure 14-3). These results are consistent with the idea that we are motivated to meet a certain standard of performance that we have set for ourselves. Without feedback, we cannot determine how well we are doing and, consequently, we cannot easily assess whether we need to put forth more effort, to persevere, or even to analyze our behavior.

Self-Set Goals, Assigned Goals, and Commitment

Bandura and others have argued that self-set goals tend to produce greater motivation than assigned goals do. There are at least two reasons for this. First, we are in the best position to create an optimal goal because

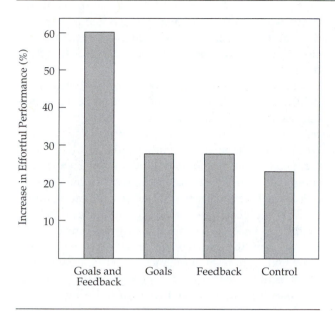

Figure 14-3. Mean percentage change in level of motivation under four conditions: goals with performance feedback, goals alone, feedback alone, and none of these factors (control). (From "Self-Evaluative and Self-Efficacy Mechanisms Governing the Motivational Effects of Goal Systems," by A. Bandura & D. Cervone, *Journal of Personality and Social Psychology*, 1983, 45, 1017–1028. Copyright © 1983 by the American Psychological Association. Reprinted with permission.)

we are the best judges of our own capacity for a given task. Second, we tend to be more committed to decisions that we have made ourselves. Thus, it makes sense that self-set goals will maximize motivation.

Research by Locke and Latham (1990) indicates that assigned difficult goals can motivate people, but only when people become committed to the goal. Much of their research has been done in a work setting, where people are already committed to putting in time. In that situation, committing to a difficult goal may simply be perceived as an opportunity for greater satisfaction. Additionally, the assignment of a difficult goal may communicate to workers the idea that their boss is confident in their ability to complete the task. As we know (Chapter 13), people are more inclined to select difficult goals if they perceive that they have ability to attain those goals. Similarly, teachers often set difficult goals for students, so that their high expectations communicate belief that their students have the ability to achieve such difficult goals.

The Need for Challenging Goals

It was popular for a time to tell people to do their best rather than to assign difficult goals. As we saw in Chapter 13, this approach grew out of a model in which self-esteem is assumed to depend on the sum total of positive and negative events. This model suggests that reducing negative events will improve self-esteem and hence performance.

Research shows that individuals told to do their best do no better than those with no goals (Locke & Latham, 1990). It appears that, when people are told to do their best, they interpret these instructions to mean stay the course. Unless they are challenged, they assume that they are doing their best. As we see in the next section, if a goal is to motivate behavior, it must create a discrepancy. It appears that saying "Do your best" fails to do that.

Discrepancy Hypotheses

Most goal-setting theories argue that goals create a discrepancy between where the individual is and where the individual would like to be and that the tension created by this discrepancy leads to action. However, the theories think of this discrepancy in different ways.

1. **Large Discrepancy.** According to discrepancy theory, which typically focuses on proximal goals, people need to create a discrepancy large enough to motivate them to action. The larger the discrepancy, the greater the motivation. While there is some evidence that effort increases as goal difficulty increases, there is obviously an upper limit (Locke & Latham, 1990).
2. **Optimal Discrepancy.** Optimal-discrepancy theory emerged to define more precisely what kinds of proximal goals motivate behavior. According to optimal-discrepancy theory, a task should be neither so difficult that the individual cannot hope to achieve it nor so easy that it does not challenge the individual. Most optimal-discrepancy theories are concerned with what challenges an individual. They have their roots in cognitive processing theory, which describes how people process information and develop competence.

Optimal-discrepancy theories assume that mastery involves the incremental development of the motor and/or cognitive structures that underlie competence (Dember & Earl, 1957; Bandura, 1991a).

3. **Normative Discrepancy.** It is sometimes suggested that people with a performance or ego orientation are motivated to achieve a level of a skill that will meet normative standards (Locke & Latham, 1990). According to this approach, people are motivated by the discrepancy between where they are and some level of skill possessed by an important referent group. In sports, for example, there are important standards that participants must meet in order to win.

Self-Efficacy Theory

Bandura (1991) has put forth a comprehensive overview of goal setting, as follows. First, the individual assesses whether the distal goal will provide some desired reward or satisfaction. (For example, "If I lose weight will I really be more attractive or healthier?") Bandura describes this step in terms of *outcome expectations,* defined as "a person's estimate that a given behavior will lead to certain outcomes." If outcome expectations are low, then the individual will not be motivated to select that goal. If they are high, the individual may then move to the next step—assessing whether he or she can mobilize the resources necessary to achieve the desired outcome. If I have become convinced that the only way to achieve my weight objectives is through exercise, I must then assess whether I can put in the time and effort required to achieve that goal. Bandura calls this judgment *feelings of self-efficacy,* defined as "the conviction that one can successfully execute the behavior required to produce the outcomes." In research, participants are simply asked if they believe they can do something. The resulting judgment can be thought of as a measure of *subjective difficulty.* While one person might foresee little difficulty in pursuing an exercise program, another might find the idea almost impossible.

Feelings of self-efficacy are assumed to be stable across time, but they are not stable across different situations. Unlike global feelings of competency, self-efficacy is situation-specific. Thus, it is necessary to measure feelings of self-efficacy for each new situation.

According to Bandura's theory, then, behavior is governed both by feelings of self-efficacy and by outcome expectations. If I have strong outcome expectations and strong feelings of self-efficacy, I will be inclined to put forth the effort necessary to achieve the desired outcome.

Bandura argues that goal-directed behavior is driven by the discrepancy between outcome expectations and where the individual is now, but the anticipated satisfaction is mediated by feelings of self-efficacy. If feelings of self-efficacy are low, I will not be inclined to make an effort or persist in the face of poor progress towards the goal. Note that feelings of self-efficacy will obviously be affected by outcome expectations. If my goals are very high, my efficacy feelings might well be lower as a result. If my outcome expectations are low, then my feelings of self-efficacy are likely to be higher. In tests of the theory, self-efficacy ratings are typically used to predict performance. Most tests have shown that such feelings tend to be a good predictor of a wide range of behaviors.

According to Bandura, discrepancies are reduced through a process called concept matching. When we set a goal, we create an image of the anticipated outcome. Failure to match the image sustains our motivation. Once the image has been matched, Bandura suggests, the motivation will subside. If my image is a slim and athletic torso, I would be inclined to maintain my efforts longer than if my image is only a moderately lean and athletic torso. What makes Bandura's theory so elegant is that it incorporates the idea that people have different goals and different beliefs about their ability to attain those goals. As a result, the theory can predict the wide individual differences that we typically observe when studying motivational processes.

Self-efficacy theory has proven very powerful in predicting a wide variety of behaviors such as adherence to exercise programs and stop-smoking programs (Schwarzer & Fuchs, 1995), complex decision-making (Bandura & Jourden, 1991), and even self-empowerment (Ozer & Bandura, 1990). The theory was originally proposed to account for the effectiveness of programs for the treatment of anxiety. In these programs, people were given specific skills to deal with specific anxiety-provoking or fearful situations. Thus, a person anxious about public speaking would be provided with the skills to effectively handle such a situation—for instance, how to structure a talk, how to speak clearly and dramatically, and how to manage any accompanying anxiety. Studies show that, once they have

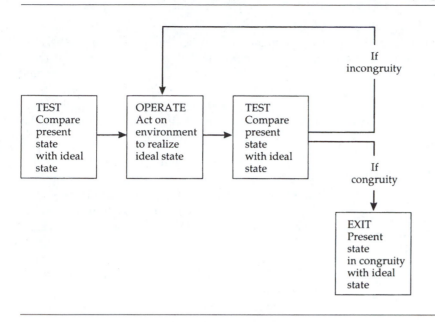

Figure 14-4. The TOTE unit. The TOTE model suggests that people compare their present state with an ideal state (TEST) to determine if there is need for action. If there is a discrepancy, they are motivated to act on the environment (OPERATE). If the discrepancy remains (if there is incongruity), they will be motivated to continue acting on the environment to realize the ideal state. Once the discrepancy is removed (there is congruity), they will cease acting on the environment (EXIT). (From *Understanding Motivation and Emotion* by J. M. Reeve, p. 182. Copyright © 1992 by Holt, Rinehart and Winston, Inc. Reprinted with permission.)

the skills they need, people are less anxious and their self-efficacy typically increases. In short, when people perceive that they have the skills to deal with a specific situation, they feel empowered and self-confident.

Strategy Development: Making Plans and Making Adjustments

Early versions of motivation theory analyzed goal attainment in terms of effort, persistence, and direction of behavior. Cognitive motivation theory introduced the idea that individuals may approach the attainment of a goal in intelligent or ill-conceived ways. Four aspects of an intelligent approach to goal attainment have been identified.

1. **Designing routes to goals.** Planning is essential if we are to achieve our goals. That involves time management—in particular, setting aside the time necessary to accomplish specific goals—and breaking our goals into manageable units or subgoals, which become the focus of our attention. In other words, we need immediate goals.

Miller, Galanter, and Pribram (1960) have proposed the TOTE (test, operate, test, exit) model to describe how people gain congruence between a goal (an ideal) and a behavior (Figure 14-4). According to their

model, an individual creates a plan, activates the plan, and then monitors feedback to determine whether there is congruity or incongruity. Bandura would say that the individual decides whether there is a match. If there is congruity with an ideal goal state, the individual exits the TOTE unit, and the motivation subsides; otherwise, the individual adjusts behavior to eliminate the incongruity.

2. **Adjustment and fine-tuning.** Most contemporary researchers (e.g., Campion & Lord, 1982; Carver & Scheier, 1981) view plans as adjustable and subject to frequent modification. In other words, the plan is as likely to change as the individual's action sequence. People who succeed rarely do so on the first try. Colonel Sanders, the founder of Kentucky Fried Chicken, is said to have knocked on more than 1600 doors before he found a buyer for his famous chicken recipe. What often differentiates people who succeed from those who do not is persistence—the kind of persistence in which people systematically change one thing and then another until they have achieved their goal. Japanese industrialists have adopted the concept of continuous improvement: They keep searching for ways to improve their products by 1% here and 1% there. In other words, rather than trying something totally different, they attempt to improve something that is already good.

Some people respond to failure by totally abandoning their goal and moving on to something else. Had Thomas Edison used that approach, he never would have invented the light bulb. Like Thomas Edison, top athletes work to improve one small thing, thereby creating an edge over their competitors. The best way to change something is to decide in advance what needs to be changed and then to search for a route to achieve that change. If we have a clear concept of what we want to achieve, it is much easier to make the necessary adjustments.

3. **Using mental rehearsal.** The use of mental rehearsal is commonplace in athletics. For Greg Louganis, who won the gold medal for diving at the 1988 Olympics, the first step in learning a new dive was to rehearse the dive over and over in his mind. Once he had a clear image, he would mount the ladder and try the dive. At the precise moment that he left the board, he would run the mental image in his mind and let it guide his behavior. Initially, his attempts were less than perfect but, with successive attempts, he found that he could match his behavior to the mental image he had created. This is a good example of how the TOTE model works.

Why does mental rehearsal work? Any response is made up of many smaller components. When we think of each of these components, we fire a neural process in the brain that is responsible for that component. There is even evidence that, when we think about certain things, blood flows to that area of the brain. By repeatedly creating the same image, we force the brain to connect these various neural firings into a sequence. In this way, the behavior takes on an automatic quality.

Elizabeth Manley, who won the silver medal for figure skating in the 1988 Winter Olympics, was considered a distant contender for third place, at best. Just days before the competition, she had a breakthrough in her mental imagery: She could see herself performing her routine flawlessly. When it came time for her to perform, she did just that.

Athletes often want to do different things—for instance, different dives—that involve different sequences of the same basic components. By rehearsing the image corresponding to the desired behavior just before attempting it, the athlete informs the brain which neural pattern to run. This is precisely what Jack Nicklaus, the golfer, does before making a shot.

4. **Using advisors and coaches.** Asking experts is a very good way to determine whether we are doing something correctly. Harvey McKay is the CEO of a large company, a marathon runner, and the author of a best-selling book called *Swim with the Sharks without Being Eaten Alive*. Each time McKay sets out to accomplish another goal, he first located the best experts he could find and asked them to coach him. On the basis of their experience, they helped him to break down the larger goal into manageable subgoals.

All of these examples illustrate that motivation involves attempts to match some action to an anticipated image or outcome. In setting goals, there are two problems: how to create the correct image or desired state; and how to find a route. Distal goals should remain relatively abstract; they exist to provide the motivation and the direction for behavior. Thomas Edison knew he wanted to create a light bulb (a distal goal), but he didn't know exactly how to construct it. Therefore, he had to imagine prototypes that might work (proximal goals). Eventually, one of the prototypes constructed did match the desired image (distal goal), and today we have a commercial light bulb. To achieve distal goals often involves creativity. We need to generate alternatives (or prototypes) and then see if one of these alternatives will work. Usually, the routes we devise don't work exactly as we planned. Often a great deal of trial and error is involved. That is why persistence is so important. However, when we encounter frustration and failure, we think about giving up. Consequently, managing our moods (self-reactions) is a critical part of self-regulation. That's our next topic.

Managing Emotions, Moods, and Self-Doubt

Self-efficacy beliefs are affected by mood. Kavanaugh and Bower (1985) demonstrated that self-efficacy beliefs may be dramatically different when people are in a positive, neutral, or negative mood state (Figure 14-5). According to Bower's affective priming theory, past successes and failures are stored as memories along with affect. When a particular mood is aroused, the memories associated with that mood are also aroused. These memories serve as the data base for making judgments about the likelihood of succeeding—that is, self-efficacy judgments. Therefore, it is important to manage our moods—in particular, to work on becoming more optimistic.

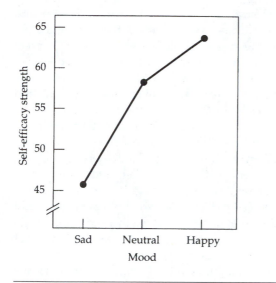

Figure 14-5. Mean strength of self-perceived efficacy across heterosexual, social, and athletic domains of functioning when efficacy judgments were made in a positive, neutral, or negative mood state. (From "Mood and Self-Efficacy: Impact on Job and Sadness on Perceived Capabilities," by D. J. Kavanagh & G. H. Bower, *Cognitive Therapy and Research,* 1985, 9, 507–525. Copyright © 1985 by Plenum Publishing Corporation. Reprinted with permission.)

Virtually everybody suffers from self-doubt. Some people, however, are able to manage self-doubt and do not let it overwhelm them. As Bandura (1991a) noted, "You cannot prevent the birds of worry and care from flying over your head. But you can stop them from building a nest in your head" (p. 135).

Self-doubt often results when we cannot turn off negative thoughts that intrude into our thinking. Sarason (1975) has found that intrusive thinking is one of the major components of test anxiety. It prevents us from focusing our attention on the task at hand. Apparently, what produces this stress is not the intrusive thoughts themselves nor their frequency but, rather, our inability to turn them off (Churchill & McMurray, 1990; Kent, 1987). Evidence from many sources indicates that dwelling on our coping deficiencies not only causes distress but impairs our level of functioning and performance (Bandura, 1988; Lazarus & Folkman, 1984; Meichenbaum, 1977). Failure to control intrusive

thinking can also result in depressive rumination, which again impairs performance and also diminishes perceptions of competency (Chapter 10).

Research indicates that people with strong self-efficacy beliefs are less troubled by self-doubt, tend to handle adversity better, and tend to organize their thinking better (Bandura, 1991a). In other words, they do not need to spend as much time managing negative thinking.

Within Bandura's theory, there is a dual route to emotional control: through our perception that we have the ability or skills to cope with a specific situation; and through our perception that we can deal with intrusive negative thoughts. As discussed earlier (Chapter 11), research by Ozer and Bandura (1990) showed that negative thoughts not only lead to feelings of anxiety but to avoidant behavior. In their research, which focused on empowering women who were fearful of sexual assault, they found that mastery training greatly reduced negative thoughts. Are there other ways to decrease negative thought? Various theorists have argued that it is often possible to gain control over negative thoughts by employing various self-regulation processes.

Dealing with Self-Doubt

Ellis and Greiger (1977) have suggested three methods of gaining control over negative intrusive thoughts: monitoring self-talk; cognitive restructuring; and substituting other thoughts.

Monitoring Self-Talk

People often engage in self-talk when they are trying to accomplish a task (Helmstetter, 1986). They may say to themselves, for instance, "This is too hard for me"; "I'm never going to make it"; "If I can just get around the next corner, I'm home free"; or "I think I'm going to win this one." Where does this self-talk come from, and what does it mean? It obviously comes from our assessment of our abilities relative to the difficulty of the task. Because self-talk changes quite dramatically as we proceed from the beginning of a task to the end, it is obviously not a stable estimate of our abilities. For example, people will start by saying, "I think I am going to do well"; then, when things get tough, they say, "I don't think I can do this"; and, towards the end, they say, "If I can just hang in there, I'll make it."

Motivation is typically at a low point when our self-talk becomes negative. Negative self-talk generally reflects a momentary downward shift in feelings of self-efficacy. As a result, we are inclined to give up because the discrepancy between perceived abilities and goals is no longer optimal. Can we learn to control our self-talk, in order to prevent a slump in our motivation? It appears so. We must learn first to monitor our self-talk and then to alter it so that it is more congruent with goal-directed behavior. In short, we need to engage in positive self-talk—"I know I can do it, I know I can succeed," for example.

Cognitive Restructuring

Once we have learned to substitute positive for negative self-talk, the next step is to become aware of the dynamics of success. If we are aware, for example, that we tend to experience self-doubt when we push ourselves, we can regard the emergence of self-doubt as an indicator that we are indeed pushing ourselves to new heights. When athletes—especially body builders—want to overcome plateaus, they will often remind themselves, "No pain, no gain." It appears that many of the limits on our performance that we accept are purely psychological. After Roger Bannister broke the four-minute mile, for instance, many other athletes matched his achievement. Obviously, it wasn't their bodies that were limiting them, but their minds.

Substituting Other Thoughts

One reason that competing against other people can push us to new levels is that our attention shifts away from our pain and fatigue and towards the idea of winning. Considerable evidence indicates that, when we are thinking pleasant thoughts, our body responds favorably. The trick is to learn to control our thinking so that we do not fall prey to lower motivation.

Developing Good Thinking Habits

One route towards the self-regulation of motivation is to develop good thinking habits. As Seligman (1990) has noted, "Habits of thinking need not be forever. One of the most significant findings in psychology in the last twenty years is that individuals can choose the way they think" (p. 8). Because all of us—no matter how skilled we are or how carefully we plan—will en-

counter frustrations and setbacks, we need to learn to become optimistic. We examined the differences between optimists and pessimists at length in Chapters 10 and 11, along with ways of becoming an optimist. The important point is that becoming an optimist, like becoming a constructive thinker, is a self-regulation process—a process that we can learn.

Ellen Langer (1990) has made a similar point in her book *Mindfulness.* She argues people often allow themselves to be guided by images that they have stored in their unconscious. When we become old, for example, we may allow ourselves to be guided by images that we have stored earlier about what old people can and cannot do, never questioning whether these images are accurate or useful. As a result, we may do things that reflect what we think we should do and not what we are capable of doing. On the basis of her research she has argued that one reason people act old, such as not making decisions or not carrying heavy things, is not because they cannot make decisions or are not capable of carrying heavy things but because their images tell them they can't. In one experiment, she induced older men to adopt a more youthful set of images and found that this manipulation produced not only many outward changes, such as a younger posture and gait, but several more basic changes such as improved eyesight, better mental functioning, and improved memory (Langer, 1989).

Langer argues that people need to question the images they have about how to behave in certain situations or at different ages and, if necessary, to change those images so that they are congruent with a happy and productive life. She argues that we do not have to behave mindlessly; we can become mindful by reflecting on our own behavior.

Dreams, Images, and Visualization

Some theorists believe that the process of motivation is not governed by our rational system but rather comes out of a system that is based more on images (visual or auditory) or perhaps emotions (pleasure and pain)—for example, the experiential system proposed by Epstein. Whereas the rational system uses abstract symbols, words, and numbers, the experiential system uses concrete images, metaphors, and narratives (Epstein, 1990).

For instance, Levinson (1978) describes human motivation in terms of what he calls the *dream*—an imagined self associated with a variety of goals, aspirations, and values. He suggests that, as we mature, the dream becomes cognitively refined and more motivationally powerful.

Nuttin (1984) has criticized psychology for talking about the impersonal, instinctual, or unconscious nature of human motivation. He has argued that personalized motivation transforms the activity of goal-setting into concrete intentions and plans. Dreams and visualization are one way of personalizing motivation. They also make things seem real. But dreams and visualization may do more. They may serve to access those systems that are directly concerned with creating action.

As Markus and Nurius (1986) point out, we rarely think about our goals in abstract terms; our goals are part of a very personal drama, in which we play the central role.

Research by Taylor (1983) has shown that, when people with cancer can gain a sense of mastery, their ability to cope improves, and so does their health. Markus and Nurius (1986) suggest that, for this to happen, the desire for health must be translated into a "vision of the self as healthy, active, and strong and must be accompanied by specific plans and strategies for becoming these possible selves" (p. 961). In other words, people need to create an image that is both focused (specific) and real (pertaining to their needs).

Others who have worked with mental images agree that focusing on clear, realistic mental images—preferably visual images—of the goals they want to attain is a powerful motivational tool (e.g., Cratty, 1989). The image should be as detailed as possible, incorporating as many senses as possible (Samuels & Samuels, 1975). Recently, Crick and Koch (1992) have

Practical Application 14-1

Preparing for Setbacks and Hard Work

We often fail to appreciate that people who have succeeded also experienced periods of self-doubt, thought about quitting, experienced failure along the way, or wondered whether the time they were putting in was worth it. One of the best ways to prepare for setbacks is to collect stories about the struggles that people we admire went through. A good starting point would be John White's (1982) book *Rejection*, which presents numerous stories about eminent people who experienced many rejections before they prevailed. Gertrude Stein submitted poems to editors for 20 years before she had one accepted. James Joyce's *Dubliners* was rejected by 22 publishers. Rodin was repeatedly rejected by the École des Beaux-Arts. Decca Records turned down the Beatles. In the academic world, John Garcia, whose pioneering work demonstrated that there are limitations to learning, was told by one reviewer of his oft-rejected manuscripts that the phenomenon he described was no more likely than the discovery of bird droppings in a cuckoo clock (Bandura, 1989). When Martin Seligman first attempted to report his pioneering research on learned helplessness, he was told by a senior professor in his department, who had been editor of the

Journal of Experimental Psychology for 20 years, that the article made him "physically sick."

Start collecting your own stories and look for clues to what made it possible for these people to prevail in spite of overwhelming odds. Things don't just happen; nor is success an accident. Success comes from learning to deal with adversity.

Humans are often inclined to assume that other people succeed because they are more intelligent, more talented, or luckier. In fact, what makes the difference is the individual's ability to prevail. In a study, people were asked to judge the intelligence of scientists who had made an important discovery. One group was told about the process that led the scientists to their discovery, while the other group was not. Those subjects told about the process judged the scientists to be less intelligent (Langer & Thompson, 1987). Once you understand that achievement simply involves systematically approaching a goal and then prevailing, you won't become overwhelmed by the belief that only the talented succeed. Zig Zigler likes to describe how he met a janitor with an IQ of 160. Unless you set goals and prevail, it doesn't matter how gifted you are.

provided evidence that, when people create mental images, they actually stimulate neurons in the brain to fire. If that is so, those images are real, and can have real behavioral consequences.

Aspirations as Distal Goals

Psychologists have traditionally described distal goals as aspirations. The word *aspiration* is a good word because it captures the idea of goals being in the future, that such goals are broad rather than narrow, and that effort may well be involved in their attainment. To aspire is to want something. If I aspire to become an actor, I don't just see myself playing a single part in a particular play; rather, I see myself as having a set of skills or competencies that will enable me to do many things over a long period of time. The concept of possible selves, which we will turn to shortly, incorporates both the abstract quality of an aspiration and the more personal quality of a dream.

Summary

Self-regulation of behavior is an outgrowth of social-cognitive theories. Self-regulation involves three steps: (1) self-observation (self-monitoring); (2) self-evaluation (self-judgment); and (3) self-reaction (self-incentive). According to goal-setting theory, goals (1) arouse effort; (2) give rise to persistence; (3) provide direction; and (4) motivate strategy development. A distinction has been made between distal and proximal goals. While both are important, they serve different functions. As a general rule, people should set difficult but attainable goals. The motivation to work towards assigned goals appears to be mediated by commitment. Interestingly, people who are instructed to do their best do no better than people with no goals. According to goal-setting theory, there should be optimal discrepancy; that is, the task should be neither so difficult as to be unachievable nor so easy as to be no challenge.

Self-efficacy theory involves two major constructs: outcome expectations; and feelings of self-efficacy. According to the theory, motivation is created by self-set goals. The mechanism that governs the termination of motivation is concept matching. A key component of goal attainment is strategy development, which involves designing routes to goals and the fine-tuning of behavior. Many athletes rely on mental rehearsal and good coaching to perfect their behavior. Managing our emotions is important for goal attainment. We can learn to manage self-doubt by managing intrusive thinking. According to Bandura, there is a dual route to emotional control. Accordingly, people need to learn how to control their thinking and also how to develop coping skills. Self-defeating thoughts may be managed by monitoring self-talk, by cognitive restructuring, and by substituting positive thoughts.

Several theorists have advocated the importance of creating vivid images, such as dreams, to enhance the motivational processes associated with goal setting. In the final analysis, behavior is motivated by our aspirations—abstract conceptualizations of what we want in the future. This concept encompasses the idea of developing competencies.

Self-Regulation and the Self-Concept

Research shows that our success is not predicted by our intelligence but rather by how we think about the world (Epstein, 1991; Seligman, 1990). Some people have learned to think in ways that lead them to succeed; others think in more destructive ways that ultimately result in failure.

Many theorists believe that our self-concept ultimately determines the goals that we set, how we evaluate progress towards those goals, and the impact of success and failure on our future goal-directed behavior. In short, the self is the cornerstone of self-regulation. Certain individuals, for example, are inclined to set difficult goals for themselves because their self-concept allows them to entertain the belief that they can reach those goals. Perhaps their self-concept incorporates the idea they have the capacity to learn, or the capacity to work hard, or the capacity to find the right path. Armed with such beliefs, they can visualize themselves reaching their goals, and they decide to put forth effort.

The self-concept can be conceptualized as self-knowledge. It embraces how we think about the external world and how we think about our ability to deal with it. Growing out of our attempts to make sense of our own behavior, our self-concept represents the past, the present, and the future. It determines, for instance, how we process information, the feelings we experience, the dreams we have, our motivation to act, our reactions to feedback, and how we reflect on success and failure (Deci & Ryan, 1991; Dweck, 1991; Markus & Wurf, 1987).

The self-concept may or may not be conscious; that is, we may or may not be aware of the principles by which it operates. For example, we may or may not be aware that we ascribe to an entity theory of intelligence or an incremental theory of intelligence. Nevertheless, having decided at some level of consciousness to endorse one of these theories, we will behave in highly predictable ways. If we believe in an incremental theory, for example, we will be more inclined to put forth effort.

The self-concept has three main functions.

1. **To provide information.** The self-concept provides information that will enable us to make judgments about what we can or cannot do. The information contained in the self-concept, however, is not always well-grounded in reality, and much of it has not been confirmed by social experience (Markus & Nurius, 1986). Individuals whose self-concept underestimates their skills and talents may find it difficult and even impossible to develop aspirations that might motivate them to set difficult goals.

2. **To provide context.** Humans are inclined to view feedback regarding their behavior in the context of their enduring aspirations and goals. Receiving a grade of B may mean very little for someone whose only wish is to graduate but a great deal for someone who wants to be admitted to medical school. Similarly, a broken lunch date may have very different implications for us, depending on whether we feel lonely or we simply hoped to gain some interesting information from our prospective companion.

3. **To provide integration.** The self-concept is not only a storehouse of information about the self but provides the global integration of that information (Higgins, 1996). From that integration of information comes our sense of identity. As Erikson (1950) points out, our sense of identity provides us with the ability to experience the self as something that has both continuity and sameness. Interestingly, this sense of continuity and sameness may make it difficult for us to change,

because changing means that we must give up, at least momentarily, the sense of who we are or who we are destined to be.

According to many current theorists, the self is both learned and constructed (Deci & Ryan, 1991). It is learned by internalizing the beliefs and attitudes of those around us, such as our parents and teachers; it is constructed by developing new beliefs as a result of our interactions with the environment. Even though my parents were not concerned about the environment, I may learn to care because of what I see happening around me. Politically, I may have learned from my parents to favor government social programs but, because of my perceptions about the growing national debt, I may come to favor fewer and less generous government programs.

Self-Knowledge and Self-Regulatory Functions

Self-knowledge is unique because it pertains to our survival and also because it must be continually regulated so as to be as current as possible, again for reasons of survival (Higgins, 1996). It is also selective; it tends to keep track of those aspects that are important for survival, such as our strengths and weaknesses. In the final analysis, the self exists for the purpose of helping us to interact with the environment.

Three components of the self with three distinct self-regulatory functions have been distinguished: (1) the instrumental self; (2) the expectant self; and (3) the monitored self.

1. **The instrumental self.** The instrumental self provides information about what will happen if we behave or fail to behave in certain ways—for instance, "If I don't give this phone message to my boss, she'll get annoyed" or "If I reciprocate the generosity of a friend, the friendship will endure." This information often pertains to the consequences of meeting—or failing to meet—the desires and expectations of significant others—for example, "Being kind to others would please my mother" or "If I procrastinate, I know my father will be upset." Thus, in a work setting, for instance, our behavior will be influenced not only by what we think is important and appropriate there but also by what we carry with us from our past (Higgins, 1996).

2. **The expectant self.** The expectant self provides information about what is likely to happen if we engage in a certain activity. Should I ask someone for a date, for example, I will expect a certain outcome, depending on a variety of factors, on the basis of my experience in the past. Similarly, should I get involved in a game of tennis, I will have some idea of what is going to happen, again depending on the context. Representation of certain competencies has a clear survival function. By knowing what to expect, I can prepare myself for the outcome. If I expect failure, for example, I will know what to do next.

The expectant self is more than just a summary of our past experiences. It provides the motivation for contingency plans—for instance, the tendency to shift to a less difficult task when we begin failing at an easy task. Higgins (1996) suggests that the expectant self should be conceptualized as a dispositional state. It gives rise to action, but the specific action is determined by other parts of the self.

3. **The monitored self.** The monitored self provides information about how well we are doing in relation to some goal or desired state. In other words, the monitored self exists to help reduce the discrepancy between the current and ideal selves. Should a person develop a new desired self, perhaps because of a new intimate relationship, the monitored self would become involved in creating this new *emergent self.* The survival value of a monitored self is obvious. Because the discrepancy between the ideal and the existing is assumed to motivate behavior, insuring that the individual focuses on this discrepancy would serve to facilitate the achievement of a particular goal (Higgins, 1996).

These three selves are complementary. The instrumental self provides information about how the world responds to us, the expectant self provides information about how we respond to the world, and the monitored self provides information about how we are doing in relation to certain desires and demands. Each of these pieces of information enables us to choose the most appropriate action in the given circumstances. The existence of these more or less distinct systems should enhance our survival.

Two Aspects of the Self

William James (1890) made a distinction between the "I" and the "me" of the self. Deci and Ryan (1991) char-

acterized these two aspects of the self as, respectively, an agent and a repository (a storage place) of society's values. The repository part of the self (the "me") involves values, such as family, justice, and sharing, and regulatory processes, such as persisting, following rules, and abstaining from aggression. We internalize both values and regulatory processes because, as social beings, we have a need for relatedness. To gain that sense of relatedness or acceptance, we internalize the beliefs of people who are important to us, such as our parents and friends. The agent side (the "I") is autonomous and needs to be in control. When the autonomous side of the self is allowed to develop skills and competence by mastering the environment, the individual gains a sense of self-determination. The agent side is responsible for actively integrating information (as opposed to absorbing it) and for generating rules and principles to guide our actions. According to this distinction, the repository side is actively constructed by the agent side. Over time, I will adjust my values and my self-regulatory processes so that they are congruent with the self-determined part of the self. I may decide, for example, to give up the idea that I must have children, because it is inconsistent with my desire to pursue certain plans I have selected, such as sailing around the world.

Self-Discrepancy Theory

According to Higgins' (1987, 1996) self-discrepancy theory, there is a discrepancy between the *actual self,* which represents the attributes we think we possess, and the *ideal self,* which represents our hopes, wishes, and aspirations. In this model, the ideal self is viewed as a *self-guide;* it gives us direction. It is also a source of affect; while living up to an ideal can be a source of positive affect—for instance, self-satisfaction—failure to live up to an ideal can be a source of negative affect. This model suggests that there is a single core self and a single ideal self. However, other theorists have suggested that there may be many ideal selves and that they may have their roots in rethinking the core self (Higgins, 1996).

Possible Selves

Self-knowledge, by itself, does not automatically lead to growth and development. According to Markus and Nurius (1986), the possible selves that we construct for

When we try on new hats, we are symbolically trying on possible selves to see how they fit.

ourselves create motivation and are therefore the basis for change. These possible selves are closely linked to our self-concept. When we think about what we might become, we draw heavily upon self-knowledge. We ask ourselves, for example, whether we have the skill or ability to do something; whether we can develop that skill or ability; whether we are willing to put forth the effort and persist; and whether we are willing to give up other activities. In other words, we don't arbitrarily pull possible selves out of the air; rather, we create them from information contained in the self. These images are very real, because they come out of very personal information—our self-knowledge. Like aspirations, however, they have an abstract, conditional quality. They are possibilities that might follow from certain actions.

Possible selves are created selectively on the basis of our experience in a given domain of expertise. As we become aware of our own abilities or talents, we develop an enduring sensitivity to tasks in which those abilities or talents might be relevant (Nicholls, 1990). If we know that we are smart in school, for example, we will remain sensitive to issues of intelli-

gence and achievement in school. If we know that we are good at dealing with others, we will remain sensitive to occupations in which we can make use of those talents. The self also contains sociocultural and historical information (Stryker, 1984). This information can be both liberating and limiting. If I am from a poor background and I learn that someone with a similar background became President of the United States, I may realize that, despite my background, I don't have to set limits on my goals. It I know that no one from my family has ever experienced great success, however, I may unconsciously conclude that I cannot hope for success.

Possible Selves and Goals

It has been suggested that possible selves link the self-concept to goals (Markus & Nurius, 1986; Markus, Cross, & Wurf, 1990): "The inclusion of a sense of what is possible within the self-concept allows it to become dynamic" (Markus & Nurius, 1990, p. 960).

Possible selves represent the future-oriented component of the self-concept. They range from the ideal self that we would like to become—the successful self, the creative self, the rich self, the thin self, the loved self, the respected self—to the self that we are afraid we might become: the alone self, the depressed self, the incompetent self, the alcoholic self, the unemployed self. If we're aware that we enjoy using drugs, for example, a possible self might be a drug addict. If we're aware that we cannot make decisions, a possible self might be a person who depends on others to get through life.

Possible selves may or may not be an immediate source of motivation. Sometimes we have no real intention of acting on a certain possible self. The impetus that pushes us from possible selves to creating aspirations is not altogether clear. It may be as simple as a word of encouragement from another person or as complex as a careful assessment of the pros and cons. In the final analysis, it involves making a decision.

Developing a Range of Possible Selves

Individuals who wish to achieve great things need to develop a self-concept that will permit the elaboration of a range of possible selves. As Markus and Nurius (1986) point out, possible selves do not simply happen; rather, they grow out of a well-defined self-concept. There are at least three characteristics of a well-defined self-concept: It is highly differentiated, positive, and linked to perceptions of competencies. Let's look at each of these aspects in turn.

1. **A highly differentiated self-concept.** As we saw in Chapter 13, people with highly differentiated or diverse self-concepts tend to be more likely to achieve difficult goals. Markus and Nurius (1986) suggest that individuals who view themselves as having numerous categories for the self (numerous possible selves) are able to achieve more goals, because they perceive that they can assume more roles. Linville (1987) has suggested that people who have *self-complexity*—that is, a range of conceptions of their identity—are better able to achieve goals and to deal with a wide variety of negative events. Because they can see themselves in a wide variety of situations, they can rise to new challenges and cope with new situations. Campbell (1990) argues that people with high self-esteem have greater clarity of self-concept. Using confidence measures, she has found that people with high self-esteem are more certain of self-attributes. Baumgardner (1990) suggests that it is important to have depth or certainty about a

particular trait dimension. Certainty about a trait—being athletic or creative, for instance—is important, she argues, because it is the basis for self-esteem, which, in turn, is the basis for attempting new and different things. As we have already noted, Baumgardner (1990) concludes that "to know oneself is to like oneself" (p. 1062). She argues that a strong self-concept, characterized by depth or certainty, promotes a sense of control over future outcomes and thus leads to positive affect and self-confidence.

2. **A positive self-concept.** Campbell (1990) found that people with high self-esteem describe themselves with more positive attributes. Extensive research has shown that people with high self-esteem not only possess attributes that are linked to success but tend to cope well with change and stress. For example, children identified as having high self-esteem are characterized by two sets of attributes: (1) confidence, curiosity, independence, and self-initiative; and (2) the ability to adapt to change and stress. Children with low self-esteem, in contrast, are characterized by (1) failure to show confidence, curiosity, independence, and initiative; and (2) inability to adapt to change (Harter, 1990). A consistent theme in the self-concept literature is that people with good self-concepts are motivated by challenges and can deal with stress (e.g., Epstein, 1992). Another common theme in the experimental literature is that people with good self-esteem tend to react positively to new challenges (Seligman, 1990). Substantial evidence suggests that, in order to be positive, people need to view the world as benevolent. In a benevolent world, people can take risks.

3. **A self-concept linked to perceptions of competencies.** Ultimately, the self-concept is linked to competencies (Nicholls, 1990) and perceptions of competencies (Langer & Park, 1990). If we have a clear perception that we are competent in a given domain, we are likely to set more difficult goals for ourselves. There is some reason to believe that taking an optimistic view of our competencies is a good idea (Seligman, 1990). Those who believe that they can do something will often try and, in the process of trying, they will often succeed. That is what it means to be an optimist.

The Creation of Possible Selves

Possible selves do not just happen. They result from combining and recombining elements of the self in new ways. Sometimes, they emerge from acts of fantasy in which we entertain a wide variety of images of ourselves. Sometimes they are constructed on the basis of decisions about what we should or should not do. Those decisions may be shaped by values that we hold or principles that we have come to accept as important. Deciding that we'd prefer a long life to an exciting life, for example, might affect our selection of an occupation (Kendall, Learner, & Craighead, 1984; Learner, 1982).

If possible selves are created and constructed, we can take personal responsibility for motivating ourselves to change. Many theorists take the position that possible selves are only the starting point for change. In the final analysis, we need to set clearly defined goals for ourselves. However, those goals, it appears, must be congruent with our values or else we are unlikely to achieve them. A study by Langer and Thompson (cited in Langer, 1989) illustrates that people find it difficult to change behaviors that they value. The study participants were presented with a list of negative traits—such as rigid, grim, and gullible—and asked whether they had tried to change these behaviors and if they had succeeded or failed. Later, the participants were asked how much they valued such traits as consistency, seriousness, and trust. The researchers found that the participants had difficulty changing certain negatively phrased traits if they valued those traits. For example, people generally do not like to see themselves as rigid but, if they value consistency, they may find it difficult to become spontaneous. Similarly, people generally don't like to see themselves as gullible but, if they value trust, they may have difficulty becoming suspicious or cynical.

Although our possible selves are closely linked to our self-concept, we can begin to create new possible selves (Practical Application 14-2).

Implicit Theories

The self houses our implicit theories. We have many implicit theories about many things. Two classes of implicit theories are relevant to goal setting: implicit theories about the world; and implicit theories about ability. These are sometimes called simply world theories and self theories. Let's examine these in turn.

Implicit Theories about the World

A number of self theorists suggest that everyone develops an implicit theory of reality (e.g., Epstein, 1990; Dweck & Leggett, 1988). It appears that people not only have a world theory and a self theory, but also have beliefs and ideas about the relationship between the self and the world. For example, they may believe that, because they live in a bad world, they cannot control most things that happen to them or that, because it is a good world, events are controllable (Epstein, 1990). In this section, we consider three prototypes of how people conceptualize the world and how those concepts shape their ideas about what they can or should do.

Prototype 1: The world as threatening or malevolent. Some people are inclined to view the world in negative terms (Epstein, 1990; Watson & Clark, 1984). They see the world as threatening or malevolent. When they wake up each morning, they dread to enter the world that waits outside their front doors. Apprehensive that the world is going to harm them, they experience stress in preparation for fight or flight. Their hearts may speed up and their blood pressure may rise. Sometimes they are angry, on the unspoken assumption that, in a hostile world, the best defense is an offense. Alternatively, they may become very passive, in the hope of being left alone.

These people are pessimists. They expect bad things to happen and sometimes seem pleased when bad things happen to others, because such events confirm their view of the world and their survival strategy. These people have little sense of agency or control; they are reactive. They think in terms of survival of the fittest in a dog-eat-dog world.

At least two dimensions characterize this implicit theory of the world. First, these people tend to have what Watson and Clark (1984) called a disposition towards negative affectivity. All their experiences are focused around deprivation and defeat. They are anxious, fearful, unhappy, and distressed. According to Watson and Clark (1984), a wide variety of personality scales that purport to measure trait anxiety, neuroticism, repression-sensitization, ego strength, and general maladjustment appear to measure the same underlying personality trait—the disposition toward negative affectivity. Following up on this work, it has been suggested that people who are anxious and fearful tend to view the world as threatening (Franken, Gibson, & Rowland, 1992). They are inclined to limit their interactions with the world because it is a threat to their physical and psychological well-being.

People who are anxious also tend to have low self-esteem (Franken, Gibson, & Rowland, 1992). For example, they are easily discouraged; they are inclined to give up when things aren't working; they get nervous in new situations; they have poor opinions of themselves; they do not see life as satisfying; and they often wish they were someone else.

Second, people who view the world as threatening tend to be aware only of limited possibilities. For example, people who are anxious do not select new or different activities but rather select activities that are

Practical Application 14-2

How to Create Possible Selves

Sometimes people get into a rut. Because their parents told them they should become a doctor like Uncle George, they never entertain any other alternative. Years ago, I had a friend who had decided, with encouragement from his parents, to emulate his uncle by pursuing a career in engineering. Not having the aptitude, he struggled and failed. At that point, he had to face the possibility that his chosen career might not be right for him. When he began to explore other options, he suddenly realized that his interests were in the social sciences. Once success followed another and eventually, after graduating from Oxford, he set up his own research institute.

How do you go about creating possible selves without having to wait for failure? Start by making a list of things that you are good at doing or things that you have done well. Make sure this list contains things that are not part of your school experiences, such as bargaining or making friends. Also, write down some of the skills that you think you might acquire with some effort. For example, perhaps you think you could learn how to repair a bicycle or to play an instrument.

Next, find the category under which such a skill could be found. For example, if you have worked at a swimming pool and been left in charge from time to time, the corresponding category is manager. If you have organized a school dance, you would put that in the category of producer or organizer. If you have won an athletic contest, you would call yourself a winning athlete. Take each of these category names and put them into a new list. The purpose of this exercise is to get you to think in broader terms. When

you do that, a whole new world will open up for you. You will say to yourself, I'm a manager, an organizer, and an athlete. Often people do not realize that the skills they acquire in one task will generalize to other situations. Armed with these new categories, you can suddenly see yourself doing many things.

With this new list, think of things that you might do. Write down all of them, even if they wouldn't make money or make you famous. Over the next weeks or even month, write down other things that come to mind. From this list, generate as many possible selves as you can. It is not important whether you actually want to pursue them. The point of this exercise is to make you aware that there are many possibilities. You might be surprised to see many options that you have never considered before.

A very good technique is to ask your friends what they think a person with the skills from your category list might do. We are often blind to new alternatives, because our self-concept works hard to prevent us from entertaining new alternatives. In fact, when presented with a new alternative, we often say, "That isn't me." Nevertheless, when people make suggestions, we tend to incorporate those ideas into our unconscious. It is amazing how a simple act of encouragement can alter our motivation. If someone else can believe we can do it, why can't we? Psychologists have known about this phenomenon for some time and systematically use suggestions and encouragement to get people to try new things. Often, when people try new things, they succeed, which is the basis for further strivings.

more familiar to them (e.g., Berlyne, 1960; White, 1959). There is also evidence that people who can be characterized as fearful perceive more activities as dangerous and risky and therefore psychologically unavailable to them (Franken, Gibson, & Rowland, 1992).

Prototype 2: The world as benevolent. Some people have the disposition to view the world in positive terms (Seligman, 1990; Scheier & Carver, 1985, 1988; Snyder et al., 1991). They see the world as benevolent—as good and generous. When these people wake up in the morning, they are convinced that good things are going to happen to them; they are optimists. They exude confidence and seem unaffected by setbacks. Their sense of agency is highly developed. They feel that they have the ability to find the right path and to claim their rightful reward. They think, "This is my day" or "Something good is going to happen to me today."

Again, two dimensions characterize these people. First, they have a disposition to experience positive affect. They see themselves not only as successful but as happy people. Seligman (1990) views optimism as the opposite of depression. Whereas depression is characterized by negative mood and negative affect, optimism is characterized by positive mood and positive affect.

Second, these people believe that the world offers many positive opportunities or possibilities. For instance, research on anxiety shows that people who are low in anxiety are more inclined to explore their environment, more inclined to respond to new stimulations, and more inclined to try new activities (e.g., Berlyne, 1960; White, 1959). There is also research on optimism and hope that indicates optimists are open to new experiences and challenges (Seligman, 1990), and that people who are hopeful tend to have a strong sense of agency (goal-directed determination) and awareness of pathways (ability to plan routes to goals) and are able to set not only more goals but more difficult goals (Synder et al., 1991).

Further evidence comes from work with sensation seekers—people who are motivated by the need for novel and complex stimulation and are willing to take risks to experience such stimulation (Zuckerman, 1979). My colleagues and I did a study with sensation seekers to explore their tendency to take risks. Risk is defined by Webster's dictionary as the possibility of loss or injury. If an activity is perceived to be risky, it follows that we should avoid it. But what makes some-

thing risky? Is there some objective measure of risk? Perhaps everything we do is risky if viewed from a certain perspective. It is clear from our research that some people willingly participate in activities traditionally labeled as dangerous. It is important to remember that the labeling of something as dangerous or risky is based on norms. If we were to use only anxious people to define what is risky, then the norms for what is risky would be very different than if we used nonanxious people or sensation seekers. If very anxious people were the norm, leaving the house at all might be viewed as a risky activity.

My colleagues and I wanted to explore why some people are willing to engage in activities that have traditionally been labeled as risky while others are not. In our study, we gave participants Zuckerman's Sensation Seeking Scale, Wolpe and Lange's Fear Schedule Survey, a Danger Assessment Questionnaire, and an Attitudes Towards Risk Questionnaire. The Attitudes Toward Risk Questionnaire asked people to indicate on a five-point scale whether items were "like me" or "not like me." A factor analysis of this scale identified two distinct factors: one that pertained to taking psychological risks, which we called *disregard of social approval;* another that pertained to taking physical risks, which we called *disregard of danger.* The items for the two factors are presented in Table 14-1.

We found that people high in the sensation-seeking motive tended to be less fearful, tended to perceive a variety of activities as less dangerous, and indicated that they like to take both physical and psychological risks (Franken, Gibson, & Rowland, 1992). These results indicate that fear, danger, and risk may be in the eye of the beholder.

Prototype 3: The world as benign. There are people who view the world as neither threatening nor benevolent. For these people, pleasure and satisfaction are not the result of something good happening or of preventing something bad from happening but rather derive from their own actions—more precisely, from exercising competence. These people wake up in the morning with a goal they want to accomplish. Perhaps they have decided that they want a bigger house in a new location. In time, they buy an old house, tear it down, and build their dream house.

Thus, for these people, pleasure comes from operating on the world and changing it. In order to do so,

Table 14-1. Items from the Attitudes Towards Risk Questionnaire. In the original scale administered to the study participants, the items were mixed together; they have been rank-ordered in this table according to which item loaded greatest on that particular factor.

Factor 1: Psychological Risks: Disregard of Social Approval

1. While I don't deliberately seek out situations or activities that society disapproves of, I find that I often end up doing things that society disapproves of.
2. I often do things that I know my parents would disapprove of.
3. I often think about doing things that are illegal.
4. I do not let the fact that something is considered immoral stop me from doing it.
5. I often think about doing things that I know my friends would disapprove of.
6. I often seek out situations or activities that society does not approve of.
7. I do not let the fact that something is illegal stop me from doing it.
8. I often think about doing things that I know my parents would disapprove of.
9. I often think about doing things that I know society would disapprove of.
10. I often think about doing things that are immoral.

Factor 2: Physical Risks: Disregard of Danger

11. I like the feeling that comes with taking physical risks.
12. I consider myself a risk-taker.
13. Being afraid of doing something new often makes it more fun in the end.
14. The greater the risk, the more fun the activity.
15. I like to do things that almost paralyze me with fear.
16. I like the feeling that comes with taking psychological or social risks.
17. While I don't deliberately seek out situations or activities that involve physical risk, I often end up doing things that involve physical risk.
18. I like the feeling that comes from entering a new situation.
19. I often think about doing activities that involve physical risk.
20. I often think about doing things that would arouse a great deal of fear or anxiety in me.

Source: Reprinted from "Sensation Seeking and the Tendency to View the World as Threatening," by R. E. Franken, K. J. Gibson, & G. L. Rowland, *Personality and Individual Differences,* 1992, *12,* 31–38 (Appendix 3, p. 37). Copyright © 1992. Reprinted with kind permission from Pergamon Press Ltd, Headington Hill Hall, Oxford OX3 OBW, UK).

they must develop skills or competence. Through exercising skills and competence, they experience satisfaction. They say to themselves, "I will develop the skills so that I can make it into what I want" or "I want to be free to do it my way."

This view of the world has its origins in the philosophy of individualism. According to this philosophy, people should be treated as autonomous and self-reliant. Further, they must be given freedom to exploit the world, because it is through exercising their skills and changing things that people gain happiness.

The idea that some people view the world as benign is reflected in the theory of Deci and Ryan (1991), who suggest that people are born with three needs: the need for autonomy, the need for competence, and the need for relatedness. The satisfaction of these needs brings happiness and satisfaction.

What about the dimensions of affect and possibilities that we used to characterize the other two world theories? People who view the world as benign do not see it as the source of either positive or negative affect. They see positive and negative affect as consequences of their actions, which, in turn, are a product of their goals. The main positive emotion that Deci and Ryan talk about is pride, which results from exercising competence or gaining mastery. Negative affect results from the inability to experience autonomy and self-determination. Frustration would be one of the main negative emotions. They also talk about the need for relatedness, which, they suggest, provides the primary impetus for internalizing values and regulatory processes.

What about possibilities? Possibilities come from within the self and have little or no direct link to the external world. The self acts on the world and creates something new by molding or shaping the world according to our needs or desires. The ultimate basis for all possibilities is competence. With competence, anything is possible; without it, nothing is possible.

However, this does not mean that people who view the world as benign have nothing to fear, nor that they gain no pleasure from the external world. Deci and Ryan acknowledge that the external world can be a source of both pleasure and pain, but they do not see this as the focus of the self. It is unfortunate that we have to deal with, for instance, crime, pollution, and divorce in the course of exercising competence, but these are not of central concern to the self; they are peripheral. The self is concerned with autonomy, self-determination, and relatedness.

Self-regulation and world theories. The obvious implication of all this is that whether people will set difficult goals for themselves is linked to their implicit theory of the world. That is, the more people believe the world is benevolent or even benign, the more likely they are to construct broad and well-defined possible selves and, consequently, the more likely they are to set difficult goals.

From a survival perspective, seeing the world as malevolent is adaptive, because we are sensitized to cues that might threaten our survival. However, because of our defensive posture, we fail to set difficult goals or take risks. In short, we end up living a life of quiet desperation; always alert to danger, we never really enjoy ourselves or embrace new challenges.

In order to change, we need to view the world differently. Instead of seeing the world as a source of threat, we need to see it as a source of challenge. Numerous experiments by social psychologists show that, when people change the way they label things, their perceptions and actions change as well. Take the concept of challenge, for example. Research using a stress paradigm has shown that, if people view something as challenging, they are less likely to experience stress than if they view it as a threat (Higgins, 1996). Such research suggests that it may be possible for people to self-regulate by monitoring their thought processes and learning how to replace self-defeating views with self-facilitating views. This is often called *cognitive reframing* or *restructuring.* By taking a different view of the situation, people react to it differently. Numerous researchers, including Beck, Epstein, and Seligman, have argued that, through self-regulation, people can learn to change the way they think about their interactions with the world.

Implicit Theories of Competence

To understand how people view the self, we need to observe how they cope, adapt, shape, or embrace the external world—collectively called *strategies.* Most people do not simply react mindlessly; they respond with carefully devised strategies.

Of the many strategies that people use, two seem to be very pervasive across many situations: the *mastery strategy* and the *performance strategy.* It's helpful to think of these strategies as *orientations.* Like a disposition, an orientation points us in a certain direction.

The mastery strategy and the performance strategy have been discussed by various theorists—most notably, Dweck (Dweck, 1991; Dweck & Leggett, 1988). These concepts have their roots in the early literature on the mastery motive (e.g., White, 1959) and in Rogers' (1959) work on conditional and unconditional love.

These strategies are not rational or conscious; rather, they are implicit theories that we develop through processes such as modeling, instruction, and construction. We are not locked into one strategy or another but rather can learn to change our orientation by adjusting our focus.

The mastery strategy. The mastery strategy can be defined in terms of a general belief system that involves three interrelated beliefs: the belief that we can acquire the skills necessary to survive; the belief that we can control the environment through the development of skills; and the belief that we have the capacity to create happiness and health. In Dweck's (1991) theory, the mastery strategy grows out of the belief that intelligence is incremental. Through work and effort, people can change their intelligence and their ability to adapt to the world.

Some writers fail to emphasize that people with a strong mastery motive are typically very skilled. In addition to believing that they can control things, they actually have a large repertoire of skills that enable them to control things. For example, they often have the ability to acquire the information they need; they know how to organize the information they acquire; they know how to apply that information; and they have the social skills necessary to be truly effective. The mastery motive, in other words, combines attitudes and beliefs with a set of generalized skills.

People who develop a mastery strategy learn to take credit for their actions. Further, they come to develop a generalized belief that they can effect change through their ability to learn and develop new skills. Their continued development of new skills is rewarded and sustained by the feelings of self-efficacy that accompany the development of each new skill. Typically, they feel pride at their achievements.

The performance strategy. The performance strategy can also be defined in terms of a belief system that involves three interrelated beliefs: that we can achieve what we want by learning the rules for winning; that winning is an acceptable way to get ahead; and that happiness is the result of winning. The performance-oriented person tends to be concerned with the *outcome*, whereas the mastery orientation is concerned with the *process*. This is a very important distinction.

As we have seen, mastery-oriented individuals are sustained by the feelings of self-efficacy they gain from effectively dealing with the world; the process is the source of their motivation. Performance-oriented individuals, in contrast, are sustained by winning—that is, by the outcome. While skills are often involved in winning, performance-oriented individuals do not neces-

sarily view themselves as having skills. Rather, they see themselves as using tactics, such as undermining other people. As a result, it is more difficult for them to take credit for their successes.

This distinction does not mean that mastery types do not like to win, nor that performance types are not interested in experiencing feelings of self-efficacy, but they have a different focus or emphasis. There is considerable evidence that experiencing feelings of efficacy is the more powerful motivator of behavior in the long run (Deci & Ryan, 1991).

Self-regulation and self theories. The obvious implication of all this is that whether people will set difficult goals for themselves is linked to their implicit theories about competence. That is, the more people are mastery-oriented, the more likely they are to set difficult goals for themselves. How does a person become more mastery-oriented?

One of the most important things people can learn is that competency isn't something they have or don't have; rather, competency is something they must develop. While there are obvious biological limitations, they account for much less than people often think. In a study referred to earlier, Langer (1989) asked her students to evaluate the intelligence of scientists who had achieved an impressive intellectual outcome, such as discovering a new planet or inventing a new drug. When she described the achievement in terms of a series of steps, they judged the scientists to be less intelligent than when she simply named the achievement. When they saw the steps, the accomplishments did not seem that difficult. Thus, the key to becoming mastery-oriented is to recognize that a series of well-defined steps leads to every accomplishment. If we can discover those steps, we can become competent.

By recognizing that each achievement involves a series of steps, Japanese industrialists have made great strides in manufacturing quality products such as cars and electronic equipment. They have learned to view manufacturing as a process made up of many components. To improve the overall product, they focus their energy on trying to improve each of the components and the links between those components. Whenever they learn how to produce a better component, they introduce the change as soon as possible, whereas North American manufacturers tend to wait for a model

Success comes to those who have embraced the importance of mastery.

change. As a result, they are usually slightly ahead of their competition. As we noted earlier, this approach has come to be called continuous improvement.

The continuous improvement concept is a good metaphor for creating personal competency. Like the manufacturing process, competency is made up of a series of components. Each component can be improved and then reintroduced into the chain that makes up the competency. Athletes often use this approach. For a time, they work on one component. Having perfected that component, they reintroduce it into the chain to ensure that it harmonizes with the other components. Next, they work on another component and then reintroduce that component into the chain, and so on. While change is incremental in the short run, it is often very dramatic in the long run.

By breaking processes down into components and then reassembling them, athletes can create a wide variety of skills out of a few basic components. Standup comics use a similar approach. They have a series of components—skits and jokes—that they can string together in various ways depending on the particular audience.

The Relationship between World Theories and Self Theories

Epstein (1990) has suggested that individuals' world theories and self theories are linked by certain propositions. As yet, we don't have a clear idea of these propositions. All we really know is that world theories seem to vary independently of self theories. That is, if we know that a person has adopted the view that the world is threatening, we cannot predict whether that person has a mastery orientation or a performance orientation.

Some psychologists have suggested that world theories and self theories are linked by superordinate categories. Each of us has an underlying principle that guides our life—a guiding phrase, for example. Let's say that my guiding phrase is "I want to make this a better world." This phrase may embody the idea that, while I perceive the world as malovent—a source of pain and threat, at least for some people—my goal is to help relieve that pain, perhaps by entering politics, creating a new drug, or writing a book. Let's say that my guiding phrase is "I am going to enjoy life to the fullest." This phrase may embody the idea that it is a benevolent world and that I intend to enjoy it, by adopting either a mastery or a performance orientation.

Summary

Research on the self-regulation of behavior has led to a renewed interest in the concept of self. Our self-concept is determined both by how we view the external world and by how we view our ability to deal with it. The self can be thought of as self-knowledge that provides both information and context. Higgins has argued that the self has three distinct self-regulatory functions that correspond to three selves: an instrumental self, an expectant self, and a monitored self. Going back to William James, a distinction has been made between two aspects of the self: as a repository of information ("me") and as an agent ("I").

It has been suggested that possible selves are the link between the self-concept and goals. The first step of self-motivation, therefore, is to create possible selves. Possible selves are the future part of our self-concept. Possible selves are closely linked to the self-concept and therefore self-knowledge plays an important role in their creation. Possible selves are created selectively on the basis of our experience in a given domain of expertise, but they also contain sociocultural and historical information, which provides the necessary context. If we are to create diverse possible selves, we need a highly differentiated self, a positive self-concept, and a self that is linked closely to perceptions of competencies. Through goal setting, possible selves create action.

The psychological literature includes at least three prototypes describing how people view the external world. People who perceive the world as threatening (prototype 1) are dispositionally inclined to experience negative affect and tend to see the world as limited in opportunities or possibilities. Anxious and neurotic people are examples of this prototype. People who view the world as benevolent (prototype 2) are dispositionally inclined to experience positive affect and tend to view the world as offering many opportunities or possibilities. Optimists and hopeful people are examples of this prototype. People who view the world as benign (prototype 3) value autonomy and self-determination. In shaping the external world through the application of autonomy and self-determination, they experience the pleasure that comes with exercising competence. The outside world is neither a source of pleasure or pain, nor a source of opportunity. Individualists are examples of this prototype. Finally, a distinction may be made between people who hold a mastery orientation and those who hold a performance orientation. Whereas the mastery orientation is motivated by the process—the feelings of self-efficacy that accompany the exercise of skills—the performance orientation is motivated by outcome.

An Overview: Becoming a Process-Oriented Person

Most current motivation theorists hold that, in order to succeed, we need to focus on the process, rather than

the goal. Virtually all of the work reviewed in this chapter stresses the importance of the process, as opposed to the outcome. In his book *Flow*, Csikszentmihalyi (1990) argues that optimal experience occurs when we undertake challenging tasks with clear goals and immediate feedback. In such situations, he argues, we lose all self-doubt and experience a sense of control. That experience is so strong, he argues, that we are willing to put forth whatever effort is needed to develop the skills we require.

Many motivation writers have argued that the main reward or satisfaction from achievement is associated not with reaching the goal but with working towards the goal—not with being there but with getting there. When Torvil and Dean won their gold medal in the Olympics for pair figure skating, Dean said he felt that he had achieved his dream; it was wonderful. In the next sentence, he talked about how difficult it would be to go back to work. Achieving a dream is exciting, but the pleasure is often short-lived. In order to continue enjoying life, we need new dreams to sustain us. One of our more celebrated dreamers and achievers is Apple Computer co-founder Steve Jobs; fittingly, his biography is subtitled, *The Journey Is the Reward* (Young, 1988).

Performance goals should not be ignored in this process. If we are to make important contributions to society and to gain recognition, we must be attuned to the wants and needs of other people. Knowing that we have made a difference to our society can be a great source of self-satisfaction. Mother Teresa is a good example of a person who has learned the importance of creating something that transcends ourselves.

Main Points

1. There is growing evidence that humans can self-regulate their motivation.
2. Self-regulation involves self-observation, self-evaluation, and self-reaction.
3. Goals arouse effort, give rise to persistence, provide direction, and motivate strategy development.
4. There are two basic classes of goals: distal goals and proximal goals.
5. The goals that we set for ourselves should be difficult but attainable.

6. Feedback is critical if we are to achieve our goals.

7. Assigned goals are effective provided we commit to them.

8. It has been suggested that goals create a discrepancy, which, in turn, creates a tension state. It is that tension state that gives rise to action.

9. Within Bandura's theory, the key to self-motivation is setting difficult but attainable goals.

10. Within his theory, outcome expectations are defined as "a person's estimate that a given behavior will lead to certain outcomes."

11. In the same theory, self-efficacy is defined as "the conviction that one can successfully execute the behavior required to produce the outcomes."

12. Feelings of self-efficacy come from past performance.

13. It is important not only to make plans but to learn how to adjust behavior so that it is congruent with the plans.

14. It is also important to learn to change our plan when it does not work.

15. Many people use mental rehearsal to create a plan in their minds.

16. It is sometimes advisable to make use of advisors and coaches.

17. Since mood can affect feelings of self-efficacy, we must learn how to manage our moods.

18. Learning to manage self-doubt is important, because self-doubt tends to undermine feelings of self-efficacy.

19. Self-doubt occurs when we are unable to turn off negative thoughts that intrude into our thinking.

20. Three methods have been suggested to deal with self-doubt: monitoring self-talk, cognitive restructuring, and substituting more positive thoughts.

21. Developing good thinking habits can help us to deal with setbacks.

22. Through self-reflection, we can learn to change our thinking habits.

23. Langer's work shows how important it is for us to become mindful of the images that often guide our behavior.

24. Dreams and visualization are a means of personalizing motivation, of making goals real, and per-

haps of accessing the sensory and emotional motivation system.

25. Interest in the self-concept grew out of the observation that success is not predicted by intelligence.

26. The self-concept can be thought of as self-knowledge. It is based on our experiences in a given domain and also reflects sociocultural and historical information.

27. The self-concept provides both information and context.

28. The self-regulatory self can be conceptualized as made up of three distinct components (selves): the instrumental self, the expectant self, and the monitored self.

29. It has been suggested that the self-concept is both learned and constructed.

30. The repository side of self (the "me") involves values and regulatory processes, whereas the agent side of the self (the "I") is autonomous and needs to be in control.

31. If we are to construct diverse possible selves, we need a self-concept that is highly differentiated, positive, and closely linked to perceptions of competency.

32. Possible selves are the future-oriented component of the self-concept. They grow out of self-knowledge.

33. Possible selves are linked to action through goals.

34. The three different prototypes of self-awareness and environmental awareness are: (1) that the world is hostile and threatening; (2) that the world is benevolent; and (3) that the world is benign.

35. People develop different strategies or orientations for dealing with the world.

36. People with a mastery strategy deal with the world by developing competency; feelings of efficacy reward the development of competency.

37. People with a performance strategy deal with the world by learning the rules of winning.

38. Mastery-type individuals tend to be process-oriented; performance types tend to be outcome-oriented.

References

AARONS, L. (1976). Sleep-assisted instruction. *Psychological Bulletin, 83,* 140.

ABELSON, H., COHEN, R., HEATON, E., & SUDER, C. (1971). National survey of public attitudes toward and experience with erotic materials. In *Technical Report of the Commission on Obscenity and Pornography* (Vol. 6). Washington, DC: Government Printing Office.

ABPLANALP, J. (1983). Premenstrual syndrome: A selective review. *Women and Health, 8,* 107–124.

ABRAMSON, L. Y., METALSKY, G. L., & ALLOY, L. B. (1989). Hopelessness depression: A theory-based process-oriented subtype of depression. *Psychological Review, 96,* 358–372.

ABRAMSON, L. Y., SELIGMAN, M. E. P., & TEASDALE, J. D. (1978). Learned helplessness in humans: Critique and reformulation. *Journal of Abnormal Psychology, 87,* 49–74.

ADELSON, S. P. (1968). Changes in diets of households, 1955 to 1965. *Journal of Home Economics, 60,* 448–455.

AINSWORTH, M. D. S., BLEHAR, M. C., WATER, E., & WALL, S. (1978). *Patterns of attachment: A psychological study of the strange situation.* Hillsdale, NJ: Erlbaum.

AKERSTEDT, T., TORSVALL, L., & GILLBERG, M. (1982). Sleepiness and shift work: Field studies. *Sleep, 5,* S95–S106.

AKIL, H., MADDEN, J., IV, PATRICK, R. L., & BARCHAS, J. D. (1976). Stress induced increase in endogenous opiate peptides: Concurrent analgesia and its partial reversal by naloxone. In H. W. Kosterlitz (Ed.), *Opiates and endogenous opiate peptides.* Amsterdam: Elsevier North-Holland.

ALEXANDER, B. K., PEELE, S., HADAWAY, P. F., MORSE, S. J., BRODSKY, A., & BEYERSTEIN, B. L. (1985). Adult, infant, and animal addiction. In S. Peele, *The meaning of addiction* (pp. 73–96). Lexington, MA: Lexington Books.

ALLEN, L. S., & GORSKI, F. A. (1991). Sexual dimorphism of the anterior commissure and massa intermedia of the human brain. *Journal of Comparative Neurology, 312,* 97–104.

ALLEN, L. S., RICHEY, M. F., CHAI, Y. M., & GORSKI, R. A. (1991). Sex differences in the corpus callosum of the living human being. *Journal of Neuroscience, 11,* 933–942.

ALLOY, L. B., & ABRAMSON, L. Y. (1979). Judgement of contingency in depressed and nondepressed students: Sadder but wiser. *Journal of Experimental Psychology, General, 108,* 441–485.

American Cancer Society. (1994). Cancer facts and figures—1993. New York: Author.

American Psychiatric Association. (1994). *Diagnostic and statistical manual of mental disorders* (4th ed.). Washington, DC: Author.

AMES, C. (1987). The enhancement of student motivation. In D. A. Kleiber & M. Maehr (Eds.), *Advances in motivation and achievement* (pp. 123–148). Greenwich, CT: JAI Press.

AMES, C., & ARCHER, J. (1988). Achievement goals in the classroom: Students' learning strategies and motivation processes. *Journal of Education Psychology, 80,* 260–267.

AMSEL, A. (1958). The role of frustrative nonreward in noncontinuous reward situations. *Psychological Bulletin, 55,* 102–119.

AMSEL, A. (1962). Frustrative nonreward in partial reinforcement and discrimination learning: Some recent history and a theoretical extension. *Psychological Review, 69,* 306–328.

AMSEL, A. (1972). Behavioral habituation, counterconditioning, and a general theory of persistence. In A. H. Black & W. F. Prokasy (Eds.), *Classical conditioning: Vol. II. Current research and theory.* New York: Appleton-Century-Crofts.

ANDERSEN, B. L., KIECOLT-GLASER, J. K., & GLASER, R. (1994). A biobehavioral model of cancer stress and disease course. *American Psychologist, 49,* 389–404.

ANDERSON, J. F. (1988). *The role of hope in appraisal, goal-setting, expectancy, and coping.* Unpublished doctoral dissertation. University of Kansas, Lawrence.

ANDREWS, F. M. (1975). Social and psychological factors that influence the creative process. In I. A. Taylor and J. W. Getzels (Eds.), *Perspectives in creativity* (pp. 117–145). Chicago: Aldine.

ANGELL, M. (1985). Disease as a reflection of the psyche. *New England Journal of Medicine, 312,* 1570–1572.

APFELBAUM, M. (1975). Influence of level of energy intake on energy expenditure in man: Effects of spontaneous intake, experimental starvation, and experimental overeating. In G. A. Bray et al. (Eds.), *Obesity in perspective* (DHEW Publication No. NIH 75-708, Vol. 2). Washington, DC: U.S. Government Printing Office.

APTER, M. J. (1982). *The experience of motivation: Theory of psychological reversals.* New York: Academic Press.

ARKES, H. R., & BOYKIN, A. W. (1971). Analysis of complexity preference in Head Start and nursery school children. *Perceptual and Motor Skills, 33,* 1131–1137.

ARKIN, A. M., ANTROBUS, J. S., ELLMAN, S. J., & FARBER, J. (1978). Sleep mentation as affected by REMP deprivation. In A. M. Arkin, J. S. Antrobus, & S. J. Ellman (Eds.), *The mind in sleep: Psychology and psychophysiology.* Hillsdale, NJ: Erlbaum.

ARMITAGE, A. K., HALL, G. H., & SELLERS, C. M. (1969). Effects of nicotine on electrocortical activity and acetylcholine release from the cat cerebral cortex. *British Journal of Pharmacology, 35,* 152–160.

AROM, A., PARIS, M., & AROM, E. N. (1995). Falling in love: Prospective studies of self-concept change. *Journal of Personality and Social Psychology, 69,* 1102–1112.

ARONSON, E., & MILLS, J. (1959). The effect of severity of initiation on liking for a group. *Journal of Abnormal and Social Psychology, 59,* 181–188.

ASCHOFF, J. (Ed.). (1965). *Circadian clocks.* Amsterdam: North-Holland.

ASERINSKY, E., & KLEITMAN, N. (1953). Regularly occurring periods of eye mobility and concomitant phenomena during sleep. *Science, 118,* 273–274.

ATKINSON, J. W. (1953). The achievement motive and recall of interrupted and completed tasks. *Journal of Experimental Psychology, 46,* 381–390.

ATKINSON, J. W. (1957). Motivational determinants of risk-taking behavior. *Psychological Review, 64,* 359–372.

ATKINSON, J. W., & BIRCH, D. (1978). *An introduction to motivation* (rev. ed.). New York: Van Nostrand.

AVERILL, J. R. (1973). Personal control over aversive stimuli and its relationship to stress. *Psychological Bulletin, 80,* 286–303.

AVERILL, J. R., & BOOTHROYD, P. (1977). On falling in love in conformance with the romantic ideal. *Motivation and Emotion, 1,* 235–247.

AVERILL, J. R. (1983). Studies on anger and aggression: Implications for theorists of emotion. *American Psychologist, 38,* 1145–1160.

AX, A. F. (1953). The physiological differentiation between fear and anger in humans. *Psychosomatic Medicine, 15,* 433–442.

BAEKELAND, F. (1970). Exercise deprivation: Sleep and psychological reactions. *Archives of General Psychiatry, 22,* 365–369.

BAEKELAND, F., & LASKY, R. (1966). Exercise and sleep patterns in college athletes. *Perceptual and Motor Skills, 23,* 1203–1207.

BAILEY, J. M. (1995). Sexual orientation revolution. *Nature Genetics, 11,* 353–354.

BAILEY, J. M., GAULIN, S., AGYEI, Y., & GLADUE, B. A. (1994). Effects of gender and sexual orientation evolutionary relevant aspects of human mating psychology. *Journal of Personality and Social Psychology, 66,* 1081–1093.

BAILEY, J. M., & PILLARD, R. C. (1991). A genetic study of male homosexual orientation. *Archives of General Psychiatry, 48,* 1089–1097.

BAILEY, J. M., PILLARD, R. C., NEALE, M. C. I., & AGYEI, Y. (1993). Heritable factors influence sexual orientation in women. *Archives of General Psychiatry, 50,* 217–223.

BALES, R. F. (1946). Cultural differences in the rate of alcoholism. *Quarterly Journal of Studies on Alcohol, 6,* 380–499.

BANAJI, M. R., & STEELE, C. M. (1989). The social cognition of alcohol use. *Social Cognition, 7,* 137–151.

BANCROFT, J. (1987). A physiological approach. In J. H. Geer & W. T. O'Donohue (Eds.), *Theories of human sexuality* (pp. 411–421). New York: Plenum.

BANDURA, A. (1973). *Aggression: A social learning analysis.* Englewood Cliffs, NJ: Prentice-Hall.

BANDURA, A. (1982). The self and mechanisms of agency. In J. Suls (Ed.), *Psychological Perspectives on the Self* (Vol. 1, pp. 3–39), Hillsdale, NJ: Erlbaum.

BANDURA, A. (1986). *Social foundations of thought and action: A social cognitive theory.* Englewood Cliffs, NJ: Prentice-Hall.

BANDURA, A. (1988). Self-efficacy conceptions of anxiety. *Anxiety Research, 1,* 77–98.

BANDURA, A. (1989). Human agency in social cognitive theory. *American Psychologist, 44,* 1175–1184.

BANDURA, A. (1991a). Self-regulation of motivation through anticipatory and self reactive mechanisms. In R. A. Dienstbier (Ed.), *Perspectives on Motivation.* Nebraska Symposium on Motivation (pp. 69–164). Lincoln: University of Nebraska Press.

BANDURA, A. (1991b). Social cognitive theory of self-regulation. *Organizational Behavior and Human Decision Processes, 50,* 248–287.

BANDURA, A., & CERVONE, D. (1983). Self-efficacy mechanisms governing the motivational effects of goal systems. *Journal of Personality and Social Psychology, 45,* 1017–1028.

BANDURA, A., CIOFFI, D., TAYLOR, C. B., & BROUILLARD, M. E. (1988). Perceived self-efficacy in coping with cognitive stressors and opioid addiction. *Journal of Personality and Social Psychology, 55,* 479–488.

BANDURA, A., & JOURDEN, F. J. (1991). Self-regulatory mechanisms governing the impact of social comparison on complex decision making. *Journal of Personality and Social Psychology, 60,* 941–951.

BANDURA, A., & MISCHEL, W. (1965). Modification of self-imposed delay of reward through exposure to live and symbolic models. *Journal of Personality and Social Psychology, 2,* 698–705.

BANDURA, A., & SCHUNK, D. H. (1981). Cultivating competence, self-efficacy and intrinsic interest through proximal self-motivation. *Journal of Personality and Social Psychology, 41,* 586–598.

BANDURA, A., TAYLOR, C. B., WILLIAMS, S. L., MEFFORD, I. N., & BARCHAS, J. D. (1985). Catecholamine secretion as a function of perceived coping self-efficacy. *Journal of Consulting and Clinical Psychology, 53,* 406, 414.

BANJI, M. R., & STEELE, C. M. (1989). The social cognition of alcohol use. *Social Cognition, 7,* 137–151.

BARCHAS, P. (1986). A sociophysiological orientation to small groups. In E. Lawler, (Ed.), *Advances in group processes* (Vol. 3, pp. 209–246). Greenwich, CT: JAI Press.

BARGH, J. A., & GOLLWITZER, P. M. (1994). Environmental control of goal-directed actions: Automatic and strategic contingenices between situation and behavior. In W. D. Spaulding (Ed.). *Integrative views of motivation, cognition and emotion: Nebraska Symposium on Motivation* (Vol. 41, pp. 71–124). Lincoln: University of Nebraska Press.

BARLOW, D. H. (1988). *Anxiety and its disorders: The nature and treatment of anxiety and panic.* New York: Guilford Press.

BARLOW, D. H., CHORPITA, B. F., & TUROVSKY, J. (1996). Fear, panic, anxiety and disorders of emotion. In R. A. Dienstbier (Ed.). *Perspectives on anxiety, panic, and fear. Nebraska Symposium on Motivation* (Vol. 43, pp. 251–328). Lincoln: University of Nebraska Press.

BARNES, G. (1979). The alcoholic personality: A reanalysis of the literature. *Journal of Studies on Alcohol, 40,* 571–634.

BARNES, G. E., MALAMUTH, N. M., & CHECK, J. V. P. (1984). Personality and sexuality. *Personality and Individual Differences, 5,* 159–172.

BARON, J. (1992). The effect of normative beliefs on anticipated emotions. *Journal of Personality and Social Psychology, 63,* 320–330.

BARON, R. A. (1973). Threatened retaliation from the victim as an inhibitor of physical aggression. *Journal of Research in Personality, 7,* 103–115.

BARON, R. A. (1977). *Human aggression.* New York: Plenum.

BARR, T. (1969). *Psychopharmacology.* Baltimore: Williams & Wilkins.

BARRON, F., & HARRINGTON, D. M. (1981). Creativity, intelligence, and personality. In M. R. Rosenzweig & L. W. Porter (Eds.), *Annual review of psychology* (pp. 439–476). Palo Alto, CA: Annual Reviews.

BARRY, H., III, WAGNER, A. R., & MILLER, N. E. (1962). Effects of alcohol and amobarbital on performance inhibited by experimental extinction. *Journal of Comparative and Physiological Psychology, 55,* 464–468.

BARSALOU, L. W. (1993). Ad hoc categories. *Memory and Cognition, 11,* 211–227.

Basic Behavioral Science Task Force of the National Advisory Mental Health Council, Rockville, MD (1996). Basic behavioral science research for mental health: Perception, attention, learning, and memory. *American Psychologist, 51,* 133–142.

BASOW, S. A. (1992). *Stereotypes and Roles (3rd ed.).* Pacific Grove, CA: Brooks/Cole.

BAUMEISTER, R. F., & LEARY, M. R. (1995). The need to belong: Desire for interpersonal attachments as a fundamental human motivation. *Psychological Bulletin, 117,* 497–529.

BAUMGARDNER, A. H. (1990). To know oneself is to like oneself: Self-certainty and self-affect. *Journal of Personality and Social Psychology, 58,* 1062–1072.

BEACH, F. A. (1976). Hormonal control of sex-related behavior. In F. A. Beach (Ed.), *Human sexuality in four perspectives* (pp. 247–267). Baltimore: Johns Hopkins University Press.

BEARY, J. F., BENSON, H., & KLEMCHUK, H. P. (1974). A simple psychophysiologic technique which elicits the hypometabolic changes in the relaxation response. *Psychosomatic Medicine, 36,* 115–120.

BECK, A. T. (1967). *Depression: Clinical, experimental, and theoretical aspects.* New York: Harper & Row.

BECK, A. T. (1976). *Cognitive theory and emotional disorders.* New York: International Universities Press.

BECK, A. T. (1983). Cognitive therapy of depression: New approaches. In P. Clayton & J. Barrett (Eds.), *Treatment of depression: Old and new approaches* (pp. 265–290). New York: Raven Press.

BECK, A. T. (1985). Theoretical perspectives on clinical anxiety. In A. H. Tuma & J. D. Maser (Eds.), *Anxiety and anxiety disorders.* Hillsdale, NJ: Erlbaum.

BECK, A. T. (1991). Cognitive therapy: A 30-year retrospective. *American Psychologist, 46,* 368–375.

BECK, A. T., WEISSMAN, A., & KOVACS, M. (1976). Alcoholism, hopelessness, and suicidal behavior. *Journal of Studies on Alcohol, 37,* 66–77.

BECK, A. T., & YOUNG, J. E. (1978, April). College blues. *Psychology Today,* pp. 80–92.

BECKER, M. (Ed.). (1974). *The health belief model and personal health behavior.* Thorofare, NJ: Charles B. Slack.

BELL, A., WEINBERG, M. S., & HAMMERSMITH, S. K. (1981). *Sexual preference: Its development in men and women.* Bloomington: Indiana University Press.

BELL, P. A. & BYRNE, D. (1978). Repression-sensitization. In H. London & J. E. Exner, Jr. (Eds.), *Dimensions of personality.* New York: Wiley.

BELLAH, R. N., MADSEN, R., SULLIVAN, W. M., SWIDLER, A., & TIPTON, S. M. (1985). *Habits of the Heart.* New York: Harper & Row.

BEM, D. J. (1967). Self-perception: An alternative interpretation of cognitive dissonance phenomenon. *Psychological Review, 74,* 183–200.

BENBOW, C. P., & STANLEY, J. C. (1983). Sex differences in mathematical reasoning ability: More facts. *Science, 222,* 1029–1031.

BENBOW, C. P., & STANLEY, J. C. (1980). Sex differences in mathematical ability: Fact or artifact? *Science, 210,* 1029–1031.

BENET, V., & WALLER, N. G. (1995). The big seven factor model of personality description: Evidence for its cross-cultural generality in a Spanish sample. *Journal of Personality and Social Psychology, 69,* 701–718.

BENSON, H. (1975). *The Relaxation Response.* New York: Avon Books.

BENSON, H. (1987). *Your Maximum Mind*. New York: Avon Books.

BENSON, H., & WALLACE, R. K. (1972). Decreased blood pressure in hypertensive subjects who practiced meditation. *Circulation,* Suppl. 2, 516.

BERENBAUM, S. A., & HINES, M. (1992). Early androgens are related to childhood sex-typed toy preferences. *Psychological Sciences, 3,* 203–206.

BERKOWITZ, L. (1962). *Aggression: A social psychological analysis.* New York: McGraw-Hill.

BERKOWITZ, L. (1969). The frustration-aggression hypothesis revised. In L. Berkowitz (Ed.), *Roots of aggression* (pp. 29–34). New York: Atherton Press.

BERKOWITZ, L. (1989). Frustration-aggression hypothesis: Examination and reformulation. *Psychological Bulletin, 106,* 59–73.

BERKOWITZ, L. (1990). On the formation and regulation of anger and aggression: A cognitive-neoassociationistic analysis. *American Psychologist, 45,* 494–503.

BERKOWITZ, L. (1993). *Aggression: Its causes, consequences, and control.* New York: McGraw-Hill.

BERKOWITZ, L. (1994). Guns and youth. In L. Eron, J. H. Gentry, & P. Schlegel (Eds.), *Reason to hope: A psychosocial perspective on violence and youth* (pp. 251–279). Washington, DC: American Psychological Association.

BERKOWITZ, L., & GEEN, R. G. (1966). Film violence and the cue properties of available targets. *Journal of Personality and Social Psychology, 3,* 525–530.

BERLYNE, D. E. (1958). The influence of complexity and novelty in visual figures on orienting responses. *Journal of Experimental Psychology, 55,* 289–296.

BERLYNE, D. E. (1960). *Conflict, arousal, and curiosity.* New York: McGraw-Hill.

BERLYNE, D. E. (1969). The reward value of indifferent stimulation. In J. T. Tapp (Ed.), *Reinforcement and behavior.* New York: Academic Press.

BERLYNE, D. E. (1971). *Aesthetics and psychobiology.* New York: Appleton-Century-Crofts.

BERLYNE, D. E., KOENIG, I. D. V., & HIROTA, T. (1966). Novelty, arousal, and the reinforcement of diversive exploration in the rat. *Journal of Comparative and Physiological Psychology, 62,* 772–796.

BERREBI, A. S., FITCH, R. H., RALPHE, D. L., DENENBERG, J. O., FRIEDRICH, V. L., JR., & DENENBERG, V. H. (1988). Corpus-callosum: Region-specific effects of sex, early experience and age. *Brain Research, 438,* 216–224.

BETTELHEIM, B. (1950). *Love is not enough: The treatment of emotionally disturbed children.* Glencoe, IL: Free Press.

BEXTON, W. H., HERON, W., & SCOTT, T. H. (1954). Effects of decreased variation in the sensory environment. *Canadian Journal of Psychology, 8,* 70–76.

BIEBER, I., DAIN, H. J., DINCE, P. R., DRELLICH, M. G., GRAND, H. G., GUNLACH, R. H., KREMERS, M. V., WILBUR, C. B., & BIEBER, T. B. (1962). *Homosexuality: A psychoanalytic study.* New York: Vintage.

BINDRA, D. A. (1974). Motivational view of learning, performance, and behavior modification. *Psychological Review, 81,* 199–213.

BIRNEY, R. C., BURDICK, H., & TEEVAN, R. C. (1969). *Fear of failure.* New York: Van Nostrand.

BIXLER, E. O., KALES, A., SOLDATOS, C. R., VELA-BUENO, A., JACOBY, J. A., & SCARONE, S. (1982). Sleep apnea in a normal population. *Research Communications in Chemical Pathology and Pharmacology, 36,* 141–152.

BLATT, S. J. (1995). The destructiveness of perfectionism: Implications for the treatment of depression. *American Psychologist, 50,* 1003–1020.

BLOCK, J. (1995). On the relation between IQ, impulsivity and delinquency. *Journal of Abnormal Psychology, 104.*

BLOOM, G., VON EULER, U. S., & FRANKENHAEUSER, M. (1963). Catecholamine excretion and personality traits in paratroop trainees. *Acta Physiologica Scandinavica, 58,* 77–89.

BLOOMFIELD, H. H., CAIN, M. P., JAFFE, D. T., & KORY, R. B. (1975). *TM: Discovering inner energy and overcoming stress.* New York: Dell.

BLUM, K., HAMILTON, M. L., & WALLACE, J. E. (1977). Alcohol and opiates: A review of common neurochemical and behavioral mechanisms. In K. Blum (Ed.), *Alcohol and opiates: Neurochemical and behavioral mechanisms.* New York: Academic Press.

BOLGER, N. (1990). Coping as a personality process: A prospective study. *Journal of Personality and Social Psychology, 59,* 525–537.

BOLGER, N., & ECKENROLE, J. (1991). Social relationships, personality, and anxiety during a major stressful event. *Journal of Personality and Social Psychology, 61,* 440–449.

BOLLES, R. C. (1970). Species-specific defense reactions and avoidance learning. *Psychological Review, 77,* 32–48.

BOLLES, R. C., & FANSELOW, M. S. (1982). Endorphins and behavior. *Annual Review of Psychology, 33,* 87–101.

BONANNO, G. A., & SINGER, J. L. (1990). Repressive personality style: Theoretical and methodological implications for health and pathology. In J. L. Singer (Ed.), *Repression and dissociation* (pp. 435–470). Chicago: University of Chicago Press.

BONNET, M. H. (1985). Effect of sleep disruption on sleep, performance, and mood. *Sleep, 8,* 11–19.

BONNET, M. H., & ROSA, R. R. (1987). Sleep and performance in young adults and older normals and insomniacs during sleep loss and recovery. *Biological Psychology, 25,* 153–172.

BONVALLET, M., & ALLEN, M. B., JR. (1963). Prolonged spontaneous and evoked reticular activation following discrete bulbar lesions. *Electroencephalography and Clinical Neurophysiology, 15,* 969–988.

BORDEN, R. J., BOWEN, R., & TAYLOR, S. P. (1971). Shock-setting behavior as a function of physical attack and extrinsic reward. *Perceptual and Motor Skills, 33,* 563–568.

BORING, E. G. (1950). *A history of experimental psychology* (2nd ed.). New York: Appleton-Century-Crofts.

BOWLBY, J. (1969). *Attachment and Loss: Vol. 1. Attachment.* New York: Basic Books.

BOWLBY, J. (1973). *Attachment and Loss: Vol. 2. Separation: Anxiety and Anger.* New York: Basic Books.

BOWLBY, J. (1979). *The making and breaking of affectional bonds.* London: Tavistock.

BOWLBY, J. (1980). *Attachment and Loss: Vol. 3. Loss: Sadness and Depression.* New York: Basic Books.

BRADY, J. V. (1967). Emotion and sensitivity of psychoendocrine systems. In D. C. Glass (Ed.), *Neurophysiology and emotion* (pp. 70–95). New York: Rockefeller University Press.

BRADY, J. V. (1975). Towards a behavioral biology of emotion. In L. Levi (Ed.), *Emotions: Their parameters and measurement.* New York: Raven Press.

BRAIN, P. H. (1984). Biological explanations of human aggression and the resulting therapies offered by such approaches: A critical evaluation. In R. J. Blanchard & D. C. Blanchard (Eds.), *Advances in the study of aggression* (Vol. 1, pp. 63–102). San Diego, CA: Academic Press.

BRAY, G. A. (1992). Pathophysiology of obesity. *American Journal of Clinical Nutrition, 55,* 488S–494S.

BREMER, J. (1959). *Asexualization: A follow-up study of 244 cases.* New York: Macmillan.

BRIEF, A. P., BUTCHER, A. H., GEORGE, J. M., & LINK, K. E. (1994). Integrating bottom-up and top-down theories of subjective well-being: The case of health. *Journal of Personality and Social Psychology, 64,* 646–653.

BROCKNER, J. (1979). The effects of self-esteem, success-failure, and self consciousness on task performance. *Journal of Personality and Social Psychology, 37,* 1732–1741.

BROOKS-GUNN, J., & FURSTEMBERG, F. F., JR. (1989). Adolescent sexual behavior. *American Psychologist, 44,* 249–257.

BROWN, G. M. (1983). Endocrine alterations in anorexia nervosa. In P. L. Darby, P. E. Garfinkel, D. M. Garner, & D. V. Coscina, *Anorexia nervosa: Recent developments in research* (pp. 231–247). New York: Alan R. Liss.

BROWNELL, K. D., & RODIN, J. (1994). The dieting maelstrom: Is it possible and advisable to lose weight? *American Psychologist, 49,* 781–791.

BRUNER, J. (1992). Another look at New Look 1. *American Psychologist, 47,* 780–783.

BRUNER, J. S., MATTER, J., & PAPANEK, M. L. (1955). Breadth of learning as a function of drive level and mechanization. *Psychological Review, 62,* 1–10.

BUCHSBAUM, M. S., GERNER, R., & POST, R. M. (1981). The effects of sleep deprivation on average evoked potentials in depressed patients and normals. *Biological Psychiatry, 16,* 351–363.

BURNSTEIN, E., & WORCHEL, P. (1962). Arbitrariness of frustration and its consequences for aggression in a social situation. *Journal of Personality, 30,* 528–540.

BUSHMAN, B. J. (1995). Moderating role of trait aggressiveness in the effects of violent media on aggression. *Journal of Personality and Social Psychology, 69,* 950–960.

Business Week, Special 1989 Bonus Issue (1989). *Innovation in America.*

BUSS, A. H. (1963). Physical aggression in relation to different frustrations. *Journal of Abnormal and Social Psychology, 67,* 1–7.

BUSS, A. H., & DURKEE, A. (1957). An inventory for assessing different kinds of hostility. *Journal of Consulting Psychology, 21,* 343–349.

BUSS, A. H., & PERRY, M. (1992). The aggression questionnaire. *Journal of Personality and Social Psychology, 63,* 452–459.

BUSS, D. M. (1994). *The evolution of desire.* New York: Basic Books.

BUTLER, R. A. (1953). Discrimination learning by rhesus monkeys to visual-exploration motivation. *Journal of Comparative and Physiological Psychology, 46,* 95–98.

BUUNK, B. P., DOOSJE, B. J., JANS, L. G. J. M., & HOPSTAKEN, L. E. M. (1993). Perceived reciprocity, social support, and stress at work: The role of exchange and communal orientation. *Journal of Personality and Social Psychology, 65,* 801–811.

CAHALAN, D., & ROOM, R. (1974). *Problem drinking among American men* (Monograph 7). New Brunswick, NJ: Rutgers Center of Alcohol Studies.

CAIN, E. N., KOHORN, E. I., QUINLAN, D. M., LATIMER, K., & SCHWARTZ, P. E. (1986). Psychosocial benefits of a cancer support group. *Cancer, 57,* 183–189.

Calgary (1989). Comments at a concert. June 23, 1997.

CAMPBELL, J. D. (1990). Self-esteem and clarity of the self-concept. *Journal of Personality and Social Psychology, 59,* 538–549.

CAMPION, M. A., & LORD, R. G. (1982). A control systems conceptualization of the goal-setting and changing process. *Organization Behavior and Performance, 30,* 265–287.

CARLSON, E. R., & COLEMAN, C. E. H. (1977). Experiential and motivational determinants of the richness of an induced sexual fantasy. *Journal of Personality, 45,* 528–542.

CARLSON, S., FELTEN, D. L., LIVNAT, S., & FELTEN, S. Y. (1987). Alternations of monoamines in specific autonomic nuclei following immunization in mice. *Brain, Behavior, and Immunity, 1,* 52–64.

CARROLL, J. L. (1992). The relationship between humor appreciation and perceived physical health. *Psychology, 27,* 34–37.

CARROLL, J. L., & SHMIDT, J. L., JR. (1990). Correlation between humorous coping style and health. *Psychological Reports, 70,* 402.

CARRUTHERS, M. E. (1974). *Western way of death: Stress, tension, and heart attacks.* New York: Pantheon.

CARSKADON, M. A., & DEMENT, W. C. (1977). Sleepiness and sleep state on a 90-min schedule. *Psychophysiology, 14,* 127–133.

CARSKADON, M. A., & DEMENT, W. C. (1981). Cumulative effects of sleep restriction on daytime sleepiness. *Psychophysiology, 18,* 107–113.

CARTWRIGHT, R. (1990). A network model of dreams. In R. R. Bootzin, J. F. Kihlstrom, & D. L. Schacter (Eds.), *Sleep and cognition* (pp. 179–189). Washington, DC: American Psychological Association.

CARTWRIGHT, R. D., LLOYD, S., BUTTERS, E., WEINER, L., McCARTHY, L., & HANCOCK, J. (1975). Effects of REM time on what is recalled. *Psychophysiology, 12,* 561–568.

CARTWRIGHT, R. D., MONROE, L. J., & PALMER, C. (1967). Individual differences in response to REM deprivation. *Archives of General Psychiatry, 16,* 297–303.

CARTWRIGHT, R. D., & RATZEL, R. (1972). Effects of dream loss on waking behaviors. *Archives of General Psychiatry, 27,* 277–280.

CARVER, C. S. (1979). A cybernetic model of self-attention processes. *Journal of Personality and Social Psychology, 37,* 1251–1281.

CARVER, C. S., BLANEY, P. H., & SCHEIER, M. F. (1979a). Focus of attention, chronic expectancy, and responses to a feared stimulus. *Journal of Personality and Social Psychology, 37,* 1186–1195.

CARVER, C. S., BLANEY, P. H., & SCHEIER, M. F. (1979b). Reassertion and giving up: The interactive role of self-directed attention and outcome expectancy. *Journal of Personality and Social Psychology, 37,* 1859–1870.

CARVER, C. S., & SCHEIER, M. F. (1981). *Attention and self-regulation: A control theory approach to human behavior.* Chicago: Springer.

CARVER, C. S., SCHEIER, M. F., & WEINTRAUB, J. K. (1989). Assessing coping strategies: A theoretically based approach. *Journal of Personality and Social Psychology, 56,* 267–283.

CASS, V. C. (1990). The implication of homosexual identity formation for the Kinsey model and scale of sexual preference. In D. P. McWhiter, S. A. Sanders, & J. M. Reinisch (Eds.), *Homosexuality/heterosexuality: concepts of sexual orientation* (pp. 239–266). New York: Oxford University Press.

CASTALDO, V., & KRYNICKI, V. (1973). Sleep patterns and intelligence in functional mental retardation. *Journal of Mental Deficiency Research, 17,* 231–235.

CASTALDO, V., KRYNICKI, V., & GOLDSTEIN, J. (1974). Sleep stages and verbal memory. *Perceptual and Motor Skills, 39,* 1023–1030.

CATTELL, R. B. (1946). *The description and measurement of personality.* NY: World Book.

CATTELL, R. B. (1971). *Abilities: Their structure, growth and action.* Boston, MA: Houghton Mifflin.

CAUL, W. F., BUCHANAN, D. C., & HAYS, R. C. (1972). Effects of unpredictability of shock on incidence of gastric lesions and heart rate in immobilized rats. *Physiology and Behavior, 8,* 669–672.

CAUTHEN, N. R., & PRYMAK, C. A. (1977). Meditation versus relaxation: An examination of the physiological effects of relaxation training and of different levels of experience with transcendental meditation. *Journal of Consulting and Clinical Psychology, 45,* 496–497.

CHAMBLESS, D. L., & GRACELY, E. J. (1989). Fear of fear and the anxiety disorders. *Cognitive Therapy and Research, 13,* 9–20.

CHANDRA, R. K., & NEWBERNE, P. M. (1977). *Nutrition, immunity, and infection: Mechanisms of interaction.* New York: Plenum.

CHASSLER, S. (1988, December). What teen boys think about sex. *Parade,* p. 1617.

CHRISTIANSEN, K., & KNUSSMANN, R. (1987). Sex hormones and cognitive functioning in men. *Neuropsychobiology, 18,* 27–36.

CHURCHILL, A. C., & McMURRAY, N. E. (1990). *Self-efficacy and unpleasant intrusive thought.* Manuscript submitted for publication.

CIBA Foundation Symposium. (1979). *Sex hormones and behavior.* Amsterdam: Excerpta Medica.

CLARKE, D. H. (1975). *Exercise physiology.* Englewood Cliffs, NJ: Prentice-Hall.

CLONINGER, C. R., SIGVARDSSON, S., & BOHMAN, M. (1988). Coping, expectancies, and alcohol abuse: A test of social learning formulations. *Journal of Abnormal Psychology, 97,* 218–230.

COCCARO, E. F., BERGEMAN, C. S., & McCLEARN, G. E. (1993). Heritability of irritable impulsiveness: A study of twins reared together and apart. *Psychiatry Research, 48,* 229–242.

COHEN, D. B. (1977). Neuroticism and dreaming sleep: A case for interactionism in personality research. *British Journal of Social and Clinical Psychology, 16,* 153–163.

COHEN, D. B. (1979). Dysphoric affect and REM sleep. *Journal of Abnormal Psychology, 88,* 73–77.

COHEN, L. (1982). Life change and the sensation seeking motive. *Personality and Individual Differences, 3,* 221–222.

COHEN, S., & McKAY, G. (1984). Social support, stress and the buffering hypothesis: A theoretical analysis. In A. Baum, J. E. Singer, & S. E. Taylor (Eds.), *Handbook of psychology and health* (Vol. 4, pp. 253–267). Hillsdale, NJ: Erlbaum.

COHEN, S. TYRRELL, D. A., & SMITH, A. P. (1991). Psychological stress in humans and susceptibility to the common cold. *New England Journal of Medicine, 325,* 606–612.

COHEN, S., & WILLIAMSON, G. M. (1991). Stress and infectious disease in humans. *Psychological Bulletin, 109,* 5–24.

COLDITZ, G. A. (1992). Economic costs of obesity. *American Journal of Clinical Nutrition, 55,* 503S–507S.

COLEMAN, M. (1971). Serotonin levels in whole blood of hyperactive children. *Journal of Pediatrics, 78,* 985–990.

COLEMAN, R. M. (1986). *Wide Awake at 3:00 A.M.: By choice or by chance.* New York: W. H. Freeman.

COLLAER, M. L., & HINES, M. (1995). Human behavioral sex differences: A role for gonadal hormones during early development. *Psychological Bulletin, 118,* 55–107.

COLLINS, D. L., BAUM, A., & SINGER, J. E. (1983). Coping with chronic stress at Three Mile Island: Psychological and biochemical evidence. *Health Psychology, 2,* 149–166.

CONDRY, J. C. (1977). Enemies of exploration: Self-initiated versus other-initiated learning. *Journal of Personality and Social Psychology, 35,* 459–477.

CONDRY, J. C., & CHAMBERS, J. (1978). Intrinsic motivation and the process of learning. In M. R. Lepper & D. Greene (Eds.), *The hidden costs of rewards: New perspectives on the psychology of human motivation.* (pp. 61–84). Hillsdale, NJ: Erlbaum.

COOPER, J. R., BLOOM, F. E., & ROTH, B. H. (1982). *The biochemical basis of neuropharmacology* (4th ed.). New York: Oxford University Press.

COOPER, M. L., FRONE, M. R., RUSSELL, M., & MUDAR, P. (1995). Drinking to regulate positive and negative emotions: A motivational model of alcohol use. *Journal of Personality and Social Psychology, 69,* 990–1005.

COOPERSMITH, S. (1967). *The antecedents of self-esteem.* San Francisco: W. H. Freeman.

COSTELLO, C. G. (1976). *Anxiety and depression: The adaptive emotions.* Montreal: McGill-Queens University Press.

COSTRA, P. T., JR., & McCRAE, R. R. (1992). Four ways five factors are basic. *Personality and Individual Differences, 13,* 653–665.

COX, W. M., & KLINGER, E. (1988). A motivational model of alcohol use. *Journal of Abnormal Psychology, 97,* 168–180.

COYNE, J. C., & LAZARUS, R. S. (1980). Cognitive style, stress perception, and coping. In I. L. Kutash & L. B. Schlesinger (Eds.), *Handbook on stress and anxiety: Contemporary knowledge, theory, and treatment* (pp. 144–158). San Francisco: Jossey-Bass.

CRANDALL, C. S. (1994). Prejudice against fat people: Ideology and self-interest. *Journal of Personality and Social Psychology, 66,* 882–894.

CRATTY, B. J. (1989). *Psychology in contemporary sport.* Englewood Cliffs, NJ: Prentice Hall.

CRICK, C., & MITCHISON, G. (1983). The function of dream sleep. *Nature, 304,* 111–114.

CRICK, C., & MITCHISON, G. (1986). REM sleep and neural nets. *The Journal of Mind and Behavior, 7,* 229–250.

CRICK, F., & KOCH, C. (1992, September). The problem of consciousness. *Scientific American,* pp. 153–159.

CROYLE, R., & COOPER, J. (1983). Dissonance arousal: Physiological evidence. *Journal of Personality and Social Psychology, 45,* 782–791.

CSIKSZENTMIHALYI, M. (1990). *Flow: The psychology of optimal experience.* New York: Harper & Row.

CULBERSTON, F. M. (1997). Depression and gender. *American Psychologist, 52,* 25–31.

CUTHBERT, B., KRISTELLER, J., SIMONS, R., HODES, R., & LANG, P. J. (1981). Strategies of arousal control: Biofeedback, meditation, and motivation. *Journal of Experimental Psychology: General, 110,* 518–546.

CZAYA, J., KRAMER, M., & ROTH, T. (1973). *Changes in dream quality as a function of time into REM.* Paper presented at the meeting of the Association for the Psychophysiological Study of Sleep, San Diego, CA.

DALTON, K. (1960). Schoolgirls' misbehaviour and menstruation. *British Medical Journal, 2,* 1647–1649.

DALTON, K. (1961). Menstruation and crime. *British Medical Journal, 3,* 1752–1753.

DALTON, K. (1964). *The premenstrual syndrome.* Springfield, IL: Charles C Thomas.

DALTON, K. (1977). *The premenstrual syndrome and progesterone therapy.* London: Heinman.

DANK, B. (1971). Coming out in the gay world. *Psychiatry, 34,* 180–197.

DARWIN, C. (1859). *The origin of species by means of natural selection: Or, the preservation of favored species in the struggle for life.* New York: Collier.

DARWIN, C. (1872). *The expression of the emotions in man and animals.* Chicago: University of Chicago Press, 1965.

DAVIS, B. (1973). *Norepinephrine and epinephrine secretions following rest and exercise in trained and untrained males.* Unpublished doctoral dissertation. University of Illinois at Urbana-Champaign.

DAVIS, C. M. (1928). Self selection of diet by newly weaned infants. *American Journal of Diseases of Children, 36,* 651–679.

DAVIS, D. H., GOODWIN, D. W., & ROBINS, L. N. (1975). Drinking amid abundant illicit drugs. *Archives of General Psychiatry, 32,* 230–233.

DAVIS, V. E., & WALSH, M. J. (1970). Alcohol, amines, and alkaloids: A possible biochemical basis for alcohol addiction. *Science, 167,* 1005–1007.

D'EMILIO, J., & FREEDMAN, E. B. (1988). *Intimate matters: A history of sexuality in America.* New York: Harper & Row.

DENGERINK, H. A., & MYERS, J. D. (1977). The effects of failure and depression on subsequent aggression. *Journal of Personality and Social Psychology, 35,* 88–96.

DE RIVERA, T. (1982). *A structural theory of emotions.* New York: International University Press.

DE TOCQUEVILLE, A. (1969). *Democracy in America* (G. Lawrence, Trans.; J. P. Mayer, Ed.). New York: Doubleday, Anchor Books. (Original work published 1835)

DE WIED, D. (1966). Inhibitory effects of ACTH and related peptides on extinction of conditioned avoidance behavior in rats. *Proceedings of the Society for Experimental Biology and Medicine, 122,* 28–32.

DE WIED, D. (1967). Opposite effects of ACTH and glucocorticoids on extinction of conditioned emotional behavior. In L. Martini, F. Fraschini, & M. Motta (Eds.), *Proceedings of the second international congress on hormonal steroids* (pp. 945–951). Amsterdam: Excerpta Medica.

DE WIED, D. (1980). Pituitary-adrenal system hormones and behavior. In H. Selye (Ed.), *Selye's guide to stress research* (Vol. 1) (pp. 252–279). New York: Van Nostrand Reinhold.

DeBONO, E. (1970). *Lateral thinking.* London: Penguin Books.

DeBONO, E. (1987). *Six thinking hats.* New York: Penguin Books.

DECI, E. L. (1972). Effects of externally mediated rewards on intrinsic motivation. *Journal of Personality and Social Psychology, 22,* 113–120.

DECI, E. L. (1975). *Intrinsic motivation.* New York: Plenum.

DECI, E. L., & RYAN, R. M. (1985). *Intrinsic motivation and self-determination in human behavior.* New York: Plenum.

DECI, E. L., & RYAN, R. M. (1991). A motivational approach to self: Integration in personality. In R. A. Dienstbier (Ed.), *Perspectives on motivation* (pp. 237–288). *Nebraska Symposium on Motivation.* Lincoln: University of Nebraska Press.

DEMBER, W. N. (1956). Response by the rat to environmental change. *Journal of Comparative and Physiological Psychology, 49,* 93–95.

DEMBER, W. N., & EARL, R. W. (1957). Analysis of exploratory, manipulatory, and curiosity behaviors. *Psychological Review, 64,* 91–96.

DEMBROSKI, T. M., & COSTA, P. T. (1987). Coronary prone behavior: Components of the Type A pattern and hostility. *Journal of Personality, 55,* 212–235.

DEMENT, W. C. (1960). The effect of dream deprivation. *Science, 131,* 1705–1707.

DEMENT, W. C. (1969). The biological role of REM sleep (circa 1968). In A. Kales (Ed.), *Sleep: Physiology and pathology.* Philadelphia: Lippincott.

DEMENT, W. C. (1972). *Some must watch while some must sleep.* San Francisco: W. H. Freeman.

DEMENT, W. C., & CARSKADON, M. A. (1982). Current perspectives on daytime sleepiness. *Sleep, 5,* S56–S66.

DEMENT, W. C., & VILLABLANCA, J. (1974). Clinical disorders in man and animal model experiments. In O. Petre-Ouadens & J. Schlag (Eds.), *Basic sleep mechanisms.* New York: Academic Press.

DENENBERG, V. H. (1967). Stimulation in infancy, emotional reactivity, and exploratory behavior. In D. C. Glass (Ed.), *Neurophysiology and emotion.* New York: Rockefeller University Press & Russell Sage Foundation.

DENGERINK, H. A., & BERTILSON, H. S. (1974). The reduction of attack instigated aggression. *Journal of Research in Personality, 8,* 254–262.

DENGERINK, H. A., & LEVENDUSKY, P. G. (1972). Effects of massive retaliation and balance of power on aggression. *Journal of Experimental Research in Personality, 6,* 230–236.

DENGERINK, H. A., & MYERS, J. D. (1977). The effects of failure and depression on subsequent aggression. *Journal of personality and Social Psychology, 35,* 88–96.

DEY, F. (1970). Auditory fatigue and predicted permanent hearing defects from rock-and-roll music. *New England Journal of Medicine, 282,* 467–469.

DIAMOND, M. C. (1988). The interaction between sex hormones and environment. In M. C. Diamond (Ed.), *Enriching heredity* (pp. 115–177). New York: Free Press.

DIAMOND, M. C., DOWLING, G. A., & JOHNSON, R. E. (1981). Morphologic cerebral cortical asymmetry in male and female rats. *Experimental Neurology, 71,* 261–268.

DILALLA, L. F., & GOTTESMAN, I. I. (1991). Biological and genetic contributions to violence: Widom's untold tale. *Psychological Bulletin, 109,* 125–129.

DINGES, D. F. (1989). The nature of sleepiness: Cause, contexts, and consequences. In A. J. Stunkard & A. Baum (Eds.), *Perspectives in behavioral medicine: Eating, sleeping, and sex* (pp. 147–179). Hillsdale, NJ: Erlbaum.

DINGES, D. F., & KRIBBS, N. B. (1991). Performing while sleepy: Effects of experimentally induced sleepiness. In T. M. Monk (Ed.), *Sleep, sleepiness and performance* (pp. 97–127). New York: Wiley.

DODGE, K. A. (1993). Social cognitive mechanisms in the development of conduct disorder and depression. *Annual Review of Psychology, 44,* 559-584.

DOHLER, K.-D., COQUELIN, A., DAVIS, F., HINES, M., SHRYNE, J. E., & GRRSKI, R. A. (1984). Pre- and postnatal influence of testosterone propionate and diethylstilbestrol on differentiation of the sexually dimorphic nucleus of the preoptic area in male and female rats. *Brain Research, 302,* 291–295.

DOLE, V. P. (1980). Addictive behavior. *Scientific American, 240*(6), 138–150.

DOMINICK, J. R., & GREENBERG, B. S. (1971). Attitudes toward violence: The interaction of television exposure, family attitudes, and social class. In G. A. Comstock & E. A. Rubinstein (Eds.), *Television and social behavior: Vol. 3. Television and adolescent aggressiveness* (pp. 314–335). Washington, DC: Government Printing Office.

DONNERSTEIN, E. L., & LINZ, D. G. (1986). The question of pornography. *Psychology Today, 20,* 56–59.

DOOB, A. N., & CLIMIE, R. J. (1972). Delay of measurement and the effects of film violence. *Journal of Experimental Social Psychology, 8,* 136–142.

DOWLING, C. (1989). *Perfect women: Daughters who love their mothers but don't love themselves.* Pocket Books.

DUBBERT, P. M. (1992). Exercise in behavioral medicine. *Journal of Consulting and Clinical Psychology, 60,* 613–618.

DURDEN-SMITH, J., & DE SIMONE, D. (1983). *Sex and the brain.* New York: Warner.

DWECK, C. S. (1986). Motivational processes affecting learning. *American Psychologist, 41,* 1040–1048.

DWECK, C. S. (1991). Self-theories and goals: Their role in motivation, personality, and development. In R. A. Dienstbier (Ed.), *Perspectives on Motivation.* Nebraska Symposium on Motivation (pp. 199–235). Lincoln: University of Nebraska Press.

DWECK, C. S., & LEGGETT, E. L. (1988). A social-cognitive approach to motivation and personality. *Psychological Review, 95,* 256–273.

DWECK, C. S., & LICHT, B. (1990). Learned helplessness and intellectual achievement. In J. Garber and M. Seligman (Eds.). *Learned helplessness: Theory and application* (pp. 197–222).

DYKSTRA, L. (1992). Drug Action. In J. Grabowski and G. R. Vanden Bos (Eds.), *Psychopharmacology: Basic mechanisms and applied interventions* (pp. 59–66). Washington, DC: American Psychological Association.

EAGLY, A. H. (1995). The science and politics of comparing women and men. *American Psychologist, 50,* 145–158.

EAGLY, A. H., & STEFFEN, V. J. (1986). Gender and aggressive behavior: A metaanalytic review of the social psychological literature. *Psychological Bulletin, 100*, 309–330.

EARL, R. W. (1957). *Problem solving and motor skill behaviors under conditions of free choice.* Unpublished doctoral dissertation, University of Michigan, Ann Arbor.

EARL, R. W., FRANKEN, R. E., & MAY, R. B. (1967). Choice as a function of stimulus change. *Perceptual and Motor Skills, 24*, 183–189.

EASTERBROOK, J. A. (1959). The effect of emotion on cue utilization and the organization of behavior. *Psychological Review, 66*, 183–201.

EDEN, A. (1975). *Growing up thin.* New York: David McKay.

EDWARDS, W. (1961). Behavioral decision theory. In P. R. Farnsworth (Ed.), Annual review of psychology (Vol. 12, pp. 473–498). Palo Alto, CA: Annual Reviews.

EHRHARDT, A. A., & MEYER-BAHLBURG, H. F. L. (1981). Effects of prenatal sex hormones on gender-related behavior. *Science, 211*, 1312–1318.

EHRHARDT, A. A., MEYER-BAHLBURG, H. F. L., ROSEN, L. R., FELDMAN, J. F., VERIDIANO, N. P., ZIMMERMAN, L., & McEWEN, B. S. (1985). Sexual orientation after prenatal exposure to exogenous estrogen. *Archives of Sexual Behavior, 14*, 57–77.

EISENBERGER, R., & CAMERON, J. (1996). Detrimental effects of reward: Reality or myth? *American Psychologist, 51*, 1153–1166.

EISENBERGER, R., & SELBST, M. (1994). Does reward increase or decrease creativity? *Journal of Personality and Social Psychology, 66*, 1116–1127.

EKMAN, P. (1994). Strong evidence for universals in facial expression: A reply to Russell's mistaken critique. *Psychological Bulletin, 115*, 268–287.

EKMAN, P., LEVENSON, R. W., & FRIESEN, W. V. (1983). Autonomic nervous system activity distinguishes among emotions. *Science, 221*, 1208–1210.

ELISE, A., & GRIEGER, R. (1977). *Handbook of rational emotive therapy.* New York: Springer.

ELKIN, R., & LEIPPE, M. (1986). Physiological arousal, dissonance, and attitude change: Evidence for a dissonance arousal link and a "don't remind me" effect. *Journal of Personality and Social Psychology, 51*, 55–65.

ELLIOT, A. J., & DEVINE, P. G. (1994). On the motivational nature of cognitive dissonance: Dissonance as psychological discomfort. *Journal of Personality and Social Psychology, 67*, 382–394.

ELLMAN, S. J., SPIELMAN, A. J., LUCK, D., STEINER, S. S., & HALPERIN, R. (1991). REM deprivation: A review. In S. J. Ellman & J. S. Antrobus (Eds.), *The mind in sleep: Psychology and psychophysiology* (2nd ed., pp. 329–376). New York: Wiley.

ELLMAN, S. J., & WEINSTEIN, L. N. (1991). REM sleep and dream formation: A theoretical integration. In S. J. Ellman & J. S. Antrobus (Eds.), *The mind in sleep: Psychology and psychophysiology* (2nd ed., pp. 466–488). New York: Wiley.

ELLMAN, S. J., & STEINER, S. S. (1969a). *The effect of electrical self-stimulation on REM rebound.* Paper presented at the meeting of the Association for the Psychophysiological Study of Sleep, Boston.

ELLMAN, S. J., & STEINER, S. S. (1969b). *The effect of REM deprivation on intracranial self-stimulation.* Paper presented at the meeting of the Association for the Psychophysiological Study of Sleep, Boston.

EMMONS, R. A. (1992). The repressive personality social support. In H. S. Friedman (Ed.), *Hostility, coping and health* (pp. 141–150). Washington, DC: American Psychological Association.

EMRICK, C. D., & HANSEN, J. (1983). Assertions regarding effectiveness of treatment of alcoholism: Fact or fantasy. *American Psychologist, 38*, 1078–1088.

ENGLE, K. B., & WILLIAMS, T. K. (1972). Effect of an ounce of vodka on alcoholics' desire for alcohol. *Quarterly Journal of Studies on Alcohol, 33*, 1099–1105.

EPSTEIN, S. (1972). The nature of anxiety with emphasis upon its relationship to expectancy. In C. D. Spielberger (Ed.), *Anxiety: Current trends in theory and research* (Vol. 2, pp. 292–334). New York: Academic Press.

EPSTEIN, S. (1990). Cognitive-experiential self-theory. In L. A. Pervin (Ed.), *Handbook of personality: Theory and research* (pp. 165–191). New York: Guilford Press.

EPSTEIN, S. (1991). Cognitive-experiential self-theory: An integrative theory of personality. In R. Curtis (Ed.), *The relational self convergences in psychoanalysis and social psychology* (pp. 111–137). New York: Guilford Press.

EPSTEIN, S. (1992). Coping ability, negative self-evaluation, and overgeneralization: Experiment and theory. *Journal of Personality and Social Psychology, 62*, 826–836.

EPSTEIN, S., LIPSON, A., HOLSTEIN, C., & HUH, E. (1992). Irrational reactions to negative outcomes: Evidence for two conceptual systems. *Journal of Personality and Social Psychology, 62*, 328–339.

EPSTEIN, S., & MEIER, P. (1989). Constructive thinking: A broad coping variable with specific components. *Journal of Personality and Social Psychology, 57*, 332–350.

ERIKSON, E. H. (1950). *Childhood and society.* New York: Norton.

ERON, L. D., GENTRY, J. H., & SCHLEGEL (Eds.). (1994). *Reason to hope: A psychosocial perspective on violence and youth.* Washington, DC: American Psychological Association.

ERON, L. D., HUESMANN, L. R., LEFKOWITZ, M. M., & WALDER, L. Q. (1972). Does television violence cause aggression? *American Psychologist, 27*, 253–263.

ERSKINE, H. (1973). The polls: Hopes, fears, and regrets. *Public Opinion Quarterly, 37*, 132–145.

EVANS, G. E., SHAPIRO, D. H., & LEWIS, M. (1993). Specifying dysfunctional mismatches between different control dimensions. *British Journal of Psychology, 84*, 255–274.

EYSENCK, H. J. (1967). *The biological basis of personality.* Springfield, IL: Charles C Thomas.

EYSENCK, H. J. (1973). Personality and the maintenance of the smoking habit. In W. L. Dunn (Ed.), *Smoking behavior:*

Motives and incentives (pp. 113–146). Washington, DC: Winston.

EYSENCK, H. J. (1976). *Sex and personality.* London: Open Books.

EYSENCK, H. J. (1988). Personality and stress as causal factors in cancer and coronary heart disease. In M. P. Janisse (Ed.), *Individual differences, stress, and health psychology* (pp. 129–145). New York: Springer.

EYSENCK, H. J. (1991). Dimensions of personality: 16, 5, or 3? Criteria for a taxonomic paradigm. *Personality and Individual Differences, 12,* 773–790.

FALK, J. L. (1983). Drug dependence: Myth or motive? *Pharmacology Biochemistry and Behavior, 19,* 385–391.

FARKAS, G. M., & ROSEN, R. C. (1976). Effect of alcohol on elicited male sexual response. *Journal of Studies on Alcohol, 37,* 265–272.

FARLEY, F. H. (1986, May). The big T in personality. *Psychology Today,* pp. 44–52.

FAUSTO-STERLING, A. (1985). *Myths of gender: Biological theories about women and men.* New York: Basic Books.

FEINBERG, I., KORESKO, R. L., HELLER, N., & STEINBERG, H. R. (1973). Sleep EEG and eye-movement patterns in young and aged normal subjects and in patients with chronic brain syndrome. In W. B. Webb (Ed.), *Sleep: An active process.* Glenview, IL: Scott, Foresman.

FELDMAN, R. S., & BERNSTEIN, A. G. (1978). Primacy effects in self-attribution of ability. *Journal of Personality, 46,* 732–742.

FENIGSTEIN, A. (1979). Does aggression cause a preference for viewing media violence? *Journal of Personality and Social Psychology, 37,* 2307–2317.

FENWICK, P. B., DONALDSON, S., GILLIS, L., BUSHMAN, J., FENTON, G. W., PERRY, L., TILSLEY, C., & SERAFINOWICZ, H. (1977). Metabolic and EEG changes during transcendental meditation: An explanation. *Biological Psychology, 5,* 101–118.

FENZ, W. D., & EPSTEIN, S. (1969, September). Stress: In the air. *Psychology Today,* pp. 28–29, 58–59.

FERN, R. W. (1976). Hearing loss caused by amplified pop music. *Journal of Sound and Vibration, 46,* 462–464.

FESHBACH, N. D. (1987). Parental empathy and child adjustment/maladjustment. In N. Eisenberg & J. Strayer (Eds.), *Empathy and its development* (pp. 271–291). New York: Cambridge University Press.

FESTINGER, L. (1957). *A theory of cognitive dissonance.* Evanston, IL: Row, Peterson.

FEY, S. G., & LINDHOLM, E. (1978). Biofeedback and progressive relaxation: Effects on systolic and diastolic blood pressure and heart rate. *Psychophysiology, 15,* 239–247.

FINCHER, J. (1979, January). Natural opiates in the brain. *Human Behavior,* pp. 28–32.

FISCHMAN, J. (1987, February). Type A on trial. *Psychology Today,* pp. 42–50.

FISHER, C., & DEMENT, W. (1962). *Dreams and psychosis.* Paper presented at the meeting of the Western New England Psychoanalytic Society, New Haven, CT.

FISHER, H. (1992). *Anatomy of love: The natural history of monogamy, adultery and divorce.* New York: Norton.

FISHER, W. A., & BYRNE, D. (1978). Sex differences in response to erotica? Love versus lust. *Journal of Personality and Social Psychology, 36,* 117–125.

FLESHNER, M., LAUDENSLAGER, M. L., SIMONS, L., & MAIER, S. F. (1989). Reduced serum antibodies with social defeat in rats. *Physiological Behavior, 45,* 1183–1187.

FLORIAN, V., MIKULINCER, M., & TAUBMAN, O. (1995). Does hardiness contribute to mental health during a stressful real-life situation? The roles of appraisal and coping. *Journal of Personality and Social Psychology, 68,* 687–695.

FOLGER, R. (1991). Justice as worth. In J. Meindl (Chair), Justice in the workplace: Interpersonal processes (II). Symposium conducted at the Third International Conference on Social Justice, Utrecht, the Netherlands, July.

FOLKMAN, S. (1984). Personal control and stress and coping processes: A theoretical analysis. *Journal of Personality and Social Psychology, 46,* 839–852.

FOLKMAN, S., & LAZARUS, R. S. (1985). If it changes it must be a process: Study of emotion and coping during three stages of a college examination. *Journal of Personality and Social Psychology, 48,* 150–170.

FOLKMAN, S., LAZARUS, R. S., DUNKEL-SCHETTER, C., DELONGIS, A., & GRUEN, R. J. (1986). Dynamics of a stressful encounter: Cognitive appraisal, coping and encounter outcomes. *Journal of Personality and Social Psychology, 50,* 992–1003.

FOLKMAN, S., SCHAEFER, C., & LAZARUS, R. S. (1979). Cognitive processes as mediators of stress and coping. In V. Hamilton & D. M. Warburton (Eds.), *Human stress and cognition: An information processing approach* (pp. 265–298). New York: Wiley.

FOULKES, D. (1962). Dream reports from different stages of sleep. *Journal of Abnormal and Social Psychology, 65,* 14–25.

FOULKES, D. (1966). *The psychology of sleep.* New York: Scribners.

FOULKES, D., SPEAR, P. S., & SYMONDS, J. D. (1966). Individual differences in mental activity at sleep onset. *Journal of Abnormal Psychology, 71,* 280–286.

FOULKES, D., & VOGEL, G. (1965). Mental activity at sleep onset. *Journal of Abnormal Psychology, 70,* 231–243.

FRANKEN, R. E. (1987). *Sensation seeking and beliefs and attitudes.* Unpublished manuscript, University of Calgary, Canada.

FRANKEN, R. E. (1988). Sensation seeking, decision making styles, and preference for individual responsibility. *Personality and Individual Differences, 9,* 139–146.

FRANKEN, R. E. (1990). Thinking styles of sensation seekers. Unpublished manuscript, University of Calgary, Canada.

FRANKEN, R. E. (1992). Sensation seeking, optimism, hope, instrumentality and self-esteem. Unpublished research.

FRANKEN, R. E. (1993). Sensation seeking and keeping your options open. *Personality and Individual Differences, 14,* 247–249.

FRANKEN, R. E., & BROWN, D. J. (1995). Why do people like competition? The motivation for winning, putting forth effort, improving one's performance, performing well, being instrumental, and expressing forceful/aggressive behavior. *Personality and Individual Differences, 19*, 175–184.

FRANKEN, R. E., & BROWN, D. J. (1996). The need to win is not adaptive: The need to win, coping strategies, hope and self-esteem. *Personality and Individual Differences, 20*, 805–808.

FRANKEN, R. E., & PRPICH, W. (1996). Dislike of competition and the need to win: Self-image concerns, performance concerns and the distraction of attention. *Journal of Behavior and Personality, 11*, 695–712.

FRANKEN, R. E., GIBSON, K., & MOHAN, P. (1990). Sensation seeking and disclosure to close and casual friends. *Personality and Individual Differences, 11*, 829–832.

FRANKEN, R. E., GIBSON, K. J., & ROWLAND, G. L. (1992). Sensation seeking and the tendency to view the world as threatening. *Personality and Individual Differences, 13*, 31–38.

FRANKEN, R. E., & STRAIN, A. (1974). Effect of increased arousal on response to stimulus change in a complex maze. *Perceptual and Motor Skills, 39*, 1076–1078.

FRANKENHAEUSER, M. (1980). Psychoneuroendocrine approaches to the study of stressful person-environment transactions. In H. Selye (Ed.), *Selye's guide to stress research* (Vol. 1). New York: Van Nostrand Reinhold.

FRANKENHAEUSER, M., DUNNE, E., & LUNDBERG, U. (1976). Sex differences in sympathetic-adrenal medullary reactions induced by different stressors. *Psychopharmacology, 476*, 1–5.

FRANKENHAEUSER, M., & JOHANSSON, G. (1976). Task demand as reflected in catecholamine excretion and heart rate. *Journal of Human Stress, 2*, 15–23.

FRANKENHAEUSER, M., LUNDBERG, U., & FORSMAN, L. (1980). Dissociation between sympathetic-adrenal and pituitary-adrenal responses to an achievement situation characterized by high controllability: Comparison between Type A and Type B males and females. *Biological Psychology, 10*, 79–91.

FRENCH, E. G. (1956). Motivation as a variable in work-partner selection. *Journal of Abnormal and Social Psychology, 53*, 96–99.

FREUD, S. (1934). *A general introduction to psychoanalysis.* New York: Washington Square Press. (Original work published 1915)

FREUD, S. (1947). The ego and the id. In *The standard edition of the complete psychological works of Sigmund Freud* (Vol. 19). London: Hogarth Press. (Original work published 1923)

FREUD, S. (1949). Formulations regarding the two principles of mental functioning. In *Collected papers of Sigmund Freud* (Vol. 4). London: Hogarth Press. (Original work published 1911)

FREUD, S. (1949). Instincts and their vicissitudes. In *Collected papers of Sigmund Freud* (Vol. 4). London: Hogarth Press. (Original work published 1915)

FREUD, S. (1953). *The interpretation of dreams.* London: Hogarth Press. (Original work published 1900)

FRIEDLAND, N., KEINAN, G., & REGEV, Y. (1992). Controlling the uncontrollable: Effects of stress on illusory perceptions of controllability. *Journal of Personality and Social Psychology, 63*, 923–931.

FRIEDMAN, H. S. (1991). *Self-healing personality: Why some people achieve health and others succumb to illness.* New York: Henry Holt.

FRIEDMAN, H. S. (1992). Understanding hostility, coping, and health. In H. S. Friedman (Ed.), *Hostility, coping and health* (pp. 3–9). Washington, DC: American Psychological Association.

FRIEDMANN, J., GLOBUS, G., HUNTLEY, A., MULLANEY, D., NAITOH, P., & JOHNSON, L. (1977). Performance and mood during and after gradual sleep reduction. *Psychophysiology, 14*, 245–250.

FRIEDMAN, M., & ROSENMAN, R. H. (1974). *Type A behavior and your heart.* New York: Knopf.

FRIEDMAN, M. I., & STRICKER, E. M. (1976). The physiological psychology of hunger: A physiological perspective. *Psychological Review, 83*, 409–431.

FRIJDA, N. H. (1988). The laws of emotion. *American Psychologist, 43*, 349–353.

FROHMAN, L. A., GOLDMAN, J. K., & BERNARDIS, L. L. (1972). Metabolism of intravenously injected 14C-glucose in weanling rats with hypothalamic obesity. *Metabolism: Clinical and Experimental, 21*, 799–805.

FROST, R. O., GOOLKASIAN, G. A., ELY, R. J., & BLANCHARDS, F. A. (1982). Depression, restraint, and eating behavior. *Behavioral Research and Therapy, 20*, 113–121.

FUNKENSTEIN, D. H., KING, S. H., & DROLETTE, M. E. (1974). The direction of anger during a laboratory stress-inducing situation. *Psychosomatic Medicine, 16*, 404–413.

FUSTER, J. M. (1958). Effects of stimulation of brain stem on tachistoscopic perception. *Science, 127*, 150.

GACKENBACH, J., & BOSVELD, J. (1989a). *Control your dreams.* New York: Harper & Row.

GACKENBACH, J., & BOSVELD, J. (1989b, October). Take control of your dreams. *Psychology Today*, pp. 27–32.

GAGNON, J. H. (1974). Scripts and the coordination of sexual conduct. In J. K. Cole & R. Diensteiber (Eds.), *Nebraska Symposium on Motivation* (Vol. 21, pp. 27–59). Lincoln: University of Nebraska Press.

GAGNON, J. H. (1977). *Human Sexualities.* Glenview, IL: Scott, Foresman.

GAGNON, P., DE KONINCK, J., & BROUGHTON, R. (1985). Reappearance of electroencephalogram slow waves in extended sleep with delayed bedtime. *Sleep, 8*, 118–128.

GARCIA, J., & KOELLING, R. A. (1966). Relation of cue to consequence in avoidance learning. *Psychonomic Science, 4*, 123–124.

GARCIA, J., McGOWAN, B. K., ERVIN, F. R., & KOELLING, R. A. (1968). Cues: Their relative effectiveness as a function of the reinforcer. *Science, 160,* 794–795.

GARLAND, A. F., & ZIGLER, E. (1993). Adolescent suicide prevention: Current research and social policy implications. *American Psychologist, 48,* 169–182.

GARN, S. M., & CLARK, D. C. (1976). Trends in fatness and the origins of obesity. *Pediatric, 57,* 443–455.

GARNER, D. M., & WOOLEY, S. C. (1991). Confronting failure of behavioral and dietary treatments for obesity. *Clinical Psychology Review, 11,* 729–780.

GARRITY, T. F., STALLONES, L., MARX, M. B., & JOHNSON, T. P. (1989). Pet ownership and attachment as supportive factors in the health of the elderly. *Anthrozoos, 3,* 35–44.

GARROW, J. (1978). The regulation of energy expenditure. In G. A. Bray (Ed.), *Recent advances in obesity research* (Vol. 2). London: Newman.

GEBHARD, P. H. (1973). Sex differences in sexual responses. *Archives of Sexual Behavior, 2,* 201–203.

GEEN, R. G. (1968). Effects of frustration, attack, and prior training in aggressiveness upon aggressive behavior. *Journal of Personality and Social Psychology, 9,* 316–321.

GEEN, R. G. (1976). Observing violence in the mass media: Implications of basic research. In R. G. Geen & E. C. O'Neal (Eds.), *Perspectives on aggression.* New York: Academic Press.

GEEN, R. G. (1990). *Human Aggression.* Pacific Grove, CA: Brooks/Cole.

GEER, J. H., & BROUSSARD, D. B. (1990). Scaling sexual behavior and arousal: Consistency and sex differences. *Journal of Personality and Social Psychology, 58,* 664–671.

GEER, J. H., DAVISON, G. C., & GATCHEL, R. J. (1970). Reduction of stress in humans through nonveridical perceived control of aversive stimulation. *Journal of Personality and Social Psychology, 16,* 731–738.

GENTRY, W. D. (1985). Relationship of anger-coping styles and blood pressure among black Americans. In M. A. Chesney and R. H. Roseninan (Eds.), *Anger and hostility in cardiovascular and behavioral disorders* (pp. 139–147). Washington, DC: Hemisphere.

GENTRY, W. D., CHESNEY, A. P., GARY, H. E., HALL, R. P., & HARBURG, E. (1982). Habitual anger-coping styles: I. Effect on men's blood pressure and risk for essential hypertension. *Psychosomatic Medicine, 44,* 195–202.

GERNER, R. H., POST, R. M., GILLIN, J. C., & BUNNEY, W. E. (1979). Biological and behavioral effects of one night's sleep deprivation in depressed patients and normals. *Journal of Psychiatric Research, 15,* 21.

GERRARD, M. (1987). Sex, sex guilt, and contraceptive use revisited: The 1980s. *Journal of Personality and Social Psychology, 52,* 975–980.

GESCHWIND, N., & GALABURDA, A. M. (1987). *Cerebral lateralization: Biological mechanisms, associations, and pathology.* Cambridge, MA: MIT Press.

GETZELS, J. W., & JACKSON, P. W. (1962). *Creativity and intelligence: Exploration with gifted students.* New York: Wiley.

GIBBONS, F. X., & McCOY, S. B. (1991). Self-esteem, similarity, and reactions to active versus passive downward comparison. *Journal of Personality and Social Psychology, 60,* 414–424.

GIBSON, K. J., FRANKEN, R. E., & ROWLAND, G. L. (1989). Sensation seeking and marital adjustment. *Journal of Sex and Marital Therapy, 15,* 57–61.

GIESE, H., & SCHMIDT, A. (1968). *Student sexuality.* Hamburg: Rowohlt.

GILBERT, D. G. (1979). Paradoxical tranquillizing and emotion-reducing effects of nicotine. *Psychological Bulletin, 86,* 643–661.

GILBERT, R. M. (1981). Drug abuse as an excessive behavior. In H. Shaeffer and M. E. Burglass, *Classic contributions in the addictions.* New York: Brunner/Mazel.

GILLBERG, M., & ÅKERSTEDT, T. (1982). Body temperature and sleep at different times of day. *Sleep, 5,* 378–388.

GILLIN, J. C., & WYATT, R. J. (1975). Schizophrenia: Perchance a dream. *International Review of Neurobiology, 17,* 297–342.

GILOVICH, T., & MEDVEC, V. H. (1995). The experience of regret: What, when, and why. *Psychological Review, 102,* 379–395.

GLADUE, B. A. (1991). Aggressive behavioral characteristics, hormones, and sexual orientation in men and women. *Aggressive Behavior, 17,* 313–326.

GLANZER, M. (1953). The role of stimulus satiation in spontaneous alternation. *Journal of Experimental Psychology, 45,* 387–393.

GLASS, D. C. (1977a). *Behavior patterns, stress, and coronary disease.* Hillsdale, NJ: Erlbaum.

GLASS, D. C. (1977b). Stress, behavior patterns, and coronary disease. *American Scientist, 65,* 177–187.

GLASSER, W. (1976). *Positive addiction.* New York: Harper & Row.

GLASSMAN, A. (1969). Indolamines and affective disorder. *Psychosomatic Medicine, 31,* 107–114.

GLAUBMAN, H., ORBACH, J., AVIRAM, O., FRIEDER, J., FRIEMAN, M., PELLED, O., & GLAUBMAN, R. (1978). REM deprivation and divergent thinking. *Psychophysiology, 15,* 75–79.

GLAUBMAN, H., ORBACH, L., GROSS, Y., AVIRAM, O., FRIEDER, L., FRIEMAN, M., & PELLED, O. (1979). The effect of presleep focal attention load on subsequent sleep patterns. *Psychophysiology, 16,* 467–470.

GOLDMAN, J. K., SCHNATZ, J. D., BERNARDIS, L. L., & FROHMAN, L. A. (1970). Adipose tissue metabolism of weanling rats after destruction of ventromedial hypothalamic nuclei: Effect of hypophysectomy and growth hormone. *Metabolism: Clinical and Experimental, 19,* 995–1005.

GOLDMAN, J. K., SCHNATZ, J. D., BERNARDIS, L. L., & FROHMAN, L. A. (1972a). Effects of ventromedial hypothalamic destruction in rats with preexisting streptozotocin-induced diabetes. *Metabolism: Clinical and Experimental, 21,* 132–136.

GOLDMAN, J. K., SCHNATZ, J. D., BERNARDIS, L. L., & FROHMAN, L. A. (1972b). The vivo and in vitro metabolism in hypothalamic obesity. *Diabetologia, 8,* 160–164.

GOLDMAN, R., JAFFA, M., & SCHACHTER, S. (1968). Yom Kippur, Air France, dormitory food, and eating behavior of obese and normal persons. *Journal of Personality and Social Psychology, 10,* 117–123.

GOLEMAN, D. (1976, February). Meditation helps break the stress spiral. *Psychology Today,* pp. 82–86, 93.

GOODENOUGH, D. R. (1978). Field dependence. In H. London & J. E. Exner, Jr. (Eds.), *Dimensions of personality* (pp. 165–216). New York: Wiley.

GOODNER, C. J., & RUSSELL, J. A. (1965). Pancreas. In T. C. Ruch & H. D. Patton (Eds.), *Physiology and biophysics.* Philadelphia: Saunders.

GORDON, H. W., & LEE, P. (1986). A relationship between gonadotropins and visuospatial function. *Neuropsychologia, 24,* 563–576.

GORSKI, R. A. (1974). The neuroendocrine regulation of sexual behavior. In G. Newton and A. H. Riesen (Eds.), *Advances in Psychobiology* (Vol. 2, pp. 1–58). New York: Wiley.

GORSKI, R. A. (1985). Sexual dimorphisms of the brain. *Journal of Animal Science, 61,* 38–61.

GORSKI, R. A. (1988). Hormone-induced sex differences in hypothalamic structure. *Bull TMIN, 16,* Suppl. 3, 67–90.

GORSKI, R. A. (1991). Sexual differentiation of the endocrine brain and its control. In M. Motta (Ed.), *Brain endocrinology* (2nd ed., pp. 71–104).

GOUGH, H. G. (1976). Studying creativity by means of word association tests. *Journal of Applied Psychology, 61,* 348–353.

GOY, R. W., & McEWEN, B. S. *(1980). Sexual differentiation of the brain.* Cambridge, MA: MIT Press.

GRAY, J. A. (1982). *The neuropsychology of anxiety: An enquiry in the functions of the septo-hippocampal system.* Oxford: Oxford University Press.

Gray, J. A., & McNaughton, N. (1996). The activation and regulation of fear and anxiety. In R. A. Dienstrier (Ed.). *Perspectives on anxiety, panic, and fear. Nebraska Symposium on Motivation* (Vol. 43, pp. 61–134). Lincoln: University of Nebraska Press.

GREENBERG, R., & PEARLMAN, C. A. (1974). Cutting the REM nerve: An approach to the adaptive role of REM sleep. *Perspectives in Biology and Medicine, 17,* 513–521.

GREENBERG, R., PILLARD, R., & PEARLMAN, C. (1972). The effect of dream (stage REM) deprivation on adaptation to stress. *Psychosomatic Medicine, 34,* 257–262.

GREENE, D., & LEPPER, M. R. (1974). Effects of extrinsic rewards on children's subsequent intrinsic interest. *Child Development, 45,* 1141–1145.

GREENE, R., & DALTON, K. (1953). The premenstrual syndrome. *British Medical Journal, 1,* 1007–1014.

GREISER, C., GREENBERG, R., & HARRISON, R. H. (1972). The adaptive function of sleep: The differential effects of

sleep and dreaming on recall. *Journal of Abnormal Psychology, 80,* 280–286.

GREIST, J. H., KLEIN, M. H., EISCHENS, R. R., FARIS, J., GURMAN, A. S., & MORGAN, W. P. (1979). Running as treatment for depression. *Comprehensive Psychiatry, 20,* 41–54.

GRESHAM, S. C., AGNEW, H. W., JR., & WILLIAMS, R. L. (1978). The sleep of depressed patients. *Archives of General Psychiatry, 15,* 447–450.

GRIFFIN, S. J., & TRINDLER, J. (1978). Physical fitness, exercise, and human sleep. *Psychophysiology, 15,* 447–450.

GRIFFITH, W., MAY, J., & VEITCH, R. (1974). Sexual stimulation and interpersonal behavior. Heterosexual evaluative responses, visual behavior, and physical proximity. *Journal of Personality and Social Psychology, 30,* 367–377.

GRINSPOON, L., & BAKALAR, J. B. (1993). Marihuana: The forbidden medicine. New Haven, CT: Yale University Press.

GRINSPOON, L., & HEDBLOM, P. (1975). *The speed culture: Amphetamine use and abuse in America.* Cambridge, MA: Harvard University Press.

GROSSMAN, S. P. (1967). *A textbook of physiological psychology.* New York: Wiley.

GROSVENOR, A., & LACK, L. C. (1984). The effect of sleep before or after learning on memory. *Sleep, 7,* 155–167.

GRUNBERG, N. E., & STRAUB, R. O. (1992). The role of gender and taste class in the effects of stress on eating. *Health Psychology, 11,* 97–100.

GUILFORD, J. P. (1967). *The nature of human intelligence.* New York: McGraw-Hill.

GUY, R. F., RANKIN, B. A., & NORVELL, M. J. (1980). The relation of sex-role stereotyping to body image. *Journal of Psychology, 105,* 167–173.

HADDAD, N. F., McCULLERS, J. C., & MORAN, J. D. (1976). Satiation and the detrimental effects of material rewards. *Child Development, 47,* 547–551.

HAESSLER, H. A., & CRAWFORD, J. D. (1967). Fatty acid composition and metabolic activity of depot fat in experimental obesity. *American Journal of Physiology, 213,* 255–261.

HALL, J. B., & BROWN, D. A. (1979). Plasma glucose and lactic acid alterations in response to a stressful exam. *Biological Psychology, 8,* 179–188.

HALPERN, D. F., & CASS, M. (1994). Laterality, sexual orientation, and immune system functioning: Is there a relationship? *International Journal of Neuroscience, 77,* 167–180.

HAMER, D. H., & COPELAND, P. (1994). *The science of desire.* New York: Simon & Schuster.

HAMER, D. H., HU, S., MAGNUSON, V. L., HU, N., & PATTATUCCI, A. M. L. (1993). A linkage between DNA markers on the X chromosome and sexual orientation. *Science, 261,* 321–327.

HAMMOND, W. R., & YUNG, B. (1993). Psychology's role in the public health response to assaultive violence among young African American men. *American Psychologist, 48,* 142–154.

HANSEN, J. R., STØA, K. F., BLIX, A. S., & URSIN, H. (1978). Urinary levels of epinephrine and norepinephrine in parachutist trainees. In H. Ursin, E. Baade, and S. Levine (Eds.), *Psychobiology of stress: A study of coping men.* New York: Academic Press.

HARBURG, E., BLAKELOCK, E. H., & ROEPER, P. J. (1979). Resentful and reflective coping with arbitrary authority and blood pressure. *Psychosomatic Medicine, 41,* 189–202.

HARLOW, H. F. (1953). Mice, monkeys, men, and motives. *Psychological Review, 60,* 23–32.

HARLOW, H. F., & HARLOW, M. K. (1969). Effects of various mother-infant relationships on rhesus monkey behaviors. In B. M. Foss (Ed.), *Determinants of infant behavior* (Vol. 4, pp. 63–74). London: Methuen.

HARRINGTON, D. M. (1981). Creativity, analogical thinking and muscular metaphors. *Journal of Mental Imagery, 6,* 121–126.

HARRIS, C. B. (1988). *Hope: Construct definition and the development of an individual differences scale.* Unpublished doctoral dissertation, University of Kansas, Lawrence.

HARTER, S. (1990). Causes, correlates, and the functional role of global self worth: A life-span perspective. In R. J. Sternberg & J. Kolligian, Jr. (Eds.), *Competence considered* (pp. 67–97). New Haven, CT: Yale University Press.

HARTER, S. (1993). Visions of the self: Beyond the me in the mirror. In J. E. Jacobs (Ed.), *Nebraska symposium on motivation: Vol. 40. Developmental perspectives on motivation. Current theory and research in motivation* (pp. 99–144). Lincoln: University of Nebraska Press.

HARTMANN, E. L. (1973). *The functions of sleep.* New Haven, CT: Yale University Press.

HARTMANN, E. L. (1974). The functions of sleep. *Annual of Psychoanalysis, 2,* 271–289.

HARTMANN, E. L., BAEKELAND, F., & ZWILLING, G. R. (1972). Psychological differences between long and short sleepers. *Archives of General Psychiatry, 26,* 463–468.

HARTMANN, E. L., & STERN, W. C. (1972). Desynchronized steep deprivation: Learning deficit and its reversal by increased catecholamines. *Physiology and Behavior, 8,* 585–587.

HARTSE, K. M., ROTH, T., & ZORICK, F. J. (1982). Daytime sleepiness and daytime wakefulness: The effect of instruction. *Sleep, 5,* S107–S118.

HASELTINE, F. P., & OHNO, S. (1981). Mechanisms of gonadal differentiation. *Science, 211,* 1272–1278.

HASHIM, S. A., & VAN ITALLIE, T. B. (1965). Studies in normal and obese subjects with a monitored food dispensary device. *Annals of the New York Academy of Science, 131,* 654–661.

HASSENFELD, I. N. (1993). Psychophysiology and psychoneuroimmunology. In F. S. Duerkesm (Ed.), *Behavioral science for medical students* (pp. 399–407). Baltimore: Williams & Wilkins.

HAUG, M., BRAIN, P. F., & KAMIS, A. B. (1985). A brief review comparing the effects of sex steroids on two forms of aggression in laboratory mice. *Neurological Science and Behavioral Reviews, 10,* 463–467.

HAWKE, C. C. (1950). Castration and sex crimes. *American Journal of Mental Deficiency, 55,* 220–226.

HAWKINS, R. C., JR., TURELL, S., & JACKSON, L. J. (1983). Desirable and undesirable masculine and feminine traits in relation to students' dietary tendencies and body image dissatisfaction. *Sex Roles, 9,* 705–724.

HAYWOOD, H. C. (1971). Individual difference in motivational orientations: A trait approach. In H. Day, D. E. Berlyne, & D. E. Hunt (Eds.), *Intrinsic motivation: A new direction in education.* Toronto: Holt, Rinehart & Winston.

HEATH, R. G. (1963). Electrical self-stimulation of the brain in man. *American Journal of Psychiatry, 120,* 571–577.

HEATHER, N., WINTON, M., & ROLLNICK, S. (1982). An empirical test of "a cultural delusion of alcoholics." *Psychological Reports, 50,* 379–382.

HEATHERTON, T. F., & POLIVY, J. (1991). Development and validation of a scale measuring state self-esteem. *Journal of Personality and Social Psychology, 60,* 895–910.

HEATHERTON, T. F., & POLIVY, J. (1991). Chronic dieting and eating disorders: A spiral model. In J. H. Crowther, S. E. Hobfall, M. A. P. Stephens, & D. L. Termenbaum (Eds.), *The etiology of bulimia: The individual and familial context* (pp. 86–108). Washington, DC: Hemisphere.

HEBB, D. O. (1955). Drive and the C.N.S. (conceptual nervous system). *Psychological Review, 62,* 243–254.

HEILMAN, M. E., & SARUWATARI, L. R. (1979). When beauty is beastly: The effects of appearance and sex on evaluations of job applicants for managerial and nonmanagerial jobs. *Organizational Behavior and Human Performance, 23,* 360–372.

HEIMAN, J. R. (1975, April). Women's sexual arousal. *Psychology Today,* pp. 91–94.

HEIMAN, J. R. (1977). A psychophysiological exploration of sexual arousal patterns in females and males. *Psychophysiology, 14,* 266–274.

HELMREICH, R. L., BEANE, W. E., LUCKER, G. W., & SPENCE, J. T. (1978). Achievement motivation and scientific attainment. *Personality and Social Psychology Bulletin, 4,* 222–226.

HELMREICH, R. L., SPENCE, J. T., BEANE, W. E., LUCKER, G. W., & MATTHEWS, K. A. (1980). Making it in academic psychology: Demographic and personality correlates of attainment. *Journal of Personality and Social Psychology, 39,* 896–908.

HELMSTETTER, S. (1986). *What to say when you talk to yourself.* New York: Simon & Schuster.

HENNIGAN, K. M., DEL ROSARIO, M. L., HEATH, L., COOK, T. D., WHARTON, J. D., & CALDER, B. J. (1982). The impact of the introduction of television on crime in the United States. *Journal of Personality and Social Psychology, 42,* 461–477.

HERMAN, C. P. (1974). External and internal cues as determinants of smoking behavior of light and heavy smokers. *Journal of Personality and Social Psychology, 30,* 664–672.

HERMAN, C. P., & MACK, D. (1975). Restrained and unrestrained eating. *Journal of Personality, 43,* 646–660.

HERMAN, C. P., & POLIVY, J. (1984). A boundary model for the regulation of eating. In A. J. Stunkard & E. Stellar (Eds.), *Eating and its disorders* (pp. 141–156). New York: Raven Press.

HERON, W. (1957). The pathology of boredom. *Scientific American, 196,* 52–56.

HIGGINS, E. T. (1987). Self-discrepancy: A theory relating self and affect. *Psychological Review, 94,* 319–340.

HIGGINS, E. T. (1996). Self-knowledge serving self-regulatory functions. *Journal of Personality and Social Psychology, 71,* 1062–1083.

HILL, H., SORIANO, F. I., CHEN, A., & LaFRAMBOISE, T. D. (1994). Sociocultural factors in the etiology and prevention of violence among ethnic minority youth. In L. D. Dron, J. H. Gentry, & P. Schegel (Eds.). *Reason to hope: A psychosocial perspective on violence & youth* (pp. 59–97). Washington, DC: American Psychological Association.

HINES, M. (1990). Gonadal hormones and human cognitive development. In J. Balthazart (Ed.), *Hormones, brains, and human behaviors in vertebrates: Vol. 1. Sexual differentiation, neuroatotomical aspects, neurotransmitters, and neuropeptides* (pp. 51–63). Basel, Switzerland: Karger.

HINES, M., ALLEN, L. S., & GORSKI, R. A. (1992). Sex differences in subregions of the medial nucleus of the amygdala, and the bed nucleus of the stia terminalis of the rat. *Brain Research, 579,* 321–326.

HINES, M., ALSUM, P., ROY, M. et al. (1987). Estrogenic contribution to sexual differentiation in the female guinea pig: Influences of diethylstibestrol and tamoxifen on neural behavior and ovarian development. *Hormones and Behavior, 21,* 402–417.

HINES, M., CHIU, L., McADAMS, L. A., BENTLER, P. M., & LIPCAMON, J. (1992). Cognition and the corpus callosum: Verbal fluency, visuospatial ability, and language lateralization related to midsagittal surface areas of the callosal subregions. *Behavioral Neurosciences, 106,* 3–14.

HIROTO, D. S. (1974). Locus of control and learned helplessness. *Journal of Experimental Psychology, 102,* 187–193.

HIROTO, D. S., & SELIGMAN, M. E. P. (1975). Generality of learned helplessness in man. *Journal of Personality and Social Psychology, 31,* 311–327.

HIRSCH, J., KNITTLE, J. L., & SALANS, L. B. (1966). Cell lipid content and cell number in obese and nonobese human adipose tissue. *Journal of Clinical Investigation, 45,* 1023.

HITE, S. (1976). *The Hite report: A nationwide survey of female sexuality.* New York: Macmillan.

HOBSON, J. A. (1988). *The dreaming brain.* New York: Basic Books.

HOCKEY, G. R. J., DAVIES, S., & GRAY, M. M. (1972). Forgetting as a function of sleep at different times of day. *Quarterly Journal of Experimental Psychology, 24,* 386–393.

HOFFMAN, M. L. (1970a). Conscience, personality, and socialization techniques. *Human Development, 13,* 90–126.

HOFFMAN, M. L. (1970b). Moral development. In P. H. Mussen (Ed.), *Handbook of child psychology* (Vol. 2, 3rd ed.). New York: Wiley.

HOFFMAN, M. L. (1982). *Development of prosocial behavior.* New York: Academic Press.

HOKANSON, J. E., & BUTLER, A. C. (1992). Cluster analysis of depressed college students' social behaviors. *Journal of Personality and Social Psychology, 62,* 273–280.

HOKANSON, J. E., DeGOOD, D. E., FORREST, M. S., & BRITTAIN, T. M. (1971). Availability of avoidance behaviors in modulating vascular-stress responses. *Journal of Personality and Social Psychology, 19,* 60–68.

HOLLON, S. D., DeRUBEIS, R. J., & EVANS, M. D. (1990). Combined cognitive therapy and pharmacology in the treatment of depression. In D. Manning and A. Francis (Eds.), *Combination drug and psychotherapy in depression.* Washington, DC: American Psychiatric Press.

HOLMES, D. S. (1984). Meditation and somatic arousal reduction. *American Psychologist, 39,* 1–10.

HOOKER, E. (1957). The adjustment of the male overt homosexual. *Journal of Projective Techniques, 21,* 18–31.

HOPSON, J. L. (1987, August). Boys will be boys, girls will be. . . . *Psychology Today,* pp. 60–66.

HOROWITZ, M. J. (1976). *Stress response syndromes.* New York: Jacob Aronson.

HOROWITZ, M. J. (1979). Psychological response to serious life events. In V. Hamilton & D. Warburton (Eds.), *Human stress and cognition: An information processing approach* (pp. 237–263). New York: Wiley.

HOTH, C. C., REYNOLDS, C. F., HOUCK, P. R., HALL, F., et al. (1989). Predicting mortality in mixed depression and dementia using EEG sleep variables. *Journal of Neuropsychiatry and Clinical Neurosciences, 14,* 366–371.

HOUSE, J. S., LANDIS, K., & UMBERSON, D. (1988). Social relationships and health, *Science, 241,* 540–545.

HOWLEY, E. T. (1976). The effect of different intensities of exercise on the excretion of epinephrine and norepinephrine. *Medicine and Science in Sports, 8,* 219–972.

HOYENGA, K. B., & HOYENGA, K. T. (1979). *The question of sex differences: Psychological, cultural, and biological issues.* Boston: Little, Brown.

HOYLE, R. H., & CRAWFORD, A. M. (1996). Use of individual-level data to investigate group phenomena: Issues and strategies. *Small Group Research.*

HOYT, M. F., & SINGER, J. L. (1978). Psychological effects of REM ("dream") deprivation upon waking mentation. In A. M. Arkin, J. S. Antrobus, and S. J. Ellman (Eds.). *The mind in sleep: Psychology and psychophysiology.* Hillsdale, NJ: Erlbaum.

HU, S., PATTATUCCI, M. L., PATTERSON, C., LI, L., FULKER, D. W., CHERNY, S. S., KRUGLYAK, L., & HAMER, D. H. (1995). *Nature Genetics, 11,* 248–256.

HUBA, G. J., NEWCOMB, M. D., & BENTLER, P. M. (1981). Comparison of canonical correlation and interbattery factor analysis on sensation seeking and drug use domains. *Applied Psychological Measurement, 5,* 291–306.

HULL, C. L. (1943). *Principles of behavior.* New York: Appleton-Century-Crofts.

HULL, J. G., & BOND, C. F. (1986). Social and behavioral consequences of alcohol consumption and expectancy: A meta-analysis. *Psychological Bulletin, 99,* 347–360.

HULL, J. G., VAN TREUREN, R. R., & VIRNELLI, S. (1987). Hardiness and health: A critique and alternative approach. *Journal of Personality and Social Psychology, 53,* 518–530.

HUNT, J. McV. (1963). Motivation inherent in information processing. In O. J. Harvey (Ed.), *Motivation and social interaction: Cognitive determinants.* New York: Ronald Press.

HUTT, C. (1996). Exploration and play in children. In P. A. Jewell & C. Loizos (Eds.), *Play, exploration, and territory in mammals* (pp. 61–81). Symposia of the Zoological Society of London (No. 18). New York: Academic Press.

HYDE, J. S. (1986). Gender differences in aggression. In J. S Hyde & M. C. Linn (Eds.), *The psychology of gender: Advances through meta-analysis* (pp. 51–66). Baltimore: Johns Hopkins University Press.

HYDE, J. S., & LINN, M. (1988). Gender differences in ability: A meta-analysis. *Psychological Bulletin, 104,* 53–69.

HYDE, J., FENNEMA, E., & LAMON, S. J. (1990). Gender differences in mathematics performance: A meta-analysis. *Psychological Bulletin, 107,* 139–155.

IMPERATO-McGINLEY, J., GUERRERO, L., GAUTIER, T., & PETERSON, R. E. (1974, December). Steroid 5 alpha-reductase deficiency in man: An inherited form of male pseudohermaphroditises, *Science, 186,* 1213–1215.

IMPERATO-McGINLEY, J., PETERSON, R. E., GAUTIER, T., & STURLA, E. (1979). Androgen and the evolution of male-gender pseudohermaphroditises with 5 alpha-reductase deficiency. *New England Journal of Medicine, 300,* 1233–1237.

ISEN, A. M., DAUBMAN, K. A., & NOWICKI, G. P. (1987). Positive affect facilitates creative problem solving. *Journal of Personality and Social Psychology, 52,* 1122–1131.

IVEY, M. E., & BARDWICK, J. M. (1968). Patterns of affective fluctuation in the menstrual cycle. *Psychosomatic Medicine, 30,* 336–345.

IZARD, C. E. (1977). *Human emotions.* New York: Plenum.

IZARD, C. E. (1990). Facial expressions and the regulation of emotions. *Journal of Personality and Social Psychology, 58,* 487–498.

IZARD, C. E., LIBERO, D. Z., PUTNAM, P., & HAYNES, O. M. (1993). Stability of emotion experiences and their relations to traits of personality. *Journal of Personality and Social Psychology, 64,* 847–860.

IZARD, C. E., & TOMKINS, S. S. (1966). Affect and behavior: Anxiety as negative affect. In C. D. Spielberger (Ed.), *Anxiety and behavior.* New York: Academic Press.

JACOBS, B. L. (1987). How hallucinogenic drugs work. *American Scientist, 75,* 386–392.

JACOBS, B. L., & TRULSON, M. E. (1979). Mechanisms of action of LSD. *American Scientist, 67,* 396–404.

JACOBSON, R. C., & ZINBERG, N. E. (1975). *The social basis of drug prevention* (Publication SS-5). Washington, DC: Drug Abuse Council.

JAFFE, J. H., & MARTIN, W. R. (1990). Opioid analgesics and antagonists. In A. G. Gilman, T. W. Rall, A. S. Nies, & P. Taylor (Eds.), *Goodman and Glimmer's "The pharmacological basis of therapeutics"* (pp. 485–521). New York: Pergamon Press.

JAMES, W. (1890). *The principles of psychology.* New York: Holt.

JANOWSKY, J. S., OVIATT, S. K., & ORWOLL, E. S. (1994). Testosterone influences spatial cognition in older men. *Behavioral Neurosciences, 108,* 325–332.

JEFFERY, R. W., WING, R. R., THORSON, C., BURTON, L. R., RAETHER, C., HARVEY, J., & MULLEN, M. (1993). Strengthening behavioral interventions for weight loss: A randomized trial of food provision and monetary incentive. *Journal of Consulting and Clinical Psychology, 61,* 1038–1045.

JEFFREY, D. B., & KATZ, R. G. (1977). *Take it off and keep it off.* Englewood Cliffs, NJ: Prentice-Hall.

JENSEN-CAMPBELL, L. A., GRAZIANO, W. G., & WEST, S. G. (1995). Dominance, prosocial orientation, and female preferences: Do nice guys really finish last? *Journal of Personality and Social Psychology, 68,* 427–440.

JESSOR, R. (1979). Marijuana: A review of recent psychosocial research. In R. L. Dupont, A. Goldstein, and J. O'Donnell (Eds.), *Handbook on drug abuse.* Rockville, MD: National Institute on Drug Abuse.

JEVNING, R., WILSON, A. F., & DAVIDSON, J. M. (1978). Adrenocortical activity during meditation. *Hormones and Behavior, 10,* 54–60.

JOHNSON, E. H., SPIELBERGER, C. D., WORDEN, T. J., & JACOBS, G. A. (1987). Emotional and familial determinants of elevated blood pressure in black and white adolescent males. *Journal of Psychosomatic Research, 31,* 287–300.

JOHNSON, D. W., & JOHNSON, R. T. (1985). Motivation processes in cooperative, competitive, and individualistic learning situations. In C. Ames & R. Ames (Eds.), *Research on Motivation in Education* (Vol. 2). New York: Academic Press.

JOSEPHS, R. A., LARRICK, R. P., STEELE, C. M., & NISBETT, R. E. (1992). Protecting the self from the negative consequences of risky decisions. *Journal of Personality and Social Psychology: 62,* 26–37.

JOUVET, M. (1967, February). The states of sleep. *Scientific American,* pp. 62–72.

JOYCE, C. R. B. (1970). Cannabis. *British Journal of Hospital Medicine, 4,* 162–166.

JULIEN, R. M. (1975). *A primer of drug action.* San Francisco: W. H. Freeman.

JURASKA, J. M., & KOPCIK, J. R. (1988). Sex and environmental influences on the size and ultrastructure of the rat corpus callosum. *Brain Research, 450,* 1–8.

KAGAN, J. (1984). *Establishing a morality: The nature of the child.* New York: Basic Books.

KAGAN, J., & SNIDMAN, N. (1991). Temperamental factors in human development. *American Psychologist, 46,* 856–862.

KAHA, C. W. (1983). The creative mind: Form and process. *Journal of Creative Behavior, 17,* 84–94.

KAHNEMAN, D. (1973). *Attention and effort.* Englewood Cliffs, NJ: Prentice-Hall.

KALANT, O. J. (1973). *The amphetamines: Toxicity and addiction* (2nd ed.). Toronto: University of Toronto Press.

KALAT, J. W. (1995). *Biological psychology.* Pacific Grove, CA: Brooks/Cole.

KALES, A., BIXLER, E. O., SOLDATOS, C. R., VELA-BUENO, A., CALDWELL, A. B., & CADIEUX, R. J. (1982). Role of sleep apnea and nocturnal myoclonus. *Psychosomatics, 23,* 589–595, 600.

KAMEN, L., RODIN, J., SELIGMAN, M. E. P., & DWYER, J. (1991). Explanatory style and cell-mediated immunity in elderly men and women. *Health Psychology, 10,* 229–235.

KAMIN, L. J. (1968). Attention-like processes in classical conditioning. In M. R. Jones (Ed.), *Miami symposium on the prediction of behavior: Aversive stimuli* (pp. 9–34). Coral Gables, FL: University of Miami Press.

KANDEL, D. B. (1984). Marijuana users in young adulthood. *Archives of General Psychiatry, 41,* 200–209.

KANDEL, D. B., KESSLER, R. C., & MARGULIES, R. Z. (1978). Antecedents of adolescent initiation into stages of drug use: A developmental analysis. In D. B. Kandel (Ed.), *Longitudinal research on drug abuse* (pp. 73–99). Washington, DC: Hemisphere.

KANDEL, D. B., & YAMAGUCHI, K. (1985). Developmental patterns of the use of legal, illegal, and prescribed drugs. In C. L. Jones & R. J. Battjes (Eds.), *Etiology of drug abuse* (pp. 193–235). Rockville, MD: National Institute on Drug Abuse.

KAPLAN, R. M. (1990). Behavior as the central outcome in health care. *American Psychologist, 45,* 1211–1220.

KARLI, P. (1991). *Animal and human aggression.* New York: Oxford University Press.

KATZ, J. L. (1990). Testimony to Maryland Governor's Prescription Drug Commission.

KATZ, L., & EPSTEIN, S. (1991). Constructive thinking and coping with laboratory-induced stress. *Journal of Personality and Social Psychology, 61,* 789–800.

KAVANAUGH, D. J., & BOWER, G. H. (1985). Mood and self-efficacy: Impact of job and sadness on perceived capabilities. *Cognitive Therapy and Research, 9,* 507–525.

KEESEY, R. E., & POWLEY, T. L. (1975). Hypothalamic regulation of body weight. *American Scientist, 63,* 558–565.

KEINAN, G. (1987). Decision making under stress: Scanning of alternative under controllable and uncontrollable treats. *Journal of Personality and Social Psychology, 52,* 639–644.

KELLER, M. (1970). The great Jewish drink mystery. *British Journal of Addiction, 64,* 287–295.

KELLY, A. E., & KAHN, J. (1994). Effect of suppression of personal intrusive thoughts. *Journal of Personality and Social Psychology, 66,* 998–1006.

KEMLER, D., & SHEPP, B. (1971). The learning and transfer of dimensional relevance and irrelevance in children. *Journal of Experimental Psychology, 90,* 120–127.

KENDALL, P. C., LEARNER, R. M., & CRAIGHEAD, W. E. (1984). Human development and intervention in childhood psychotherapy. *Child Development, 55,* 71–82.

KENDLER, K. S., HEATH, A., MARTIN, N. G., & EAVES, L. J. (1986). Symptoms of anxiety and depression in a volunteer population. *Archives of General Psychiatry, 43,* 213–221.

KENDLER, K. S., HEATH, A. C., MARTIN, N. G., & EAVES, L. J. (1987). Symptoms of anxiety and symptoms of depression: Same genes, different environments? *Archives of General Psychiatry, 44,* 451–457.

KENT, G. (1987). Self-efficacious control over reported physiological, cognitive and behavioral symptoms of anxiety. *Behaviour Research and Therapy, 25,* 341–347.

KERNIS, M. H., BROCKNER, J., & FRANKEL, B. S. (1989). Self-esteem and reactions to failure: The mediating role of overgeneralization. *Journal of Personality and Social Psychology, 57,* 707–714.

KERNIS, M. H., GANNEMANN, B. D., & BARCLAY, L. C. (1989). Stability and level of self-esteem as predictors of anger arousal and hostility. *Journal of Personality and Social Psychology, 56,* 1013–1022.

KESSLER, R. C., KENDLER, K. S., HEATH, A., NEALE, M. C., & EAVES, L. J. (1992). Social support, depressed mood, and adjustment to stress: A genetic epidemiologic investigation. *Journal of Personality and Social Psychology, 62,* 257–272.

KIECOLT-GLASER, J. K., & GLASER, R. (1992). Psychoneuroimmuninology: Can psychological interventions modulate immunity? *Journal of Consulting and Clinical Psychology, 60,* 569–575.

KIESLER, C. A., & PALLAK, M. S. (1976). Arousal properties of dissonance manipulations. *Psychological Bulletin, 83,* 1014–1025.

KIMURA, D. (1992). Sex differences in the brain. *Scientific American, 267,* 118–125.

KINSEY, A. C., POMEROY, W. B., & MARTIN, C. E. (1948). *Sexual behavior in the human male.* Philadelphia: Saunders.

KINSEY, A. C., POMEROY, W. B., & MARTIN, C. E. (1953). *Sexual behavior in the human female.* Philadelphia: Saunders.

KIRSCH, I. (1985). Response expectancy as a determinant of experience and behavior. *American Psychologist, 40,* 1189–1202.

KLAUSNER, S. Z., FOULKES, E. F., & MOORE, M. H. *(1980). The Inupiat: Economics and alcohol on the Alaskan North Slope.* Philadelphia: Center for Research on the Acts of Man, University of Pennsylvania.

KLECK, R. E., & RUBENSTEIN, C. (1975). Physical attractiveness, perceived attitude similarity, and interpersonal attraction in an opposite-sex encounter. *Journal of Personality and Social Psychology, 31,* 107–114.

KLEIN, R., & ARMITAGE, R. (1979). Rhythms in human performance: 1¹/₂ hour oscillation in cognitive style. *Science, 204,* 1326–1328.

KLEIN, R., & BIERHOFF, H. W. (1992). Responses to achievement situations: The mediating function of perceived fairness. Manuscript submitted for publication.

KLEINGINNA, P. R., JR., & KLEINGINNA, A. M. (1981a). A categorized list of emotion definitions, with suggestions for a consensual definition. *Motivation and Emotion, 5,* 345–379.

KLEINGINNA, P. R., JR., & KLEINGINNA, A. M. (1981b). A categorized list of motivation definitions, with suggestions for a consensual definition. *Motivation and Emotion, 5,* 263–291.

KLEITMAN, N. (1963). *Sleep and wakefulness.* Chicago: University of Chicago Press.

KLINGER, E. (1975). Consequences of commitment to and disengagement from incentives. *Psychological Review, 82,* 1–25.

KOBASA, S. C. (1979a). Personality and resistance to illness. *American Journal of Community Psychology, 7,* 413–423.

KOBASA, S. C. (1979b). Stressful life events, personality, and health: An inquiry into hardiness. *Journal of Personality and Social Psychology, 37,* 1–11.

KOBASA, S. C. (1982). Commitment and coping in stress among lawyers. *Journal of Personality and Social Psychology, 42,* 707–717.

KOBASA, S. C., MADDI, S. R., & KAHN, S. (1982). Hardiness and health: A prospective study. *Journal of Personality and Social Psychology, 42,* 168–177.

KOBASA, S. C., & PUCCETTI, M. C. (1983). Personality and social resources in stress-resistance. *Journal of Personality and Social Psychology, 45,* 839–850.

KOHN, A. (1986). *No contest: The case against competition.* Boston, MA: Houghton-Mifflin.

KOLB, L. (1962). *Drug addiction: A medical problem.* Springfield, IL: Charles C Thomas.

KORIDZE, M. G., & NEMSADZE, N. D. (1983). Effect of deprivation of paradoxical sleep on the formation and differentiation of conditioned reflexes. *Neuroscience and Behavioral Psychology, 82,* 369–373.

KOULACK, D., PREVOST, F., & DE KONINCK, J. (1985). Sleep, dreaming, and adaptation to a stressful intellectual activity. *Sleep, 8,* 244–253.

KRAINES, S. H. (1957). *Mental depressives and their treatment.* New York: Macmillan.

KRAMER, M. (1982). The psychology of the dream: Art or science? *Psychiatric Journal of the University of Ottawa, 7,* 87–100.

KRAMER, M. (1990). Nightmares (dream disturbances) in posttraumatic stress disorder: Implications for a theory of dreaming. In R. R. Bootzin, J. F. Kihlstrom, & D. L. Schacter (Eds.), *Sleep and cognition* (pp. 190–202). Washington, DC: American Psychological Association.

KRAMER, M., CZAYA, J., ARAND, D., & ROTH, T. (1974). *The development of psychological content across the REMP.* Paper presented at the meeting of the Association for the Psychophysiological Study of Sleep, Jackson Hole, WY.

KRANTZ, D. S., & SCHULZ, R. (1980). A model of life crisis, control, and health outcomes: Cardiac rehabilitation and relocation of the elderly. In A. Baum & J. E. Singer (Eds.), *Advances in environmental psychology: Vol. 2. Applications of personal control* (pp. 23–57). Hillsdale, NJ: Erlbaum.

KRAUT, R. (1979). Two components of happiness. *Philosophical Review, 87,* 167–196.

KUHL, J. (1981). Motivational and functional helplessness: The moderating effect of state versus action-orientation. *Journal of Personality and Social Psychology, 40,* 155–170.

KUHN, D. Z., MADSEN, C. H., & BECKER, W. C. (1967). Effects of exposure to an aggressive model and "frustration" on children's aggressive behavior. *Child Development, 38,* 739–745.

KUMANYIKA, S. (1990). Diet and chronic disease issues for minority populations. *Journal of Nutrition Education, 22,* 89–96.

LABERGE, S. (1985). *Lucid dreaming.* New York: Ballantine Books.

LACEY, B. C., & LACEY, J. I. (1978). Two-way communication between the heart and the brain: Significance of time within the cardiac cycle. *American Psychologist, 33,* 99–113.

LACEY, J. I., KAGAN, J., LACEY, B. C., & MOSS, H. A. (1963). The visceral level: Situational determinants and behavioral correlates of autonomic response. In P. Knapp (Ed.), *Expression of the emotions in man* (pp. 161–205). New York: International Universities Press.

LACEY, J. I., & LACEY, B. C. (1970). Some autonomic-central nervous system interrelationships. In P. Black (Ed.), *Physiological correlates of emotion.* New York: Academic Press.

LADER, M. H. (1975). *Psychophysiology of mental illness.* London: Routledge & Kegan Paul.

LADER, M. H. (1980a). Psychophysiological studies in anxiety. In G. D. Burrows & D. Davies (Eds.), *Handbook of studies on anxiety.* Amsterdam: Elsevier/North Holland.

LADER, M. H. (1980b). The psychophysiology of anxiety. In H. van Praag, M. H. Lader, O. Rafaelsen, & E. Sachar (Eds.), *Handbook of biological psychiatry.* New York: Marcel Dekker.

LAGERSPETZ, K., & VIEMERO, V. (1989). Television and aggressive behavior among Finnish children. In L. R. Huesmann & L. D. Eron (Eds.), *Television and the aggressive child: A cross-national comparison* (pp. 81–118). Hillsdale, NJ: Erlbaum.

LANGELLE, C. (1989). *An assessment of hope in a community sample.* Unpublished master's thesis, University of Kansas, Lawrence.

LANGER, E. J. (1989). *Mindfulness.* Reading, MA: Addison Wesley.

LANGER, E. J., & PARK, K. (1990). Incompetence: A conceptual consideration. In R. J. Sternberg and J. Kolligian, Jr. (Eds.), *Competence considered*. New Haven, CT: Yale University Press.

LANGER, E., & RODIN, J. (1976). The effects of enhanced personal responsibility for the aged: A field experiment in an institutionalized setting. *Journal of Personality and Social Psychology, 34*, 191–198.

LANGLEY, P. W., SIMON, H. A., BRADSHAW, G. F., & ZYTKOW, J. M. (1986). *Scientific discovery: Computational exploration of the creative process*. Cambridge, MA: MIT Press.

LARSON, L. A., & MICHELMAN, H. (1973). *International guide to fitness and health: A world survey of experiments in science and medicine applied to daily living*. New York: Crown.

LASAGNA, L., MOSTELLER, F., VON FELSINGER, J. M., & BEECHER, H. K. (1954). A study of the placebo response. *American Journal of Medicine, 16*, 770–779.

LAW, A., LOGAN, H., & BARON, R. S. (1994). Desire for control, felt control, and stress inoculation training during dental treatment. *Journal of Personality and Social Psychology, 67*, 926–936.

LAW, D. J., PELLEGRINO, J. W., & HUNT, E. B. (1993). Comparing the tortoise and the hare: Gender differences and experience in dynamic spatial reasoning tasks. *Psychological Science, 4*, 35–40.

LAZARUS, R. S. (1981). The stress and coping paradigm. In C. Eisdorfer, D. Cohen, A. Kleinman, & P. Maxim (Eds.), *Models for clinical psychopathology* (pp. 177–214). New York: Spectrum.

LAZARUS, R. S. (1991). Cognition and motivation in emotion. *American Psychologist, 46*, 352–367.

LAZARUS, R. S. (1991). *Emotion and adaptation*. New York: Oxford University Press.

LAZARUS, R. (1991). Progress on a cognitive-motivational-relational theory of emotion. *American Psychologist, 46*, 819–834.

LAZARUS, R. S., & FOLKMAN, S. (1984). *Stress, appraisal, and coping*. New York: Springer.

LAZARUS, R. S., & LAUNIER, R. (1978). Stress-related transactions between person and environment. In L. A. Pervin & M. Lewis (Eds.), *Perspectives in interactional psychology* (pp. 287–327). New York: Plenum.

LEAN, M. E., POWRIE, J. K., ANDERSON, A. S., & GARTHWAITE, P. H. (1990). Obesity, weight loss and prognosis in type II diabetes. *Diabetic Medicine, 7*, 228–233.

LEARNER, R. M. (1982). Children and adolescents as producers of their own development. *Developmental Review, 2*, 342–370.

LeDOUX, J. E. (1986). Sensory systems and emotion. *Integrative Psychiatry, 4*, 237–248.

LeDOUX, J. E. (1992). Emotions and the limbic system. *Concepts in Neuroscience, 2*, 169–199.

LeDOUX, J. E. (1993). Emotional memory systems in the brain. *Behavior and Brain Research, 58*, 69–79.

LeDOUX, J. (1996). *The emotional brain: The mysterious underpinnings of emotional life*. New York: Simon & Shuster.

LEDWIDGE, B. (1980). Run for your mind: Aerobic exercise as a means of alleviating anxiety and depression. *Canadian Journal of Behavioral Science, 12*, 126–140.

LEFCOURT, H. M., MARTIN, R. A., & SALEH, W. E. (1984). Locus of control and social support: Interactive moderator of stress. *Journal of Personality and Social Psychology, 47*, 378–389.

LEFCOURT, H. M., MILLER, R. S., WARE, E. E., & SHERK, D. (1981). Locus of control as a modifier of the relationship between stressors and moods. *Journal of Personality and Social Psychology, 41*, 357–369.

LEHMAN, H. C. (1966). The most creative years of engineers and other technologists. *Journal of Genetic Psychology, 108*, 263–270.

LEPPER, M. R., & GREENE, D. (1975). Turning play into work: Effects of adult surveillance and extrinsic rewards on children's intrinsic motivation, *Journal of Personality and Social Psychology, 31*, 479–486.

LEPPER, M. R., GREENE, D., & NISBETT, R. E. (1973). Undermining children's intrinsic interest with extrinsic reward: A test of the "overjustification" hypothesis. *Journal of Personality and Social Psychology, 28*, 129–137.

LERNER, J. V., & LERNER, R. M. (1986). *Temperament and social interaction in infants and children*. San Francisco: Jossey-Bass.

LERNER, M. J. (1977). The justice motive: Some hypotheses as to its origin and forms. *Journal of Personality, 45*, 1–52.

LERNER, R. M. (1984). *On the nature of human plasticity*. New York: Cambridge Press.

LEVAY, S. (1991). A difference in hypothalamic structure between heterosexual and homosexual men. *Science, 253*, 1034–1037.

LEVENSON, H. (1981). Differentiating among internality, powerful others, and chance. In H. M. Lefcourt (Ed.), *Research with the locus of control construct: Assessment methods* (Vol. 1, pp. 15–63). New York: Academic Press.

LEVINE, S. (1960, May). Stimulation in infancy. *Scientific American*, pp. 80–86.

LEVINE, S. (1971, January). Stress and behavior. *Scientific American*, pp. 26–31.

LEVINSON, D. J. (1978). *The seasons of a man's life*. New York: Ballantine.

LEWIN, K. (1938). *The conceptual representation and the measurement of psychological forces*. Durham, NC: Duke University Press.

LEWIN, K., DEMBO, T., FESTINGER, L., & SEARS, P. S. (1944). Level of aspiration. In J. McV. Hunt (Ed.), *Personality and behavior disorders* (Vol. 1, pp. 33–38). New York: Roland Press.

LEWIN, L., & GLAUBMAN, H. (1975). The effect of REM deprivation: Is it detrimental, beneficial, or neutral? *Psychophysiology, 12*, 349–353.

LIEBOWITZ, S. F. (1994). Specificity of hypothalamic peptides in the control of behavioral and physiological processes. Models of neuropeptide action. *Annals of the New York Academy of Sciences, 739,* 12–35.

LIND, S. K., & MUMFORD, M. D. (1987, March). *Values as predictor of job performance and advancement potential.* Paper presented at the meeting of the Southeastern Psychological Association, Atlanta, GA.

LINVILLE, P. W. (1987). Self-complexity as a cognitive buffer against stress-related illness and depression. *Journal of Personality and Social Psychology, 52,* 663–676.

LINZ, D., DONNERSTEIN, E., & PENROD, S. (1987). The findings and the recommendations of the Attorney General's Commission on Pornography. *American Psychologist, 42,* 946–953.

LLOYD, C. W. (1964). Problems associated with the menstrual cycle. In C. W. Lloyd (Ed.), *Human reproduction and sexual behavior.* Philadelphia: Lea & Febiger.

LOCKE, E. A., & LATHAM, G. P. (1990). *A theory of goal setting and task performance.* Englewood Cliffs, NJ: Prentice Hall.

LOCKE, E. A. (1968). Toward a theory of task motivation and incentives. *Organizational Performance and Human Performance, 3,* 157–189.

LORE, R. K., & SCHULTZ, L. A. (1993). Control of human aggression. *American Psychologist, 48,* 16–25.

LOSCH, M., & CACIOPPO, J. (1990). Cognitive dissonance may enhance sympathetic tonis, but attitudes are change to reduce negative affect rather than arousal. *Journal of Personality and Social Psychology, 26,* 289–304.

LOWELL, E. L. (1952). The effect of need for achievement on learning and spread of performance. *Journal of Psychology, 33,* 31–40.

LOWTHER, W. (1979, August 6). Marriage running down. *Maclean's,* p. 43.

LUNDBERG, U., & FRANKENHAEUSER, M. (1978). Psychophysiological reactions to noise as modified by personal control over noise intensity. *Biological Psychology, 6,* 51–59.

MacKINNON, D. W. (1962). The nature and nurture of creative talent. *American Psychologist, 17,* 484–495.

MACON, D. A. (1987, March). *Age, climate and personality as predictors of scientific productivity.* Paper presented at the meeting of the Southern Psychological Association, Atlanta, GA.

MacVICAR, M., WINNINGHAM, M., & NICKEL, J. (1989). Effects of aerobic interval training on cancer patients' functional capacity. *Nursing Research, 38,* 348–351.

MAEHR, M. L., & STALLINGS, W. M. (1972). Freedom from external evaluation. *Child Development, 43,* 177–185.

MAHONEY, M. J., & MAHONEY, K. (1976). *Permanent weight control.* New York: W. W. Norton.

MAIER, S. F. (1970). Failure to escape traumatic shock: Incompatible skeletal motor responses or learned helplessness? *Learning and Motivation, 1,* 157–170.

MAIER, S. F., LAUDENSLAGER, M., & RYAN, S. M. (1985). Stressor controllability, immune function, and endogamous opiates. In F. R. Brush & J. B. Overmier (Eds.),

Affect, conditioning, and cognition: Essays on the determinants of behavior. Hillsdale, NJ: Erlbaum.

MAIER, S. F., & SELIGMAN, M. E. P. (1976). Learned helplessness: Theory and evidence. *Journal of Experimental Psychology, 105,* 3–46.

MAIER, S. F., SELIGMAN, M. E. P., & SOLOMON, R. L. (1969). Pavlovian fear conditioning and learned helplessness. In B. A. Campbell & R. M. Church (Eds.), *Punishment.* New York: Appleton-Century-Crofts.

MAIER, S. F., WATKINS, L. R., & FLESHNER, M. (1994). Psychoneuroimmuninology: The interface between behavior, brain, and immunity. *American Psychologist, 49,* 1004–1007.

MALAMUTH, N. M., & DONNERSTEIN, E. (1984). *Pornography and sexual aggression.* New York: Academic Press.

MANDERLINK, G., & HARACKIEWICZ, J. M. (1984). Proximal versus distal goal setting and intrinsic motivation. *Journal of Personality and Social Psychology, 47,* 918–928.

MARCO, C. A., & SULS, J. (1993). Daily stress and the trajectory of mood: Spillover, response assimilation, contrast, and chronic negative affectivity. *Journal of Personality and Social Psychology, 64,* 1053–1063.

MARGULES, D. L. (1979). Beta-endorphin and endoloxone: Hormones of the autonomic nervous system for the conservation or expenditure of bodily resources and energy in anticipation of famine or feast. *Neuroscience and Biochemical Reviews, 3,* 155–162.

MARKUS, H., & NURIUS, P. (1986). Possible selves. *American Psychologist, 41,* 954–969.

MARKUS, H., & WOLF, E. (1987). The dynamic self-concept: A social psychological perspective. *Annual Review of Psychology, 38,* 299–337.

MARKUS, H., CROSS, S., & WURF, E. (1990). The role of the self system in competence. In R. J. Sternberg & J. Kolligian, Jr. (Eds.), *Competence considered* (pp. 205–225). New Haven, CT: Yale University Press.

MARSHALL, G. N., WORTMAN, C. B., KUSULAS, J. W., HERVIG, L. K., & VICKERS, R. R., JR. (1992). Distinguishing optimism from pessimism: Relations to fundamental dimensions of mood and personality. *Journal of Personality and Social Psychology, 62,* 1067–1074.

MARTIN, R. A., & LEFCOURT, H. M. (1983). The sense of humor as a moderator of the relation between stressors and moods. *Journal of Personality and Social Psychology, 45,* 1313–1324.

MASCOLO, M. F., & FISCHER, K. W. (1995). Developmental transformations in appraisals for pride, shame, and guilt. In J. P. Tangney, & K. W. Fischer (Eds.) *Self-conscious emotions: The psychology of shame, guilt, embarrassment, and pride.* New York: Guilford Press.

MASLOW, A. H. (1943). A theory of human motivation. *Psychological Review, 50,* 370–396.

MASLOW, A. H. (1954). *Motivation and personality.* New York: Harper & Row.

MASLOW, A. H. (1970). *Motivation and personality* (2nd ed.). New York: Harper & Row.

MASON, J. W. (1975). Emotions as reflected in patterns of endocrine integration. In L. Levi (Ed.), *Emotions: Their parameters and measurement*. New York: Raven Press.

MASON, J. W., BRADY, J. V., & TOLSON, W. W. (1966). Behavioral adaptations and endocrine activity. In R. Levine (Ed.), *Endocrines and the central nervous system: Proceedings of the Association for Research in Nervous and Mental Diseases* (pp. 227–250). Baltimore: Williams & Wilkins.

MASON, J. W., MAHER, J. T., HARTLEY, L. H., MOUGEY, E. H., PERLOW, M. J., & JONES, L. G. (1976). Selectivity of corticosteroid and catecholamine responses to various natural stimuli. In G. Serban (Ed.), *Psychopathology of human adaptation* (pp. 147–172). New York: Plenum.

MASSERMAN, J. H., & YUM, K. S. (1946). An analysis of the influence of alcohol on experimental neuroses in cats. *Psychosomatic Medicine, 8*, 36–52.

MASTERS, W. H., & JOHNSON, V. E. (1966). *Human sexual response*. Boston: Little, Brown.

MASTERS, W. H., & JOHNSON, V. E. (1975). *The pleasure bond: A new look at sexuality and commitment*. Boston: Little, Brown.

MASTERS, M. S., & SANDERS, B. (1993). Is the gender difference in mental rotation disappearing? *Behavior Genetics, 23*, 337–341.

MATTHEWS, G., DAVIES, D. R., & LEES, J. L. (1990). Arousal, extraversion, and individual differences in resource availability. *Journal of Personality and Social Psychology, 59*, 150–168.

MATTHEWS, K. A., GLASS, D. C., ROSENMAN, R. H., & BORTNER, R. W. (1977). Competitive drive, pattern A, and coronary heart disease: A further analysis of some data from the Western Collaborative Group Study. *Journal of Chronic Disease, 30*, 489–498.

MAY, R. B. (1963). Stimulus selection of preschool children under conditions of free choice. *Perceptual and Motor Skills, 16*, 203–206.

MAY, R. (1983). *The meaning of anxiety*. New York: Norton.

MAYER, J. (1955). Regulation of energy intake and the body weight: The glucostatic theory and lipostatic hypothesis. *Annals of the New York Academy of Sciences, 63*, 15–43.

McARDLE, W. D., KATCH, F. I., & KATCH, V. L. (1991). *Exercise physiology*. Philadelphia: Lea & Febiger.

McCLELLAND, D. C. (1985). *Human motivation*. Glenview, IL: Scott, Foresman.

McCLELLAND, D. C. (1989). Motivational factors in health and disease. *American Psychologist, 44*, 675–683.

McCLELLAND, D. C., ATKINSON, J. W., CLARK, R. A., & LOWELL, E. L. (1953). *The achievement motive*. New York: Appleton-Century-Crofts.

McCLELLAND, D. C., & PILON, D. A. (1983). Sources of adult motives in patterns of parent behavior in early childhood. *Journal of Personality and Social Psychology, 44*, 564–574.

McCLELLAND, D. C., ROSS, G., & PATEL, V. (1985). The effect of an academic examination on salivary norepineph-rine and immunoglobulin levels. *Journal of Human Stress, 11*, 52–59.

McCRAE, R. R. (1987). Creativity, divergent thinking and openness to experience. *Journal of Personality and Social Psychology, 52*, 1258–1265.

McCRAE, R. R., & COSTA, P. T., JR. (1987). Validation of the five-factor model of personality across instruments and observers. *Journal of Personality and Social Psychology, 52*, 81–90.

McFARLAND, C., ROSS, M., & DeCOURVILLE, N. (1989). Women's theories of menstruation and biases in recall of menstrual symptoms. *Journal of Personality and Social Psychology, 57*, 522–531.

McGRATH, M. J., & COHEN, D. B. (1978). REM sleep facilitation of adaptive waking behavior. A review of the literature. *Psychological Bulletin, 85*, 24–57.

McGRAW, K. O., & McCULLERS, J. C. (1974). The distracting effect of material reward: An alternative explanation for superior performance of reward groups in probability learning. *Journal of Experimental Child Psychology, 18*, 149–158.

McGRAW, K. O., & McCULLERS, J. C. (1975, September). *Some detrimental effects of reward on laboratory task performance*. Paper presented at the meeting of the American Psychological Association, Chicago.

McNALLY, R. J. (1996). Cognitive bias in the anxiety disorders. In R. A. Dienstier (Ed.). *Perspectives on anxiety, panic, and fear. Nebraska Symposium on Motivation* (Vol. 43, pp. 211–250). Lincoln: University of Nebraska Press.

McPARTLAND, R. J., & KUPFER, D. J. (1978). Rapid eye movement sleep cycle, clock time, and sleep onset. *Electroencephalography and Clinical Neurophysiology, 45*, 178–185.

MEICHENBAUM, D. H. (1977). *Cognitive-behavior modification: An integrative approach*. New York: Plenum Press.

MEYER, L. B. (1961). *Emotion and meaning in music*. Chicago: University of Chicago Press.

MEYER, W. U. (1982). Indirect communications about perceived ability estimates. *Journal of Educational Psychology, 74*, 888–897.

MIKULA, G., PETRI, B., & TANZER, N. (1989). What people regard as unjust: Types and structures of everyday experiences of injustice. *European Journal of Social Psychology, 20*, 133–149.

MILGRAM, S. (1963). Behavioral study of obedience. *Journal of Abnormal and Social Psychology, 67*, 371–378.

MILGRAM, S. (1974). *Obedience to authority*. New York: Harper & Row.

MILLER, D. G., GROSSMAN, Z. D., RICHARDSON, R. L., WISTOW, B. W., & THOMAS, F. D. (1978). Effect of signaled versus unsignaled stress on rat myocardium. *Psychosomatic Medicine, 40*, 432–434.

MILLER, G. A. (1956). The magical number seven, plus or minus two: Some limits on our capacity for processing information. *Psychological Review, 63*, 81–97.

MILLER, G. A., GALANTER, E., & PRIBRAM, K. H. (1960). *Plans and structure of behavior.* New York: Holt.

MILLER, I. W., III, & NORMAN, W. H. (1979). Learned helplessness in humans: A review and attribution-theory model. *Psychological Bulletin, 86,* 93–118.

MILLER, L. B., & ESTES, B. W. (1961). Monetary reward and motivation in discrimination learning. *Journal of Experimental Psychology, 61,* 501–504.

MILLER, N. E. (1941). The frustration-aggression hypothesis. *Psychological Review, 48,* 337–342.

MILLER, N. E. (1951). Learnable drives and rewards. In S. S. Stevens (Ed.), *Handbook of experimental psychology* (pp. 435–472). New York: Wiley.

MILLER, N. E. (1980). Effects of learning on physical symptoms produced by psychological stress. In H. Selye (Ed.), *Selye's guide to stress research* (Vol. 1). New York: Van Nostrand Reinhold.

MILLER, P. A., & EISENBERG, N. (1988). The relation of empathy to aggressive and externalizing/antisocial behavior. *Psychological Bulletin, 103,* 324–344.

MILLER, W. R. (1983). Controlled drinking: A history and critical review. *Journal of Studies on Alcohol, 44,* 68–83.

MILLER, W.. R., & MUÑOZ, R. F. (1976). *How to control your drinking.* Englewood Cliffs, NJ: Prentice-Hall.

MILLER, W. R., & SELIGMAN, M. E. P. (1975). Depression and learned helplessness in man. *Journal of Abnormal Psychology, 84,* 228–238.

MILLS, J. H. (1975). Noise and children: A review of literature. *Journal of Acoustical Society of America, 58,* 767–779.

MILLS, J. H. (1978). Effects of noise on young and old people. In D. M. Lipscomb (Ed.), *Noise and audiology* (pp. 229–241). Baltimore: University Park Press.

MILSTEIN, R. M. (1980). Responsiveness in newborn infants of overweight and normal weight parents. *Appetite, 1,* 65–74.

MINEKA, S. (1985). Animal models of anxiety-based disorders: Their usefulness and limitations. In A. Tuma & J. Maser (Eds.), *Anxiety and anxiety disorders* (pp. 199–244). Hillsdale, NJ: Erlbaum.

MISCHEL, W. (1961). Delay of gratification, need for achievement, and acquiescence in another culture. *Journal of Abnormal and Social Psychology, 62,* 543–552.

Models of addiction [Special issue]. (1988, May). *Journal of Abnormal Psychology.*

MOISEEVA, N. I. (1979). The significance of different sleep states for the regulation of electrical brain activity in man. *Electroencephalography and Clinical Neurophysiology, 46,* 371–381.

MONEY, J. (1980). *Love and love sickness.* Baltimore, MD: Johns Hopkins University Press.

MONEY, J. (1987a). Propaedeutics of diecious G-I/R: Theoretical foundations for understanding dimorphic gender-identity/role. In J. Reinisch, L. A. Rosenblum, & S. A. Sanders (Eds.), *Masculinity/femininity: Basic perspectives* (pp. 13–28). New York: Oxford University Press.

MONEY, J. (1987b). Sin, sickness, or status: Homosexual gender identity and psychoneuroendocrinology. *American Psychologist, 42,* 384–399.

MONEY, J., SCHWARTZ, M., & LEWIS, V. (1984). Adult erotosexual status and fetal hormonal masculinization and demasculinization: 46 XX congenital virilizing adrenal hyperphasia and 46 XY androgen-insensitivity syndrome compared. *Psychoneuroendocrinology, 9,* 203–207.

MOOK, D. G. (1963). Oral and postingestional determinants of the intake of various solutions in rats with esophageal fistulas. *Journal of Comparative and Physiological Psychology, 56,* 645–659.

MORGAN, W. P., & HORSTMAN, D. H. (1976). Anxiety reduction following acute physical activity. *Medicine and Science in Sports, 8,* 62.

MORGANE, P. J., & STERN, W. C. (1975). The role of serotonin and norepinephrine in sleep-waking activity. *National Institute on Drug Abuse, Research Monograph Series,* No. 3, 37–61.

MORRIS, D. (1969). *The naked ape.* New York: Dell.

MORRISON, A. R. (1983). A window on the sleeping brain. *Scientific American, 248,* 94–102.

MORSE, D. R., MARTIN, J. S., FURST, M. L., & DUBIN, L. L. (1977). A physiological and subjective evaluation of meditation, hypnosis, and relaxation. *Psychosomatic Medicine, 39,* 304–324.

MORTON, J. H., ADDITION, H., ADDISON, R. G., HUNT, L., & SULLIVAN, J. J. (1953). A clinical study of premenstrual tension. *American Journal of Obstetrics and Gynecology, 65,* 1182–1191.

MORUZZI, G., & MAGOUN, H. W. (1949). Brain stem reticular formation and activation of the EEG. *Electroencephalography and Clinical Neurophysiology, 1,* 455–473.

MOSES, J. M., JOHNSON, L. C., NAITOH, P., & LUBIN, A. (1975). Sleep stage deprivation and total sleep loss: Effects on sleep behavior. *Psychophysiology, 12,* 141–146.

MOSES, J. M., LUBIN, A., NAITOH, P., & JOHNSON, L. C. (1978). Circadian variation in performance, subjective sleepiness, sleep, and oral temperature during an altered sleep-wake schedule. *Biological Psychology, 6,* 301–308.

MOSES, J. M., NAITOH, P., & JOHNSON, L. C. (1978). The REM cycle in altered sleep/wake schedules. *Psychophysiology, 15,* 569–575.

MOSHER, D. L., & ABRAMSON, P. R. (1955). Subjective sexual arousal to films of masturbation. *Journal of Consulting and Clinical Psychology, 45,* 796–807.

MOSSHOLDER, K. W. (1980). Effects of externally mediated goals setting on intrinsic motivation: A laboratory experiment. *Journal of Applied Psychology, 65,* 202–210.

MOUNT, G. R., WALTERS, S. R., ROWLAND, R. W., BARNES, P. R., & PAYTON, T. I. (1978). The effects of relaxation techniques on normal blood pressure. *Behavioral Engineering, 5(1),* 1–4.

MOYER, K. E. (1976). *The psychobiology of aggression.* New York: Harper & Row.

MOYER, K. (1987). *Violence and aggression. A physiological perspective.* New York: Paragon House.

MULLANEY, D. J., JOHNSON, L. C., NAITOH, P., FRIEDMANN, J. K., & GLOBUS, G. G. (1977). Sleep during and after gradual sleep reduction. *Psychophysiology, 14,* 237–244.

MUMFORD, M. D., & GUSTAFSON, S. B. (1988). Creativity syndrome: Integration, application, and innovation. *Psychological Bulletin, 103,* 27–43.

MUNSINGER, H., & KESSEN, W. (1964). Uncertainty, structure, and preference. *Psychological Monographs, 78* (9, Whole No. 586).

MURRAY, H. A. (1938). *Explorations in personality.* New York: Oxford University Press.

NACHMAN, M. (1970). Learned taste and temperature aversions due to lithium chloride sickness after temporal delays. *Journal of Comparative and Physiological Psychology, 73,* 22–30.

NAKAZAWA, Y., KOTORII, M., KOTORII, T., TACHIBANA, H., & NAKANO, T. (1975). Individual differences in compensatory rebound of REM sleep with particular reference to their relationship to personality and behavioral characteristics. *Journal of Nervous and Mental Disease, 161,* 18–25.

National Academy of Sciences, National Research Council. (1989). *Diet and health: Implications for reducing chronic disease risk.* Washington, DC: National Academy Press.

National Advisory Mental Health Council. (1995). Basic behavioral science research for mental health: A national investment: Emotion and motivation. *American Psychologist, 50,* 838–845.

National Commission on the Causes and Prevention of Violence. (1970). *Crime.* Washington, DC: U.S. Government Printing Office.

NAVON, D., & GOPHER, D. (1979). On the economy of the human processing system. *Psychological Review, 86,* 214–255.

NEISS, R. (1988). Reconceptualizing arousal: Psychological states in motor performance. *Psychological Bulletin, 103,* 345–366.

NEISSER, U., BOODOO, G., BOUCHARD, T. J., JR., BOYKIN, A. W., BRODY, N., CECI, S. J., HALPERN, D. F., LOEHLIN, J. C., PERLOFF, R., STERNBERG, R. J., & URBINA, S. (1996). Intelligence: Knowns and unknowns. *American Psychologist, 51,* 77–101.

NEZU, A. M., NEZU, C. M., & BLISSETT, S. E. (1988). Sense of humor as a moderator of the relation between stressful events and psychological distress: A prospective analysis. *Journal of Personality and Social Psychology, 54,* 520–525.

NICHOLLS, J. G. (1984). Achievement motivation: Conceptions of ability, subjective experience, task choice, and performance. *Psychological Review, 91,* 328–346.

NICHOLLS, J. (1989). *The competitive ethos and democratic education.* Cambridge, MA: Harvard University Press.

NICHOLLS, J. G. (1990). What is ability and why are we mindful of it? A developmental perspective. In R. J. Sternberg & J. Kolligian, Jr. (Eds.), *Competence considered* (pp. 11–40). New Haven, CT: Yale University Press.

NICHOLS, J. R. (1965). How opiates change behavior. *Scientific American, 212*(2), 80–88.

NISBETT, R. E. (1968). Taste, deprivation, and weight determinants of eating behavior. *Journal of Personality and Social Psychology, 10,* 107–116.

NISBETT, R. E., & SCHACHTER, S. (1966). Cognitive manipulation of pain. *Journal of Experimental Social Psychology, 2,* 227–236.

NISHIHARA, K., MORI, K., ENDO, S., OHTA, T., & KENSHIRO, O. (1985). Relationship between sleep efficiency and urinary excretions of catecholamines in bed-rested humans. *Sleep, 8,* 110–117.

NOLEN-HOEKSEMA, S. (1987). Sex differences in depression: Theory and evidence. *Psychological Bulletin, 101,* 259–282.

NOLEN-HOEKSEMA, S. (1990). *Sex differences in depression.* Stanford: Stanford University Press.

NORMAN, D. A., & BOBROW, D. B. (1975). On data-limited and resource-limited processes. *Cognitive Psychology, 7,* 44–64.

NOVACO, R. W. (1985). Anger and its therapeutic regulation. In M. A. Chesney and R. H. Rosenman (Eds.), *Anger and hostility in cardiovascular and behavioral disorders* (pp. 139–147). Washington, DC: Hemisphere.

NUTTIN, J. R. (1984). *Motivation, planning and action: A relational theory of behavior dynamics.* Hillsdale, NJ: Erlbaum.

O'BRIEN, M. (1987). *Vince: A personal history of Vince Lombardi.* New York: Morrow.

O'LEARY, A. (1990). Stress, emotion, and human immune function. *Psychological Bulletin, 108,* 363–382.

OLDS, J. (1955). Physiological mechanisms of reward. In M. R. Jones (Ed.), Nebraska Symposium on Motivation (Vol. 3). Lincoln: Nebraska.

OLDS, J., & MILNER, P. (1954). Positive reinforcement produced by electrical stimulation of the septal area and other regions of the rat brain. *Journal of Comparative and Physiological Psychology, 47,* 419–427.

ONIANI, T. N. (1984). Does paradoxical sleep deprivation disturb memory trace consolidation? *Physiology and Behavior, 33,* 687–692.

ORNSTEIN, R., & SOBEL, D. (1987, March). The healing brain. *Psychology Today,* pp. 48–52.

ORY, M., & GOLDBERG, E. (1983). Pet ownership and life satisfaction in elderly women. In A. H. Katcher & A. Beck (Eds.), *New perspectives on our life with companion animals* (pp. 803–817). Philadelphia: University of Pennsylvania Press.

OSBORN, C. A., & POLLACK, R. H. (1977). The effects of two types of erotic literature on physiological and verbal measures of female sexual arousal. *Journal of Sex Research, 13,* 250–256.

OSBORNE, F. E. (1996). *Self: An eclectic approach.* Boston: Allyn & Bacon.

OSTROVE, N. (1978). Expectations for success on effort-determined tasks as a function of incentive and performance feedback. *Journal of Personality and Social Psychology, 36,* 909–916.

OVERMIER, J. B., & SELIGMAN, M. E. P. (1967). Effects of inescapable shock on subsequent escape and avoidance responding. *Journal of Comparative and Physiological Psychology, 63,* 28–33.

OWENS, W. A. (1969). Cognitive, noncognitive and environmental correlates of mechanical ingenuity. *Journal of Applied Psychology, 53,* 199–208.

OZER, E., & BANDURA, A. (1990). Mechanisms governing empowerment effects: A self-efficacy analysis. *Journal of Personality and Social Psychology, 58,* 472–486.

PADILLA, A. M., PADILLA, C., KETTERER, T., & GIACALONE, D. (1970). Inescapable shocks and subsequent escape/avoidance conditioning in goldfish *(Carassius auratus). Psychonomic Science, 20,* 295–296.

PALLAK, M., & PITTMAN, T. (1972). General motivational effects of dissonance arousal. *Journal of Personality and Social Psychology, 21,* 349–358.

PAMUK, E. R., WILLIAMSON, D. F., SERDULA, M. K., MADANS, J., & BYERS, T. E. (1993). Weight loss and subsequent death in a cohort of U.S. adults. *Annals of Internal Medicine, 119,* 744–748.

PANKSEPP, J., SIVIY, S. M., & NORMANSELL, L. A. (1985). Brain opioids and social emotions. In M. Reite & T. Field (Eds.), *The psychobiology of attachment and separation* (pp. 3–49). New York: Academic Press.

PARKES, K. R. (1984). Locus of control, cognitive appraisal, and coping in stressful episodes. *Journal of Personality and Social Psychology, 46,* 655–668.

PARLEE, M. B. (1973). The premenstrual syndrome. *Psychological Bulletin, 80,* 454–465.

PARMEGGIANI, P. L. (1977). Interaction between sleep and thermoregulation. *Waking and Sleeping, 1*(2), 123–132.

PATON, W. D. M., & CROWN, J. (Eds.). (1972). *Cannabis and its derivatives: Pharmacology and experimental psychology: Symposium proceedings.* London: Oxford University Press.

PATTERSON, G. R. (1976). The aggressive child: Victim and architect of a coercive system. In E. J. Mash, L. A. Hamerlynck, & L. C. Handy (Eds.), *Behavior modification and families* (pp. 267–316). New York: Brunner/Mazel.

PATTERSON, G. R. (1980). Mothers: The unacknowledged victims. *Monograph of the Society for Research in Child Development,* No. 45.

PATTERSON, G. R., DeBARYSHE, B. D., & RAMSEY, E. (1989). A developmental perspective on antisocial behavior. *American Psychologist, 44,* 329–335.

PAVLOV, I. P. (1927). *Conditioned reflexes* (G. V. Anrep, Trans.). New York: Dover.

PECK, M. S. (1988). *The different drum: Community making and peace.* Simon & Schuster.

PEDERSEN, N. L., GATZ, M., PLOMIN, R., NESSELROADE, J. R., & McCLEARN, G. E. (1989). Individual differences in locus of control during the second half of the life span for identical and fraternal twins reared apart and reared together. *Journal of Gerontology, 44,* 100–105.

PEELE, S. (1982). Love, sex, drugs and other magical solutions to life. *Journal of Psychoactive Drugs, 14,* 125–131.

PEELE, S. (1983, September/October). Out of the habit trap. *American Health,* pp. 42–47.

PEELE, S. (1984). The cultural context of psychological approaches to alcoholism. *American Psychologist, 39,* 1337–1351.

PEELE, S. (1985). *The meaning of addiction.* Lexington, MA: Lexington.

PEELE, S. (1989). *Diseasing of America: Addiction treatment out of control.* Lexington, MA: Lexington.

PEELE, S., & BRODSKY, A. (1991). *The truth about addiction and recovery.* New York: Fireside.

PELHAM, B. W., & NETER, E. (1995). The effect of motivation of judgment depends on the difficulty of the judgment. *Journal of Personality and Social Psychology, 68,* 581–594.

PENDERY, M. L., MALTZMAN, L. M., & WEST, L. J. (1982). Controlled drinking by alcoholics? Findings and a reevaluation of a major affirmative study. *Science, 217,* 160–175.

PENNEBAKER, J. W. (1989). Confession, inhibition, and disease. In L. Berkowitz (Ed.), *Advances in experimental social psychology* (Vol. 22, pp. 211–244). Orlando, FL: Academic Press.

PENNEBAKER, J. W. (1990). *Opening up: The healing power of confiding in others.* New York: Avon Books.

PENNEBAKER, J. W. (1992). Inhibition as the linchpin. In H. S. Friedman (Ed.), *Hostility, coping and health* (pp. 127–139). Washington, DC: American Psychological Association.

PERVIN, L. A. (Ed.). (1989). Goal concepts in personality and social psychology. Hillsdale, NJ: Erlbaum.

PETERS, T. J., & WATERMAN, R. H., JR. (1982). *In search of excellence.* New York: Harper & Row.

PETERSEN, A. C., COMPAS, B. E., BROOKS-GUNN, J., STEMMLER, M., EY, S., & GRANT, K. E. (1993). Depression in adolescence. *American Psychologist, 48,* 155–168.

PETERSEN, C., & SELIGMAN, M. (1984). Causal explanations as a risk factor for depression: Theory and evidence. *Psychological Review, 91,* 347–374.

PETERSON, C., SELIGMAN, M., & VAILLANT, G. (1988). Pessimistic explanatory style as a risk factor for physical illness: A thirty-five-year longitudinal study. *Journal of Personality and Social Psychology, 55,* 23–27.

PETERSEN, S. E., FOX, P. T., POSNER, M. L., MINTUN, M., & RAICHLE, M. E. (1988). Positron emission tomography studies of the cortical anatomy of single-world processing. *Nature, 331,* 585–589.

PFAFFMAN, C. (1960). The pleasures of sensation. *Psychological Review, 67,* 253–268.

PIAGET, J. (1970). Piaget's theory. In P. H. Mussen (Ed.), *Carmichael's manual of child psychology* (Vol. 1, 3rd ed., pp. 703–732). New York: Wiley.

PIAGET, J. (1952). *The origins of intelligence in children.* New York: International Universities Press.

PICKENS, R. (1968). Self administration of stimulants by rats. *International Journal of Addiction, 3,* 215–221.

PIETROPINTO, A., & SIMENAUER, J. (1977). *Beyond the male myth: What women want to know about men's sexuality.* New York: Times Books.

PINEL, J. P. J. (1993). *Biopsychology.* Boston: Allyn & Bacon.

PITTS, F. N., JR. (1969). The biochemistry of anxiety. *Scientific American, 220*(2), 69–75.

PIVIK, T., & FOULKES, D. (1966). Dream deprivation: Effects on dream content. *Science, 153,* 1282–1284.

PLOTKIN, W. B. (1978). Long-term eyes-closed alpha-enhancement training: Effects on alpha amplitudes and on experiential state. *Psychophysiology, 15,* 40–52.

POLIVY, J. (1976). Perception of calories and regulation of intake in restrained and unrestrained subjects. *Addictive Behavior, 1,* 237–243.

POLIVY, J., & HERMAN, C. P. (1983). *Breaking the diet habit: The natural weight alternative.* New York: Basic Books.

POLIVY, J., HERMAN, C. P., HACKETT, R., & KULESHNYK, I. (1986). The effects of self-attention and public attention on eating in restrained and unrestrained subjects. *Journal of Personality and Social Psychology, 50,* 1253–1260.

POSNER, M. I.; PETERSON, S. E., FOX, P. T., & RAICHLE, M. E. (1988). Localization of cognitive operations in the human brain. *Science, 240,* 1627–1631.

POST, R. M., LAKE, C. R., JIMERSON, D. C., BUNNEY, W. E., WOOD, J. H., ZIEGLER, M. C., & GOODWIN, E. K. (1978). Cerebrospinal fluid norepinephrine in affective illness. *American Journal of Psychiatry, 135,* 907–912.

POWERS, P. S. (1982). Obesity: Psychosomatic illness review: No. 2. *Psychosomatics, 23,* 1027–1039.

PRIBRAM, K. H. (1976). Self-consciousness and intentionality. In G. E. Schwartz & D. Shapiro (Eds.), *Consciousness and self-regulation: Advances in research* (Vol. 1). New York: Plenum.

QUADAGNO, D. M., BRISCO, R., & QUADAGNO, J. S. (1977). Effects of perinatal gonadal hormones on selected nonsexual behavior patterns: A critical assessment of the nonhuman and human literature. *Psychological Bulletin, 82,* 62–80.

QUIRCE, C. M., ODIO, M., & SOLANO, J. M. (1981). The effects of predictable and unpredictable schedules of physical restraint upon rats. *Life Sciences, 28,* 1897–1902.

RABINOWITZ, D., & ZIERLER, K. L. (1962). Forearm metabolism in obesity and its response to intra-arterial insulin: Characterization of insulin resistance and evidence for adaptive hyperinsulinism. *Journal of Clinical Investigation, 41,* 2173–2181.

RAICHLE, M. I. (1988). Modern imaging approaches to human learning and memory: Establishing a basis for understanding the damaged brain. In *Plasticity and Path-ology in the Damaged Brain.* The Second Annual Bristol-Myers Squibb Symposium on Neuroscience Research. University of California, San Diego. Raven Health Care Communications.

RAMÍREZ, E., MALDONADO, A., & MARTOS, R. (1992). Attributions modulate immunization against learned helplessness in humans. *Journal of Personality and Social Psychology, 62,* 139–146.

RAPOPORT, J. L. (1989a, March). The biology of obsessions and compulsions. *Scientific American.*

RAPOPORT, J. L. (1989b). *The boy who couldn't stop washing: The experience and treatment of obsessive-compulsive disorder.* New York: E. P. Dutton.

RAYNOR, J. O. (1974). Future orientation in the study of achievement motivation. In J. W. Atkinson & J. O. Raynor (Eds.), *Motivation and achievement* (pp. 121–154). Washington, DC: Winston.

REICHE, R., & DANNECKER, M. (1977). Male homosexuality in West Germany: A sociological investigation. *Journal of Sex Research, 13,* 35–53.

REID, R. L., & YEN, S. S. (1983). Premenstrual syndrome. *American Journal of Obstetrics and Gynecology, 139,* 85–104.

REISENZEIN, R. (1994). Pleasure-arousal theory and the intensity of emotions. *Journal of Personality and Social Psychology, 67,* 525–539.

RELICH, J. D. (1983). *Attribution and its relation to other affective variables in predicting and inducing arithmetic achievement.* Unpublished doctoral dissertation, University of Sydney, Australia.

RESCORLA, R. A. (1988). Pavlovian conditioning: It's not what you think it is. *American Psychologist, 43,* 151–169.

RESNICK, S. M., BERENBAUM, S. A., GOTTESMAN, I. I., & BOUCHARD, T. J., JR. (1986). Early hormonal influences on cognitive functioning in congenital adrenal hyperphasia. *Developmental Psychology, 22,* 191–198.

RICHARDSON, G. S., CARSKADON, M. A., ORAV, E. J., & DEMENT, W. C. (1982). Circadian variations in elderly and young adult subjects. *Sleep, 5,* S82–S94.

ROBERTS, G. C., & TREASURE, D. C. (1994). Parental goal orientations and beliefs about the competitive-sports experience. *Journal of Applied Social Psychology, 24,* 631–645.

ROBINS, L. N., DAVIS, D. H., & GOODWIN, D. W. (1974). Drug use by U.S. Army enlisted men in Vietnam: A follow-up on their return home. *American Journal of Epidemiology, 99,* 235–249.

ROBINS, L. N., & PRZYBECK, T. R. (1985). Age of onset of drug use as a factor in drug and other disorders. In C. L. Jones & R. J. Battjes (Eds.), *Etiology of drug abuse* (pp. 178–192). Rockville, MD: National Institute of Drug Abuse.

RODIN, J. (1981). Current status of the internal-external hypothesis for obesity. *American Psychologist, 36,* 361–372.

RODIN, J. (1984). Effects of food choice on amount of food eaten in a subsequent meal: Implications for weight gain. In J. Hirsch and T. B. Van Itallie (Eds.), *Recent advances in obesity research* (Vol. 4). Lancaster, PA: Technomic.

RODIN, J., & LANGER, E. J. (1977). Long-term effects of a control-relevant intervention with the institutionalized aged. *Journal of Personality and Social Psychology, 35,* 897–902.

RODIN, J., & SLOCHOWER, J. (1976). Externality in the nonobese: Effects of environmental responsiveness on weight. *Journal of Personality and Social Psychology, 33,* 338–344.

RODIN, J., SLOCHOWER, J., & FLEMING, B. (1977). Effects of degree of obesity, age of onset, and weight loss on responsiveness to sensory and external stimuli. *Journal of Comparative and Physiological Psychology, 91,* 586–597.

ROGERS, C. R. (1951). *Client-centered therapy: Its current practice, implications, and theory.* Boston: Houghton Mifflin.

ROGERS, C. R. (1959). A theory of therapy, personality, and interpersonal relationships, as developed in the client-centered framework. In S. Koch (Ed.), *Psychology: A study of a science. Study 1: Conceptual and systematic: Vol. 3. Formulations of the person and the social context* (pp. 184–256). New York: McGraw-Hill.

ROOS, P. E., & COHEN, L. H. (1987). Sex roles and social support as moderators of life stress adjustment. *Journal of Personality and Social Psychology, 52,* 576–585.

ROSE, G. A., & WILLIAMS, R. T. (1961). Metabolic studies on large and small eaters. *British Journal of Nutrition, 15,* 1–9.

ROSEN, B. C., & D'ANDRADE, R. G. (1959). The psychological origins of achievement motivation. *Sociometry, 22,* 185–218.

ROSEN, R. (1979). Some crucial issues concerning children of divorce. *Journal of Divorce, 3,* 19–25.

ROSENFELD, A. H. (1985, June). Depression: Dispelling despair. *Psychology Today, 85,* 29–34.

ROSENMAN, R. H., BRAND, R. J., JENKINS, C. D., FRIEDMAN, M., STRAUS, R., & WURM, M. (1975). Coronary heart disease in the Western Collaborative Group Study: Final follow-up experience of 8½ years. *Journal of the American Medical Association, 233,* 872–877.

ROSENMAN, R. H., FRIEDMAN, M., STRAUS, R., JENKINS, C. D., ZYZANSKL, S. J., & WURM, M. (1970). Coronary heart disease in the Western Collaborative Group Study: A follow-up experience of 4½ years. *Journal of Chronic Disease, 23,* 173–190.

ROSENMAN, R. H., FRIEDMAN, M., STRAUS, R., WURM, M., JENKINS, D., & MESSINGER, H. B. (1966). Coronary heart disease in the Western Collaborative Group Study: A follow-up experience of two years. *Journal of the American Medical Association, 195,* 86–92.

ROSENTHAL, R., & JACOBSON, L. (1968). *Pygmalion in the classroom: Teacher expectations and pupils' intellectual development.* New York: Holt, Rinehart & Winston.

ROSLER, A., & KOHN, G. (1983). Male pseudohermaphroditism due to 17B-hydroxysteroid dehydrogenase deficiency. *Journal of Steroid Biochemistry, 19,* 663–674.

ROSSIER, J., BLOOM, F. E., & GUILLEMIN, R. (1980). Endorphins and stress. In H. Selye (Ed.), *Selye's guide to stress research* (Vol. 1). New York: Van Nostrand Reinhold.

ROTH, T., KRAMER, M., & LUTZ, T. (1976). The effects of sleep deprivation on mood. *Psychiatric Journal of the University of Ottawa, 1,* 136–139.

ROTHBART, M. K., & AHADI, S. A. (1994). Temperament and the development of personality. *Journal of Abnormal Psychology, 103,* 55–66.

ROTTER, J. B. (1954). *Social learning and clinical psychology.* Englewood Cliffs, NJ: Prentice-Hall.

ROTTER, J. B. (1966). Generalized expectancies for internal versus external control of reinforcement. *Psychological Monographs, 80,* 1–28.

ROTTER, J. B. (1972). An introduction to social learning theory. In J. B. Rotter, J. E. Chance, & E. J. Phares (Eds.), *Applications of a social learning theory of personality.* New York: Holt, Rinehart & Winston.

ROUTTENBERG, A. (1968). The two-arousal hypothesis: Reticular formation and limbic system. *Psychological Review, 75,* 51–80.

ROUTTENBERG, A. (1978, November). The reward system of the brain. *Scientific American,* pp. 154-164.

ROWLAND, G. L., FRANKEN, R. E., & HARRISON, K. (1986). Sensation seeking and participation in sporting activities. *Journal of Sports Psychology, 8,* 212–220.

RUBIN, R. T., REINISCH, J. M., & HASKETT, R. F. (1981). Postnatal gonadal steroid effects on human behavior. *Science, 211,* 1318–1324.

RUDERMAN, A. J. (1986). Dietary restraint: A theoretical and empirical review. *Psychological Bulletin, 99,* 247–262.

RULE, B. G., & NESDALE, A. R. (1976). Moral judgments of aggressive behavior. In R. G. Geen & E. C. O'Neal (Eds.), *Perspectives on aggression* (pp. 37–60). San Diego, CA: Academic Press.

RUSHTON, J. P., FULKER, D. W., NEALE, M. C., NIAS, D. K. B., & EYSENCK, H. J. (1986). Altruism and aggression: The heritability of individual differences. *Journal of Personality and Social Psychology, 50,* 1192–1198.

RUSSELL, J. A. (1995). Facial expressions of emotion: What lies beyond minimal universality? *Psychological Bulletin, 118,* 379–391.

SACKETT, G. P. (1965). Effects of rearing conditions upon the behavior of rhesus monkeys *(Macaca mulata). Child Development, 36,* 855–868.

SALKOVSKIS, P. M., CLARK, D. M., & HACKMANN, A. (1991). Treatment of panic attacks using cognitive therapy with exposure or breathing restraining. *Behavior Research and Therapy, 29,* 161–166.

SALTUS, R. (1990, July 6). Sleep. *Calgary Herald.*

SAMUELS, M., & SAMUELS, N. (1975). *Seeing with the mind's eye.* New York: Random House.

SANDAY, P. R. (1981). The sociocultural context of rape: A cross-cultural study. *Journal of Social Issues, 37,* 5–27.

SARASON, B. R., PIERCE, G. R., & SARASON, I. G. (1990). Social support: The sense of acceptance and the role of relationships. In B. R. Sarason, I. G. Sarason, & G. R. Pierce (Eds.), *Social support: An interactional view* (pp. 97–128). New York: Wiley.

SARASON, I. G. (1984). Stress, anxiety, and cognitive interference: Reactions to tests. *Journal of Personality and Social Psychology, 46*, 929–938.

SAUNDERS, D. (1978). *The relationship of attitude variables and explanations of perceived and actual career attainment in male and female businesspersons.* Unpublished doctoral dissertation, University of Texas at Austin.

SCHACHTER, J. (1957). Pain, fear, and anger in hypertensives and normotensives. *Psychosomatic Medicine, 19*, 17–29.

SCHACHTER, S. (1971a). *Emotion, obesity, and crime.* New York: Academic Press.

SCHACHTER, S. (1971b). Some extraordinary facts about obese humans and rats. *American Psychologist, 26*, 129–144.

SCHACHTER, S. (1977). Nicotine regulation in heavy and light smokers. *Journal of Experimental Psychology: General, 106*, 5–12.

SCHACHTER, S., GOLDMAN, R., & GORDON, A. (1968). Effects of fear, food deprivation, and obesity on eating. *Journal of Personality and Social Psychology, 10*, 91–97.

SCHACHTER, S., & GROSS, L. P. (1968). Manipulated time and eating behavior. *Journal of Personality and Psychology, 10*, 98–106.

SCHACHTER, S., KOZLOWSKI, L. T., & SILVERSTEIN, B. (1977). Effects of urinary pH on cigarette smoking. *Journal of Experimental Psychology: General, 106*, 13–19.

SCHACHTER, S., SILVERSTEIN, B., & PERLICK, D. (1977). Psychological and pharmacological explanations of smoking under stress. *Journal of Experimental Psychology. General, 106*, 31–40.

SCHACHTER, S., & SINGER, J. E. (1962). Cognitive, social, and physiological determinants of emotional states. *Psychological Review, 69*, 379–399.

SCHEIER, M. F., & CARVER, C. S. (1985). Optimism, coping and health: Assessment and implications of generalized outcomes expectancies. *Health Psychology, 4*, 210–247.

SCHEIER, M. F., & CARVER, C. S. (1988). A model of behavioral self-regulation: Translating intention into action. In L. Berkowitz (Ed.), *Advances in Experimental Social Psychology* (Vol. 21, pp. 303–346). New York: Academic Press.

SCHEIER, M. F., MATTHEWS, K. A., OWENS, J. F., MAGOVERN, G. J., SR., LEFEBVRE, R. C., ABBOTT, R. A., & CARVER, C. S. (1989). Dispositional optimism and recovery from coronary artery bypass surgery: The beneficial effects on physical and psychological well being. *Journal of Personality and Social Psychology, 57*, 1024–1040.

SCHEIER, M. F., MATTHEWS, K. A., OWENS, J. F., MAGOVERN, G. J., SR., LEFEBVRE, R. C., & SCHIFF, S. R. (1982). Conditioned dopaminergic activity. *Biological Psychiatry, 17*, 135–154.

SCHILDKRAUT, J. J., & KETY, S. S. (1967). Biogenic amines and emotion. *Science, 156*, 21–30.

SCHLEISER-STROPP, B. (1984). Bulimia: A review of the literature. *Psychological Bulletin, 95*, 247–257.

SCHUSTER, T. L., KESSLER, R. C., & ASELTINE, R. H., JR. (1990). Positive interactions, negative interactions, and depressed mood. *American Journal of Community Psychology, 18*, 423–438.

SCHWARTZ, B. (1990). The creation and destruction of value. *American Psychologist, 45*, 7–15.

SCHWARTZ, G. E. (1974, April). The facts of transcendental meditation: Part II. TM relaxes some people and makes them feel better. *Psychology Today*, pp. 39–44.

SCHWARTZ, G. E., DAVIDSON, R. J., & GOLEMAN, D. J. (1978). Patterning of cognitive and somatic processes in the self-regulation of anxiety: Effects of meditation versus exercise. *Psychosomatic Medicine, 40*, 321–328.

SCHWARZER, R., & FUCHS, R. (1995). Changing risk behaviors and adopting health behaviors: The role of self-efficacy beliefs. In A. Bandura (Ed.), *Self-efficacy in changing societies* (pp. 259–288). Cambridge University Press.

SCHWARZER, R., DUNKEL-SCHETTER, C., & KEMENY, M. (1994). The multidimensional nature of received social support in gay men at risk of HIV infection and AIDS. *American Journal of Community Psychology, 22*, 319–339.

SCRIMA, L. (1982). Isolated REM sleep facilitates recall of complex associative information. *Psychophysiology, 19*, 252–259.

SCRIMA, L., BROUDY, M., NAY, K. N., & COHN, M. A. (1982). Increased severity of obstructive sleep apnea after bedtime alcohol ingestion: Diagnostic potential and proposed mechanism of action. *Sleep, 5*, 318–328.

SELIGMAN, M. E. P. (1971). Phobias and preparedness. *Behavior Therapy, 23*, 307–320.

SELIGMAN, M. E. P. (1975). *Helplessness: On depression, development, and death.* San Francisco: W. H. Freeman.

SELIGMAN, M. E. P. (1988, October). Boomer blues. *Psychology Today*, pp. 50-55.

SELIGMAN, M. E. P. (1989). *Why is there so much depression today? The waxing of the individual and the waning of the commons* (G. Stanley Hall Lecture Series, No. 9). Washington DC: American Psychological Association.

SELIGMAN, M. E. P. (1990). *Learned optimism.* New York: Alfred A. Knopf.

SELIGMAN, M. E. P., & MAIER, S. F. (1967). Failure to escape shock. *Journal of Experimental Psychology, 74*, 1–9.

SELIGMAN, M. E. P., MAIER, S. F., & SOLOMON, R. L. (1971). Unpredictable and uncontrollable aversive events. In F. R. Brush (Ed.), *Aversive conditioning and learning* (pp. 347–400). New York: Academic Press.

SELIGMAN, M. E. P., & SCHULMAN, P. (1986). Explanatory style as a predictor of performance as a life insurance agent. *Journal of Personality and Social Psychology, 50*, 832–838.

SELYE, H. (1974). *Stress without distress.* Philadelphia: Lippincott.

SHAINESS, N. A. (1961). A reevaluation of some aspects of femininity through a study of menstruation: A preliminary report. *Comprehensive Psychiatry, 2*, 20–26.

SHAPIRO, D. H., SCHWARTZ, C. E., & ASTIN, J. A. (1996). Controlling ourselves, controlling our world: Psychology's role in understanding positive and negative consequences of seeking and gaining control. *American Psychologist, 51*, 1213–1230.

SHAW, J. (1982). Psychological androgyny and stressful life events. *Journal of Personality and Social Psychology, 43*, 145–153.

SHAYWITZ, B. A., SHAYWITZ, S. E., PUGH, K. R., CONSTABLE, R. T., SKUDLARSKI, P., FULBRIGHT, R. K., BRONEN, R. A., FLETCHER, J. M., SHANKWELLER, D. P., KATZ, L., & GORE, J. C. (1995). Sex differences in the functional organization of the brain for language. *Nature, 373*, 607–609.

SHER, K. J., WALITZER, K. S., WOOD, P. K., & BRENT, E. E. (1991). Characteristics of children of alcoholics: Putative risk factors, substance abuse, and psychopathology. *Journal of Abnormal Psychology, 100*, 427–448.

SHERMAN, I. W., & SHERMAN, V. G. (1989). *Biology: A human approach.* New York: Oxford University Press.

SHODA, Y., MISCHEL, W., & PEAKE, P. K. (1990). Predicting adolescent cognitive and self-regulatory competencies from preschool delay of gratification. *Developmental Psychology, 26*, 978–986.

SHORTELL, J., EPSTEIN, S., & TAYLOR, S. P. (1990). Instigation to aggression as a function of degree of defeat and capacity for massive retaliation. *Journal of Personality, 38*, 313–328.

SHOWERS, C. (1992). Compartmentalization of positive and negative self-knowledge: Keeping bad apples out of the bunch. *Journal of Personality and Social Psychology, 62*, 1036–1049.

SHRAUGER, J. S. (1972). Self-esteem and reactions to being observed by others. *Journal of Personality and Social Psychology, 23*, 192–200.

SIEGEL, J. M. (1979). Reticular formation activity and REM sleep. In R. Drucker-Colin, M. Shkurovich, & M. B. Sterman (Eds.), *The functions of sleep* (pp. 73–97). New York: Academic Press.

SIEGEL, J. M. (1990). Stressful life events and use of physician services among the elderly: The moderating role of pet ownership. *Journal of Personality and Social Psychology, 58*, 1081–1086.

SIEGEL, S. (1979). The role of conditioning in drug tolerance and addiction. In J. D. Keehn (Ed.), *Psychopathology in animals: Research and clinical implications* (pp. 143–168). New York: Academic Press.

SIEGEL, S. (1983). Classical conditioning, drug tolerance, and drug dependence. In R. G. Smart, F. B. Glasser, Y. Israel, H. Kalant, R. E. Popham, & W. Schmidt (Eds.), *Research advances in alcohol and drug problems.* New York: Plenum.

SIGMON, S. T., & SNYDER, C. R. (1990). *Positive and negative affect as a counterexplanation for the relationship between hope and coping strategies.* Unpublished manuscript, University of Kansas, Department of Psychology, Lawrence.

SILVERSTEIN, B., KOZLOWSKI, L. T., & SCHACHTER, S. (1977). Social life, cigarette smoking, and urinary pH. *Journal of Experimental Psychology: General, 106*, 20–23.

SIMON, H. A. (1994). The bottleneck of attention: Connecting thought with motivation. In W. D. Spaulding (Ed.). *Integrative views of motivation, cognition and emotion: Nebraska Symposium on Motivation* (Vol. 41, pp. 1–21). Lincoln: University of Nebraska Press.

SIMON, W., & GAGNON, J. H. (1986). Sexual scripts: Permanence and change. *Archives of Sexual Behavior, 15*, 97–120.

SIMPSON, M. T., OLEWINE, D. A., JENKINS, C. D., RAMSEY, F. H., ZYZANSKI, S. J., THOMAS, G., & HAMES, C. G. (1974). Exercise-induced catecholamines and platelet aggregation in the coronary-prone behavior pattern. *Psychosomatic Medicine, 36*, 476–487.

SKINNER, B. F. (1938). *The behavior of organisms: An experimental analysis.* New York: Appleton-Century-Crofts.

SKINNER, B. F. (1948). *Walden two.* New York: Macmillan.

SKINNER, B. F. (1969). *Contingencies of reinforcement: A theoretical analysis.* New York: Appleton-Century-Crofts.

SKINNER, B. F. (1971). *Beyond freedom and dignity.* New York: Knopf.

SKINNER, H. A., GLASER, F. B., & ANNIS, H. M. (1982). Crossing the threshold: Factors in self-identification as an alcoholic. *British Journal of Addiction, 77*, 51–64.

SLADECZEK, I., & DOMINO, G. (1985). Creativity, sleep and primary process thinking in dreams. *Journal of Creative Behavior, 19*, 38–46.

SLATER, E., & SHIELDS, J. (1969). Genetic aspects of anxiety. *British Journal of Psychiatry, 3*, 62–71.

SMART, R. G. (1965). Effects of alcohol on conflict and avoidance behavior. *Quarterly Journal of Studies on Alcohol, 26*, 187–205.

SMITH, C., & BUTLER, S. (1982). Paradoxical sleep at selective times following training is necessary for learning. *Physiology and Behavior, 29*, 469–473.

SMITH, C., & YOUNG, J. (1980). Reversal of paradoxical sleep deprivation by amygdaloid stimulation during learning. *Physiology and Behavior, 24*, 1035–1039.

SMITH, G. F., & DORFMAN, D. D. (1975). The effect of stimulus uncertainty on the relationship between frequency of exposure and liking. *Journal of Personality and Social Psychology, 31*, 150–155.

SMITH, J. E., CO, C., FREEMAN, M. E., SANDS, M. P., & LANE, J. D. (1980). Neurotransmitter turnover in rat striatum is correlated with morphine self-administration. *Nature, 287*, 152–154.

SMITH, R. E., PTACEK, J. T., & SMOLL, F. L. (1992). Sensation seeking, stress, and adolescent injuries: A test of stress-buffering, risk-taking, and coping skills hypothesis. *Journal of Personality and Social Psychology, 62*, 1016–1024.

SMITH, T. W., & FROHM, K. D. (1985). What's so unhealthy about hostility? Construct validity and psychosocial correlates of the Cook and Medely Ho Scale. *Health Psychology, 4*, 503–520.

SMOLLER, J. W., WADDEN, T. A., & STUNKARD, A. J. (1987). Dieting and depression: A critical review. *Journal of Psychosomatic Research, 31,* 429–440.

SNYDER, C. R., HARRIS, C., ANDERSON, J. R., HOLLERAN, S. A., IRVING, L. M., SIGMON, S. T., YOSHINOBU, L., GIBB, J., LANGELLE, C., & HARNEY, P. (1991). The will and the ways: Development and validation of an individual-differences measure of hope. *Journal of Personality and Social Psychology, 60,* 570–585.

SNYDER, F., SCOTT, J., KARACAN, I., & ANDERSON, D. (1968). Presumptive evidence on REMS deprivation in depressive illness. *Psychophysiology, 4,* 382.

SNYDER, M. (1979). Self-monitoring processes. In L. Berkowitz (Ed.), *Advances in experimental social psychology* (Vol. 12, pp. 85–128). New York: Academic Press.

SNYDER, M., SIMPSON, J. A., & GANGESTAD, S. (1986). Personality and sexual relations. *Journal of Personality and Social Psychology, 51,* 181–190.

SNYDER, S. (1977a). The brain's own opiates. *Chemical and Engineering News, 55*(48), 26–35; 266-271.

SNYDER, S. (1977b). Opiate receptors and internal opiates. *Scientific American, 236*(3), 44–56.

SOBELL, M. B., & SOBELL, L. C. (1976). Second year treatment outcome of alcoholics treated by individualized behavior therapy: Results. *Behavior Research Therapy, 14,* 195–215.

SOLOMON, R. L. (1980). The opponent-process theory of acquired motivation: The costs of pleasure and the benefits of pain. *American Psychologist, 35,* 691–712.

SOLOMON, R. L., & CORBIT, J. D. (1974). An opponent process theory of motivation: I. Temporal dynamics of affect. *Psychological Review, 81,* 119–145.

SORRENTINO, R. M., & HEWITT, E. C. (1984). The uncertainty-reducing properties of achievement tasks revisited. *Journal of Personality and Social Psychology, 47,* 884–899.

SOSTEK, A. J., SOSTEK, A. M., MURPHY, D. L., MARTIN, E. B., & BORN, W. S. (1981). Cord blood amine oxidase activities relate to arousal and motor functioning in human newborns. *Life Sciences, 28,* 2561–2568.

SPEALMAN, R. D., MADRAS, B. K., & BERGMAN, J. (1989). Effects of cocaine and related drugs in nonhuman primates. II. Stimulant effects on schedule-controlled behavior. *Journal of Pharmacology and Experimental Therapeutics, 251,* 142–149.

SPENCE, J. T. (1970). The distracting effects of material reinforcers in the discrimination learning of lower- and middle-class children. *Child Development, 41,* 103–111.

SPENCE, J. T., & HELMREICH, R. L. (1983). Achievement-related motives and behavior. In J. T. Spence (Ed.), *Achievement and achievement motives* (pp. 7–74). San Francisco: W. H. Freeman.

SPIELBERGER, C. D. (1983). *Manual for the State-Trait Anxiety Inventory* (Form V). Palo Alto, CA: Consulting Psychologists Press.

SPIELBERGER, C. D. (1985). Anxiety, cognition, and affect. A state-trait perspective. In A. H. Tuma & J. D. Maser (Eds.), *Anxiety and the anxiety disorders* (pp. 109–130). Hillsdale, NJ: Erlbaum.

SPIELBERGER, C., CRASSER, S. S., & SOLOMON, E. P. (1988). The experience, expression, and control of anger. In M. P. Janisse (Ed.), *Health Psychology: Individual Differences and Stress.* New York: Springer-Verlag.

SPINKS, J. A., BLOWERS, G. H., & SHEK, D. T. L. (1985). The role of the orientating response in the anticipation of information: A skin conductance response study. *Psychophysiology, 22,* 385–394.

STAUB, E. (1996). Cultural-societal roots of violence: The examples of genocidal violence and of contemporary youth violence in the United States. *American Psychologist, 51,* 117–132.

STEELE, C. M., & JOSEPHS, R. A. (1990). Alcohol myopia: Its prized and dangerous effects. *American Psychologist, 45,* 921–933.

STEELE, C. M., & SOUTHWICK, L. (1985). Alcohol and social behavior: 1. The psychology of drunken excess. *Journal of Personality and Social Psychology, 48,* 18–34.

STEIN, L. (1980). The chemistry of reward. In A. Routtenberg (Ed.), *Biology of reinforcement: Facets of brain stimulation reward.* New York: Academic Press.

STEIN, M. I. (1968). Creativity. In F. Bogarta & W. W. Lambert (Eds.), *Handbook of personality theory and research* (pp. 67–89). Chicago: Rand McNally.

STENBERG, C. R., & CAMPOS, J. J. (1990). The development of anger expressions in infancy. In N. Stein, B. Leventhal, & T. Trabasso (Eds.), *Psychological and biological approaches to emotion* (pp. 247–282). Hillsdale, NJ: Erlbaum.

STEPANSKI, E., LAMPHERE, J., BADIA, P., ZORICK, F., & ROTH, T. (1984). Sleep fragmentation and daytime sleepiness. *Sleep, 7,* 18–26.

STERNBERG, R. J. (1991). *Love: The way you want it.* New York: Bantam.

STEWART, J., & KOLB, B. (1988). Cerebral asymmetry and sex. *Behavior and Neural Biology, 49,* 344–360.

STOKOLS, D. (1992a). Conflict-prone and conflict-resistant organizations. In H. S. Friedman (Ed.), *Hostility, coping and health* (pp. 65–75). Washington, DC: American Psychological Association.

STOKOLS, D. (1992b). Establishing and maintaining healthy environments. *American Psychologist, 47,* 6–22.

STORM, C., & STORM, T. (1987). A taxonomic study of the vocabulary of emotions. *Journal of Personality and Social Psychology, 53,* 805–816.

STRICKLAND, B. R. (1989). Internal-external control expectancies: From contingency to creativity. *American Psychologist, 44,* 1–7.

STRIGEL-MOORE, R. H., SILBERSTEIN, L. R., & RODIN, J. (1986). Toward understanding risk factors for bulimia. *American Psychologist, 41,* 246–263.

STROEBE, W., & STROEBE, M. (1987). *Bereavement and health: The psychological and physical consequences of partner loss.* New York: Cambridge University Press.

STROEBE, W., STROEBE, M., ABAKOUMKIN, G., & SCHUT, H. (1996). The role of loneliness and social support in adjustment to loss: A test of attachment theory versus stress theory. *Journal of Personality and Social Psychology, 70,* 1241–1249.

STRYKER, S. (1984). Identity theory: Developments and extensions. In *Self and social structure. Conference on self and identity.* Symposium conducted at the meeting of the British Psychological Society, University College, Cardiff, Wales.

STUART, R. B. (1978). *Act thin, stay thin.* New York: Norton.

STUNKARD, A. J. (1959). Obesity and the denial of hunger. *Psychosomatic Medicine, 21,* 281–289.

STUNKARD, A. J., FOCH, T. T., & HRUBEC, Z. (1986). A twin study of human obesity. *JAMA, 256,* 52–54.

STUNKARD, A. J., SORENSON, T. I. A., HANIS, C., TEASDALE, T. W., CHAKRABORTY, R., SCHULL, W. J., & SCHULSINGER, E. (1986). An adoption study of human obesity. *New England Journal of Medicine, 314,* 193–198.

STURUP, G. K. (1960). Sex offenses: The Scandinavian experience. *Law and Contemporary Problems, 25,* 361–365.

STURUP, G. K. (1968). Treatment of sexual offenders in Herstedvester, Denmark: The rapist. *Acta Psychiatrica Scandinavica, 44*(Suppl. 204).

SUEDFELD, P. (1975). The benefits of boredom: Sensory deprivation reconsidered. *American Scientist, 63,* 60–69.

SUEDFELD, P., & KRISTELLER, J. L. (1982). Stimulus reduction as a technique in health psychology. *Health Psychology, 1,* 337–357.

SULLOWAY, F. J. (1996). *Born to rebel: Birth order, family dynamics and creative lives.* New York: Pantheon Books.

SVEBAK, S., & MURGATROYD, S. (1985). Metamotivational dominance: A multimethod validation of reversal theory constructs. *Personality and Social Psychology, 48,* 107–116.

SWAAB, D. F., & FLIERS, E. A. (1985). A sexually dimorphic nucleus in the human brain. *Science, 228,* 1112–1115.

SWANN, W. B., JR. (1983). Self-verification: Bringing social reality into harmony with the self. In J. Suls & A. G. Greenwals (Eds.), *Social psychological perspectives on the self* (Vol. 2, pp. 33–66). Hillsdale, NJ: Erlbaum.

SWANN, W. B. (1996). *Self-traps: The elusive quest for higher self-esteem.* New York: W. H. Freeman.

SWEENEY, P., ANDERSON, K., & BAILEY, S. (1986). Attributional style in depression: A meta-analytic review. *Journal of Personality and Social Psychology, 50,* 974–991.

SWINSON, R. P., & EAVES, D. (1978). *Alcoholism and addiction.* Estover, Plymouth, England: MacDonald & Evans.

SWITZKY, H. N., & HAYWOOD, H. C. (1974). Motivational orientation and the relative efficacy of self-monitored and externally imposed reinforcement systems in children. *Journal of Personality and Social Psychology, 30,* 360–366.

SYLVA, K., BRUNER, J. S., & GENOVA, P. (1976). The role of play in the problem-solving of children 3–5 years old. In J. S. Bruner, A. Jolly, & K. Sylva (Eds.), *Play: Its role in development and evolution* (pp. 244–257). New York: Penguin.

TAGGART, P., & CARRUTHERS, M. E. (1971). Endogenous hyperlipidaemia induced by emotional stress of race driving. *Lancet, 1,* 363–366.

TALLMAN, J. F., PAUL, S. M., SKOLNICK, P., & GALLAGER, D. W. (1980). Receptors for the age of anxiety: Pharmacology of the benzodiazepines. *Science, 207,* 274–281.

TANGNEY, J. P., BURGGRAF, S. A., & WAGNER, P. E. (1995). Shame-proneness, guilt-proneness, and psychological symptoms. In J. P. Tangney & K. W. Fischer (Eds.), *Self-conscious emotions: The psychology of shame, guilt, embarrassment, and pride* (pp. 343–367). New York: Guilford Press.

TANGNEY, J. P., MILLER, R. S., FLICKER, L., & BARLOW, D. H. (1996). Are shame, guilt, and embarrassment distinct emotions? *Journal of Personality and Social Psychology, 70,* 1256–1269.

TARLER-BENLOLO, L. (1978). The role of relaxation in biofeedback training: A critical review of the literature. *Psychological Bulletin, 85,* 727–755.

TARTER, R. E. (1988). Are there inherited behavior traits that predispose to substance abuse? *Journal of Consulting and Clinical Psychology, 56,* 189–196.

TARTER, R. E., MOSS, H. B., & VANYUKOV, M. M. (1995). Behavior genetic perspective of alcoholism etiology. In H. Begleiter & B. Kissin (Eds.), *Alcohol and alcoholism* (Vol. 1, pp. 294–326). New York: Oxford University Press.

TAUB, J. M. (1977). Behavioral and psychological correlates of a difference in chronic sleep duration. *Biological Psychology, 5,* 29–45.

TAUB, J. M., HAWKINS, D. R., & VAN DE CASTLE, R. L. (1978). Personality characteristics associated with sustained variations in the adult human sleep/wakefulness rhythm. *Waking and Sleeping, 2*(1), 7–15.

TAVRIS, C. (1989). *Anger: The misunderstood emotion.* New York: Simon & Schuster.

TAVRIS, C. (1992). *The mismeasure of woman.* New York: Simon & Schuster.

TAVRIS, C., & WADE, C. (1984). *The longest war: Sex differences in perspective* (2nd ed.). San Diego: Harcourt Brace Jovanovich.

TAYLOR, C. W. (1972). Can organizations be creative too? In C. W. Taylor (Ed.), *Climate for creativity* (pp. 1–15). New York: Pergamon Press.

TAYLOR, S. E. (1983). Adjustment to threatening events: A theory of cognitive adaptation. *American Psychologist, 38,* 1161–1173.

TAYLOR, S. E. (1989). *Positive illusions: Creative self-deception and the healthy mind.* New York: Basic Books.

TAYLOR, S. E. (1990). Health psychology: The science and the field. *American Psychologist, 45,* 40–50.

TAYLOR, S. E., KEMENY, M. E., ASPINWALL, L. G., SCHNEIDER, S. G., RODRIGUEZ, R., & HERBERT, M. (1992). Optimism, coping, psychological distress, and high-risk sexual behavior among men at risk for acquired immunodeficiency syndrome (AIDS). *Journal of Personality and Social Psychology, 63,* 460–473.

TAYLOR, S. P. (1967). Aggressive behavior and physiological arousal as a function of provocation and the tendency to inhibit aggression. *Journal of Personality, 35,* 297–310.

TAYLOR, S. P., & PISANO, R. (1971). Physical aggression as a function of frustration and physical attack. *Journal of Social Psychology, 84,* 261–267.

TEDESCHI, J. T., & FELSON, R. B. (1994). *Violence, aggression and coercive action.* Washington, DC: American Psychological Association.

TEGANO, D. W., MORAN, D. J., III, & SAWYERS, J. K. (1991). *Creativity in early childhood classrooms.* Washington, DC: National Education Association.

TEITELBAUM, P. (1961). Disturbances in feeding and drinking behavior after hypothalamic lesions. In M. R. Jones (Ed.), *Nebraska Symposium on Motivation* (Vol. 9, pp. 39–68). Lincoln: University of Nebraska Press.

TELLEGEN, A., BOUCHARD, T. J., WILCOX, K. J., SEGAL, N. L., LYKKEN, D. T., & RICH, S. (1988). Personality similarities in twins reared apart and together. *Journal of Personality and Social Psychology, 54,* 1031–1039.

TERRACE, H. S. (1969). Extinction of a discriminative operant following discrimination learning with and without errors. *Journal of the Experimental Analysis of Behavior, 12,* 571–582.

TESSER, A., & PAULHUS, D. L. (1976). Toward a causal model of love. *Journal of Personality and Social Psychology, 34,* 1095–1105.

THARP, G. D. (1975). The role of glucocorticoids in exercise. *Medicine and Science in Sports, 7,* 6–11.

THOMAS, A., CHESS, S., & BIRCH, H. G. (1970, August). The origins of personality. *Scientific American, 223,* 102–109.

THOMAS, H. (1966). Preference for random shapes: Ages six through nineteen years. *Child Development, 37,* 843–859.

THOMPSON, R. A. (1990). Emotion and self-regulation. In *Nebraska Symposium on Motivation 1988: Socioemotional development* (Vol. 36, pp. 367–467). Lincoln: University of Nebraska Press.

THORNDIKE, E. L. (1913). *Educational psychology: The psychology of learning* (Vol. 2). New York: Teachers College Press.

TIGER, L. (1979). *Optimism: The biology of hope.* New York: Simon & Schuster.

TILLEY, A. J. (1985). Recovery sleep at different times of the night following loss of the last four hours of sleep. *Sleep, 8,* 129–136.

TILLICH, P. (1965). The right to hope. *The University of Chicago Magazine, 58,* 16–22.

TOCH, H. (1969). *Violent men.* Chicago: Aldine.

TOCH, H. (1992). *Violent men: A psychological inquiry into the psychology of violence.* Washington, DC: American Psychological Association.

TOLMAN, E. C. (1932). *Purposive behavior in animals and men.* New York: Appleton-Century-Crofts.

TOMAKA, J., & BLASCOVICH, J. (1994). Effects of justice beliefs on cognitive appraisal of, and subjective, physiological, and behavioral responses to, potential stress. *Journal of Personality and Social Psychology, 67,* 732–740.

TOMPOROWSKI, P. D., & ELLIS, N. R. (1986). Effects of exercise on cognitive processes: A review. *Psychological Bulletin, 99,* 338–346.

TORRENCE, E. P. (1965). *Rewarding creative behavior.* Englewood Cliffs, NJ: Prentice-Hall.

TRACY, R. L., & TRACY, L. N. (1974). Reports of mental activity from sleep stages 2 and 4. *Perceptual and Motor Skills, 38,* 647–648.

TROGERSEN, S. Genetic factors in anxiety disorders. *Archives of General Psychiatry, 40,* 1085–1089.

TROLLINGER, L. M. (1979). *A study of the* biographical and personality factors of creative women in music. Unpublished doctoral dissertation, Temple University, Philadelphia, PA.

TURKINGTON, C. (1992). Depression seen induced by decline in NE levels. *APA Monitor, 13,* 11.

TSUDA, A., & HIRAI, H. (1975). Effects of the amount of required coping response tasks on gastrointestinal lesions in rats. *Japanese Psychological Research, 17,* 119–132.

TYLER, L. E. (1978). *Individuality.* San Francisco: Jossey-Bass.

UNGER, R. K. (1985). Personal appearance and social control. In M. Safir, M. Mednick, L. Dafna, & J. Bernard (Eds.), *Women's worlds: From the new scholarship* (pp. 142–151). New York: Praeger.

VAILLANT, G. E. (1983). *The natural history of alcoholism.* Cambridge: Harvard University Press.

VAILLANT, G. L. (1977). *Adaptation to life.* New York: Wiley.

VAN DYKE, C., & BYCK, R. (1982). Cocaine. *Scientific American, 246,* 128–141.

VAUX, A. (1992). Assessment of social support. In H. O. F. Veiel & U. Baumann (Eds.), *The meaning and measurement of social support* (pp. 193–216). New York: Hemisphere.

VEIEL, H. O. F., & BAUMANN, U. (1992). The many meanings of social support. In H. O. F. Veiel & U. Baumann (Eds.), *The meaning and measurement of social support* (pp. 1–9). New York: Hemisphere.

VEREBY, V., & BLUM, K. (1979). Alcohol euphoria, possible mediation via endorphinergic mechanisms. *Journal of Psychedelic Drugs, 11,* 305–311.

VERNIKOS-DANELLIS, J., & HEYBACH, J. P. (1980). Psychophysiologic mechanisms regulating the hypothalamic-pituitary-adrenal response to stress. In H. Selye (Ed.), *Selye's guide to stress research* (Vol. 1, pp. 206–251). New York: Van Nostrand Reinhold.

VEZINA, P., KALIVAS, P. W., & STEWART, J. (1987). Sensitization occurs to the locomotor effects of morphine and the specific μ opioid receptor agonist DAGO, administered repeatedly to the ventral tegmental area but not to the nucleus accumbens. *Brain Research, 417,* 51–58.

VISINTAINER, M., VOLPICELLI, J., & SELIGMAN, M. (1982). Tumor rejection in rats after inescapable and escapable shock. *Science, 216,* 437–439.

VITZ, P. (1966a). Affect as a function of stimulus variation. *Journal of Experimental Psychology, 71,* 74–79.

VITZ, P. (1966b). Preference for different amounts of stimulus complexity. *Behavioral Science, 11,* 105–114.

VOGEL, G. W. (1975). A review of REM sleep deprivation. *Archives of General Psychiatry, 32,* 749–761.

VOGEL, G. W. (1978). Sleep-onset mentation. In A. M. Arkin, J. S. Antrobus, & S. J. Ellman (Eds.), *The mind in sleep: Psychology and psychophysiology* (pp. 97–108). Hillsdale, NJ: Erlbaum.

VOGEL, G. W. (1979). A motivational theory of REM sleep. In R. Drucker-Colin, M. Shkurovich, & M. B. Sterman (Eds.), *The functions of sleep* (pp. 233–250). New York: Academic Press.

VOLPICELLI, J. R. (1987). Uncontrollable events and alcohol drinking. *British Journal of Addiction, 82,* 385–396.

VOYER, D., VOYER, S., & BRYDEN, M. P. (1995). Magnitude of sex differences in spatial abilities: A meta-analysis and consideration of critical variables. *Psychological Bulletin, 117,* 250–270.

VREVEN, R., & NUTTIN, J. R. (1976). Frequency perception of successes as a function of results previously obtained by others and by oneself. *Journal of Personality and Social Psychology, 34,* 734–745.

WALKER, E. L. (1974, September). *Psychological complexity and aesthetics, or the hedgehog as an aesthetic mediator (HAM).* Invited address to American Psychological Association convention, New Orleans.

WALKER, L. E. A. (1989). Psychology and violence against women. *American Psychologist, 44,* 695–702.

WALLACE, R. K., & BENSON, H. (1972, February). The physiology of meditation. *Scientific American,* pp. 84–90.

WALLACE, R. K., BENSON, H., & WILSON, A. F. (1971). A wakeful hypometabolic physiologic state. *American Journal of Physiology, 221,* 795–799.

WANNAMETHEE, G., & SHAPER, A. G. (1990). Weight changes in middle-aged British men: Implications for health. *European Journal of Clinical Nutrition, 44,* 133–142.

WATERMAN, A. S. (1993). Two conceptions of happiness: Contrasts of personal expressiveness (eudaimonia) and hedonic enjoyment. *Journal of Personality and Social Psychology, 64,* 678–691.

WATSON, D., & CLARK, L. A. (1984). Negative affectivity: The disposition to experience aversive emotional states. *Psychological Bulletin, 96,* 465–490.

WATSON, J. B., & MORGAN, J. J. B. (1917). Emotional reactions and psychological experimentation. *American Journal of Psychology, 28,* 163–174.

WEBB, W. B. (1975). *Sleep: The gentle tyrant.* Englewood Cliffs, NJ: Prentice-Hall.

WEBB, W. B. (1979). Theories of sleep functions and some clinical implications. In R. Drucker-Colin, M. Shkurovich, & M. B. Sterman (Eds.), *The functions of sleep* (pp. 19–35). New York: Academic Press.

WEBB, W. B., & AGNEW, H. W., JR. (1975a). Are we chronically sleep deprived? *Bulletin of the Psychonomic Society, 6,* 47–48.

WEBB, W. B., & AGNEW, H. W., JR. (1975b). Sleep efficiency for sleep-wake cycles of varied length. *Psychophysiology, 12,* 637–641.

WEBB, W. B., & AGNEW, H. W., JR. (1977). Analysis of the sleep stages in sleep-wakefulness regimens of varied length. *Psychophysiology, 14,* 445–450.

WEBB, W. B., & FRIEL, J. (1971). Sleep stage and personality characteristics of "natural" long and short sleepers. *Science, 171,* 587–588.

WEBB, W. B., & LEVY, C. M. (1982). Age, sleep deprivation, and performance.

WEGNER, D. M. (1989). *White bears and other unwanted thoughts.* New York: Viking/Penguin.

WEIDNER, G., SEXTON, G., McLELLARN, R., CONNOR, S. L., & MATARAZZO, J. D. (1987). The role of Type A behavior and hostility in an elevation of plasma lipids in adult women and men. *Psychosomatic Medicine, 49,* 136–145.

WEINER, B. (Ed.). (1972a). *Attribution: Perceiving the causes of behavior.* Morristown, NJ: General Learning Press.

WEINER, B. (1972b). *Theories of motivation: From mechanism to cognition.* Chicago: Markham.

WEINER, B. (Ed.). (1974). *Achievement motivation and attribution theory.* Morristown, NJ: General Learning Press.

WEINER, B. (1979). A theory of motivation for some classroom experiences. *Journal of Educational Psychology, 71,* 3–25.

WEINER, B. (1991). On perceiving the other as responsible. In R. A. Dienstbier (Ed.), *Nebraska Symposium on Motivation (1990): Perspectives on Motivation* (pp. 165–198). Lincoln: University of Nebraska Press.

WEINER, B. (1995). *Judgments of responsibility.* New York: Guilford Press.

WEINER, B., FRIEZE, I., KUKLA, A., REED, L., REST, S., & ROSENBAUM, R. M. (1971). *Perceiving the causes of success and failure.* Morristown, NJ: General Learning Press.

WEINER, B., & KUKLA, A. (1970). An attributional analysis of achievement motivation. *Journal of Personality and Social Psychology, 15,* 1–20.

WEINER, B., & POTEPAN, P. A. (1970). Personality characteristics and affective reactions towards exams of superior and failing college students. *Journal of Educational Psychology, 61,* 144–151.

WEINGBERGER, D. A. (1990). The construct validity of the repressive coping style. In J. L. Singer (Ed.), *Repression and dissociation* (pp. 337–386). Chicago: University of Chicago Press.

WEISS, J. M. (1968). Effects of coping responses on stress. *Journal of Comparative and Physiological Psychology, 65,* 251–260.

WEISS, J. M. (1970). Somatic effects of predictable and unpredictable shock. *Psychosomatic Medicine, 32,* 397–408.

WEISS, J. M. (1971a). Effects of coping behavior in different warning signal conditions on stress pathology in rats. *Journal of Comparative and Physiological Psychology, 77*, 1–13.

WEISS, J. M. (1971b). Effects of punishing the coping response (conflict) on stress pathology in rats. *Journal of Comparative and Physiological Psychology, 77*, 14–21.

WEISS, J. M. (1971c). Effects of coping behavior with and without a feedback signal on stress pathology in rats. *Journal of Comparative and Physiological Psychology, 77*, 22–30.

WEISS, J. M., GLAZER, H. L., & POHORECKY, L. A. (1976). Coping behavior and neurochemical changes: An alternative explanation of the original "learned helplessness" experiments. In G. Serban & A. Kling (Eds.), *Animal models in human psychobiology* (pp. 141–173). New York: Plenum.

WEISS, J. M., GLAZER, H. L., POHORECKY, L. A., BRICK, J., & MILLER, N. E. (1975). Effects of chronic exposure to stressors on avoidance-escape behavior and on brain norepinephrine. *Psychosomatic Medicine, 37*, 522–534.

WEISS, J. M., STONE, E. A., & HARRELL, N. W. (1970). Coping behavior and brain norepinephrine level in rats. *Journal of Comparative and Physiological Psychology, 72*, 153–160.

WEISS, M. (1958). Alcohol as a depressant of psychological conflict in rats. *Quarterly Journal of Studies on Alcohol, 19*, 226–237.

WEISSMAN, M. M., LEAR, P. F., HOLZER, C. E., III, MEYERS, J. K., & TISCHLER, G. L. (1984). The epidemiology of depression: An update on sex differences in rates. *Journal of Affective Disorders, 7*, 179–188.

WENDER, P. H., KETY, S. S., ROSENTHAL, D., SCHULSINGER, F., ORTMANN, J., & LUNDE, I. (1986). Psychiatric disorders in the biological and adoptive families of adopted individuals with affective disorders. *Archives of General Psychiatry, 43*, 923–929.

WHALEN, R. E. (1976). Brain mechanisms controlling sexual behavior. In F. A. Beach (Ed.), *Human sexuality in four perspectives* (pp. 215–246). Baltimore: Johns Hopkins University Press.

WHITAM, F. L. (1977). The homosexual role. A reconsideration. *Journal of Sex Research, 13*, 1–11.

WHITAM, F. L., & MATHY, R. M. (1986). *Male homosexuality in four societies.* New York: Praeger.

WHITE, A., HANDLER, P., & SMITH, E. L. (1964). *Principles of biochemistry* (3rd ed.). New York: McGraw-Hill.

WHITE, J. (1982). *Rejection.* Reading, MA: Addison-Wesley.

WHITE, J. A., ISMAIL, A. H., & BOTTOMS, G. D. (1976). Effects of physical fitness on the adrenocortical response to exercise stress. *Medicine and Science in Sports, 8*, 113–118.

WHITE, R. W. (1959). Motivation reconsidered: The concept of competence. *Psychological Review, 66*, 297–333.

WICKENS, C. D. (1984). Processing resources in attention. In R. Parasuraman & D. R. Davies (Eds.), *Varieties of attention* (pp. 63–102). New York: Academic Press.

WIDOM, C. S. (1989a). Does violence beget violence? A critical examination of the literature. *Psychological Bulletin, 106*, 3–28.

WIDOM, C. S. (1989b). The cycle of violence. *Science, 224*, 160–166.

WIEBE, D. J. (1989). Hardiness and stress moderation: A test of proposed mechanisms. *Journal of Personality and Social Psychology, 60*, 89–99.

WIKLER, A. (1980). *Opioid dependence.* New York: Plenum.

WILLIAMS, G. C., GROW, V. M., FREEDMAN, Z. R., RYAN, R. M., & DECI, E. L. (1996). Motivational predictors of weight loss and weight-loss maintenance. *Journal of Personality and Social Psychology, 70*, 115–126.

WILLIAMS, R. (1989). *The trusting heart: Great news about Type A behavior.* New York: Random House.

WILLIAMS, R. H. (1960). Hypoglycemosis. In R. H. Williams (Ed.), *Diabetes.* New York: Hoeber.

WILLS, T. (1981). Downward comparison principles in social psychology. *Psychological Bulletin, 90*, 245–271.

WILLS, T. (1991). Similarity and downward comparison. In J. Suls & T. Wills (Eds.), *Social comparison: Contemporary theory and research* (pp. 51–78). Hillsdale, NJ: Erlbaum.

WILLS, T. A., DuHAMEL, K., & VACCARO, D. (1995). Activity and mood temperament as predictors of adolescent substance use: Test of a self-regulation mediational model. *Journal of Personality and Social Psychology, 68*, 901–916.

WILLS, T. A., VACCARO, D., & McNAMARA, G. (1992). The role of life events, family support, and competence in adolescent substance use: A test of vulnerability and protective factors. *American Journal of Community Psychology, 20*, 349–374.

WILLS, T. A., VACCARO, D., & McNAMARA, G. (1994). Novelty seeking, risk taking, and related constructs as predictors of adolescent substance use: An application of Cloninger's theory. *Journal of Substance Abuse, 6*, 1–20.

WILM, E. C. (1925). *The theories of instinct: A study of the history of psychology.* New Haven, CT: Yale University Press.

WILSON, G. T. (1981). The effect of alcohol on human sexual behavior. In N. Mello (Ed.), *Advances in substance abuse: Behavioral and biological research.* Greenwich, CT: JAI Press.

WILSON, J. D. (1981). The hormonal control of sexual development. *Science, 211*, 1278–1284.

WILSON, T. D., & LINVILLE, P. W. (1985). Improving the performance of college freshmen with attributional techniques. *Journal of Personality and Social Psychology, 49*, 287–293.

WILSON, T. D., & SCHOOLER, J. W. (1991). Thinking too much: Introspection can reduce the quality of preferences and decisions. *Journal of Personality and Social Psychology, 60*, 181–192.

WINTERBOTTOM, M. R. (1958). The relation of need for achievement to learning experiences in independence and mastery. In J. W. Atkinson (Ed.), *Motives in fantasy, action, and society* (pp. 453–478). Princeton, NJ: Van Nostrand.

WISE, C. D., & STEIN, L. (1969). Facilitation of brain self-stimulation by central administration of norepinephrine. *Science, 163*, 299–301.

WISE, R. A. (1988). The neurobiology of craving: Implications for the understanding and treatment of addiction. *Journal of Abnormal Psychology, 97*, 118–132.

WISE, R. A., & BOZARTH, M. A. (1987). A psychomotor stimulant theory of addiction. *Psychological Review, 94*, 469–492.

WOLFGANG, M. E., & STROHM, R. B. (1956). The relationship between alcohol and criminal homicide. *Quarterly Journal of Studies on Alcohol, 17*, 108–123.

WOLPE, J. (1969). *The practice of behavior theory.* New York: Pergamon Press.

WONG, W. P. T., & WEINER, B. (1981). When people ask "why" questions, and the heuristics of attributional search. *Journal of Personality and Social Psychology, 40*, 650–663.

WONNACOTT, S. (1992). Bath University, England.

WOOD, J. V., SALTZBERG, J. A., NEALE, J. M., STONE, A. A., & RACHMIEL, T. B. (1990). Self-focused attention, coping responses, and distressed mood in everyday life. *Journal of Personality and Social Psychology, 58*, 1027–1036.

WOODS, J. H., KATZ, J. L., & WINGER, G. (1987). Abuse liability of benzodiazepines. *Pharmacological Review, 39*, 251–413.

WOOLEY, S. C., & GARNER, D. M. (1991). Obesity treatment: The high cost of false hope. *Journal of the American Dietetic Association, 91*, 1248–1251.

WORICK, W. W., & SCHALLER, W. E. (1977). *Alcohol, tobacco, and drugs: Their uses and abuses.* Englewood Cliffs, NJ: Prentice-Hall.

WRIGHT, R. A., TOI, M., & BREHM, J. W. (1984). Difficulty and interpersonal attraction. *Motivation and Emotion, 8*, 327–341.

WURTMAN, R. J. (1982). Nutrients that modify brain function. *Scientific American, 246*, 50–59.

YATES, W. R., PERRY, P., & MURRAY, S. (1992). Aggression and hostility in anabolic steroid users. *Biological Psychiatry, 31*, 1232–1234.

YOSHINOBU, L. R. (1989). Construct validation of the Hope Scale: Agency and pathways components. University of Kansas, Lawrence.

YOUNG, J. P. R., FENTON, G. W., & LADER, M. H. (1971). Inheritance of neurotic traits: A twin study of the Middlesex Hospital Questionnaire. *British Journal of Psychiatry, 119*, 393–398.

YOUNG, J. S. (1988). *Steve Jobs: The Journey is the Reward.* Glenview, IL: Scott, Foresman.

YOUNG, P. T. (1975). *Understanding your feelings and emotions.* Englewood Cliffs, NJ: Prentice-Hall.

ZAHN-WAXLER, C., & KOCHANSKA, G. (1990). The origins of guilt. In *Nebraska Symposium on Motivation (1988): Socioemotional Development* (Vol. 36, pp. 183–258). Lincoln: University of Nebraska Press.

ZEKI, S. (1992, September). The visual image in mind and brain. *Scientific American,* pp. 69–76.

ZENTALL, S. S., & ZENTALL, T. R. (1983). Optimal stimulation: A model of disordered activity and performance in normal and deviant children. *Psychological Bulletin, 94*, 446–471.

ZILBERGELD, B. (1978). *Mate sexuality: A guide to sexual fulfillment.* Boston: Little Brown.

ZILLMAN, D., KATCHER, A. H., & MILAVSKY, B. (1972). Excitation transfer from physical exercise to subsequent aggressive behavior. *Journal of Experimental Social Psychology, 8*, 247–259.

ZIMBARDO, P. G. (1969). The human choice: Individuation, reason, and order versus deindividuation, impulse, and chaos. In W. J. Arnold & D. Levine (Eds.), *Nebraska Symposium on Motivation* (Vol. 17, pp. 237–307). Lincoln: University of Nebraska Press.

ZIMBARDO, P. G. (1972). Pathology of imprisonment. *Society, 9*, 4–8.

ZUCKERMAN, H. (1974). The scientific elite: Nobel laureates' mutual influence. In R. S. Albert (Ed.), *Genius and eminence* (pp. 171–186). New York: Pergamon Press.

ZUCKERMAN, M. (1978a, February). The search for high sensation. *Psychology Today,* pp. 38–46; 96–99.

ZUCKERMAN, M. (1978b). Sensation seeking. In H. London & J. E. Exner, Jr. (Eds.), *Dimensions of personality* (pp. 487–559). New York: Wiley.

ZUCKERMAN, M. (1979). *Sensation seeking: Beyond the optimal level of arousal.* Hillsdale, NJ: Erlbaum.

ZUCKERMAN, M. (1983). *Biological bases of sensation seeking, impulsivity, and anxiety.* Hillsdale, NJ: Erlbaum.

ZUCKERMAN, M. (1994). *Behavioral expressions and biosocial bases of sensation seeking.* Cambridge: Cambridge University Press.

ZUCKERMAN, M., BUCHSBAUM, M. S., & MURPHY, D. L. (1980). Sensation seeking and its biological correlates. *Psychological Bulletin, 88*, 187–214.

Author Index

Aarons, L., 146
Abakoumkin, G., 257
Abelson, H., 88
Abplanalp, J., 215
Abramson, P. R., 88
Abramson, L. Y., 289, 291, 318
Addison, R. G., 215
Addition, H., 215
Adelson, S. F., 61
Agnew H. W., Jr., 50, 148, 150, 160, 169, 170
Agyei, .Y, 85, 105
Ahadi, S. A., 180, 181
Ainsworth, M. D. S., 330
Åkerstedt, T., 148, 151
Akil, H., 246
Alexander, R., 183, 186
Allen, L. S., 102, 103, 105
Allen, M. B., Jr., 130
Alloy, L. B., 291, 318
Allred, K. D., 263
American Cancer Society, 267
American Psychiatric Association, 291
Amsel, A., 6, 13, 219, 240
Andersen, B. L., 247, 267, 268, 269
Anderson, A. S., 77
Anderson, D., 156
Anderson, J. R., 326
Anderson, K., 291
Andrews, F. M., 356
Angell, M., 330
Annis, H. M., 201
Antrobus, J. S., 167
Apfelbaum, M., 75
Apter, M. J., 119, 120, 122, 142
Arand, D., 165
Arkes, H. R., 341
Arkin, A. M., 167
Armitage, A. K., 194
Aron, A., 94
Aron, E. N., 94
Aronson, E., 44
Aschoff, J., 147
Aseltine, R. H., Jr., 329
Aserinsky, E., 145
Astin, J. A., 366
Atkinson, J. W., 25, 46, 240, 370, 373, 374
Averill, J. R., 94, 227, 250, 366
Ax, A. F., 233

Baekeland, F., 49, 149
Badia, P., 172
Bahlburg, 106
Bailey, J. M., 85, 105, 108
Bailey, S., 291
Bakalar, J. B., 194
Bales, R., 202
Banaji, M. R., 200
Bancroft, J. A., 98
Bandura, A., 2, 14, 21, 39, 48, 104, 221, 240, 266, 308, 309, 312–317, 366, 369–370, 381, 392–396, 399, 401, 402
Banji, M. R., 225
Barchas, J. D., 246
Barchas, P., 314, 315, 327
Barclay, L. C., 387
Bardwick, J. M., 214
Bargh, J. A., 44, 47
Barlow, D. H., 118, 119, 121, 125, 126, 128, 274, 276, 297, 316, 383
Barnes, G., 179
Barnes, G. E., 92
Barnes, P. R., 261
Baron, R. A., 210–211, 219
Baron, R. S., 270
Barr, T., 188
Barron, F., 356
Barry, H., III, 198
Barsalou, L. W., 362
Basic Behavioral Science Task Force of the National Advisory Mental Health Council, 37
Basow, S. A., 91, 215
Baum, A., 255
Baumann, U., 257
Baumetister, R. F., 326
Baumgardner, A. H., 386, 406
Beach, F. A., 99, 102
Beane, W. E., 137, 139
Beary, J. F., 261
Beck, A. T., 127, 128, 280, 281, 292–296, 301, 320, 411
Becker, M., 203
Becker, W. C., 219
Beecher, H., 184
Bell, A., 107
Bell, P. A., 160
Bellah, R. N., 282
Bem, D. J., 134

Benbow, C. P., 99, 100
Benet, V., 18
Benson, H., 124, 192, 261, 262, 270
Bentler, P. M., 102, 352
Berenbaum, S. A., 106
Bergeman, C. S., 214
Bergman, J., 188
Berkowitz, L., 14, 209, 212, 219–220, 221, 229
Berlyne, D. E., 18, 53, 117, 118, 131, 240, 306, 310, 341, 342, 343, 344, 347, 353, 355, 371, 409
Bernardis, L. L., 66
Bernstein, A. G., 377
Berrebi, A. S., 103
Bertilson, H. S., 211
Bettelheim, B., 327
Bexton, W. H., 118
Bieber, I., 107
Bierhoff, H. W., 227
Bindra, D. A., 189
Birch, D., 25, 240
Birch, H. G., 339
Bixler, E. O., 172
Blakelock, E. H., 234
Blanchards, F. A., 67
Blaney, P. H., 383
Blascovich, J., 269
Blatt, S. J., 280, 293
Blehar, M. C., 330
Blissett, S. E., 265
Blix, A. S., 306
Bloom, F. E., 130, 191, 246
Bloom, G., 251
Bloomfield, H. H., 261
Blowers, G. H., 131
Blum, K., 196
Blumenthal, J. A., 234
Bobrow, D. B., 33, 37
Bohman, M., 180
Bolger, N., 135, 257
Bolles, R. C., 183, 246, 287
Bonanno, G. A., 257
Bond, C. F., 197
Bonnet, M. H., 152, 153
Bonvallet, M., 130
Boothroyd, P., 94
Borden, R. J., 211
Boring, E. G., 12

Born, W. S., 2
Bortner, R. W., 233
Bosveld, J., 164
Bottoms, G. D., 49
Bouchard, T. J., Jr., 106
Bowen, R., 211
Bower, G. H., 398, 399
Bowlby, J., 257, 330
Boykin, A. W., 341
Bozarth, M. A., 194
Bradshaw, G. F., 357
Brady, J. V., 250, 288, 308, 309, 311
Brain, P. F., 214
Brain, P. H., 216
Bray, G. A., 56, 77
Brehm, J. W., 94
Bremer, J., 214
Brent, E. E., 179
Brick, J., 251
Brickman, P., 377
Brief, A. P., 279, 280
Brittain, T. M., 288
Brockner, J., 383, 388
Brodsky, A., 187
Brooks-Gunn, J., 91
Broudy, M., 172
Broughton, R., 149
Brouillard, M. E., 312
Broussard, D. B., 90
Brown, D. A., 134
Brown, D. J., 124, 138, 139, 254
Brown, J. D., 261
Brownell, K. D., 56, 76, 77
Bruner, J. S., 44, 348
Bryden, M. P., 99
Buchanan, D. C., 250
Buchsbaum, M. S., 153, 188
Bunney, W. E., 153
Burggraf, S. A., 381
Burnstein, E., 219
Bushman, B. J., 222
Business Week, 358
Buss. A. H., 213, 216, 219, 235
Buss, D. M., 7, 209
Butcher, A. H., 279, 280
Butler, A. C., 293, 338
Butler, S., 157
Buunk, B. P., 254
Byck, R., 188, 189
Byers, T. E., 77
Byrne, D., 88, 91, 160

Cacioppo, J. T., 133
Cahalan, D., 198
Cain, E. N., 261, 269
Cameron, J., 346, 356
Campbell, J. D., 386, 406
Campion, M. A., 397
Campos, J. J., 209
Carlson, E. R., 88
Carlson, N. R., 285, 286
Carlson, S., 248

Cass, M., 106
Carroll, J. L., 35
Carruthers, M. E., 234, 306
Carskadon, M. A., 150, 151, 155
Cartwright, R., 164
Cartwright, R. D., 158, 159, 167
Carver, C. S., 139, 318, 324, 326, 383, 397, 409
Cass, V. C., 109
Castaldo, V., 158, 159
Cattell, R. B., 17, 353
Cauthen, N. R., 261
Cervone, C., 394, 395
Chai, Y. M., 102
Chambers, J., 346
Chambless, D. L., 277
Chandra, R. K., 268
Chassler, S., 91
Check, J. V. P., 92
Chen, A., 229
Chesney, A. P., 233
Chess, S., 339
Chiu, L., 102
Chorpita, B. F., 118, 125, 276
Christiansen, K., 99
Churchill, A. C., 399
Cioffi, D., 312
Clark, D. C., 67
Clark, D. M., 277
Clark, L. A., 4, 119, 127, 277, 407
Clark, R. A., 370, 373
Clarke, D. H., 49
Climie, R. J., 222
Cloninger, C. R., 180
Coccaro, E. F., 214
Cohen, D. B., 152, 157, 158, 160, 164
Cohen, L., 264
Cohen, L. H., 263
Cohen, R., 88
Cohen, S., 204, 205, 243, 246, 329
Cohn, M. A., 172
Colditz, G. A., 77
Coleman, C. E. H., 88
Coleman, R. M., 153
Collins, D. L., 255
Condry, J. C., 346, 348
Conger, J. J., 197–199
Connor, S. L., 233
Cooper, J., 133
Cooper, J. R., 130, 191
Cooper, M. L., 178
Coopersmith, S., 385–386
Copeland, P. M., 105
Corbit, J. D., 50, 176
Costa, P. T., Jr., 17, 233
Costello, C. G., 284
Cox, W. M., 202, 205
Coyne, J. C., 254
Craighead, W. E., 407
Crandall, C. S., 77
Cratty, B. J., 137, 401
Crawford, A. M., 327

Crawford, J. D., 66
Crick, C., 164
Crick, F., 35, 42, 401–402
Crolye, R., 133
Cross, S., 405
Crown, J., 193
Csikszentmihalyi, M., 414
Culbertson, F. M., 292
Cuthbert, B., 262
Czaya, J., 165

D'Andrade, R. G., 372
D'emilio, J., 90
Dalton, K., 215
Dank, B., 107
Dannecker, M., 107
Darwin, C., 9, 10
Daubman, K. A., 356
Davidson, J. M., 261
Davies, D. R., 117
Davies, S., 158
Davis, B., 49, 65, 188
Davis, C. M., 61
Davis, D. H., 185
Davis, V. E., 196
Davison, G. C., 257
De Courville, N., 215
De Koninck, J., 149, 160
De Rivera, T., 25, 240
De Simone, D., 99
De Tocqueville, A., 282
De Wied, D., 245
DeBaryshe, B. D., 181
Debono, E., 354, 355, 359, 360, 361
Deci, E. L., 6, 76, 282, 346, 349, 380, 387, 403, 404, 410, 411, 412
DeGood, D. E., 288
Delongis, A., 254
Dember, W. N., 18, 337, 341, 342, 346, 371, 396
Dembroski, T. M., 233, 234
Dement, W. C., 145, 150, 151, 155, 156, 169
Denenberg, V. H., 339
Dengerink, H. A., 211
Derubeis, R. J., 281
Descartes, R., 8, 9
Devine, P. G., 133
Dey, F., 52
Diamond, M. C., 101, 102
Dilalla, L. F., 221
Dinges, D. F., 151, 152, 153, 154
Dodson, J. D., 117
Dodge, K. A., 280
Dohler, K-D., 106
Dole, V. P., 184, 185
Dominick, J. R., 222
Domino, G., 361
Donnerstein, E. I., 222, 223
Doob, A. N., 222
Doosje, B. J., 253
Dorfman, D. D., 340, 341
Dowling, C., 79

Dowling, G. A., 101
Drolette, M. E., 233
Dubbert, P. M., 268
Dubin, L. L., 251
DuHamel, K., 180, 181
Dunkel-Schetter, C., 254, 257
Dunne, E., 312
Durden-Smith, J., 99
Durkee, A., 213
Dweck, C. S., 44, 140, 324, 375, 376–378,
    382, 385–386, 403, 407, 411, 412
Dwyer, J., 367
Dykstra, L., 183, 191

Eagly, A. H., 103, 104, 216
Earl, R. W., 18, 337, 338, 341, 342, 346,
    371, 396
Easterbrook, J. A., 120, 121, 123, 124, 131,
    142, 348
Eaves, D., 175, 176, 188, 193, 199, 281
Eaves, L. J., 124, 196, 329
Eden, A., 67
Edwards, W., 21
Ehrhardt, A. A., 106, 109
Eisenberg, N., 231
Eisenberger, R., 346, 356
Ekman, P., 241, 265
Elkin, R., 123, 131, 141
Elliot, A. J., 133
Elliott, E. E., 377
Ellis, A., 320, 321, 399
Ellis, N. R., 50
Ellman, S. J., 154, 155, 157, 162, 167
Ely, R. J., 67
Emmons, R. A., 257
Emrick, C. D., 201, 204
Endo, S., 148
Engle, K. B., 197
Epstein, S., 44, 211, 242, 257, 258, 259, 260,
    266, 269, 274, 300, 301, 313, 400, 402,
    406, 407, 411, 413
Erikson, E. H., 403
Eron, L. D., 222, 229
Erskine, H., 310
Ervin, F. R., 62
Estes, B. W., 346
Evans, G. E., 368
Evans, M. D., 281
Eysenck, H. J., 17, 50, 91, 92, 117, 124, 125,
    128, 143, 194, 197, 213, 257

Falk, J. L., 187
Fanselow, M. S., 183, 246
Farber, J. 167
Farkas, G. M., 198
Farley, F. H., 350, 351, 352
Fausto-Sterling, A., 105, 215
Fava, M., 183
Feinberg, I., 159
Feldman, R. S., 377
Felson, R. B., 209, 213, 220, 223, 225, 229
Felten, D. L., 248

Felten, S. Y., 248
Fenigstein, A., 221, 222
Fennema, E., 99
Fenton, G. W., 124
Fenwick, P. B., 261
Fenz, W. D., 313
Fern, R. W., 52
Feshbach, S., 231
Festinger, L., 44, 133, 134, 349
Fey, S. G., 261, 262
Fincher, J., 184
Fischer, K. W., 380, 381
Fischman, J., 234
Fisher, H., 93
Fisher, W. A., 88
Fishman, S. M., 192
Fleming, B., 71
Fleshner, M., 246, 247
Flicker, L., 297
Fliers, E. A., 101
Florian, V., 263, 269
Foch, T. T., 64
Folger, R., 226
Folkman, S., 136, 137, 140, 254, 255,
    258, 399
Forrest, M. S., 288
Forsman, L., 245
Foulkes, D., 156, 160, 165, 166
Foulkes, E. F., 203
Fox, P. T., 115
Frankel, B. S., 388
Franken, R. E., 94, 124, 136, 138, 139, 140,
    191, 253, 264, 316, 338, 344, 245,
    351–353, 355, 356, 383, 384, 387,
    408–410
Frankenhaeuser, M., 245, 251, 268, 312
Freedman, E. B., 90
Freedman, Z. R., 76
Freeman, A., 320
Freeman, M. E., 246
French, E. G., 370
Freud, S., 10, 11, 163
Friedland, N., 270
Friedman, H. S., 243
Friedman, M., 232, 233
Friedman, M. I., 56, 57
Friedmann, J., 149, 150
Friel, J., 149
Friesen, W. V., 265
Frijda, N. H., 240, 242, 295, 300, 301
Frohm, K. D., 234
Frohman, L. A., 66
Frone, M. R., 178
Frost, R. O., 67
Fuchs, R., 396
Fulker, D. W., 213
Funkenstein, D. H., 233
Furst, M. L., 261
Furstenberg, F. F., Jr., 91
Fuster, J. M., 113

Gackenbach, J., 165

Gagnon, J. H., 88, 89, 90
Gagnon, P., 149
Galaburda, A. M., 106
Galanter, E., 397
Gallager, D. W., 130
Gangestad, S., 92
Garcia, J., 62
Garland, A. F., 281
Garn, S. M., 67
Garner, D. M., 76
Garrity, T. F., 256
Garrow, D. J. S., 75
Garthwaite, P. H., 77
Gary, H. E., 233
Gatchel, R. J., 257
Gatz, M., 367
Gaulin, S., 85
Gebhard, P. H., 88
Geen, R. G., 210, 219, 221, 234
Geer, J. H., 90, 257
Genova, P., 348
Gentry, W. D., 233
Gentry, J. H., 229
George, J. M., 279, 280
Gerner, R. H., 153
Gerrard, M., 91
Geschwind, N., 106
Getzels, J. W., 357
Giacolone, D., 285
Gibbons, F. X., 384
Gibson, K. J., 94, 191, 264, 353, 408–410
Giese, H., 91
Gilbert, R. M., 194, 203
Gillberg, M., 148, 151
Gillin, J. C., 153, 159
Gilovich, T., 310, 312
Gladue, B. A., 85, 214, 216
Glanzer, M., 337
Glaser, F. B., 201
Glaser, R., 247, 267, 268, 367
Glass, D. C., 233, 367
Glasser, W., 175
Glassman, A., 281
Glaubman, R., 146, 158
Glazer, H. I., 250, 251
Globus, G. G., 150
Goldman, R., 66, 69, 70
Goldstein, J., 158
Goleman, D., 261
Gollwitzer, P. M., 44, 47
Goodenough, D. R., 159
Goodner, C. J., 56
Goodwin, D. W., 185
Goolkasian, G. A., 67
Gopher, D., 33, 37
Gordon, A., 70
Gordon, H. W., 99
Gorski, R. A., 101, 102, 103, 105
Gottesman, I. I., 106, 221
Gough, H. G., 361
Goy, R. W., 99
Gracely, E. J., 277

Grannemann, B. D., 387
Gray, J. A., 125, 274, 275, 276
Gray, M. M., 158
Graziano, W. G., 86
Green, R., 108
Greenberg, B. S., 222
Greenberg, R., 158, 159, 160
Greene, R., 215, 346
Greiser, C., 159, 160, 164
Gresham, S. C., 50
Grieger, R., 399
Griffin, J. E., 50
Griffith, W., 88
Grinspoon, L., 188, 194
Gross, J., 69
Grossman, S. P., 217, 250
Grosvenor, A., 157
Grow, V. M., 76
Grunberg, N. E., 68
Guilford, J. P., 354
Guillemin, R., 246
Gur, R., 115
Gustafson, S. B., 353, 355, 357
Guy, R. F., 78

Hackett, R., 74
Hackmann, A., 277
Haddad, N. F., 346
Haessler, H. A., 66
Hall, G. H., 194
Hall, J. B., 134
Hall, R. P., 233
Halperin, R., 157
Halpern, D. F., 106
Hamer, D. H., 105
Hamilton, M. L., 196
Hammersmith, S. K., 107
Hammond, W. R., 231
Handler, P., 246
Haney, T. L., 234
Hansen, J. R., 306, 312
Hansen, J., 201, 204
Harackiewicz, J. M., 348
Harburg, E., 233, 234
Harlow, H. F., 306, 338
Harlow, M. K., 306
Harrell, N. W., 309
Harrington, D. M., 355, 356
Harris, C. B., 325
Harrison, K., 316, 351
Harrison, R. H., 159
Harter, S., 380, 381, 388, 406
Hartmann, E. L., 32, 160, 168
Hartse, K. M., 151
Haseltine, F. P., 99, 101, 102, 103, 105
Hashim, S. A., 61
Haskett, R. F., 99
Hassenfeld, I. N., 367
Haug, M., 214
Hawke, C. C., 214
Hawkins, D. R., 148
Hawkins, R. C., Jr., 79

Haynes, O. M., 124
Hays, R. C., 250
Haywood, H. C., 347
Heath, A., 124, 281
Heath, A. C., 329
Heath, R. G., 306
Heather, N., 201
Heatherton, T. F., 70, 381
Heaton, E., 88
Hebb, D. O., 53, 117, 118
Hedblom, P., 188
Heider, F., 47
Heilman, M. E., 78
Heiman, J. R., 88
Helmreich, R. L., 136, 137, 138, 139, 264
Helmstetter, S., 399
Heller, N., 159
Hennigan, K. M., 222
Herman, C. P., 72, 73, 74, 75, 195
Heron, W., 118, 119
Hervig, L. K., 319
Hewitt, E. C., 376
Heybach, J. P., 245, 246
Higgins, E. T., 403–405, 411
Hill, H., 229
Hines, M., 99, 102, 103, 106, 108
Hirai, H., 251
Hirota, T., 344
Hiroto, D. S., 285, 286, 287, 288
Hirsch, J., 67
Hite, S., 90
Hobson, J. A., 161, 162, 163, 164, 359, 360
Hockey, B., 158
Hodes, R., 262
Hoffman, M. L., 298, 299, 300, 366
Hokanson, J. E., 288, 293
Hollon, S. D., 281, 291, 320
Holmes, D. S., 261
Holstein, C., 301
Holzer, C. E., III, 281
Hooker, E., 106
Hopson, J. L., 216
Hopson, J. A., 182, 183
Hopstaken, L. E. M., 254
Horowitz, M. J., 131, 257, 262
Horstman, D. H., 49
Hoth, C. C., 154
House, J. S., 329
Howley, E. T., 49, 188
Hoyenga, K. B., 97, 245, 246
Hoyenga, K. T., 97, 245, 246
Hoyle, R. H., 327
Hoyt, M. F., 168
Hrubec, Z., 64
Hu, N., 105
Hu, S., 105
Huba, G. J., 352
Huesmann, L. R., 222
Huh, E., 301
Hull, C. L., 12, 14, 15, 44, 240, 337
Hull, J. G., 197, 263
Hunt, E. B., 99

Hunt, J. McV., 52
Hunt, L., 215
Hutt, C., 338
Hyde, J. S., 99, 216

Imperato-McGinley, J., 108
Isen, A. M., 356
Ismail, A. H., 49
Ivey, M. E., 214
Izard, C. E., 124, 241, 274, 282, 298

Jackson, L. J., 79
Jackson, P. W., 357
Jacobs, B. L., 193
Jacobs, G. A., 233
Jacobson, R. C., 202
Jaffa, M., 69
Jaffe, J. H., 183, 261
James, W., 404
Janowsky, J. S., 99
Jans, L. G. J. M., 253
Jasper, H. H., 115
Jeffrey, D. B., 76
Jensen-Campbell, L. A., 86
Jessor, R., 203
Jevning, R., 261
Johansson, G., 312
Johnson, D. W., 138
Johnson, E. H., 233
Johnson, L. C., 148, 150, 160
Johnson, R. E., 101
Johnson, R. T., 138
Johnson, T. P., 256
Johnson, V. E., 83, 84, 85, 86, 87, 88, 93, 98
Josephs, R. A., 199–201, 225, 394
Jourden, F. J., 396
Jouvet, M., 129, 147
Joyce, C. R. B., 193
Juraska, J. M., 103

Kagan, J., 124, 125, 128, 130, 297, 339
Kaha, C. W., 359
Kahn, J., 278
Kahn, S., 262
Kahneman, D., 33, 37
Kalant, O. J., 188
Kalat, J. W., 32
Kales, A., 172
Kalivas, P. W., 190
Kamen, L., 367
Kamis, A. B., 214
Kandel, D. B., 179, 202, 203
Kaplan, R. M., 331
Karacan, I., 156
Karli, P., 214
Katch, F. I., 79
Katch, V. L., 79
Katz, J. L., 124, 190, 191
Katz, L., 260
Katz, R. G., 76
Kavanaugh, D. J., 398, 399

Keesey, R. E., 65, 66
Keinan, G., 252, 270
Keller, M., 202
Kelly, A. E., 278
Kelly, G. F., 107
Kemeny, M., 257
Kemler, D., 287
Kendall, P. C., 407
Kendler, K. S., 124, 281, 329
Kenshiro, O., 148
Kent, G., 399
Kernis, M. H., 387
Kessen, W., 339, 340, 341
Kessler, R. C., 202, 329
Ketterer, T., 285
Kety, S. S., 49, 50, 281, 311
Keys, A. B., 328
Kiecolt-Glaser, J. K., 247, 267, 268, 367
Kiesler, C. A., 160
Kimura, D., 99, 100, 102
King, S. H., 233
Kinsey, A. C., 83
Kirsch, I., 197
Klausner, S. Z., 203
Kleck, R. E., 94
Klein, R., 227
Kleinginna, A. M., 25, 240, 243
Kleinginna, P. R., Jr., 25, 240, 243
Kleitman, N., 145, 170
Klemchuk, H. P., 261
Klinger, E., 202, 205, 284
Knittle, J. L., 67
Knussmann, R., 99
Kobasa, S. C., 262, 263, 331
Koch, C., 35, 42, 401, 402
Kochanska, G., 296, 298
Koelling, R. A., 62
Koenig, I. D. V., 344
Kohn, A., 138
Kohn, G., 108
Kohorn, E. I., 269
Kolb, B., 102
Kolb, L., 177
Kopcik, J. R., 103
Koresko, R. L., 159
Koridze, M. G., 157
Kotorii, M., 160
Kotorii, T., 160
Koulack, D., 160
Kory, R. B., 261
Kozlowski, L. T., 194, 195
Kraines, S. H., 50
Kramer, M., 152, 164, 165
Krantz, D. S., 257
Krasner, S. S., 234
Kraut, R., 307
Kribbs, N. B., 151
Kristeller, J. L., 131, 262
Krynicki, V., 158, 159
Kuhl, J., 291
Kuhn, D. Z., 219
Kukla, A., 374, 375

Kuleshnyk, I., 74
Kusulas, J. W., 319

Laberge, S., 164, 166
Lacey, B. C., 130, 143
Lacey, J. I., 130, 143
Lack, L. C., 157
Lader, M. H., 124
LaFromboise, T. D., 229
Lamon, S. J., 99
Lamphere, J., 172
Landis, K., 329
Lane, J. D., 246
Lang, P. J., 262
Langelle, C., 325
Langer, E. J., 35, 43, 44, 196, 256, 270, 331, 332, 354, 355, 359, 360, 367, 400, 406, 407, 412
Langley, P. W., 357
Larrick, R. P., 394
Larson, L. A., 49
Lasagna, L., 184
Lasky, R., 49
Latham, G. P., 5, 21, 131, 240, 274, 312, 349, 376, 392–396
Katimer, K., 269
Laudenslager, M. L., 247
Laudenslager, M., 330
Launier, R., 254, 312
Law, A., 270
Law, D. J., 99
Lazarus, R. S., 136, 137, 140, 240, 241, 254, 255, 258, 259, 269, 274, 279, 296, 299, 300, 306, 307–309, 312, 368, 380, 399
Lear, P. F., 281
Learner, R. M., 407
Leary, M. R., 326
LeDoux, J. E., 4, 5, 6, 217–218, 252, 269
Ledwidge, B., 49, 50, 190
Lee, P., 99
Lees, J. L., 117
Lefcourt, H. M., 263, 264, 329
Lefkowitz, M. M., 222
Leggett, E. L., 140, 375, 376–377, 407, 411
Leibling, B., 195
Leippe, M., 123, 133, 141
Lepper, M. R., 346
Lerner, J. V., 179
Lerner, M. J., 225
Lerner, R. M., 42, 179, 407
Levay, S., 101, 104, 105
Levendusky, P. G., 211
Levenson, H., 369
Levenson, R. W., 265
Levine, S., 115, 116
Levinson, D., 400–401
Levy, C. M., 151
Lewin, I., 158
Lewin, K., 20
Lewis, M., 66, 368
Lewis, V., 106
Libero, D. Z., 124

Licht, B., 324
Liebowitz, S. F., 58
Lind, S. K., 356
Lindholm, E., 261, 262
Lindsley, D. B., 114
Link, K. E., 279, 280
Linn, M., 99
Linsenmeier, J. A. W., 377
Linville, P. W., 377, 406
Linz, D. G., 222, 223
Lipcamon, J., 102
Lipson, A., 301
Livnat, S., 248
Locke, E. A., 5, 21, 131, 240, 274, 312, 349, 376, 392–396
Logan, H., 270
Lord, R. G., 397
Lore, R. K., 220
Losch, M., 133
Lowell, E. L. 370, 373
Lowther, W., 51
Lubin, A., 148, 160
Luck, D., 157
Lucker, G. W., 137, 139
Lundberg, U., 245, 263, 312
Lutz, T., 152

MacDougall, J. M., 234
Mack, D., 73
Mackinnon, D. W., 353, 360
Macon, D. A., 362
MacVicar, M., 268
Madans, J., 77
Madden, J., IV, 246
Maddi, S. R., 262
Madras, B. K., 188
Madsen, C. H., 219
Madsen, R., 282
Maehr, M. L., 346, 347
Magnuson, V. L., 105
Magoun, H. W., 30
Mahoney, K., 76
Mahoney, M. J., 76
Maier, S. F., 246, 248, 249, 284, 285, 288, 330
Malamuth, N. M., 92, 222
Maldonado, A., 288
Maltzman, I. M., 202
Manderlink, G., 348
Marco, C. A., 277
Margules, D. L., 66, 68, 75
Margulies, R. Z., 202
Markus, H., 7, 386, 401, 403, 404–405, 406
Marshall, G. N., 319
Martin, C. E., 83
Martin, E. B., 2
Martin, J. S., 261
Martin, N. G., 124, 281
Martin, R. A., 263, 264, 329
Martin, W. R., 183, 281
Martindale, 185
Martos, R., 288

Marx, M. B., 256
Mascolo, M. F., 380, 381
Maslow, A. H., 15, 17, 19, 20, 326, 327–329, 355
Mason, J. W., 308, 309, 311
Masserman, J. H., 197
Masters, M. S., 99
Masters, W. H., 83, 84, 85, 86, 87, 88, 93, 98
Matarazzo, J. D., 233
Mathy, R. M., 105
Matter, J., 348
Matthews, G., 117
Matthews, K. A., 137, 233
May, J., 88
May, R. B., 338
May, R., 274
Mayer, J., 56
McArdle, W. D., 79
McCareins, A. G., 377
McClearn, G. E., 214, 367
McClelland, D. C., 15, 16, 40, 135, 329, 370, 372–374, 384
McCoy, S. B., 384
McCrae, R. R., 17, 283, 356
McCullers, J. C., 346
McDougall, W., 10
McEwen, B. S., 99
McFarland, C., 215
McGrath, M. J., 157, 158
McGraw, K. O., 346
McKay, G., 329
McLellarn, R., 233
McMurray, N. E., 399
McNally, R. J., 278, 279
McNamara, G., 180, 181
McNaughton, N., 274, 275
Medvec, V. H., 310, 312
Mefford, I. N., 314, 315
Meichenbaum, D. H., 399
Meier, P., 258, 259, 260
Metalsky, G. I., 291
Meyer, L. B., 52, 377
Mayer-Bahlburg, H. F., 106
Meyers, J. K., 281
Michelman, H., 49
Mikula, G., 226
Mikulincer, M., 263, 269
Milgram, S., 210, 213
Miller, D. G., 250
Miller, G. A., 130, 397
Miller, I. W., III, 289
Miller, L. B., 346
Miller, N. E., 198, 219, 251, 274
Miller, P. A., 231
Miller, R. S., 263, 297
Miller, W. R., 199, 201, 287
Mills, J., 44
Mills, J. H., 52
Milner, P., 28, 306
Milstein, R. M., 64
Mineka, S., 275
Mintun, M., 115

Mischel, W., 2, 320, 370
Mitchison, G., 164
Mohan, P., 94, 264, 353
Moiseeva, N. I., 168
Meisset, R., 66
Money, J., 97, 104, 106, 109. 214
Monroe, L. J., 159, 167
Mook, D. G., 56
Moore, M. H., 203
Moran, D. J., III, 346
Morgan, J. J. B., 12
Morgan, W. P., 49
Morgane, P. J., 147
Mori, K., 148
Morris, D., 84, 98
Morrison, A. R., 146
Morse, D. R., 261
Morton, J. H., 215
Moruzzi, G., 30
Moses, J. M., 148, 160
Mosher, D. L., 88
Moss, H. B., 130, 180
Mossholder, K. W., 348
Mosteller, F., 184
Mount, G. R., 261
Moyer, K., 217
Moyer, K. E., 209, 217
Mudar, P., 178
Mullaney, D. J., 150
Mumford, M. D., 353, 355, 357
Muñoz, R. F., 199, 201
Munsinger, H., 339, 340, 341
Murgatroyd, S., 120
Murphy, D. L., 2, 188
Murray, H. A., 5, 15, 25, 370
Murray, S., 214
Myers, J. D., 211

Nachman, M., 62
Naitoh, P., 148, 150, 160
Nakano, T., 160
Nakazawa, Y., 160
National Advisory Mental Health Council, 281
National Commission on the Causes & Prevention of Violence, 197
National Research Council, 56
Navon, D., 33, 37
Nay, K. N., 172
Neale, J. M., 266
Neale, M. C., 105, 213, 329
Neiss, R., 113, 122, 142
Neisser, U., 100
Nemsadze, N. D., 157
Nesdale, A. R., 227
Nesselroade, J. R., 367
Neter, E., 137
Newberne, P. M., 268
Newcomb, M. D., 352
Nezu, A. M., 265
Nezu, C. M., 265
Nias, D. K. B., 213

Niaura, R. S., 196
Nicholls, J. G., 19, 378, 405, 406
Nichols, J. R., 184, 185
Nickel, J., 268
Nisbett, R. E., 47, 48, 61, 346, 394
Nishihara, K., 148
Nolen-Hoeksema, S., 291, 292
Norman, W. H., 33, 37, 289
Normansell, L. A., 327
Norvell, M. J., 78
Nowicki, G. P., 356
Nurius, P., 7, 386, 401, 403, 404–405, 406
Nuttin, J. R., 377, 401

O'Brien, M., 138
Odio, M., 250
Ohno, S., 99, 101, 102, 103, 105
Ohta, T., 148
Olds, J., 28, 306
Oniani, T. N., 157
Ornstein, R., 330
Orwoll, E. S., 99
Osborn, C. A., 88
Osborne, F. E., 381, 383, 384, 387, 388
Ostrove, N., 377
Overmier, J. B., 284
Oviatt, S. K., 99
Owens, J. F., 362
Ozer, E., 313, 314, 315, 316, 318, 369, 396, 399

Padilla, A. M., 285
Padilla, C., 285
Pallak, M. S., 159
Pallak, M., 134
Palmer, C., 159, 167
Pamuk, E. R., 77
Panksepp, J., 183, 327
Papanek, J. L., 348
Parecki, A., 380
Paris, M., 94
Park, K., 406
Parkes, K. R., 263
Parlee, M. B., 215
Parmeggiani, P. L., 148
Patel, V., 135
Paton, W. D. M., 193
Patrick, R. L., 246
Pattatucci, A. M. L., 105
Patterson, G. R., 181, 211, 212, 221
Paul, S. M., 130
Paulhus, D. L., 94
Pavlov, I. P., 36
Payton, T. I., 261
Peake, P. K., 2
Pearlman, C., 158, 160
Peck, M. S., 326
Pedersen, N. L., 367
Peele, S., 179, 184, 185, 187, 190, 199, 201–205
Pelham, B. W., 137
Pellegrino, J. W., 99

Pendery, M. L., 202
Pennebaker, J. W., 262
Penrod, S., 223
Perlick, D., 195
Perry, M., 213, 216
Perry, P., 214, 235
Pert, C., 66
Pervin, L. A., 240
Peters, T. J., 352
Petersen, A. C., 280, 281
Petersen, S. E., 115
Peterson, C., 270, 289, 324
Petri, B., 226
Pfaffman, C., 306
Piaget, J., 18, 20, 41, 43, 339, 344, 371
Pickens, R., 189
Pierce, G. R., 326
Pietropinto, A., 91
Pillard, R., 158
Pillard, R. C., 105, 108
Pilon, D. A., 372
Pinel, J. P. J., 231
Pisano, R., 219
Pitts, F. N., Jr., 49
Pittman, T., 134
Pivik, T., 160
Plomin, R., 367
Pohorecky, L. A., 250, 251
Polivy, J., 72, 73, 74, 75, 79, 381
Pollack, R. H., 88
Pomeroy, W. B., 83
Posner, M. I., 115
Post, R. M., 49, 153
Potepan, P. A., 375
Powers, P. S., 64
Powley, T. L., 65, 66
Powrie, J. K., 77
Prevost, F., 160
Pribram, K. H., 217, 397
Prpich, W., 124, 136, 140, 383, 384, 387
Prymak, C. A., 261
Przybeck, T. R., 179
Ptacek, J. T., 264
Puccetti, M. C., 263
Putnam, P., 124

Quadagno, D. M., 106
Quadagno, D., 91
Quadagno, J. S., 106
Quinlan, D. M., 269
Quirce, C. M., 250

Rabinowitz, D., 75
Rachmiel, T. B., 266
Raichle, M. E., 114, 115
Ramírez, E., 288
Ramsey, E., 181
Rankin, B. A., 78
Rapoport, J. L., 26, 27
Ratzel, R., 167
Raynor, J. O., 25, 240
Reeve, J. M., 397
Regev, Y., 270

Reiche, R., 107
Reid, R. L., 215
Reinisch, J. M., 99
Reisenzein, R., 122
Relich, J. D., 377
Rescorla, R. A., 37
Resnick, S. M., 106
Richardson, G. S., 149
Richardson, R. L., 250
Richey, M. F., 102
Robins, L. N., 179, 185
Rodin, J., 56, 64, 71, 72, 75, 76, 77, 104, 256, 331, 367
Roeper, P. J., 234
Rogers, C. R., 19, 20, 382, 385, 411
Rollnick, S., 201
Room, R., 198
Roos, P. E., 263
Rosa, R. R., 153
Rose, G. A., 65
Rosen, B. C., 372
Rosen, R., 327
Rosen, R. C., 198
Rosenfeld, A. H., 52, 280
Rosenman, R. H., 232, 233
Rosler, A., 108
Ross, G., 135
Ross, M., 215
Rossier, J., 246
Roth, B. H., 130, 191
Roth, T., 151, 152, 164, 172
Rothbart, M. K., 180, 181
Rotter, J. B., 212, 286, 367–369
Routtenberg, A., 188, 306, 307
Rowland, G. L., 191, 261, 264, 316, 351, 353, 408–410
Rubenstein, C., 94
Rubin, R. T., 99
Ruderman, A. J., 74
Rule, B. G., 227
Rushton, J. P., 213
Russell, J. A., 56, 241
Russell, M., 178
Ryan, R. M., 6, 76, 282, 346, 349, 380, 387, 403, 404, 410, 411, 412
Ryan, S. M., 330

Sackett, G. P., 341
Salans, L. B., 67
Saleh, W. E., 263, 329
Salkovskis, P. M., 277
Saltus, R. S., 154
Saltzberg, J. A., 266
Samuels, M., 401
Samuels, N., 401
Sanday, P. R., 231
Sanders, B., 99
Sands, M. P., 246
Sarason, B. R., 326
Sarason, I. G., 124, 135, 136, 326, 399
Saruwatari, L. R., 78
Saunders, D., 136
Sawyers, J. K., 346

Schachter, J., 233
Schachter, S., 47, 48, 53, 61, 62, 69, 70, 121, 194, 195, 104, 312, 313
Schaller, W. E., 175
Scheier, M. F., 139, 318, 325, 383, 397, 409
Schiff, B. B., 188, 189
Schildkraut, J. J., 49, 50, 281, 311
Schleiser-Stropp, B., 78
Schmidt, A., 91
Schmidt, J. L., Jr., 35
Schnartz, B., 66
Schooler, J. W., 360
Schulman, P., 322
Schultz, L. A., 220
Schulz, R. A., 256
Schunk, D. H., 393
Schuster, T. L., 329
Schut, H., 256
Schwartz, C. E., 366
Schwartz, G. E., 261
Schwartz, M., 106
Schwartz, P. E., 269
Schwarzer, R., 257, 396
Scott, J., 156
Scott, T. H., 118
Scrima, L., 157, 172
Selbst, M., 356
Seligman, M. E. P., 6, 35, 46, 127, 128, 192, 240, 263, 269, 270, 275, 279–291, 294, 301, 318–324, 356, 366, 367, 369, 387, 400, 401, 402, 406, 409, 411
Sellers, C. M., 194
Selye, H., 266
Serdula, M. K., 77
Sexton, G., 233
Shainess, N. A., 214
Shaper, A. G., 77
Shapiro, D. H., 366, 367, 368
Shaw, J., 263
Sheehan, D. V., 192
Shek, D. T. L., 131
Shepp, B., 287
Sher, K. J., 179
Sherk, D., 263
Sherman, I. W., 57, 58
Sherman, V. G., 57, 58
Shibuya, H., 66
Shields, J., 124
Shoda, Y., 2
Shortell, J., 211
Showers, C., 387
Shrauger, J. S., 140
Siegel, J. M., 146, 256
Siegel, S., 184
Sigmon, S. T., 325
Sigvardsson, S., 180
Silberstein, L. R., 75
Silverstein, B., 194, 195
Simenauer, J., 91
Simon, H. A., 36, 357
Simon, N. G., 214
Simon, W., 88, 89
Simons, L., 247, 262

Simpson, J. A., 92
Simpson, M. T., 234
Singer, J. E., 53, 122, 255, 312, 313
Singer, J. L., 168, 257
Siviy, S. M., 327
Skinner, B. F., 12, 13, 14, 15, 46
Skinner, H. A., 201
Skolnick, P., 130
Sladeczek, I., 361
Slater, E., 124
Slochower, J., 71
Smart, R. G., 197
Smith, A. P., 246
Smith, C., 157
Smith, E. L., 246
Smith, G. F., 340, 341
Smith, J. E., 246
Smith, R. E., 264
Smith, T. W., 234
Smith, T., 263
Smoll, F. L., 264
Smoller, J. W., 68
Snidman, N., 124, 125, 339
Snyder, C. R., 6, 240, 318, 324, 325, 387, 409
Snyder, F., 156
Snyder, M., 48, 92
Snyder, S., 183
Sobel, D., 330
Sobell, L. C., 201–202
Sobell, M. B., 201–202
Solano, J. M., 250
Solomon, E. P., 234
Solomon, R. L., 50, 176, 177
Soriano, F. I., 229
Sorrentino, R. M., 376
Sostek, A. J., 2
Sostek, A. M., 2
Spealman, R. D., 188
Spear, P. S., 166
Spence, J. T., 136, 137, 138, 139, 264, 346
Spielberger, C. D., 123, 126, 233, 234
Spielman, A. J., 157
Spinks, J. A., 131
Sprague, J., 91
Stallings, W. M., 346, 347
Stallones, L., 256
Stanley, J. C., 99, 100
Staub, E., 228, 229, 230, 231
Steele, C. M., 199–201, 225, 394
Steffen, V. J., 216
Stein, L., 188, 306
Stein, M. I., 357
Steinberg, H. R., 159
Steiner, S. S., 155, 157
Stenberg, C. R., 209
Stern, W. C., 168
Stepanski, E., 172
Stern, W. C., 32, 146
Sternberg, R. J., 94, 95, 96, 97, 366
Stewart, J., 102, 190
Stoa, K. F., 306
Stokols, D., 252, 253, 331
Stone, A. A., 266

Stone, E. A., 309
Storm, C., 380
Storm, T., 380
Strain, A., 344, 345
Straub, R. O., 68
Stricker, E. M., 56, 57
Strickland, B. R., 355, 360
Striegel-Moore, R. H., 75
Stroebe, M., 257
Stroebe, W., 257
Strohm, R. B., 225
Stryker, S., 405
Stuart, R. B., 65, 67
Stunkard, A. J., 64, 68, 69
Sturup, G. K., 214
Suder, C., 88
Suedfeld, P., 34, 131
Sullivan, J. J., 215
Sullivan, W. M., 282
Sulloway, F. J., 355, 357
Suls, J., 277
Svebak, S., 120
Swaab, D. F., 101
Swann, W. B., 381, 382
Swann, W. B., Jr., 382
Sweeny, P., 291
Swidler, A., 282
Swinson, R. P., 175, 176, 188, 193, 196, 199
Switzky, H. N., 347
Sylva, K., 348
Symonds, J. D., 166

Tachibana, H., 160
Taggart, P., 306
Tallman, J. F., 130, 191
Tangney, J. P., 297, 381
Tanzer, N., 226
Tarler-Benlolo, L., 261
Tarter, R. E., 179, 180
Taub, J. M., 148
Taubman, O., 263, 269
Tavris, C., 103, 108, 235, 236
Taylor, C. B., 312, 314, 315
Taylor, C. W., 356
Taylor, S. E., 263, 270, 318, 329, 330, 331, 401
Taylor, S. P., 211, 219
Taylor, S., 270
Teasdale, J. D., 288, 289
Tedeschi, J. T., 209, 213, 220, 223, 225, 229
Teevan, R. C., 203
Tefler, E., 307
Tegano, D. W., 346
Tellegen, A., 214
Terrace, H. S., 376
Tesser, A., 94
Tharp, G. D., 49
Thomas, A., 339
Thomas, F. D., 250
Thomas, H., 339
Thompson, R. A., 296
Thorndike, E. L., 241

Tiger, L., 182, 319
Tilley, A. J., 160
Tillich, P., 318
Tipton, S. M., 282
Tischler, G. L., 281
Toch, H., 212
Toi, M., 94
Tolman, E. C., 20
Tolson, W. W., 308, 309, 311
Tomaka, J., 269
Tomkins, S. S., 274
Tomporowski, P. D., 50
Torrence, E. P., 355
Torsvall, L., 151
Tracy, L. N., 165
Tracy, R. L., 165
Trinder, J., 50
Trulson, M. E., 193
Tsuda, A., 251
Turell, S., 79
Turkington, C., 283
Turovsky, J., 118, 125, 276
Tyler, L. E., 354
Tyrrell, D. A., 246

Umberson, D., 329
Unger, R. K., 78
Ursin, H., 306

Vaccaro, D., 180, 181
Vaillant, G. E., 197, 202–204, 270, 362
Valiant, G., 270
Van De Castle, R. L., 148
Van Dyke, C., 188, 189
Van Itallie, T. B., 61
Van Treuren, R. R., 263
Vanyukov, M. M., 180
Vaux, A., 257
Veiel, H. O. F., 257
Veitch, R., 88
Vereby, V., 196
Vernikos-Danellis, J., 245, 246
Vezina, P., 190
Vickers, R. R., Jr., 319
Villablanca, J., 169
Virnelli, S., 263
Visintainer, M., 324
Vitz, P., 341
Vogel, G. W., 145, 157, 159, 165, 166
Volpicelli, J., 324
Volpicelli, J. R., 183, 197
Von Euler, U. S., 251
Von Felsinger, J. M., 184
Voyer, D., 99
Voyer, S., 99
Vreven, R., 377

Wadden, T. A., 68
Wade, C., 108
Wagner, A. R., 198
Wagner, P. E., 381
Walder, L. Q., 222
Walitzer, K. S., 179

Walker, E. L., 52
Walker, L. E. A., 228
Wall, S., 330
Wallace, J. E., 196
Wallace, R. K., 261, 262
Waller, N. G., 18
Walsh, A., 93
Walsh, M. J., 196
Walters, S. R., 261
Wannamethee, G., 77
Ware, E. E., 263
Waterman, A. S., 307, 308
Waterman, R. H., Jr., 352
Waters, W. F., 330
Watkins, L. R., 246
Watson, D., 4, 119, 127, 277, 407
Watson, J. B., 12, 14, 20
Webb, W. B., 145, 148, 149, 150, 151, 154, 160, 169, 170
Wegner, D. M., 278
Weidner, G., 233, 234
Weinberg, M. S., 107
Weiner, B., 25, 227, 240, 289, 291, 374, 375, 386
Weingberger, D. A., 257
Weinstein, L. N., 154, 155
Weintraub, J. K., 139
Weiss, J. M., 250, 251, 309
Weiss, M., 198
Weissman, M. M., 281
West, L. J., 202
West, S. G., 86
Whalen, R. E., 98, 214
Whitam, F. L., 105, 107
White, A., 246
White, J. A., 49
White, J., 401

White, R. W., 5, 18, 39, 339, 344, 370, 371, 409, 411
Wickens, C. D., 33, 37
Widom, C. S., 221, 230
Wiebe, D. J., 263
Wikler, A., 184
Williams, G. C., 76
Williams, R., 234
Williams, R. B., 234
Williams, R. H., 75
Williams, R. L., 50
Williams, R. T., 65
Williams, S. L., 314, 315
Williams, T. K., 197
Williamson, D. F., 77
Williamson, G. M., 243
Wills, T. A., 180, 181
Wills, T., 384
Wilson, A. F., 261
Wilson, G. T., 197
Wilson, J. D., 99, 101, 102, 103, 105
Wilson, T. D., 360, 377
Winger, G., 191
Winningham, M., 268
Winterbottom, M. R., 372, 373
Winton, M., 201
Wise, C. D., 188
Wise, R. A., 190, 194, 195, 196
Wistow, B. W., 250
Wolfgang, M. E., 225
Wolpe, J., 11, 409
Wong, W. P. T., 227
Wonnocott, S., 194
Wood, J. V., 266
Woods, J. H., 191
Wooley, S. C., 76
Worchel, P., 219

Worden, T. J., 233
Worick, W. W., 175
Wortman, C. B., 319
Wright, R. A., 94
Wurf, E., 403, 406
Wurtman, R. J., 57
Wyatt, R. J., 159

Yamaguchi, K., 179
Yates, W. R., 214
Yen, S. S., 215
Yerkes, R. M., 117
Yoshinobu, L. R., 325
Young, J., 157
Young, J. E., 280, 281
Young, J. P. R., 124
Young, J. S., 358, 414
Young, P. T., 306
Yum, K. S., 197
Yung, B., 231

Zahn-Waxler, C., 296, 298
Zeki, S., 114
Zentall, S. S., 179
Zentall, T. R., 179
Zierler, K. L., 75
Zigler, E., 281
Zilbergeld, B., 90
Zillmann, D., 141
Zimbardo, P. G., 211
Zinberg, N. E., 202
Zorick, F. J., 151, 172
Zuckerman, H., 357
Zuckerman, M., 2, 4, 25, 94, 180, 188, 306, 313, 347–352, 355, 409
Zwilling, G. R., 149

Subject Index

Ability, 374–377, 385, 386, 407, 412
Accommodation, 41, 164, 371
Achievement, 16, 39, 136, 203, 347, 356, 357, 369–377, 385, 412, 414
  see also Need to achieve
Acquired motives, 39
Action, 25, 28
Acts of commission, 296, 299-300, 310
Acts of omission, 296, 299–300, 310
Adaptation, 247, 341
Addictive personality, 202
Adipose tissue, 57, 63, 65–66
Adrenal cortex, 59, 245, 261
Adrenal glands, 98, 148, 216, 245
Adrenal medulla, 59, 115, 245, 251
Adrenocortical response, 49
Adrenocorticotropic hormone (ACTH), 245–246
Adventure, 91
Adventure seeking, 348
Adversity, 35, 41, 270, 320, 380
Affect, 6, 28–29, 117, 176, 307, 342, 356, 404, 411
  see also Hedonic tone
Affective disorder, 281
Agency, 324–325, 329, 370, 380, 388, 409
Aggression, 14, 209–236
  definition, 210, 212
Alarm reaction, 267, 276
Alcohol, 32, 35, 57, 169–170, 178–179, 183, 196–204, 225, 268, 352
Alcoholic, 42, 197, 199–200
Alcohol use:
  beliefs about control, 200–201
  cultural differences, 199, 202
  and depression, 197
  moderators, 202–203
  and quitting, 200–205
  situational factors, 198
Alienation, 109, 203
Alprazolam, 190–191
Alternation behavior, 336–338
Alternatives, 21, 45, 323, 324, 354–355
  see also Possibilities
Altruism, 297
Ambiguity, 279, 356, 359–361
Amino acids, 57, 63

Amphetamines, 28, 49–50, 147, 170, 188–190, 306
Amygdala, 103, 124, 217–218, 229, 270
  see also Limbic system
Anabolism, 75
Androgens, 97–98, 99 100, 102, 214–215
Androstenedione, and aggression, 215–216
Anger, 5, 212–213, 220–221, 227–228, 233–236, 241
Anorexia nervosa, 65, 66, 74, 78–80
Antianxiety drugs, 190, 275, 278
Antidepressants, 27, 32, 153, 157, 170, 281, 282, 283, 291
Anxiety, 3, 32, 49, 51, 91, 118–119, 123–128, 135–136, 182, 190–191, 241, 274, 275–280, 288, 298, 309, 313, 314, 316, 339, 345, 348, 383
  trait, 124–128, 274
Appraisal, 127, 128, 242–243, 254, 269
Arousal, 47, 49, 52–53, 94, 113, 115, 117–134, 136–137, 141–142, 148, 179, 194, 228, 313, 316, 342–345, 347–349
Aspirations, 393, 402, 405
Assimilation, 371
Attachment, 183, 257, 326–327, 329–331
Attention, 21, 33–36, 40, 44, 48, 113, 120–121, 124, 125, 128, 131–132, 134, 142, 339, 344, 348
  see also Vigilance
Attitudes, 41–43, 46, 48, 90–91, 412
Attraction, 94
Attribution:
  and aggression, 227
  and depression, 289
Attribution theory, 47–48
Automatic behavior, 44–45, 48, 349, 354
Automatic thoughts, 294–295
Autonomic Nervous System (ANS), 113, 115, 125
Autonomous types, 293
Autonomy, 16, 356–357
Avoidance learning, 285

Basal metabolic rate (BMR), 64–65
Beliefs, 21, 41–44, 46, 48, 91, 270, 412
  and alcohol, 197, 200
  and self-control, 187

Belongingness, 326–328, 330
Benign view of the world, 269, 409, 411
Benzodiazepines, 190–192
Binge eating, 74, 77, 80
Biogenic amines, 147
Bipolar depression, *see* Manic-depressive disorder
Bisexuality, 105–106
Blame, 227, 290
Blood pressure, 59, 85, 87, 233–234, 261, 267, 288
Boredom, 349
Boundary theory, 72
Bulimia, 56, 78–79

Caloric thrift, *see* Anabolism
Caloric waste, *see* Catabolism
Calories, 57–58, 64, 73, 75
Cancer, 56, 57, 63, 77, 246–247, 257, 267–269, 324, 401
Cannabis, *see* Hallucinogenics
Carbohydrates, 56, 58, 63
Cardiovascular disorders, 77, 233
Catabolism, 75
Catecholamine hypothesis, 281
Catecholamines, 168, 188, 234, 263, 268, 269, 281, 282, 308, 311, 312, 314, 330
Categories, 42–43, 48, 358–360, 387
Catnaps, 153–154
Cerebral cortex, 101–103
Challenge, 19, 254–255, 262, 265, 376–378, 395, 406, 409, 411
Chance meeting, 94
Chloridazepoxide, 190
Chlorpromazine, 306
Choice, *see* Decisions
Circadian rhythm, 147–148, 150–153
Classical conditioning, 12, 36–39, 48, 184, 275
Claustrophobia, 37, 275
Clitoris, 84–85, 99, 216
Cocaine, 32, 188–190, 350, 352
Cognition, definition, 40
Cognitive dissonance, 43–44, 48, 123, 132–134, 160
Cognitive incongruity, 274
Cognitive restructuring, 399, 400, 411

Cognitive experiential self-theory (CEST), 258
Collative variables, 343
Commitment, 21, 92, 94–95, 262, 331, 352
Communication, 353
Community, 326, 330, 331
Compartmentalization, 388
Compassion, 241
Competence, 2, 282, 325, 346, 369–371, 375, 378, 386, 394, 396, 406, 410–413
Competition, 136, 138
Competitiveness, 124, 136–138
Complexity, 33, 94, 338–343
Compliance, 269
Concept matching, 396
Conditional love, 19, 385
Confidence, 406
Conflict, 234, 343
Conflict-prone organization, 252–253
Conflict-resistant organization, 252–253
Congenital adrenal hyperphasis (CAH), 105–106
Conscious behavior, 44–45, 163, 300, 403
Consistency, 43, 354, 355
Constructive thinking, 258, 260, 270, 294–295
Consummate love, 96
Context:
　and behavior, 185, 403
　and conditioning, 37
　and control, 47–48
Continuous improvement, 397–398, 413
Control, 2, 37, 40, 42, 45, 60, 67, 73, 76, 113, 181, 231, 255–256, 262, 269, 279, 285–288, 312, 366–370, 404
　and aggression, 212
　and power, 228
　and stress, 34, 254–256
Conventionality, 299, 355
Coping, 127–128, 139, 180–181, 233, 250–251, 254–255, 258, 260–262, 269, 270, 308, 312, 368
Core relational themes, 241, 307
Coronary heart disease (CHD), 232–234
Corpus callosum, 102–103, 307
Cortical activity, *see* EEG activity
Corticosteroids, 256, 330
Corticosterone, 245, 250, 268
Corticotropin releasing factor (CRF), 245, 248
Counterconditioning, 38, 276
Creativity, 353–362
Criticism, 356
Curiosity, 40, 338–339, 354, 406
Cynical hostility, 234

Danger, 409
　see also Fear; Threat
Decisions, 45–46, 352, 360
Deliquency, 351, 352
Dependency, 175

Depression, 28, 32, 34, 49–51, 127, 157, 269, 280–284, 288, 289, 291–296, 301, 326, 409
　and eating disorders, 67–68
Desensitization, 376
Destructive thinking, 258, 260
Diabetes, 56, 58, 63, 77
Diazepam, *see* Valium
Diethylstibestrol affected (DES), 106
Differentiation, 406
Dihydrotestosterone, 99, 108
Direction, 14, 15, 47, 357, 393
Discipline, 299
Discrepancy, 18, 19, 343, 395, 396, 404
Disease, and stress, 246, 267
Disgust, 241
Disinhibited eater, 68, 73–74
Disinhibition, 196–197, 225, 348, 355
Disposition, 5, 14, 18, 19, 25, 28, 30, 58, 63, 92, 124, 128, 212, 407, 409, 411
Disputation, 321–323
Dissonance, *see* Cognitive dissonance
Distraction, 140, 292, 321
Distress, 243
Divergent thinking, 355
Dominance, 86
Dopamine, 32, 49–51, 93, 188–189, 281, 306
Dopamine system, 188, 190
Dopanergic system, 194, 196
Doubt, *see* Self-doubt
Dreaming, theory of, 163–165
Dreams, 162–165, 168, 400
Drive, 12, 14, 15, 18, 44, 240, 348
Drug addiction, definition, 175

EEG activity, 146–147
Effectance motivation, 39, 370, 371
Effort, 21, 374, 375, 377, 386, 393, 394
Ego strength, 408
Elavil, 281
　see also Antidepressants
Emotion, 28, 37, 240–243, 274, 307
　theories of, 240
Emotion-focused coping, 254–255, 260–262
Empathetic distress, 298, 300
Empathetic guilt, 298
Empathy, 231, 296
Empowerment, 397
Endocrine system, 115
Endogenous morphine, *see* Endorphins
Endorphins, 32, 93, 182–184, 196–197, 246, 263, 269, 319, 327, 330
Energy, 14, 15, 25, 30, 56–57, 58, 64, 68, 75, 248–249, 309
Entity theory, 375–378, 394
Envy, 241
Epinephrine, 59, 115, 148, 233, 245, 288, 308, 311, 312, 313, 315, 349
Escape learning, 285
Esteem needs, 329

Estradiol, 97, 99, 214
Estrogen, 97–98, 99, 105, 106
　and aggression, 214
Euphoria, 28, 32, 34, 49, 93, 182, 188, 189, 193, 246, 281, 319
Evolution, 10
Excitement, 84, 87, 89, 119
Exercise, 49–50, 53, 64, 182–183, 261, 268
Expectations, 14, 20, 21, 44, 52, 179, 184, 186, 189–190, 197, 396
Experience seeking, 348, 351
Experiential system, 44, 258, 301, 400
Explanatory style, 289, 301, 319, 324, 374
Exploratory behavior, 18, 32, 336–342, 344, 347, 348, 350, 354
External causation, 13, 40, 41, 44, 46–48, 64, 288, 367
　see also Internal/external causation
Extinction, 6, 36, 38
Extraversion, 17, 91, 124–125, 148, 319, 339
Extrinsic motivation, 346

Facial expression, 241, 298
Failure, 128, 204–205, 287, 289, 374–378, 381–384, 388
Falling in love, 89, 93–94
Famine hypothesis, 66–67, 74
Fantasy, 88–89, 149, 407
Fat cells, *see* Adipose tissue
Fatigue, 50, 150
Fats, 56–57, 63
Fatty acids, 56, 58, 246, 250
Fear, 28, 37–38, 70, 274–276, 310, 347, 376, 383
Fear-based guilt, 298
Fear of failing, 374
Feedback, 151, 325, 376, 382, 387, 388, 394
Feelings of efficacy, 370, 396
Fight-or-flight response, 217–218, 229, 243–245, 249, 270, 275, 276
"Flow," 414
Follicle-stimulating hormone (FSH), 98
Food preference, 61–62
Fright, 241
Fructose, 72
Frustration, 219–220, 229–230, 411

GABA (Gamma-amino butyric acid), 32, 130, 191
Gastrointestinal tract, 56
Gender schema, 109
Gender identity, 104, 107
Genital stimulation, 84–86
Glucocorticoids, 59, 245–246, 249, 268
Glucose, 56–58, 65–66, 72, 115, 196, 246, 250
Glycogen, 57
Goal-directed behavior, 5, 6, 297, 302, 308, 318, 325, 396, 402

Goals, 5, 94, 242, 274, 324–325, 349, 378, 392–397, 401, 402, 406, 407, 409, 412, 414
  paratelic, 120
  telic, 119
Gonadotropic hormones, 98
Growth motivation, 18, 19
Guilt, 241, 296–301, 376

Habits, 12, 14, 44–45, 51, 56, 400
Habitual behavior, 354, 361
  see also Automatic behavior
Habituate, 301
Hallucinations, 118, 162, 193
Hallucinogenics, 188, 193–194
Happiness, 46, 241, 279, 282, 295, 306–308, 310, 411, 412
Hardwired behavior, 26–28
Hardy personality, 262–263, 331
Harm, 210, 223, 269
Health, 35, 140, 183, 205, 232–236, 243, 256, 263, 264, 267–270, 324, 329, 331, 366, 367
Heart rate, 34, 47, 69, 85, 87, 97, 130, 233
Hedonic enjoyment, 307–308
Hedonic happiness, 307–308, 313
Hedonic tone, 120, 342, 344
Hedonism, 306, 307
Helplessness, 231, 279, 286, 288, 324, 378
  see also Learned helplessness
Heroin, 32, 37, 182–186, 188
Hippocampus, *see* Limbic system
Homosexuality, 27, 104–109
Hope, 139–140, 241, 270, 290, 318–319, 324, 325, 388
Hopelessness, 290
Hostility, 213, 229, 230–231, 233–235
Humanistic theories, 19
Humor, 236, 264–265
Hunger, 56, 58–59, 60, 63, 66, 68–69, 71–76
Hyperactivity, 34, 179–180
Hyperinsulin response, 75
Hypertension, 56, 77, 131, 233
Hypothalamus, 59, 66, 98, 101, 103–105, 115, 148, 245, 248, 307

Image construction, 52, 300, 358–359, 400
Imitation, and aggression, 14, 221
Immune response, 246, 248–249, 262, 268–270, 324, 329, 330
Immune system, 35, 93, 106, 183, 246–249, 263, 267–269, 330
Immunization, 288
Implicit theories, 44, 46, 48, 127, 128, 242, 269, 280, 407–413
Impulsivity, 2, 125, 179, 214, 218
Incentive, 39, 44
Incongruity, and arousal, 343
Incremental theory, 375, 376, 378
Independence, 372, 373, 406
Individualism, 282, 368

Induction, socialization by, 299
Inescapable shock, conditioning by, 284, 309
Inferiority, 79
Information, 30, 32–36, 40, 42–43, 130, 132, 162, 225, 257, 339, 340, 342, 343, 344, 348–349, 357–359, 403, 404
Initiative, 406
Inner dialogue, *see* Self-talk
Insomnia, 169–172, 261, 267
Instinct, 8, 10, 11, 12
Instrumental aggression, 210, 213
Instrumental learning, 12, 38–39
Instrumentality, 263–264
Insulin, 56, 58–60, 63, 71–72, 75
Intelligence, 258–259, 357, 358, 378, 412
Intercourse, 83, 88, 91
Internals, 286, 288, 301, 367, 374
Internal/external causation, 47, 290
  and obesity, 68–70, 74
  see also Locus of control theory, 47, 263
Intimacy, 91–93, 94–96
Intrinsic motivation, 6, 39, 346–349, 356
Introversion, 125, 148
Intrusive thinking, 124, 135, 136, 278, 399

Jealousy, 241
Jet lag, and sleep deprivation, 150

Knowledge, 357, 358

Labels, 42, 48–49
Lateral hypothalamus (LH), 65
Lateral thinking, 359, 360
Laughter, and endorphins, 183
Learned helplessness, 284–289
Lesbians, *see* Homosexuality
Leuteinizing hormone (LH), 98
Librium, 190–191
Limbic system, 29, 52, 125, 193
Lipids, 66
Locus coeruleus, 129, 147, 274, 283, 307
Locus of control theory, 47, 263
Love, 91, 92, 93–96, 183, 241, 328
Love withdrawal, 183, 299
Lucid dreaming, 165
Lysergic Acid Diethylamide (LSD), 147, 193–194
  see also Hallucinogenics

Magic mushrooms, *see* Hallucinogenics 193
Malnutrition, 61
Management of anger, 235–236
Manic-depressive disorder, 281, 291
Marijuana, 185, 193, 202, 352
  see also Hallucinogenics
Marital satisfaction, 93, 353
Mastery strategy/orientation, 19, 139, 383, 385, 386, 411, 412

Mastery, 18, 30, 39, 46, 136–137, 315, 316, 349, 366, 369–373, 378, 396
Masturbation, 88, 90, 91, 105
Mathematical abilities, 99
Meditation, 124, 260–262, 270
Memory, 32, 40, 42, 151, 162, 218, 343
Menopause, 98
Mental images, 141, 401
Mental rehearsal, 398
Metabolism, 64, 66, 268
Methadone, 184
Microsleeps, and sleep deprivation, 151
Migraine headaches, 262
Mindfulness, 45, 331, 332
Mineralcorticoids, 245
Modeling, 12–13, 28, 41, 43–44, 88, 127, 221, 356, 372, 412
Monoamine oxidase (MAO), 157, 180, 282, 283, 349, 350
Monoamine oxidase inhibitors (MAOI), 281–283
Morphine, 32, 93, 182–185
Motives, 40, 242
Myopia, and alcohol, 200, 225

Narcolepsy, 146, 171
Nardil, 282
Narplan, 282
Need to achieve, 15, 119, 370, 372–374, 385
Need to avoid failure, *see* Fear of failing
Need to communicate, *see* Communication
Needs, 5, 15, 17, 19, 22, 25, 163, 229–230, 240, 328–329, 411
Neurotic behavior, 11, 125, 135, 179, 328
Neuroticism, 17, 22, 124, 125, 135, 160, 319, 408
Neurotransmitters, 27, 30–35, 57–58, 63, 129–189, 246, 283, 349
Nicotine, 194–196, 268
Norepinephrine, 32, 49–51, 53, 57, 59, 93, 115, 129, 147, 183, 188–189, 217, 233, 245, 251, 265, 281–283, 288, 306, 308, 309, 312–315
Novelty, 2, 18, 94, 119, 125, 180, 274, 311, 338, 339, 342, 343, 350
NREM, 159, 168
NREM dreams, 149, 165
Nutrition, 61–62

Obesity, 26–27, 56, 58, 60–61, 63–68, 69, 75–76, 78
Obsessive-compulsive disorder, 26, 278
Openness, 356, 357, 359
Opponent process theory, 37, 50, 176–177
Optimal arousal, 179
  see also arousal
Optimal stimulation, 117, 119, 125
Optimism, 46, 263, 270, 289–290, 318–323, 324, 325, 388, 409
Orgasm, 83–85, 87, 89–90, 93

Outcome orientation, 412
Ovaries, 98–99
Overgeneralization, 128, 293, 388
Overweight, *see* Obesity
Oxytocin, 93

Pacer range, 341–342
Panic, 182, 276–278
Parnate, 282
Partial reinforcement effect, 38
Passion, 83, 95, 96
Pathways, 324–325, 380, 387, 409
Patterns, 359
Penis, 84, 86, 99, 108
Perceptual speed, 99
Performance strategy/orientation, 377,
     381, 383, 386, 396, 411, 412
Permanence, 289–290, 301
Persistence, 6, 13, 14, 15, 21, 47, 377, 378,
     380, 386, 393, 397
Personal control, 312
Personalization, 289, 290
Pervasiveness, evaluation of, 289–290, 301
Pessimism, 270, 280, 289–292, 296, 319, 388
Pet ownership, 256, 326
Petting, 83, 89
Phenylethylanine (PEA), 93
Phobia, 124, 275
Pituitary, 98, 245–246
Pituitary adrenal response, 245, 248
Plasma lipids, 234
Play, used to suspend judgment, 360
Pleasure bond, 98
Pornography, 88, 222–223
Positron Emission Tomography (PET), 114
Positive self-regard, 19, 385, 386
Possibilities, 359, 411
     see also Alternatives
Possible selves, 405, 406, 407, 411
Power, 45, 135
Predictability, 250, 354, 355, 360, 366, 382
Premenstrual syndrome (PMS), 214–215
Prewired behavior, 27–28, 120
Pride, 109, 241, 309, 376, 380, 381, 383, 411
Problem solving, 130, 292, 346, 353, 355,
     361
Problem-focused coping, 254–255, 266
Process orientation, 295, 414
Progesterone, and aggression, 214–215
Progestins, 97–98, 101
Proteins, 25, 32, 57–58, 64
Prozac, 282
Psilocybin, 193
     see also Hallucinogenics
Psychoactive drugs, 175
Psychoanalytic theory, 107
Punishment, 10, 14, 38, 88, 125, 275, 298,
     350, 356, 376

Rage, 220
Raphe nuclei, 129, 147, 193, 274
Rational system, 258, 300–301, 400

Reactive inhibition, 337
Redundancy, 359
Relatedness, 404, 410
Relaxation response, 124, 261
Relaxed awareness, 34, 183
Relief, 241, 309
REM deprivation, 150, 152, 154–160,
     167–168
     see also REM sleep
REM dreams, 149, 156, 165–166
REM rebound, 155, 159–160, 167
REM sleep:
     and adaptation to stress, 158, 160
     and consolidation of learning, 160
     and creativity, 158
     and field independence/dependence,
          159
     and individual differences, 159
     and learning, 157–158
     and neuroticism, 160
     and paralysis, 145–146, 154
     theories of, 155–160, 168
     see also REM deprivation
Remote associations, 360–362
Repressive personality, 257
Repressors, 160
Responsibility, 290
Restrained eater, 68, 72, 73–74, 80
Restricted environmental stimulation,
     130–131
Restricted orientation, 92
Retaliation in like kind, 211
Reticular activating system (RAS), 30,
     113–115, 130, 146–147, 193
Reward centers of the brain, 28, 306, 349,
     350
Rigidity, 355
Risk, 313, 347, 351, 409
Rock music, 51–53
Romance, 88, 92, 95
Rumination, 291–292, 301, 360, 388, 399
Running, 49–51, 53, 183

Sadness, 241
Satiation, 337
     see also Stimulus satiation 338
Satiety, 60, 63, 65, 71–72, 73, 74, 78
Scrotum, 87
Self-actualization, 355
Self-awareness, and eating, 80
Self-concept, 19, 20, 94, 159–160, 231, 299,
     382, 386, 389, 402, 403, 405, 406
Self-confidence, 51–52, 331, 356, 357
Self-determination, 346, 349, 368, 388, 404,
     411
Self-disclosure, 94
Self-discrepancy, 404
Self-doubt, 22, 266, 315, 381, 383, 384, 388,
     399, 414
Self-efficacy, 21, 94, 204, 309, 313–316,
     396–398, 412
     see also feelings of efficacy

Self-esteem, 46, 80, 94, 140, 290, 377,
     379–389, 394, 395, 406, 408
Self-image, 51, 109, 124, 140, 356, 385
Self-initiated, 187
Self-injury, 182
Self-knowledge, 387, 402, 403, 405
Self-limiting behavior, 294–295
Self-monitor, 2, 48, 92
Self-referent, *see* self-reflection
Self-reflection, 155, 299–300, 360
Self-regulation, 2, 8, 22, 41, 48, 181, 392,
     400, 402, 411, 412
Self-reliance, 282
Self-satisfaction, 307, 310, 312, 392, 394,
     414
Self-statement, 263, 294–295
     see also Self-talk
Self-talk, 399–400
Self-worth, 226–228, 326, 381, 388
Sensation seeking, 94, 180, 264, 306,
     336–353, 355, 409
Sensory deprivation, 34, 118–119, 347
Sensory overload, 123, 130–132
Sensory/narrative based system, 301
Septum, *see* Limbic system
Serotonin, 32, 57, 129, 147, 183, 188, 193,
     214, 281, 282, 283
Setpoint theory, 66–67
Sex hormones, 97–102
Sex assignment, 107–108
Sexual arousal, 83, 84, 87–90
Sexual dimorphism, 101–104
Sexual orientation, 27, 103–109
Sexual scripts, 88–90
Shame, 241, 296–297, 299–301, 376, 381,
     383, 388
Shift work, 152–153
Signaled shock, 250
Sleep deprivation, 148, 150–153
Sleep disorders, 169–172
Sleep reduction, 149
     see also Sleep deprivation
Sleepiness, 150–152
Slow-wave sleep (SWS), 50, 149, 152, 160,
     168–170
Social support, 257, 268, 326, 329–331
Sociotropic types, 293
Softwired behavior, 26–28
Spatial abilities, 98, 101, 106
Specific dynamic action (SDA), 64
Spiral model of eating disorder, 79–80
Stage of resistance, 267
Status, 86
Stereotype, 43, 48, 108
Stimulus change, 337
Stimulus satiation, 337
Strategies, 21, 411
Stress, 2, 32, 34–35, 49, 67–68, 77, 123, 132,
     139–140, 191, 194–195, 243–270, 277,
     283, 312, 366, 367, 411
Substance abuse, definition, 175
Substitution, 196

Suicide, 280–281, 293
Surprisingness, 343
Sympathetic adrenal response, 244–245
Sympathetic nervous system, 115–116,
    189, 276
Synthesis, 359, 360

Tactile, 83, 306
Task difficulty, 374–375
Temporal lobes, 216–217
Testes, 87, 98
Testosterone, 97–103, 105, 108, 350
    and aggression, 214–216
Threat, 3–5, 19, 28, 30, 230–231, 254, 269,
    270, 278, 279, 408, 411

Thrill seeking, 306, 313, 316, 348
Tofranil, 281
Tolerance, 109, 176
Type A behavior, 232–233

Ulcers, 250, 267, 288
Uncertainty, 310–312, 360
    see also Unpredictability
Unconditional love, 20, 385, 386
Unconscious, 163, 300, 354
Uncontrollable events, 255, 283–286, 311,
    330, 368
Unconventional, 356, 357
Unpredictability, 250, 312
Unrestrained eater, 72

Unrestricted orientation, 92
Urinary acidity, 194–195

Vagina, 85, 98, 99
Valium, 175, 190–191
Values, 41–43, 46, 48, 331, 382, 404
Variety, *see* Complexity
Vasocongestion, 84, 85
Ventromedial nuclei (VMN), 65–66
Vigilance, 151, 234
Violence, 221–223, 229
Visual images, 35
Visualization, 21, 401

Yo-yo effect, 66–67, 77, 80

Photo Credits

This page constitutes an extension of the copyright page. We have made every effort to trace the ownership of all copyrighted material and to secure permission from copyright holders. In the event that any question arises as to the use of any material, we will be pleased to make the necessary corrections in future printings.

Chapter 1: 1, Corbis/Bettmann; **4,** Stock, Boston/John Elk III; **9,** Mary Evans Pictures, Corbis/Bettmann; **11,** Photo Researchers, Inc.; **13,** Christopher Johnson/Stock, Boston; **24,** Pamela R. Schuyler/Stock, Boston. **Chapter 2: 41,** Corbis/Bettmann; **50,** Roberto Soncin Gerometta/Photo 20-20; **55,** Michael Newman/PhotoEdit. **Chapter 3: 60,** Jeff Greenberg/PhotoEdit; **76,** Michael Newman/PhotoEdit. **Chapter 4: 82,** Michael Newman/PhotoEdit; **89,** Elizabeth Crews/Stock, Boston. **Chapter 5: 112,** David Young-Wolff/PhotoEdit; **129,** Rudi Von Briel/PhotoEdit; **135,** Arthur Grace/Stock, Boston. **Chapter 6: 144,** Nita Winter/The Image Works; **156,** Michael Weisbrot/Stock, Boston; **161,** M. Richards/PhotoEdit; **163,** kofoto. **Chapter 7: 174,** Charles Gatewood/The Image Works; **180,** Michael Newman/PhotoEdit; **186,** UPI/Corbis Bettmann; **198,** Bachmann/PhotoEdit. **Chapter 8: 208,** Akos Szilvasi/Stock, Boston; **211,** Copyright 1965 by Stanley Milgram, from the film OBEDIENCE, distributed by the Pennsylvania State University, PCR. By permission of Mrs. Alexandra Milgram; **222,** Shelley Boyd/PhotoEdit, **232,** Lionel Delevingne/Stock, Boston. **Chapter 9: 239,** Jim Mahoney/The Image Works. **Chapter 10: 273,** Jean-Claude Lejeune/Stock, Boston; **292,** Esbin-Anderson/Photo 20-20; **297,** Robert Brenner/PhotoEdit. **Chapter 11: 305,** Myrleen Ferguson/PhotoEdit; **317,** Jeff Greenberg/PhotoEdit; **327,** Tony Freeman/PhotoEdit. **Chapter 12: 335,** Lee Snider/The Image Works; **354,** Jeff Greenberg/PhotoEdit; **358,** Esbin-Anderson/Photo 20-20. **Chapter 13: 365,** Christopher Brown/Stock, Boston, **367,** Dennis MacDonald/PhotoEdit; 380, Peter Southwick/Stock, Boston; **387,** Myrleen Ferguson/PhotoEdit. **Chapter 14: 391,** Courtesy of Canadian Space Agency; **405,** David Young-Wolff/PhotoEdit; **413,** Michael Newmann/PhotoEdit.